P9-DIW-586

TAKING SIDES

Clashing Views in

Adolescence

SECOND EDITION

TAKING SIDES

Clashing Views in

Adolescence

SECOND EDITION

Selected, Edited, and with Introductions by

B.J. Rye
St. Jerome's University at the University of Waterloo

and

Maureen T.B. Drysdale
St. Jerome's University at the University of Waterloo

McGraw-Hill
Higher Education

Boston   Burr Ridge, IL   Dubuque, IA   New York   San Francisco   St. Louis
Bangkok   Bogotá   Caracas   Kuala Lumpur   Lisbon   London   Madrid   Mexico City
Milan   Montreal   New Delhi   Santiago   Seoul   Singapore   Sydney   Taipei   Toronto

The McGraw·Hill Companies

**McGraw-Hill
Higher Education**

TAKING SIDES: CLASHING VIEWS IN ADOLESCENCE, SECOND EDITION

1 2 3 4 5 6 7 8 9 0 DOC/DOC 0 9 8

MHID: 0-07-351536-1
ISBN: 978-0-07-351536-6
ISSN: 1933-0499

Managing Editor: *Larry Loeppke*
Senior Managing Editor: *Faye Schilling*
Senior Developmental Editor: *Jill Peter*
Editorial Assistant: *Nancy Meissner*
Production Service Assistant: *Rita Hingtgen*
Permissions Coordinator: *Shirley Lanners*
Senior Marketing Manager: *Julie Keck*
Marketing Communications Specialist: *Mary Klein*
Marketing Coordinator: *Alice Link*
Senior Project Manager: *Jane Mohr*
Design Specialist: *Tara McDermott*
Cover Graphics: *Kristine Jubeck*

Compositor: ICC Macmillan Inc.
Cover Image: © Patrick Sheandell/Photo Alto

www.mhhe.com

Preface

Adolescence is a critical developmental period in everyone's life. In order for us to become adults, we have to "survive" adolescence. For some, this stage of life is characterized by "storm-and-stress," while others glide through the transition unscathed. Most of us have some fond memories of pleasant and exciting experiences coupled with recollections of embarrassing and awkward experiences. Some events that occur during adolescence are universal—such as puberty, physical growth, and psychological maturation—whereas other phenomena are a function of environmental forces—such as cultural context, family structure, school organization, and peer group practices.

How do these different forces and contexts influence the development of adolescents in Western society today? The purpose of this book is to examine some of the issues that may have an impact on adolescents in a didactic, dialectic fashion. To this end, *Taking Sides: Clashing Views in Adolescence* has been developed to foster critical and incisive thinking about issues that may have a significant impact on adolescent development in the twenty-first century. We have included interdisciplinary writings (e.g., from psychology, sociology, medicine, law, and religious studies domains) representing issues relevant to the period of adolescence in developed "Western" societies (e.g., Australia, Canada, and the United States). *Taking Sides: Clashing Views in Adolescence* presents yes/no perspectives in response to 19 questions. Consequently, 38 lively readings written by opponents who sit on different sides of the various topics under consideration are included. Each issue involves:

- A *question* that attempts to capture the essence of the debate.
- An *introduction* whereby information is presented that can be used by the reader as a background to the issue. Also available is some information about the essay authors of the debate as this may help to explain the perspective from which the writer comes.
- Two *essays* where one supports the "yes" side of the controversy while the other speaks to the "no" side of the question.
- A *postscript* presents additional information, which may help to elucidate the issue further, raises additional and thought-provoking questions, and synthesizes the two authors' perspectives.

It is important to note that no issue is truly binary. There are always "gray" areas that fall in between the "yes" and the "no" perspectives. The *Recommended Readings* section provides more references for the interested individual; some readers will wish to delve into particular topics in greater detail. This section was included to give some additional direction for that purpose. At the end of the book, the *Contributors to This Volume* provides information about each essay author. A person's training, career track, and life situation colors her/his perspective on any issue; no one is completely objective. Also, the *Internet References* presents some useful Web site addresses (URLs) that are relevant to the issues discussed in each part.

As you read the different perspectives, you may find that you disagree with one side or both viewpoints. Regardless, it is important to read each selection carefully and critically and respect the opinions of others. This format of the textbook necessarily challenges the reader to face her or his own biases, beliefs, and values about the controversial topics presented. Two of the most important tools that a student can develop in her or his scholarly pursuits is (1) to be able to keep an open mind such that you may consider dissenting views while respecting the opinions of those who disagree with your perspective and (2) to become a critical thinker and evaluate arguments from many different angles and viewpoints. We encourage you to challenge your own perspective so that you can develop these crucial skills.

A word to the instructor An *Instructor's Resource Guide*, with issue synopses, suggestions for classroom discussion, and test questions (multiple choice and essay), is available from McGraw-Hill/Contemporary Learning Series. A general guidebook, *Using Taking Sides in the Classroom*, which discusses methods and techniques for integrating the pro/con approach into any classroom setting, is also available. An online version of *Using Taking Sides in the Classroom* and a correspondence service for *Taking Sides* adopters can be found at http://www.mhcls.com/usingts.

Taking Sides: Clashing Views in Adolescence is one of the many titles in the Taking Sides series. If you are interested in seeing the table of contents for any of the other titles, please visit the Taking Sides Web site at http://www.mhcls.com/takingsides.

Acknowledgments First, and foremost, we would like to thank our families for their patience with us during this *Taking Sides* project. Thanks to Fraser Drysdale, Mallory Drysdale, Adam Drysdale, and Megan Drysdale as well as to Scott Campbell Rye, Barbara Campbell, and Donald Campbell. Your unconditional support during this *Taking Sides* undertaking was greatly appreciated.

A special thank you goes to St. Jerome's University for providing financial support for this project through the Academic Dean's Research Fund. Without this financial support, we could have never undertaken this project.

For expert assistance with researching the issues, editing, and further fine-tuning, we wish to express our heart-felt thanks to Mary-Jean Costello who was instrumental to this process. Additional thanks to Rachel Brown, Megan Drysdale, Fraser Drysdale, Glenn Meaney, Nadia Palarchio, Mallory Drysdale, and Artella Oh for their contributions to this book.

Thanks to McGraw-Hill/Contemporary Learning Series staff for their work on this project: Marcy Mealia, Tim McLeary, and Jill Peter.

In short, thank you to the rich network of colleagues, family, and friends who helped us at various stages of this project. Your support was and is greatly appreciated!

Contents In Brief

UNIT 1   Adolescent Health   1

Issue 1.   Should Adolescents Be Taking Selective Serotonin Reuptake Inhibitors (SSRIs) for Depression?   2

Issue 2.   Should Adolescents Be Allowed to Drink Alcohol?   25

Issue 3.   Should Parental Consent Be Required for Adolescents Seeking Abortions?   41

Issue 4.   Do Boys Worry about an Ideal Body Image as Much as Girls Do?   69

Issue 5.   Should the Human Papillomavirus (HPV) Vaccine Be Mandatory for Early Adolescent Girls?   92

Issue 6.   Is the Use of Nicotine Replacement Therapy (NRT) an Appropriate Cessation Aid for Adolescents Wishing to Quit Smoking?   101

UNIT 2   Sex and Sexuality   131

Issue 7.   Does Engaging in Early Sexual Activity Cause Depressive Symptoms in Adolescents?   132

Issue 8.   Is There Cause for Concern About an "Oral Sex Crisis" for Teens?   155

Issue 9.   Is Comprehensive Sex Education for Adolescents Too Liberal?   169

Issue 10.   Does a Traditional or "Strong" Double Standard with Respect to Sexual Behavior Exist Among Adolescents?   197

Issue 11.   Is Female Sexual Orientation More Fluid than Male Sexual Orientation During Adolescence?   224

UNIT 3   Relationships   253

Issue 12.   Does Divorce or Disruption in Family Structure During Adolescence Have a Detrimental Effect on Development?   254

Issue 13.   Does Dating Impede Developmental Adjustment for Adolescents?   277

Issue 14.   Do Online Friendships Hinder Adolescent Well-Being?   301

UNIT 4   Problem Behaviors   325

Issue 15.   Should Adolescents Who Commit Serious Offenses Be Tried and Convicted as Adults?   326

Issue 16.   Are Girls Bigger Bullies than Boys?   349

UNIT 5   Media   369

Issue 17. Does Sex on TV Negatively Impact Adolescent
Sexuality?   370

Issue 18. Do Video Games Impede Adolescent Cognitive
Development?   393

Issue 19. Are Social Networking Sites (SNSs), such as Facebook, a
Cause for Concern among Adolescents?   410

Contents

Preface   v

Correlation Guide   xvii

Introduction   xix

UNIT 1   ADOLESCENT HEALTH   1

Issue 1.   Should Adolescents Be Taking Selective Serotonin Reuptake Inhibitors (SSRIs) for Depression?   2

YES: **Christopher J. Kratochvil et al.**, from "Selective Serotonin Reuptake Inhibitors in Pediatric Depression," *Journal of Child and Adolescent Psychopharmacology* (vol. 16, no. 1/2, 2006)   4

NO: **Tamar Wohlfarth et al.**, from "Antidepressants Use in Children and Adolescents and the Risk of Suicide," *European Neuropsychopharmacology* (vol. 16, 2006)   17

Christopher Kratochvil M.D., an associate professor of psychiatry at the University of Nebraska Medical Center, and colleagues in the United States, examined recent data from meta-analyses and re-assessed the risk/benefit relationship associated with the use of SSRIs for pediatric depression. They conclude that SSRIs play a role in the treatment of pediatric depression. Tamar Wohlfarth, a clinical assessor, and colleagues in the Netherlands assessed antidepressant use in pediatric patients and report an increased risk for events related to suicidality among those taking antidepressants. They caution the use of all SSRIs and NSRAs in the pediatric population.

Issue 2.   Should Adolescents Be Allowed to Drink Alcohol?   25

YES: **Rutger C.M.E. Engels, et al.**, from "Peer Group Reputation and Smoking and Alcohol Consumption in Early Adolescence," *Addictive Behaviors* (vol. 31, 2006)   27

NO: **Sandra A. Brown**, from "Providing Substance Abuse Prevention and Treatment Services to Adolescents," Testimony Before the U.S. Senate, Subcommittee on Substance Abuse and Mental Health Services (June 15, 2004)   33

Engels and colleagues, researchers in the Netherlands, suggest that substance use, while potentially problematic, may serve beneficial developmental functions for adolescents. Particularly, adolescents who drink alcohol appeared to be more self-confident and sociable than those who abstained based on peer evaluations. Researcher Sandra Brown, a psychiatrist from the University of California–San Diego, argues that early onset of alcohol and drug use put youth at greater risk for neurological damage, alcohol related injuries (e.g., from drinking and driving), and future substance dependence.

Issue 3.   Should Parental Consent Be Required for Adolescents Seeking Abortions?   41

YES: **Teresa Stanton Collett,** from Testimony Before the Subcommittee on the Constitution, Committee on the Judiciary, U.S. House of Representatives (September 6, 2001)   *43*

NO: **Nancy E. Adler, Emily J. Ozer, and Jeanne Tschann,** from "Abortion Among Adolescents," *American Psychologist* (March 23, 2003)   *55*

Teresa Stanton Collett, law professor at the University of St. Thomas School of Law in Minnesota, analyzes the reasons for parental notification laws such as the Child Interstate Abortion Notification Act. She advocates parental involvement in a minor's decision to terminate a pregnancy. Nancy Adler, a professor of medical psychology at the University of California-San Francisco, and colleagues argue that the empirical data do not support the assumptions that adolescents are at a higher risk of psychological harm from abortion and are unable to make an adequately informed decision. In fact, studies suggest a relatively low risk associated with abortion, and adolescents seeking abortion appear to make an informed choice.

Issue 4.   Do Boys Worry about an Ideal Body Image as Much as Girls Do?   69

YES: **Diane C. Jones and Joy K. Crawford,** from "The Peer Appearance Culture During Adolescence: Gender and Body Mass Variations," *Journal of Youth and Adolescence* (vol. 35, no. 2, 2006)   *71*

NO: **Duane A. Hargreaves and Marika Tiggemann,** from "Idealized Media Images and Adolescent Body Image: 'Comparing' Boys and Girls," *Body Image* (vol. 1, 2004)   *82*

Diane Jones, an associate professor in educational psychology at the University of Washington, and Joy Crawford, a doctoral student in human development and cognition at the University of Washington, suggest that adolescent boys experience more appearance pressure and teasing than adolescent girls. They also argue that boys discuss muscle building more than girls discuss dieting. Duane Hargreaves and Marika Tiggemann, researchers in the School of Psychology at Flinders University, state that adolescent girls are more vulnerable to body image pressures than boys. They argue that the glamorization of eating disorders among female celebrities and the media play a significant role.

Issue 5.   Should the Human Papillomavirus (HPV) Vaccine Be Mandatory for Early Adolescent Girls?   92

YES: **Cruise, E.,** from "Writing for PRO position: Should the HPV vaccine be mandatory for early adolescent girls?" *The American Journal of Maternal Child Nursing, 32(4),* 208, 2007   *94*

NO: **Anderson, T.L.,** from "Writing for CON position: Should the HPV vaccine be mandatory for early adolescent girls?" *The American Journal of Maternal Child Nursing, 32(4),* 209, 2007   *96*

Erin Cruise, an instructor of nursing at Radford University in Virginia, lists many of the reasons that public health personnel are in favor of the HPV vaccination being legislated as mandatory for young girls. She discusses the sexuality-related issues as well as a financial cost-benefit analysis associated with mandatory HPV vaccination. Tamika L. Anderson, a public health nurse and child care nurse consultant with the Davidson County Health Department in Lexington, North Carolina, argues against the implementation of a mandatory HPV vaccination for female adolescents. Some of the concerns identified are safety, choice, and cost.

Issue 6. Is the Use of Nicotine Replacement Therapy (NRT) an Appropriate Cessation Aid for Adolescents Wishing to Quit Smoking? 101

YES: Karen Hanson, Sharon Allen, Sue Jensen, and Dorothy Batsukami, from "Treatment of Adolescent Smokers with the Nicotine Patch," *Nicotine & Tobacco Research* (August, 2003) *103*

NO: William P. Adelman, from "Tobacco use Cessation for Adolescents," *Adolescent Medicine Clinics* (October, 2006) *112*

Karen Hanson and colleagues, from the Tobacco Use Research Center at the University of Minnesota, present the results of an empirical study where they had adolescent smokers use a nicotine-replacement patch or a placebo patch (i.e., a patch with no nicotine unbeknownst to the participant). The results suggested that, with cognitive-behaviorial therapy and an incentive program (money for not smoking), the patch was effective at reducing withdrawal symptoms and cravings and there was some indication that the patch helped adolescents reduce the amount they smoked. Hanson et al. concluded that the patch may be helpful for adolescent smokers who attempt to quit. William P. Adelman, a physician who is a member of the Department of Adolescent Medicine at the National Naval Medical Center in Bethesda, Maryland, in a review article, argues that there are "teen" patterns of smoking and "adult" patterns of smoking and that use of nicotine replacement therapy is appropriate only for adolescents who exhibit adult-type smoking behavior. He calls for caution in the use of nicotine replacement therapy as it could be a "gateway" substance that leads to use of other controlled substances or results in other unintended negative physiological consequences.

UNIT 2 SEX AND SEXUALITY 131

Issue 7. Does Engaging in Early Sexual Activity Cause Depressive Symptoms in Adolescents? 132

YES: Robert E. Rector, Kirk. A. Johnson, and Lauren R. Noyes, from "Sexually Active Teenagers are More Likely to Be Depressed and to Attempt Suicide," *A Report of the Heritage Center for Data Analysis* (CDA03-04, Heritage Foundation, 2003) *134*

NO: Joseph J. Sabia, from "Does Early Adolescent Sex Cause Depressive Symptoms?" *Journal of Policy Analysis and Management* (Autumn, 2006) *142*

Robert Rector and colleagues from the Heritage Foundation, a conservative think tank in Washington, D.C., contend that teens who are sexually active are significantly more likely to be depressed or suicidal than virgins. Joseph J. Sabia, a University of Georgia economics professor, analyzed the same data set as Rector et al. but found that, by considering other variables, the relationship between sexual intercourse and depression disappeared.

Issue 8.   Is There Cause for Concern About an "Oral Sex Crisis" for Teens?   155

YES: Sharon Jayson, from "Teens Define Sex in New Ways," http://www.USAToday.com (October 19, 2005)   *157*

NO: Alexander McKay, from "Oral Sex Among Teenagers: Research, Discourse, and Education," *Canadian Journal of Human Sexuality* (Fall/Winter 2004)   *162*

Journalist Sharon Jayson argues that more than half of 15- to 19-year-olds are engaging in oral sex. She reports some experts are becoming increasingly worried that adolescents who approach this intimate behavior so casually might have difficulty forming healthy intimate relationships later on. Alexander McKay, research coordinator of the Sex Information and Education Council of Canada, argues that the discourse about oral sex is somewhat exaggerated but may be used as a vehicle for increasing discussions with teens about their motives for sexual activity, which, in turn, can help guide sex education initiatives.

Issue 9.   Is Comprehensive Sex Education for Adolescents Too Liberal?   169

YES: Aida Orgocka, from "Perceptions of Communication and Education About Sexuality Among Muslim Immigrant Girls in the US," *Sex Education* (October 2004)   *171*

NO: John Santelli et al., from "Abstinence and Abstinence-Only Education: A Review of U.S. Policies and Programs," *Journal of Adolescent Health* (vol. 38, 2006)   *182*

Aida Orgocka, a gender and development expert at the University of Illinois, presents a qualitative study of Illinois mothers' and daughters' perceptions of the sexual health school curriculum from a Muslim perspective. The participants tended to find the sex education curriculum at odds with Muslim values such that many of the girls opted to forgo the school-based sexual health classes. John Santelli, a professor of clinical population, family health, and clinical pediatrics at the Mailman School of Public Health in Columbia University, and colleagues review current U.S. policies encouraging abstinence-only sexual health education and discuss the potential negative impact and ethical considerations arising from these policies on adolescent sexual practices.

Issue 10.   Does a Traditional or "Strong" Double Standard with Respect to Sexual Behavior Exist Among Adolescents?   197

YES: Mary Crawford and Danielle Popp, from "Sexual Double Standards: A Review and Methodological Critique of Two Decades of Research," *Journal of Sex Research* (February 2003)   *199*

NO: Michael J. Marks and R. Chris Fraley, from "The Sexual Double Standard: Fact or Fiction?" *Sex Roles* (February 2005)   *213*

Mary Crawford, a psychology professor at the University of Connecticut, and her graduate student Danielle Popp present evidence suggesting the double standard that males are socially rewarded and females socially derogated for sexual activity exists among adolescents as it does among adults. Researchers Michael Marks and Chris Fraley oppose the above claim and suggest that there is little evidence that the traditional double standard exists among adolescents or even among adults.

Issue 11.   Is Female Sexual Orientation More Fluid than Male Sexual Orientation During Adolescence?   224

YES: Lisa M. Diamond, from "A New View of Lesbian Subtypes: Stable versus Fluid Identity Trajectories over an 8-year Period," *Psychology of Women Quarterly* (vol. 29, no. 2, 2005)   *226*

NO: Margaret Rosario, Eric W. Schrimshaw, Joyce Hunter, and Lisa Braun, from "Sexual Identity Development Among Lesbian, Gay, and Bisexual Youths: Consistency and Change Over Time," *The Journal of Sex Research* (February 2006)   *238*

Lisa Diamond, an assistant professor of psychology and women's studies at the University of Utah, presents the results of an 8-year study that compared women who were "stable" versus "fluid" in their sexual orientation self-labeling and found that those who were "fluid" had more fluctuation in their physical and emotional attractions as well as sexual behavior and romantic relationships. She argues for acknowledging the important role of female plasticity in sexual orientation research. Researchers Rosario and colleagues oppose the hypothesis that females are more sexually fluid than males. They argue that female youth were less likely to change their sexual identity than males.

UNIT 3   RELATIONSHIPS   253

Issue 12.   Does Divorce or Disruption in Family Structure During Adolescence Have a Detrimental Effect on Development?   254

YES: Paul R. Amato, from "The Impact of Family Formation Change on the Cognitive, Social, and Emotional Well-Being of the Next Generation," *The Future of Children* (Fall 2005)   *256*

NO: Eda Ruschena et al., from "A Longitudinal Study of Adolescent Adjustment Following Family Transitions," *Journal of Child Psychology and Psychiatry* (vol. 46, no. 4, 2005)   *264*

Sociology professor Paul Amato presents evidence that children growing up in stable, two-parent families are less likely to experience cognitive, emotional, and social problems than those who do not. Eda Ruschena, a psychologist at the Catholic Education Office in Melbourne, and her colleagues from the University of Melbourne claim that adolescents do not necessarily experience negative social, emotional, or psychological outcomes during family transitions.

Issue 13.   Does Dating Impede Developmental Adjustment for Adolescents?   277

YES: Deborah P. Welsh, Catherine M. Grello, and Melinda S. Harper, from "When Love Hurts: Depression and Adolescent Romantic Relationships," in Paul Florsheim, ed., *Adolescent Romantic Relations and Sexual Behavior* (Lawrence Erlbaum, 2003)   *279*

NO: **Wyndol Furman and Laura Shaffer,** from "The Role of Romantic Relationships in Adolescent Development," in Paul Florsheim, ed., *Adolescent Romantic Relations and Sexual Behavior* (Lawrence Erlbaum, 2003) *289*

Researchers Welsh, Grello, and Harper, while not arguing that all teen romantic relationships are detrimental, demonstrate how such relationships can be a catalyst for teens who are at risk to develop depression. Wyndol Furman, a child clinical psychologist at the University of Denver, and Laura Shaffer make the case for areas where romantic relationships can impact teen development. While many of their arguments are speculative or supported only by correlational research, they make a compelling case for the benefits of teenage romances.

Issue 14. Do Online Friendships Hinder Adolescent Well-Being? 301

YES: **Lauren Donchi and Susan Moore,** from "It's a Boy Thing: The Role of the Internet in Young People's Psychological Wellbeing," *Behavior Change* (vol. 21, no. 2, 2004) *303*

NO: **Patti M. Valkenburg and Jochen Peter,** from "Online Communication and Adolescent Well-Being: Testing the Stimulation Versus the Displacement Hypothesis," *Journal of Computer-Mediated Communication* (vol. 12, 2007) *312*

Psychologists Lauren Donchi and Susan Moore suggest that adolescent boys who rate their online friendships as very important are more likely to have lower self-esteem and to be lonely. Those with more face-to-face friendships are higher on self-esteem and less lonely. Professors Patti Valkenburg and Jochen Peter, in the Amsterdam School of Communications Research at the University of Amsterdam, argue that online communication enhances well-being through its positive effect on time spent with friends and quality of friendships.

UNIT 4 PROBLEM BEHAVIORS 325

Issue 15. Should Adolescents Who Commit Serious Offenses Be Tried and Convicted as Adults? 326

YES: **Daniel P. Mears,** from "Getting Tough with Juvenile Offenders: Explaining Support for Sanctioning Youths as Adults," *Criminal Justice and Behavior* (April 2001) *328*

NO: **Laurence Steinberg and Elizabeth S. Scott,** from "Less Guilty by Reason of Adolescence: Developmental Immaturity, Diminished Responsibility, and the Juvenile Death Penalty," *American Psychologist* (December 2003) *336*

Daniel Mears, an associate professor for the College of Criminology and Criminal Justice at Florida State University, reports that for serious offenses, there is widespread support for sanctioning youths as adults. He points to a conservative group, fearful of crime, worrying about social order and public safety. Laurence Steinberg, distinguished university professor at Temple University, and Elizabeth Scott, law professor at the University of Virginia, argue that adolescents often lack the capabilities to make mature judgments, control impulses, and resist coercion from peers and therefore should not be held to the same standards of criminal conduct as adults.

Issue 16. Are Girls Bigger Bullies than Boys? 349

YES: Melanie J. Zimmer-Gembeck, Tasha C. Geiger, and Nicki R. Crick, from "Relational and Physical Aggression, Prosocial Behavior, and Peer Relations: Gender Moderation and Bidirectional Association," *Journal of Early Adolescence* (November 2005) *351*

NO: Christina Salmivalli and Ari Kaukiainen, "'Female Aggression' Revisited: Variable- and Person-Centered Approaches to Studying Gender Differences in Different Types of Aggression," *Aggressive Behavior* (vol. 30, 2004) *360*

Melanie Zimmer-Gembeck, an assistant professor of psychology at Griffith University in Australia, and her colleagues report gender differences in levels of relational aggression, which is a type of bullying. In early adolescence, girls are more relationally aggressive than boys. The authors argue that girls may use relational aggression to gain and keep friends. Christina Salmivalli, professor of applied psychology, and psychologist Ari Kaukiainen, both from University of Turku, argue that boys use all types of aggression more than girls in early adolescence. This included direct aggression, verbal aggression, and indirect or relational aggression.

UNIT 5 MEDIA 369

Issue 17. Does Sex on TV Negatively Impact Adolescent Sexuality? 370

YES: Rebecca L. Collins et al., from "Watching Sex on Television Predicts Adolescent Initiation of Sexual Behavior," *Pediatrics* (September 3, 2004) *372*

NO: Rebecca L. Collins et al., from "Entertainment Television as a Healthy Sex Educator: The Impact of Condom-Efficacy Information in an Episode of *Friends*," *Pediatrics* (November 5, 2003) *382*

Rebecca Collins and colleagues from the RAND Corporation present evidence from a longitudinal survey that adolescents who viewed more sexual content at baseline were more likely to initiate intercourse and progress to more advanced sexual activities during the subsequent year. Collins and colleagues in an earlier study suggested that entertainment television can also serve as a healthy sex educator and can work in conjunction with parents to improve adolescent sexual knowledge.

Issue 18. Do Video Games Impede Adolescent Cognitive Development? 393

YES: Philip A. Chan and Terry Rabinowitz, from "A Cross-Sectional Analysis of Video Games and Attention Deficit Hyperactivity Disorder Symptoms in Adolescents," *Annals of General Psychiatry* (vol. 5, 2006) *395*

NO: Jing Feng, Ian Spence, and Jay Pratt, from "Playing an Action Video Game Reduces Gender Differences in Spatial Cognition," *Psychological Science* (vol. 18, no. 10, 2007) *401*

Philip Chan, from Lifespan at Rhode Island Hospital, and Terry Rabinowitz, from the University of Vermont College of Medicine, report a significant association between playing video games and inattention and may lead to problems in school. Jing Feng, Ian Spence, and Jay Pratt, from the University of Toronto, report that playing video games can enhance spatial attention, which have been associated with success in mathematics and science courses.

Issue 19. Are Social Networking Sites (SNSs), such as Facebook, a Cause for Concern among Adolescents? 410

YES: **Ralph Gross and Alessandro Acquisti,** from "Information Revelation and Privacy in Online Social Networks (The Facebook Case)," *In Proceedings of the 2005 ACM Workshop on Privacy in the Electronic Society,* ACM Press, New York (2005) *412*

NO: **Nicole B. Ellison, Charles Steinfield, and Cliff Lampe,** from "The Benefits of Facebook 'Friends': Social Capital and College Students' Use of Online Social Network Sites," *Journal of Computer-Mediated Communication* (vol. 12, 2007) *422*

Ralph Gross, and Alessandro Acquisti, Carnegie Mellon University, argue that participation in social networking sites, such as Facebook, exposes users to both physical and cyber risks. Researchers Nicole Ellison, Charles Steinfield, and Cliff Lampe from the Department of Telecommunication, Information Studies, and Media, at Michigan State University present evidence suggesting a strong positive association between Facebook and social capital, self-esteem, and life satisfaction.

Contributors 434

Correlation Guide

The *Taking Sides* series presents current issues in a debate-style format designed to stimulate student interest and develop critical thinking skills. Each issue is thoughtfully framed with an issue summary, an issue introduction, and a postscript. The pro and con essays—selected for their liveliness and substance—represent the arguments of leading scholars and commentators in their fields.

Taking Sides: Clashing Views in Adolescence, 2/e is an easy-to-use reader that presents issues on important topics such as *adolescent health, sex and sexuality,* and *antisocial behavior.* For more information on *Taking Sides* and other *McGraw-Hill Contemporary Learning Series* titles, visit www.mhcls.com.

This convenient guide matches the issues in **Taking Sides: Adolescence, 2/e** with the corresponding chapters in three of our best-selling McGraw-Hill Adolescence textbooks by Santrock and Steinberg.

Taking Sides: Adolescence, 2/e	Adolescence, 12/e by Santrock	Adolescence, 8/e by Steinberg
Issue 1: Should Adolescents Be Taking Selective Serotonin Reuptake Inhibitors (SSRIs) for Depression?	**Chapter 13:** Problems in Adolescence and Emerging Adulthood	**Chapter 13:** Psychosocial Problems in Adolescence
Issue 2: Should Adolescents Be Allowed to Drink Alcohol?	**Chapter 13:** Problems in Adolescence and Emerging Adulthood	**Chapter 7:** Work, Leisure, and Mass Media
Issue 3: Should Parental Consent Be Required for Adolescents Seeking Abortions?	**Chapter 6:** Sexuality	**Chapter 11:** Sexuality
Issue 4: Do Boys Worry about an Ideal Body Image as Much as Girls Do?	**Chapter 2:** Puberty, Health, and Biological Foundations	**Chapter 1:** Biological Transitions **Chapter 10:** Intimacy
Issue 5: Should the Human Papillomavirus (HPV) Vaccine be Mandatory for Early Adolescent Girls?		**Chapter 11:** Sexuality
Issue 6: Is the Use of Nicotine Replacement Therapy (NRT) an Appropriate Cessation Aid for Adolescents Wishing to Quit Smoking?	**Chapter 13:** Problems in Adolescence and Emerging Adulthood	**Chapter 13:** Psychosocial Problems in Adolescence
Issue 7: Does Engaging in Early Sexual Activity Cause Depressive Symptoms in Adolescents?		**Chapter 11:** Sexuality
Issue 8: Is There Cause for Concern About an "Oral Sex Crisis" for Teens?	**Chapter 6:** Sexuality	**Chapter 11:** Sexuality

Taking Sides: Adolescence, 2/e	Adolescence, 12/e by Santrock	Adolescence, 8/e by Steinberg
Issue 9: Is Comprehensive Sex Education for Adolescents Too Liberal?	**Chapter 6:** Sexuality	**Chapter 11:** Sexuality
Issue 10: Does a Traditional or "Strong" Double Standard with Respect to Sexual Behavior Exist among Adolescents?	**Chapter 5:** Gender **Chapter 6:** Sexuality	**Chapter 8:** Identity **Chapter 11:** Sexuality
Issue 11: Is Female Sexual Orientation More Fluid than Male Sexual Orientation During Adolescence?	**Chapter 6:** Sexuality	**Chapter 11:** Sexuality
Issue 12: Does Divorce or Disruption in Family Structure During Adolescence Have a Detrimental Effect on Development?	**Chapter 8:** Families	**Chapter 4:** Families
Issue 13: Does Dating Impede Developmental Adjustment for Adolescents?	**Chapter 9:** Peer and Romantic Relationships	**Chapter 10:** Intimacy
Issue 14: Do Online Friendships Hinder Adolescent Well-Being?	**Chapter 12:** Culture	**Chapter 7:** Work, Leisure, and Mass Media
Issue 15: Should Adolescents Who Commit Serious Offenses Be Tried and Convicted as Adults?		**Chapter 3:** Social Transitions **Chapter 13:** Psychosocial Problems in Adolescence
Issue 16: Are Girls Bigger Bullies than Boys?	**Chapter 10:** Schools	**Chapter 5:** Peer Groups
Issue 17: Does Sex on TV Negatively Impact Adolescent Sexuality?	**Chapter 12:** Culture	**Chapter 7:** Work, Leisure, and Mass Media
Issue 18: Do Video Games Impede Adolescent Cognitive Development?	**Chapter 12:** Culture	**Chapter 7:** Work, Leisure, and Mass Media
Issue 19: Are Social Networking Sites (SNSs), such as Facebook, a Cause for Concern among Adolescents?	**Chapter 12:** Culture	**Chapter 7:** Work, Leisure, and Mass Media

Introduction

Adolescence is a period of development marked by a transition spanning the second decade of life. Developmentally, adolescence begins at approximately age 10 and lasts into the early twenties, although from eighteen or nineteen onwards, the period is referred to as "emerging adulthood" (Arnett, 2004). Adolescence is a period of time when individuals leave the security of childhood to meet the demands of the adult world. They pull away from the structure of family in search of independence. This involves finding an identity, making a commitment, and carving out a responsible place in society. Although the transition is very individual (i.e., occurring in different ways and at different rates), it involves dealing with three sets of developmental challenges or tasks. The challenges involve the biological, psychological, and social changes occurring during this crucial period of development. The biological changes are the most visible, with puberty and hormones driving the changes in body appearance. Adolescents must learn to cope and accept these changes. The psychological changes involve advances in cognitions and enhanced emotional development, leading to stronger decision making, mature judgment, better planning, and advanced perspective taking. The task here is to cope with these new characteristics and to use them to adapt to the transition and find a place in the world. The third challenge is to find a responsible role in society and commit to a revised sense of self. The social changes (i.e., relationships, newfound independence) taking place during this time permit the adolescent to explore different roles. Taken together, the challenges and changes result in children becoming adults.

History of Adolescence

Historically, the period between childhood and adulthood has been recognized as distinct; however, it was not researched or given a specific name until the twentieth century. In ancient Greek times, Plato, Socrates, and Aristotle had specific views of adolescence. Plato, for example, recognizing the advances in thinking and judgment during the second decade of life, believed that formal education should only start at this time. Socrates, also aware of the advances in cognitions, argued that the stronger thinking skills allowed youth to become better at arguing. In addition, he recognized the down side to this developmental advancement, arguing that youth were inclined to contradict their parents and tyrannize their teachers. Aristotle argued that the most important aspect of this period of development was the ability to choose. He believed that human beings became capable of making rational choices and good decisions during the second decade. Aristotle also recognized that, although youth exhibited gains in thinking, they were still immature and different from adults.

His strong opinion and knowledge about youth is stated clearly in the following passage:

> "The young are in character prone to desire and ready to carry any desire they may have formed into action. Of bodily desires it is the sexual to which they are most disposed to give way, and in regard to sexual desire they exercise no self-restraint. They are changeful, too, and fickle in their desires, which are as transitory as they are vehement; for their wishes are keen without being permanent, like a sick man's fits of hunger and thirst. They are passionate, irascible, and apt to be carried away by their impulses. They are the slaves, too, of their passion, as their ambition prevents their ever brooking a slight and renders them indignant at the mere idea of enduring an injury. They are charitable rather than the reverse, as they have never yet been witnesses of many villainies; and they are trustful, as they have not yet been often deceived. They are sanguine, too, for the young are heated by nature as drunken men by wine, not to say that they have not yet experienced frequent failures. Their lives are lived principally in hope. They have high aspirations; for they have never yet been humiliated by the experience of life, but are unacquainted with the limiting force of circumstances. Youth is the age when people are most devoted to their friends, as they are then extremely fond of social intercourse. If the young commit a fault, it is always on the side of excess and exaggeration, for they carry everything too far, whether it be their love or hatred or anything else" (Aristotle 4th Century B.C.).

The early philosophical views such as those mentioned above were unchallenged for many centuries. However, by the late nineteenth century/ early twentieth century, this changed, and the age of adolescence was recognized. It was argued that children and youth were not miniature adults and, therefore, should not be treated in the same way as adults, especially with respect to labor and family responsibility. As a result, child labor laws were implemented, followed by mandatory schooling until age 16. Basically, children were being protected and not permitted to work; however, they could not be left unsupervised, aimlessly wandering about, getting into trouble. The solution: "Keep them in school until they can work." With these changes in the early 1900s, the concept of adolescence became more defined. Adolescents were not children and were not yet adults, resulting in the recognition that they were unique in their development and, as such, deserved special attention.

At this time (i.e., circa 1900), G. Stanley Hall began studying adolescence in terms of their behaviors, their emotions, and their relationships. Known as the father of adolescent research, he concluded that children went through turmoil and upheaval during their second decade of life and, as such, were in a state of constant *storm-and-stress*, a term he coined from the German "sturm und drang." Hall identified three key aspects of adolescent storm-and-stress: risky behaviors, mood disruptions, and conflict with parents. Hall argued that the physical changes occurring during this period of the lifespan (e.g., growth spurts, sexual maturation, and hormonal changes) resulted in psychological turbulence. He further argued that the turmoil was both universal and biologically based. In other words, it was inevitable regardless of other factors. To disseminate these arguments, Hall published *Adolescence* (1904), the first text on adolescent development, making the study of adolescence both scientific and scholarly. Since the time of Hall's book, research on adolescence has attracted attention from many disciplines such as psychology, sociology, anthropology, and medicine.

Soon after Hall's view of adolescence, Margaret Mead published *Coming of Age in Samoa* (1928), which challenged Hall's view of universal adolescent storm-and-stress. After conducting observational research in Samoa (a distinctly different culture than Western society), Mead explained how Samoan adolescents experienced a gradual and smooth transition to adulthood because of the meaningful connections made between their roles during adolescence and the roles they would perform as adults. She argued that the transition through adolescence was not simply biological, but rather sociocultural, and the turmoil identified by Hall was environmentally and culturally specific and certainly not universal. Some cultures, she stated, provided a smooth, gradual transition that allowed adolescents to experience minimal, if any, storm-and-stress.

For many years, Mead was alone in arguing against Hall's view. Most social scientists based their research on what Richard Lerner (a current and eminent developmental researcher) called Hall's deficit model of adolescence where developmental deficits caused turmoil resulting in problem behaviors such as alcohol use, drugs, school failure, teen pregnancy, crime, and depression. Essentially, Hall's deficit model and view of storm-and-stress as universal was not disputed or challenged until the 1960s when it was realized that not all adolescents had a turbulent time during the transition from childhood to adulthood. Research in the 1960s began providing evidence to support Mead's perspective, arguing that many adolescents had good relationships and strong core values with few, if any, problem behaviors. Researchers, in supporting Mead, were not necessarily disputing Hall. They recognized that, while some adolescents did in fact experience an intense period of storm-and-stress, many had a smooth and uneventful transition. This led to the more recent view of a *modified storm-and-stress* period of development. From this perspective, conflict with parents, mood disruptions, and risky behaviors are on a continuum dependent on many psychological, sociological, cultural, and environmental factors.

Theories of Adolescent Development

During the twentieth century, many theories have been proposed to explain human development. A simple overview of a few of the key theories is provided with a particular emphasis on the period of adolescence.

Psychoanalytic theory states that development is unconscious and dependent on early experiences with parents. It is predicated on the premise that personality is comprised of three mostly unconscious psychological constructs: the Id, where raw desires, urges, and drives are housed (e.g., sexual desires, hunger, thirst); the Ego, which "manages" the desires and tries to appease or satisfy the wants of the Id, while working within the constraints of the real world (e.g., satisfying unacceptable sexual desires with fantasies or substituted behaviors); and the Superego, which is the social conscience of the personality (e.g., where parental and societal values reside). Within the framework of psychoanalytic theory, these three hypothesized constructs must work in harmony in order for the person to be well-adjusted and to function effectively within society. The development of these structures arises out of different psychosexual stages, which are a series of sexual obstacles the child must overcome in order to proceed to the next stage of development. Sigmund Freud (1938) and daughter Anna Freud (1958) argued that the balance previously achieved between the Id, the Ego, and the Superego is destroyed during adolescence because of the new pressures on the ego. As a result, the sexual drives brought on by puberty and hormonal changes affect an adolescent's sense of reality and subsequent behavior. From a psychoanalytic point of view, a positive sense of self, prosocial behavior, and overall healthy development can occur only if psychosexual development was not restricted in earlier years. Essentially, the sexual reawakening during adolescence (i.e., the genital stage) leads to healthy adult sexuality and overall well-being if children are not restricted during any of the previous psychosexual stages (i.e., oral, anal, phallic, and latency).

From a *cognitive perspective*, human development is a bidirectional process, explained in terms of an individual's action on the environment and the action of the environment on the individual. As a child matures, he or she becomes more active in his or her environment and more advanced cognitively. Jean Piaget, a pioneer of cognitive developmental theory, proposed that children proceed through a sequence of distinct developmental stages: the sensorimotor stage (birth to age 2), the preoperational stage (ages 2 to 5), the concrete operational stage (age 6 to early adolescence), and the formal operational stage (early adolescence to adulthood). Piaget argued that, between the ages of 11 and 15, adolescents enter the formal operational stage. Abstract and hypothetical thinking emerges during this stage, and as a result, children attain the ability to see that reality (e.g., how others treat them) and their thoughts about reality (e.g., how others "should" treat them) are different. They gain the ability to generate and recognize hypotheses about reality. The ability to think abstractly also allows adolescents to project themselves into the future, distinguish present reality from possibility, and think about what *might* be. Piaget also argued that adolescents, once in the formal operational stage, gain competence in formal reasoning, which is marked by a transition from inductive reasoning (e.g., "Jane had unprotected sex and did not get pregnant; therefore, if I have unprotected sex, I will not get pregnant.") to deductive reasoning (e.g., "There are risks involved when having unprotected sex, and because Jane did not get pregnant, does not mean that I will not get pregnant."). This transition means that adolescents are not only able to systemize their ideas and critically deal with their own thinking to construct theories, but they are also able to test their theories logically and to discover the truth scientifically. They can devise many interpretations of an observed outcome (e.g., pregnancy may be the result of unprotected sex, failed contraception, or in vitro fertilization), and they can anticipate many possibilities prior to an actual event (e.g., unprotected sex may lead to pregnancy, an STI, or HIV/AIDS).

Currently, there is debate as to whether Piaget was correct in saying that adolescents gain the competencies cited above by age 15. Neuroscientists argue that the adolescent brain may not be fully developed until late adolescence or early adulthood. Neuroimaging indicates that the prefrontal cortex (the home of the executive functions) is the last part of the human brain to develop, not reaching full maturity until the early twenties or later. This would mean that, until the brain has reached maturity, adolescents would not be competent in planning, setting priorities, organizing thoughts, suppressing impulses, weighing out consequences, and formal reasoning. Without these competencies in place, adolescents may have a difficult time with decision making. Neuroscientists therefore tend to attribute bad decisions to an underdeveloped brain (see Issue 15 for more on this argument).

Social cognitive theory (Bandura, 2005) is another approach to understanding adolescent development and behavior. From this perspective, adolescent development is understood in terms of how adolescents reason about themselves, others, and the social world around them. Theorists such as David Elkind (1967; 1978) describe adolescent reasoning and thinking in terms of the advances in metacognition. With the ability to "think about their own thinking" (metacognition), adolescents spend most of their time focused on themselves. They daydream more and, as they become preoccupied with their own thoughts, they come to believe that others are or should be as preoccupied with them as they are with themselves. As a result, they think everyone notices them. A typical example is the adolescent who cannot possibly go to school because of a facial blemish. To the distraught adolescent, everyone will notice and criticize them. David Elkind uses the term adolescent egocentrism to describe these changes in behavior and thought.

Moving toward a more social perspective is Erik Erikson's (1959) *psychosocial theory* of ego development, which encompasses the entire life span. He describes development from birth to old age as occurring in eight stages with each stage characterized by a crisis between two opposing forces (e.g., trust versus mistrust) that must be resolved successfully. According to Erikson, the resolution of a crisis is dependent on the successful resolution of all previous crises. For example, the adolescent crisis of *identity formation* versus *role confusion* can only be resolved if adolescents were successful in resolving the previous four crises of childhood (i.e., having a sense of trust vs. mistrust, autonomy vs. shame and doubt, initiative vs. guilt, and industry vs. inferiority). In addition, the resolution of the adolescent identity crisis will affect the resolution of future crises. Resolving the identity crisis means showing commitment toward a role—personal, sexual, occupational, and ideological (i.e., a concept about human life that involves a set of beliefs and values). Once complete, the established identity is a distinctive combination of personality characteristics and social style by which the adolescent defines himself/herself and by which he or she is recognized by others.

The last theory presented here is Urie Bronfenbrenner's *ecological systems theory* (1979), which examines the role of five different environments on an individual's development and well-being. Imagine the adolescent at the center of a large circle with each system radiating outward. The first system immediately surrounding the adolescent is the microsystem. This is the setting in which a person lives and includes one's family, peers, school, and neighbourhood. The second system, called the mesosystem, consists of the relationships between the different microsystems. An example is the relationship between an adolescent's family and school. According to Bronfenbrenner, the relationship between these two microsystems has a different effect on the individual than each microsystem separately. The third system is the exosystem, which comprises the linkages between different settings that indirectly involves the adolescent. An example is the relation between the home and a parent's workplace. Outside the exosystem is the macrosystem. This is, essentially, the cultural and social influence on an individual, such as belief systems, material resources, customs, and lifestyles, which are embedded in each of the previous inner systems. Finally, there is the chronosystem, which involves environmental events and transitions over time. For example, adolescents who were directly involved in a major trauma such as 9/11 or hurricane Katrina will have different life experiences affecting their development than adolescents who were not directly involved.

The theories presented above provide only an introduction to understanding human behavior and, in particular, adolescent behavior. Other theories exist and contribute to the interdisciplinary approach currently used to enhance our understanding of adolescence. For a more comprehensive discussion of these theories, refer to the suggested readings list at the end of this introduction.

Adolescence in the Twentieth Century

Adolescence in and of itself is a period of human development marke by many changes, transitions, and both positive and negative behaviors. Since the study of adolescence first began in the early twentieth century, researchers have examined how particular events and issues affected adolescent attitudes and behaviors. In this third section of the introduction, we provide an overview of how events shaped the way adolescents behaved and how they dealt with particular issues. For example, in the 1920s, when the period of adolescence was officially recognized, North American youth responded with a sense of newfound freedom. They were essentially given permission to stay young and have fun while they could. The decade became known as the Roaring Twenties, with increased autonomy and freedom. An interesting effect was that many adults responded to the behaviors of the young by adopting a similar appealing lifestyle with more music, dancing, and partying. This was short-lived, however, with the Great Depression of the 1930s followed by World War II in the 1940s. Irresponsibility and the age of adolescence were put on hold during these difficult times. Many young people were forced to seek employment or to serve their country in the war. The exposure to poverty, family struggles, war, violence, and death resulted in a drive for stability and security following the war. The 1950s were a time when adults focused on ensuring this security and stability for their families. During this time, adolescents were considered to be the "silent generation" because life seemed perfect. They had only their futures upon which to focus. In North American society, getting an education, finding a good job, getting married, and raising a family were the goals for the adolescents of the fifties.

In the 1960s, there was once again disruption to stability and security with the Vietnam War and the assassinations of North American politicians and leaders. Many adolescents reacted with anger and frustration. They did not trust politicians or decision makers because they were seen as disrupting their perceived ideal world and sense of security. They held political protests to voice their views of idealism. They challenged authority and promoted peace, love, and freedom with drug use, loosening of sexual behavior, and cohabitation. This peace movement of the sixties is remembered with phrases such as "make love not war" and "reject authority." For most, there was no focus on working hard and establishing a stable career. Attending university was as much about fun and freedom from parents as it was about studying.

The sexual revolution of the 1960s lasted into the 1970s, with adolescents becoming more focused on their own needs and goals but not without further struggles. Adolescent girls and young women, aware of the opportunity differential and stereotyped careers for men and women, began the long and difficult fight for equality. The previous argument that women would have babies and be unreliable was no longer valid. Thanks to the contraceptive pill, which was introduced in the sixties, women gained control over their reproduction and the freedom to choose if and when they would have a family. Gender inequality was no longer an issue of biology. The success of the Women's Movement in the seventies and eighties resulted in many more young women attending college and university—eventually bridging the gender gap in many professions such as medicine, law, and engineering. With more women attending to their careers, and postponing childbearing or deciding to be childless, two-income families became more popular. Small families, large homes, travel, and material possessions such as the "best" home computers became the goals. This way of life has had a profound effect on children born since 1980. For example, a carryover effect from the sixties and seventies is the notion that if you want something badly enough, you can get it. Parents have become so involved in their childrens' lives, providing material possession upon material possession, that kids have come to expect it. Large screen televisions, personal computers, electronic devices, cell phones, and disposable income are common expectations among many of today's youth. The adolescents of the twenty-first century, known as the Millennials, are unique and different from adolescents of the past.

Adolescence in the Twenty-First Century

Today's adolescents have unique experiences and issues not encountered by previous generations. There are many factors contributing to this. For instance, the advances in technology have been influential in shaping the lives of adolescents today. Many carry a cell phone, an MP3 player, and have their own personal computer, enabling them to communicate with anyone—regardless of where they are. These devices also give them instant access to music, computer games, and information. Essentially, we have technologically savvy adolescents who spend much of their time alone with inanimate objects.

A second factor contributing to the uniqueness of today's adolescents is their perceived sense of entitlement. Parents have protected and given so much to their children that, once they leave home for university or work, they come to expect the same. Parents, having had to fight for rights in the sixties and seventies, have taught their children "if you want something, it's your right to have it." As university educators, we have seen firsthand the effect this has had. For example, Millennial students are often more demanding and persistent in their demands compared to previous cohorts of the eighties and nineties. A typical example is demanding an exam be rescheduled because of personal travel plans. Millennials are also more likely to have their parents involved in their post-secondary education, making calls to professors and administrators requesting information or favors for their adolescent.

A third unique factor contributing to the novel experiences of the youth of the Millennial age involves sexual freedom. That is, youth of today experience a more open sexual discourse because of significant social events including the Sexual Revolution and Women's Movement of the 1960s and 1970s, the Gay Rights Movement of the 1970s and 1980s, as well as the HIV/AIDS crisis of the 1980s and onward. Different forms of media have also played a large role in opening up knowledge and discussion about sexuality; for example, the Internet has made many sexually oriented Web sites accessible to youth despite efforts to provide filters. Some of these Web sites are informational, while others would be characterized as obscene or pornographic. Television, films, as well as magazines and books tend to involve more overt sexuality, as regulations regarding these media have been relaxed over recent decades. These changes have had an impact on social programs including more explicit and precise sexual health education in the school system—although this has involved considerable controversy. All of this cumulates in a more sexually savvy adolescent than perhaps was the case in previous generations.

The Millennial cohort is probably more aware of pregnancy and STI prevention as well as issues surrounding sexual violence—more so than previous generations. According to a recent report published by the Centers for Disease Control and Prevention (Abma, Martinez, Mosher, & Dawson, 2004), the teenage pregnancy rate has dropped from 1990 to 2000. From 1982 and 1995 to 2002, teen intercourse has decreased (i.e., there has been an increased rate of adolescent "virginity"). Among sexually active teen girls, there has been increased condom use and decreased "no protection" during intercourse, as well. All of these changes might be positive side-effects of the increased openness and more positive attitudes toward the sexuality of adolescents.

Not only has sexual behaviors of adolescents changed across the generations, but gender roles have also changed significantly. This involves the roles of girls and boys in relation to "feminine" and "masculine" traits. Gender rigidity has declined, and greater tolerance for gender variation has increased, although early adolescence is known as a time when youth are less understanding of violations of gender rules. Regardless, this has made the youth of the twentieth century more accepting of lesbian, gay, bisexual, and transgender people (Ponton & Judice, 2004). In sum, sexual behaviors, attitudes, and roles have changed dramatically for the Millennial generation and, while always an important aspect of adolescent development, these topics have become more central in adolescent research.

The introduction thus far has provided an overview of adolescence from when the term was first coined to the present. Through the twentieth century, adolescents were faced with many hurdles and issues that affected their development and overall transition from childhood to adulthood. The goal of this book is to present issues facing adolescents in the first decade of the twenty-first century. We address controversies such as adolescent use of antidepressants, alcohol consumption, and youth justice. We debate adolescent consent for abortions, mandatory HPV vaccinations, and comprehensive sex education. We also cover divorce and family disruption, body image, cyber-friendships, sex on television, sexual behavior, sexual orientation, and bullying.

These issues will shape the behaviors of tomorrow's adolescents and guide future research. As is evident from the issues listed above, this book presents adolescence as an interdisciplinary topic. We have selected issues that can be used in a variety of disciplines and courses.

References and Suggested Readings

Abma, J.C., Martinez, G.M., Mosher, W.D., & Dawson, B.S. (2004). Teenagers in the United States: Sexual activity, contraceptive use, and childbearing, 2002. National Center for Health Statistics. *Vital Health Stat* 23(24).

Arnett, J. (2004). *Adolescence and emerging adulthood*, 2nd edition. New Jersey: Prentice Hall.

Bandura, A. (2005). The evolution of social cognitive theory. In Ken G. Smith & Michael A. Hitt (Eds.). *Great minds in management. The process of theory development* (pp. 9–35). New York: Oxford University Press.

Bronfenbrenner, U. (1979). *The ecology of human development*. Cambridge, MA: Harvard University Press.

Elkind, D. (1967). Egocentrism in adolescence. *Child Development*, 38, 1025–1034.

Elkind, D. (1978). Understanding the young adolescent. *Adolescence*, 13, 127–134.

Erikson, E. (1959). Identity and the life cycle. *Psychological Issues*, 1, 1–171.

Freud, A. (1958). Adolescence. *Psychoanalytic Study of the Child*, 13, 255–278.

Freud, S. (1938). *An outline of psychoanalysis*. London: Hogarth Press.

Hall, G.S. (1904). *Adolescence*. New York: Appleton.

Lerner, R. Brown, J., & Kier, C. (2005). *Adolescence: Development, diversity, context, and application*. Toronto: Prentice Hall.

Mead, M. (1928). *Coming of age in Samoa*. New York: Morrow.

Ponton, L.E., & Judice, S. (2004). Typical adolescent sexual development. *Child & Adolescent Psychiatric Clinics of North America*, 13(3), 497–511.

Santrock, J. (2005). *Adolescence*, 10th edition. New York: McGraw-Hill.

Steinberg, L. (2004). *Adolescence*. New York: McGraw-Hill.

Internet References . . .

Canadian Health Network

Administered by the Public Health Agency of Canada, this Web site has sections dedicated to various demographic groups; of interest is the section on youth. Topics are presented in an A-to-Z index and include areas such as mental and physical health, sexuality, violence prevention, healthy eating, and active living.

http://www.canadian-health-network.ca

Canadian Paediatric Society

This Web site, from the national association of paediatricians, includes several publications regarding adolescent health issues including adolescent dieting, pregnancy, emergency contraception, sexual abuse, and eating disorders, among other topics.

http://www.cps.ca/english/publications/AdolesHealth.htm

Centre for Addiction and Mental Health

The Centre for Addiction and Mental Health (CAMH) is Canada's leading addiction and mental health teaching hospital as well as a highly respected research institute. This page is the portal to CAMH's Child, Youth, and Family Resources section and provides information on CAMH's health promotion and substance use prevention programs and products as well as treatment programs and research studies. This includes links to their research and "best advice" papers.

**http://www.camh.net/About_Addiction_Mental_Health/Child_Youth_
Family_Resources/index.html**

National Institute on Alcohol Abuse and Alcoholism

National Institute on Alcohol Abuse and Alcoholism is part of the National Institutes of Health. They provide information on alcohol and its related health issues as well as pamphlets, brochures, and posters. The Underage Drinking Research Initiative page provides statistics on underage drinking, research reports and surveys, print resources, and literature reviews regarding underage drinking.

**http://www.niaaa.nih.gov
http://www.niaaa.nih.gov/AboutNIAAA/NIAAASponsoredPrograms/
underage.htm**

National Abortion Federation

This Web site, an association of abortion providers in North America, presents general information, research, and publications about abortion.

http://www.prochoice.org

National Right to Life

The National Right to Life Committee is an organization that opposes abortion, euthanasia, and infanticide. The Web site provides information on relevant legislation and reports, and is updated with current writings opposing abortion.

http://www.nrlc.org

Adolescent Health

*A*dolescent physical and psychological health has important implications for future well-being. An adolescent who is both mentally and physically fit has a better chance to develop into a strong, productive, and happy adult. There are a multitude of adolescent health-related issues that could have an influence on the healthy development of a teen. In the following part, six issues that relate to different aspects of adolescent health are examined.

- Should Adolescents Be Taking Selective Serotonin Reuptake Inhibitors (SSRIs) for Depression?

- Should Adolescents Be Allowed to Drink Alcohol?

- Should Parental Consent Be Required for Adolescents Seeking Abortions?

- Do Boys Worry about an Ideal Body Image as Much as Girls Do?

- Should the Human Papillomavirus (HPV) Vaccine Be Mandatory for Early Adolescent Girls?

- Is the Use of Nicotine Replacement Therapy (NRT) an Appropriate Cessation Aid for Adolescents Wishing to Quit Smoking?

ISSUE 1

Should Adolescents Be Taking Selective Serotonin Reuptake Inhibitors (SSRIs) for Depression?

YES: Christopher J. Kratochvil et al., from "Selective Serotonin Reuptake Inhibitors in Pediatric Depression," *Journal of Child and Adolescent Psychopharmacology* (vol. 16, no. 1/2, 2006)

NO: Tamar Wohlfarth et al., from "Antidepressants Use in Children and Adolescents and the Risk of Suicide," *European Neuropsychopharmacology* (vol. 16, 2006)

ISSUE SUMMARY

YES: Christopher Kratochvil M.D., an associate professor of psychiatry at the University of Nebraska Medical Center, and colleagues in the United States, examined recent data from meta-analyses and re-assessed the risk/benefit relationship associated with the use of SSRIs for pediatric depression. They conclude that SSRIs play a role in the treatment of pediatric depression.

NO: Tamar Wohlfarth, a clinical assessor, and colleagues in the Netherlands assessed antidepressant use in pediatric patients and report an increased risk for events related to suicidality among those taking antidepressants. They caution the use of all SSRIs and NSRAs in the pediatric population.

An estimated 4–8% of adolescents suffer from depression, and that the lifetime prevalence for major depressive disorder (MDD) by adolescence ranges between 15 and 20% (American Academy of Child and Adolescent Psychiatry, 1998). Depressive disorders are generally chronic among adolescents with an average episode lasting eight months. Unfortunately, adolescents with clinical depression often go untreated, and untreated depression is a major risk factor for substance abuse, school failure, impaired relationships, and personality disorders. Depression is also the strongest predictor of suicidal ideation, attempts, and completions; completions now being the third leading cause of death in 15–19-year-olds (Anderson, 2002).

Given the serious nature of the disorder for adolescents, early recognition and effective treatment is crucial. Effective treatments for adolescents with depressive disorders most often include psychotherapy and antidepressant medications. Studies have indicated that a combination of both treatments is most effective, although studies have also found antidepressants alone to convey almost as much benefit as the combined treatment.

Antidepressants introduced since 1990, especially selective serotonin re-uptake inhibitors (SSRIs) have become a preferred treatment option for adolescents with depression. Compared to their predecessors, the tricyclic antidepressants (TCAs), SSRIs such as fluoxetine (Prozac), sertraline (Zoloft), paroxetine (Paxil), and citalopram (Celexa) are better tolerated, have a lower frequency of cardiac events and sudden death, fewer anticholonergic effects (e.g., dry mouth), and superior efficacy (Hamrin & Scahill, 2005). SSRIs work by blocking the reuptake of serotonin (5HT), a neurotransmitter in the central nervous system involved in a range of physiological and behavioral functions including sleep, wakefulness, appetite, emotional response, and thought process. Although the etiology of depression is unknown, serotonin is believed to play an important role: Depression may be associated with reduced serotoninergic function. Therefore, antidepressants such as SSRIs appear to be effective in treating the disorder. However, the safety of prescribing antidepressants to adolescents has been the subject of increasing concern. Specifically, these drugs may be associated with an increased risk of suicidal ideation and behavior (suicidality) in pediatric patients.

The controversy about the safety and efficacy of antidepressants, particularly SSRIs and newer antidepressants such as selective norepinephrine reuptake inhibitors (SNRIs), began in June 2003. At that time, the U.S. Food and Drug Administration (FDA) conducted an investigation of antidepressants, including citalopram, fluoxetine, fluvoxamine (Luvox), nefazodone (Serzone), sertraline, and paroxetine. The meta-analysis of 24 SRI trials resulted in the FDA issuing a black box warning describing an increased risk of worsening of depression and suicidality for all current and future antidepressants used in those under the age of 18. The FDA investigation resulted in only fluoxetine receiving approval for major depression in children and adolescents. Of note, however, is that of the data reviewed by the FDA, no completed suicides were reported in any of the randomized controlled trials (RCTs) of adolescents taking any of the above medications.

The controversial black-box warning describing the possible link between use of the antidepressants and suicide in adolescents has since led to an active debate regarding the appropriate treatment of depression in younger patients. How safe and effective are SSRIs? Do antidepressants, such as SSRIs, increase the risk of suicidal behavior? Ecological studies provide mixed evidence on the risks and benefits of SSRIs—some show that increases in SSRI use are associated with reductions in suicide rates, while others show the opposite to be true.

In the selections that follow, Christopher Kratochvil et al. provide clear evidence for prescribing SSRIs for moderate to severe depressive disorders. They argue that the available research does not support the hypothesis that the risks of taking SSRIs outweigh the benefits. On the other hand, Tamar Wohlfarth and colleagues are firm in their argument against the use of SSRIs among adolescents due to the increased risk of suicidality and other related behaviors.

YES  Christopher J. Kratochvil et al.

Selective Serotonin Reuptake Inhibitors in Pediatric Depression: Is the Balance Between Benefits and Risks Favorable?

Introduction

The use of the selective serotonin reuptake inhibitors (SSRIs) has grown significantly in the treatment of pediatric major depressive disorder (MDD), owing, in part, to efficacy data in adults, ease of dosing, and perception of good tolerability and safety in overdose. However, concerns have arisen intermittently over the past decade regarding the safety of the SSRIs in the treatment of MDD. Whereas in adults the well-documented efficacy of SSRIs ensures a favorable risk/benefit balance, the paucity of information in the pediatric population has made it difficult for clinicians and regulators to reach the same conclusion in youths. The recent availability of meta-analyses completed by regulatory agencies of published and unpublished industry-sponsored trials, epidemiological studies of youth suicide and medication use, and the Treatment for Adolescents with Depression Study (TADS) (TADS Team 2004) have expanded our knowledge-base regarding the efficacy and safety of SSRIs in young patients. Based on currently available data, we provide in this paper a critical discussion of potential risks and benefits of SSRIs in the treatment of children and adolescents with depression.

Background and Context

Fluoxetine, the first SSRI approved in the United States for the treatment of MDD, was made commercially available in 1987. As early as 1991, the U.S. Food and Drug Administration (FDA) held a public meeting to address concerns that fluoxetine was potentially contributing to suicidal behaviors in adults. . . . Subsequently, reviews of clinical trials submitted to the FDA involving nine antidepressants and 48,000 subjects (77 of whom completed suicide) did not find a statistically significant difference in the risk

From *Journal of Child and Adolescent Psychopharmacology*, vol. 16, no. 1/2, March 2006, excerpts from pp. 11–24. Copyright © 2006 by Mary Ann Liebert, Inc. Reprinted by permission via Rightslink.

for suicide or suicide attempt between SSRIs and placebo, or between SSRIs and other types of antidepressants (Khan et al. 2003).

The early pediatric literature on the treatment of MDD with SSRIs was primarily limited to case reports and small, open-label trials. It wasn't until 1997 that the first randomized, double-blind, placebo-controlled trial showing the efficacy of fluoxetine in children and adolescents (age, 7–18 years) with MDD was published (Emslie et al. 1997). In this National Institute of Mental Health (NIMH)-funded study, 56% of the subjects in the fluoxetine group had improved at the end of the 8-week trial compared with 33% in the placebo group ($p < 0.05$). In 1998, based, in part, on that trial, the practice guidelines published by the American Academy of Child and Adolescent Psychiatry (AACAP) recommended SSRIs as initial therapy in the acute phase of MDD (Birmaher et al. 1998). This was followed by an increase in prescribing SSRIs for youths. . . .

With the advent of the FDA Modernization Act (U.S. Congress 1997), . . . the number of industry-sponsored MDD studies in children and adolescents grew (Emslie et al. 2002; Wagner et al. 2004). . . . Following two positive randomized clinical trials involving 315 youths 8–18 years of age (Emslie et al. 2002; Emslie et al. 1997), the FDA approved fluoxetine for the treatment of pediatric MDD in January 2003. Fluoxetine remains the only drug that is FDA-approved for the treatment of depression in children and adolescents. . . .

Then, in mid-2003, the Medicine and Health Care Products Regulatory Agency the (MHRA) of the British Department of Health issued a report concluding that paroxetine was contraindicated in patients with MDD under the age of 18. . . .

The MHRA notice proved to be the first in a series of notices by both the FDA and MHRA expressing concerns regarding antidepressants in the treatment of pediatric depression. It also marked the beginning of extensive analyses conducted by both regulatory agencies and two public hearings in 2004 regarding SSRIs and suicidality, this time with a focus on the pediatric population.

In December 2003, the MHRA completed a summary analysis of their data regarding antidepressant use in pediatric depression. They reported that there was no evidence of efficacy for any SSRI in pediatric depression, except for fluoxetine. Additionally, the MHRA described a rate of adverse events that exceeded those of placebo in many trials, with specific concerns regarding suicidality. . . .

In February 2004, the FDA convened a joint meeting of their Psychopharmacologic Advisory Committee and Pediatric Subcommittee of the Anti-Infective Drugs Advisory Committee in order to evaluate the use of antidepressants in children and adolescents. . . . The FDA was particularly concerned with examining the adverse events data regarding the emergence or occurrence of suicide-related events. . . . In the course of this review, it became apparent that there were marked differences in methods of data collection, coding, and analyses of adverse event data across studies. This necessitated a review and reclassification of the suicidality adverse events in order to accurately assess the available data. In March 2004, as these analyses were being conducted, the FDA issued a public health advisory, as an interim step, asking manufacturers of 10 different antidepressant drugs to include in their label a warning section recommending close scrutiny for worsening depression or emergence of suicidality in adult and pediatric patients treated with these agents (FDA 2004a).

In September 2004, the results of a meta-analysis of 24 controlled clinical trials of nine antidepressants in approximately 4400 pediatric patients were presented at a public hearing. . . . Although no completed suicides occurred in these trials, the cumulative risk for suicidality when adverse events were collected by spontaneous report was approximately 4% on active medication versus approximately 2% on placebo. . . . When data was systematically collected utilizing rating scales at baseline and routinely throughout the trials, the overall rates of treatment-emergent suicidality and suicidal worsening were higher than was reported using spontaneous adverse event reports, but there was no difference between the rates in the placebo and active drug groups (Hammad 2004).

Based on the recommendations of the committee, the FDA took the following four actions (FDA 2004b). They issued a "black box" warning that antidepressant use in children was accompanied by an increased risk for suicidality. . . . Secondly, they required a medication guide to accompany all prescriptions. . . . Thirdly, they established guidelines for frequency of monitoring when initiating antidepressants. . . . And finally, they initiated unit-of-use packaging to ensure that every patient receives the medication guide each time a prescription is filled.

The findings regarding suicidality have forced clinicians to carefully consider the existing data on (1) the efficacy of antidepressants in this population, (2) the potential harm of these medications, and (3) what the implications are for the treatment of children and adolescents in their own practice.

Efficacy Data

In 2004, the FDA reviewed both published and unpublished data on the efficacy of SSRIs in pediatric depression and concluded that only 3 (two fluoxetine and one citalopram) of 15 pediatric MDD trials showed evidence of efficacy, defined as a statistically significant ($p < 0.05$) superiority of active medication over placebo on the primary outcome measure. . . . Three other trials were believed to provide some suggestion of potential benefit, but they did not meet FDA guidelines for a "positive" efficacy study. The trial of paroxetine was positive on several secondary endpoints, though not on the primary outcome, while the two trials of sertraline showed a positive primary endpoint only when their data were pooled and analyzed.

These data provide support for the FDA indication of fluoxetine for pediatric depression. The summary of these data also highlight the fact that the majority of studies conducted to date on pediatric depression were unpublished and that all of the unpublished studies were negative studies (i.e., did not demonstrate a benefit of active medication compared to placebo on the primary outcome measure).

Published Versus Unpublished Data

Clinicians and the general public receive their information on clinical trials through published data. A meta-analysis assessed conclusions based on published data and contrasted those to conclusions reached by combining published and unpublished data.

Five published, acute, randomized, placebo-controlled trials of SSRIs in pediatric depression were compared with all unpublished data. . . . All of the fluoxetine trials had been published, and two trials (Emslie et al. 2002; Emslie et al. 1997) supported its efficacy in pediatric major depression, suggesting a favorable risk/benefit profile. The published results of one paroxetine trial and two sertraline trials suggested equivocal or weakly positive efficacy which, in the case of paroxetine, was not supported by two other then-unpublished trials (Berard et al. 2006). Likewise, efficacy of citalopram was supported by one published trial (Wagner et al. 2004) but not by an unpublished one. . . . For venlafaxine and mirtazapine, two unpublished trials for each compound did not demonstrate efficacy. . . .

The discrepancies between published and unpublished data highlight the potential for biased reporting of positive versus negative results. Whittington et al. (2005) expressed concerns that clinical guideline development and clinical decisions regarding treatment are largely dependent on the evidence base established through peer-reviewed journals and that non-publication of trials could lead to erroneous recommendations for treatment.

TADS Data

The Treatment for Adolescents with Depression Study (TADS) is an NIMH-sponsored multisite trial comparing fluoxetine, cognitive behavioral therapy (CBT), their combination, and placebo in 439 adolescents with a primary diagnosis of major depression (TADS Team 2004). . . . TADS is significant in that it was the largest acute treatment study of depression in youths. Additionally, TADS had a psychosocial treatment arm, both stand alone and in combination with fluoxetine, which had not been included in previous antidepressant trials.

TADS had two primary outcome measures, the scalar Children's Depression Rating Scale—Revised (CDRS-R; Poznanski and Hartmut 1996) total score and the end-of-treatment response rate defined by a categorical Clinical Global Impression—Improvement (CGI-I) score of much or very much improved. CDRS-R adjusted mean (standard deviation) scores at baseline, week 6, and week 12 were: CBT with fluoxetine 60.79 (4.85), 38.10 (7.78), 33.79 (8.24); fluoxetine alone 58.94 (4.00), 39.80 (7.37), 36.30 (8.18); CBT alone 59.64 (4.52), 44.63 (8.30), 42.06 (9.18); placebo 61.18 (4.27), 44.90 (7.32), 41.77 (7.99). Pairwise contrasts on the CDRS-R regression slope coefficients showed that combination treatment with fluoxetine and CBT was statistically superior to placebo ($p = 0.001$), CBT ($p = 0.001$), and fluoxetine ($p = 0.02$), whereas fluoxetine alone was statistically superior to CBT ($p = 0.01$) but not placebo ($p = 0.10$). Supporting analyses performed on the week 12 CDRS-R adjusted means demonstrated fluoxetine with CBT ($p = 0.001$) and fluoxetine alone ($p = 0.002$) to be superior to placebo, whereas CBT alone was not ($p = 0.97$). Fluoxetine with CBT was superior to CBT alone ($p = 0.001$) but not to fluoxetine alone ($p = 0.13$), whereas fluoxetine alone was superior to CBT alone ($p = 0.001$). The other primary efficacy outcome measure, the CGI–I-defined rates of response, showed that more patients were responders to combination therapy (71%) or fluoxetine (61%) than to CBT (43%) or placebo (35%; $p \leq 0.01$) (TADS Team 2004).

Thus, on one of the two primary analyses, fluoxetine approached statistical significance compared to placebo, although it was significantly better than CBT. However, the preponderance of the evidence from the other positive primary analysis and supporting analyses, using end-of-treatment CDRS-R scores, supports the use of fluoxetine alone in decreasing depressive symptoms.

The clinical impact of treatment on outcome was evaluated by calculating the effect size and the number needed to treat (NNT) to each additional responder, based on the adjusted means. The effect size derived from the CDRS-R was 0.98 for fluoxetine with CBT, 0.68 for fluoxetine alone, and –0.03 for CBT alone. Effect sizes from the odds ratio (OR) for the dichotomized CGI-I were 0.84 for fluoxetine with CBT, 0.58 for fluoxetine alone, and 0.20 for CBT alone. The NNT for the dichotomized CGI-I for fluoxetine and CBT was 3 (95% Confidence Interval [CI], 2–4), for fluoxetine alone was 4 (95% CI, 3–8), and for CBT alone 12 (95% CI, 5–23). Thus, the largest study to date of adolescent depression provided clear evidence of fluoxetine's efficacy in adolescents with moderate to severe depression.

Summary
Based upon these clinical trials, fluoxetine does appear to have efficacy in the treatment of pediatric depression, with the majority of the trials demonstrating positive results. . . .

Safety Data

Risk of Treatment
In September 2004, when the FDA presented results of their meta-analysis of 25 trials plus TADS, safety data were presented in addition to the efficacy data (Hammad 2004). In order to make the clinical trial datasets more uniform with respect to adverse event reporting, an independent team of experts utilized a novel approach developed by researchers at Columbia University to evaluate and recode all adverse events for suicidal and self-injurious behaviors (suicide attempt, preparatory acts, suicidal ideation, and so forth). Following reclassification, 78 of the approximately 4400 subjects from these datasets (1.7%) were coded as experiencing either suicidal behavior ($n = 33$) or suicidal ideation ($n = 45$). Once a uniform

classification was applied, relative risks for suicidal ideation and behavior were calculated by drug and by study indication. . . . There were no completed suicides, and only venlafaxine and fluoxetine in TADS exhibited a statistically significant signal for suicidality (suicide attempts or suicidal ideation). The overall relative risk (RR) for suicidality was 1.66 (95% CI; 1.02, 2.68) for MDD trials and 1.95 (1.28, 2.98) for all trials, all indications. The authors of the analysis concluded that: "Although the difference is small, it seems likely that the effect is real, because the findings were statistically significant in aggregate and are consistent across multiple studies of various agents" (Brent 2004).

This issue can be analyzed in terms of "risk difference," which provides an estimate of the absolute increase in risk of the event of interest attributable to treatment, in this case, suicidality. This is calculated by subtracting the risk in the placebo group from the risk in the active drug group. The overall risk difference for the SSRIs in the MDD trials is approximately 2%. In other words, 2 patients of 100 treated with an SSRI for major depression would be expected to have an increase in suicidality during short-term treatment attributable to the drug. Suicidality, when it did occur, was primarily ideation, with only a minority of events involving actual suicide attempts (27 suicide attempts, 6 "preparatory actions)," and 45 suicidal ideation events). Additional risk beyond that is inherent in the disorder being treated (Hammad 2004).

In addition to an increase in the risk of suicidality, SSRIs are almost twice as likely as placebo to cause increased agitation and hostility during acute treatment. . . . At this time, it is unclear whether the increased risk for suicidality associated with these medications is mediated by the agitation and hostility symptoms, but it is important for patients and families to be aware of this potential.

FDA Conclusions Regarding Risk

The advisory committee to the FDA concluded that the adverse events reported voluntarily during clinical trials in aggregate did indicate an increased risk of treatment-emergent suicidality. Although there was variability in the adverse event data, the committee was unable to conclude that any single antidepressant was free of risk. The committee suggested additional research is needed to further delineate the risks and benefits of these drugs in pediatric patients with psychiatric illness. . . . Long-term trials using placebo and fluoxetine as controls . . . would better inform clinicians how to diagnose and treat pediatric depression. The risks associated with pharmacological and non-pharmacological interventions, as well as the risks of not treating depressed children and adolescents, should also be assessed (FDA 2004b).

Since the FDA's October 2004 "black box" warning and additional recommendations regarding antidepressant use in children, other regulatory bodies have also released warnings. In April 2005, the European Medicines Agency issued a press release regarding their review of SSRI and SNRI medicines in children and adolescents. . . . They recommended: ". . . strong warnings across the whole of the European Union to doctors and parents about these risks. . . .

TADS Data Pertaining to Risk

TADS provided a systematic approach to collecting data on suicidality, beginning at baseline and continuing to all subsequent endpoints, which allows for a longer-term assessment of the role of various treatments on suicide. At baseline, clinically significant suicidal thinking was present in 29% of the sample, as measured by the CDRS-R suicide item and the Suicidal Ideation Questionnaire-Junior High School Version (SIQ-Jr; Reynolds 1987). Suicidality declined significantly in all four treatment groups with fluoxetine plus CBT showing the greatest reduction ($p = 0.02$). There were no completed suicides in the course of the study but 24 (5.5%) of the 439 TADS patients experienced a suicide-related event. Seven (7) of the 24 suicide-related events were suicide attempts (1.6% of the total sample). Four (4) of the attempts were by patients assigned to fluoxetine and CBT, 2 to fluoxetine alone, and 1 to CBT alone. None of the subjects taking placebo attempted suicide.

Harm-related events, which included thoughts or behaviors related to harm of self as well as harm to others, occurred in 11.9% of those assigned to fluoxetine alone, 8.4% fluoxetine with CBT, 4.5% CBT alone, and 5.4% placebo.

Overall, suicidality decreased with treatment. Improvement was greatest for those receiving combination treatment and least for those receiving fluoxetine alone. It is important to note that, though fluoxetine did not appear to increase suicidal ideation, the harm-related adverse events did occur more frequently in fluoxetine-treated patients (TADS Team 2004).

Epidemiological and Observational Data

Although no causality can be determined, non-experimental studies using community or observational data offer a perspective complementary to the information from controlled clinical trials of antidepressant use in children and adolescents.

Whereas the pediatric use of antidepressants has substantially increased throughout the previous decade, the overall youth suicide rates had been declining. During 1992–2001, for example, the overall suicide rate among persons 10–19 years of age declined from 6.2 to 4.6 per 100,000 population (CDC 2004). A significant inverse relationship was also found between regional rates of antidepressant medication use and suicide rates of 10- to 19-year-old youths in the United States in 1990–2000. Each 1% increase in antidepressant use was associated with a decrease of 0.23 suicides per 100,000 adolescents per year.

Valuck et al. assessed antidepressant use in youth by analyzing a large database of insurance claims from both commercial and Medicaid plans. They examined claims filed (January 1997 to March 2003) from various regions across the United States on adolescents newly diagnosed with MDD who had at least 6 months of follow-up data (Valuck et al. 2004). The database of 24,119 adolescents revealed crude suicide attempt rates, ranging from 0.0% to 2.3%. Treatment with SSRIs, . . . other antidepressants, . . . or multiple antidepressants . . . after index MDD diagnosis resulted in no statistically significant increase in risk of suicide attempt. Thus, whereas the SSRIs were associated with a numerically higher risk of suicide attempt . . . the increase failed to reach statistical significance. Treatment with an antidepressant medication for at least 180 days reduced the likelihood of a suicide attempt, as compared to treatment courses of less than 55 days. . . . The authors concluded that antidepressants had no statistically significant effects on the likelihood of suicide attempts.

A review of National Vital Statistics from the Centers for Disease Control and Prevention analyzed records of all U.S. individuals at the counts level who committed suicide between 1996 and 1998, examining the association between antidepressant prescription and suicide rate. . . . The data demonstrated lower suicide rates in association with increased use of selective serotonin reuptake inhibitors and new-generation non-SSRIs, compared to TCA use. Suicide rates tended to be higher in counties with larger proportions of TCA prescriptions. As the authors point out, this type of data cannot demonstrate causal relationships because the higher number of TCA prescriptions may simply be a marker for counties with more limited access to mental health care. The higher rates of suicides with TCA prescriptions may also reflect the greater toxicity in overdose of TCAs. After adjusting for age, gender, race, income, and county-to-county variability in suicide rates, the overall relationship between all prescribed antidepressants and suicide rate was not statistically significant ($p = 0.14$).

Jick et al. conducted an evaluation of antidepressant prescriptions utilizing a matched case control design based on patients' prescriptions/diagnoses in the U.K. General Practice Research Database (GPRD), 1993–1999 (Jick et al. 2004). Data were collected on patients 10–69 years of age treated with amitriptyline, fluoxetine, paroxetine, and dothiepin (reference group), assessing cases of nonfatal suicide behavior (ideation or attempts) ($n = 555$), suicides ($n = 17$), and controls ($n = 2062$) without suicidal behavior. Compared to dothiepin, there was no statistically significant difference in suicidality with one antidepressant compared to another, with a range for the relative risk (RR) for nonfatal suicide behavior of 0.83–1.29. Results were similar for patients 10–19 years of age, although the sample of adolescent cases was small. There were no suicides in the 10–19 year olds prescribed medication in this study population. However, in reviewing the entire GPRD population from 1993 to 1999, 15 persons in this age group had committed suicide, none of whom had received an antidepressant drug.

Jick et al.'s evaluation of the time-course of suicidal events is also of clinical interest. The RR of nonfatal suicidal behavior/suicide was highest for patients within 1–9 days of the antidepressant being prescribed (*versus* 90 days or more). The RR for nonfatal suicidal behavior during this earlier time period was 4.07 (95% CI, 2.89–5.74), whereas the RR for suicide was 38.0 (95% CI, 6.2–231). Although this could indicate an exacerbation of suicidality during the initiation of treatment, it could also be related to the acuity that prompted the initiation of the treatment. It has been reported, even prior to the antidepressant era, that people were most likely to commit suicide as they were coming out of a depressive episode.

Also, though it has been hypothesized that abrupt discontinuation of antidepressants may play a role in exacerbation of symptoms and suicidality, there was no statistically significant association between discontinuation of an antidepressant and nonfatal suicidal behavior.

Another way to determine whether SSRIs are implicated in completed suicides is through toxicological analysis of individuals dying from suicide. A study of suicide in more than 5000 adults found that, most often, antidepressants had not been taken immediately before death, even though the majority of the persons had been depressed. A study of 14,857 suicides and 26,422 other deaths in Sweden (Isacsson et al. 2005) found that none of the 15 suicides below the age of 15 years had an SSRI detected on toxicology. In 15- to 19-year-old suicide victims, SSRIs had a lower relative risk in suicides compared with non-SSRIs. These findings do not support the suggestion that SSRIs are triggering suicides in adults or youth.

In a study of 49 adolescent suicides in Utah, 24% had been prescribed antidepressants, but none had tested positive for SSRIs at the time of death (Gray et al. 2003). In a postmortem study conducted on 66 suicides among persons under 18 years of age in New York City from 1993 through 1998 (Leon et al. 2004), 54 (81.8%) had serum toxicological analysis for antidepressants and an injury-death interval of 3 days or less. Imipramine was detected in 2 victims and fluoxetine in another 2 (total 10%). None of the other 90% of suicides had antidepressants detected. . . .

Risk of Nontreatment

When weighing the potential risks and benefits of treatment, it is also important to consider the risk of not treating MDD. Suicide is the third-leading cause of death among adolescents 15–19 years of age, and fourth-leading cause of death among 10- to 14-year-olds (Anderson 2002). . . .

Weissman et al. also found an elevated risk of suicide and co-morbidity in long-term follow-up studies of depression. During a period spanning approximately 10 years between adolescence and early adulthood, they estimated a 5-fold increased likelihood of suicide attempt associated with pediatric depression (Weissman et al. 1999a; Weissman et al. 1999b). Prepubertal children with an earlier age of MDD onset are also at increased risk for substance abuse, conduct disorder, overall impaired functioning, and need for long-term psychiatric and medical services (Weissman et al. 1999b). Clinical outcomes in adulthood of adolescent onset MDD demonstrated a high rate of suicide (7.7%) and a 5-fold increase for a first suicide attempt (Weissman et al. 1999a).

Unfortunately, the available treatment interventions have limited data on acute efficacy and unproven effectiveness in improving the long-term outcome of the disorder. Nonetheless, fluoxetine remains the most effective acute intervention, either alone or in combination with psychotherapy, for decreasing depressive symptoms in adolescents suffering from moderate to severe depression. However, specialized psychotherapy alone does not seem to be a valid therapeutic option for these moderately to severely depressed patients (TADS Team 2004).

Summary

Analyses of suicidality adverse events collected in the pediatric antidepressant trials have demonstrated an elevation in suicidality when placebo was compared to active medication. Systematic and repeated assessments of suicidality using symptom rating scales, however, have not supported this finding. In fact, when these data were collected in TADS at baseline, 6 weeks, and 12 weeks, all four treatment groups demonstrated a decline in suicidality, with the greatest decline occurring in the group receiving fluoxetine with CBT. Also of interest are the epidemiological and observational data, which demonstrate an increase in the use of SSRIs in the pediatric population but no corresponding increase in completed suicides. In fact, studies have generally identified an inverse correlation, both nationally and regionally with suicide and antidepressant usage.

Discussion

. . . Considerable evidence supports the use of fluoxetine for pediatric MDD. However, even fluoxetine carries risks, which must be considered in the risk/benefit analysis and treatment planning. The TADS Team concluded that: "The combination of fluoxetine with CBT offered the most favorable tradeoff between benefit and risk for adolescents with major depressive disorder" (TADS Team 2004). Combination therapy may be the best treatment for teenagers with major depression, especially when the depression is moderate to severe and there is a history of past or present suicidality. Whereas CBT alone was not better than placebo, and, by most measures, was inferior to combination treatment or fluoxetine alone, it proved to be a useful adjunct to pharmacotherapy. CBT also demonstrated usefulness, both alone and in combination with fluoxetine, in the reduction of suicidal thoughts and behaviors. Because nearly 40% of depressed teens do not respond to fluoxetine and others aren't able to tolerate it, treatments other than fluoxetine should continue to be studied and be made available.

What We Still Do Not Know

Despite a recent expansion of data, our knowledge-base about the efficacy and safety of SSRIs remains limited, with many unanswered questions:

- Are there clinically significant differences between prepubertal and adolescent depression with respect to antidepressant treatment efficacy and safety? If so, what are the underlying causes of such differences?
- Are there clinically significant differences among SSRIs and similarly related antidepressants with respect to efficacy and/or safety?

- What accounts for the apparent discrepancy between the efficacy of SSRIs in adult depression and the much weaker and inconsistent data in the pediatric population? Is pediatric depression a substantively different condition than depression in adults? . . .
- How can one best interpret "negative" trials of antidepressants? It is important to note that negative studies do not necessarily prove a lack of efficacy. . . .
- Are there real differences in safety of SSRIs between children/adolescents and adults? Why is an association between SSRIs and suicidality detectable in pediatric data, but not in the much larger database of adult studies? Will closer examination of adult data reveal that youth are not specifically at risk and the risk regarding suicidality is ubiquitous across developmental stages?
- Which subgroup of depressed youths are the best candidates for antidepressant treatment and which ones are likely to respond to non-pharmacological interventions?
- What is the most effective way to monitor patients for safety during treatment with antidepressants? . . .
- How can a clinician distinguish suicidality that is causally related to the treatment delivered from suicidality that emerges as a result of the underlying illness? . . .

The recent concerns about SSRIs have illustrated the value of having conducted 15 randomized clinical trials in pediatric depression in a relatively short period of time. Without data from these trials, no assessment of benefit and risk could have been even attempted. However, studies with small sample sizes, such as those conducted to date, will never answer important safety questions where the outcomes of interest occur infrequently. It is not practical to design a randomized clinical trial with suicide as an endpoint, owing to the sample size and duration of a study necessary to evaluate the risk of such an uncommon event. Moreover, establishing relative risk by drug, drug class, subgrouping (e.g., age, gender, disorder) and understanding some aspect of mechanism (e.g., activation) requires very large samples. Hence, practical clinical trials (March et al. 2005) are essential if we are to learn more about predictors and management of risk. It is extraordinary that no one has risen to this challenge, to address this significant public health issue, and advocates for depressed youths shouldn't avoid saying so.

References

Anderson RN: Deaths: Leading causes for 2000. Natl Vital Stat Rep 50:1–85, 2002.

Berard R, Fong R, Carpenter DJ, Thomason C, Wilkinson C: An international, multicenter, placebo-controlled trial of paroxetine in adolescents with major depressive disorder. J Child Adolesc Psychopharmacol 16: 2006.

Birmaher B, Brent DA, Benson RS: Summary of the practice parameters for the assessment and treatment of children and adolescents with depressive disorders. J Am Acad Child Adolesc Psychiatry 37:1234–1238, 1998.

Brent DA: Antidepressants and pediatric depression—the risk of doing nothing. N Engl J Med 351:1598–1601, 2004.

CDC: Methods of suicide among persons aged 10–19 years—United States, 1992–2001. Morb Mortal Wkly Rep 53:471–474, 2004.

Emslie GJ, Heiligenstein JH, Wagner KD, Hoog SL, Ernest DE, Brown E, Nilsson M, Jacobson JG: Fluoxetine for acute treatment of depression in children and adolescents: A placebo-controlled, randomized clinical trial. J Am Acad Child Adolesc Psychiatry 41:1205–1215, 2002.

Emslie GJ, Rush AJ, Weinberg WA, Kowatch RA, Hughes CW, Carmody T, Rintelmann J: A double-blind, randomized, placebo-controlled trial of fluoxetine in children and adolescents with depression. Arch Gen Psychiatry 54:1031–1037, 1997.

Gray D, Moskos M, Keller T: Utah Youth Suicide Study New Findings. Santa Fe, New Mexico, Annual Meeting of the American Association of Suicidology, April 23–26, 2003 (abstract).

Hammad TA: Results of the Analysis of Suicidality in Pediatric Trials of Newer Antidepressants. Psychopharmacology Drugs Advisory Committee and the Pediatric Advisory Committee, September 13–14, 2004. . .

Isacsson G, Holmgren P, Ahlner J: Selective serotonin reuptake inhibitor antidepressants and the risk of suicide: A controlled forensic database study of 14,837 suicides. Acta Psychiatr Scand 111:286–290, 2005.

Jick H, Kaye JA, Jick SS: Antidepressants and the risk of suicidal behaviors. JAMA 292:338–343, 2004.

Khan A, Khan S, Kolts R, Brown WA: Suicide rates in clinical trials of SSRIs, other antidepressants, and placebo: Analysis of FDA reports. Am J Psychiatry 160:790–792, 2003.

Leon AC, Marzuk PM, Tardiff K, Teress JJ: Paroxetine, other antidepressants, and youth suicide in New York City: 1993 through 1998. J Clin Psychiatry 65:915–918, 2004.

March JS, Silva SG, Compton S, Shapiro M, Califf R, Krishnan R: The case for practical clinical trials in psychiatry. Am J Psychiatry 162:836–846, 2005.

Poznanski EO, Hartmut BM: Children's Depression Rating Scale—Revised (CDRS-R). Los Angeles, Western Psychological Services, 1996.

Reynolds WM: Professional Manual for the Suicidal Ideation Questionnaire. Odessa Florida, Psychological Assessment Resources Inc., 1987.

TADS Team: Fluoxetine, cognitive-behavioral therapy, and their combination for adolescents with depression: Treatment for Adolescents with Depression Study (TADS) randomized, controlled trial. JAMA 292:807–820, 2004.

U.S. Food and Drug Administration: Summary Minutes of the CDER Psychopharmacological Drugs Advisory Committee and the FDA Pediatric Advisory Committee. September 13–14, 2004(a). . . .

U.S. Food and Drug Administration: FDA Launches a Multipronged Strategy to Strengthen Safeguards for Children Treated with Antidepressant. October 15, 2004(b). . . .

Valuck RJ, Libby AM, Sills MR, Giese AA, Allen RR: Antidepressant treatment and risk of suicide attempt by adolescents with major depressive disorder: A propensity-adjusted retrospective cohort study. CNS Drugs 18:1119–1132, 2004.

Wagner KD, Robb AS, Findling RL, Jin J, Gutierrez MM, Heydorn WE: A randomized, placebo-controlled trial of citalopram for the treatment of major depression in children and adolescents. Am J Psychiatry 161:1079–1083, 2004.

Weissman MM, Wolk S, Goldstein RB, Moreau D, Adams P, Greenwald S, Klier CM, Ryan ND, Dahl RE, Wickramaratne P: Depressed adolescents grown up. JAMA 281:1707–1713, 1999a.

Weissman MM, Wolk S, Wickramaratne P, Goldstein RB, Adams P, Greenwald S, Ryan ND, Dahl RE, Steinberg D: Children with prepubertal-onset major depressive disorder and anxiety grown up. Arch Gen Psychiatry 56:794–801, 1999b.

Whittington CJ, Kendall T, Pilling S: Are the SSRIs and atypical antidepressants safe and effective for children and adolescents? Curr Opin Psychiatry 18:21–25, 2005.

NO

Antidepressants Use in Children and Adolescents and the Risk of Suicide

1. Introduction

An increasing number of children and adolescents are treated with antidepressants. However, evidence to support such treatment in this age group is lacking. In fact, most pharmacological treatments of paediatric patients in most fields of medicine lack supportive empirical evidence. Regulatory authorities in Europe and the US have undertaken various measures, including guidelines (EMEA, 1999) and legislation (FDA, 1997) in order to try and correct for this situation. These efforts have led to the initiation of numerous randomised clinical studies in paediatric patients, including studies of antidepressants medications.

As the results of these studies have become available, an apparent signal with respect to suicide-related events has begun to emerge, first with respect to paroxetine and later with respect to other antidepressants. These findings have instigated renewed attention to the question whether SSRIs have the potential to induce suicidality. . . . The review of the results of clinical trials in children by Whittington et al. (2004) concluded that the risk involved in the treatment with SSRIs of children with depression outweighs the benefit except for fluoxetine.

Examining a partly overlapping data set, regulatory authorities have concluded that all antidepressants that were examined are associated with a signal of suicidality, and hence recommended issuing a warning against the use of all antidepressants in children and adolescents (EMEA, 2004a; FDA, 2004). The purpose of this paper is to describe the evidence these recommendations were based on. . . .

2. Methods

Altogether 22 short-term randomised double-blind placebo-controlled clinical trials are examined. These studies were conducted and submitted to the registration authorities for the purpose of obtaining a registration for the treatment of depression and anxiety disorders in children and adolescents. . . .

From *European Neuropsychopharmacology,* October 10, 2005, excerpts from pp. 79–83. Copyright © 2005 by European College of Neuropsychopharmacology. Reprinted by permission of Elseveir Health Sciences via Rightslink.

The studies involved eight different pharmaceutical products and included over 4000 paediatric patients. Pharmacodynamically, these products were selective serotonin and/or noradrenerge reuptake inhibitors: SSRIs and NSRIs.

The studies were conducted between 1984 and 2002. Most studies, however, were of recent date. Most trials (15) included patients with major depressive disorders (MDD), four trials were of patients with obsessive–compulsive disorder (OCD), two with generalised anxiety disorder (GAD), and one with social anxiety disorder (SAD).

Diagnoses were made by psychiatrists and were based on DSM-III or DSM-IV criteria, depending on the time period in which the trial was performed. The design of the trials varied with respect to instruments used to measure efficacy. However, most depression trials used the revised version of the Children Depression Rating Scale (CDRS-R) and all OCD studies used the Child Yale-Brown Obsessive Compulsive Scale (CY–BOCS). The mean severity scores at baseline indicated that most patients included in the studies suffered from moderate to severe disorders. Trials varied with respect to the age range of patients, with some including only children, some only adolescents and some both age groups. The duration of the trials varied between 6 and 12 weeks.

The study reports were searched for descriptions of adverse events that could indicate suicide or events related to suicidality. The following strings were searched for: 'suic-', 'self-', 'harm', 'injury', 'injurious', 'intentional', 'non-accidental', 'hostility', 'emotional' and 'lability'. Event descriptions that included the string 'suic-' were defined as adverse events related to suicidality. Events that included any of the other terms but not the term 'suic-' were classified as 'self-harm', 'hostility' or 'emotional lability', unless clearly indicated that these were accidental. Case reports that were identified were counted so that each patient could be counted only once in each category. . . .

2.1. Data Analysis

No tests of significance were performed on event rates in the individual studies, as the studies were not powered in order to detect differences between treatment groups in the rates of these rare events. Instead, for each study, the existence of a signal for suicidality was defined as any rate observed in the treatment group that was higher than that seen in placebo. In addition, where possible, point estimates for the relative risk (RR) were calculated (i.e. if the rate in the placebo group was not zero).

A random effect meta-analysis was conducted over all the studies. The ORs and RDs (with 95% confidence intervals) were calculated based on a random effect model. . . .

3. Results

. . . No completed suicides were reported in any of the studies. . . .

[Events] (including self-harm, hostility and emotional lability), which are thought to have the same underlying mechanism as suicide-related events, occurred more frequently in the treatment groups compared to the placebo groups. . . .

Signals appeared in studies of longer duration (i.e. 10–12 weeks) as well as in studies of shorter duration (i.e. 6–8 weeks) and in studies that included only adolescents as well as in studies that included both children and adolescents. Therefore, it was concluded that there is no association between the appearance of the suicidality signal and the duration of the studies or with the age range of the patients included. Furthermore, an examination of the cases with suicide-related events in studies that included both children and adolescents indicated that an equal number of children and adolescents were involved in these behaviours.

A meta-analysis for the MDD studies showed an overall significant odds ratio (OR) of 1.67 (95% CI: 1.05–2.65, $\chi^2_{(13)\ heterogeneity} = 8.93$, $p = 0.78$) and a significant risk difference (RD) of 1.4% (95% CI: 0.36%–2.46%, $\chi^2_{(14)\ heterogeneity} = 11.25$, $p = 0.66$).

Results for the anxiety disorders studies showed an overall non-significant OR . . . and a non-significant RD. . . .

Meta-analysis of the MDD trials indicated that efficacy results are heterogeneous across trials and hence an overall measure of efficacy could not be meaningfully interpreted. Furthermore, examination of the design of the trials indicated that there were significant differences between the trials in the methods used to select patients into the trials that are likely to lead to differences in the included patient populations. Thus, heterogeneity between the trials with respect to design and with respect to efficacy makes it difficult to derive an overall statement about efficacy with respect to MDD. Because efficacy could be detected in some trials that used more stringent inclusion procedure (e.g. placebo run-in), it may be that some of these compounds are efficacious in a subgroup of children and adolescents who suffer from more severe and more persistent depression.

The trials of the various anxiety disorders were positive in some but not all products. The meta-analysis for the anxiety trials indicated no significant heterogeneity across trials . . . and an overall effect size of 0.39 (95% CI: 0.27–0.51), indicating a small to medium overall effect.

4. Discussion

The review of all trials that were submitted to the European registration authorities has shown that no completed suicide was reported in any of these trials. However, a signal pertaining to suicidality and related behaviours was detected in all products that were examined.

The combined OR for events related to suicidality in all the depression studies (1.67) has reached statistical significance while the OR in the anxiety disorders studies was weaker (1.33) and did not reach statistical significance. However, the existence of a risk for suicidality in patients treated for anxiety cannot be ruled out. Failure to reach statistical significance may be because the studies were not powered to detect differences in this rare event.

The conclusion from the clinical trials data, therefore, is that in children and adolescents, there is an association between the use of all the antidepressants that were examined and suicide-related events.

No relationship to patients' age, gender or duration of the study was detected, although the numbers are too small to allow any definitive conclusions with regard to these factors.

The evidence concerning efficacy seems to suggest that the MDD trials were heterogeneous with respect to both efficacy and methodology, specifically the methods used to recruit patients. Trials that used long and extensive diagnostic procedure and placebo run-in had better efficacy results than trials that did not. These results may indicate that these compounds may be efficacious in a select group of patients who suffer from more severe and more persistent depression. Efficacy results were stronger and more homogeneous in the anxiety trials, indicating that antidepressants may be effective in treating anxiety disorders in children and adolescents. . . .

The FDA has reached similar conclusions to the ones arrived at in this review (FDA, 2004). Two sets of analyses, using different case ascertainment strategies to define suicide-related events, were run by the FDA. The first used cases of suicide-related behaviours that were identified by the sponsors of the studies. The second analysis relied on events that were classified as suicide-related by a group of suicide experts, under the coordination of researchers at Columbia University. Despite this and other differences in the methods, the two analyses arrived at similar results and reached similar conclusions and recommendations. The analyses presented in this paper are similar to the first FDA analysis in the way cases were identified, but differ in that the number of patients rather than the number of person years at risk were used for the denominators. In addition to other technical differences, the analysis in this paper is based on a slightly different set of studies, corresponding to antidepressants that are registered in Europe. In spite of all these differences, similar conclusions were arrived at, namely that all antidepressants are associated with suicide-related events. . . .

Another source of information that may be relevant to the issue at hand is the General Practice Research Database (GPRD), a computerised database of longitudinal clinical records from 777 GP practices covering about 5% of the UK population. Analyses of the GPRD data set (Martinez et al., 2005) have suggested that suicidality in paediatric patients is associated with the use of SSRIs. However, it is known that patients who are at higher risk for suicidality are more commonly prescribed SSRIs as opposed to TCAs. Hence, the observed association might be due to this selection process rather than to a relatively high risk associated with SSRIs compared to TCAs.

Yet another source of evidence outside RCTs are ecological studies investigating co-occurring time trends in the prescription of SSRIs and suicide rates. Several studies have demonstrated that increases in the use of SSRIs are associated with reductions in suicide rates in the total population, among adults (Isacsson, 2000) as well as among male adolescents (Olfson et al., 2003). These findings provide indirect evidence suggesting that, on the group level, SSRIs may be beneficial in their effect on suicidality. However, these findings should be interpreted with caution, as reduction in suicide rates may be due to other trends in risk factors.

In summary, there are grounds for concerns regarding the use of antidepressants in the paediatric population due to the increased risk of suicidality and related behaviours. Although the signal that is detected is weak, the fact that it is consistently found in a large number of studies indicates that this might not be a chance finding. The fact that a signal was detected in studies of all products that were examined suggests that the process responsible for this phenomenon (although the nature of this process is, as of as now, unclear) may be operating in all instances of antidepressants use in paediatrics and not only in those products for which data happened to be available. Hence, the evidence indicates that a warning concerning the use of antidepressants in the paediatric population is called for. While the evidence for efficacy is inconsistent, especially with respect to the treatment of MDD, this does not necessarily indicate that those antidepressants are ineffective in all cases of depression in children or adolescents. Negative results may be due to failures in the design of the studies (e.g. not stringent enough inclusion criteria).

Altogether these results call for caution in the use of all the examined SSRIs and NSRIs in the treatment of paediatric patients. The need for caution also applied to other types of antidepressants (e.g. tricyclic antidepressants). As long as no contradictory information is available, it is safer to assume that the same risks apply to these medications as well. . . .

References

European Agency for the Evaluation of Medicinal products (EMEA), 1999. Committee for Proprietary Medicinal Products: Guidelines for studies in children (CPMP)/(ICH/2711/99), Topic E11 Note for Guidance on Clinical Investigation of Medicinal Products in the Paediatric Population. . . .

European Agency for the Evaluation of Medicinal products (EMEA), 2004a. Press release on Paroxetin. London, 22 April 2004a. Doc. Ref. EMEA/ D/11206/04/ Final. . . .

Food and Drug Administration (FDA), 1997. Modernization Act, enacted Nov. 21, 1997. . . .

Food and Drug Administration (FDA), 2004. . . .

Isacsson, G., 2000. Suicide prevention: a medical breakthrough? Acta Psychiatr. Scand. 102, 113–117.

Martinez, C., Rietbrock, S., Wise, L., Ashby, D., Chick, J., Moseley, J., Evans, S., Gunnell, D., 2005. Antidepressant treatment and the risk of fatal and non-fatal self harm in first episode depression: nested case-control study. BMJ 330, 373–374.

Olfson, M., Shaffer, D., Marcus S.C., Greenberg, T., 2003. Relationship between antidepressant medication treatment and suicide in adolescents. Arch. Gen. Psychiatry 60, 978–982.

Whittington, C.J., Kendall, T., Fonagy, P., Cottrell, D., Cotgrove, A., Boddington, E., 2004. Selective serotonin reuptake inhibitors in childhood depression: systematic review of published versus unpublished data. Lancet 363, 1341–1345.

POSTSCRIPT

Should Adolescents Be Taking Selective Serotonin Reuptake Inhibitors (SSRIs) for Depression?

Major depression is a serious illness in children and adolescents and, therefore, it is important to identify safe and effective medications for the treatment of this disorder in our youth. Recent warnings of the potential serious negative effects of antidepressants, especially SSRIs, raise questions about the risk-benefit ratio of these drugs. Arguments against their use focus on the increased risk of suicidal behaviors, while those in favor argue that untreated adolescents are at greater risk for long-term psychiatric problems and suicide.

The two selections for this issue are excellent examples of these opposing views. Wohlfarth and colleagues, for example, argue that empirical evidence outlining the benefits of treating adolescent depression with SSRIs is lacking. Although no completed suicides were reported in their meta-analysis of 24 RCTs, self-harming behaviors (related to suicidality) occurred more frequently in all treatment groups (i.e., all antidepressant products) compared to placebo groups. They concluded that, for children and adolescents, there is a significant association between the use of all antidepressants and suicide-related events. Wohlfarth et al.'s conclusions are consistent with results from previous meta-analytical studies such as the Whittington et al. study (2004) and Jureidini et al. (2004). Further, their results also support the warnings made by the FDA in 2003.

Alternatively, Kratochvil and colleagues argue that the warnings are not necessarily based on sound published data. They examined both the efficacy data and safety data and found that the majority of studies conducted were unpublished studies with negative results. All fluoxetine studies were published and had positive outcomes indicating a favorable risk/benefit profile. Furthermore, the largest study on adolescent depression (Treatment for Adolescents with Depression Study, TADS) provided strong support for fluoxetine efficacy for the treatment of moderate to severe depression. TADS also indicated suicidality decreased with treatment. Kratochvil and his colleagues conclude that the data from the studies do not support the argument that SSRIs add to suicide risk. In fact, many studies report a decrease in suicide ideation while taking SSRIs—this decrease must be considered an improvement in the depressed condition. Kratochvil et al.'s conclusions are similar to those reported by Lapierre (2003) and Hamrin and Scahill (2005).

There are obvious opposing views on this issue but perhaps with future publications of methodologically sound clinical trials, the costs and benefits of SSRIs will become clearer. In the meantime, these selections raise awareness of adolescent depression and, given that suicide is a risk in the context of depression, they also strengthen the argument that safe and effective treatment is essential.

References/Further Readings

American Academy of Child and Adolescent Psychiatry. (1998). Practice parameters for the assessment and treatment of children and adolescents with depressive disorders. *Journal of the American Academy of Child and Adolescent Psychiatry, 37*(suppl.), 63S–83S.

Anderson, R. (2002). Deaths: Leading causes for 2000. *National Vital Statistics Report, 50,* 1–85.

Emslie, G., Kratochvil, C., Vitiello, B., Silva, S., Mayes, T., McNulty, S., Weller, E., Waslick, B., Casat, C., Walkup, J., Pathak, S., Rohde, P., Posner, K., March, J., The Columbia Suicidality Classification Group, & the TADS Team. (2006). Treatment for adolescents with depression study (TADS): Safety results. *Journal of the American Academy of Child and Adolescent Psychiatry, 45,* 1440–1455.

Hamrin, V., & Scahill, L. (2005). Selective serotonin reuptake inhibitors for children and adolescents with major depression: Current controversies and recommendations. *Issues in Mental Health Nursing, 26,* 433–450.

Jureidini, J., Doecke, C., Mansfield, P., Haby, M., Menkes, D., & Tonkin, A. (2004). Efficacy and safety of antidepressants for children and adolescents. *British Medical Journal, 328,* 879–883.

Lapierre, Y. D. (2003). Suicidality with selective serotonin reuptake inhibitors: Valid claim? *Journal of Psychiatry & Neuroscience, 28,* 340–347.

Wallace, A., Neily, J., Weeks, W., & Friedman, M. (2006). A cumulative meta-analysis of selective serotonin reuptake inhibitors in pediatric depression: Did unpublished studies influence the efficacy/safety debate? *Journal of Child and Adolescent Psychopharmacology, 16,* 37–58.

Whittington, C., Kendall, T., Fonagy, P., Cottrell, D., Cotgrove, A., & Boddington, E. (2004). Selective serotonin reuptake inhibitors in childhood depression: Systematic review of published versus unpublished data. *The Lancet, 363,* 1341–1345.

U.S. Food and Drug Administration (2004). FDA launches a multipronged strategy to strengthen safeguards for children treated with antidepressant medication. *PDA News,* retrieved Thursday, June 22, 2006 from: www.fda.gov/bbs/topics/news/2004/NEW01124.html.

ISSUE 2

Should Adolescents Be Allowed to Drink Alcohol?

YES: Rutger C.M.E. Engels, et al., from "Peer Group Reputation and Smoking and Alcohol Consumption in Early Adolescence," *Addictive Behaviors* (vol. 31, 2006)

NO: Sandra A. Brown, from "Providing Substance Abuse Prevention and Treatment Services to Adolescents," Testimony Before the U.S. Senate, Subcommittee on Substance Abuse and Mental Health Services (June 15, 2004)

ISSUE SUMMARY

YES: Engels and colleagues, researchers in the Netherlands, suggest that substance use, while potentially problematic, may serve beneficial developmental functions for adolescents. Particularly, adolescents who drink alcohol appeared to be more self-confident and sociable than those who abstained based on peer evaluations.

NO: Researcher Sandra Brown, a psychiatrist from the University of California–San Diego, argues that early onset of alcohol and drug use put youth at greater risk for neurological damage, alcohol-related injuries (e.g., from drinking and driving), and future substance dependence.

Alcohol use prevention may not seem like it should be a controversial issue. After all, alcohol use is strictly regulated and illegal for adolescents. Substance abuse can create a host of social, health, and legal problems; therefore, adolescent prohibition is easily justified. Organizations such as MADD (Mothers Against Drunk Driving) and AA (Alcoholics Anonymous) attest to the potential harm of alcohol use; this harm is more detrimental for adolescents than adults. So, what makes alcohol use among adolescents a controversial issue?

The majority of youth will try alcohol at some point during their adolescence. Among youth, the prevalence of current alcohol use increased with age, from 3 percent at age 12 to about 70 percent of persons 21 or 22 years old; however, among adults, the prevalence of alcohol use decreased with increasing age, from 62 percent among 26- to 29-year-olds to 34 percent among people aged 65 or older (Substance Abuse and Mental Health Services Administration, 1999; 2003). Further, the highest prevalence of both binge and heavy drinking was for young adults aged 18 to 25 (42 and 15 percent, respectively), with the peak rate of both measures occurring at age 21. Of concern, however, is that about 80 percent of adult respondents receiving alcohol treatment reported that they first became intoxicated before the age of 18, although not all youth who experiment with alcohol will become dependent as adults (Substance Abuse and Mental Health Services Administration, 1999; 2003). This finding suggests that youth drinking patterns may have a significant impact on future alcohol dependence.

Most countries have regulations governing the use and sale of alcohol, called alcohol control measures. One common control measure is an "age of majority." This age differs from place-to-place; for example, in Wisconsin, the age of majority for drinking alcohol is 21 years, while in Quebec, it is 18 years of age. In some European countries (e.g., France), 14-year-olds can drink wine but not hard liquor. These laws have been demonstrated as effective at reducing youth alcohol consumption; for example, in communities where youth perceived stores to be supportive of enforcing age of majority as well as a likelihood of being caught by police when drinking were much less likely to have youth engage in underage drinking (Carpenter et al., 2007; Dent, Grube, & Biglan, 2005).

Regardless of these alcohol control measures, North American data consistently demonstrate that a large number of adolescents engage in underage drinking (e.g., Johnston et al., 2006; Paglia-Boak & Adlaf, 2006). The motivation underlying this illicit drinking may be social (Piko et al., 2007); there are drinking norms to which adolescents must conform or risk being labeled as less social, less mature, or even deviant. Adolescents who abstain from drinking may suffer social sanctions (e.g., stigma) from their peers. Particularly, males may have their masculinity called into question if they do not drink alcohol. This could perhaps explain the gender difference in alcohol consumption. Thus, there are many reasons (e.g., social pressure) for adolescents to consume alcohol despite the many deterrents (e.g., laws prohibiting consumption and restricted access to alcohol).

In the following selections, Engels et al. suggest that there may be some significant social benefits for adolescents who drink alcohol. They suggest that *not* drinking in youth can be indicative of some significant developmental social problems (e.g., issues with developing intimate relationships with peers). In contrast, Brown's paper—where she reviews some of the negative consequences of alcohol use by youth such as neurological deficits caused by early alcohol consumption—is disturbing and alarming and seems to suggest that groups such as parents, schools, healthcare professionals, and government should ban or eradicate alcohol consumption by youth. As you read the two selections, consider how these two viewpoints could be reconciled.

YES

Rutger C.M.E. Engels et al.

Peer Group Reputation and Smoking and Alcohol Consumption in Early Adolescence

1. Introduction

National surveys in Western societies, such as the United States, Great Britain, and the Netherlands have shown that experimentation with risk behaviors, such as cigarette smoking, marijuana use and alcohol consumption is rather normal among adolescents. The widespread uptake of alcohol in adolescence focuses attention on the developmental tasks to be realized in the teenage years. The transition from adolescence to adulthood is characterized by intensified contacts with peers and an entrance into new social contexts and activities. The relevance for adolescents to achieve intimacy goals, such as closeness and trust, shifts from parents towards peers. It is essential for young people to establish contact with new friends or to strengthen existing affiliations. In this way they can reflect their own ideas and opinions. From 14, 15 years on, youngsters spend more time with friends outside the parental home in comparison with children and early adolescents. Going out to pubs, discos and parties is considered to be important for the development and maintenance of friendships as well as romantic relationships. Since some leisure time activities take place in settings, such as bars, discos and parties, in which certain risk behaviors (e.g., smoking, drinking) and the development of peer relations come together, some risk behaviors can be assumed to facilitate peer group integration. We will discuss three lines of research that reflect this reasoning.

First, research has shown that compared to drinkers, abstainers are less sociable, spend less time with their friends and are less likely to have a chumship, and have less adequate social skills. With prospective and concurrent analyses, Maggs and Hurrelmann (1998) found small but consistent support for the positive effects of substance use (including smoking) on peer relations. In addition, findings from a few longitudinal studies suggested that abstaining late adolescents and young adults are less likely to develop a steady intimate relationship than drinkers.

Second, when youngsters are asked what motives they endorse for their drinking or smoking behavior, they often mention the social aspects of substance use. It seems to make parties more fun, it makes one more relaxed, makes it easier to approach others, or to share feelings and experiences. The literature on drinking motives, for instance, illustrates that people who endorse enhancement (i.e., drinking to feel relaxed and at ease) and social motives (i.e., drinking to celebrate, to have a good time with friends), are more likely to report high drinking levels in social contexts. Research on alcohol expectancies has shown that the expected reinforcing social elements of drinking are related to, and predictive of, frequency and quantity of adolescent alcohol use. Apparently in the eyes of the beholder (i.e., youngsters themselves), substance use is interconnected with sociability and associated with social interactions.

Third, research on social images, stereotypes and self-other identification, and substance use strongly relies on the assumption that people value smoking or drinking peers positively. For example, people may have self-consistency and self-enhancement motives for using cigarettes; not only those who perceive their self-image to be similar to a smoking stereotype (peer smoker) are more likely to initiate smoking, but also those who value the characteristics of a typical smoking peer (stereotype) higher than their own image are more likely to start smoking. In sum, people who link substance use to desired social characteristics that are represented in peers are more likely to be engaged in substance use.

These three lines of research [support] the assumption that substance use has social benefits, or that young people at least perceive that this is the case. However, the overwhelming majority of studies used self-report data on social performance in relations. A limitation of self-reports is that there might be discrepancies in how people think they act in social encounters, and how others perceive them interacting. It is therefore essential to gather data among an individual's peers. If the social or psychological functions of substance use are primarily in the eyes of the beholder, and peer group members do *not* associate social skills or performance with substance using peers, this might be essential and valuable information for challenging prevailing distorted cognitions of substance using early adolescents on the social consequences of their behavior. Further, it might be possible that, though substance use is related to social benefits, it is also associated with negative behaviors, such as aggression, inattentiveness, and poor school performance. Therefore, it is relevant to get a more comprehensive picture by gathering information on traits and behaviors of substance using and non-using early adolescents from their immediate peer group members.

In the present study, we examined the association between peer group reputation and substance use. As is the case in sociometric research, members of a specific group (i.e., pupils in a school class) are asked to nominate class members who have specific characteristics that are related to social behavior, such as sociability, aggression, achievement motivation, withdrawal, emotional stability, and self-confidence. When the findings confirm that drinkers and smokers possess certain positive *social* characteristics, and not negative characteristics, such as aggression, emotional instability or loss of control, as perceived by their own peers, we have gained more insight into the etiology of adolescents' uptake of substance use. . . .

2. Method

2.1. Participants

Participants were 3361 adolescents (1430 girls, 1931 boys) attending 17 first (n = 361, mean age 12.5 years), 42 second (n = 1032, 13.4 years), 44 third (n = 983, 14.5 years), and 45 fourth and fifth (n = 985, 15.6 years) grade secondary school classes in the Arnhem-Nijmegen region in The Netherlands. The age of the students ranged from 12 years to 18 years. . . .

2.2. Measures

2.2.1. Substance Use
The average number of cigarettes smoked per day over the past month was measured using a 9-point scale (0, 1, 2, 3, 4, 5, 6–10, 11–20, >20). The average number of glasses of alcohol (i.e., beer, wine, mixed drinks) consumed over the past month was measured using a 10-point scale (0, 1–2, 3–4, 5–6, 7–10, 11–15, 16–20, 21–30, 31–50, >50).

2.2.2. Peer Group Reputation
Peer group reputation was based on 20 "Guess who" peer nomination items. The 20 items concerned attributes of an individual's peer group functioning. Per item, the students had to nominate three to five classmates. To correct for unequal numbers of nominating students per class, all of the nominations received from all nominating classmates on a particular item were summed and transformed per class into probability scores (p-scores) for each subject. . . .

The 20 items comprise . . . five . . . peer group reputation factors: *Aggression–Inattentiveness* (e.g., being perceived as quarrelsome, lazy, absent-minded, irritable), *Achievement–Withdrawal* (e.g., being perceived as persistent, hard working, shy, reserved, withdrawn), *Self-confidence* (e.g., being perceived as sensible, secure, steady, sincere), *Sociability* (e.g., being perceived as enthusiastic and considerate), and *Emotionality–Nervousness* (e.g., being perceived as emotional, anxious, nervous, uncreative). . . .

3. Results

3.1. Descriptives

Of all adolescents, 67% had never smoked. The adolescents who smoked had smoked on average 4 cigarettes a day during the past month, with 25% of them reporting having smoked on average more than 10 cigarettes a day. No differences existed between boys and girls in smoking. With respect to drinking, 38% of all adolescents reported that they had not consumed any alcohol during the past month. Adolescents who drank had consumed on average between 6 and 10 glasses. Gender differences indicated that boys had consumed significantly more than girls. . . .

3.2. Variable-Centered Approach

First, we calculated . . . correlations between peer group reputation scores and substance use. It appeared that all five peer group reputation measures were . . . associated with smoking and alcohol use. Respondents who were evaluated by their class members as being high on aggression–inattentiveness, self-confidence and sociability were more likely to smoke and drink. In contrast, respondents who were evaluated as being high on achievement–withdrawal and emotionality–nervousness were less likely to smoke and drink. . . . In addition, boys were more likely to report higher levels of alcohol use and lower levels of smoking as compared to girls. Age was associated with increased substance use.

3.3. Person-Centered Approach

. . . [Cluster] analyses were computed and four clusters were obtained. [Cluster analysis identifies similar groups of people based on the peer reputation variables. A cluster might be thought of as a profile of traits or characteristics.] Adolescents in cluster 1 ($n = 961$) were characterized by high scores on self-confidence and sociability and low to moderate scores on achievement–withdrawal and emotionality–nervousness. Cluster 2 adolescents ($n = 432$) were characterized by high scores on aggression–inattentiveness and emotionality–nervousness, and low scores on self-confidence, achievement–withdrawal and sociability. Adolescents in cluster 3 ($n = 1169$) had high scores on emotionality–nervousness and achievement–withdrawal. Finally, adolescents in cluster 4 ($n = 772$) were characterized by moderate scores on all five peer group reputation scores. . . .

In a second step, we calculated the scores on smoking and drinking for the four clusters. . . . [The] four groups [clusters] of adolescents [were compared] on smoking and drinking. . . . [The groups (clusters) were significantly different in terms of their alcohol use and cigarette smoking.] Highest scores on alcohol and cigarette use were found for cluster 1, with respondents high on self-confidence and sociability. Lowest likelihood of engagement in substance use was found for cluster 3, with respondents characterized by emotionality–nervousness and achievement–withdrawal. Hardly any differences were found between smoking and drinking across the different clusters. Apparently, students do not attribute different traits or behaviors to either substance. . . .

4. Discussion

Variable- and person-centered approaches employed in the present study demonstrate that students draw distinctions between substance using and non-using classmates. According to the variable-centered approach, drinkers and smokers appear to be more self-confident, sociable and aggressive, and less nervous, emotional, oriented on achievement and withdrawn. The person-centered approach provides a more precise picture, demonstrating that particularly pupils who are self-confident and sociable, but are low on nervousness and achievement–withdrawal according to their class mates, are engaged most strongly in smoking and drinking. It is important to mention that students who combine high aggressiveness–inattentiveness and emotionality–nervousness are also likely to engage in more smoking and drinking when compared to those who score moderately low on all peer group reputation measures or those who combine particularly high scores on achievement–withdrawal and emotionality–nervousness.

These findings are in line with research showing that adolescents who drink report that they are more sociable, have more friends and spend more time with their friends. Apparently, these self-perceptions are in line with the opinions of others in the direct social environment of adolescents. On the other hand, it is quite clear that those who drink or smoke score lower on achievement and school performance, and score higher on aggression and inattentiveness. The groups identified with the person-centered approach show that two categories of early adolescents drink and smoke more than others: those who are sociable and self-confident, and those who are aggressive and emotionally insecure. In particular concerning alcohol use, it would be interesting [to know] whether especially the latter category is associated with the negative consequences of binge drinking and alcohol misuse in adolescence. Drinking in adolescence, especially riskful drinking patterns, such as binge drinking or problem drinking, is not only a predictor of alcohol misuse and problem drinking in adulthood, but drinking in adolescence is also related to car accidents, suicide, delinquency, aggression, and sexual assaults. It would be interesting to know whether in particular early starting, aggressive and emotional drinkers experience negative consequences of drinking later on.

A limitation of the current study is that we could not carry out a longitudinal investigation. We could not test the long term association of engagement in substance use by adolescents and peer reputation. This affects the generalizability of our results. For instance, it might be possible that our findings are limited to early adolescence, and that if we would interview all respondents in late adolescence, the reputation of substance users among their peers is different. Thus, some of the differences in social and emotional development could disappear if our sample were reinterviewed later on. It is also crucial to understand that we do not make causal inferences from our data. We do not imply that smoking leads to self-confidence and social acceptance. It is possible that those who start to drink and smoke in early adolescence have a high social status in the group, and therefore positive social and personal attributions are made by others. Or that sociable and self-confident adolescents are more likely to spend time with friends at parties where they consume alcohol. Longitudinal research should reveal whether substance use leads to specific peer reputation scores, the other way around, or both. Since the main result of this study could be viewed as encouraging smoking and drinking, it should be stressed that the main goal was to explore the social reputation of drinkers and smokers in the eyes of their peers.

It is questionable to what extent our findings can be generalized to other countries and cultures. The legal age for entering public drinking places in the Netherlands is 16 years. At this age, youngsters are allowed to order soft alcoholic beverages, such as beer and wine. The legal age to purchase cigarettes is also 16 years of age. Since in some Western countries the legal age for pub-going, alcohol use and cigarette smoking is substantially higher, attention must be paid to the significance of age groups and comparability of findings across countries.

Nevertheless, our findings illustrate that early adolescents who engage in smoking and drinking are not only perceived as self-confident and sociable, but also with less interest in school and academic performance, emotionality and nervousness, and aggression. Further, some subgroups of higher engagement are distinguished. Although part of these patterns is already reported in the literature using self-reports, this is, to our knowledge, the first study employing reports by peers (i.e., classmates) on adolescents' social and personal development.

Reference

Maggs, J. L., & Hurrelmann, K. (1998). Do substance use and delinquency have differential associations with adolescents peer relations? *International Journal of Behavioural Development, 22,* 367–388.

Sandra A. Brown  **NO**

Providing Substance Abuse Prevention and Treatment Services to Adolescents

Introduction

Recent research supported by the National Institutes of Health and other agencies is leading to a common understanding about the critical role of age of onset of addictive disorders in their course, consequences and progression. Researchers are finding that these disorders often begin during adolescence and sometimes even during childhood; therefore early intervention may prevent many of the social, behavioral, health, and economic consequences caused by alcohol and drug abuse as well as provide an opportunity to treat problems before they become full blown and damage in the lives of our youth.

Early Onset

NIAAA [National Institute on Alcohol Abuse and Alcoholism] and NIDA [National Institute on Drug Abuse] supported researchers are finding that alcohol and other drug addictions commonly start earlier than previously understood, and the earlier youth start the greater the lifetime risk for dependence. New findings regarding early patterns of abuse and dependence dramatically underscore the importance of reducing underage drinking and drug use. The age of most prevalent tobacco dependence onset is 15 and for alcohol dependence age 18 is the most common period of first diagnosis of dependence. It is now clear that most cases of alcohol dependence begin before age 25. After that age, new cases drop off precipitously. The epidemiological research message is obvious: youth is a critical window of opportunity for preventing alcohol, tobacco and other drug disorders. Previous studies have suggested that this is so, but the new research findings, corroborated by independent sources, have confirmed these findings.

Ongoing research may reveal a cause-and-effect relationship between early use and subsequent dependence, or it may reveal that common biological and environmental factors drive the risk for both use and dependence,

APA Testimony before the U.S. Senate, Subcommittee on Substance Abuse Prevention and Treatment Services to Adolescents, June 15, 2004.

as well as other addictive and psychiatric disorders. In either case, these new data are a powerful indicator of the need for more effective preventive interventions for youth.

Given the new epidemiologic findings, the fact that alcohol use is so widespread among children and adolescents is troubling. Alcohol is the primary substance of abuse among American children and adolescents.

- 47 percent of 8th graders, 67 percent of 10th graders, and 78 percent of 12th graders have used alcohol.
- 11 percent of 6th graders have reported binge drinking (5 or more drinks per occasion for males; 4 for females) in the past 2 weeks.
- 30 percent of high-school seniors have reported binge drinking at least once a month.
- 44 percent of college students have reported binge drinking in the past 2 weeks.
- 23 percent have reported that they binge drink frequently.
- Youth who drink alcohol before age 14 are 4 times more likely to become alcohol dependent in their lifetime than those who wait until age 21 or older.

Neurodevelopmental Studies

A series of recent studies indicate that exposure to drugs of abuse during adolescence may produce more adverse effects than exposure during adulthood in part because of the important changes occurring in the brain during adolescent development. Advances in science have now brought us to a point where researchers can use new animal models, modern brain imaging technology and other neurobehavioral assessment tools to probe the effects of alcohol, tobacco and other drugs on the developing brain and determine immediate as well as its long-term behavioral consequences.

Emerging findings from neuroimaging studies demonstrate that brain structures change during adolescence to become more specialized and efficient in their functioning. Our developmentally focused research indicates important neurocognitive disadvantages among adolescents with alcohol and drug use disorders as compared to teens without substance involvement. For example, even after three weeks of abstinence, alcohol dependent youth display a 10% decrement in delayed memory functions. Neuropsychological testing of these youth followed up to eight years demonstrates that continued heavy drinking during adolescence is associated with diminished memory of verbal and nonverbal material, and poorer performance on tests requiring attention skills. Alcohol and drug withdrawal over the teen years appears to uniquely contribute to deterioration in functioning in visuospatial tasks. Recent brain imaging studies of alcohol and drug using youth compared to youth without such experience have also shown reduced hippocampal volumes, white matter microstructure irregularities, and brain response abnormalities while performing cognitive tasks among those with early alcohol/drug exposure. Additionally, youth who have extensive experience with alcohol have increased brain response when viewing alcohol advertisements compared to other beverage advertisements.

Animal studies are consistent with the findings that alcohol or drug exposure during adolescence has more adverse consequences than delayed (adult) exposure. In these investigations, adolescent alcohol exposure is associated with more frontal lobe damage and poorer spatial memory. Further research is needed to understand how age of drinking or drug use onset and duration of abstinence at the time of assessment affect cognitive and behavioral findings. Longitudinal studies are needed to clarify neuromaturational changes associated with early alcohol and drug exposure and patterns of resiliency. Although the magnitude of effects observed in adolescents' neurocognition is modest, the implications are major given the prevalence of alcohol involvement, and the important educational, occupational, and social transitions that occur during adolescence.

These new directions in adolescent research will help to inform us on important aspects of cognition, decision-making, motivation, emotional regulation, and risk perception during adolescence, and will help us determine how these factors play a role in the use and consequences of alcohol and drugs. Armed with new knowledge about how adolescents make decisions, control their impulses and desires, and what motivates their behavior, researchers and agencies will be poised to design better preventions and interventions to reduce alcohol, tobacco and other drug experimentation, abuse and dependence, as well as other risky behaviors. Adolescents have in common unique neurobiological and neurocognitive developmental factors that affect risk and resiliency vis-à-vis substance use. Few studies have addressed these developmentally specific neurobiological and neurocognitive mechanisms and consequences of heavy drinking/use in this group despite the importance of these for long-term development.

Vulnerability

While early initiation of substance involvement is a powerful predictor of subsequent dependence, not everyone who uses at a young age later develops abuse or dependence. Even among youth with two alcoholic parents, only about one-half become alcohol dependent. The outcome is determined largely by the interplay of environmental and genetic/biological factors.

Environmental factors have the biggest influence on whether a child first uses alcohol, tobacco or other substances. However, genetic factors have an influence on whether a child continues to use. Understanding how these factors result in initiation and continuation of use or make resolution of drinking/drug use more difficult is essential to disrupting the developmental process of addictive behavior. Thus, a focus on genetic/biological aspect of use may clarify how variations in genes result in differences in how our bodies absorb, distribute, and eliminate substances and variability in tolerance.

Binge Drinking

Binge drinking, episodes of heavy drinking (5 or more drinks for males; 4 or more drinks for females), is a problem for people in any age group, whether or not the drinker is addicted to alcohol. An alarming number of children and adolescents binge drink and that it is increasing. Drinking too much, too fast in this manner carries additional risks especially for youth. They include car crashes, injury, death, property damage, encounters with the justice system, and family, school, and workplace problems. Each drink increases the fatal crash risk more for youth than for adults. At a blood alcohol level of 0.08% in every age and gender group there is at least an 11-fold increase in single vehicle fatal crash risk. Among males 16–20 at a blood alcohol level of 0.08% there is a 52-fold increase in single vehicle crash risk compared to sober drivers the same age.

Epidemiology studies have shown beyond doubt that genes play a role in risk of alcohol, tobacco and other drug dependence. Research toward discovering which genes are involved, what biochemical pathways they influence in brain cells, and how these pathways translate into specific behaviors is the next step to this line of investigation. Such findings provide information about genetic/molecular events in the brain that influence use, and provide potential targets for pharmacological intervention. For example, new findings about a naturally occurring marijuana-like substance in the brain also provide potential new molecular targets for pharmacological intervention.

Prevention of Abuse and Dependence

Prevention of alcohol and substance use problems among youth need to be understood as a continuum of services and consequently research needs to span this continuum. This continuum ranges from **universal** prevention (those appropriate for all children and adolescents who might use alcohol, tobacco or other drugs) to **selective** preventative measures for subgroups with risk factors for abuse or dependence, to **indicated** preventative measures for those individually at high risk for the disorder. Preventive interventions for alcohol, tobacco, and other drug use disorders and related problems can be improved through early detection and diagnosis, and through testing of new behavioral strategies at the individual, family, and community levels. Of particular interest are longitudinal data on children entering the age of risk, adolescents and young adults in high-risk environments (college and the military), youth who resolve use/problems without formal treatment, and women of childbearing age. New interventions to prevent early-onset of use can be gleaned through studies that identify developmental and environmental features as well as biological factors that stimulate or suppress addictive behavior.

It is important to evaluate prevention programs on an ongoing basis as well as disseminate research findings to communities, educators, parents, and healthcare providers who are the first line of defense against alcohol, drugs and other risky behaviors. Both NIAAA and NIDA offer free educational materials designed to help students learn about the impact of alcohol and drugs on the brain and body. Parents, educators, and community leaders can use these materials to help guide their thinking, planning, selection, and delivery of drug abuse prevention programs at the community level. NIAAA and NIDA also have websites that offer science-based information specifically designed for teens. *The Leadership to Keep Children Alcohol-Free* has recruited 33 Governors' spouses to spearhead a national prevention campaign which influences both public policy and local practices. *The Task Force on College Drinking* has brought together university presidents and researchers, and is making headway in efforts to reduce the seemingly intractable problem of drinking by college students.

Clearly, alcohol and substance use disorders are the result of a complex combination of genetic and environmental interactions that influence how people respond to the substance and their initial propensity for using alcohol and drugs. Longitudinal studies of these genetic and environmental factors are crucial for understanding (1) early initiation of drinking and drug use, (2) transition to harmful use, abuse, and dependence, and (3) remission and abatement of alcohol and drug related problems in untreated populations. This is particularly critical for youth as some resolve problematic use without treatment and research in this area can teach us how to facilitate changes in alcohol and drug involvement in ways that are most developmentally appropriate and acceptable to youth. Developmentally specific research in these areas has potential to help identify mechanisms of vulnerability and protection which can be used in prevention.

Improving Effectiveness of Treatment

Findings from the National Household Survey on Drug Abuse indicate that about 10 percent of 12- to 17-year-olds (about 2.3 million) are heavy users of alcohol or drugs, yet only 187,000 (8%) received services. Although estimates of the cost-effectiveness of early intervention are speculative, research suggests that early treatment has the potential to be cost-effective, especially in comparison with incarceration or treatment for a long-term abuse problem. For instance, cost benefit research on drug and alcohol treatment generally (Office of National Drug Control Policy, 2001) suggests that the range of savings is between $2.50 and $9.60 for every dollar spent on treatment. Unfortunately, only one person in seven who would qualify for treatment was admitted to treatment in 1999 (National Institute on Drug Abuse Community Epidemiology Work Group, 1999). The proportion of youth who are admitted to treatment is even smaller.

Much progress has been made in developing behavioral/psychosocial interventions for alcohol and other substance use disorders, but much remains to be investigated. Controlled research trials provide evidence that several psychosocial treatment approaches may be effective in reducing alcohol and other drug use while also improving associated behavioral, familial, and psychosocial outcomes. These outcomes are enhanced when a combination of modalities are offered in a comprehensive, integrated treatment plan that addresses alcohol and drug abuse and a broad range of biopsychosocial problems, skills deficits, and comorbid psychiatric problems. For example, having families involved in the treatment program increases the likelihood of success in youth. Brief Strategic Family Therapy (BSFT) and Cognitive Behavioral Interventions are examples of promising youth specific treatment already in the field. The evaluation and dissemination of more evidence-based interventions in a variety of community venues, including schools, healthcare settings, and prisons, should be a high priority. Developing, evaluating, and improving efficacy and cost-effectiveness of treatments is a central goal in alcohol, tobacco and drug research. Adolescent focused treatment research lags behind adult treatment research. Studies are needed to develop and test new behavioral therapies; conduct clinical trials in existing treatment settings; examine cost-effectiveness of behavioral and pharmaceutical therapies; clarify mechanisms of action that make effective treatments successful; and conduct trials of dissemination strategies, to test how effective they are at introducing behavioral and pharmacological treatments into real-world clinical practice.

Alcohol, tobacco and other drugs affect genders and subpopulations differently, and some groups suffer more adverse effects of alcohol, tobacco and drugs than other groups. For treatment of these youth problems to be optimally effective, research to study the role of gender, ethnicity, socio-economic status, and other variables in determining the effects of various substance abuse interventions is sorely needed. For example, we need to support studies on specific facilitators and barriers to alcohol and drug treatment in minority and rural populations.

Clearly multifaceted longitudinal research is sorely needed to fully understand the development and resolution of alcohol and drug use disorders in the context of child and adolescent development. Through such focused process research (e.g., changes in brain structure and recovery of functioning, decision making process, social and family dynamics) can improved prevention and intervention policies emerge.

POSTSCRIPT

Should Adolescents Be Allowed to Drink Alcohol?

The two selections presented here do not necessarily contradict each other because the phenomena and issues surrounding adolescent drinking are complex. Brown's paper clearly speaks to potential negative effects of adolescent alcohol use, while Engels et al. found some social benefits of drinking for many teens. However, Engels et al. also found that users of alcohol and cigarettes were perceived by their peers as highly aggressive, nervous, insecure, and lacking in sociability. Engels et al. speculated that this group *might* be at risk for longer-term, more negative outcomes of substance use (e.g., adult alcohol problems). This may be a group at whom specific prevention and intervention efforts need to be aimed.

A key question still remains: Can we differentiate adolescents who will "benefit" from alcohol use from those who may suffer long-term harm so as to intervene with the latter group? Brown calls this approach selective prevention. Or, should we simply be more conservative and maintain the ban on adolescent alcohol use (which is as high as 21 years in some U.S. states)? Alternatively, would it be more advantageous to allow youth to drink alcohol legally and therefore, less covertly, in order to avoid the potential problems associated with youth prohibition (i.e., drinking in unsafe, unsupervised environments)? Then, we can intervene with those who are actually experiencing the negative consequences of alcohol use. Brown calls this approach indicative intervention.

Some harm-reduction programs have been developed to educate youth on alcohol use. Such programs are not necessarily aimed at eradicating adolescent drinking but are designed to foster safer alcohol-related attitudes, reduce how often and how much youth drink, and reduce unsupervised drinking, which is correlated with alcohol-related injuries. For example, McBride et al. (2004) demonstrate the sustained effects of a harm-reduction program: The intervention group continued to demonstrate more positive effects relative to a control group 17 months after completion of the intervention. Like McBride et al., others have argued that promoting complete abstinence in adolescent drinking through intervention is likely to be ineffective and unsuccessful.

Alcohol education can be effective when presented within a harm-reduction framework. This would be consistent with Brown's universal prevention while also perhaps maintaining some of the potential benefits of adolescent drinking as identified by such researchers as Engels et al. However, Engels et al. and Brown would agree that it is critical that selective prevention and indicative intervention programs exist for those youth who demonstrate problems or who are at increased risk for alcohol abuse-related problems.

Regardless of what approach we take, programs aimed at reducing alcohol consumption should be part of a broader societal response. Youth attitudes about alcohol likely reflect the modeling of adult attitudes and behavior.

References/Further Readings

Alcohol & Public Policy Group (2003). Alcohol: No ordinary commodity. *Addiction, 98,* 1343–1350.

Babor, T.F., Caetano, R., Casswell, S., Edwards, G., Giebrecht, N., Graham, K., Grube, J., Gruenewald, P., Hill, L., Holder, H., Homel, R., Osterberg, E., Rehm, J., Room, R., & Rossow, I. (2003). *Alcohol: No Ordinary Commodity—Research and Public Policy.* Oxford & London: Oxford University Press.

Carpenter, C.S., Kloska, D.D., O'Malley, P.M., & Johnston, L.D. (2007). Alcohol control policies and youth alcohol consumption: Evidence from 28 years of Monitoring the Future. *The B.E. Journal of Economic Analysis & Policy, 7*(1), Article 25.

Dent, C.W., Grube, J.W., & Biglan, A. (2005). Community level alcohol availability and enforcement of possession laws as predictors of youth drinking. *Preventive Medicine, 40,* 355–362.

Hill, L., Hamilton, G., Roche, A., Anderson, P., & McBride, N. (2004). Commentaries on McBride et al. *Addiction, 99,* 292–298.

Johnston, L.D., O'Malley, P.M., Bachman, J.G., & Schulenberg, J.E. (2007). *Monitoring the Future national survey results on drug use, 1975–2006: Volume I, Secondary school students* (NIH Publication No. 07-6205). Bethesda, MD: National Institute on Drug Abuse. Available: http://www.monitoringthefuture.org/pubs/monographs/vol1_2006.pdf

McBride, N., Farringdon, F., Midford, R., Meuleners, L., & Phillips, M. (2004). Harm minimization in school drug education: Final results from the School Health and Alcohol Harm Reduction Project (SHAHRP). *Addiction, 99,* 278–291.

Paglia-Boak, A. & Adlaf, E. (2006). Substance use and harm in the general youth population. In Canadian Centre on Substance Abuse's (CCSA). *Substance use in Canada: Youth in focus.* (pp. 4–13). Ottawa, ON: CCSA, Health Canada. Available: http://www.ccsa.ca/NR/rdonlyres/5D418288-5147-4CAC-A6E4-6D09EC6CBE13/0/ccsa0115212007e.pdf

Piko, B.F., Wills, T.A., & Walker, C. (2007). Motives for smoking and drinking: Country and gender differences in samples of Hungarian and US high school students. *Addictive Behavior, 32* 2087-2098.

Substance Abuse and Mental Health Services Administration, Office of Applied Studies (2003). National Survey on Drug Use and Health: Results. Rockville, MD: Department of Health and Human Services. Retrieved on June 23, 2006 from: http://oas.samhsa.gov/NHSDA/2k3NSDUH/2k3results.htm#ch3.

Substance Abuse and Mental Health Services Administration (1999). Treatment of Adolescents with Substance Abuse Disorders, Treatment Improvement Protocol (TIP), Series 32. Rockville, MD: Department of Health and Human Service.

ISSUE 3

Should Parental Consent Be Required for Adolescents Seeking Abortions?

YES: Teresa Stanton Collett, from Testimony Before the Subcommittee on the Constitution, Committee on the Judiciary, U.S. House of Representatives (September 6, 2001)

NO: Nancy E. Adler, Emily J. Ozer, and Jeanne Tschann, from "Abortion Among Adolescents," *American Psychologist* (March 23, 2003)

ISSUE SUMMARY

YES: Teresa Stanton Collett, law professor at the University of St. Thomas School of Law in Minnesota, analyzes the reasons for parental notification laws such as the Child Interstate Abortion Notification Act. She advocates parental involvement in a minor's decision to terminate a pregnancy.

NO: Nancy Adler, a professor of medical psychology at the University of California-San Francisco, and colleagues argue that the empirical data do not support the assumptions that adolescents are at a higher risk of psychological harm from abortion and are unable to make an adequately informed decision. In fact, studies suggest a relatively low risk associated with abortion, and adolescents seeking abortion appear to make an informed choice.

In 1973 the United States Supreme Court decision *Roe v. Wade* guaranteed a woman's right to access abortion without restriction during the first trimester. The decision did not mention, however, the age of the woman seeking the abortion. A number of individual states, therefore, have statutes that require a girl under the age of 18 to either receive one or both parents' or legal guardians' consent in order to obtain an abortion, or to notify one or both parents. In Canada, abortion was illegal until 1969, when Parliament amended the Criminal Code to allow abortion to be legal under certain circumstances. Then, in 1988, the Supreme Court of Canada struck down the amended law involving the "certain conditions" as unconstitutional (called the Morgentaler decision). Currently, Canada has no laws surrounding abortion, and it is treated like any other medical procedure. Canada has no age restrictions, and nothing similar to the U.S. parental notification/consent laws is required when adolescents seek abortion.

A U.S. Supreme Court decision, *Belotti v. Baird,* upheld the rights of states to place these restrictions on girls—provided there is an option for a "judicial bypass." This means that a girl can appear before a judge and either demonstrate that she is mature enough to make the decision to have an abortion or explain why notifying her parents would be detrimental to her. As the *Belotti* decision says, "[if] the court decides the minor is not mature enough to give informed consent, she must be given the opportunity to show that the abortion is in her best interest. If she makes this showing, the court must grant her bypass petition." As of February 2008, 35 states required parental involvement with an adolescent's decision to have an abortion (Guttmacher Institute, 2008). All of these states allow for judicial bypass.

Any discussions around abortion rights are rooted in the fundamental support or opposition to abortion itself. It can be challenging, therefore, to separate out the question of abortion from the question of whether or not minors can make an informed decision. Even adults who consider themselves to be pro-choice may support an adult woman's right to choose whether to carry or terminate a pregnancy, while feeling differently about girls under the age of 18 being able to make this decision for themselves. Others are clear on their belief that abortion is wrong regardless of the circumstance or age of the girl or woman involved. And still others believe that any girl or woman, regardless of age, is able and has the right to make this personal decision for herself. Specific to the debate around parental notification is the issue of someone other than a parent facilitating an abortion for a girl under the age of 18.

Because the Canadian legal situation is quite different from that of the United States, parental notification is not an issue. When considering abortion and receiving sexual health counseling, teen girls are encouraged by counselors to communicate with their parents *if* the girl has raised the issue of parental discussion. When having a therapeutic abortion, a teen typically has a support person accompany her to the appointment, and this is sometimes a parent. Sexual health counselors and abortion counselors, when discussing abortion with a young person, are legally bound to report to authorities (e.g., Child and Family Services and/or police) in exceptional circumstances outlined by the Criminal Code of Canada. These circumstances include: (1) when the client is under the legal age to consent to sexual activity (i.e., the girl is under 14 years of age and her sexual partner is not her peer—this means that he is at least 2 years older than the girl), (2) when there is reported child abuse or neglect or a violation of an authority relationship (e.g., a teacher having an affair with a 15-year-old student), or (3) when the client expresses intent to harm herself or others. Thus, there is no mandatory parental notification in Canada, but there is reporting to authorities in the circumstances outlined above.

Theresa Stanton Collett describes the rationale for parental involvement laws, focusing in particular on the Child Custody Protection Act and the Child Interstate Abortion Notification Act. Nancy Adler et al. discuss key issues raised by, and often used to justify, parental involvement laws. These authors do not believe these reasons are sufficient to warrant laws enforcing parental notification and/or consent.

YES

Teresa Stanton Collett

Transporting Minors for Immoral Purposes: The Case for the Child Custody Protection Act and the Child Interstate Abortion Notification Act

. . . [Activists] opposing federal legislation ensuring compliance with state laws that require parental involvement in a minor's decision to obtain an abortion ignore the reality that minors obtaining secret abortions return to the homes of their parents, at least until they attain majority. Consider the testimony of . . . Joyce Farley:

> My daughter was a victim of several horrible crimes between the ages of [twelve] and [thirteen]. My child was provided alcohol, raped and then taken out of state by a stranger . . . [the rapist's mother, who] arranged and paid for an abortion to be performed on my child.

⁕

> . . . The plan was to keep the rape and abortion a secret. If I had not contacted the State police on the morning of August 31, 1995, when I found my child missing, she might not be alive today. Severe pain and bleeding revealed complications from an incomplete abortion. . . .

Unfortunately, studies confirm that the experience of Mrs. Farley's daughter is not unique. "Younger teenagers are especially vulnerable to coercive and nonconsensual sex. . . . National studies reveal "[a]lmost two-thirds of adolescent mothers have partners older than [twenty] years of age."[1] . . . In a study of over 46,000 pregnancies by school-age girls in California, researchers found that

> 71 [percent], or over 33,000, were fathered by adult post-high-school men whose mean age was 22.6 years, an average of [five] years older than the mothers. . . . Even among junior high school mothers aged [fifteen] or younger, most births are fathered by adult men [six to seven] years their senior. *Men aged [twenty-five] or older father more births among California school-age girls than do boys under age [eighteen].*[2]

From *Health Matrix*, vol. 16, 2006, excerpts from pp. 108–116, 119–130, 132–134, 136–145. Copyright © 2006 by Teresa Stanton Collett. Reprinted by permission of the author.

. . . [A] number of young girls who obtained abortions without their parents' knowledge were encouraged to do so by a sexual partner who could be charged with statutory rape.

Abortion providers are reluctant to report information indicating a minor is the victim of statutory rape.[3] Yet, failure to report statutory rape may result in the minor returning to an abusive relationship. For example, a Planned Parenthood affiliate in Arizona was found civilly liable for failing to report the fact that the clinic had performed an abortion on a twelve-year-old girl who had been impregnated by her foster brother. The abortion provider did not report the crime as required by law, and the girl returned to the foster home where she was raped and impregnated a second time. . . .

Secret abortions do nothing to expose these men's wrongful conduct. In fact, by aborting the pregnancy, abusive partners destroy the public evidence of their misconduct and are licensed to continue the abuse. Furthermore, by failing to preserve fetal tissue the abortion providers may make effective prosecution of the rape difficult or impossible since the defendant's paternity cannot be established through the use of DNA testing.

Concerns such as these, as well as recognition of the medical benefits to minors from parental involvement, have persuaded legislators and citizens of forty-five states to enact some form of parental involvement legislation. However, not all of these laws are in effect. Of the laws in effect, some have little impact due to broad waiver provisions or broad definitions of who is to receive notice or give consent on behalf of the minor. Parents in twenty-eight states are effectively guaranteed the right to be involved in their minor daughters' decisions to obtain abortions in most cases where the abortions are obtained in the minor's state of residence. The Child Custody Protection Act (CCPA) and its companion legislation, the Child Interstate Abortion Notification Act (CIANA), are designed to ensure that these state law protections of minors continue, whether the minor obtains the abortion in her home state or elsewhere.

I. Crossing State Lines

It is difficult to know how often minors or others influencing them seek to evade the protections of effective parental involvement laws since official statistics are somewhat unreliable.[4] There are some indications that taking minors across state lines to avoid parental knowledge or consent is a significant problem. For example, . . . from 2000 to 2002, out-of-state minors obtained approximately one-third of all abortions obtained by minors in Delaware.[5] David Greenberg, past president and CEO of Planned Parenthood of Delaware, explained the reasons minors come to Delaware to obtain abortions:

> Sometimes, it's because the Delaware provider is closer or cheaper. Delaware requires parental notification for teens [fifteen] and younger. Delaware also has several 'bypasses.' One lets a teen's grandmother bring her. Another allows a licensed mental health worker to sign a statement if the girl cannot involve her parents.

This last exception ensures that minors need not experience the discomfort of revealing the consequences of their sexual activity to their parents, who, more likely than not, will be less than pleased to learn of their daughters' pregnancies.

. . . In contrast, Indiana, which has a parental consent law and is surrounded by Michigan, Ohio, Kentucky, Illinois, and Wisconsin, all of which, with the exception of Illinois, have parental involvement laws, reported only twenty-eight of 630 abortions were performed on non-resident minors in 2002.

The advertising of abortion clinics located in states with no parental involvement laws in effect or with liberal bypass provisions reinforces the statistical and anecdotal evidence suggesting that minors cross state lines to evade parental notification or consent requirements. In addition to the Hope Clinic's (located near St. Louis), attempt to attract Missouri citizens, "Yellow Pages in Pennsylvania carry display ads promoting abortion clinics in New Jersey and Maryland with this eye-catching marketing phrase: 'No Parental Consent Required.'" Abortion rights organizations also reinforce this message: "Usually you can get around telling your parents *by going to a clinic in a state without these restrictions* or, explaining your situation to a judge. But this can take time, so call right away."

All of this evidence supports the conclusion that abortion providers and others seeking to conceal minors' pregnancies from the minors' parents encourage minors to cross state lines to avoid the requirements of parental involvement laws. It is this conduct that the CCPA is designed to address.

II. Terms of the CCPA and CIANA

The CCPA would make it a federal crime to circumvent a home-state law requiring notification or consent of one or both parents prior to an abortion by transporting a minor across state lines to obtain an abortion. If found guilty, the defendant could be fined or imprisoned for not more than one year, or both. Any parent who suffers harm from a violation of the Act may obtain appropriate relief in a civil action as well. . . .

On April 27, 2005, the House of Representatives passed the companion bill, the CIANA, by a vote of 270-157. Like the CCPA, CIANA amends the federal criminal code to prohibit transporting a minor across a state line to obtain an abortion to avoid parental involvement laws in a minor's home state. CIANA also requires an abortion provider who performs an abortion on a minor who is a resident of a state other than that in which the abortion is performed to provide at least twenty-four hours actual notice (in person) to a parent of the minor before performing the abortion (or if actual notice is not possible after a reasonable effort, twenty-four hours constructive notice by certified mail). Transporting a minor with intent to evade parental involvement laws or performing an abortion without complying with CIANA's requirements may result in a criminal fine or imprisonment up to one year or both. Civil relief is also available to any parent who suffers harm from a violation of the Act. Like the CCPA, CIANA provides an affirmative defense to criminal and civil actions if the abortion provider reasonably believed the parent had consented or been notified as required by the law of the minor's home state or that the minor had obtained a judicial bypass of parental involvement in her home state.

Opponents of the CCPA and CIANA argue that any federal intervention in this area is misguided because a majority of teens already involve a parent in their decisions to obtain abortions, and those who do not often have good reasons for not doing so—including fear for their personal safety. Relying upon the fact that numerous medical associations oppose parental involvement laws, they argue that teens will delay or avoid needed care, sometimes resorting to dangerous self-treatments or "back-alley abortions." Finally, abortion rights activists argue that it is not the role of the federal government to involve itself in an issue that is first and foremost a matter of family law, historically an area regulated by the states. These are powerful arguments if true, but careful examination reveals them to be false.

III. Teens' Involvement of a Parent and the Consequences

The claim that a majority of teens have involved a parent in their decision to obtain abortions uniformly originates from a study by Stanley Henshaw and Kathryn Kost.[6] The methodology of the study itself is subject to several criticisms. While it purports to be "based on a nationally representative sample of more than 1,500 unmarried minors having an abortion," no respondents from the twenty-one states requiring parental involvement at that time were included. Therefore, no respondent was impacted by a parental consent or notification law. Further, the sample included only respondents who obtained abortions—there is no information from adolescents who decided to continue their pregnancies.

Even more importantly, the study is based only on a survey of adolescents with no attempt to gain information from the parents of the minors. To obtain an accurate understanding of the impact and value of parental involvement in minors' abortion decisions, it is necessary to have information from both the adolescents and their parents. Without information obtained directly from parents of those adolescents who responded to survey questions about their parents, there is no basis for assessing the accuracy of the adolescents' perceptions regarding their parents' knowledge, behavior, and attitudes.

Researcher bias is most evident in the design of the survey. Minors whose parents knew of their pregnancy were asked whether they experienced any of eleven possible "adverse" consequences from their parents finding out, but were not asked about any possible positive outcomes. At a minimum, balanced research would require asking respondents to also report benefits of parents finding out about their intended abortion and whether the minors are glad that their parents were involved in the decision-making process.

Notwithstanding these obvious flaws, the study is extensively relied upon in the debate regarding parental involvement laws. Opponents of such laws commonly cite the study for the proposition that "most teens voluntarily involve their parents in their abortion decision," relying on the fact that 61 percent of minors surveyed claimed a parent knew of their decision to obtain an abortion. Yet according to the study, only 45 percent of the minors had informed a parent of their pregnancy and abortion plans. The remaining parents had learned of the pregnancy and abortion plans from someone other than the minor.[6]

Of the girls under age sixteen whose parents were unaware of their pregnancy, only 47 percent involved "any adult" in their abortion decision or arrangements. For girls ages sixteen and seventeen, the percentage involving "any adult" only went up to 52 percent. "By the definitional parameters of Dr. Henshaw's study, the 'involvement' which the 'any adult' had in the girl's abortion 'arrangements' may have involved only paying for the abortion or driving to the clinic.[6] 'Involvement' did not necessarily include any sort of 'counsel' or emotional support."

With parental involvement laws in effect, the increase in parental involvement is dramatic. . . . For example, in Texas, parental involvement in abortion decision-making by minor girls significantly increased, from 69 percent to approximately 95 percent, immediately after enactment of that state's parental notification law. . . . With the encouragement of parental involvement laws, a substantial majority of minors include their parents in deciding how to respond to an unexpected pregnancy.

Contrary to the concerns expressed by opponents of CCPA and CIANA, the Henshaw and Kost study found that the primary reason minors avoided telling their parents was not fear of physical violence or abandonment, but a desire to avoid parental disappointment.

. . . Adolescents are often reluctant to inform their parents about any action that they know would displease or disappoint them. . . . But such fear does not justify empowering an adolescent to disregard the very people in her life who can provide her with informed, experienced input and sincere, selfless support while responding to an unplanned pregnancy.

The study also identified some effects of parental involvement for those minors who indicated that a parent knew of their intention to obtain an abortion. The most commonly reported effect was that parents' stress increased. Parental stress upon learning of a child's problem is hardly uncommon or indicative of family dysfunction. Another "adverse" result was that parents forced the respondent to stop seeing her boyfriend. It is not clear whether this consequence was harmful. . . . "[P]arents whose daughters told them about the pregnancy were understanding and supportive as often as they were upset and disappointed."[6] . . .

These results comport with the experience in states having parental involvement laws in effect. As part of the preparation for litigation related to the Minnesota parental involvement law, Minnesota Attorney General . . . in 1989, stated that "after some five years of the statute's operation, the evidence does not disclose a single instance of abuse or forceful obstruction of abortion for any Minnesota minor" and there was no evidence of any increase in medical complications which could be attributed to the law. . . .

IV. Objections by Professional Associations

Medical associations opposing the CCPA* assume that teens will not seek necessary health care if they know that their parents must consent. . . . However, the only study to actually test behavior of teens, rather than merely their opinions, rendered a different outcome. In establishing their family practice, an Israeli group of physicians sent some invitations to only teens and some invitations to teens after obtaining parental consent. The spontaneous response rate . . . was higher if parents were involved.[7] . . .

Recent research indicates that parental involvement is fundamental to the well-being of teens. . . . Their importance in the lives of their teens is strongly supported in research, particularly current research on resiliency.[8] . . . "[g]reater parental supervision and involvement is related to girls being more sexually assertive, delaying sexual initiation, using dual contraception, and being less likely to become pregnant or acquire an STD."[9]

In a study of 609 teenagers . . . recruited from high-risk neighborhoods . . ., the girls who reported less parental monitoring were 2.5 times more likely to become pregnant in the six month follow-up period than those who reported greater parental involvement. This finding led researchers to conclude "interventions designed to increase parental monitoring or adolescent females' perceptions of their parents' monitoring may be effective components of pregnancy prevention programs designed for minority youth."[10] . . .

These conclusions are consistent with studies finding that parental involvement laws reduce both teen pregnancy rates and teen abortion rates.[11, 12]

V. Anticipated Injuries from Self-Induced or Illegal Abortions

Some opponents . . . object on the basis of what they agree would be a rare case of a minor who might injure herself by attempting to self-induce an abortion or seek an illegal abortion.

Similar arguments have been asserted before in debates regarding other abortion regulations. They ultimately have proven groundless. When . . . restricted governmental funding for abortions was first being considered, Dr. Willard Cates, representing the Centers for Disease Control Abortion

---

*The American Medical Association (AMA) and the American Academy of Pediatrics (AAP) oppose parental involvement laws.

Surveillance Branch, predicted a total of seventy-seven excess deaths to women who would seek illegal abortions and an additional five excess deaths due to delays in seeking abortion.[13] . . . No such increase in mortality or morbidity had occurred.[14] . . .

This experience, combined with the experience of states having parental involvement laws with no ill effects on the well-being of minors—some for over two decades—suggests that injuries from self-induced or illegal abortions is largely a phantom fear.

VI. Medical Benefits of Parental Involvement

Testimony regarding families' experiences absent parental involvement laws, as well as the medical literature concerning women's health, suggest that there are many medical benefits from requiring parental involvement.

First and foremost, parental involvement laws ensure that parents have adequate knowledge to assist their daughters in responding to any post-abortion complications that may arise. When considering the Texas Parental Notification Act, legislators heard several stories of parents whose ability to respond to their daughters' medical crises were limited by not knowing of their daughters' abortions. Leslie French, a nineteen year-old student at the University of Texas testified regarding "Amy," who was fifteen and pregnant. Amy obtained an abortion on Friday, suffered terrible complications, and subsequently died on Sunday. Because Amy's parents did not know of her abortion, they delayed taking her to hospital until she was unconscious. . . .

At the same hearing Dr. Michael Love, an obstetrician and gynecologist practicing in Austin, Texas, testified to the value of parental knowledge of a minor's abortion:

> I know from my own personal experience—I have dealt with septic abortion. And it was a young lady that I cared for. She chose to go to one of the local reproductive clinics here in town, obtain their services, and if it were not for her parents knowing about what happened and caring for her, she probably would have died, because by the time I was notified about her, she already had an elevated temperature of 104—, she was obtunded, didn't know who she was, where she was, and if not for the concern of her parents who were able to bring her to the emergency room for treatment and subsequent surgery, there is a strong possibility that she would have died, much as the [fifteen]-year-old girl who died at Ben Taub hospital in the mid 90's [sic].

The credibility of Dr. Love's testimony was increased by the fact that he had previously worked in a clinic that performed elective abortions. . . .

Both Congress and the federal courts have received similar testimony; . . . CCPA and CIANA are aimed at preventing such tragedies.

By aborting their pregnancies, women lose the health benefits that childbirth and its accompanying lactation bring, including reduced risk of breast, ovarian, and endometrial cancer.[15, 16, 17]

. . . Furthermore, women who have had abortions experience "varying degrees of emotional distress" and are more likely to exhibit self-destructive behaviors, including suicide.[18] Two studies, one from the United States and the other from Finland, have shown surprising increased rates of suicide following abortion.[15] This phenomenon is not seen after miscarriage.[15] . . . Of particular concern is a survey study of Minnesota high school students that found adolescent girls were ten times more likely to attempt suicide in the six months after an abortion than adolescents who did not have abortions.[19] . . . Regardless of whether there is a causal link, the observation of the association between abortion and suicide "suggests careful screening and follow-up for depression and anticipatory guidance/precautions for women who choose elective abortion."[15]

At least forty-nine studies have demonstrated a statistically significant increase in premature births or low birth weight risk in women with prior induced abortions.[20]

. . . While it is often said that abortion is significantly safer than completing the pregnancy, the fact is we simply don't have the statistical information to know. Abortion providers have conceded this fact in the published literature.[21] Yet any attempts to remedy this critical lack of public health information are fought by abortion-rights advocates.[22]

VII. Federalism Concerns

The final argument that opponents of the CCPA and CIANA raise is related to the proper limits on federal power:

> Allowing a state's laws to extend beyond its borders runs completely contrary to the state sovereignty principles on which this country is founded. For example, gambling using slot machines is legal in the state of Nevada, but not in California. Residents of Nevada are prohibited from gambling while in California, while California residents of those states are permitted to gamble while in Nevada. Forcing citizens of California to carry their home state's law into Nevada, thereby prohibiting them from using slot machines while in Nevada, would be inconsistent with federalism principles. Requiring compliance within the borders of one state with the different and possibly conflicting law of another state would be even more ludicrous in the case of abortion—a constitutionally protected right—then it would be in the case of casino gambling, which is not a constitutionally protected activity.

Inherent in this argument are a number of assumptions, chief among them that a minor's obtaining a secret abortion is a "constitutionally protected activity" and that this activity trumps the historically recognized constitutional right of parents to direct the care and upbringing of their minor children. . . .

In *H.L. v. Matheson*, the Court specifically rejected the idea that "every minor, regardless of age or maturity, may give effective consent for termination of her pregnancy." . . . In contrast, "the fundamental right of parents to make decisions concerning the care, custody, and control of their children" is one of the oldest interests protected by American law. . . . Within this right is the right of a parent to direct the medical care of a minor. . . . Laws requiring parental involvement prior to the performance of an abortion on a minor are merely a limited application of this general rule to a specific surgical procedure. . . .

Given that states clearly have the constitutional authority to enact parental involvement laws, the only question posed by the CCPA and CIANA is whether Congress can pass legislation giving them extraterritorial effect. . . .

> First, [the CCPA] can be conceptualized as a federal law extension to state law that functions to increase the state law's efficacy. So under-stood, [the CCPA] does not extend the operation of state law extrater-ritorially, but simply is federal law that operates across state borders, as federal law often does.
>
> Second, the criticism that [the CCPA] unlawfully extends state laws is based on the misconception that one state's regulatory author-ity ends at its borders. . . . Today, state laws regularly apply to persons, transactions, and occurrences that occur outside the state's borders. Thus scholarly restatements of the law and the Model Penal Code both understand that states may regulate their citizens out-of-state activities, and may even criminalize out-of-state activity that is permissible in the state where it occurs.
>
> Third, . . . the Effects Clause and the Commerce Clause both can serve to extend states' regulatory powers. The Effects Clause gives Con-gress the power to alter the extraterritorial effect that one state's public acts, records and judicial proceedings have in other states. Thus before Congress enacted the Violence Against Women Act's full faith and credit provision, it was uncertain whether a protective order issued in State A would have effect in State B, whose laws differed from State A. . . . The federal act provided that State B was required to give effect to State A's protective order. Similarly, while states on their own may not enact protectionist legislation that disallows goods from other states to cross their borders, the Commerce Clause allows Congress to grant states such powers to discriminate against goods from other states. As a structural matter, a federal government that umpires the sister states' regulatory powers vis-a-vis one another is eminently sensible, and several consti-tutional provisions—including the Effects Clause and the Commerce Clause—empower Congress to serve this function.

In short, both state and federal governments have the ability to extend the reach of state laws that protect the welfare of the citizens of the states.

This principle clearly applies to CCPA. CIANA, however, goes beyond the extraterritorial enforcement of individual state's parental involvement laws and adds a national requirement of twenty-four hour notification to a parent of the minor's intent to obtain an abortion in cases where the minor has crossed state lines to obtain an abortion, absent a declaration of abuse by the minor, a medical emergency, an order of judicial bypass from the minor's home state, or compliance with the requirements of any parental involvement law from the minor's state of residence. If the minor's home state has no parental involvement law and the minor crosses state lines to obtain an abortion, the law would require notification of the minor's parent. . . .

The constitutional authority for Congress to enact such a law lies in its power to regulate interstate commerce. It seems beyond dispute that the provision of abortion services is within the channels of commerce, and therefore within the congressional power to regulate interstate commerce, particularly when considering that the CCPA and the CIANA are, in part, responding to interstate advertising by abortion providers. . . .

Conclusion

Experience has shown that parental involvement laws decrease teen pregnancy and increase the ability of responsible parents to guide and support their minor daughters during this difficult time. They protect the health of minors by ensuring that parents had adequate information to monitor and respond knowledgably to any post-abortion complications that arise. Such laws also assure the ability of parents to intervene in cases where their young daughters are being victimized by adult males who seek to conceal the consequences of their sexual conduct by persuading the girls to obtain secret abortions. Legislators in forty-five states have recognized the value of parental involvement in a minor's decision to obtain an abortion and have passed some form of parental involvement law. The CCPA and the CIANA simply further the ability of states to protect their minor citizens and the rights of parents to be involved in the decisions of their daughters who are facing unplanned pregnancies. . . .

References

1. American Academy of Pediatrics Committee on Adolescence, *supra* note 5, at 518. *See also* U.S. Dep't of Health and Hum. Serv., Report to Congress on Out-of-Wedlock Childbearing, DHHS Pub. No. 95-1257, at x (1995). . . .

   In fact, data indicate[s] that, among girls [fourteen] or younger when they first had sex, a majority of these first intercourse experiences were nonvoluntary. Evidence also indicates that among unmarried teenage mothers, two-thirds of the fathers are age [twenty] or older, suggesting that differences in power and status exist between many sexual partners.

   Id.

2. Mike A, Males, *Adult Involvement in Teenage Childbearing and STD*, 346 Lancet 64, 64–65 (1995) (emphasis added). . . .

3. Patricia Donovan, *Caught Between Teens and the Law: Family Planning Programs and Statutory Rape Reporting*, The Guttmatcher Report on Public Policy, June 1998, at 5.

4. *See* Rebekah Saul, *Abortion Reporting in the United States: An Examination of the Federal-State Partnership,* 30 Fam. Plan. Persp. 244, 245 (1998).

5. Jim Kessler et al., The Demographics of Abortion: The Great Divide Between Abortion Rhetoric and Abortion Reality 12 (2005). . . .

6. Stanley K. Henshaw & Kathryn Kost, *Parental Involvement in Minors' Abortion Decisions,* 24 Fam. Plan. Persp. 196, 205 (1992).

7. Barry Knishkowy et al., *Adolescent Preventative Health Visits: A Comparison of Two Invitation Protocols,* 13 J. Am. Board Fam. Prac. 11 (2000).

8. Minn. Dep't. of Health, Healthy Minnesotans: Strategies for Public Health, Vol. 2, at Category: Child and Adolescent Growth and Development 6 (2002).

9. Mary B. Short & Susan L. Rosenthal, *Helping Teenaged Girls Make Wise Sexual Decisions,* 48 Contemporary OB/GYN 84, 88 (2003).

10. Richard A. Crosby et al., *Low Parental Monitoring Predicts Subsequent Pregnancy Among African-American Adolescent Females,* 15 J. Pediatric & Adolescent Gynecology 43, 45 (2002).

11. *See* Michael J. New, Analyzing the Effect of Pro-Life Legislation on the Incidence of Abortion Among Minors 8 (June 15, 2005) (unpublished manuscript on file with author) (finding that "parental involvement laws on average reduce the number of abortions performed on teens by around 15 percent").

12. James L. Rogers et al., *Impact of the Minnesota Parental Notification Law on Abortion and Birth,* 81 Am. J. Pub. Health 294 (1991).

13. Diana B. Pettiti & Willard Cates, Jr., *Restricting Medicaid Funds for Abortions: Projections of Excess Mortality for Women of Childbearing Age,* 67 Am. J. Pub. Health 860, 861 (1977).

14. Center for Disease Control, *Health Effects of Restricting Federal Funds for Abortion—United States,* 28 MMWR: Morbidity and Mortality Wkly. Rep. 37, 37 (1979).

15. *See* John M. Thorp, Jr. et al., *Long-Term Physical and Psychological Health Consequences of Induced Abortion: Review of the Evidence,* 58 Obstetrical & Gynecological Surv. 67, 67 (2003).

16. Valerie Beral et al., *Does Pregnancy Protect Against Ovarian Cancer?,* Lancet, May 20, 1978, at 1083 ("pregnancy—or some component of the childbearing process—protects directly against ovarian cancer").

17. Grethe Albrektsen et al., *Is the Risk of Cancer of the Corpus Uteri Reduced by a Recent Pregnancy? A Prospective Study of 765,756 Norwegian Women,* 61 Int'l. J. Cancer 485 (1995).

18. Elizabeth Ring-Cassidy & Ian Gentles, Women's Health After Abortion 17 (2nd ed. 2003).

19. B. Garfinkel et al., Stress, Depression and Suicide: A Study of Adolescents in Minnesota, Responding to High Risk Youth 43–55 (1986).

20. Brent Rooney & Byron C. Calhoun, *Induced Abortion and Risk of Later Premature Births,* 8 J. Am. Physicians & Surgeons 46, 46 (2003). . . .

21. J. Richard Udry et al., *A Medical Record Linkage Analysis of Abortion Underreporting,* 28 Fam. Plan. Persp. 228, 228 (1996). . . .

22. Stanley K. Henshaw, *Unintended Pregnancy and Abortion: A Public Health Perspective, in* A Clinician's Guide to Medical and Surgical Abortions 11, 20 (Maureen Paul et al., eds. 1999).

Nancy E. Adler, Emily J. Ozer, and
Jeanne Tschann

 **NO**

Abortion Among Adolescents

Issues of abortion for adolescents are embedded in the status and meaning of abortion in the country in which they are living. For adolescents in
much of the world, particularly in developing countries, the major problem is access to safe, legal abortion. One quarter of women in the world
live in countries in which abortion is either completely prohibited or permitted only to save the woman's life. These restrictions are not limited to
adolescents but apply to women of all ages. . . . In the United States, safe,
legal abortion is available, but access is more limited for adolescents than
for adults. The most common restriction is the requirement in some states
for parental involvement or consent.

Worldwide, there has been a move toward liberalizing abortion laws.
In the second half of the 20th century, most industrialized nations and
many developing countries reformed and eased their abortion laws. As
legal abortion becomes more widely available, issues of adolescents' access
become more salient. Most of the available research on adolescent abortion is from the United States but may be useful for other countries that are
contemplating potential consent requirements. Below, we review the current status of abortion laws pertaining to adolescents worldwide, examine
questions raised by parental involvement laws in the United States and by
the relevant psychological research, and discuss the issues facing adolescents seeking abortions in the United States and internationally.

Parental Involvement Laws

Out of 158 countries in which legal abortion is available, 55 countries
permit abortion only when necessary to save the life of the woman. Parental
authorization for abortion is required in 28 countries, including 5 countries in which abortions may only be performed to save the woman's life.
Cuba, Denmark, Italy, Norway, Turkey, and most Eastern European countries require written parental consent for adolescents to have an abortion,
and in Turkey, married women must have the consent of their husbands.
In several Western countries, including Denmark, Italy, and Norway, a
court or hospital committee may bypass this parental consent restriction.

From *American Psychologist,* vol. 58, no. 3, March 2003, excerpts from pp. 211–217. Copyright
© 2003 by American Psychological Association. Reprinted by permission via Rightslink.

As of 2001, France no longer requires parental consent for adolescents but does require an adult of the minor's choice to be involved in the abortion process.

Thirty-two states [34 as of February 2008] in the United States currently restrict adolescents' access to abortion. Parental notification laws require that one or both parents be notified prior to the adolescent having her abortion; parental consent laws require explicit permission from one or both parents. Fifteen states enforce parental notification laws; 17 enforce parental consent laws. Several states permit another adult family member such as a grandparent to give consent instead of a parent. As of 2001, all but 4 states with parental consent or notification laws allow for an alternative judicial bypass of parental involvement. This is granted by a judge if (a) the minor is deemed capable of giving informed consent or (b) the abortion is in the best interests of the adolescent and parental involvement would likely cause harm or abuse of the minor.

Issues Raised by Parental Involvement Laws

The stated purposes of most parental involvement laws in the United States are to protect adolescents from making a harmful decision and to promote family functioning by assuring that parents become involved in their daughters' decision making and/or care. Parents of legal minors are responsible for their children's well-being, including the authorization of medical treatment. However, adolescents are allowed to make some decisions regarding reproductive health independently; for example, all 50 U.S. states and the District of Columbia allow minors to consent to testing and treatment for sexually transmitted diseases. Such testing and treatment are considered to be *sensitive services*. Laws regarding sensitive services recognize that such services are inextricably bound to issues of adolescents' sexuality and that minors may be hesitant to seek them if they have to inform their parents. A recent survey confirmed that parental notification can have adverse effects on service utilization and on health. [One study] found that almost 60% of current female patients under the age of 18 said that their utilization of services would change if parental notification were required. Anticipated adverse effects included delay and discontinuation of services, including sexual health care and STD testing. Most states do not require parental involvement for prenatal care or delivery if adolescents decide to continue their pregnancies. Thirty-four states and the District of Columbia explicitly permit a minor mother to place her child for adoption without her own parents' permission or knowledge. Eleven states make no distinction between minor and adult parents.

Parental involvement laws differentiate abortion from other sensitive services on the premise that this is a high-risk decision. . . . Below, we examine the three key rationales for restrictive laws regarding adolescents: (a) that abortion poses a significant risk, (b) that adolescents are incapable of making an adequately informed decision, and (c) that adolescents benefit from parental involvement that results from notification or consent. . . .

Risk of Harm From Abortion

Abortion itself carries relatively few medical risks, especially compared with the risks of childbearing. Although overall pregnancy-related mortality rates in the United States are 9.2 per 100,000 live births, the mortality rate is 0.3 per 100,000 legal abortions. In other countries where abortion is safe and legal, rates are comparably low compared with pregnancy-related deaths.

Well-designed studies of psychological responses following abortion have consistently shown that risk of psychological harm is also low. Some women experience psychological dysfunction following an abortion, but postabortion rates of distress and dysfunction are lower than preabortion rates. Moreover, the percentage of women who experience clinically relevant distress is small and appears to be no greater than in general samples of women of reproductive age. A recent study . . . showed not only that rates of disorders such as depression and posttraumatic stress disorder (PTSD) were not elevated in a large sample of 442 abortion patients followed for two years but also that the incidence of PTSD was actually lower in patients postabortion than are rates in the general population.

Although overall risks of psychological harm from abortion are low, one might still worry that adolescents are at heightened risk. The empirical data, however, do not support this. The best study of adolescent abortion followed 360 adolescents over two years after they had been interviewed when seeking a pregnancy test (Zabin, Hirsch, & Emerson, 1989). Some adolescents had a negative test, some were pregnant and carried to term, and some were pregnant and aborted their pregnancy. The adolescents who underwent an abortion showed significant drops in anxiety and significant increases in self-esteem and internal locus of control from baseline to two years later. In addition, the abortion patients appeared to be functioning as well as—or even better than—adolescents who had had a negative pregnancy test or who had carried to term. Two years after baseline, the abortion group showed lower trait anxiety than the other two groups, had higher self-esteem than the negative pregnancy group, and had a stronger internal locus of control than the childbearing group. They were also more likely than those in the other groups to be in school or to have graduated from high school, more likely to be at grade level if they were in school, and less likely to have a subsequent pregnancy, as well as having higher economic well-being.

Recent studies have examined directly whether legal minors are at greater risk of negative psychological responses following abortion than are older patients. Quinton, Major, and Richards (2001) compared responses of 38 abortion patients under age 18 versus 402 adult patients. On . . . a standardized measure of depression, there were no differences either one month or two years postabortion. One month postabortion, the minors reported somewhat less satisfaction and benefit in relation to their abortion than did the adults, but over time, minors' ratings became more positive, and two years later there were no differences by age. Thus, the minors increasingly reported having benefited from the abortion, whereas the adults reported such benefits at both time periods. Even at the one-month assessment, the mean levels for adolescents were in the positive range. Similar results were obtained [in another] one-month-[study comparing] postabortion functioning of 23 patients under 18 years of age with that of 40 patients ages 18–21 years. There were no significant age differences on standardized measures of depression, self-esteem, anxiety, or positive states of mind or on emotional responses to abortion. [Minors] reported less comfort than adult patients with their decision one month postabortion, but the absolute values signified that most minors were comfortable with their decision. In this sample, there was no difference by age in patients' feelings about whether abortion was the right decision. Notably, results suggested that adolescents were not harmed by the abortion experience; in fact, there were significant decreases in scores on the Beck Depression Inventory and on negative emotions, and there was a significant increase in positive emotions from preabortion levels to one month postabortion.

In sum, the available data show that mean postabortion scores on psychological measures are well within normal bounds for minors as well as for adults. The data do not suggest that legal minors are at heightened risk of serious adverse psychological responses compared with adult abortion patients or with peers who have not undergone abortion.

Informed Consent

A second rationale for restrictive laws is that adolescents are not capable of making an adequately informed choice. Although adolescents are often viewed as irrational and less capable of informed action than adults, the empirical data suggest a more complex view. Studies examining the extent to which adolescents believe themselves to be invulnerable to bad outcomes have concluded that adolescents are no more biased in their perceptions than are adults. Other research has found that adolescents are consistent in their reasoning and decision making, behaving in ways that conform to rational models of decision making. [One study] found that young adolescents age 14 did not differ significantly from adults in their responses to hypothetical treatment choices; they were no different in their understanding of treatment options or the reasonableness of their decision as evaluated by health professionals. Koocher and DeMaso (1990), in discussing children's competence in relation to medical procedures in general, noted that "children are often more capable of expressing preferences and participating in making major life decisions than is generally recognized in medical settings or under the law" (p. 68).

Competence is domain specific; performance in one sector does not necessarily generalize to performance in other sectors, and there is no single measure of competence. This limits the extent to which research in areas other than health can be applied to evaluating adolescents' capacity to give informed consent for abortion. For example, one area where there is substantial discussion of competency regards the competency of adolescents to stand trial as adults. Research on adjudicative competence cannot be readily applied to competency to consent for abortion, however. For one thing, the competencies needed to make decisions regarding one's legal defense in a trial are markedly different from those needed to decide about pregnancy. Components of adjudicative competence include such things as the ability to work collaboratively with an attorney, to testify at trial, and to understand the sequence of pretrial and trial events. These place different demands than does the abortion decision. In addition, adolescents involved in these two domains are different in important ways. As discussed below, adolescents who are seeking abortion may have more psychological and social resources and be more capable of making an informed choice than are their peers. The reverse is likely to be true for adolescents facing prosecution for criminal activities, who have higher than average rates of mental disorders.

Studies examining the quality of adolescents' reasoning regarding hypothetical or real decisions about abortion provide further caution about applying findings on adolescent reasoning in general to understanding adolescents' abilities to consent to abortion. In a study of 90 female adolescents in their first trimester of pregnancy who had decided to have an abortion, [there were] differences in global moral reasoning between younger (12–14 years) and older (17–19 years) adolescents but [no] differences in reasoning about abortion. [College] students anticipated a different process of seeking advice and consultation in deciding about an abortion than they would for other types of decisions. Among other differences, the students reported that they were relatively more likely to consult with their significant other for an abortion decision than for a medical, a career or educational, or an interpersonal decision. They also showed different patterns with respect to consulting family members, friends, and professionals for abortion than for other decisions.

Ambuel and Rappaport (1992) . . . examined the decision making of 75 patients seeking a pregnancy test, comparing legal adults ages 18–21 years with two groups of younger adolescents: ages 14–15 years and ages 16–17 years. Some were considering abortion, and some planned to carry to term. Patients' interviews with a pregnancy counselor were evaluated on four indicators of competence: (a) volition, or the voluntary and independent nature of the decision; (b) global quality of reasoning; (c) awareness of consequences of the decision; and (d) the types of considerations expressed regarding the decision. Neither younger nor older adolescents considering abortion differed from legal adults on any of the components of competency. Among patients not considering abortion, there was no difference in competency between those ages 16–17 and those ages 18–21, but the youngest adolescents who planned to carry to term were significantly lower in volition, awareness of consequences, and global quality of the decision.

An earlier study of 26 adults and 16 adolescents seeking a pregnancy test also found little difference in the decision-making processes of adolescents ages 13–17 and adults ages 18–25.

The findings by Ambuel and Rappaport (1992) are consistent with the view that adolescents seeking abortion are relatively more capable than their peers of making an informed choice. The youngest adolescents who planned to carry to term showed lower quality decision making than legal adults, whereas same-aged adolescents considering abortion did not differ from adults in their decision processes. Similarly, among teens studied by Zabin et al. (1989), those who subsequently had an abortion differed in key ways from those who subsequently carried to term. At baseline, adolescents who subsequently chose abortion had higher educational achievement, had more-educated mothers, and were from families in better economic circumstances; all of these factors are likely to be associated with greater competence. . . .

In sum, this research suggests that under current conditions, adolescent abortion patients may represent a subgroup that is more competent than pregnant adolescents who are not considering abortion. The actual experience in judging adolescents' competence and justification for abortion supports this view. Where it has been studied, it appears that virtually all adolescents' requests for judicial bypass are granted by judges assessing their competence and reasons for requesting bypass of parental consent.

Consequences of Parental Involvement in the Abortion Decision

Although parental involvement laws aim to promote family communication and functioning, there is little empirical data about whether they actually do so. Forcing communication between parents and children around the abortion decision may not have the desired positive effects. Health care providers and investigators have voiced concern about possible physical or emotional harm to adolescents who are forced to involve their parents in their abortion decision. Many, if not most, adolescents voluntarily tell their parents. Studies have reported widely varying numbers ranging from 35% to 91% of adolescents who inform their parents even when parental consent is not mandated; younger adolescents are more likely to inform their parents than are older adolescents. Adolescents who do not tell parents about their pregnancy cite fear of disappointing their parents, fear of anger, concern that their parents would punish them, and worries that a parent might become physically violent.

Young women who do not tell their parents about their pregnancy appear to have different family circumstances than those who do. Those who do not involve their parents perceive their family communication to be less open, feel less free to talk about feelings in general, and are less comfortable talking to their parents about sex than are young women who tell their parents about their pregnancy. Zabin and Sedivy (1992) found no differences in satisfaction with the decision to terminate or to continue to term between adolescents who consulted with a parent who supported their decision and adolescents who did not consult with a parent. However, adolescents who consulted with a parent who did not support their decision were less happy than were either those who never consulted their parents or those who consulted their parents and received support. Zabin and Sedivy concluded that "the small number who did not communicate made a responsible decision" (Zabin & Sedivy, 1992, p. 323).

One problem with mandatory parental notification is that young women with serious concerns about the consequences of notifying their parents may pursue other avenues to obtain abortions. As a result, some adolescents subject themselves to risk of injury and death by seeking an illegal abortion. For example, Becky Bell, a teenager in Indiana, died from the complications of an illegal abortion. She underwent this procedure because under Indiana law she would have had to obtain consent from one of her parents for a legal abortion, and she did not want to disappoint them. Parental consent requirements may also cause adolescents to seek legal abortions in another state. In some states, within-state abortions among minors decreased by as much as 50% after passage of parental consent laws, while out-of-state abortions obtained by minors in states not requiring parental consent increased in the same period.

Research by Henshaw and Kost (1992) provides indirect-evidence about the potential harm in forcing adolescents to notify parents of their pregnancy. In that study, adolescents whose parents found out about their pregnancy without the adolescent telling them reported more adverse consequences due to parental knowledge compared with adolescents who voluntarily told their parents about the pregnancy. These adverse consequences included parents making them have an abortion, physical violence, and being forced to leave home.

Current Debate in the United States

Debate in the United States about adolescent abortion is occurring largely in the courts in the context of legal challenges to parental consent legislation. The American Psychological Association has filed several amicus briefs arguing against restrictions on adolescents' access to abortion. This is an area where legal and scientific arguments and conventions are not well aligned. [Research] cannot prove "no difference"; not finding a difference between adolescent and adult competence (or psychological response) is not equivalent to proving that there are no differences. This dilemma derives from the difficulty of proving the null hypothesis. In the current situation, where several studies have not found a difference in psychological functioning or in competency, one can at least say that the scientific evidence does not provide justification for the assumptions on which restrictive legislation is built. Though one cannot say there is no difference, one can say with some confidence that the available data are consistent with the view that there are no meaningful differences between adolescents and adults.

One challenge to this view is that the null findings could result from inadequate statistical power in studies with small numbers of participants. However, although it would be helpful to have large-scale studies of representative samples, this may not be necessary to draw some conclusions. A key issue is the clinical significance, not simply the statistical significance, of a difference between groups. Studies with large samples can result in statistically significant differences even when the effect size is quite small. For example, with large numbers of participants, a half-point difference on the Beck Depression Inventory between adolescents and adults could be statistically significant. However, such a small difference would have few implications for mental health because the vast majority of both adolescents and adults score well below the cutoff for moderate or severe depression. Only where there are large enough effects to have public health implications should one demand policy intervention. If adolescents are markedly less competent than adults or if adolescents show substantially worse psychological outcomes after abortion than do adults, this should show up as a medium or large effect, which would not require a large sample to show a difference between groups.

U.S. and International Issues

Adolescents throughout the world are having abortions, but their experiences vary dramatically depending on where they live. A major determinant is the legal status of abortion for all women; a secondary one is the restrictions placed on adolescents. Even within the United States, there are marked differences by state and region. An urban teen in New York or California, where parental consent is not required and public and private providers are available, will have a much easier time than adolescents who live in states such as North Dakota or Mississippi, which require consent of both parents, or who live in a rural area where there are no providers. There are some countries, notably the Scandinavian countries, where abortions may be easier to obtain than in the United States and may carry less stigma, in part because adolescent sexual activity is itself less stigmatized. Yet, in many parts of the world, teens seeking to terminate their pregnancies face far greater risks and obstacles than do their counterparts in the United States.

Unfortunately, there are few comparative data on adolescents from other countries. Among industrialized countries with similar or less restrictive abortion laws, the small number of psychologically oriented studies have focused largely on adolescents' attitudes toward abortion or on the psychological effects of abortion (Quinton et al., 2001). With few exceptions, research on adolescents and abortion in developing countries has mainly been concerned with basic issues of access and safety. It seems likely that psychological responses would be more negative in countries and states where adolescents experience greater risk, in terms of both physical safety and social stigma, in terminating an unwanted pregnancy.

The legal and social status of abortion within countries is often closely tied to predominant religious teachings. Agostino and Wahlberg (1991) studied adolescents in Italy and Sweden. The majority of Italian adolescents in that study indicated that abortion is only justified on medical grounds, whereas most Swedish adolescents in the study believed that nonmedical reasons also provide sufficient grounds for abortion. The authors attributed this difference in attitudes to greater Catholic influence in Italy and its prohibition of abortion. Yet countries with the same predominant religion may vary with respect to abortion laws. In Islamic law, for example, the killing of a soul is strictly prohibited, and the fetus is generally considered to develop a soul at the time of quickening, when the mother can detect fetal movements. However, although some Islamic countries permit abortion prior to quickening, others prohibit abortions completely. Thus, adolescents in other countries are likely to be affected both by secular laws and by their own religious beliefs about abortion, similar to the U.S. political and religious debate over when life begins.

It is important to note critical differences in the social roles of adolescent women across the industrialized and developing world. Although adolescent urban elites in many developing countries occupy social roles similar to those of many U.S. adolescents with respect to pursuing higher education and career experience prior to marriage, large numbers of adolescents from rural or less elite backgrounds marry and begin families as adolescents. In these countries, adolescent pregnancy does not necessarily imply single parenthood, as is more often the case in the United States. In India, for example, roughly 30% of rural female adolescents are married by age 15, and 40% of all women ages 15–19 are married, despite laws prohibiting marriage before age 18 for females. Early marriage is often accompanied by strong pressures to quickly prove fertility because a young woman's security in the home of her husband's family may be largely determined by her ability to bear children—particularly a son. Adolescent women in such cultural and familial settings may experience little real power in decisions regarding abortion; those in rural settings must further contend with limited access to reproductive health services.

In sum, the overriding issue regarding abortion for adolescents in the international context is that abortion is frequently completely prohibited. Other issues are the age at which young women marry and are considered adults, the power that women have to determine their own fertility, the availability of safe abortion, and the stigma associated with abortion due to societal norms and religious beliefs. If the international trend toward liberalization of abortion laws continues in both industrialized and developing nations, the issues that currently are of concern in the United States may become more central in those countries. Within the United States, the focus of debate on adolescent abortions has been on the need for parental involvement and/or consent. Although it seems obvious that it is better to have parents involved in their minor daughter's decision making and care, there is little evidence that adolescents benefit from having this mandated. Moreover, there is reason to be concerned about the potential adverse effects of legislating parental involvement. Parental consent legislation has also been predicated on the assumption that it is needed because adolescents are at high risk for adverse responses to abortion and are not capable of making an adequately informed choice. Research to date provides no backing for these assumptions.

It is tempting to end this article by calling for research on adolescents' decision making about abortion and their psychological responses in the United States and internationally, and such research would certainly be useful. In the United States, for example, it would be informative to compare adolescents' experience with and responses to abortion in states with different parental consent laws. This could assess whether hypothesized benefits of parental notification or consent (e.g., involvement of parents in their daughter's care, better medical and psychosocial outcomes, increased communication within the family, and strengthened relationships between parents and children) occur more often in states with consent laws. Similarly, the relative prevalence of potential hazards (e.g., increased rates of abuse, increased conflict between parents and children, increased stress for adolescents who have to go through a court hearing, more midtrimester abortions, and more adolescents going out of state or seeking illegal abortions) should be examined. Some of these effects have been studied, but there is too little information to allow for a comprehensive analysis of costs versus benefits. At this time, there is no evidence that parental consent is either needed or beneficial. Further debate and policy discussion would benefit from studies that directly test the consequences of requiring parental notification or consent for abortion.

At the same time, the research suggested above is not the most critical need. In all countries, abortion generally represents the failure to prevent an unwanted pregnancy. In some countries, this is due to lack of access to effective contraception; in others, it may be due to high rates of rape, incest, or other coerced intercourse. In still other countries, abortion rates may be affected by a preference for male children. While all women, including adolescents, who need to terminate an unwanted pregnancy should have access to safe, legal abortion, it is also necessary to focus on the conditions that lead to the need for abortion.

References

Agostino, M. B., & Wahlberg, V. (1991). Adolescents' attitudes to abortion in samples from Italy and Sweden. *Social Science and Medicine, 33,* 77–83.

Ambuel, B., & Rappaport, J. (1992). Developmental trends in adolescents' psychological and legal competence to consent to abortion. *Law and Human Behavior,* 16, 129–154.

Henshaw, S. K., & Kost, K. (1992). Parental involvement in minors' abortion decisions. *Family Planning Perspectives,* 24, 196–213.

Koocher, G. P., & DeMaso, D. R. (1990). Children's competence to consent to medical procedures. *Pediatrician,* 17, 68–73.

Quinton, W., Major, B., & Richards, C. (2001). Adolescents and adjustment to abortion: Are minors at greater risk? *Psychology, Public Policy, and Law, 7,* 491–514.

Zabin, L. S., Hirsch, M. B., & Emerson, M. R. (1989). When urban adolescents choose abortion: Effects on education, psychological status and subsequent pregnancy. *Family Planning Perspectives, 21,* 248–255.

Zabin, L. S., & Sedivy, V. (1992). Abortion among adolescents: Research findings and the current debate. *Journal of School Health, 62,* 319–324.

POSTSCRIPT

Should Parental Consent Be Required for Adolescents Seeking Abortions?

The abortion debate, like many other controversies, is often viewed in extremes. One is pro-choice or one is anti-choice. There is no gray area in between. At the same time, however, introducing a minor into the discussion often alters the discussion—particularly the younger the girl is who is seeking the abortion. In some cases, the younger a girl is, the more protection adults may feel she needs. In other cases, the younger she is, the more likely some abortion opponents might be to make an exception, citing a preference for the "necessary evil" of abortion over letting a 14-year-old girl become a parent.

An important factor to keep in mind is the fact that not everyone has sexual intercourse by choice. While many abortion opponents will make an exception for pregnancies that are caused by rape or incest, others maintain that a pregnancy is a pregnancy and that no potential life should be punished even if it were conceived in a violent manner. If a state law requires that a parent be notified, and the parent who is notified is the one who caused the pregnancy, then parental notification may have stopped an abortion only to put a girl's safety or life in jeopardy. On the other hand, in cases of incest, parental notification could help to bring rape or incest—which are all too frequently hidden or kept private—out into the open so that it will not happen again, and the perpetrator, if known, can be arrested and the abuse stopped.

Legislating personal decisions is, as always, a slippery slope. How far do we go? How do laws legislating one behavior or type of procedure affect others? For example, parental consent is currently not required in order for a minor to obtain birth control. Controversy remains around one particular type of birth control, Emergency Contraception, formerly known as the "morning-after" pill. A form of emergency contraception, Plan B (levonorgestrel), is dispensed by a pharmacist without a prescription in Canada. Emergency Contraception is not an abortion; it prevents pregnancy from happening. In fact, if a woman is pregnant without knowing it, has unprotected intercourse, and then takes Emergency Contraception, her pregnancy should not be affected by the Emergency Contraception. At the same time, however, since one of the ways in which Emergency Contraception works is by preventing a fertilized egg from implanting, those who believe that life begins at conception argue that Emergency Contraception is the same thing as abortion. Therefore, the door that is open to parental notification and consent laws remains open to support for parental notification or consent before Emergency Contraception can be dispensed. This in turn could lead to legislation requiring parental notification or consent for birth control pills and condoms. How would such notification be enacted and enforced within a pharmacy as condoms and emergency contraception pills (in Canada) are relatively easily accessible?

In an ideal world, people would not have sex before they are old enough and established enough in their lives to be able to manage the potential consequences of being in a sexual relationship. In an ideal world, abortion would not be necessary because no pregnancy would be unplanned or come as the result of rape or incest. However, we do not live in an ideal world. People, regardless of age, have unprotected sex or use contraception incorrectly. People, regardless of age, are raped and sexually abused. Women, regardless of age, have pregnancies that may need to be terminated for medical reasons. In some households, the revelation of an unplanned pregnancy can result in violence against the pregnant teen and/or her partner.

Is there a solution between these two extremes that could enable parents to show their care and support of their adolescents while at the same time letting them make their own decisions? Where do feelings about abortion, in general, come into play in one's thoughts and opinions on this particular matter?

It is important to note that studies do indicate that many adolescents seek the advice of parents or trusted adults when considering abortion. In fact, as many as 9 out of 10 girls seeking an abortion consult with a parent. This figure was higher for younger girls, girls who live with their parents, and girls who have good communication with their parents. In summary, it appears that regardless of the legislation, the majority of adolescent girls consult with a parent regarding their abortion decision. This perhaps is indicative of an adequate level of maturity and competence in making important life decisions regarding abortion.

References/Further Reading

Alford, S. (January 2003). *Adolescents and abortions: The facts*. Washington, D.C.: Advocates for Youth. Available online at: http://www.advocatesforyouth.org/publications/factsheet/fsabortion.htm.

Benson, M. J. (2004). After the adolescent pregnancy: Parents, teens, and families. *Child & Adolescent Social Work Journal*, 21(5), 435–455.

Center for Reproductive Rights (January 2006). The Teen Endangerment Act: Harming young women who seek abortions. Available online at: http://www.reproductiverights.org/pub_fac_ccpa.html.

Earll, C.G. (2000). Frequently asked questions: Parental involvement in minor abortions. *Citizen Link: Focus on Social Issues*. Colorado Springs, CO: Focus on the Family. Available online at: http://www.family.org/cforum/fosi/bioethics/faqs/a0027733.cfm.

Finken, L. (2005). The role of consultants in adolescents' decision making: A focus on abortion decisions. In J.E. Jacobs & P. A. Klaczynski (Eds.), pp. 255–278. *The development of judgment and decision making in children and adolescents.* Mahwah, NJ: Lawrence Erlbaum.

Guttmacher Institute (February 2008). State policies in brief: Parental involvement in minors' abortions. New York: Guttmacher Institute. Available online at: http://www.guttmacher.org/statecenter/spibs/spib_PIMA.pdf.

Hull, N. E. H., & Hoffer, P. C. (2001). *Roe v. Wade: The Abortion Rights Controversy in American History* (University Press of Kansas).

Jones, R. K., Purcell, A., Singh, S., & Finer, L. B. (2005). Adolescents' reports of parental knowledge of adolescents' use of sexual health services and their reactions to mandated parental notification for prescription contraception. *Journal of the American Medical Association, 293*(3), 340–348.

Klick, J., & Stratmann, T. (2008, spring). Abortion access and risky sex among teens: Parental involvement laws and sexually transmitted Diseases. *Journal of Law, Economics, & Organization, 24*(1).

Scott, E. S., & Woolard, J. L. (2004). The legal regulation of adolescence. In R.M. Lerner, Richard M & L. Steinberg (Eds.), pp. 523–550. *Handbook of adolescent psychology* (2nd ed.). Hoboken, NJ: Wiley & Sons.

ISSUE 4

Do Boys Worry about an Ideal Body Image as Much as Girls Do?

YES: **Diane C. Jones and Joy K. Crawford**, from "The Peer Appearance Culture During Adolescence: Gender and Body Mass Variations," *Journal of Youth and Adolescence* (vol. 35, no. 2, 2006)

NO: Duane A. Hargreaves and Marika Tiggemann, from "Idealized Media Images and Adolescent Body Image: 'Comparing' Boys and Girls," *Body Image* (vol. 1, 2004)

ISSUE SUMMARY

YES: Diane Jones, an associate professor in educational psychology at the University of Washington, and Joy Crawford, a doctoral student in human development and cognition at the University of Washington, suggest that adolescent boys experience more appearance pressure and teasing than adolescent girls. They also argue that boys discuss muscle building more than girls discuss dieting.

NO: Duane Hargreaves and Marika Tiggemann, researchers in the School of Psychology at Flinders University, state that adolescent girls are more vulnerable to body image pressures than boys. They argue that the glamorization of eating disorders among female celebrities and the media play a significant role.

Many young adolescents are dissatisfied with their bodies. Research maintains that 50–70% of adolescent girls participate in dieting, and an even higher number maintain a feeling of dissatisfaction with their body and a longing to be thin. It is also reported that body weight dissatisfaction and affiliated weight-loss strategies may be a precondition for developing an eating disorder (Tomori and Rus-Makovec, 2000). Research also indicates that adolescent boys have concerns about their bodies. Specifically, it is estimated that one third of adolescent boys desire a thinner body while another third desire a larger more muscular build. McCabe and Ricciardelli (2001) report that as many as 50% of boys are trying to lose weight while just as many are engaged in muscle-building strategies.

These statistics indicate that physical appearance is on the minds of many adolescents. In fact, for both boys and girls, satisfaction with one's body is an important developmental issue during adolescence. It plays a significant role in predicting self-esteem, physical appearance self-concept, emotional distress, depression, eating disorders, and overall psychological adjustment. For this reason, it is important to understand the variables that affect body image and to examine whether the risk factors and rates differ for boys and girls.

The role of sociocultural pressures regarding the ideal thin body has been researched extensively among adolescent girls and although many factors can contribute greatly to unhealthy beliefs regarding adolescents' weight, and shape, one particularly significant factor is the media. The media play a powerful role in bombarding girls with images of acceptable and unacceptable body shapes. In magazines and on television, the ideal female body is tall, thin, and perhaps even prepubescent looking. Research has indicated that as girls progress through adolescence, they become more aware of the sociocultural ideal and as a result, increase their attempts to achieve it (McCabe & Ricciardelli, 2005). Essentially, there is a "drive for thinness" amongst many adolescent girls. In reality, few girls have the genetic makeup for the ideal body type portrayed in the media.

Little research, however, has examined the increasing number of ideal male body images in the media and the effects on male body satisfaction. As with females, there is a clear sociocultural ideal for males, specifically a V-shaped, lean, and muscular build. Where there is a drive for thinness for females, one could say there is a drive for muscularity among males. However, is the drive for muscularity for males similar to the drive for thinness for females? The drive for thinness has been associated with weight loss strategies such as excessive dieting and exercise, while the drive for muscularity has been associated with muscle-building strategies such as excessive exercise, body-building, and anabolic steroid use (Ricciardelli & McCabe, 2003). Do these similarities mean that boys and girls worry equally about an ideal body image or are girls more influenced by the sociocultural pressures regarding an ideal body type?

As previously mentioned, body image and psychosocial adjustment has been well documented for girls and women; however, the relationship is less clear for boys and men. The increase in boys' and men's magazines depicting the ideal lean and muscular body has led to a need to examine the effects on male body image. As such, many researchers are including a sample of boys in their research design.

Two such studies examining body image satisfaction among boys and girls are presented below. In the first selection, Jones and Crawford suggest that adolescent boys are just as likely to experience body image dissatisfaction. In the second selection, Hargreaves and Tiggemann report that adolescent girls are more vulnerable to body image pressures than boys.

**Diane Carlson Jones
and Joy K. Crawford**

The Peer Appearance Culture During Adolescence: Gender and Body Mass Variations

Gender and Body Image

Gender has figured prominently in the study of body image. The focus has typically been on females who have reported greater body dissatisfaction compared to males (McCabe and Ricciardelli, 2005). The extent of body dissatisfaction among adolescent girls has been frequently explained by the greater sociocultural emphasis upon physical attractiveness for women and an increasingly prominent "culture of thinness." The cultural ideal of thinness has glorified low body weight as a central attribute and has become a defining feature of feminine beauty.

Although body dissatisfaction has typically been less evident among males, there is increasing recognition of the sociocultural pressures on body image and adjustment for adolescent boys. The desire to develop muscularity has emerged as an important issue that has been associated with higher levels of depression and lower self-esteem (McCreary and Sasse, 2000). Furthermore, body dissatisfaction and strategies to gain muscle among boys have been linked to heightened concern with muscularity. Thus muscularity has been the primary appearance ideal associated with body image among males.

Body Mass and Body Image

Body mass has also been identified as an important factor in the development of body image based on its role as a risk factor for body image disturbances and psychological adjustment for both girls and boys. Body mass index (BMI) has been a standard measure of relative physical status with larger values indicating greater adiposity. In the literature on adolescent girls, a positive, linear relationship between BMI and body dissatisfaction has been reported frequently (Stice and Whitenton, 2002).

For boys, the pattern has been more inconsistent. In some cases, BMI has not been a significant predictor of body image dissatisfaction among

From *Journal of Youth and Adolescence*, April 2006, vol. 35, no. 2, pp. 257–266. Copyright © 2006 by Springer Science + Business Media. Reprinted by permission via Rightslink and by Diane Carlson Jones.

boys (Jones, 2004). However, the majority of the evidence has shown that higher BMI scores are related to greater body dissatisfaction and weight related concerns.

At the same time, there is reason to be concerned about being either underweight or overweight for boys. . . . For example, in a study of high school senior boys, a curvilinear relationship best described the relationship between BMI and body dissatisfaction: body dissatisfaction was greatest for the boys in the lowest and the highest BMI levels (Presnell *et al.*, 2004). Furthermore, low BMI values for boys have been indicated as a risk factor for body dissatisfaction and use of drugs to enhance muscularity. . . .

The Peer Appearance Culture

Overall, the evidence supports relationships among gender, body mass, and body image dissatisfaction. However, there has been little investigation of the ways in which the peer appearance culture may vary across different levels of body mass and the role of gender in shaping the variation. We investigated three general domains: appearance culture among friends (appearance conversations and diet/muscle talk), peer evaluations (peer appearance pressure, appearance teasing, and vicarious peer teasing) and peer standing (appearance-dependent acceptance, peer social comparison).

Appearance Culture Among Friends

. . . In this study, we explored two aspects of the appearance culture that are manifested among friends: appearance conversations and body change talk.

Appearance Conversations with Friends
Conversations about appearance are verbal exchanges that focus attention on general appearance-related issues, reinforce the value and importance of appearance to close friends, and promote the construction of appearance ideals. . . . Previous research has verified that girls and boys who reported more frequent conversations with their friends about appearance also reported greater internalization of appearance ideals and body dissatisfaction (Jones, 2004).

Body Change Talk: Dieting/Muscle Building
We also explored conversations that focused on the specific aspects of dieting for girls and muscle building for boys. The more focused conversations on the specific topic of dieting have been related to body image dissatisfaction among adolescent girls and are reported more often by adolescent girls than boys. However, since boys have been more likely to engage in muscle-building strategies than dieting (McCabe and Ricciardelli, 2003a), a more gender-appropriate indicator of the appearance culture among boys would be to assess their perceptions of how often they talk with their friends about muscle building.

. . . Because of the greater centrality of appearance for girls, we predicted that adolescent girls would be more likely to engage in the appearance conversations. Likewise, we expected that girls would engage in more diet talk than boys would report muscle-building talk.

The relationship between BMI and the appearance culture among friends has not been previously investigated. There is evidence, however, that girls with higher BMI are more likely to report dieting. Therefore, we expected that BMI would be positively associated with more "diet talk" among the girls. For boys, we examined the possibility of heightened appearance concerns and muscle-building talk among boys who were either underweight or overweight.

Appearance Evaluation

Peer Appearance Pressure

Peers provide pointed or implied social pressure when they make suggestions for body change strategies. Messages such as "You should lose some weight" or "You'd look better if you had more muscles" can have a direct impact on body satisfaction, weight loss strategies, and eating pathology for girls and boys. . . . The pressure generated by peers was identified as a significant longitudinal predictor of body dissatisfaction for adolescent girls (Stice and Whitenton, 2002). In a similar manner, the longitudinal prediction of body change strategies was related to pressure from same-gender best friends for both boys and girls (McCabe and Ricciardelli, 2003b).

Appearance Teasing

. . . It is important to consider peer teasing because it has been a significant correlate of body dissatisfaction for boys and girls in cross-sectional research.

Gender differences in appearance teasing have not been as clearly documented. Certainly, both adolescent girls and boys experience appearance teasing. In a survey of a midwestern city, 30% of adolescent girls and 25% of adolescent boys reported that peers teased them about weight. However, weight concerns are only one facet of appearance teasing that can include critical comments about muscularity as well. When more comprehensive measures of peer teasing about weight and shape have been used, boys have reported more teasing and critical appearance comments than girls.

Additionally, BMI has been clearly implicated in the experience of peer teasing. Adolescents who are heavier are more likely to report appearance and weight teasing (Faith *et al.*, 2002). . . .

Vicarious Appearance Teasing

Students also experience negative evaluations vicariously. . . . The positive and negative experiences that happen to others can become sources of learning for those who observe or vicariously experience the event.

We apply this concept to the arena of appearance teasing by suggesting that adolescents are attune to the appearance teasing that other peers encounter. In these vicarious experiences, students are learning that physical characteristics are subject to explicit and critical teasing by peers. . . . Teasing, whether experienced personally or vicariously, identifies appearance attributes that are violations of expectations and thus help to establish and reinforce normative and ideal standards.

Our predictions regarding gender and appearance evaluation were that girls would report feeling more appearance pressure (McCabe and Ricciardelli, 2005; Presnell *et al.*, 2004), but boys would perceive more appearance teasing. For BMI effects, we hypothesized that adolescents with higher BMI levels would report more peer appearance pressure and teasing. Furthermore, we expected that underweight boys would also be likely targets for appearance teasing because of the deviation from the muscularity ideal. Underweight girls more closely exemplify the thin ideal for females and would not be as likely to experience the disapproval or pressure of norm violation.

Peer Acceptance Concerns

Appearance-Based Acceptance
Peer acceptance is one of the central concerns of adolescents. Most of the research linking appearance to perceived peer acceptance has investigated girls' body image. The general finding has been that girls who think that their peer relationships would improve through weight loss have been more likely to be more dissatisfied with their body images (Gerner and Wilson, 2005). . . .

In the present study, we examined the degree to which perceived acceptance by peers was based on a salient appearance attribute for girls (thinness) and for boys (muscularity). Because appearance and social acceptance have been considered especially important in the lives of adolescent girls, we predicted that girls, especially those with elevated BMIs, would endorse higher levels of appearance-based peer acceptance. We predicted that both overweight and underweight boys would be more likely to believe that their relationships with peers would improve as a result of appearance changes.

Peer Appearance Comparisons
Appearance social comparison refers to the cognitive judgments that people make about their own appearance relative to others. These comparisons are pivotal to self-evaluations and are a means of gathering information about highly valued attributes, social expectations, and norms. Research on adolescents has revealed that peers are frequent targets of appearance comparisons for both boys and girls. . . .

How do gender and BMI relate to comparisons within the peer appearance culture? Based on previous research, we expected appearance comparisons to be more frequently reported by girls than by boys. The frequency of social comparison is theoretically predicted to rise when there is greater self-uncertainty or when an attribute is particularly salient to one's relative standing. These conditions are especially relevant for girls who have lower body esteem and for whom appearance is important. We, therefore, predicted that higher BMI level would be associated with more frequent appearance comparison among girls than among boys.

Summary of Hypotheses

Overall experiences within the peer appearance culture were expected to vary based on gender, BMI, and their interaction. We predicted that adolescent girls compared to boys would be more likely to report engaging in the appearance conversations, body change talk, and appearance comparisons. We also expected that girls would report feeling more appearance pressure, but that boys would perceive more appearance teasing. In regards to BMI, we hypothesized that adolescents with higher BMI levels would report more body change talk, peer appearance pressure, and teasing. We also examined the interaction of gender and BMI to distinguish the perceived experiences for overweight girls and under- and overweight boys.

Method

Participants

The sample included 415 adolescents who were either in 7th grade (90 girls and 82 boys) or 10th grade (125 girls and 118 boys). The students were primarily from middle to upper-middle-class backgrounds based on school district characteristics and student-reported parental education levels. The self-reported ethnic background of the participants was European American (68%), African American (1%), Asian American (19%), and Hispanic (3%).

Measures

Body Mass Index Categories
Body mass was based on the students' self-reported height and weight. . . . The students were then categorized into one of four groups: underweight, BMI < 25th percentile; low average, BMI $\geq$ 25 < 50th percentile; high average, BMI $\geq$ 50 < 85th percentile; overweight, BMI $\geq$ 85th percentile. . . .

Appearance Conversations
Five items assessed the frequency with which students reported talking about their bodies and appearance enhancements with their friends. The scale included items such as "My friends and I talk about what we can do to look our best." . . . Responses were rated on a scale from "1" (never) to "5" (very often). The alphas for the current study were adequate (girls, α = .89; boys, α = .88).

Body-Change Strategies: Diet/Muscle Talk
A five-item scale was newly devised for this study to evaluate the frequency with which students reported body-change strategies. The focus for boys

was on muscle-building talk and included items such as "My friends and I talk about building our muscles." . . . Items for the girls reflected concern with dieting: "My friends and I talk about losing weight." . . . The internal consistency was excellent for girls (α = .93) and boys (α = .93).

Peer Appearance Pressure

Eight items assessed the frequency with which students reported being pressured by peers to either diet (girls) or build their muscles (boys) from same- and other-gender friends and other peers. . . . Items presented to the girls included "Girls who are my friends say that I should go on a diet." . . . Sample item for the boys: "Boys who are my friends say that I should build up my muscles." . . . Higher summary scores represented greater perceived peer pressure. The internal consistency of the scale was adequate (girls, α =.92; boys, α = .89).

Appearance Teasing

Items that measured teasing from girls and boys about body size and shape were derived from previous research (Jones, 2004). The original items were adapted to distinguish between the teasing initiated by friends and by other peers about body size. . . . Items were summed to form one scale that had adequate reliability for the boys (α = .89) and girls (α = .88). Higher scores indicated greater perceived teasing about size and shape of body.

Vicarious Appearance Teasing

. . . In this newly created scale, two items for both girls and boys focused on weight teasing, e.g., "I hear students make fun of other kids because of their weight." Two additional items referred to teasing about shape (girls) or build (boys): "I hear students make fun of other kids because of their shape (girls)/build (boys). . . . Alphas were adequate for the girls' scale (.92) and the boys' (.89).

Appearance Dependent Acceptance

Eight items of the Likeability scale (Oliver and Thelen, 1996) were adapted to assess students' perceptions that changes in their appearance would influence their acceptance among peers. . . . The statements presented to the girls were identical to those in the original scale which emphasized thinness. . . . For the boys, statements were adapted to reflect a focus on muscularity. . . . Higher scores indicated that perceived acceptance among peers would be enhanced by either becoming thinner (girls) or more muscular (boys) (girls, α = .96; boys, α = .92).

Peer Social Comparisons

The peer items from the social comparison to models and peers scale (SCMP; Jones, 2001) assessed how frequently participants reported comparing themselves to same-sex peers on a series of physical and social attributes. Only the physical attributes are included here. Girls rated the frequency with which they compared themselves to girls at school in terms of weight, shape, hips, stomach, and thighs. The physical appearance attributes rated by the boys included weight, build, chest/pec muscles, stomach, and biceps. . . . Higher scores indicated greater self-reported social comparison on the appearance attributes. The scales had excellent internal reliability (girls, α = .98; boys, α = .89).

Body Image Dissatisfaction

The Body Dissatisfaction subscale from the Eating Disorder Inventory (Garner *et al.*, 1983) was used to measure body image dissatisfaction. . . . Two of the original items (hips and thighs) were altered for the boys to assess their satisfaction with chest and bicep size. . . . The final scales had adequate internal reliability for girls (α = .89) and boys (α = .79).

Results

We first ran a principal component factor analysis using varimax rotation to verify the structure of the peer appearance culture scales. . . . Eight factors emerged with eigenvalues greater than 1 accounting for 74% of the variance. The factor loadings indicated that each peer scale loaded on a separate factor with the exception of appearance-dependent acceptance which loaded on two factors. However, some items had cross-loadings on the two factors so that we combined the items to form one scale.

We next evaluated the relative distribution for the BMI categories. Chi-square analyses revealed that there were no significant gender or age differences in the percentage of students in each category ($ps > .05$). The majority of the students were in the high average BMI level. . . .

The intercorrelations were moderate to strong for both girls and boys for most measures. Because the pattern of relationships appeared to be somewhat distinct for the different measures for boys and girls, we chose not to reduce the number of peer culture indicators in our analyses but adjusted our analyses using Bonferroni's correction. We evaluated mean differences for the peer appearance culture measures in a series of 2 (gender) × 2 (grade) × 4 (BMI category) ANOVAs. We set a significance level of $p < .006$ based on Bonferroni's correction. Significant interaction effects were investigated in follow-up analyses. Tukey's post-hoc analyses ($p < .05$) were used to evaluate significance between BMI categories. Paired t-tests determined gender and grade differences.

Appearance Culture Among Friends

Analyses of the two friends' appearance culture variables revealed differences for gender, grade, and BMI category. . . . The hypothesis that girls would report more appearance conversations with friends was confirmed, $F(1, 399) = 40.82, p < .001$. However, contrary to predictions, it was the boys who reported talking more about body-change strategies with their friends than the girls did, $F(1, 399) = 13.38, p < .001$.

Variations across the BMI categories were also significant, but only for diet/muscle talk, $F(1, 399) = 8.45, p < .001$. The post-hoc analyses revealed three significantly different groups. The adolescents in the underweight category were the least likely ($M = 8.56$) and those in the overweight category were the most likely ($M = 13.26$) to report diet/muscle talk. The low-average ($M = 10.6$) and high-average ($M = 11.3$) BMI categories emerged as a similar subset that was significantly different from the other two groups.

Grade differences emerged such that appearance conversations and diet/muscle talk were more frequent among 10th graders than 7th graders (appearance conversations, $F(1, 399) = 40.82, p < .001$; diet/muscle talk, $F(1, 399) = 70.18, p < .001$).

Appearance Evaluations

Gender differences emerged for two types of appearance evaluations. Boys reported more peer appearance pressure and appearance teasing than did the girls (peer appearance pressure, $F(1, 399) = 34.45, p < .001$; appearance teasing, $F(1, 399) = 7.15, p < .003$).

The gender differences for appearance peer pressure were qualified by interactions for gender × BMI, $F(3, 399) = 7.01, p < .001$. The interaction term was further broken down by gender for interpretation. Variations in peer appearance pressure by BMI category were evident for both girls and boys in the follow-up analyses (girls, $F(3, 214) = 3.54, p < .02$; boys, $F(3, 196) = 4.62, p < .01$). Girls in the overweight category perceived more peer pressure to diet than did girls in the other categories (although the difference with the high average group was not significant). For the boys, however, it was the underweight respondents compared to the other three groups who perceived the most pressure to develop their muscles.

The differences for peer appearance teasing were also further qualified by significant differences between BMI categories, $F(3, 399) = 10.29, p < .001$, and the near-significant interaction of BMI and gender, $F(3, 399) = 3.97, p < .008$. In the follow-up analyses the BMI factor was significant for girls, $F(3, 207) = 4.34, p < .005$, and for boys, $F(3, 192) = 8.31, p < .001$. The pattern of means and post-hoc tests indicated that girls in the overweight category were most likely to report appearance teasing, but in this case, the level was not significantly different from the teasing level for underweight girls. Among the boys, it was once again the underweight boys who reported the most appearance teasing by peers compared to the other groups of boys.

Grade interacted with gender also to account for differences in peer appearance pressure, $F(1, 399) = 10.60, p < .001$. Follow-up analyses within gender revealed that it was the 10th grade boys ($M = 12.96$) who perceived more peer appearance pressure than 7th grade boys ($M = 10.00, t(201) = -4.02, p < .001$). There were no grade differences in peer appearance pressure among the girls.

Peer Acceptance Concerns

Appearance-based acceptance and peer social comparison revealed complex patterns of significance. Appearance-based acceptance was the only measure to display a significant three-way interaction, $F(3, 398) = 4.48$, $p < .004$ as well as significant effects for, gender $\times$ grade, $F(1, 398) = 8.40$, $p < .004$, and gender $\times$ BMI, $F(3, 398) = 13.32, p < .001$. In order to understand the interactions, grade and BMI effects were evaluated for girls and boys separately using grade (2) $\times$ BMI (4) ANOVAs.

Among the girls, BMI was significant, $F(3, 207) = 20.57, p < .001$. . . . Girls who were overweight were most likely to feel that peers would be more accepting if they were thinner. The girls in the underweight category were least likely to perceive their acceptance linked to being thinner.

The grade $\times$ BMI analyses among the boys indicated that grade was the only significant factor, $F(3, 191) = 11.02, p < .001$. It was the older boys ($M = 16.40$) compared to the younger ones ($M = 14.08$) who thought that their peer acceptance was linked more strongly to having a muscular build.

Variations in peer social comparisons were also confirmed by main effects for BMI, $F(3, 395) = 10.24, p < .001$, gender (marginal) $F(1, 395) = 6.08, p < .01$, and their interaction, $F(3, 395) = 5.87, p < .001$. However, the within gender follow-up analyses produced a significant BMI effect only among the girls, $F(3, 206) = 13.71, p < .001$. . . . Girls in the overweight category reported that they compared their appearance with peers more often than did the girls in the other BMI categories. . . .

Peer social comparison also varied by grade, $F(1, 395) = 21.23, p < .001$. Peer social comparisons were more frequently reported by 10th graders than 7th graders.

Body dissatisfaction varied by gender, $F(1, 399) = 12.55, p < .001$, BMI, $F(3, 399) = 23.30, p < .001$, and their interactions, $F(3, 399) = 11.84$, $p < .001$. BMI categories significantly distinguished body dissatisfaction among the girls, $F(3, 206) = 29.60, p < .001$, and boys, $F(3, 192) = 3.05$, $p < .03$. For the boys, the overweight respondents felt most dissatisfied with their body image, but their dissatisfaction scores were only significantly greater than the low average group. Among the girls, the significant distinctions revealed three groups: the overweight girls were the most dissatisfied among the girls; the low and high average girls were more dissatisfied than the underweight girls.

Discussion

Adolescent Girls

The evidence clearly indicates that girls are embedded in an appearance culture and, as predicted, report more appearance conversations with friends than the boys. At the same time, there were similar levels of appearance conversations across the BMI categories. . . .

. . . The differences that emerged for the girls among the BMI categories indicate that specific elements of the "culture of thinness" are more frequently a part of the lives of the girls with the highest BMI levels. Girls in the overweight category are talking about dieting more frequently than are the girls in the other BMI categories. They perceive more negative appearance evaluation as revealed by the scores for peer appearance pressure and appearance teasing. The overweight girls are seemingly in a place of uncertainty, as they feel that acceptance in the peer world is dependent on conforming more closely to the thin ideal. . . . The fact that there were no differences for vicarious appearance teasing suggests that the heightened appearance pressure and teasing are not merely a function of a greater sensitivity to appearance issues. Thus it is the overweight girls who feel the greatest burden in the peer appearance culture. . . .

Adolescent Boys

The results from this study demonstrate that boys as well as girls experience a great deal of pressure from their peers related to appearance. There are two findings that give special definition to the appearance culture among the boys. First, boys perceive more appearance pressure than the girls and admit that they talk with their friends about muscle building at a rate greater than girls talk about dieting. These findings are contrary to our predictions and are particularly interesting because appearance issues are considered to be of greater importance for girls. Certainly girls reported higher levels of general appearance conversations. The contribution of this research is to document that boys clearly are participants in appearance related exchanges with their peers when the focus is on muscularity.

. . . Male friendships tend to be more activity oriented and muscle-building talk is about a shared activity that friends can do together. . . . Our findings suggest that appearance topics and teasing may be part of these exchanges. In these ways, muscle-building talk and appearance pressure give insight into the male appearance culture that is aligned with elements of muscularity (McCreary and Sasse, 2000).

Second, we do not find support for a uniform curvilinear relationship between BMI and the boys' peer appearance culture. Rather the general pattern is for underweight and overweight boys to have appearance concerns that depend on particular aspects of the appearance culture. For example, an overall BMI effect for body change strategies suggests that it is the boys in the overweight category who more frequently discuss muscle building with friends, not the underweight boys. However, it is the underweight boys who are more frequently on the receiving end of negative messages from peers about muscularity via peer appearance pressure and appearance teasing. . . .

The Role of Development

Grade differences also emerge as an important aspect of the peer appearance culture. The older adolescents report more frequent appearance conversations, diet/muscle talk, and appearance comparisons. Furthermore, unlike other research (McCabe and Ricciardelli, 2005), we do not find decreases with age in the importance of body image issues for boys. Rather the older boys give evidence that peer appearance pressure is greater in high school than in middle school, a result that may implicate the effects of the later onset of pubertal changes for boys. Also the older boys report that their acceptance by peers is more likely linked to their appearance. Certainly the achievement of sexual maturity amid the greater attention to romantic relationships, sports, and popularity in the high school culture are possible reasons that the older boys are more embedded in the peer appearance culture. In these ways, appearance issues appear to be more salient with age, especially for boys.

Overall, this research contributes to the literature on the development of body image by providing evidence on multiple aspects of the peer appearance culture for both boys and girls. . . . Appearance issues are seemingly as important to boys as to girls. Still the pattern of results indicates that it is primarily the overweight girls and underweight boys who disproportionately experienced the negative evaluations and pressures of the peer appearance culture. . . .

References

Faith, M. S., Leone, M. A., Ayers, T. S., Heo, M., and Pietrobelli, A. (2002). Weight criticism during physical activity, coping skills, and reported physical activity in children. *Pediatrics* 110: 1–8.

Garner, D. M., Olmstead, M. P., and Polivy, J. (1983). Development and validation of a multidimensional eating disorder inventory for anorexia nervosa and bulimia. *Int. J. Eating Disord.* 2: 15–34.

Gerner, B., and Wilson, P. H. (2005). The relationship between friendship factors and adolescent girls' body image concern, body dissatisfaction, and restrained eating. *Int. J. Eating Disord.* 37: 313–320.

Jones, D. C. (2001). Social comparison and body image: Attractiveness comparison to models and peers among adolescent girls and boys. *Sex Roles* 45: 645–664.

Jones, D. C. (2004). Body image among adolescent girls and boys: A longitudinal study. *Dev. Psychol.* 40: 823–835.

McCabe, M. P., and Ricciardelli, L. A. (2003a). A longitudinal study of body change strategies among adolescent males. *J. Youth Adolesc.* 32: 105–113.

McCabe, M. P., and Ricciardelli, L. A. (2003b). Sociocultural influences on body image and body changes among adolescent boys and girls. *J. Soc. Psychol.* 143: 5–26.

McCabe, M. P., and Ricciardelli, L. A. (2005). A prospective study of pressures from parents, peers, and the media on extreme weight change behaviors among adolescent boys and girls. *Behav. Res. Therapy* 43: 653–668.

McCreary, D. R., and Sasse, D. K. (2000). An exploration of the drive for muscularity in adolescent boys and girls. *J. Am. Coll. Health* 48: 297–304.

Oliver, K. K., and Thelen, M. H. (1996). Children's perceptions of peer influence on eating concerns. *Behav. Therapy* 27: 25–39.

Presnell, K., Bearman, S. K., and Stice, E. (2004). Risk factors for body dissatisfaction in adolescent boys and girls: A prospective study. *Int. J. Eating Disord.* 36: 389–401.

Stice, E., and Whitenton, K. (2002). Risk factors for body dissatisfaction in adolescent girls: A longitudinal investigation. *Dev. Psychol.* 38: 669–678.

**Duane A. Hargreaves and
Marika Tiggemann**

 **NO**

Idealized Media Images and Adolescent Body Image: "Comparing" Boys and Girls

Introduction

Body dissatisfaction, which is common among women of all ages, is especially prevalent during adolescence when body image is [a very] important component of adolescent girls' self-esteem (Levine & Smolak, 2002). Arguably the most likely cause of body dissatisfaction among adolescent girls is the current unrealistic standard of female beauty which places an inordinate emphasis on thinness, and which is unattainable for most girls (Ackard & Peterson, 2001). This ideal standard of beauty is conveyed to individuals via a number of sources including family, peers and the mass media. . . .

A small number of studies have examined the impact of media images on the body image of adolescents. Correlational studies show that adolescent girls who read more magazines and watch more television report greater body dissatisfaction (Hofchire & Greenberg, 2002). Experimental studies show that exposure to idealised media images leads to increased state body dissatisfaction for girls. To date, however, . . . few correlational studies have included boys (Botta, 2003). While a small number of experimental studies have found a negative impact of muscular-ideal magazine images on college-aged men (Leit, Pope, & Gray, 2002), no experimental studies of the media's immediate impact on the body image of adolescent boys have been conducted. Although boys' body dissatisfaction is typically less severe than for girls, they too express dissatisfaction with their body weight and appearance (Levine & Smolak, 2002; Ricciardelli & McCabe, 2001). Such dissatisfaction has been linked to a number of negative consequences including the development of dieting, excessive exercise, and low self-esteem.

Like girls, the most likely cause of body dissatisfaction among boys is an unrealistic appearance ideal. The current ideal male body is lean but highly muscular, characterised by a "well-developed chest and arms, with wide shoulders tapering down to a narrow waist" (Pope et al., 2000, p. 30).

From *Body Image*, vol. 1, October 2004, excerpts from pp. 351–361. Copyright © 2004 by Elsevier Health Sciences. Reprinted by permission via Rightslink.

Images of this ideal have become increasingly common in the media. For example, compared to 25 years ago, men are now more often bare chested in magazines, in accord with increased sexual objectification of male bodies in mainstream advertising (Rohlinger, 2002). Repeated exposure to images of unrealistically muscular male ideals may cause men to feel insecure about their own bodies, parallel to the way in which exposure to images of unrealistically thin models promotes body dissatisfaction among girls.

The purpose of the present experiment was to examine the impact of televised images of idealised male attractiveness, in addition to female attractiveness, on adolescent body image. Effects on the underlying process, and individual differences in reaction, were also examined. Social comparison theory (Festinger, 1954) would suggest that the mechanism by which media exposure influences body image is appearance-related social comparison. Specifically, . . . viewing television, or reading magazines, prompts individuals to evaluate their own appearance by comparison to the salient and highly attractive models who pervade such media. Because this process leads most individuals to find themselves wanting, such upward social comparison produces a negative evaluation of one's own physical appearance, resulting in a state-like increase in body dissatisfaction.

In addition there are likely to be stable individual differences in comparison tendency relating to appearance (Wood, 1989). Such differences might predict who engages in "state" appearance-related social comparison to media images, and is therefore most vulnerable to the media's effect on body image. Recent evidence suggests girls are more likely to engage in appearance-related social comparison than boys (Jones, 2001). Moreover, individuals who have a trait-like tendency to engage in appearance-related social comparison or who are more strongly invested in their appearance, sometimes referred to as appearance schematics, may be particularly likely to engage in appearance comparison to media images. We propose that these stable individual difference variables (e.g., trait social comparison, appearance schematicity, and gender) interact with characteristics of the media image (e.g., salience of the model's attractiveness) to predict when media exposure will prompt appearance-related comparison and increased body dissatisfaction.

To date this perspective has been investigated only for women and girls. . . . We believe this perspective is equally applicable to an understanding of men's and boys' body image. The present study used a 2 × 2 between subjects experimental design to investigate the effects of commercial condition (thin ideal, muscular ideal, non-appearance control) and instructional set (appearance-focus, distracter) on boys' and girls' appearance-related social comparison and state body dissatisfaction. . . . It was predicted that boys (girls) would report greater body dissatisfaction and appearance comparison after viewing muscular-ideal (thin-ideal) commercials than non-appearance commercials, and that adolescents high on trait social comparison and appearance schematicity would be most strongly affected.

Method

Participants

The participants were 595 adolescent students (310 girls, 285 boys [, mean age 14.3 years)] . . . of medium socio-economic status. . . . Participants were [randomly] allocated to the thin-ideal, muscular-ideal, or non-appearance commercial condition by . . . class group (n = 42), and were randomly allocated to the instructional set conditions on an individual basis. This procedure resulted in a total of 153 girls in the thin-ideal commercial condition, 157 girls in the non-appearance commercial condition, 146 boys in the muscular-ideal commercial condition, and 139 boys in the non-appearance commercial condition.

Materials

State Mood and Body Dissatisfaction

A number of visual analogue scales (VAS) were used as measures of body dissatisfaction and mood. Participants were asked to indicate how they feel "right now" on a series of four mood dimensions: "Happy"; "Worried"; "Confident"; and "Angry"; and four dimensions of body satisfaction: "Fat"; "Strong"; "Dissatisfied (unhappy) with weight and shape" and "Dissatisfied (unhappy) with overall appearance." Each participant completed the VAS on two occasions: 5 min before commercial viewing and immediately after commercial viewing. . . .

Three of the four body dissatisfaction VAS were significantly intercorrelated . . . and so were combined to form a composite state body dissatisfaction variable. . . . Intercorrelations between the four mood VAS were also significant . . . and so were combined to form a composite mood variable (happy and confident were reverse coded, such that higher scores reflect greater negative affect). . . . The composite state body dissatisfaction and negative mood variables were significantly positively correlated. . . .

State Appearance Comparison

A series of self-report items . . . assessed appearance-related social comparison during commercial viewing. Participants were asked to use a Likert scale ranging from 1 = *not at all* to 7 = *very much* to indicate what they had thought about while viewing the commercials. The five items assessed how much they: (1) thought about the qualities of the commercials; (2) thought about the effectiveness of the commercials; (3) thought about the attractiveness of the people in the commercials; (4) compared their own appearance to the actors in the commercials; and (5) wanted to be like the actors in the commercials. Questions 2 and 3 served as a manipulation check of the instructional set which asked participants to rate the "effectiveness of the commercials" (Question 2) or the "attractiveness of actors in the commercials" (Question 3). Responses to Question 4 formed the single-item state appearance comparison variable.

Appearance Schematicity
The Appearance Schemas Inventory (ASI) (Cash & Labarge, 1996) was used to measure appearance schematicity. Using a five-point Likert scale ranging from 1 = *strongly disagree* to 5 = *strongly agree*, respondents indicate their level of agreement with 14 statements (e.g., "What I look like is an important part of who I am"), . . . such that high scores reflect higher appearance schematicity. . . .

Trait Social Comparison
The Physical Appearance Comparison Scale (PACS) (Thompson et al., 1991) measures the degree to which individuals tend to compare their appearance with others. Participants indicate their agreement with five statements (e.g., "In social situations, I compare my figure to the figure of other people") using a five-point scale ranging from 1 = *never* to 5 = *always*. . . . Both trait social comparison and appearance schematicity were measured approximately 15 min after participants completed the dependent measures.

Experimental Manipulation: Videotape Stimulus

Three sets of video stimulus materials were compiled, each containing 18 television commercials. [The first set (thin-ideal commercials)] . . . contained female actors who "epitomise societal ideals of thinness and attractiveness" for women. . . . The second set . . . (muscular-ideal commercials) . . . contained images of men who epitomise societal ideals of muscularity and attractiveness. . . . The third set of commercials contained no actors who epitomised either the thin ideal for women or the muscular ideal for men. To ensure that these commercials (control condition) were of equal interest to viewers, they were matched to the first two sets on both effectiveness and product category.

[A pilot tape of 145] commercials were collected from Australian primetime television [and were tested] according to the following criteria: (1) "to what extent do the actors epitomise the current thin ideal for women?" (2) "to what extent do the actors epitomise the current muscular-attractiveness ideal for men?" and (3) "how effective is the commercial?" [The] 15 commercials that most epitomised the muscular ideal for men were chosen first [followed by the] 15 commercials that most epitomised the thin ideal for women. . . . [Finally] 15 commercials that contained women and men of "normal" appearance were matched to these commercial sets. . . . A further three non-appearance commercials were selected and included in all three commercial sets to help disguise the purpose of the study.

Experimental Manipulation: Instructional Set

Instructions for viewing the commercials were manipulated using a commercial rating task. Half the participants were asked to rate the attractiveness of the actors (appearance focus condition) in each commercial. . . . In contrast, the other half of participants (distracter condition) were asked to rate the overall effectiveness of each commercial. . . .

Results

The Effect of Television Commercials on Girls' and Boys' Body Dissatisfaction

The results [showed] significant main effects of gender, $F(1, 586) = 25.20$, $p < 0.001$, . . . commercial condition, $F(1, 586) = 5.34$, $p < 0.05$, . . . and instructional set, $F(1, 586) = 11.87$, $p < 0.05$. . . . The appearance focus instructions produced more body dissatisfaction than the distracter instructions. The main effects of gender and commercial condition were modified by a significant Gender × Commercial condition interaction, $F(1, 586) = 12.26$, $p < 0.001$. . . . As predicted, girls viewing thin-ideal commercials had significantly greater body dissatisfaction $(M = 32.7)$ than those viewing the non-appearance commercials $(M = 27.7)$, $F(1, 307) = 16.08$, $p < 0.001$. . . . In contrast, boys in the muscular-ideal condition did not report greater body dissatisfaction $(M = 25.1)$ than boys in the non-appearance condition $(M = 26.1)$, $F(1, 282) < 1$, $p > 0.05$. There were no further significant two- or three-way interactions. . . .

The Effect of Television Commercials on Girls' and Boys' State Mood

. . . [The results showed] that girls $(M = 23.5)$ reported greater negative mood than boys $(M = 20.3)$, $F(1, 586) = 16.46$, $p < 0.001$, . . . and that girls and boys in the ideal appearance condition reported significantly greater negative mood $(M = 23.1)$ than girls and boys in the non-appearance condition $(M = 20.7)$, $F(1, 586) = 9.98$, $p < 0.01$. . . . There were no further significant effects. . . .

The Effect of Television Commercials on Girls' and Boys' Appearance Comparison

[Results] revealed a main effect of gender whereby, irrespective of experimental condition, girls engaged in greater appearance comparison $(M = 2.51$, $SD = 1.70)$ than boys $(M = 2.07$, $SD = 1.35)$, $F(1, 583) = 14.38$, $p < .001$. . . . There was also a significant main effect of commercial condition whereby participants in the ideal appearance condition engaged in greater appearance comparison $(M = 2.72)$ than participants in the non-appearance condition $(M = 1.88)$, $F(1, 583) = 45.81$, $p < 0.001$. . . . But the main effects of gender and commercial condition should be interpreted in light of a significant Gender × Commercial condition interaction, $F(1, 183) = 9.20$, $p < 0.01$. . . . [Idealized] appearance commercials led to greater appearance comparison for girls than for boys, $F(1, 296) = 17.39$, $p < 0.001$, . . . but . . . girls and boys did not differ in the non-appearance condition, $F(1, 291) < 1$, $p > 0.05$. There was no significant main effect of instructional set, . . . nor significant interaction of instructional set with either gender or commercial condition. . . .

Trait Social Comparison and Appearance Schematicity as Moderating Variables

Appearance schematicity and trait social comparison were highly correlated for both girls, $r = 0.68$, . . . and boys, $r = 0.60$. . . . Thus, the two scales were averaged to form a single appearance investment variable. [Analysis] showed that girls reported greater appearance investment . . . than boys ($t(589) = 5.28$, $p < .001$). . . . [Participants] were then divided into tertiles based on their appearance investment score. Participants in the low appearance investment group (102 girls and 125 boys) scored between 1 and 2.24, participants in the medium group (98 girls and 101 boys) scored between 2.25 and 2.99, and participants in the high investment group (103 girls and 54 boys) scored between 3.00 and 5.00.

. . . The results for body dissatisfaction show a significant main effect of gender, $F(1, 570) = 22.19$, $p < 0.001$, . . . commercial condition, $F(1, 570) = 6.33$, $p < 0.05$, . . . and appearance investment, $F(2, 570) = 9.07$, $p < 0.001$, . . . and a significant Gender × Commercial condition interaction, $F(2, 570) = 7.65$, $p < 0.01$. . . . There were no other significant [interactions]. A second ANCOVA for mood showed a significant main effect of gender, $F(1, 570) = 10.84$, $p < 0.001$, . . . and commercial condition, $F(1, 570) = 8.09$, $p < 0.01$, . . . but not appearance investment. . . .

Lastly, . . . results [showed] a significant main effect of gender, $F(1, 567) = 6.36$, $p < 0.05$, . . . commercial condition, $F(1, 567) = 53.32$, $p < 0.001$, . . . and appearance investment, $F(2, 567) = 50.10$, $p < 0.001$, . . . and significant two-way interactions between Gender and Commercial condition, $F(2, 567) = 6.41$, $p < 0.05$, . . . and Appearance investment and Commercial condition, $F(2, 567) = 7.24$, $p < 0.001$. . . . [Participants] high on appearance investment reported greater appearance-related social comparison with the commercials than participants in the medium and low appearance investment groups. . . . [This] effect was larger in the ideal condition . . . than in the non-appearance condition. . . .

Discussion

The present study has replicated the results of previous research for adolescent girls. As predicted, exposure to thin-ideal commercials led to significantly greater body dissatisfaction and negative affect among girls than non-appearance commercials. Although the effect sizes were only small, the results are consistent with the conclusion that exposure to thin-ideal media has a small and reliable negative effect on girls.

But the main purpose of the study was to examine the effect of idealized images of male attractiveness on adolescent boys, which has been largely neglected in previous research. The results show that muscular-ideal television commercials had only a limited impact on boys' body image, and on average, exposure to muscular-ideal commercials did not lead to increased body dissatisfaction. This finding was in contrast to some previous studies that found a negative impact of muscular-ideal magazine images on college-aged men (Leit et al., 2002). It could be that males do not develop a vulnerability to muscular-ideal media images until late adolescence or early adulthood, perhaps due to developmental changes in the salience of muscularity concerns.

A second important purpose of the study was to examine the role of social comparison processes for understanding the media's impact. While exposure to thin-ideal and muscular-ideal commercials did lead to increased appearance comparison, this effect was stronger for girls. These results suggest that, in general, girls seem to process self-related appearance information more deeply and more automatically than boys. . . .

Overall the results suggest that the media's immediate impact on body image is both stronger and more normative for girls than boys. This pattern of results reflects the general pattern of gender differences in the body image literature (Levine & Smolak, 2002), suggesting that boys' body image experiences mirror those of girls but are typically less prevalent, and when present, less severe.

In summary, the present results suggest that unrealistic ideals of beauty in the media are an important source of social comparison, and a possible cause of body dissatisfaction among certain girls and boys. It remains unclear how these short-lasting effects might generalize to real world media exposure. However, as a whole, the results support the usefulness of social comparison theory, which proposes appearance comparison as an underlying process by which the media can increase body dissatisfaction, and appearance schematicity/trait social comparison as explanations as to why some adolescents are more vulnerable than others to the media's immediate effect. . . .

References

Ackard, D. M., & Peterson, C. B. (2001). Association between puberty and disordered eating, body image, and other psychological variables. *International Journal of Eating Disorders 29*, 187–194.

Botta, R. A. (2003). For your health? The relationship between magazine reading and adolescents' body image and eating disturbances. *Sex Roles, 48*, 389–399.

Cash, T. F., & Labarge, A. S. (1996). Development of the appearance schemas inventory: A new cognitive body image assessment. *Cognitive Therapy and Research, 20*, 37–50.

Festinger, L. (1954). A theory of social comparison processes. *Human Relations, 7*, 117–140.

Hofshire, L. J., & Greenberg, B. S. (2002). Media's impact on adolescents' body dissatisfaction. In J. D. Brown, J. R. Steele & K. W. Walsh-Childers (Eds.), *Sexual teens, sexual media: Investigating media's influence on adolescent sexuality*. New Jersey: Erlbaum.

Jones, D. (2001). Social comparison and body image: Attractiveness comparisons to models and peers among adolescent girls and boys. *Sex Roles, 45*, 645–664.

Leit, R. A., Pope, H. G., Jr., & Gray, J. J. (2002). Cultural expectations of muscularity in men: The evolution of Playgirl centerfolds. *International Journal of Eating Disorders, 29,* 90–93.

Levine, M. P., & Smolak, L. (2002). Body image development in adolescence. In T. F. Cash & T. Pruzinsky (Eds.), *Body image: A handbook of theory, research, and clinical practice* (pp. 74–82). New York: Guilford Press.

Pope, H. G., Phillips, K. A., & Olivardia, R. (2000). *The Adonis complex: The secret crisis of male body obsession.* New York: Free Press.

Ricciardelli, L. A., & McCabe, M. P. (2001). Children's body image concerns and eating disturbance: A review of the literature. *Clinical Psychology Review, 21,* 325–344.

Rohlinger, D. A. (2002). Eroticizing men: Cultural influences on advertising and male objectification. *Sex Roles, 46,* 61–74.

Thompson, J. K., Heinberg, L. J., & Tantleff, S. T. (1991). The physical appearance comparison scale (PACS). *The Behavior Therapist, 14,* 174.

Wood, J. V. (1989). Theory and research concerning social comparisons of personal attributes. *Psychological Bulletin, 106,* 231–248.

POSTSCRIPT

Do Boys Worry about an Ideal Body Image as Much as Girls Do?

Diane Jones and Joy Crawford examined boys' and girls' body image in terms of appearance culture, peer evaluations, and peer acceptance. They found that girls were indeed embedded in an appearance culture, with overweight girls burdened the most by a culture of thinness. However, they also found that boys were similarly burdened by an appearance culture defined by muscularity. In fact, boys, compared to girls, experienced more appearance pressure and had more conversations with peers regarding muscle building than girls talked about dieting. They concluded that body image issues are as important for boys as for girls. In particular, underweight (low BMI) and overweight (high BMI) boys are as concerned as overweight girls (high BMI).

In a previous article by Jones and Crawford (2005), they report that weight and muscularity concerns have distinct pathways to body dissatisfaction. The "weight-body dissatisfaction" pathway indicates that males with the highest BMIs (i.e., significantly heavier boys) are more likely to attribute body dissatisfaction to weight and dieting concerns. Whereas the "muscularity-body dissatisfaction" pathway indicates that males with lower BMIs (significantly lighter boys) are more concerned about muscle-weight-gaining behaviors. They conclude that BMI (both low and high) plays a significant role in predicting body satisfaction for boys.

Hargreaves and Tiggemann examined the effects of ideal body images in commercials on adolescent girls and boys. Commercials included the thin ideal for women, and the muscular ideal for men. After viewing the commercials, body dissatisfaction increased and appearance comparison was stronger for girls than for boys, suggesting stronger body image vulnerability for girls.

The above studies provide evidence for the consistent findings examining body image concerns for girls; however, they also provide evidence for the mixed findings with respect to body image concerns among boys. It could be that the female ideal is more prevalent in society. Boys may be as anxious but are not as comfortable expressing their dissatisfaction. This could explain the findings by Hargreaves and Tiggemann as well as those reported by McCabe and Ricciardelli (2004, 2005) indicating that girls experience higher levels of body dissatisfaction than boys. McCabe and Ricciardelli further argue that age may play a part. Specifically, they found that opposite of girls, as boys progressed through adolescence; they became less concerned with body importance and therefore were less likely to engage in either weight-loss or muscle-building strategies. Interestingly, Jones and Crawford found older adolescent boys were more likely to believe that peer acceptance was linked to muscles.

In summary, it appears the mixed findings might be explained in terms of age and BMI. More studies examining these variables are recommended.

References/Further Readings

Jones, D. C., & Crawford, J. K. (2005). Adolescent boys and body image: Weight and muscularity concerns as dual pathways to body dissatisfaction. *Journal of Youth and Adolescence*, 34, 629–636.

McCabe, M. P., & Ricciardelli, L. A. (2001). Body image and body change techniques among young adolescent boys. *European Eating Disorders Review*, 9, 335–347.

McCabe, M. P., & Ricciardelli, L. A. (2004). A longitudinal study of pubertal timing and extreme body change behaviors among adolescent boys and girls. *Adolescence*, 39, 145–166.

McCabe, M. P., & Ricciardelli, L. A. (2005). A prospective study of pressures from parents, peers, and the media on extreme weight change behaviors among adolescent boys and girls. *Behaviour Research and Therapy*, 43, 653–668.

McCreary, D. P., & Sasse, D. K. (2002). Gender differences in high school students' dieting behavior and their correlates. *International Journal of Men's Health*, 1, 195.

Ricciardelli, L. A., & McCabe, M. P. (2003). Sociocultural and individual influences on muscle gain and weight loss strategies among adolescent boys and girls. *Psychology in the Schools*, 40, 209–224.

Tomori, M., & Rus-Makovec, M. (2000). Eating behaviour, depression, and self-esteem in high school students. *Journal of Adolescent Health*, 26, 361–367.

ISSUE 5

Should the Human Papillomavirus (HPV) Vaccine Be Mandatory for Early Adolescent Girls?

YES: Cruise, E., from "Writing for PRO position: Should the HPV vaccine be mandatory for early adolescent girls?" *The American Journal of Maternal Child Nursing, 32(4)*, 208, 2007

NO: Anderson, T.L., from "Writing for CON position: Should the HPV vaccine be mandatory for early adolescent girls?" *The American Journal of Maternal Child Nursing, 32(4)*, 209, 2007

ISSUE SUMMARY

YES: Erin Cruise, an instructor of nursing at Radford University in Virginia, lists many of the reasons that public health personnel are in favor of the HPV vaccination being legislated as mandatory for young girls. She discusses the sexuality-related issues as well as a financial cost-benefit analysis associated with mandatory HPV vaccination.

NO: Tamika L. Anderson, a public health nurse and child care nurse consultant with the Davidson County Health Department in Lexington, North Carolina, argues against the implementation of a mandatory HPV vaccination for female adolescents. Some of the concerns identified are safety, choice, and cost.

Cervical cancer is largely a preventable cancer; it is the second most common cancer among women worldwide. It is generally accepted by the medical community to be caused by human papillomavirus (HPV), which is the virus that causes genital warts. HPV is considered the most common sexually transmitted infection in both Canada and the United States with an estimated 75% of sexually active people being infected with HPV at some point in their lives, and that percentage is higher for adolescents and young adult women. Rates for adolescent and young men are not as definite and the severe health consequences of HPV infection for males (e.g., penile cancer) are less common occurrences relative to females. Adolescent and young women—relative to older adults and males—may be more prone to contracting HPV because of biological reasons associated with the developing cervix. The good news is that, in healthy younger individuals, the immune system can "clear" the body of HPV infection in many cases (Moscicki, 2005).

In 2006, Merck & Co., a major pharmaceutical company, introduced the first vaccine for HPV. There are almost 200 types of HPV; the vaccine has been demonstrated as effective at preventing the strains of HPV that cause 70% of cervical cancers. While some people question the safety of the vaccine, the existing studies warrant global introduction (Agosti & Goldie, 2007) and the Society of Obstetricians and Gynaecologists of Canada calls it ". . . one of the most extensively tested vaccine[s] to ever come [on] the . . . market" (2007). The major safety concern is that the drug has been studied in highly controlled laboratory conditions but needs to demonstrate "real world" success (Borgmeyer, 2007). The American Association of Family Physicians has characterized mandates for vaccinations as "premature" because of the need for further data on the longer term effects of the vaccination, yet they have included the HPV vaccination on their recommended schedule of immunizations for adolescents.

Some of the issues associated with the widespread implementation of a mandatory vaccination program include the cost of the drug. Requiring three doses, the total cost in the United States is estimated to be $360 (over €250) per person vaccinated, while the cost in Canada is approximately $450 per person. In some cases, parents would have to pay for the drugs or their daughter would be prohibited from attending school. This is not a concern in Canada where HPV vaccination is currently voluntary. A major concern of conservative groups is that a mandatory HPV vaccination will cause girls to view this as adults condoning teenage sexuality (Sprigg, 2007). This worry is not likely to be realized given that fear of other sexually transmitted infections such as HIV or herpes or unintended pregnancy are more immediate risks associated with sexual behavior, yet sex education and condom distribution programs have not been shown to be associated with an increase in sexual activity (Charo, 2007). Also, vaccination for hepatitis B has not resulted in rampant sexual activity or drug use (Borgmeyer, 2007). Others worry that vaccinated women will no longer value Pap smears and, as a result, will neglect their gynecological health (Zimet, 2005; Zimmerman, 2006). A further concern is that the government is mandating HPV vaccinations as a result of underlying pressure by and financial weight of the pharmaceutical companies (Sprigg, 2007). Thus, the mandating program is viewed as nefariously financial.

While most people do not debate the value of the HPV vaccination, per se, the controversy lies in the *mandating* of vaccination. By creating conditions where children will not be allowed to attend school unless they are vaccinated for HPV creates a lack of parental rights regarding their children's health care (Charo, 2007). The mandatory HPV vaccination program becomes a question of more complex politics and moral objections rather than simply a public health issue.

In the following selections, Cruise presents facts about adolescent sexual behavior and sexually transmitted infection rates as a basis for the need for the HPV vaccination. As well, she indicates that, while the initial cost of mandatory vaccination may be large, the financial savings in treatment, as well as the reduction in human suffering, justifies the initial expense. Anderson, while not anti-vaccination, argues against the mandatory nature of the proposed HPV vaccination program. She raises the issue of the safety of the vaccination as longer term studies have not been conducted. She questions the financial accessibility of the vaccination to all girls. As you consider these two viewpoints, is there a compromise between the two positions?

YES

Erin Cruise

Should the HPV Vaccine Be Mandatory for Early Adolescent Girls?

From a public health perspective, my opinion is that it is important to mandate the human papillomavirus (HPV) vaccine for young girls. This stirs debate, despite the fact that there has been a real decline in many serious communicable diseases because of mass immunization. These are the facts: Research conducted on more than 11,000 female patients between the ages of 16 and 26 demonstrated nearly 100% efficacy of the newly approved HPV vaccine without serious side effects (CDC, 2006). This fact alone should convince skeptics of mandatory vaccination, because this vaccine has the potential to eradicate a disease that disproportionately burdens women. There are many other reasons to support adding HPV to the list of mandatory immunizations for school-aged girls, however.

More than 6 million people in the United States are newly infected with HPV each year, making it the most common sexually transmitted infection (STI). Estimates are that 50% to 80% of people who are sexually active will contract at least one of the more than 100 types of HPV during their lives. Although HPV is most frequently transmitted by vaginal or anal sex, other nonpenetrative sexual activities also may result in infection (CDC, 2006). Approximately 47% of teens in 9th through 12th grades are already sexually active, with 14% indicating that they have had at least four sexual partners (CDC, 2006). These rates have remained fairly constant for the past 10 years. Many adolescents experiment with alcohol and drugs, which are associated with risky sexual behaviors, increasing the risk of contracting HPV (CDC, 2006). Immunizing girls at the age of 11 or 12 years old, before they become sexually active, could significantly reduce the rates of HPV infection and prevent cervical cancer.

Two types of HPV cause nearly 70% of all cases of cervical cancer, which affected approximately 10,000 women in 2006 and resulted in nearly 4,000 deaths. The newly approved HPV vaccine targets these viruses and viruses that cause 90% of genital warts. Opponents cite the estimated $900 million annual cost of immunizing 11- to 12-year-old girls (Borgmeyer, 2004).

However, these costs could be appreciably offset by decreasing the more than $2 billion expended for cervical cancer treatment each year, not to mention reducing time lost from work by women enduring illness and avoiding associated loss of life.

Some of the controversy surrounding the HPV vaccine seems to be related to the sexual nature of the infection. However, the hepatitis B virus is also primarily sexually transmitted, and a vaccine was made mandatory for infants in most states a decade ago with far less outcry. Surveys indicate that parents are generally supportive of the HPV vaccine and many religious groups support its use, provided that administration is accompanied by education promoting premarital abstinence and monogamy within marriage (Zimmerman, 2006). Healthcare providers also must continue to provide education about the continued risks of contracting other types of HPV or STI and the need for ongoing routine Pap tests. The fact that the vaccine is currently recommended only for girls also seems to stimulate significant debate. Vaccine efficacy studies have not supported the introduction of immunization for males, however, and life-threatening health effects for males with HPV are rare (CDC, 2006).

Finally, mandating immunizations for school attendance has been shown to increase immunization rates, thus protecting everyone, particularly individuals who cannot receive vaccines because of contraindications (Zimmerman, 2006). This protection against the disease is the most compelling reason for mandatory vaccination. Girls usually receive other immunizations, such as the combined DPT and the meningococcal vaccine, between the ages of 11 and 12, so adding the HPV vaccine should not result in significant inconvenience to families. Mandatory vaccines are more likely to be covered by private insurance and state immunization programs, which removes cost as a barrier to compliance and acceptance.

References

Borgmeyer, C. (2004). *Many states are moving to require HPV vaccination for school entry: AAFP calls such mandates "premature."* Retrieved February 24, 2007. . . .

Centers for Disease Control and Prevention (CDC). (2006). *Human papillomavirus: HPV information for clinicians.* Retrieved February 25, 2007. . . .

Zimmerman, R. K. (2006). Ethical analysis of HPV vaccine policy options [Electronic version]. *Vaccine, 24,* 4812–4820.

Tamika L. Anderson  **NO**

Should the HPV Vaccine Be Mandatory for Early Adolescent Girls?

The human papillomavirus (HPV) vaccine, newly approved by the FDA, should not be a mandatory vaccine for young girls for several critical reasons. The first reason pertains to safety, because this is a new vaccine that has undergone phase III clinical trials testing the efficacy of the vaccine among 17,500 young women (Merck, 2007). There are data about the short-term (2–4 years) efficacy of the vaccine, but there are no accumulated data on the long-term safety of the vaccine or its long-term immunogenic qualities. Although the side effects of this vaccine are reported as minimal, these reports are based on documented side effects that occurred among the women participating in the clinical trials. We have no idea what adverse responses may occur when administered to millions of young girls. A few years ago, a vaccine to prevent rotavirus gastroenteritis among infants was approved as a recommended vaccine after successful clinical trials, only to be pulled from the market after administration to hundreds of thousands of infants because of an association with an increased incidence of intussusception after immunization. In my opinion, effectiveness trials of the HPV vaccine should be conducted in the real world as opposed to the tightly controlled research environment of phase III trials to further establish safety and help to determine duration of antibody response before mandating that the vaccine be administered to all young girls.

Another reason to think twice about mandatory HPV vaccination is that not all young women are at risk for acquiring the particular types of HPV associated with genital warts, cervical dysplasia, and an increased risk of cervical cancer. There are more than 100 identified strains of HPV; this vaccine prevents the four most common types. For most young women who acquire HPV, there are no symptoms and the virus will clear from their immune systems in a short period of time (Hilliard & Kahn, 2005).

I do not suggest that young girls be counseled to avoid vaccination but rather that the immunization be voluntary. The decision whether to receive the vaccine should be made in consultation with their healthcare provider and parents. For young women who choose life-long abstinence

From *American Journal of Maternal Child Nursing*, vol. 32, no. 4, July/August 2007, p. 209. Copyright © 2007 by Lippincott, Williams & Wilkins/Wolters Kluwer Health. Reprinted by permission.

for religious or other personal reasons, a mandated vaccine would violate their autonomy. There has also been discussion that public health nurses should administer the mandatory vaccine to young girls in the school setting. Even with parental consent, I believe that nurses would not be able to provide the necessary patient education under these circumstances.

Some proponents of mandating this vaccine have argued that other vaccines are already mandated, and adding another vaccine to the schedule would not be problematic. This view fails to recognize that all of the other childhood vaccines prevent communicable diseases that are easily spread from respiratory or casual contact routes and cannot be avoided. HPV is different; it is acquired through sexual contact. In my opinion, from a public health perspective, it is logical to mandate protection from diseases acquired through airborne transmission but not mandate a vaccine that prevents a disease transmitted through lifestyle choice.

A final reason for not mandating the vaccine is the economic cost. To be fully immunized, the HPV vaccine must be administered in a three-dose series, and estimates of costs to fully immunize all 11-year-old girls exceed $850 million per year (Elbasha, Dasbach, & Insinga, 2007). The government's Vaccine for Children Program would pay for the vaccine ($120/dose) for children who are uninsured or Medicaid eligible, and it is likely that most private insurers would cover the vaccine if mandated. For families who do not have health insurance that covers vaccines, however, affording the vaccine may be beyond their reach. The HPV vaccine should not be mandated for preadolescent girls until issues of safety, autonomy, and coverage for the uninsured are resolved.

References

Elbasha, E. H., Dasbach, E. J., & Insinga, R. P. (2007). Model for assessing human papilloma vaccination strategies. *Emerging Infectious Diseases, 13*, 28–41.

Hilliard, P. J., & Kahn, J. A. (2005). Understanding and preventing human papillomavirus infection during adolescence and young adulthood. *Journal of Adolescent Health, 37*, S1–S2.

Merck (2007). Gardasil demonstrated high prophylactic efficacy in girls and young women. . . .

POSTSCRIPT

Should the Human Papillomavirus (HPV) Vaccine Be Mandatory for Early Adolescent Girls?

An ounce of prevention is worth a pound of cure. . . . Who would disagree that we should prevent cervical cancer in women as opposed to treating it after cancer has occurred? A mandatory program of HPV vaccination of 11- to 12-year-old girls would go a long way toward reducing the incidence of cervical cancer. However, some people argue that the costs to personal autonomy are too high to implement a mandatory HPV vaccination program. Mandatory vaccination legislation is often a function of the *reasonableness* of the vaccine. That is, a risk-benefit analysis must take place: personal autonomy can be justified when there is ample risk. For example, when voluntary vaccination programs are unsuccessful, when people are unaware of the risks of the infection, or when the virus is widespread and easily transmitted, the benefits of mandatory vaccination outweigh the threats to personal autonomy (e.g., akin to speed limits or drunk driving laws, which are also threats to personal independence yet are warranted for public safety).

Does HPV constitute one of the exceptional cases that justify overruling personal choice to participate? Most of the diseases for which vaccines have been mandated are airborne—such as measles and smallpox. HPV infection is often considered to be a result of a "lifestyle choice," that is, to be sexually active. Some, such as Anderson, argue that this is why a mandated vaccination is unjustified. Others, such as Cruise, argue that the benefits of the mandated vaccination outweigh the costs.

The two authors subscribe to different theoretical frameworks in order to make their cases. One predominant perspective within the public health field is called *utilitarianism* (Zimmerman, 2006). In this theoretical paradigm, the rightness or wrongness of a particular action is based on a cost-benefit analysis. In this case, the many benefits of universal mandated HPV vaccination (e.g., prevention of cancer with consequent reduced human suffering, health care cost savings) outweigh the costs in terms of minor side effects (e.g., pain at the injection site). As well, from a compliance perspective, school-based mandatory vaccinations are very successful (Zimmerman, 2006). As a theory used to implement mandatory vaccination, utilitarianism has many pitfalls including infringing on individual freedoms as well as providing a rationale for unfair treatment of minorities (cf. HIV/AIDS, gay men, and blood donation policies).

Another theoretical perspective that is prominent within the bioethics of public health field involves the cardinal principles of beneficence (i.e., do good), nonmaleficence (i.e., do no harm), justice, and autonomy (Zimmerman, 2006). Mandatory HPV vaccinations meet the principle of beneficence in that it prevents cervical cancer. The principle of nonmaleficence is not met when one considers possible negative side effects of potentially increased unsafe sexual activity resulting from mandatory vaccination (e.g., which are theoretically possible if a girl believes adults are condoning early sexual activity and is confused about the protection offered by the vaccination) and/or reduced gynecological care (e.g., erroneous belief that, with HPV vaccination, there is no need for cervical cancer screening/Pap smears). In terms of the principle of justice, there is a "low middle class" for whom the vaccine might be less available due to financial hardship (i.e., those who are not eligible for Medicaid or similar programs yet who do not have private health care coverage of mandatory vaccinations). Finally, the issue of autonomy is violated by mandating HPV vaccination.

When reading Cruise's analysis favoring mandatory HPV vaccinations, it appears that she subscribes to a utilitarian theoretical perspective. In contrast, Anderson's discussion of the reasons against mandatory HPV vaccinations seems to appeal to the bioethical principles of beneficence, nonmaleficence, justice, and autonomy. Perhaps there is some middle ground: To redeem mandatory vaccination programs, there may be "opt out" clauses or creation of financial programs that alleviate the costs. In Ontario, Canada, for example, HPV vaccination is publically funded for grade 8 girls and vaccination is completely voluntary. With education campaigns, the girls and their parents can decide if they want to participate in this program. By making the program more universal as opposed to mandatory, reducing financial barriers, and preserving individual choice, the HPV vaccination for young women may become less controversial.

References/Further Reading

Agosti, J.M. & Goldie, S.J. (2007). Introducing HPV vaccine in developing countries—Key challenges and issues. *New England Journal of Medicine, 356(19)*, 1908–1910.

Borgmeyer, C. (2007). Many states are moving to require HPV vaccination for school entry: AAFP calls such mandates "premature." *American Association of Family Physicians News Now* available: www.aafp.org/online/en/home/publications/news/news-now/clinical-care-research/20070214hpvvaccine.html (accessed December 10, 2007).

Brewer, N.T., Cuite, C.L., Herrington, J.E., & Weinstein, N.D. (2007). Risk compensation and vaccination: "Can getting vaccinated cause people to engage in risky behaviors?" *Annals of Behavioral Medicine, 34(1)*, 95–99.

Charo, R.A. (2007). Politics, parents, and prophylaxis—Mandating HPV vaccination in the United States. *New England Journal of Medicine, 356(19)*, 1905–1908.

Lo, B. (2006). Editorial: HPV vaccine and adolescents' sexual activity. *British Medical Journal, 332*, 1106–1107.

Moscicki, A.-B. (2005). Impact of HPV infection in adolescent populations. *Journal of Adolescent Health, 37*, S3–S9.

Society of Obstetricians and Gynaecologists of Canada (14 August 2007). *Positioning Statements & Guidelines: SOGC Statement on CMAJ Commentary, "Human papillomavirus, vaccines and women's health: Questions and cautions,"* http://www.sogc.org/media/guidelines-hpv-commentary_e.asp (accessed December 11, 2007).

Sprigg, P. (2007). Don't mandate HPV vaccine—Trust parents. *Family Research Council Opinion Editorial,* http://www.frc.org/get.cfm?i=PV07D03 (accessed December 10, 2007).

Zimet, G.D. (2005). Improving adolescent health: Focus on HPV vaccine acceptance. *Journal of Adolescent Health, 37*, S17–S23.

Zimmerman, R. (2006). Ethical analysis of HPV vaccine policy options. *Vaccine, 24(22)*, 4812–4820.

ISSUE 6

Is the Use of Nicotine Replacement Therapy (NRT) an Appropriate Cessation Aid for Adolescents Wishing to Quit Smoking?

YES: Karen Hanson, Sharon Allen, Sue Jensen, and Dorothy Batsukami, from "Treatment of Adolescent Smokers with the Nicotine Patch," *Nicotine & Tobacco Research* (August, 2003)

NO: William P. Adelman, from "Tobacco use Cessation for Adolescents," *Adolescent Medicine Clinics* (October, 2006)

ISSUE SUMMARY

YES: Karen Hanson and colleagues, from the Tobacco Use Research Center at the University of Minnesota, present the results of an empirical study where they had adolescent smokers use a nicotine-replacement patch or a placebo patch (i.e., a patch with no nicotine unbeknownst to the participant). The results suggested that, with cognitive-behaviorial therapy and an incentive program (money for not smoking), the patch was effective at reducing withdrawal symptoms and cravings and there was some indication that the patch helped adolescents reduce the amount they smoked. Hanson et al. concluded that the patch may be helpful for adolescent smokers who attempt to quit.

NO: William P. Adelman, a physician who is a member of the Department of Adolescent Medicine at the National Naval Medical Center in Bethesda, Maryland, in a review article, argues that there are "teen" patterns of smoking and "adult" patterns of smoking and that use of nicotine replacement therapy is appropriate only for adolescents who exhibit adult-type smoking behavior. He calls for caution in the use of nicotine replacement therapy as it could be a "gateway" substance that leads to use of other controlled substances or results in other unintended negative physiological consequences.

T obacco was responsible for 20% of deaths at the turn of this century (Koplan, 2007). Young cigarette smoking is a major health concern as the lifetime complications associated with smoking are severe and most smoking (80%) is initiated during adolescence (USDHHS, 1994). Adolescent smoking is a prevalent phenomenon with as many as a quarter of US high school students reporting tobacco use (Marshall et al., 2006) and one in five younger North and South American teens (13–15) using some tobacco product. America (and European) teens smoke more than teens in other places in the world (Mochizuki-Kobayashi et al., 2006). While primary prevention is ideal, what methods are best for intervening with youth who already smoke?

Nicotine Replacement Therapy is a quit-smoking aide where nicotine is delivered to the body through gum or a patch applied to the arm or shoulder (transdermal nicotine). NRT methods are accessible to North American youth because they do not require a prescription (unlike smoking cessation drugs) and NRT is sold over-the-counter.

The efficacy of these pharmacological treatments is well-established. The typical experimental design is called a randomized control (or placebo-controlled) study; one group of "quitters" is randomly given the active drug/NRT while a placebo group of "quitters" is randomly assigned to receive inert pills, patches, or gum. The participants are "blind," meaning that they do not know whether they are receiving the drug/NRT or the placebo. Often, the researcher is blind to which condition the participant is assigned; this is called a double-blind. This is done to ensure that quitting efforts are influenced *only* by the drug/NRT. Most studies are conducted with adults and generally find that the participants who receive the active drug are significantly more successful at quitting smoking relative to the placebo group (see USDHHS, 2000).

How effective is NRT with the teen population? Can we extrapolate from the studies that show that NRT is effective with adults to youth? There are few studies of NRT with adolescents. The ones that exist have mixed findings and can be interpreted as *either* supporting or failing to support NRT use with teens (e.g., Killen et al., 2004).

Hanson et al. (2003), using randomized control methodology, investigated the efficacy of NRT with youth. Those teens who received an active patch had lower cravings for cigarettes and had fewer withdrawal symptoms than those assigned the placebo patch. Most teens wore the patch; there were few "adverse events" (e.g., headaches) from NRT use; and the NRT patch was rated as "helpful" for quitting and smoking reduction attempts. Hanson et al. view teen NRT use as a promising treatment.

Adelman asserts that the existing evidence indicates that NRT would not be an effective smoking-cessation aide for youth. He argues that tobacco use by adolescents is qualitatively different than adult use. He contends that some youth smoke for normative reasons—and that interventions to get these teens to cease using tobacco should take behavioral rather than pharmacological forms. As you read these two pieces, consider how the assumptions that the authors have about NRT may color the manner in which they interpret the empirical evidence.

YES

Karen Hanson, Sharon Allen, Sue Jensen, Dorothy Hatsukami

Treatment of Adolescent Smokers with the Nicotine Patch

Introduction

. . . Researchers have published relatively few studies on smoking cessation treatment for adolescents (Adelman, Duggan, Hauptman, & Joffe, 2001; Aveyard et al., 1999; Greenberg & Deputat, 1978; Hollis, Vogt, Stevens, Biglan, Severson, & Lichtenstein, 1995; Horn, Fernandes, Dino, Massey, & Kalsekar, 2003; Hurt, Croghan, Beede, Wolter, Croghan, & Patten, 2000; Lotecka & MacWhinney, 1983; Pallonen et al., 1998; Patten, Ames, Ebbert, Wolter, Hurt, & Gauvin, 2001; Perry, Killen, Telch, Slinkard, & Danaher, 1980; Perry, Telch, Killen, Burke, & Maccoby, 1983; Prince, 1995; Riley, Jerome, Behar, & Zack, 2002; Smith et al., 1996; St. Pierre, Shute, & Jaycox, 1983; Sussman, Dent, Burton, Stacy, & Flay, 1995; Sussman, Dent, & Lichtman, 2001; Weissman, Glasgow, Biglan, & Lichtenstein, 1987).

These studies have been conducted in the community at clinics, at a physician's office, and in schools. The treatment content of these studies has varied but has been focused predominantly on psychosocial aspects of smoking cessation, education on health consequences, physical dependence on nicotine, and coping strategies for smoking cessation. Only twelve studies used biochemical verification to validate participants' self-report of tobacco status. Quit smoking studies among adolescents have generally produced low success rates (USDHHS, 1994). In the twelve studies with end-of-treatment assessments, the range of end-of-treatment abstinence was 9.1%–59.0% (mean 22.5%). Eleven studies reported follow-up assessments varying from 1- to approximately 5-years posttreatment. The follow-up abstinence rates ranged from 0.0% to 52.0% (mean 16.0%). Few controlled studies have compared treatment intervention with a minimal or usual intervention. Only four out of eight of these studies have shown significantly better outcome with the active treatment intervention. One study showed significant differences in abstinence rates between the control group and the intervention group at end of treatment but not at follow-up.

From *Nicotine and Tobacco Research*, August 2003, excerpts from pp. 515–518, 521–526. Copyright © 2003 by by Society for Research on Nicotine and Tobacco. Reprinted by permission of Taylor & Francis via Rightslink.

Clearly, continued innovations are needed in the treatment of adolescent smoking. Perhaps part of the lack of efficacy is related to failure to consider adolescents' physical dependence on nicotine. Adults who used the nicotine patch experienced increased abstinence rates compared with those who received placebo patches (Fiore et al., 2000). Reducing withdrawal symptoms may help smokers to quit. Adults who wore the nicotine patch reported a reduction in withdrawal symptoms. Evidence indicates that adolescents experience withdrawal symptoms. . . . The extent of withdrawal symptom reduction in adolescents using the nicotine patch for cessation is unknown. Nicotine patch therapy has been approved for adult use and not for adolescents' use. Additionally, the nicotine patch has not yet been carefully researched with adolescents.

To date, researchers have published only two studies that have examined the effects of the nicotine patch on smoking cessation among adolescents (Hurt et al., 2000; Smith et al., 1996). Both studies used a nonrandomized, open-label design. The end-of-treatment abstinence rates were 10.9% (Hurt et al., 2000) and 13.6% (Smith et al., 1996). The 6-month follow-up rates were both only 5%. No research has been published using a double-blind, placebo-controlled, randomized study of the nicotine patch with adolescents. Furthermore, previous nicotine patch trials used minimal interventions with adolescents. A more intensive intervention may be required to sustain motivation to quit or to improve treatment outcome.

The present study design was a double-blind, placebo-controlled trial of the nicotine patch among adolescents. The research was conducted in the context of an intensive cognitive–behavioral program that used a contingency-management procedure that reinforced abstinence to increase quit rates. . . .

The purpose of the present study was to examine the following aspects of adolescent smoking cessation: (a) The effect of the nicotine patch on the signs and symptoms of withdrawal from cigarettes among adolescents, (b) adolescents' compliance with the nicotine patch, and (c) the safety of using the nicotine patch with adolescents. The secondary goal was to conduct a preliminary investigation of the short-term effectiveness of the nicotine patch in helping adolescents to quit smoking. Hypotheses regarding each of the outcomes were as follows: (a) Participants who received the active nicotine patch would experience fewer withdrawal symptoms than those who received the placebo patch, (b) participants in the active nicotine patch group would be more likely to wear the patch daily than those in the placebo group, and (c) the nicotine patch would be safe to use in most adolescent smokers. With regard to the secondary goal, cessation rates for those who received the active nicotine patch were hypothesized to be greater than the placebo system.

Methods

Participants aged 13–19 years ($N = 100$) were recruited using flyers and brochures distributed at schools and medical clinics, advertisements in school newspapers, recruiter presentations, and radio and television announcements. . . . The eligibility criteria were as follows: (*a*) Smoked at least 10 cigarettes per day for at least 6 months, (*b*) did not use any other tobacco products more than once per week, (*c*) were motivated to quit smoking, and (*d*) were not currently using nicotine replacement therapy. . . .

. . . The total study duration including the screening visit and orientation was 13 visits. Follow-up visits were conducted at 1- and 6-months posttreatment. . . .

Participants who met selection criteria completed a thorough medical screening before beginning smoking cessation treatment. . . . One week following the medical screening visit, participants attended a prequit visit. At the prequit visit, participants were randomly assigned in a double-blind manner to receive either the active nicotine patch or the placebo patch. SmithKline Beecham prepared the active nicotine patches and placebo patches, which were identical in appearance. . . . Participants were asked to wear each system on their upper torso for a 24-hr period with replacements every morning. They received a new supply of nicotine patches and returned used patches at each clinic visit. During the prequit visit, they also received a manual that offered suggestions about how to quit smoking and provided encouragement.

Participants stopped smoking 1 week after the prequit visit on the morning of visit 1. During each visit, participants received individual cognitive–behavioral counseling. . . . Participants learned about topics such as triggers for smoking, coping strategies including action and thought responses, stress management, and relapse prevention. . . . At 10 weeks postquit (end-of-treatment), participants received a discharge physical exam. . . .

Dependent Measures

Several dependent measures were obtained during each visit. Participants' heart rate, blood pressure, and body weight were measured. Expired-air carbon monoxide (CO) levels were obtained. Participants also provided salivary cotinine samples. . . .

At each visit, participants completed the Nicotine Withdrawal Symptom Checklist. They rated several withdrawal symptoms on a scale from 0 to 4, ranging from not present to severe. . . .

During all visits, adverse clinical events were described as to their nature, severity, duration, action taken, and outcome. The adverse events that participants were asked about were as follows: Joint or muscle aches; headaches; tachycardia; palpitations; dry mouth; excessive sweating; nausea/vomiting; stomachaches; sleep problems or abnormal dreams; diarrhea; lightheadedness/dizziness; and redness, itching, or swelling at the patch site. . . .

Additionally, participants were required to record on a daily basis the number of cigarettes smoked and the frequency of other tobacco products used. When participants began using nicotine patches, they also recorded the time of day that they applied the nicotine patches. Finally, at visit 10 (end-of-treatment), participants completed an Impressions of Treatment Questionnaire. . . .

Contingency-Management Procedure

A contingency-management procedure was used to reinforce abstinence from cigarettes. . . . During cessation treatment visits (1–10), participants earned points for attaining CO levels ≤8 ppm. Points were exchanged for gift certificates. . . . If participants were abstinent from cigarettes throughout the study, they received points and bonuses equivalent to US$125.00 in gift certificates. . . . Moreover, on each visit, participants had the opportunity to enter their name in a lottery to win a US$50.00 gift certificate. . . . To increase participants' motivation for attending the first two sessions, they received a US$13.00 gift certificate on both visits, for a compact disc from a music, video, and electronic store. In addition, participants were paid US$25.00 per visit for attending follow-up visits.

Results

Craving and Withdrawal Symptoms

A repeated measures analysis (a statistical technique that analyzes a person's scores over different or "repeated" times) of scores from the Nicotine Withdrawal Symptoms Checklist by craving and the total withdrawal symptoms (all symptoms except craving) was completed. These data were analyzed from the prequit visit through 2 weeks postquit (visits 0–4) for all participants. Results indicated a lower craving score and overall withdrawal symptom score in the active nicotine patch group. A time trend was found toward lower scores as time passed in craving score only for the active nicotine patch group. Neither the active nor the placebo group showed high withdrawal symptom scores. . . .

We also analyzed craving and the total withdrawal symptoms from participants who were abstinent. Participants who were abstinent in the active nicotine patch group reported significantly lower overall withdrawal symptom scores compared with those who were abstinent in the placebo patch group. No significant difference was found, however, between the active nicotine patch and placebo patch groups among those who were abstinent in craving score.

Self-Reported Nicotine Patch Use Compliance

Among subjects who completed the visits, the self-reported total compliance with use of active nicotine patches was 84.2% through 6 weeks postquit and 67.2% during the 4-week dose reduction period (visits 8–10). The self-reported total compliance with use of placebo patches was 85.0% through 6 weeks postquit and 68.5% during the 4-week dose reduction period (visits 8–10). Compliance with use of nicotine patches does not indicate that participants were abstinent.

Adverse Events

. . . Of participants, 97.9% ($n = 48$) in the active patch group vs. 93.3% ($n = 45$) in the placebo patch group experienced an adverse event. . . .

The most common adverse events reported by participants in the active vs. placebo patch groups were itching at nicotine patch site (64.5%, $n = 31$, vs. 53.3%, $n = 24$), sleep problems or abnormal dreams (62.5%, $n = 30$, vs. 51.1%, $n = 23$), joint or muscle aches (58.3%, $n = 28$, vs. 51.1%, $n = 23$), redness at nicotine patch site (54.2%, $n = 26$, vs. 42.2%, $n = 19$), light-headedness/dizziness (41.7%, $n = 20$, vs. 48.9%, $n = 22$), and stomachaches (43.8%, $n = 21$, vs. 37.8%, $n = 17$).

. . . No participants discontinued the study as a result of an adverse event. The majority of adverse events were categorized as mild.

Longest Continuous Abstinence from Quit Date

. . . No significant difference between the active nicotine patch and placebo patch groups was noted in overall time of abstinence, although for those participants quitting for at least 1 day, the active nicotine patch group's median quit time of 18 days was substantially greater than the corresponding value for the placebo group (4 days). . . . Analyses revealed no significant differences between treatment conditions using a 7-day period of abstinence, or a 30-day period of abstinence.

Predictors of Length of Abstinence from Quit Date

. . . Length of abstinence from quit date was predicted by using the following potential covariates measured at the prequit visit in the model: Age, number of alcoholic drinks consumed per month, use of caffeine, cigarettes per day, salivary cotinine level, CO level, education, gender, ethnicity, family support, Fagerström score, and years smoked. Results showed that elevated Fagerström score (a questionnaire designed to assess nicotine dependence) predicted shorter abstinence times. Conversely, older participants attained longer periods of abstinence.

Reduction in CO Levels and Cigarettes Smoked Among Nonquitters

Participants who completed the study but failed to quit for a substantial period ($n = 37$, defined as those who were not abstinent at least 9 weeks during treatment) showed a reduction in CO levels and cigarettes smoked per day. CO levels decreased from 14.2 ppm at the prequit visit to 6.2 ppm on the quit day, to 4.2 ppm at 1 week postquit, and then increased to 6.6 ppm at 10 weeks postquit. The number of cigarettes smoked per day was reduced from 16.3 at the prequit visit, to 6.0 at 1 week postquit, to 1.1 at 2 weeks postquit, and then increased to 3.7 at 10 weeks postquit.

Salivary Cotinine Levels

Prequit measures of salivary cotinine showed no significant differences by randomization group. . . .

At 1 week postquit, salivary cotinine levels differed significantly by treatment condition as would be expected. This difference diminished as time passed: 6 weeks postquit (204.7 ng/ml vs. 77.5 ng/ml), 8 weeks postquit (131.3 ng/ml vs. 103.9 ng/ml), and 10 weeks postquit (103.0 ng/ml vs. 92.4 ng/ml). The overall mean salivary cotinine levels were significantly lower at 1, 6, 8, and 10 weeks postquit compared with prequit levels. Salivary cotinine levels correlated with cigarettes smoked per day ($r = 0.41$, $p < .001$) and with expired-air CO levels ($r = 0.57$, $p = .001$) at the prequit visit.

Treatment Completion and Follow-Up Rates

Of the initial 100 participants, 53% ($n = 53$) completed treatment. Of the active nicotine patch group, 50% ($n = 25$) finished treatment, compared with 56% ($n = 28$) of the placebo patch group. . . . Most participants dropped out during the first 2 weeks postquit ($n = 23$). An additional eight participants dropped out 2–3 weeks postquit. No significant differences in dropout rate were observed across the treatment groups.

Participants' View of Treatment

Participants who attended the final treatment visit (10 weeks postquit) completed the Impressions of Treatment Questionnaire ($n = 53$). No significant differences between treatment groups were found in participants' global impressions regarding aspects of the research study except for how effective they thought the nicotine patch was in helping them to quit smoking. Participants who received the nicotine patch were more likely to rate the nicotine patch as very helpful or helpful than were those who wore the placebo patch and were unlikely to rate the nicotine patch as unhelpful or very unhelpful.

When asked which nicotine patch they thought they had worn during the study, 95.8% ($n = 23/24$) of participants in the active nicotine patch group correctly believed they had received the active nicotine patch. Of participants in the placebo group, however, one third incorrectly thought they had worn an active nicotine patch (34.5%, $n = 10/28$).

Most participants also rated the cognitive–behavioral sessions as either very helpful or helpful (84.9%, $n = 45$). Other parts of the program that participants found helpful in their attempts at quitting were as follows: Frequency of visits (96.2%, $n = 51$), accountability (86.8%, $n = 46$), and earning gift certificates. . . .

Discussion

The findings of the present study indicate that the nicotine patch may be helpful for adolescents in their quit attempts. First, consistent with other studies using the nicotine patch with adolescents (Hurt et al., 2000; Smith et al., 1996), no serious or life-threatening adverse events were reported in the present study. Additionally, as another measure of safety, the overall mean salivary cotinine levels were significantly lower throughout treatment compared with baseline smoking levels. Smoking while wearing the nicotine patch may have increased some participants' salivary cotinine levels but did not produce adverse events. . . .

Second, participants in the active nicotine patch group reported fewer withdrawal signs and symptoms including craving compared with those in the placebo group. Furthermore, participants in the active nicotine patch group who were abstinent also reported a significantly lower total withdrawal symptom score compared with those who were abstinent in the placebo patch group. No differences were found, however, between treatment groups among those who were abstinent with regard to the craving score. Participants in the two nonrandomized, open-label trials of the nicotine patch among adolescents also reported a reduction in withdrawal symptoms across time (Hurt et al., 2000; Smith et al., 1996).

Third, a significant number of participants were compliant with using the nicotine patch daily. In a nonrandomized, open-label study, researchers also found high levels of compliance (85%) with nicotine patch use during treatment (Hurt et al., 2000). Adolescents appeared to be willing to wear nicotine patches during smoking cessation attempts. Furthermore, many participants (95.8%) who completed the study believed that the nicotine patch was very helpful or helpful in their quit attempt.

Finally, although no differences between treatment groups were found with regard to abstinence rates, participants who did not quit reduced the number of cigarettes they smoked per day and CO levels by the end-of-treatment compared with baseline levels. Other researchers reported a reduction in smoking by study participants while using the nicotine patch (Hurt et al., 2000; Smith et al., 1996). . . .

The preliminary investigation of the effectiveness of the nicotine patch in helping adolescents quit smoking found no significant differences between treatment groups. This lack of difference may be associated with the overwhelming effect of the contingency-management procedure (i.e., the lottery and gift certificate program). Future studies should determine the effect of contingency-management procedures in smoking cessation. A methodological issue for researchers to consider is whether to pay participants and how much payment is optimal. In the present study, participants may have been motivated to enroll in the study to earn gift certificates rather than to quit smoking.

As consistent with the nonrandomized, open-label trials of the nicotine patch, teenage smokers in the present study attained lower rates of abstinence than those achieved by adults in other studies (Fiore et al., 1992). In the current study, 30-day point prevalence rates at the end of treatment were 20% in the active group vs. 18% in the placebo patch group. Short-term abstinence rates among adults who used the nicotine patch attained end-of-treatment rates that ranged from 18% to 77% (Fiore et al., 1992), with rates twice as high compared with adults using placebo patches (Fiore et al., 2000). Nonetheless, abstinence rates from the present study were higher than those found in the two nonrandomized, open-label trials of the nicotine patch among adolescents (Hurt et al., 2000; Smith et al., 1996). This result may indicate that an intensive treatment approach can enhance efficacy. We did not assess reasons for participants' relapse or for dropping out of the study. Researchers should determine why adolescents relapse to smoking when using the nicotine patch. This information is important for designing cessation programs. Based on the results of the present study, a larger clinical trial is warranted to examine the effect of the nicotine patch on abstinence rates.

Limitations

The present study has two limitations. First, compliance with patch use was assessed by self-report and by counting participants' used and unused patches returned at each visit. Often participants failed to return used and unused patches. We were therefore unable to determine if their self-report was accurate. In future studies, a third party, such as a parent, could verify whether participants were compliant with using medication.

Second, 47% of participants dropped out before the completion of the study. . . . Because participants in the present study were usually unwilling to return phone calls or to complete an exit visit before dropping out, we have no data regarding why participants discontinued the study.

References

Adelman, W. P., Duggan, A. K., Hauptman, P., & Joffe, A. (2001). Effectiveness of a high school smoking cessation program. *Pediatrics, 107,* E50.

Aveyard, P., Cheng, K. K., Almond, J., Sherratt, E., Lancashire, R., Lawrence, T., Griffin, C., & Evans, O. (1999). Cluster randomised controlled trial of expert system based on the transtheoretical ("stages of change") model for smoking prevention. *British Medical Journal, 319,* 948–953.

Fiore, M. C., Jorenby, D. E., Baker, T. B., & Kenford, S. L. (1992). Tobacco dependence and the nicotine patch. *Journal of the American Medical Association, 268,* 2687–2694.

Fiore, M. C., Bailey, W. C., Cohen, S. J., Dorfman, S., Goldstein, M., & Gritz, E. et al. (2000). *Treating tobacco use and dependence: Clinical practice guideline.* Rockville, MD: U.S. Department of Health and Human Services, Public Health Service.

Greenberg, J. S., & Deputat, Z. (1978). Smoking intervention: Comparing three methods in a high school setting. *The Journal of School Health, 11,* 498–502.

Hollis, J. F., Vogt, T. M., Stevens, V., Biglan, A., Severson, H., & Lichtenstein, E. (1995). The tobacco reduction and cancer control (TRACC) program: Team approaches to counseling in medical and dental settings. *National Cancer Institute Monograph, 5,* 143–168.

Horn, K., Fernandes, A., Dino, G., Massey, C. J., & Kalsekar, I. (2003). Adolescent nicotine dependence and smoking cessation outcomes. *Addictive Behaviors, 28,* 769–776.

Hughes, J. R., & Hatsukami, D. (1986). Signs and symptoms of tobacco withdrawal. *Archives of General Psychiatry, 43,* 289–294.

Hurt, R. D., Croghan, G. A., Beede, S. D., Wolter, T. D., Croghan, I. T., & Patten, C. A. (2000). Nicotine patch therapy in 101 adolescent smokers. *Archives of Pediatric and Adolescent Medicine, 154,* 31–37.

Lotecka, L., & MacWhinney, M. (1983). Enhancing decision behavior in high school "smokers." *The International Journal of the Addictions, 18,* 479–490.

Pallonen, U. E., Velicer, W. F., Prochaska, J. O., Rossi, J. S., Bellis, J. M., Tsoh, J. Y., Migneault, J. P., Smith, N. F., & Prokhorov, A. V. (1998). Computer-based smoking cessation interventions in adolescents: Description, feasibility and six-month follow-up findings. *Substance Use and Misuse, 33,* 935–965.

Patten, C. A., Ames, S. C., Ebbert, J. O., Wolter, T. D., Hurt, R. D., & Gauvin, T. R. (2001). Tobacco use outcomes of adolescents treated clinically for nicotine dependence. *Archives of Pediatric and Adolescent Medicine, 155,* 831–837.

Perry, C. L., Telch, M. J., Killen, J., Burke, A., & Maccoby, N. (1983). High school smoking prevention: The relative efficacy of varied treatments and instructors. *Adolescence, 18,* 561–566.

Prince, F. (1995). The relative effectiveness of a peer-led and adult-led smoking intervention program. *Adolescence, 30,* 188–194.

Riley, W., Jerome, A., Behar, A., & Zack, S. (2002). Feasibility of computerized scheduled gradual reduction for adolescent smoking cessation. *Substance Use and Misuse, 37,* 255–263.

Smith, T. A., House, R. F., Croghan, I. T., Gauvin, T. R., Colligan, R. C., Offord, K. P., Gomez-Dahl, L. C., & Hurt, R. D. (1996). Nicotine patch therapy in adolescent smokers. *Pediatrics, 98,* 659–667.

St. Pierre, R. W., Shute, R. E., & Jaycox, S. (1983). Youth helping youth: A behavioral approach to the self-control of smoking. *Health Education, Jan–Feb*: 28–33.

Sussman, S., Dent, C. W., & Lichtman, K. L. (2001). Project EX Outcomes of a teen smoking cessation program. *Addictive Behaviors, 26,* 425–438.

Sussman, S., Dent, C. W., Burton, D., Stacy, A. W., & Flay, B. R. (1995). *Developing school-based tobacco use prevention and cessation programs.* Thousand Oaks, CA: Sage Publications.

U.S. Department of Health and Human Services. (1994). *Preventing tobacco use among young people: A report of the surgeon general.* Atlanta, GA: Author, Public Health Service, Centers for Disease Control and Prevention, National Center for Chronic Disease Prevention and Health Promotion, Office on Smoking and Health.

Weissman, W., Glasgow, R., Biglan, A., & Lichtenstein, E. (1987). Development and preliminary evaluation of a cessation program for adolescent smokers. *Psychology of Addictive Behaviors, 1,* 84–91.

William P. Adelman  **NO**

Tobacco Use Cessation for Adolescents

$\mathbf{T}$he following are some clinical scenarios:

Case #1: A 16-year-old girl presents to the adolescent medicine provider requesting "the patch to quit smoking." She has been smoking for about a year and smokes "probably about a half pack" or 10 cigarettes per day (cpd), usually with friends before and after school. When she is at a party, she may smoke more. She does not smoke every day. She never smokes at home and says her parents "totally don't know" that she smokes. She has tried to quit "cold turkey," but it did not work.

Case #2: A 16-year-old boy presents to the adolescent medicine provider requesting "the patch to quit smoking." He has been smoking for a little more than 1 year. He smokes 18 cpd. He does most of his smoking at work (28 hours per week), where he is a mechanic's assistant. He smokes every day, even when ill. His parents know that he smokes, and he often borrows cigarettes from them. His first cigarette is smoked immediately on awakening, while he is still in bed, and he smokes at night to unwind. He has cut down from 25 cpd.

Case #3: A 16-year-old girl presents to the adolescent medicine provider for a routine physical examination. She started smoking 4 months ago. She smokes one to five cigarettes per weekend, two or three weekends per month. She smokes at parties and occasionally inhales. She smokes "to be social with friends" and because "I get a buzz." She enjoys smoking occasionally and has no interest in stopping.

. . . Clearly, these adolescents have different patterns of smoking and require individualized interventions. Evidence-based tobacco use cessation clinical practice guidelines offer clear intervention recommendations for adults but are of little assistance for adolescents. There exists a paucity of evidence regarding effective interventions for adolescent tobacco use cessation. This lack of data leaves many providers frustrated as they attempt to apply adult interventions that are unproved or simply ineffective for adolescents.

Adolescent Tobacco Use: How Is It Different from Adult Tobacco Use?

Marked differences in typology of smoking, amount of nicotine consumed, and nicotine addiction distinguish the adolescent from the adult

From *Adolescent Medicine Clinics*, vol. 17, issue 3, October 2006, excerpts from pp. 697–698, 700–712. Copyright © 2006 by Elsevier Science Ltd. Reprinted by permission.

smoker. Adolescence is notable for being the age range of initiation of tobacco use, whereas adulthood is characterized by regular use. Delay of smoking initiation until after age 18 significantly decreases the chance of becoming an established smoker [5]. The most common age for trying a first cigarette is between 14 and 15 years, and the most frequent age at which one progresses to regular smoking is between 16 and 17 years [6]. After the mid-20s, declines in smoking initiation occur [7]. An identifiable period exists between first smoking and regular use. The trajectory from initiation to daily use is sometimes described as experimental (e.g., Case #3), progressing to early regular (e.g., Case #1), and then to daily smoking (e.g., Case #2) [3]. Most health care providers for adolescents will see tobacco users when they are somewhere along this spectrum of use and addiction.

The average adult smoker consumes 19 to 20 cpd if male and 17 cpd if female [8,9]. By contrast with these stable figures, adolescent smoking increases with age. One in eleven eighth graders smokes cigarettes, compared with one in four high school seniors. Only 4.4% of eighth graders smoke daily, compared with 15% of 12th graders. Less than 2% of eighth graders, compared with 8% of 12th graders, smoke half a pack or more per day [10]. It remains unclear how best to treat adolescent smokers along the spectrum of use.

As a general rule, adult smokers are influenced most significantly by their addiction to nicotine, with more than 80% of adult tobacco users fulfilling criteria for dependence [11]. Conversely, adolescent smokers are more influenced by behavioral and environmental phenomena. For example, strong empiric evidence indicates that smoking in movies increases the rate of adolescent smoking initiation [12], and youths tend to smoke the more advertised brands of cigarettes [13]. In one study of high-risk adolescent smokers, only 20% had substantial nicotine dependence [14].

Are Adolescents Treatable?

Adolescent smokers, like their adult counterparts, are interested in quitting smoking. Seventy percent of 12- to 17-year-old smokers regret smoking [15], 85% of adolescents who smoke think about quitting [16], and 80% of current smokers who present to a primary care provider have made a cessation attempt in the past year [17]. Three of four young smokers have tried to quit at least once in adolescence and failed [18]. The need for effective youth tobacco cessation interventions has been recognized for more than a decade. . . .

The AAP (The American Association of Pediatrics), in its position statement on tobacco, clearly explains that pediatricians play a crucial role in reducing tobacco use by children, adolescents, and their parents and should rank this among their highest health prevention priorities [25]. . . . All agree that intervention in adolescent tobacco use is required. But which intervention?

What Works for Adolescent Smokers?
—A Review of the Evidence

Behavioral Therapies

Adolescent tobacco use cessation and nicotine dependence research are still new, and methodologic shortfalls that need to be addressed have been systematically described [26]. Overall, few controlled studies and only limited evidence demonstrate the efficacy of smoking cessation interventions. To date, the most effective interventions for adolescent smokers have been adolescent-specific, school- or community-based programs that teach usable social, behavioral, and coping skills. These programs are easy to implement and improve short-term outcomes, but the methods by which they were evaluated exhibited great variability, with only a few meeting rigorous, evidence-based screening criteria [27]. The long-term outcomes of these interventions are unknown, and they are not readily available in most communities.

One systematic review of controlled trials for adolescent smoking cessation reviewed 281 articles and determined that only six met selection criteria [28]. Among these, one study in pregnant adolescent girls showed a decrease in daily cigarette use and exhaled carbon monoxide levels, but not in actual cessation rates [29]. One hospital-based study [30] and one randomized, double-blind, placebo-controlled clinical study of 330 adolescent smokers who underwent either laser or sham acupuncture [31] showed no difference between intervention and control groups in smoking outcomes. In contrast, three school-based studies that were included [32–34] all reported significant impacts on smoking cessation. Only one study [32] was a randomized control trial. It incorporated biochemical validation and included school-year-long follow-up. This study looked at intermediate outcome measures in addition to cessation rates. It showed that participation in a school-based program served to assist those who failed to quit by reducing the number of cigarettes smoked per day. . . .

In another comprehensive review of adolescent tobacco use cessation trials [36], 15 of 66 trials reviewed were considered experimental by the author. Classroom programs had the highest quit rates (17%), followed by computer-based expert system programs (13%) and school-based clinics (12%). Qualities common to all the successful interventions are easy accessibility, adolescent-specificity and adolescent-friendliness (i.e., tailoring the intervention to the development and environment of the adolescent), and provision of ongoing support for cessation efforts. . . .

Psychopharmacology: Nicotine Replacement
Therapy and Antidepressants

Use of nicotine replacement therapy [NRT] among adolescents is controversial [37]. In the United States, the U.S. Food and Drug Administration labels NRTs for use by individuals at least 18 years old. NRT is a safe and effective mainstay of adult smoking cessation [38–40]; hence, current clinical practice guidelines for treating tobacco use and dependence suggest that it be a first-line treatment for adults [1,2]. These same guidelines suggest that physicians consider the use of NRT in adolescents with obvious nicotine dependence who want to quit smoking. It is imperative that practitioners who treat adolescents be aware of NRT options, because they are available over the counter, are easily accessible by minors without proof of age [41], and are often tried by adolescents before presentation to the clinician [42]. Some tobacco use researchers advocate unfettered access to NRT beginning as young as 12 years, arguing that limiting access to a potentially useful medication for tobacco use cessation based on age is arbitrary [43]. To date, NRT has not been shown to be an effective treatment for adolescent tobacco users.

It is also important that practitioners be aware of potential risks and unexplored areas of research regarding use of NRT in teenagers. NRT is effective in adults because its implementation is based on the proven assumption that adults are dependent on nicotine and therefore use tobacco to maintain a steady-state concentration of nicotine [44]. By replacing the harmful tobacco product with the relatively harmless nicotine, one may feed the addiction without the harmful health effects. One sign of nicotine addiction in adults is physiologic withdrawal. Adults who wear the nicotine patch report a reduction in withdrawal symptoms [45].

NRT would have predicted effectiveness in adolescents only if they were similarly addicted to nicotine. A currently controversial area of ongoing research is the role of nicotine addiction in smokers while still in adolescence [46,47]. Attempts to assess nicotine dependence among adolescents have resulted in various subjective criteria for definition, and widely variable sample characteristics make interpretation of the results difficult. One quarter of teenagers who try smoking ultimately will meet diagnostic criteria for nicotine dependence [48], and several studies have found evidence of nicotine dependence among some adolescent smokers [49]. Adolescents report subjective "withdrawal symptoms" when they stop smoking [50]; however, the presumption that these are signs of nicotine addiction in adolescents is unproven. In one study that examined withdrawal symptoms in adolescents who were deprived of smoking for 8 hours, adolescents received either an active 15-mg patch or a placebo patch [51]. Both groups experienced increased withdrawal symptoms compared with baseline, but there was no difference between the patch groups, suggesting that withdrawal symptoms in adolescents cannot be explained by nicotine alone. Although the degrees of influence of peer, family, internal factors, and biochemical addiction are unclear, all have been shown to play a role in the continuum of initiation to regular use. The role of nicotine addiction in childhood and adolescence is an ongoing area of vigorous study [52–55].

Does the Nicotine Patch Work for Adolescents?

The first two studies to examine the use of the nicotine patch in adolescents were open label, single group, and failed to show effectiveness [56,57]. In the first double-blind, randomized clinical trial with a primary goal of examining the effects of the nicotine patch on craving and withdrawal symptoms, safety, and compliance among adolescents, and a secondary goal of investigating the effectiveness of the patch in helping adolescents quit smoking, researchers randomized 100 13- to 19-year-olds to one-on-one cognitive treatment sessions and the patch or placebo patch. At the end of the 13-week intervention, there was no difference between groups [58]. Although it is premature to exclude NRT for all adolescents, the paltry sum of clinical evidence to date suggests that NRT is ineffective for adolescent tobacco use cessation.

Is Nicotine Replacement Therapy Safe?

NRTs are generally considered safe. Among adults, replacing the harmful tobacco with nicotine has been shown to be effective, with a favorable risk/benefit ratio. The bulk of safety studies in adults focus on cardiac outcomes [59,60]. The few adolescent studies using NRT also conclude that the modality is safe, without serious side effects. However, only short-term effects have been monitored, adolescents have different health risk profiles from adults, and most potential dangers of nicotine replacement are unexplored among adolescents. The behavioral aspects of smoking are particularly relevant to teens. Unfortunately, behavioral outcomes of nicotine replacement have yet to be explored in great depth among adolescents.

Are There Risks to Nicotine Replacement Therapy in Adolescents?

Theoretic concerns exist regarding nicotine replacement during adolescence as a cause of untoward behavioral and mental health outcomes. Animal models suggest that nicotine has detrimental effects on the adolescent brain. The translation of these findings to human adolescents is unexplored. Nicotine is a toxic substance. Adolescent nicotine exposure causes cell death and altered neurochemistry in the cortex and hippocampus [61]. . . .

Behavioral Responses to Nicotine in Adolescent Rats

Initial nicotine exposure in adolescence as opposed to adulthood affects later response to nicotine. . . . Animals first exposed to nicotine in adolescence have increased responses to the stimulating effects of nicotine as adults [62,63]. Adolescents' activity levels in response to nicotine peak at high doses. In contrast, adults' activity levels peak at medium doses. These age-related differences in sensitivity to nicotine may affect vulnerability to long-term use, because adolescents appear to have a wider dose-range of nicotine reward [64]. This evidence suggests that increased exposure to nicotine in adolescence (perhaps through NRT) may have significant effects on those who continue to smoke in adulthood.

Animal studies predict that nicotine exposure in adolescence interferes with learning. Learning to integrate stimuli in a novel environment is specifically disrupted by nicotine consumption during midadolescence [65]. Multiple human studies have identified the association between smoking and learning and school problems [66]. Rats given low doses of nicotine exposure in adolescence have higher opioid consumption as adults when compared with rats not exposed to nicotine in adolescence [67]. This association is well known in humans, as evidenced by the labeling of tobacco as a "gateway" substance, and it suggests that adult opioid use may be partly influenced by prior nicotine use [68,69].

The adolescent animal model predicts nicotine effects on anxiety. Adult rats that have been exposed to nicotine as adolescents have increased anxiety-like behaviors compared with control rats [70]. . . . Increasingly, evidence supports the presence of high rates of psychiatric comorbidity in adolescent cigarette smokers [75]. Adolescent cigarette use predicts future psychopathology, such as panic attacks and panic disorder [76], and anxiety disorders may be primarily accounted for by regular smoking in adolescence [77]. The role of nicotine replacement in the development of these symptoms is unknown.

. . . In the absence of nicotine addiction, it is possible that administration of nicotine through nicotine replacement in adolescence may lead to untoward long-term psychopharmacologic effects on behavior and biology. . . .

Does Gender Matter?

Effective interventions for adolescents have been performed primarily in mixed-gender settings. The specific role of gender in adolescent tobacco cessation is insufficiently explored. Among adults, smoking cessation trials reveal that the same interventions are effective for both women and men [86], so recommendations do not differ based on gender. However, NRT has been shown to be less efficacious in women than in men [87], and multiple reasons for differences in smoking cessation treatment effects have been posited, including physiology, psychology, and hormones [88]. It has been observed that men and women smoke differently from one another and are influenced differently by nicotine and environmental factors [89].

Interestingly, one school-based study [34] in which classes were separated by gender with same-sex leaders revealed gender-specific outcomes. It involved 10 weekly sessions, followed by four booster sessions at 2- and 4-week intervals. In a stratified analysis, cessation rates were significantly different between treatment and control groups for females (29.6% versus 8.9%, respectively) but not for males (14.4% versus 15.9%, respectively), which may lend credence to this hypothesis. At this time, there is insufficient evidence to conclude that different approaches to adolescent tobacco use cessation based on gender are warranted.

What Does This Mean to the Provider?
—A Clinical Approach to Our Cases

Recognizing that adolescent smokers are different from adults and have great patient-to-patient variability, it is clinically useful to categorize patients based on smoking patterns. Using this technique with the cases described earlier, Case #1 is a variable or "adolescent-type" smoker, Case #2 is a fixed or "adult-type" smoker, and Case #3 is an experimental smoker.

The Variable or "Adolescent-Type" Smoker

The variable smoker, on directed history, reports intermittent tobacco use. On a single day, the adolescent perhaps smokes a few cigarettes with friends before school, abstains during the school day, and does not smoke again until after school or in the evening. A different pattern of smoking emerges on the weekend, when at a party, or when away on vacation, and still further variance is found when the patient is ill or anxious or when parents are away. This "adolescent type" of smoking is driven by relationships, activities, positive and negative emotions, and social ramifications. Of course, these social and behavioral influences on the intermittent smoker are not altered with NRT, and NRT predictably fails as an effective aid in tobacco use cessation.

The Fixed or "Adult-Type" Smoker

Occasionally, the adolescent who uses tobacco like an adult confronts the physician. These adolescents vigorously pursue tobacco to maintain a steady state of nicotine, and they smoke on awakening, when ill, and even in places where smoking is forbidden. They report a consistent history of cigarettes per day that varies little. They smoke at least 10 cigarettes every day, but usually smoke closer to 20 or more. Use of a nicotine dependence score validated for adolescents will declare them dependent or highly dependent on nicotine. These adolescents, irrespective of age, are "adult-type" smokers and may benefit from pharmacotherapy such as nicotine replacement.

The Experimental Smoker

This tobacco user is early in the initiation phase. The positives of tobacco use may outweigh the negatives for this youth, so continued experimentation is anticipated. Eventually, this tobacco user will move on to more regular use.

Clinical Approach to the Adolescent Tobacco User

The adolescent tobacco user should be assessed for history of use, evidence of nicotine addiction, and willingness to quit. The key to obtaining an accurate history is to construct a 7- or 30-day smoking pattern. . . . Establishing a pattern is especially important for adolescents, because they typically have irregular smoking patterns, especially during the initiation phase of smoking, and more error is associated with variable smoking patterns than with uniform patterns [95].

A nicotine dependence score, validated for adolescents [14], can be a useful adjunct in determining when to consider nicotine replacement. This seven-question survey is simple to implement. Those who score high are highly addicted to nicotine, with good correlation to adult tobacco users who benefit from nicotine replacement. This is the subset that is most likely to benefit from pharmacotherapy.

Once a history of smoking and determination of nicotine addiction have been accomplished, if the adolescent expresses a willingness to quit smoking, mutual agreement on a treatment plan may be reached. Effective school-based programs rely on behavioral interventions that can be easy to implement in the office setting. First, the provider reviews a tobacco diary with the adolescent to identify patterns of smoking, cigarettes smoked that may be most easily discarded, and triggers that may be avoided. A teenager who smokes to make a good time better, for example before school with friends or at parties, could be encouraged to arrive at school with no time to smoke, or to socialize without tobacco. The teenager who smokes when bored or anxious may be encouraged to engage in activities where smoking is difficult (e.g., go to the movies, exercise, take a shower, write a letter, play a video game) and taught relaxation techniques such as deep breathing or progressive muscle relaxation. Building a strong partnership with the adolescent facilitates determination of a realistic plan for the individual teen. Coping skills should be taught before a quit attempt is made.

Once the reasons for smoking are clear to the adolescent, and a plan is decided on a quit date should be chosen, with ample time for the teenager to prepare his or her environment to be tobacco free. Teenagers should inform their friends and relatives that they will be quitting and recruit their help in advance. They must get rid of all their tobacco products, so access is more difficult. Menthol smokers can replace their pack of cigarettes with a tin of strong peppermints (of approximately the same size). Having done so, they may reach for their mints in place of tobacco and simulate the feel of smoking by breathing deeply after finishing a peppermint. (Concurrent use should be avoided to prevent aspiration risk.) Some teens benefit from signing a smoking contract or promising to buy a gift with money saved once they have been abstinent for a specified period. Frequent follow-up, especially in the first days and weeks after quit day, is critical to success, as is continued encouragement in the face of relapse.

Although the most effective method of adolescent tobacco use cessation is currently unknown, the least effective is the one to which the adolescent reuses to adhere. Supporting adolescents through the process of identifying the typology of smoking allows each adolescent to understand the treatment recommendation as one specific to him or her. This tactic results in a strong partnership to assist with smoking cessation.

Scenario #1

Our typical adolescent smoker states that she smokes about a half pack or 10 cpd. Based only on this history, the provider may conclude that she is a consistent daily smoker, addicted to nicotine, and a candidate for adult cessation methods. However, when we reviewed her smoking time-line, we see great variability in her smoking patterns, suggestive of environmental influences on tobacco use. On deeper exploration, she only smokes about two thirds of the month. The most she ever smokes is 11 cpd (eight times). She averages 7.7 cpd on days when she smokes, and her average daily consumption for the month is less than 5 cpd. Moreover, she is abstinent from tobacco one third of the time and went a maximum of 3 consecutive days without smoking. The significant variability in her smoking patterns is suggestive of great behavioral influence as opposed to seeking a steady state of nicotine. It is counterintuitive to expect nicotine replacement to be an effective method of tobacco cessation for her, because she has no problem abstaining from tobacco use and fails to maintain a steady level of nicotine in her body.

. . . Despite her request for the patch, nicotine replacement is not indicated for her, would predictably fail, and might lead to untoward consequences as discussed earlier. A behavioral approach is more likely to assist this patient with cessation. Recommendations for her would include identifying why she was unable to quit "cold turkey" in the past, working on those issues before picking a quit date, preparing her social environment for her quitting (informing her friends of her plans and suggesting they help), avoiding smoking enclaves at school, and perhaps skipping a couple of parties and going places where smoking is not permitted.

Scenario #2

By contrast, case #2 is striking in its lack of variability. His consumption of cigarettes varies little, irrespective of social situation, and he predictably finishes nearly the same amount of cigarettes daily. His consistent consumption of tobacco, irrespective of social situation, with no variability from weekday to weekend, suggests pursuit of a steady state of nicotine, most likely nicotine addiction, and an adult type of smoking pattern. The application of nicotine addiction survey . . . confirms our suspicion that he is highly addicted to nicotine. He is motivated to quit smoking but probably needs some assistance with his nicotine addiction to quit successfully. Recommendations for him would include beginning nicotine replacement (transdermal patch, gum, nasal spray, inhaler, lozenge) or bupropion, in addition to the behavioral modification. The decision on pharmacotherapy should be made in close discussion with the adolescent.

Smoker #1 is a variable or "adolescent-type" smoker who benefits best from behavioral interventions. Smoker #2 is a fixed or "adult-type" smoker who will most benefit from an adult approach including behavioral counseling in association with pharmacotherapy. Smoker #3 is not interested in quitting smoking.

Scenario #3

A brief motivational intervention is most appropriate for this adolescent. Brief advice from a physician leads to a spontaneous quit rate of as much as 5% among adults [96,97]. Brief motivational intervention is easy to implement and may be effective in adolescents [30,49,98]. Conversely, expending time beyond this brief intervention is detrimental, because it "turns off" the adolescent to health care messages from the provider. The author approaches such a patient as follows. He informs the patient that he sees that she uses tobacco. He asks her whether she is interested in quitting. On hearing her negative response, he simply states, "As your physician, I must inform you that the single best thing you can do for your health is to quit smoking. If you want help from me for this, do not hesitate to call me, e-mail me, or come back to see me." He follows up on the tobacco status with this patient at every visit, repeating the 15-second motivation each time. In this way, the tobacco user hears a consistent message that, it may be hoped, will help her progress to the decision to quit smoking. Once she presents ready to quit, an intervention is attempted.

Adolescent tobacco use cessation is an evolving field of research. It is imperative to recognize that adolescents are unique in their tobacco habits. . . .

References

1. Fiore MC, Bailey WC, Cohen SJ, et al. Treating tobacco use and dependence. Clinical practice guideline. Rockville (MD): US Department of Health and Human Services, Public Health Service; 2000.

2. VA/DoD clinical practice guideline for the management of tobacco use 2003. . . . Accessed December 28, 2005.

3. Pbert L, Moolchan ET, Muramoto MD, et al. The state of office-based interventions for youth tobacco use. Pediatrics 2003;11 l:e650-60.

4. Kaplan CP, Perez-Stable EJ, Fuentes-Afflick E, et al. Smoking cessation counseling with young patients. Arch Pediatr Adolesc Med 2004;158:83-90.

5. Pierce J, Gilpin EA. How long will today's new adolescent smoker be addicted to cigarettes? Am J Public Health 1996;86:253–6.

6. Kopstein A. Tobacco use in America: findings from the 1999 National Household Survey on Drug Abuse. Rockville (MD): Substance Abuse and Mental Health Services Administration, Office of Applied Studies; 2001.

7. Chassin L, Presson CC, Pitts SC, et al. Smoking cigarettes may put an individual at greater risk for developing anxiety and depression. Health Psychol 2001;9:223–31.

8. Hill DJ, White VM, Scollo MM. Smoking behaviours of Australian adults in 1995: trends and concerns. Med J Aust 1998;168:209–13.

9. Public Health Agency of Canada. Centre for Chronic Disease Prevention and Control. Smoking behaviour of Canadians: cycle 2, 1996/97 (January 1999, No. 1); 2004. . . .

10. Johnston LD, O'Malley PM, Bachman JG, et al. Monitoring the future: national results on adolescent drug use: overview of key findings, 2004 (NIH Publication #05-5726). Bethesda (MD): National Institute on Drug Abuse; 2005.

11. Shiffman S, Zettler-Segal M, Kassel J, et al. Nicotine elimination and tolerance in nondependent cigarette smokers. Psychopharmacology (Berl) 1992;109:449–56.

12. Charlesworth A, Glantz SA. Smoking in the movies increases adolescent smoking: a review. Pediatrics 2005; 166(6): 1516–28.

13. Johnston LD, O'Malley PM, Bachman JG, et al. Cigarette brands smoked by American teens: one brand predominates; three account for nearly all of teen smoking. Ann Arbor (MI): University of Michigan News and Information Services; 1999.

14. Prokhorov AV, Pallonen UE, Fava JL, et al. Measuring nicotine dependence among high-risk adolescent smokers. Addict Behav 1996;21:117–27.

15. The George H. Gallup International Institute. Teenage attitudes and behavior concerning tobacco: a report of the findings. Princeton (NJ): The George H. Gallup International Institute; 1992.

16. Zhu SH, Sun J, Billings SC, et al. Predictors of smoking cessation in US adolescents. Am J Prevent Med 1999;16:202–7.

17. Hollis JF, Polen MR, Lichtenstein E, et al. Tobacco use patterns and attitudes among teens being seen for routine primary care. Am J Health Promot 2003;17:231–9.

18. Kessler DA. Nicotine addiction in young people. N Engl J Med 1995;333: 186–90.

19. American Academy of Pediatrics Committee on Substance Abuse. Tobacco's toll: implications for the pediatrician. Pediatrics 2001;107(4):794–8.

20. Mermelstein R, Colby SM, Patten C, et al. Methodological issues in measuring treatment outcome in adolescent smoking cessation studies. Nicotine Tob Res 2002;4:395–403.

21. Sowden A, Stead L. Community interventions for preventing smoking in young people. Cochrane Database Syst Rev 2003;1:CD001291.

22. Garrison MM, Christakis DA, Ebel BE, et al. Smoking cessation interventions for adolescents: a systematic review. Am J Prev Med 2003;25(4):363–7.

23. Albrecht S, Payne L, Stone CA, et al. A preliminary study of the use of peer support in smoking cessation programs for pregnant adolescents. J Am Acad Nurse Pract 1998;1:119–25.

24. Colby SM, Monti PM, Barnett NP, et al. Brief motivational interviewing in a hospital setting for adolescent smoking: a preliminary study. J Consult Clin Psychol 1998;66:574–8.

25. Yiming C, Changxin Z, Ung WS, et al. Laser acupuncture for adolescent smokers—a randomized double-blind controlled trial. Am J Chin Med 2000;28(3–4):443–9.

26. Adelman WP, Duggan AK, Hauptman P, et al. Effectiveness of a high school smoking cessation program. Pediatrics 2001;107:e50–7.

27. Dino G, Horn K, Goldencamp J, et al. A 2-year efficacy study of note on tobacco in Florida: an overview of program successes in changing teen smoking behavior. Prev Med 2001;33:600–5.

28. Sussman S, Dent CW, Lichtman KL. Project EX: outcomes of a teen smoking cessation program. Addict Behav 2001;26:425–38.

29. Sussman S. Effects of sixty-six adolescent tobacco use cessation trials and seventeen prospective studies of self-initiated quitting. Tobacco Induced Diseases 2002;1:35–81.

30. Adelman WP. Nicotine replacement therapy for teenagers: about time or a waste of time? Arch Pediatr Adolesc Med 2004;158:205–6.

31. Fiore MC, Smith SS, Jorenby DE, et al. The effectiveness of the nicotine patch for smoking cessation: a meta-analysis. JAMA 1994;271:1940–7.

32. Cepeda-Benito A. A meta-analytic review of the efficacy of nicotine chewing gum in smoking treatment programs. J Consult Clin Psychol 1993; 61:822–30.

33. Silagy C, Mant D, Fowler G, et al. Meta-analysis on efficacy of nicotine replacement therapies in smoking cessation. Lancet 1994;343:139–42.

34. Johnson KC, Klesges LM, Somes GW, et al. Access of over-the-counter nicotine replacement therapy products to minors. Arch Pediatr Adolesc Med 2004;158:212–6.

35. Klesges LM, Johnson KC, Somes G, et al. Use of nicotine replacement therapy in adolescent smokers and nonsmokers. Arch Pediatr Adolesc Med 2003;157:517–22.

36. McNeill A, Foulds J, Bates C. Regulation of nicotine replacement therapies (NRT): a critique of current practice. Addiction 2001;96:1757–68.

37. Benowitz NL. Pharmacologic aspects of cigarette smoking and nicotine addiction. N Engl J Med 1998;319:1318–30.

38. Jorenby DE, Hatsukami DK, Smith SS, et al. Characterization of tobacco withdrawal symptoms: transdermal nicotine reduces hunger and weight. Psychopharmacology (Berl) 1996;128:130–8.

39. Henningfeld JE, Michaelides T, Sussman S. Developing treatment for tobacco addicted youth—issues and challenges. Journal of Child & Adolescent Substance Abuse 2000;9:5–26.

40. Kassel JD. Are adolescent smokers addicted to nicotine? The suitability of the nicotine dependence construct as applied to adolescents. Journal of Child & Adolescent Substance Abuse 2000;9(4):27–49.

41. Anthony JC, Warner LA, Kessler RC. Comparative epidemiology of dependence on tobacco, alcohol, and controlled substances and inhalants: basic findings from the National Comorbidity Study. Exp Clin Psychopharmacol 1994;2:244–68.

42. Schubiner H, Herrold A, Hurt R. Tobacco cessation and youth: the feasibility of brief office interventions for adolescents. Prev Med 1998;27:A47–54.

43. Colby SM, Tiffany ST, Shiffman S, et al. Are adolescent smokers dependent on nicotine? A review of the evidence. Drug and Alcohol Dependence 2000;59:583–95.

44. Killen JD, Ammerman S, Rojas N, et al. Do adolescent smokers experience withdrawal effects when deprived of nicotine? Exp Clin Psychopharmacol 2001;9:176–82.

45. Stanton WR. DSM-III-R tobacco dependence and quitting during late adolescence. Addict Behav 1995;20:595–603.

46. Buttross LS, Kastner J. A brief review of adolescents and tobacco: what we know and don't know. Am J Med Sci 2003;326:235–7.

47. DiFranza JR, Rigotti NA, McNeill AD, et al. Initial symptoms of nicotine dependence in adolescents. Tob Control 2000;9(3):313–9.

48. Winickoff JP, Pbert L, Klein JD, et al. Youth tobacco control research and activities in the United States: the current national landscape. Nicotine Tob Res 2003;5(4):435–54.

49. Smith TA, House RF, Croghan IT, et al. Nicotine patch therapy in adolescent smokers. Pediatrics 1996;98:659–67.

50. Hurt RD, Croghan GA, Beede SD, et al. Nicotine patch therapy in 101 adolescent smokers: efficacy, withdrawal symptom relief, and carbon monoxide and plasma cotinine levels. Arch Pediatr Adolesc Med 2000; 154:31–7.

51. Hanson K, Allen S, Jensen S, et al. Treatment of adolescent smokers with the nicotine patch. Nicotine Tob Res 2003;5(4):515–26.

52. Benowitz NL, Gourlay SG. Cardiovascular toxicity of nicotine: implications for nicotine replacement therapy. J Am Coll Cardiol 1997;29(7):1422–31.

53. Joseph AM, Norman SM, Ferry LH, et al. The safety of transdermal nicotine as an aid to smoking cessation in patients with cardiac disease. N Engl J Med 1996;335(24):1792–8.

54. Trauth JA, Seidler FJ, Slotkin TA. Persistent and delayed behavioral changes after nicotine treatment in adolescent rats. Brain Res 2000;880:167–72.

55. Faraday MM, Elliott BM, Phillips JM, et al. Adolescent and adult male rats differ in sensitivity to nicotine's activity effects. Pharmacol Biochem Behav 2003;74:917–31.

56. Elliott BM, Faraday MM, Phillips JM, et al. Adolescent and adult female rats differ in sensitivity to nicotine's activity effects. Pharmacol Biochem Behav 2005;80:567–75.

57. Elliott BM, Faraday MM, Phillips JM, et al. Effects of nicotine on elevated plus maze and locomotor activity in male and female adolescent and adult rats. Pharmacol Biochem Behav 2004;77:21–8.

58. Adriani W, Granstrem O, Macri S, et al. Behavioral and neurochemical vulnerability during adolescence in mice: studies with nicotine. Neuropsychopharmacology 2004;29:869–78.

59. Bryant A, Schulenberg J, Bachman JG, et al. Understanding the links among school misbehavior, academic achievement, and cigarette use; a national panel study of adolescents. Prev Sci 2000;2:71–87.

60. Klein LC. Effects of adolescent nicotine exposure on opioid consumption and neuroendocrine responses in adult male and female rats. Exp Clin Psychopharmacol 2001;9:251–61.

61. Lewisohn PM, Rohde P, Brown RA. Level of current and past adolescent cigarette smoking as predictors of future substance use in disorders in young adulthood. Addiction 1999;94:913–21.

62. Lai S, Lai H, Page JB, et al. The association between cigarette smoking and drug abuse in the United States. J Addict Dis 2000;19:11–24.

63. Slawecki CJ, Gilder A, Roth J, et al. Increased anxiety-like behavior in adult rats exposed to nicotine as adolescents. Pharmacol Biochem Behav 2003; 75:355–61.

64. Upadhyaya HP, Deas D, Brady KT, et al. Cigarette smoking and psychiatric comorbidity in children and adolescents. J Am Acad Child Adolesc Psychiatry 2003;41:1294–305.

65. Isenee B, Wittchen HU, Stein MB, et al. Smoking increases the risk of panic: findings from a prospective community study. Arch Gen Psychiatry 2003;60:692–700.

66. Boys A, Farrell M, Taylor C, et al. Psychiatric morbidity and substance use in young people aged 13–15 years: results from the child and adolescent survey of mental health. Br J Psychiatry 2003;182:509–17.

67. Gritz E, Thompson B, Emmons K, et al. Gender differences among smokers and quitters in the Working Well trial. Prev Med 1998;27:553–61.

68. Wetter D, Fiore MC, Jorenby D, et al. Gender differences in smoking. J Consult Clin Psychol 1999;67(4):555–62.

69. Gritz ER, Nielsen IR, Brooks LA. Smoking cessation and gender: the influence of physiological, psychological, and behavioral factors. J Am Med Women's Assoc 1996;51(1–2):35–42.

70. Perkins KA. Sex differences in nicotine versus nonnicotine reinforcement as determinants of tobacco smoking. Exp Clin Psychopharmacol 1996; 4(2):166–77.

71. Schwartz N. Self-reports. How the questions shape the answers. Am Psychol 1999;54:93–105.

72. Lancaster T, Stead L. Physician advice for smoking cessation. Cochrane Database Syst Rev 2004;4:CD000165.

73. Ockene JK. Physician-delivered interventions for smoking cessation: strategies for increasing effectiveness. Prev Med 1987;16(5):723–37.

74. Lampkin L, Davis B, Karen A. Rationale for tobacco cessation interventions for youth. Prev Med 1998;27(Suppl A):3–8.

POSTSCRIPT

Is the Use of Nicotine Replacement Therapy (NRT) an Appropriate Cessation Aid for Adolescents Wishing to Quit Smoking?

Hanson et al. provided evidence that the NRT patch can be useful in helping adolescents with their quit-smoking attempts by reducing cravings, withdrawal symptoms, and some biological markers of nicotine intake (i.e., measured by cotinine levels). In contrast, Adelman calls into question the state of the existing research for NRT use with adolescents. Who is right? Even major governing organizations do not agree: Clinical Practice Guideline for Treating Tobacco Use and Dependence (Fiore, Bailey, Cohen, et al., 2000) issued by the U.S. Department of Health and Human Services' Public Health Service recommend use of pharmacological techniques including NRT with adolescents who present with tobacco dependence whereas the Food and Drug Administration has not approved the use of NRT for teens (as reported in an editorial note in Barker et al., 2006 in a Center for Disease Control publication). Even health care practitioners may be very confused as to what to do about NRT vis-à-vis their teen smoking patients.

There is empirical evidence regarding the use of NRT adolescents that supports either side (e.g., Moolchan et al. 2005 found that the patch was effective for adolescents abstaining from tobacco over a 3 month period versus Hurt et al. 2000 who concluded that the NRT patch was ineffective for the treatment of adolescent smokers). It is very important to consider the motivation of the researchers (as well as clinicians' motivation when they make treatment recommendations). If researchers, for example, have strong faith in the NRT patch—but their results are mixed (i.e., no difference in quit rates but some reductions in symptoms and a reduction in number of cigarettes smoked)—they are going to emphasize the positive findings and downplay the null results. A person who wishes to argue in favor of NRT for adolescents may cite these same findings as supporting their position. One study often provides evidence for both sides.

Perhaps some might argue: Well, if it does not hurt, then why not suggest using NRT? Considering another angle: There exists the possibility of abuse of NRT by youth. Similarly, Adelman cautions about our lack of knowledge of NRT as a "gateway" substance. In one study (Klesges et al., 2003), 75% of youth smokers reported that they were using NRT but *not* for the purposes of tobacco use cessation while 18% of adolescents having tried NRT were non-smokers! This indicates a possible "abuse" of

NRT by youth. One possibility is changing the availability of NRT such that its use is monitored by a physician—in order to ensure that such misuse of NRT does not occur. In this case, NRT would have a minimum age requirement for purchase. Another alternative is to have pharmacists counsel youth who are purchasing NRT in appropriate and inappropriate usage.

Regardless of whether NRT seems to be effective or not for adolescents, there are some key points that need to be borne in mind. Most smoking cessation interventions (whether with adults or adolescents) and not very effective (e.g., with typical quit rates of around 20%). When it comes to youth, they generally *desire* self-directed smoking cessation methods (Lawrance, 2001) and most adolescents indicate that they would be most likely to try to quit on their own as opposed to using formal, mediated cessation programs (such as school-based group programs; Leatherdale & McDonald, 2007). As well, youths' attitudes toward NRT is generally positive—relative to formal, mediated cessation efforts (Leatherdale & McDonald, 2007). Further, most of the NRT and other formal smoking cessation investigations—particularly with youth—have involved some form of cognitive behavioral therapy/counselling component. Quitting rates are low regardless of use of a smoking cessation aide or "cold turkey." NRT and other smoking cessation aides will not work *unless* the individual is *motivated* to quit (that is, the person has to want to quit and has made a decision to try to quit). Regardless, it is important that, if adolescents are using NRT, they be monitored by a physician in order to ensure their safety and provide them with support in their cessation attempts.

References/Further Reading

Adelman, W.P. (2004). "Nicotine Replacement Therapy for Teenagers: About Time or a Waste of Time?" *Archives of Pediatric and Adolescent Medicine, 158,* 205–206.

Barker, D.C., Giovino, G.A, Gable, J., Tworek, C., Orleans, C.T., & Malarcher, A. (2006). "Use of Cessation Methods Among Smokers Aged 16–24 Years—United States, 2003." *Morbidity and Mortality Weekly, 55(50),* 1351–1354.

Fiore M.C., Bailey W.C., Cohen S.J., et al. (2000). *Treating Tobacco Use and Dependence. Clinical Practice Guideline.* Rockville, MD: U.S. Department of Health and Human Services, Public Health Service.

Hanson, K. Zylla, E., Allen S., Li, Z., & Hatsukami, D.K. (2008). Cigarette reduction: An intervention for adolescent smokers. *Drug and Alcohol Dependence, 95,*164–168.

Hurt, R.D., Croghan, G.A., Beede S.D., Wolter, T.D., Croghan, I.T., & Patten, C.A. (2000). Nicotine patch therapy in 101 adolescent smokers: Efficacy, withdrawal symptom relief, and carbon monoxide and plasma cotinine levels. *Archives of Pediatric Adolescent Medicine, 154* 31–37.

Killen, J.D., Robinson, T.N., Ammerman, S., Hayward, C., Rogers, J., Stone, C., Samuels, D., Levin, S.K., Green, S., & Schatzberg, A.F. (2004). "Randomized Clinical Trial of the Efficacy of Bupropion Combined with Nicotine Patch in the Treatment of Adolescent Smokers." *Journal of Consulting and Clinical Psychology, 72(4),* 729–735.

Klesges, L.M., Johnson, K.C., Somes, G., Zbikowski, S., & Robinson, L. (2003). "Use of Nicotine Replacement Therapy in Adolescent Smokers and Nonsmokers." *Archives of Pediatric Adolescent Medicine, 157,* 517–522.

Koplan, J.P. (2007). "CDC's 60th Anniversary: Director's Perspective, 1998–2002." *Morbidity and Mortality Weekly, 56(33),* 846–850.

Lawrance, K.G. (2001). "Adolescent Smokers' Preferred Smoking Cessation Methods." *Canadian Journal of Public Health, 92(6),* 423–426.

Leatherdale, S.T. & McDonald, P.W. (2007). Youth smokers' beliefs about different cessation approaches: Are we providing cessations interventions they never intend to use? *Cancer Causes Control, 18,* 783–791.

Marshall, L., Schooley, M., Ryan, H., Cox, P., Easton, A., Healton, C., Jackson, K., Davis, K.C., & Homsi, G. (2006). "Youth Tobacco Surveillance—United States, 2001–2002." *Morbidity and Mortality Weekly, Surveillance Summaries, 55(SS03)* 1–56.

Mochizuki-Kobayashi, Y., Fishburn, B., Baptiste, J., El-Awa, F., Nikogosian, H., Peruga, A., Rahman, K., Warren, C.W., Jones, N.R., Asma, S., & McKnight, L.R. (2006). "Use of Cigarettes and Other Tobacco Products Among Students Aged 13–15 Years—Worldwide, 1999–2005." *Morbidity and Mortality Weekly, 55(20),* 553–556.

Moolchan, E.T., Robinson, M.L., Ernst, M., Cadet, J.L., Pickworth, W.B., Heishman, S.J. & Schroeder, J.R. (2007). "Safety and efficacy of the Nicotine Patch and Gum for the Treatment of Adolescent Tobacco Addiction." *Pediatrics, 115 (4),* e407–14.

U.S. Department of Health and Human Services. [USDHHS] (1994). *Preventing Tobacco Use Among Young People: A Report of the Surgeon General.* Atlanta, GA: U.S. Department of Health and Human Services, Public Health Service, CDC.

U.S. Department of Health and Human Services. [USDHHS] (2000). *Reducing Tobacco Use: A Report of the Surgeon General.* Atlanta, Georgia: U.S. Department of Health and Human Services, CDC, National Center for Chronic Disease Prevention and Health Promotion, Office on Smoking and Health.

Internet References . . .

Society of Obstetricians and Gynaecologists of Canada

As one of North America's oldest national obstetrics and gynecology organizations, they provide credible and current information and education on sexual health.

http://www.sexualityandu.ca

Canadian Federation for Sexual Health/Planned Parenthood

Advocates whose mission is to advance sexual and reproductive health and rights.

http://cfsh.ca
http://www.teenwire.com

Guttmacher Institute

The Guttmacher Institute is a think tank that generates social science research, policy analysis, and public education on sexual and reproductive health.

http://www.guttmacher.org

Sexuality Information and Education Council

SIECUS/SIECCAN have the goals of promoting sexuality education and sexual health, protecting sexual rights by providing information and education, consultations, and aiding in public policy regarding sexuality.

http://www.siecus.org
http://www.sieccan.org

Resource Center for Adolescent Pregnancy Prevention

This private non-profit health education promotion website contains practical tools and information designed to help reduce sexual risk-taking behaviors.

http://www.etr.org/recapp

National Sexuality Research Center (NSRC)

The NSRC gathers and disseminates the latest accurate information and research on sexual health, education, and rights (Family & Youth section).

http://www.nsrc.sfsu.edu

The National Coalition for GLBT Youth

This website provides links to news articles, brochures, and special interests.

http://www.outproud.org

YouthResource

YouthResource takes a holistic approach to sexual issues concerning queer youth.

http://www.youthresource.com

UNIT 2

Sex and Sexuality

A *very important part of an adolescent's development is sexuality. Unfortunately, many textbooks regarding adolescents will gloss over the topics of sex and sexuality of youth because of the controversial nature of these topics. Learning about sex and sexuality is of critical importance to youth. Also, developing sexual and romantic relationships with peers is considered a critical part of youth development. Adolescence is a time when sexual identity is explored and formed. This part examines five key issues surrounding sexuality and adolescence.*

- Does Engaging in Early Sexual Activity Cause Depressive Symptoms in Adolescents?

- Is There Cause for Concern About an "Oral Sex Crisis" for Teens?

- Is Comprehensive Sex Education for Adolescents Too Liberal?

- Does a Traditional or "Strong" Double Standard with Respect to Sexual Behavior Exist Among Adolescents?

- Is Female Sexual Orientation More Fluid than Male Sexual Orientation During Adolescence?

ISSUE 7

Does Engaging in Early Sexual Activity Cause Depressive Symptoms in Adolescents?

YES: Robert E. Rector, Kirk. A. Johnson, and Lauren R. Noyes, from "Sexually Active Teenagers are More Likely to Be Depressed and to Attempt Suicide," *A Report of the Heritage Center for Data Analysis* (CDA03-04, Heritage Foundation, 2003)

NO: Joseph J. Sabia, from "Does Early Adolescent Sex Cause Depressive Symptoms?" *Journal of Policy Analysis and Management* (Autumn, 2006)

ISSUE SUMMARY

YES: Robert Rector and colleagues from the Heritage Foundation, a conservative think tank in Washington, D.C., contend that teens who are sexually active are significantly more likely to be depressed or suicidal than virgins.

NO: Joseph J. Sabia, a University of Georgia economics professor, analyzed the same data set as Rector et al. but found that, by considering other variables, the relationship between sexual intercourse and depression disappeared.

One of the most contentious issues in education in North America today is the topic of sexuality education in the school system. Liberal individuals tend to be in favor of comprehensive sex education (e.g., protection *and* abstinence). While some conservative sectors argue against any school-based sex education, many conservative individuals support abstinence-only education. Empirical support for the effectiveness of abstinence-only education is mixed (Kirby, 2001). Consequently, proponents of abstinence-only education are taking another tact: linking teen sexuality with adverse mental health effects. Even U.S. government documents (e.g., Section 510(b) of Title V of the Social Security Act which defines "abstinence education") suggest that abstinence from adolescent sexual activity is imperative: "sexual activity outside of the context of marriage is likely to have harmful psychological and physical effects" (Social Security

Act, 1996). An empirical question arises: does engaging in sexual intercourse actually result in psychological harms such as depression?

Does adolescent sexual activity result in higher levels of adolescent depression, as some sectors contend? A few studies have investigated the link between adolescent sexual activity and adolescent mental health. The results are mixed: Joyner and Udry (2000) found that adolescents who entered into a romantic relationship during the duration of the study were more likely to experience depression than were teens who did not enter such relationships. This effect was larger for females than for males. Other researchers (Hallfors et al., 2005) qualified the sex and depression link: they concluded that sex and drug/alcohol use in combination elevate risk of depression for boys and girls, and sex (not in combination with drugs/alcohol) may elevate girls' risk for depression. Finally, Meier (2007) found that only certain girls experienced depression as a result of their first sexual experience (i.e., those who had a combination of characteristics including: they were younger than most of their peers when they had sex, they had short-term relationships, and their relationship either lacked emotional commitment or was socially 'public'). The group who experienced negative outcomes as a result of first intercourse was small (14%).

These three aforementioned studies (Hallfors et al., 2005; Joyner and Udry, 2000; Meier, 2007) all used the exact same data set: the National Longitudinal Study of Adolescent Health (called Add Health). In the two papers presented here, Rector et al. (2003) as well as Sabia (2006) used the Add Health data set. Both papers address the same type of question: does adolescent sexuality result in greater depression? Rector et al. (2003) compared the percentages of those who had sex to those who had not had sex on depression and suicide attempts. They concluded that the incidence of depression and suicide attempts among adolescents differed as a function of sexual experience. Sabia approaches the question a bit differently. First, Sabia replicated the relationship found by Rector and colleagues—while also investigating how characteristics of the person (e.g., their health, their romantic relationship status, how well their family gets along) as potential "third-variable" (i.e., mediator) explanations of the relationship between teen intercourse and depression. He found the same relationship that Rector et al. did but also found that other individual-specific variables were related with both teen intercourse and depression measure (i.e., he calls this unobserved or unmeasured heterogeneity). Then, Sabia looked at the youth over time (i.e., at two time points) while also taking these individual-level variables into consideration. Sabia concluded that, when other characteristics were included in the analysis (e.g., religiosity, alcohol use, GPA), the relationship between depression and 'virginity status' disappears. In short, Sabia provides evidence that the claim that teen sexuality causes psychological harms to youth is overstated. When reading these papers, consider how the researchers attempt to answer the question might influence the results obtained.

YES ↵ Robert E. Rector, Kirk A. Johnson, and Lauren R. Noyes

Sexually Active Teenagers Are More Likely to Be Depressed and to Attempt Suicide

Teenage sexual activity is an issue of widespread national concern. Although teen sexual activity has declined in recent years, the overall rate is still high. In 1997, approximately 48 percent of American teenagers of high-school age were or had been sexually active.

The problems associated with teen sexual activity are well-known. Every day, 8,000 teenagers in the United States become infected by a sexually transmitted disease.[1] This year, nearly 3 million teens will become infected. Overall, roughly one-quarter of the nation's sexually active teens have been infected by a sexually transmitted disease (STD).[2]

The problems of pregnancy and out-of-wedlock childbearing are also severe. In 2000, some 240,000 children were born to girls aged 18 or younger.[3] Nearly all these teenage mothers were unmarried. These mothers and their children have an extremely high probability of long-term poverty and welfare dependence.

Less widely known are the psychological and emotional problems associated with teenage sexual activity. The present study examines the linkage between teenage sexual activity and emotional health. The findings show that:

- When compared to teens who are not sexually active, teenage boys and girls who are sexually active are significantly less likely to be happy and more likely to feel depressed.
- When compared to teens who are not sexually active, teenage boys and girls who are sexually active are significantly more likely to attempt suicide.

Thus, in addition to its role in promoting teen pregnancy and the current epidemic of STDs, early sexual activity is a substantial factor in undermining the emotional well-being of American teenagers.

Data Source and Methods

The data used in this analysis are taken from the National Longitudinal Survey of Adolescent Health, Wave II, 1996. This "Ad-Health" survey is a nationwide

From *Report of the Heritage Center for Data Analysis*, (CDA03–04) 2003, pp. 1–10. Copyright © 2003 by The Heritage Foundation. Reprinted by permission.

survey designed to examine the health-related behaviors of adolescents in middle school and high school. Its public-use database contains responses from approximately 6,500 adolescents, representative of teenagers across the nation. The survey is funded by the National Institute of Child Health and Human Development (NICHD) and 17 other federal agencies.

This Heritage Center for Data Analysis (CDA) analysis focuses on the link between sexual activity and emotional well-being among teens in high school years (ages 14 through 17). The Ad-Health survey asks students whether they have "ever had sexual intercourse."[4] For purposes of analysis, teens who answered yes to this question are labeled as "sexually active" and those who answered no are labeled as "not sexually active."

The survey also records the emotional health of teens. Students are asked how often, in the past week, they "felt depressed." They are provided with four possible answers to the question: They felt depressed

    (a) Never or rarely,
    (b) Sometimes,
    (c) A lot of the time, or
    (d) Most of the time or all of the time.

For purposes of analysis, the classification of "depressed" is given to those teens who answered yes to options "c" or "d"—that is, they said they felt depressed a lot, most, or all of the time. Thus, throughout the paper, the terms "depressed" or "depression" refer to this general state of continuing unhappiness rather than to a more specific sense of clinical depression.

Sexual Activity and Depression

The Ad-Health data reveal substantial differences in emotional health between those teens who are sexually active and those who are not. . . .

- A full quarter (25.3 percent) of teenage girls who are sexually active report that they are depressed all, most, or a lot of the time. By contrast, only 7.7 percent of teenage girls who are not sexually active report that they are depressed all, most, or a lot of the time. Thus, sexually active girls are more than three times more likely to be depressed than are girls who are not sexually active.
- Some 8.3 percent of teenage boys who are sexually active report that they are depressed all, most, or a lot of the time. By contrast, only 3.4 percent of teenage boys who are not sexually active are depressed all, most, or a lot of the time. Thus, boys who are sexually active are more than twice as likely to be depressed as are those who are not sexually active.

   . . . A full 60.2 percent of sexually inactive girls report that they "rarely or never" feel depressed. For sexually active teen girls, the number is far lower: only 36.8 percent. Overall, for either gender, teens who are not sexually active are markedly happier than those who are active.

The link between teen sexual activity and depression is supported by clinical experience. Doctor of adolescent medicine Meg Meeker writes, "Teenage sexual activity routinely leads to emotional turmoil and psychological distress. . . . [Sexual permissiveness leads] to empty relationships, to feelings of self-contempt and worthlessness. All, of course, precursors to depression."[5]

Sexual Activity and Attempted Suicide

The Ad-Health survey also asks students whether they have attempted suicide during the past year. . . . The link between sexual activity and attempted suicide is clear.

- A full 14.3 percent of girls who are sexually active report having attempted suicide. By contrast, only 5.1 percent of sexually inactive girls have attempted suicide. Thus, sexually active girls are nearly three times more likely to attempt suicide than are girls who are not sexually active.
- Among boys, 6.0 percent of those who are sexually active have attempted suicide. By contrast, only 0.7 percent of boys who are not sexually active have attempted suicide. Thus, sexually active teenage boys are eight times more likely to attempt suicide than are boys who are not sexually active.

Social Factors

The differences in emotional health between sexually active and inactive teens are clear. However, it is possible that the differences in emotional well-being might be driven by social background factors rather than sexual activity *per se*. For example, if students of lower socioeconomic status are more likely to be sexually active, the greater frequency of depression among those teens might be caused by socioeconomic status rather than sexual activity.

To account for that possibility, additional analysis was performed in which race, gender, exact age, and family income were entered as control variables. This means that each teen was compared to other teens who were identical in gender, age, race, and income.

The introduction of these control or background variables had virtually no effect on the correlations between sexual activity and depression and suicide. In simple terms, when teens were compared to other teens who were identical in gender, race, age and family income, those who were sexually active were significantly more likely to be depressed and to attempt suicide than were those who were not sexually active.

Teens Express Regrets Over Sexual Activity

The significantly lower levels of happiness and higher levels of depression among sexually active teens suggest that sexual activity leads to a decrease in happiness and well-being among many, if not most, teenagers.

This conclusion is corroborated by the fact that the majority of sexually active teens express reservations and concerns about their personal sexual activity.

For example, a recent poll by the National Campaign to Prevent Teen Pregnancy asked the question, "If you have had sexual intercourse, do you wish you had waited longer?"[6] Among those teens who reported that they had engaged in intercourse, nearly two-thirds stated that they wished they had waited longer before becoming sexually active. By contrast, only one-third of sexually active teens asserted that their commencement of sexual activity was appropriate and that they did not wish they had waited until they were older. Thus, among sexually active teens, those who regretted early sexual activity outnumbered those without such concerns by nearly two to one.

. . . Concerns and regrets about sexual activity are strongest among teenage girls. Almost three-quarters of sexually active teen girls (72 percent) admit they wish they had delayed sexual activity until they were older. Among sexually active teenage girls, those with regrets concerning their initial sexual activity outnumbered those without regrets by nearly three to one.

The dissatisfaction and regrets expressed by teenagers concerning their own sexual activity is striking. Overall, a majority of sexually active boys and nearly three-quarters of sexually active girls regard their own initial sexual experience unfavorably—as an event they wish they had avoided.

Discussion

While the association between teen sexual activity and depression is clear, that association may be subject to different theoretical interpretations. For example, it might be that depressed teenagers turn to sexual activity in an effort to assuage or escape their depression. In this interpretation, the link between sexual activity and depression . . . might be caused by a higher level of sexual activity among those who are already depressed before commencing sexual activity. Thus, depression might lead to greater sexual activity rather than sexual activity's leading to depression.

In limited cases, this explanation may be correct; some depressed teens may experiment with sexual activity in an effort to escape their depression. However, as a general interpretation of the linkage between depression and teen sexual activity, this reasoning seems inadequate for two reasons. First, . . . the differences in happiness and depression between sexually active and inactive teens are widespread and are not the result of a small number of depressed individuals. This is especially true for girls. Second, the fact that a majority of teens express regrets concerning their own initial sexual activity strongly suggests that such activity leads to distress and emotional turmoil among many, if not most, teens.

Hence, the most likely explanation of the overall link between teen sexual activity and depression is that early sexual activity leads to emotional stress and reduces teen happiness.

Moreover, theoretical questions about whether teen sexual activity leads to depression or, conversely, whether depression leads to teen sexual activity should not distract attention from the clear message that adult society should be sending to teens. Teens should be told that sexual activity in teen years is clearly linked to reduced personal happiness. Teens who are depressed should be informed that sexual activity is likely to exacerbate, rather than alleviate, their depression. Teens who are not depressed should be told that sexual activity in teen years is likely to substantially reduce their happiness and personal well-being.

Conclusion

Sexual activity among teenagers is the major driving factor behind the well-publicized problems of the high incidence of teenage STDs and teen pregnancy. The analysis presented in this paper also shows that sexual activity is directly connected to substantial problems among teens regarding emotional health.

- Teenagers of both genders who are sexually active are substantially less likely to be happy and more likely to be depressed than are teenagers who are not sexually active.
- Teenagers of both genders who are sexually active are substantially more likely to attempt suicide than are teenagers who are not sexually active.

Until recently, society provided teenagers with classroom instruction in "safe sex" and "comprehensive sex education."[7] In general, these curricula fail to provide a strong message to delay sexual activity, fail to deal adequately with the long-term emotional and moral aspects of sexuality, and fail to provide students with the skills needed to develop intimate loving marital relationships as adults.

Over the past five years, there has been a growth in abstinence education programs that stand in sharp contrast to "safe sex" curricula. The best abstinence education programs teach:

- The primary importance of delaying sexual activity,
- That human sexual relationships are predominantly emotional and moral rather than physical in character, and
- That teen abstinence is an important step leading toward a loving marital relationship as an adult.

Such abstinence education programs are uniquely suited to meeting both the emotional and the physical needs of America's youth.

Technical Appendix

As noted in the text, this analysis utilized Wave II data from the National Longitudinal Survey of Adolescent Health, a survey that was fielded between April and August 1996. The National Longitudinal Survey of Adolescent Health is a nationally representative survey designed to assess the health and risk behavior of America's youth. Sensitive questions of sexual activity and the like were asked in the child's home through an audio computer-assisted self-interview process. Parental consent was required before adolescents were allowed to participate. This analysis is concerned with the relationship between depression/suicide and sexual activity for individuals of ages 14 to 17 (high school–age adolescents). To that end, data from the following questions were used to gauge sexual activity, suicide attempt, and depression:

- **Sex:** Question H2CO2—"Have you ever had sexual intercourse? When we say sexual intercourse, we mean when a male inserts his penis into a female's vagina."
- **Suicide Attempt:** Question H2SU2—"During the past 12 months, how many times did you actually attempt suicide?"
- **Depression:** Question H2FS6—"How often was each of the following true during the past seven days? . . . You felt depressed."

If an adolescent responded affirmatively to the "ever had sexual intercourse" question, he or she was coded as "sexually active," and vice versa. The suicide attempt variable was recoded as a "yes/no" variable: "yes" if the respondent had attempted suicide at least once and "no" otherwise. Respondents were coded as "being depressed" if they said that they were depressed "a lot of the time" or "most of the time or all of the time." They were coded as "not depressed" if they responded that they were depressed "never or rarely" or "sometimes." The data were rejected if the respondent did not give a usable answer to any of the questions; for example, if a respondent refused to answer the "ever had sexual intercourse" question, he or she was eliminated from the analysis.

The statistical analysis took two forms. First, a basic correlation analysis showed that there is a positive and highly statistically significant relationship between sexual activity and depression/suicide attempt. Put another way, sexually active adolescents are more likely to be both depressed and suicidal. Both correlations are highly statistically significant at more than a 99.9 percent confidence level.[8]

While demonstrating that a correlation relationship exists is valuable information, more important are the differences in the observed incidences of depression and suicide attempt among these adolescents. . . . The results of the statistical analysis that compared the percentage of adolescents who had been depressed or suicidal, based on sexual activity or lack thereof . . . indicated that the difference between each pair of percentages is significant at the 95 percent level or higher. The differences are, by and large, more pronounced for young women than young men, but the relationship still holds.

As a final check of the analysis, a pair of logistic regressions was conducted to ascertain whether these results are being influenced by the socioeconomic factors of race, income, and age. When depression or attempted suicide are treated as dependent variables, and sexual activity, gender, age, race, and income are included as independent variables, the odds ratio (or predictive impact) of the sexual activity variable on the dependent variables remains statistically indistinguishable from a model that only includes the sexual activity variable. In short, sexual activity is a key independent predictor of depression and attempted suicide.

Finally, the Ad-Health survey utilizes a complex sample design in collecting the data, so any confidence interval statistic must be adjusted in order to take the sample design into consideration. To do this, the Ad-Health database was subjected to a "jackknife" procedure that corrected the standard errors of the statistics generated. In order to facilitate this analysis, the WesVar Complex Samples Version 4.2 software, developed by Westat, was used. Although the means, percentages, and correlation coefficients themselves do not change, the probability statistics (and their underlying standard errors, etc.) are corrected to take into consideration the sample design.[9]

Notes

1. Meg Meeker, *Epidemic: How Teen Sex Is Killing Our Kids* (Washington, D.C.: Regnery Publishing Company, 2002), p. 12.

2. Ibid., p. 13.

3. National Center for Health Statistics, "Births: Final Data for 2000," *National Vital Statistics Report,* Vol. 50, No. 5 (February 12, 2002), p. 46.

4. For the full wording of each question referred to in the text, see the Appendix.

5. Meeker, *Epidemic: How Teen Sex Is Killing Our Kids,* p. 64.

6. National Campaign to Prevent Teen Pregnancy, "Not Just Another Thing to Do: Teens Talk About Sex, Regret, and the Influence of Their Parents," June 30, 2000.

7. Comprehensive sex-ed and safe-sex programs are sometimes misleadingly referred to as "abstinence plus" or "abstinence-based" curricula. In reality, such programs have little or no abstinence content. See Advocates for Youth, *Transitions,* Vol. 12, No. 3 (March 2001).

8. When analysts discuss "confidence levels," it signifies that a statistical relationship exists with at least a set level of certainty. Thus, when analysts say that a correlation exists at a 99 percent confidence level, they mean there is a 99 percent chance that a relationship exists between the two factors. Put another way, they mean that there is only a 1 percent chance of claiming that a relationship exists when in reality a relationship does not exist. Most statisticians are comfortable with a confidence level of 95 percent or greater. A number of statistics books cover this subject in depth; see, for example, Edwin Mansfield, *Statistics for Business and Economics,* 4th ed. (New York: W. W. Norton & Company, 1991).

9. A number of technical reference books are available that discuss jackknife, bootstrap, and other "resampling" techniques that correct for sample design issues. For a full description of the theoretical basis of these techniques, see Bradley Efron, *The Jackknife, the Bootstrap, and Other Resampling Plans* (Philadelphia: Society for Industrial and Applied Mathematics, 1982), and Jun Shao and Dongsheng Tu, *The Jackknife and Bootstrap* (New York: Springer Verlag, 1995).

Joseph J. Sabia  **NO**

Does Early Adolescent Sex Cause Depressive Symptoms?

Introduction

A 2003 study by the Heritage Foundation (Rector, Johnson, & Noyes, 2003) splashed across the mainstream and conservative media implying evidence of a causal link between early teen sexual activity and depression. The authors of the Heritage study claimed that their findings bolstered the need for abstinence-only sex education programs in public schools. Several media outlets—including *USA Today* (Peterson, 2003), *National Review* (Pardue & Rector, 2004), and the *Washington Times* (Wetzstein, 2003)—gave extensive coverage to the Heritage study. The authors themselves contributed opinion pieces, implying a causal link between adolescent sex and depression. Writing in *National Review Online,* Melissa Pardue and Robert Rector argued:

> The dangers of early sexual activity are well documented. It leads to higher levels of child and maternal poverty, elevates the risk of sexually transmitted diseases, and often leaves teenage girls depressed, even suicidal. (NRO, January 16, 2004)

In comments appearing in a June 2003 issue of *USA Today,* Rector was more cautious, stating that the Heritage study did not definitively find a causal link between sexual activity and depression. However, he also noted that "[a causal relationship] is really impossible to prove." That is, without a randomized experiment, unmeasured heterogeneity may confound the relationship between early teen sex and depression.

Still, the authors of the Heritage report argued that their study controls for sufficient observables to conclude that "early sexual activity leads to emotional stress and reduces teen happiness" (Rector et al., 2003). While Rector and colleagues did control for a few observable characteristics that could confound the relationship between teen sex and depression, they did not adequately address the potential problems associated with unmeasured heterogeneity.

One might expect a positive relationship between early teen sex and depression for several reasons. First, as Rector and colleagues (2003) suggest, early teen sex may cause psychological trauma, as adolescents

From *Journal of Policy Analysis and Management,* vol. 25, no. 4, Autumn 2006, excerpts from pp. 803–804, 808–809, 812–814, 818–819, 821–822. Copyright © 2006 by Association for Public Policy Analysis and Management. Reprinted by permission. www.appam.org

struggle with the complicated emotions of physical intimacy at such an early age. However, it is also plausible to imagine that causality runs in the opposite direction. The onset of psychological trauma or depression may cause teens to engage in sexual intercourse in order to escape feelings of hopelessness. Finally, it may be that there is no causal link between sexual intercourse and depression, but rather a positive association due to unobserved heterogeneity. Adolescents who have the highest unobserved propensity for depression—for instance, those who have had particular childhood experiences—may be those who are most likely to engage in sexual activity.

Obtaining credible estimates of the impact of adolescent sexual intercourse on emotional health is not merely an empirical exercise. The conclusions of the Heritage study have been used by supporters of abstinence-only sex education to lobby for additional funding for such programs. However, recent work by Sabia (2006a) suggests that typical school-based sex education programs have little effect on adolescent sexual behaviors and health. Because empirical evidence on the impact of abstinence programs on teen pregnancy and sexually transmitted disease (STD) transmission is, at best, mixed (for a further review of the sex education literature, see Kirby, 2001), some proponents of abstinence programs have seized on the link between early teen sex and emotional harm as a key rationale for their policy position. . . .

Support for abstinence-only sex education is strong among many conservatives, and these views have led to significant public policy action. However, promoting abstinence will only improve the emotional well-being of adolescents if there is a causal link between early teen sex and depression. Providing credible empirical evidence on this question will be the central task of this paper. . . .

Alternative Risk and Protective Factors for Adolescent Depression: Potential Sources of Unobserved or Unmeasured Heterogeneity in the Rector et al. Study

In addition to entrance into sexual activity and romantic relationships, several demographic characteristics are theoretically hypothesized to be associated with adolescent depressive symptoms. One of the most frequently studied correlates of adolescent depression is familial relations. For example, poor relationships with parents and siblings are associated with higher rates of depression. . . . Physical health has been found to be strongly correlated to mental health. Those who rate themselves in poorer physical health tend to be more depressed (see, for example, Enns, Cox, & Martens, 2005). Being overweight may also impact mental health. . . .

There are several "protective" factors identified in the literature, believed to mediate the effects of stressors on adolescent depression. Intelligence (IQ) is one such protective factor. . . . Having a higher IQ is associated with positive mental health outcomes because adolescents with higher IQs can better cope with life's stressors. Religiosity is also viewed as a potential protective factor. . . . The literature also suggests that while lower socio-economic status may contribute to an increased likelihood of depression (Goodman et al., 2003), some cultural traits of historically disadvantaged racial communities can protect individuals from depression. For example, strong community relations among African Americans—along with strong social stigmas against suicide—may protect adolescents against depression and suicide (Gibbs & Hines, 1989; Nettles & Pleck, 1994) and promote healthy coping mechanisms (Morrison & Downey, 2000).

This study contributes to the empirical literature by providing more credible estimates of the impact of teen sex on depressive symptoms. Using difference-in-difference estimates to control for fixed individual-level unobserved heterogeneity, I am able to present more credible evidence of the nature of the relationship between losing virginity and depressive symptoms. While not achieving the internal validity of a well-designed social experiment, difference-in-difference models will produce estimates with more reasonable identification assumptions than have previously been presented in the literature. Obtaining credible estimates is critically important in informing . . . the public policy discussion over abstinence-only sex education.

Data

This analysis uses data from the National Longitudinal Study of Adolescent Health (Add Health) to estimate the relationship between teen sex and depressive symptoms. This is the same dataset used by Rector et al. (2003). The Add Health survey is a school-based nationally representative longitudinal survey that collected information from adolescents, parents, and school administrators in the 1994–95 academic year (wave 1) and again in the 1995–96 academic year (wave 2). The first wave of data is used to conduct the cross-section analysis, and waves 1 and 2 are used to conduct the difference-in-difference analysis. In the first wave, students from seventh to twelfth grade were asked questions about their mental health, personality, sexual activity, family, romantic relationships, peer groups, neighborhoods, and other health behaviors. Similar questions were posed in wave 2. Parents (mostly mothers) were also interviewed and asked about their relationships with their children, their families, and information on their backgrounds.

Outcome/Dependent Variables

. . . Three measures of mental health are constructed for use as dependent variables in this analysis. First, a measure of depression is used. Adolescents were asked the following question in both waves of data collection: *"These questions will ask about how you feel emotionally and about how you feel in general. How often was [this statement] true during the past seven days:*

You felt depressed?" This was coded as equal to 1 if the adolescent responded that she felt depressed "a lot of the time," or "most of the time or all of the time." The variable was coded as 0 if the adolescent responded that she was depressed "never or rarely" or only "sometimes." This is the same coding used in the Heritage study (Rector et al., 2003). I find that 3.7 percent of adolescent males and 7.6 percent of adolescent females aged 13–14 report being depressed. The percentages rise with age for males, to 4.7 percent of those aged 15–16 and 9.6 percent of those aged 17–18. For adolescent females, the percentages are 12.4 percent of 15–16-year-olds and 12.7 percent of 17–18-year-olds.

Second, I construct a measure of the adolescent's perceived value of life. In both waves of data, adolescents were asked, *"[During the past week], how often did you feel that your life was not worth living?"* Given the severity of this question, I code this variable . . . equal to 1 if the adolescent reports that she felt her life were not worth living "sometimes," "a lot of the time," or "most or all of the time." This variable was coded to 0 if the adolescent responded "never" or "rarely." 6.1 percent of males and 10.9 percent of females aged 13–14 reported that their life was not worth living. As with depression, the percentage rose with age for males to 8.3 percent of 15–16-year-olds, and 11.3 percent of 17–18-year-olds. For females, the percentage rose to 13.8 percent of 15–16-year-olds, and then fell to 11.6 percent of 17–18-year-olds.

Finally, I construct a measure of the adolescent's suicidal tendencies. . . . Adolescents were asked, *"During the past 12 months, did you ever seriously think about committing suicide?"* The responses for this question were a simple "yes" and "no." 7.9 percent of males and 14.4 percent of females aged 13–14 reported that they had contemplated suicide. This number rose with age for males (to 9.5 percent of 15–16-year-olds to 13.3 percent of 17–18-year-olds) and rose and fell for females (to 18.3 percent of 15–16-year-olds to 15.5 percent of 17–18-year-olds).

Quasi-Independent/Predictor Variable

. . . The survey item asks, *"Have you ever had sexual intercourse? When we say sexual intercourse, we mean when a male inserts his penis into a female's vagina."* 15.4 percent of 13–14-year-olds, 39.1 percent of 15–16-year-olds, and 58.5 percent of 17–18-year-old males reported having had sexual intercourse. The percentages are fairly similar for females (11.6 percent, 36.6 percent, and 57.8 percent, respectively).

Unobserved Heterogeneity: Other Factors That Might Account for the Relationship Between Sexual Intercourse and Depression in Adolescence

. . . In this study, it is important to disentangle the effects of being in a relationship on mental health from the effects of sexual intercourse on mental health. . . . The literature suggests that entrance into romantic relationships may be associated with increased depression, especially for females (Joyner & Udry, 2000). Hence, I include a variable measuring whether or not the adolescent reports being in a romantic or romantic-like relationship. . . . The percentage of adolescent males and females in such a relationship rose with age, from around 40 percent of 13–14-year-olds to 68 percent of 17–18-year-olds.

Attempted suicides of family members . . . or friends . . . are also expected to impact an adolescent's mental health. Family suicide attempts may reflect biological-based depression, an important correlate of adolescent depression (see, for example, Shiner & Marmorstein, 1998). Moreover, suicide attempts by family or friends can lead to greater stress and anxiety, thus increasing the likelihood of depression. . . .

Obesity may also be correlated with mental health, especially for females. . . . I include a measure of whether the adolescent perceives himself or herself to be overweight . . . as a measure of obesity and as a proxy for attractiveness to peers. . . .

Family environment may also impact adolescents' mental health. Teens with parents that frequently fight . . . or do not get along with their children . . . may be more likely to be stressed and depressed. . . . Adolescents who believe that their parents do not care . . . about them are also more likely to be depressed.

Other observable characteristics theoretically believed to be linked with adolescent depression . . . include race . . ., intelligence . . ., academic performance . . ., alcohol consumption . . ., general health . . ., household demographics . . ., mothers' depression . . . religiosity . . ., and location effects.

Methodology

This study compares two estimators (i.e., statistical methods) to examine the sensitivity of the relationship between teen sex and self-reported mental health to unobserved heterogeneity. First, I estimate a cross-section model similar to the one estimated by Rector et al. (2003) using wave 1 of the Add Health data. Each of the measures of adverse mental health, the "outcome" measures (e.g., depression, suicide), is related to a set of individual-level (e.g., being overweight, GPA) and family-level (e.g., family discord, mother's drinking) observable characteristics (i.e., features of a person that might alternatively explain the relationship between teen depression and intercourse) as well as an indicator variable measuring whether the adolescent has engaged in sexual intercourse (e.g., the predictor variable). . . . This method is called Ordinary Least Squares (OLS).

Second, to control for selection into sexual activity based on unobservable characteristics, I exploit the longitudinal nature of the Add Health data to estimate individual fixed effects models. Adolescents are interviewed in consecutive academic years (wave 1 and wave 2) and are asked questions about their sexual experiences and depressive symptoms. The difference-in-difference model . . . uses a within-person . . . strategy. In order . . . to yield an unbiased estimate of the effect of losing virginity on depression, there must be no time varying unobservables correlated with both changes in sexual behavior and with changes in depressive symptoms. This method is referred to as fixed effects or difference-in-difference.

The . . . benefit of the difference-in-difference model is that it controls for fixed individual-level unobserved characteristics (e.g., IQ, religiosity) that may be associated with both sexual activity and depressive symptoms. . . .

Approximately 10 percent of females and 8 percent of males report becoming sexually active between waves 1 and 2. Moreover, 10 to 18 percent of females reported changes in a depressive symptom between waves 1 and 2. A smaller, but significant, percentage of males (6 to 13 percent) reported changes in depressive symptoms. This descriptive evidence suggests that a difference-in-difference methodology can be credibly utilized to identify the effects of entrance into sexual intercourse on changes in depression.

Taken together, a comparison of OLS and fixed effects estimates will allow us to examine whether fixed individual-level unobserved heterogeneity upwardly biases cross-section estimates. Difference-in-difference estimators are likely to produce more credible estimates of the effect of early teen sex on adolescent mental health. . . .

Results

OLS Estimates (Ordinary Least Squares): Akin to the Technique Used by Rector et al.

. . . The OLS estimates of the relationship between teen sex and adolescent mental health, by age, used wave 1 of the Add Health data. These cross-section estimates include controls for a wide set of individual-level and family-level observables, as suggested in the theoretical literature. . . .

For those aged 13–14, I find evidence of a strong positive relationship between engaging in sexual intercourse and the likelihood of depression . . ., feelings that one's life is not worth living . . ., and serious thoughts of suicide. . . . The coefficient estimates suggest that sexual intercourse is associated with a 5 percentage-point higher probability of each of these outcomes. For 15–16-year-olds . . ., the relationships persist. Teen sex is associated with a 2.3 percentage point higher probability of depression, a 4.8 percentage point higher probability of feeling life is not worth living, and a 3.4 percentage point higher probability of having serious suicidal thoughts. However, for the oldest teens (aged 17–18), I find no evidence of a significant relationship between teen sex and mental health after controlling for observables.

The findings . . . are consistent with Rector et al. (2003) and suggest evidence of a link between teen sex and depression. Rector et al. (2003) find that the magnitude of the association between teen sex and mental health is largest for adolescent females. . . . Thus, separate models are estimated by gender. . . .

Controlling for the previously discussed control variables (e.g., x and y). . . . I find robust evidence of a significant positive relationship between sexual activity and adverse mental health for females. Sexual intercourse is associated with a 6.9 higher percentage-point probability of self-reported depression for 13–14-year-old females . . . and a 4.7 higher percentage-point probability of depression for 15–16-year-old females. Moreover, sexual intercourse is associated with higher probabilities of feeling life is not worth living for 13–14-year-olds (8.1 percentage-points) and 15–16-year-olds (5.0 percentage-points). Finally, there is a positive relationship between having sexual intercourse and the probability of having serious suicidal thoughts in the last year (6.3 percentage points for 13–14-year-old females and 4.9 percentage points for 15–16-year-old females). For the oldest teenage females (aged 17–18), there is no evidence of a significant relationship between sexual intercourse and adverse mental health after controlling for observable characteristics (e.g., support Rector, 2003). For teenage males . . ., I find little evidence of a significant relationship between sexual intercourse and depressive symptoms. Only for 15–16-year-old males, do I find that engaging in sexual intercourse is associated with a higher probability of feeling life is not worth living.

Taken together, the findings . . . confirm the central findings of the Heritage study by Rector et al. (2003).

Fixed Effects Estimates: Difference-in-Difference Analysis

. . . By time-varying covariates I am referring to variables that could change from wave 1 to wave 2 that could account for the relationship between teen depression and sexual intercourse that were *not* considered by Rector et al. The difference-in-difference models control for the following time-varying covariates: whether the adolescent is in a romantic relationship, whether a family member has attempted suicide, whether a friend has attempted suicide, whether the adolescent feels that her parents don't care about her, whether the teen perceives herself to be overweight, whether the family attends weekly religious services, whether the adolescent consumes alcohol, the adolescent's annual school grade point average, and the adolescent's perceived loneliness. . . .

For adolescent females, difference-in-difference estimates suggest consistent evidence that OLS estimates of the relationship between sexual intercourse and adverse mental health are upwardly biased due to fixed individual-level unobserved heterogeneity. After controlling for individual-level unobservables (i.e. those listed above), I find no significant relationship between losing virginity and depressive symptoms for adolescent females. . . .

For depression, for 13–14-year-old females, the coefficient estimate in the OLS model is 0.069 and is statistically significant at the 1 percent level. After controlling for unobserved heterogeneity, the coefficient falls to 0.038 and becomes insignificant. For 15–16-year-old females, the OLS estimate is positive and significant (0.047); however, the fixed effects estimate is negative and insignificant.

The findings for [not feeling that one's life is worthwhile] outcome are similar. For 13–14-year-old females, the OLS estimate is positive and significant (0.072), while the ... estimate is 60 percent smaller in magnitude and is insignificant in the difference-in-difference analysis. Moreover, while the OLS estimate of the relationship between sexual activity and feeling that life is not worth living is positive and significant for females aged 15–16, the ... difference-in-difference analysis estimate is negative and insignificant.

Most starkly, while OLS estimates of the relationship between sexual activity and serious thoughts of suicide are positive and significant for 13–14-year-old and 15–16-year-old females, difference-in-difference estimates are actually *negative* and significant. Entrance into sexual activity is associated with an 11.1 percentage point decline in suicidal thoughts for 13–14-year-old females, a 5.1 percentage point decline in suicidal thoughts for 15–16-year-olds, and a 7.7 percentage point decline in suicidal thoughts for 17–18-year-olds.

For adolescent males, difference-in-difference estimates of the relationship between sexual intercourse and mental health are statistically insignificant across all specifications, with a few positive OLS signs becoming negative after controlling for unobserved heterogeneity.

The findings of this study suggest that it is inappropriate to infer a positive causal relationship between entrance into early teen sex and depression. Rather, certain types of adolescents—those with unobserved psychological traits or childhood experiences—are simply more prone to both depression and early sexual experience. Thus, the results presented here suggest little support for the hypothesis that promoting abstinence-only sex education will ameliorate depressive symptoms.

Conclusions

Taken together with Sabia (2006a), this study suggests that recent claims about the causes and consequences of early teen sex have been overstated. Naïve interpretations of poorly designed studies have suggested that comprehensive school-based sex education programs have adverse health effects and that abstinence-only sex education can improve depressive symptoms. In fact, the evidence presented in each of these papers suggests otherwise.

This study presents consistent evidence that early entrance into sexual intercourse is not the cause of depression, but rather is an observable indicator of depression. This finding has important policy implications. In order to conclude that the adoption of abstinence-only sex education programs will improve (or hasten the onset of) adolescents' depressive symptoms, one must show (i) convincing empirical evidence that entrance into sexual intercourse causes depression, and (ii) abstinence-only sex education increases the proportion of students who abstain from sex. While the evidence on (ii) is mixed, this study suggests that it is inappropriate to infer a causal link between early teen sex and depressive symptoms. Thus, even if abstinence-only sex education did increase the proportion of students who abstained, depressive symptoms would not improve unless such a program had a direct effect on depression, independent of its effect on virginity. . . .

While the findings of this study suggest that prolonging virginity will not improve common measures of adolescent mental health, this does not preclude the presence of other health or non-health benefits to abstinence. There may be sexual, spiritual, or religious benefits to abstinence. Moreover, recent work that carefully addresses unobserved heterogeneity suggests that early teen sex might have negative educational spillovers (Sabia, 2006b). Thus, a more complete understanding of the costs of teen sex decisions would contribute to both the adolescent sex literature as well as the public policy debate over sex education.

Both this study and the proceeding study (Sabia, 2006a) shed light on important methodological and substantive shortcomings in the existing empirical literature on early teen sex. Each of these new studies suggests that recent claims about the adverse health effects of sex education and the depression-related consequences of early teen sex are exaggerated. In the context of an increasingly polarized ideological debate about how public policy could or should affect adolescents' sexual decisions, obtaining credible estimates of the causes and consequences of teen sex is critical to better informing this discussion.

References

Enns, M. W., Cox, B. J., & Martens, P. J. (2005). Investigating health correlates of adolescent depression in Canada. Canadian Journal of Public Health, 96(6), 427–431.

Gibbs, J. T., & Hines, A. M. (1989). Factors related to sex differences in suicidal behaviors among black youth. Journal of Adolescent Research, 4, 152–172.

Goodman, E., Gail, M. D., Slap, B., & Huang, B. (2003). The public health impact of socioeconomic status on adolescent depression and obesity. American Journal of Public Health, 93(11), 1844–1850.

Joyner, K., & Udry, J. R. (2000). You don't bring me anything but down: Adolescent romance and depression. Journal of Health and Social Behavior, 41, 369–391.

Kirby, D. (2001). Emerging answers: Research findings on programs to reduce teen pregnancy. Washington, DC: The National Campaign to Prevent Teen Pregnancy.

Morrison, L. L., & Downey, D. L. (2000). Racial differences in self-disclosure of suicide ideation and reasons for living: Implications for training. Cultural Diversity & Ethnic Minority Psychology, 6, 374–386.

Nettles, S. M., & Pleck, J. H. (1994). Risk, resilience, and development: The multiple ecologies of black adolescents in the United States. In R. J. Haggerty, L. R. Sherrod, N. Garmezy, & M. Rutter (Eds.), Stress, risk, and resilience in children and adolescents: Processes, mechanisms, and interventions (pp. 147–181). New York: Cambridge University Press.

Pardue, M., & Rector, R. (2004, January 16). Good money for bad advice. National Review Online.

Rector, R. E., Johnson, K. A., & Noyes, L. R. (2003). Sexually active teenagers are more likely to be depressed and to attempt suicide. A report of the Heritage Center for Data Analysis. Washington, DC: The Heritage Foundation.

Sabia, J. J. (2006a). Does sex education affect adolescent sexual behaviors and health? Journal of Policy Analysis and Management, 25(4), in press.

Sabia, J. J. (2006b). Reading, writing, and sex: Does losing virginity affect adolescent academic performance? Unpublished manuscript. Athens, GA: University of Georgia.

Shiner, R. L., & Marmorstein, N. R. (1998). Family environments of adolescents with lifetime depression: Associations with maternal depression history. Journal of the American Academy of Child and Adolescent Psychiatry, 37, 1152–1160.

Wetzstein, C. (2003, June 4). Study links teen sex to depression, suicide. The Washington Times.

POSTSCRIPT

Does Engaging in Early Sexual Activity Cause Depressive Symptoms in Adolescents?

Rector et al. conclude that teens who are sexually active are likely to be less happy, more depressed, and more likely to attempt suicide than teens who are not sexually active. In contrast, Sabia concludes that other factors, which he calls unobserved heterogeneity or individual-level observables (e.g., having had a friend who has attempted suicide, family composition), eliminate the relationship between teen sex and depression. What accounts for the contradictory conclusions based on *exact the same data set*?

The key difference between Rector et al.'s and Sabia's papers is the statistical analyses used by the authors. Rector et al. conducted a 'one-time-point' or cross-sectional study. They used a few demographic variables (i.e., race, gender, age, and family income) as control variables. In contrast, Sabia used a much longer list of variables to control for differences between sexually active and not-sexually active teens as well as considering depression over time (i.e., longitudinally). Consequently, Sabia's analyses are more statistically sophisticated.

Others have used the Add Health data and have used more statistically complicated analyses who have agreed (Meier, 2007) and disagreed (Hallfors et al., 2005; Joyner & Udry, 2000) with Sabia's conclusion. There are several possible explanations for these incongruities. Joyner and Udry investigated the relationship between *romantic relationship status* and depression—not sexual behavior. Hallfors et al. created "risk clusters" whereby the teens were classified into one of 16 'risk' groups (Hallsfors, et al. 2004); many of the groups combined sex and drug use (e.g., marijuana and sex, smokers and sex) and each teen was assigned to *only* one group. Thus, the participants who had sex or not as their only risk factor were different than the teens who had sex or not in Rector et al.'s and in Sabia's studies. Meier's analysis involved looking at those who had sex for the first time over the one year period of the study and compared them to the students who were 'virgins' during that period. Further, Rector et al. defined mental health by using one question to represent depression whereas Hallfors et al. used a 20-item instrument. Meier included self-esteem in her definition of "mental health." Different statistical techniques, methodology, and varying definitions of the grouping variable (what constitutes not-sexually-active and sexually-active) and dependent variables (e.g., depression item or scale, suicidal ideation, self-esteem) may help explain these sometimes consistent, sometimes contradictory findings.

One consistency from Rector et al., Sabia, and the other three studies (Hallfors et al., 2005; Joyner & Udry, 2000; Meier, 2007) is that we must be aware of what is called *the "third variable" problem*. Unless we conduct a well-designed experiment, it is difficult to make causal statements. Because of the nature of sexuality-related research, we often do not have the ability to conduct randomized experiments (e.g., we cannot assign people to 'sexually debut' or not). Thus, we must rely on correlational research (as did Rector et al.) or investigate prospectively, across time (as Sabia did). We need to consider what role pre-existing differences between groups may play in the phenomenon and which of these need to be 'controlled for' in our analyses. The differences in which control variables were included may also account for the differences in results.

As an informed reader, we must take into account the publication source. For many academic journals, submitted papers are vetted through a peer review process. This means that the editor finds two or three experts in the field and has them review the paper blindly (i.e., author anonymity). If the paper has logical leaps or analytic problems, these will be pointed out or the paper may be rejected for publication. While Sabia's paper was subject to this rigorous publication process and has been published in a top-ranking political science journal (Garand & Giles, 2003), Rector et al.'s paper is a technical report that has probably not been through peer review (the Education Resource Information Center does not require peer review). Peer review is a key technique in the academic publishing field.

It is incumbent upon readers to think critically about the methodology and statistical techniques used by writers, to look at the variables that are used and not used in a study, and to consider alternative explanations for the findings. The relationship between adolescent sexual activity status and depression is obviously complex.

References/Further Reading

American Academy of Child and Adolescent Psychiatry. (1998). Practice parameters for the assessment and treatment of children and adolescents with depressive disorder. *Journal of American Academy of Child and Adolescent Psychiatry, 37* (suppl.), 63S–83S.

Cornelius, J.R., Clark, D.B., Reynolds, M., Kirisci, L., & Tarter, R. (2007). Early age of first sexual intercourse and affiliation with deviant peers predict development of SUD: A prospective longitudinal study. *Addictive Behaviors, 32(4)*, 850–854.

Garand, J.C., & Giles, M.W. (2003). Journals in the discipline: A report on a new survey of American Political Scientists. *PS: Political Science & Politics*, 36, 293–s308.

Garriguet, D. (2005). Early sexual intercourse. *Health Reports, 16(3)*, 9–18 (Statistics Canada Catalogue 82–003).

Hallfors, D.D., Waller, M.W., Bauer, D., Ford, C.A., & Halpern, C.T. (2005). Which comes first in adolescence—Sex and drugs or depression? *American Journal of Preventive Medicine, 29(3),* 163–170.

Hallfors, D.D., Waller, M.W., Ford, C.A., Halpern, C.T., Brodish, P.H., & Iritani, B. (2004). Adolescent depression and suicide risk: Association with sex and drug behaviour. *American Journal of Preventive Medicine, 27(3),* 224–231.

Joyner, K., & Udry, R. (2000). You don't bring me anything but down: Adolescent romance and depression. *Journal of Health and Social Behavior, 41(4),* 369–391.

Kirby, D. (2001). *Emerging answers: Research findings on programs to reduce teen pregnancy.* Washington, D.C.: National Campaign to Prevent Teen Pregnancy.

Meier, A.M. (2007). Adolescent first sex and subsequent mental health. *American Journal of Sociology, 112(6),* 1811–1847.

Mueller, T.E., Gavin, L.E., & Kulkarni, A. (2008). The association between sex education and youths engagement in sexual intercourse, age at first intercourse and birth control use at first sex. *Journal of Adolescent Health, 42(1),* 89–96.

Social Security Act. (1996). 42 U.S.C. Title 5, § 510 (b2E). Separate Program for Abstinence Education.

ISSUE 8

Is There Cause for Concern About an "Oral Sex Crisis" for Teens?

YES: Sharon Jayson, from "Teens Define Sex in New Ways," http://www.USAToday.com (October 19, 2005)

NO: Alexander McKay, from "Oral Sex Among Teenagers: Research, Discourse, and Education," *Canadian Journal of Human Sexuality* (Fall/Winter 2004)

ISSUE SUMMARY

YES: Journalist Sharon Jayson argues that more than half of 15- to 19-year-olds are engaging in oral sex. She reports some experts are becoming increasingly worried that adolescents who approach this intimate behavior so casually might have difficulty forming healthy intimate relationships later on.

NO: Alexander McKay, research coordinator of the Sex Information and Education Council of Canada, argues that the discourse about oral sex is somewhat exaggerated but may be used as a vehicle for increasing discussions with teens about their motives for sexual activity, which, in turn, can help guide sex education initiatives.

Recently, there has been a surge in media attention given to the "problem" of teen oral sex. There are rumors of "rainbow" clubs—parties for teens where girls wear different colored lipstick and fellate boys. The "goal" is for boys to have many different colors of lipstick on their penis at the end of the party. Oral sex has been called the new "spin the bottle" of teenagers. A book for teens by Paul Ruditis entitled *Rainbow Party* (Simon & Schuster, 2005) brought with it a flurry of discussion on the topic of teen oral sex.

But is there any real cause for concern? When questioned about sex, Michael Learned, a television star of the 1970s, stated in an interview in the 1980s that she thought kids today are doing the same thing that she and her peer group were doing as kids—only the kids of the 1980s talked about their sexual activities more than her cohorts did. Is that the case with oral sex of the

Millennial teenagers? Are they simply talking about oral sex more as opposed to "doing it" more, compared to past generations?

A variety of studies have been conducted recently in North America that have gathered some preliminary information about oral sex and adolescents. Studies such as the Canadian Youth, Sexual Health and HIV/AIDS study (Boyce, Doherty, Fortin, & MacKinnon, 2003) and Centers for Disease Control and Prevention's study on sexual behavior and selected health measures of men and women aged 15–44 years (Mosher, Chandra, & Jones, 2005), both conducted in 2002, report on oral sex activity of youth. One of the major problems, however, is comparing this data to prior studies. The Canada Youth and AIDS study (King et al., 1988), which was conducted in the late 1980s and is the earlier counterpart to the Canadian 2003 study, did not ask teens about their oral sex behavior.

More recent studies have asked teenagers about their oral sex behaviors. Lisa Remez, in a study published in *Family Planning Perspectives* in December 2000, reviewed the formal research about oral sex and youth. An early study in the 1980s found that about 20 percent of 13–18 year olds had engaged in oral sex. Another early 1980s study of tenth to twelfth graders found that 24 percent of virgins had had oral sex. A mid-1990s study of "nonvirgin" university students found that many of them (between 57 to 70 percent) retrospectively reported having had engaged in oral sex prior to having intercourse. A study of ninth to twelfth graders indicated that about 10 percent of virgins had engaged in oral sex. One representative sample—the National Survey of Adolescent Males—in 1988 and again in 1995 suggested that receipt of fellatio had not increased significantly for boys aged 15–19 years, with 44 percent and 50 percent, respectively, having received oral sex. Studies in the 2000s tend to be consistent with these earlier studies with approximately 40 percent of older teens (15–17 years) having engaged in oral sexual activity (Prinstein, Meade, & Cohen, 2003) while 20 percent of younger teens (grade 9, around 14 years of age) have had oral sex (Halpern-Felsher, Cornell, Kropp, & Tschann, 2005). A recent representative study by the Canadian Association for Adolescent Health (February 2006) found that 19 percent of 14–17-year-old respondents reported having engaged in oral sex, while the average age for first oral sex and vaginal intercourse was 15 years (http://www.acsa-caah.ca/ang/pdf/misc/research.pdf).

While there may or may not be an increase in oral sexual activity from earlier generations of teens (McKay states that there is evidence for a modest increase), should sex educators and those who work with adolescents be concerned about teen oral sex activity? In the following selection, Alex McKay discusses the research around oral sex and youth, sex education about oral sex, and the health risks associated with oral sexual activity. McKay does not view oral sex as a problem, per se; rather he describes this as important opportunity for opening discussions with youth about sex education and increasing our acknowledgment of the role of pleasure in the sexual lives of adolescents. In contrast, Sharon Jayson, in a *USA Today* article, discusses some of the potential negative ramifications of, and some of the worries that adults may have about, teen oral sex.

YES

Sharon Jayson

Teens Define Sex in New Ways

The generational divide between baby-boomer parents and their teenage offspring is sharpening over sex.

Oral sex, that is.

More than half of 15- to 19-year-olds are doing it, according to a ground breaking study by the Centers for Disease Control and Prevention.

The researchers did not ask about the circumstances in which oral sex occurred, but the report does provide the first federal data that offer a peek into the sex lives of American teenagers.

To adults, "oral sex is extremely intimate, and to some of these young people, apparently it isn't as much," says Sarah Brown, director of the National Campaign to Prevent Teen Pregnancy.

"What we're learning here is that adolescents are redefining what is intimate."

Among teens, oral sex is often viewed so casually that it needn't even occur within the confines of a relationship. Some teens say it can take place at parties, possibly with multiple partners. But they say the more likely scenario is oral sex within an existing relationship.

Still, some experts are increasingly worrying that a generation that approaches intimate behavior so casually might have difficulty forming healthy intimate relationships later on.

"My parents' generation sort of viewed oral sex as something almost greater than sex. Like once you've had sex, something more intimate is oral sex," says Carly Donnelly, 17, a high school senior from Cockeysville, Md.

"Now that some kids are using oral sex as something that's more casual, it's shocking to (parents)."

David Walsh, a psychologist and author of the teen-behavior book *Why Do They Act That Way?*, says the brain is wired to develop intense physical and emotional attraction during the teenage years as part of the maturing process. But he's disturbed by the casual way sex is often portrayed in the media, which he says gives teens a distorted view of true intimacy.

Sex—even oral sex—"just becomes kind of a recreational activity that is separate from a close, personal relationship," he says.

"When the physical part of the relationship races ahead of every-thing else, it can almost become the focus of the relationship," Walsh says, "and they're not then developing all of the really important skills like trust and communication and all those things that are the key ingredients for a healthy, long-lasting relationship."

"Intimacy has been so devalued," says Doris Fuller of Sandpoint, Idaho, who, with her two teenage children, wrote the 2004 book *Promise You Won't Freak Out,* which discusses topics such as teen oral sex.

"What will the impact be on their ultimately more lasting relationships? I don't think we know yet."

Casual Attitude Is Worrying

Child psychology professor W. Andrew Collins of the University of Minnesota says a relationship "that's only about sex is not a high-quality relationship."

In a 28-year study, Collins and his colleagues followed 180 individuals from birth. His yet-to-be-published research, presented at a conference in April, suggests that emotionally fulfilling high school relationships do help teens learn important relationship skills.

The researchers did not specifically ask about oral sex, he says. But relationships that are focused more on sex tend to be "less sustained, often not monogamous and with lower levels of satisfaction."

Terri Fisher, an associate professor of psychology at Ohio State University, says oral sex used to be considered "exotic." After the sexual revolution of the 1960s, it was viewed as a more intimate sexual act than sexual intercourse, but now, in young people's minds, it's "a more casual act."

Beyond shock, many parents aren't sure what to think when they discover their children's nonchalant approach to oral sex.

"It doesn't cross your mind because it's not something you have done," Fuller says. "Most parents weren't doing this (as teenagers) in the way these kids are."

But if parents are looking for reasons to freak out, the health risk of oral sex apparently isn't one of them. Teenagers and experts agree that oral sex is less risky than intercourse because there's no threat of pregnancy and less chance of contracting a sexually transmitted disease or HIV.

"The fact that teenagers have oral sex doesn't upset me much from a public health perspective," says J. Dennis Fortenberry, a physician who specializes in adolescent medicine at the Indiana University School of Medicine.

"From my perspective, relatively few teenagers only have oral sex. And so for the most part, oral sex, as for adults, is typically incorporated into a pattern of sexual behaviors that may vary depending upon the type of relationship and the timing of a relationship."

Data Don't Tell Whole Story

A study published in the journal *Pediatrics* in April supports the view that adolescents believe oral sex is safer than intercourse, with less risk to their physical and emotional health.

The study of ethnically diverse high school freshmen from California found that almost 20% had tried oral sex, compared with 13.5% who said they had intercourse.

More of these teens believed oral sex was more acceptable for their age group than intercourse, even if the partners are not dating.

"The problem with surveys is they don't tell you the intimacy sequence," Brown says. "The vast majority who had intercourse also had oral sex. We don't know which came first."

The federal study, based on data collected in 2002 and released last month, found that 55% of 15- to 19-year-old boys and 54% of girls reported getting or giving oral sex, compared with 49% of boys and 53% of girls the same ages who reported having had intercourse.

Though the study provides data, researchers say, it doesn't help them understand the role oral sex plays in the overall relationship; nor does it explain the fact that today's teens are changing the sequence of sexual behaviors so that oral sex has skipped ahead of intercourse.

"All of us in the field are still trying to get a handle on how much of this is going on and trying to understand it from a young person's point of view," says Stephanie Sanders, associate director of The Kinsey Institute for Research in Sex, Gender and Reproduction at Indiana University, which investigates sexual behavior and sexual health.

"Clearly, we need more information about what young people think is appropriate behavior, under what circumstances and with whom," Sanders says. "Now we know a little more about what they're doing but not what they're thinking."

The $16 million study, which took six years to develop, complete and analyze, surveyed almost 13,000 teens, men and women ages 15–44 on a variety of sexual behaviors.

Researchers say that the large sample size, an increased societal openness about sexual issues and the fact that the survey was administered via head-phones and computer instead of face to face all give them confidence that, for the first time, they have truthful data on these very personal behaviors.

"There is strong evidence that people are more willing to tell computers things, such as divulge taboo behaviors, than (they are to tell) a person," Sanders says.

More Analysis Needed

Researchers cannot conclude that the percentage of teens having oral sex is greater than in the past. There is no comparison data for girls, and numbers for boys are about the same as they were a decade ago in the National Survey of Adolescent Males: Currently, 38.8% have given oral sex vs. 38.6% in 1995; 51.5% have received it vs. 49.4% in 1995.

Further analyses of the federal data by the private, non-profit National Campaign to Prevent Teen Pregnancy and the non-partisan research group Child Trends find almost 25% of teens who say they are virgins have had oral sex. Child Trends also reviewed socioeconomic and other data and found that those who are white and from middle- and upper-income families with higher levels of education are more likely to have oral sex.

Historically, oral sex has been more common among the more highly educated, Sanders says.

Is Intimacy Imperiled?

The survey also found that almost 90% of teens who have had sexual intercourse also had oral sex. Among adults 25–44, 90% of men and 88% of women have had heterosexual oral sex.

"If we are indeed headed as a culture to have a total disconnect between intimate sexual behavior and emotional connection, we're not forming the basis for healthy adult relationships," says James Wagoner, president of Advocates for Youth, a reproductive-health organization in Washington.

Oral sex might affect teenagers' self-esteem most of all, says Paul Coleman, a Poughkeepsie, N.Y., psychologist and author of *The Complete Idiot's Guide to Intimacy.*

"Somebody is going to feel hurt or abused or manipulated," he says. "Not all encounters will turn out favorably. . . . Teenagers are not mature enough to know all the ramifications of what they're doing.

"It's pretending to say it's just sexual and nothing else. That's an arbitrary slicing up of the intimacy pie. It's not healthy."

A survey of more than 1,000 teens conducted with the National Campaign to Prevent Teen Pregnancy resulted in *The Real Truth About Teens & Sex,* a book by Sabrina Weill, a former editor in chief at *Seventeen* magazine. She says casual teen attitudes toward sex—particularly oral sex—reflect their confusion about what is normal behavior. She believes teens are facing an intimacy crisis that could haunt them in future relationships.

"When teenagers fool around before they're ready or have a very casual attitude toward sex, they proceed toward adulthood with a lack of understanding about intimacy," Weill says. "What it means to be intimate is not clearly spelled out for young people by their parents and people they trust."

Although governmental and educational campaigns urge teens to delay sex, some suggest teens have replaced sexual intercourse with oral sex.

"If you say to teenagers 'no sex before marriage,' they may interpret that in a variety of ways," says Fisher.

Talk Is Crucial

Experts say parents need to talk to their kids about sex sooner rather than later. Oral sex needs to be part of the discussion because these teens are growing up in a far more sexually open society.

Anecdotal reports for years have focused on teens "hooking up" casually. Depending on the group, teens say it can mean kissing, making out or having sex.

"Friends with benefits" is another way of referring to non-dating relationships, with a form of sex as a "benefit."

But not all teens treat sex so casually, say teens from suburban Baltimore who were interviewed by USA TODAY as part of an informal focus group.

Alex Trazkovich, 17, a high school senior from Reisterstown, Md., says parents don't hear enough about teen relationships where there is a lot of emotional involvement.

"They hear about teens going to the parties and having lots and lots of sex," he says. "It happens, but it's not something that happens all the time. It's more of an extreme behavior."

Alexander McKay

 **NO**

Oral Sex Among Teenagers: Research, Discourse, and Education

The issue of teens and oral sex has appeared on the radar screens of public and media consciousness rather abruptly. The more level-headed among us may ask whether all the talk about oral sex among teens reflects a recent major shift in adolescent behaviour (i.e., a "new teen sexual revolution") or an example of unwarranted media induced anxiety, or a combination of both. It should be stated, from the onset, that nearly all the reports in the media about an "out break" of oral sex among teens, and especially young teens, are based almost entirely on anecdotal accounts and speculation. Although well-conducted survey research that allows young people to anonymously report their sexual behaviour may not always be methodologically perfect, it is almost certainly a more reliable way to obtain an accurate gage of adolescent sexual behaviour than is the television camera or journalist's interview with a group of self-selected teen informants where a social desirability bias is much more likely to be present. What does the available research tell us about oral sex among teens?

Oral Sex and Teens: What the Research Says

The *Canadian Youth, Sexual Health and HIV/AIDS Study* (Boyce, Doherty, Fortin, & MacKinnon, 2003) included a sample of just over 11,000 Canadian Grade 7, 9, and 11 students. The Grade 9 and 11 students were asked about their practice of specific sexual behaviours. The survey was conducted in 2002. At that time, 32% of Grade 9 males, 28% of Grade 9 females, 53% of Grade 11 males, and 52% of Grade 11 females reported that they had engaged in oral sex at least once (Boyce et al., 2003). How does this compare to the past? A similar study involving Canadian youth conducted in 1992 found that 27% of Grade 9 males, 21% of Grade 9 females, 48% of Grade 11 males, and 47% of Grade 11 females said they had experienced oral sex at least once (Warren & King, 1992). It should be kept in mind that in these surveys, as is typically the case, teens are asked if they have "ever" engaged in a particular behaviour. This is important because it means that the figures do not differentiate between those who have had oral sex once or twice from those who are regular practitioners. In any case, if we compare

From *The Canadian Journal of Human Sexuality,* vol. 13, no. 3–4, Fall/Winter 2004, pp. 201–202. Copyright © 2004 by SIECCAN. Reprinted by permission.

the percentages between 1992 and 2002 we might cautiously conclude that there has been a modest increase in the percentages of teens who have ever had oral sex at least once. Very few studies have assessed oral sex among younger teens. One study of 12- to 15-year-olds indicated that 18% had experienced oral sex (Boekeloo & Howard, 2002).

The popular perception is that with respect to teen oral sex, it is more likely that there is a gender discrepancy in which females are more likely to be giving (fellatio) rather than receiving (cunnilingus) oral sex from their male partners. Unfortunately, the studies mentioned above did not distinguish between who was giving and who was receiving. However, the research that is available on this point would tend to support the idea that among teens it is more likely to be the female who is giving oral sex. For example, in a large-scale study from the United States conducted in 1995, among males aged 15 to 19, 49% reported that they had received oral sex whereas 39% said that they had given oral sex (Gates & Sonenstein, 2000).

To put these statistics on oral sex in perspective, several points should be noted. First, part of the current discussion of this issue is the belief that many young people do not consider oral sex to be the "real thing," that it's not really sex, that it's not even a particularly intimate behaviour. Attitudes towards oral sex are no doubt changing but if oral sex among teens is commonly occurring on "a lark" then we should expect that oral sex will be far more common than the "real thing" (i.e., vaginal intercourse). In other words, if we put oral sex on the traditional continuum of sexual behaviours that begins with kissing, proceeds to petting above and then below the waist, moves next to oral sex, and finally ends in intercourse, then we should expect that in the new era of oral sex as "no big deal" that the traditional continuum would have become distorted. That is, that oral sex among teens would have become significantly more common relative to other sexual behaviours. However, when we look at the findings of the *Canadian Youth, Sexual Health and HIV/AIDS Study* (Boyce et al., 2003), oral sex seems to have kept its traditional place in the continuum of behaviours. For example, when we look at the sexual behaviours of Grade 9 females we see that 67% have experienced "deep, open mouth kissing," 64% have been touched above the waist, 54% have participated in touching below the waist, 28% have had oral sex, and 19% have had intercourse (Boyce et al., 2003).

A second point that we should keep in mind is that although the media and public discourse on oral sex has disproportionately focused on youth, oral sex among adults has become, over time, a normative sexual behaviour. Data from the U.S. *National Health and Social Life Survey* indicated that, for example, among 40- to 44-year-olds, 84% of men and 73% of women had given oral sex while 86% of men and 77% of women had received it (Laumann, Gagnon, Michael, & Michaels, 1994). Perhaps even more telling is a study of married and cohabiting adult couples conducted in Quebec in the late 1980s in which 80% reported engaging in oral sex in the preceding year (Samson et al., 1993). Laumann et al. (1994), in discussing their findings, suggest that "If there has been any basic change in the script for sex between women and men, it is the increase in the incidence and frequency of fellatio and cunnilingus" (p. 102). Given that oral sex has become a common, normative aspect of adult sexual behaviour, it should not come as a complete surprise that as they become sexually active, some teens will also engage in these behaviours. These statistics on oral sex can be evaluated and interpreted in a range of ways but it is probably accurate to say that while the incidence and frequency of oral sex among teens and adults alike has been increasing, albeit gradually, declarations of an "epidemic of oral sex in middle school" are probably an exaggeration.

The Current Discourse and Its Implications for Sexual Health Education

There was once a time when the urgency to provide widespread HIV/AIDS prevention education to youth and adults alike included the idea of reducing risk through "non-intercourse sex" or "non-penetrative sex" or "outer-course." These terms seem to have fallen out of the vernacular of sexual health educators but it is somewhat ironic looking back on them that the current awareness that some teens engage in oral sex should cause such apparent shock and anxiety, particularly among media commentators. There is no doubt that some of this anxiety is well placed. Clearly, as with all sexual behaviours, some teens will become involved in oral sex through manipulation or peer pressure or because they made ill-advised decisions. But it is also worth speculating about whether there is something in particular about oral sex among teens that sparks anxiety among parents, educators, and the media. And it is here that perhaps we find the silver lining in the uproar over teens and oral sex. In educating youth about sex we have tended overwhelmingly to focus on the biophysiological aspects of sexuality and reproduction. What we have tended not to talk about so much with youth, maybe because we are not so comfortable doing so, is sexual pleasure. Oral sex has nothing to do with reproduction so charts are not very helpful. In some basic respects, oral sex is about pleasure. And maybe this is at least part of what has disturbed so many people about oral sex and teens. It forces us to acknowledge that pleasure is a part of teen sexuality and the decisions that teens make about their relationships and their behaviour. Perhaps all the recent attention paid to oral sex and teens will force the issue onto the table of school-based sexual health education and parent-child discussions of sexuality. This is a good thing. Once we have calmed everybody down about the myth of an epidemic of oral sex in the middle schools we can move forward in addressing the issue of oral sex openly and honestly. This will involve a greater acknowledgement of the role of pleasure in teen sexuality. But at the same time this more holistic approach will allow us to do a much better job of helping youth make sound judgements about what is right for them, increase their skills in resisting peer pressure, and minimize their risks if and when they may choose to engage in oral sex.

Oral Sex and Pregnancy/STI/HIV Risk

Quite rightly, much of the concern around teens and oral sex relates to the potential emotional, psychosocial, and developmental consequences of young people's involvement in oral sex (Barrett, 2004). In addition, however, concern has been expressed regarding the potential health risks of oral sex. It is apparent and realistic to assume that part of the attraction to oral sex among young people is that this is a sexual behaviour that confers no risk of pregnancy. Educators need to acknowledge this as a component in teen decision-making about sexual behaviour. There is an often expressed concern that teens consider oral sex risk free and that educators need to emphasize that oral sex does carry a risk of STI transmission. However, it is not sufficient, and potentially counterproductive, to simply say that oral sex is risky. We must provide information about the STI/HIV risks of oral sex that is comprehensive and consistent with current medical knowledge. At present this suggests that we inform students that oral sex confers a lower risk of HIV and other STI infection than unprotected penile-vaginal or penileanal intercourse but that it is not risk free. Unprotected oral sex does present some level of risk for transmission of bacterial and viral STI as well as HIV (Edwards, 1998a; Edwards, 1998b; Hawkins, 2001). Students should also be informed that the use of condoms and oral dams can reduce the risk of infection from oral sex. Sexual health educators can offer further risk reduction strategies by indicating that mutual masturbation confers virtually no risk of STI/HIV transmission. These risk reduction strategies will be of particular relevance for gay, lesbian, and bisexual youth for whom oral sex may play a central role in their sexual expression.

References

Barrett, A. (2004). Teens and oral sex: A sexual health educator's perspective. *SIECCAN Newsletter, 39(1–2), in The Canadian Journal of Human Sexuality, 13,* 197–200.

Boekeloo, B.O., & Howard, D.E. (2002). Oral sexual experience among young adolescents receiving general health examinations. *American Journal of Health Behavior, 26,* 306–314.

Boyce, W., Doherty, M., Fortin, C., & MacKinnon, D. (2003). *Canadian Youth, Sexual Health and HIV/AIDS Study.* Toronto, ON: Council of Ministers of Education.

Edwards, S., & Carne, C. (1998a). Oral sex and the transmission of viral STIs. *Sexually Transmitted Infections, 74,* 6–10.

Edwards, S., & Carne, C. (1998b). Oral sex and the transmission of non-viral STIs. *Sexually Transmitted Infections, 74,* 95–100.

Hawkins, D.A. (2001). Oral sex and HIV transmission. *Sexually Transmitted Infections, 77,* 307–308.

Laumann, E.O., Gagnon, J.H., Michael, R.T., & Michaels, S. (1994). *The Social Organization of Sexuality: Sexual Practices in the United States.* Chicago, IL: The University of Chicago Press.

Sampson, J.M., Levy, J.J., Dupras, A., & Tessier, D. (1994). Active oral-genital sex among married and cohabiting heterosexual adults. *Sexological Review, 1,* 143–156.

Warren, W.K., & King, A.J. (1994). *Development and Evaluation of an AIDS/ STD/Sexuality Program for Grade 9 Students.* Kingston, ON: Social Program Evaluation Group, Queens University.

POSTSCRIPT

Is There a Cause for Concern About an "Oral Sex Crisis" for Teens?

One of the ironies of the oral sex concern debate is that, in the past, sex educators who have taken a "harm reduction" approach or who have spoken with youth about the riskiness of various sexual behaviors for HIV and sexually transmitted infections (STIs) have lauded "outercourse" as a good alternative to "intercourse" (Barrett, 2004). Thus, there is a subset of teens who have engaged in oral sex but not intercourse (see Mosher et al., 2005, who report that approximately 12 percent of teens fit in this category). Indeed, there is research to suggest that oral sex is only a theoretical risk for some sexually transmitted infections.

What is missing from the literature is a more complete understanding of why some teens engage in oral sex but not intercourse. Some may engage in oral sex because they believe (correctly) that this is a lower pregnancy risk sexual activity. Others may engage in oral sex over intercourse as an STI risk reduction activity (which is what sex educators have been espousing since the beginning of the HIV/AIDS era). According to a representative poll of teens aged 13–16 years conducted by Princeton Survey Research Associates International in 2004 (http://www.msnbc.msn.com/id/6839072), the major reasons for engaging in oral sex included because the other person wanted to have oral sex, because the teen had met the right person, and because the teen wanted to satisfy a sexual desire. Other, less important, reasons for engaging in oral sex included pregnancy prevention, curiosity, and remaining a virgin (i.e., treating oral sex as a form of abstinence).

Some theorists and thinkers in this area are concerned that the oral sex phenomenon is gender biased (e.g., Tolman, interviewed in Remez, 2000). The idea of the "rainbow party" does tend to support this contention—that it is girls fellating boys rather than boys performing cunnilingus. Research by Boekeloo and Howard (2002) suggests that heterosexual oral-sexually active boys and girls are not experiencing a disparity in receiving and giving oral sex. In their sample of 12–15 year olds who were surveyed in their physician's office, 17 percent of boys and 20 percent of girls had engaged in oral sex (giving and/or receiving).

Another concern that has been raised about the practice of oral sex by teens is that this sexual behavior is treated cavalierly, which may impede intimate relationships in the future—a point raised in the Jayson selection. A study by Halpern-Felsher et al. (2005) found that teens had a more permissive attitude toward casual oral sex than they did toward casual intercourse. However, it is noteworthy that the teens in this study disagreed with both casual oral sex and casual vaginal intercourse as permissible; they simply disagreed *more* strongly with casual vaginal intercourse.

Participation in oral sexual activities by teens is not well understood and has not been well researched. Some camps argue that this is a serious problem, an epidemic that adults must address as a serious concern. Other parties approach the teen oral sex issue as an opportunity to further the sex education of teens. Both sides agree that more conversations between adults and teens about sexuality will be beneficial for the teens.

References/Further Readings

Barrett, A. (2004). Oral sex and teenagers: A sexual health educator's perspective. *Canadian Journal of Human Sexuality,* 13(3–4), 197–200.

Boekelloo, B., & Howard, D. (2002). Oral sexual experience among young adolescents receiving general health, examinations. *American Journal of Health Behavior,* 26, 306–314.

Boyce, W., Doherty, M., Fortin, C., & MacKinnon, D. (2003). *Canadian Youth, Sexual Health & HIV/AIDS Study: Factors Influencing Knowledge, Attitudes and Behaviours.* Toronto: Council of Ministers of Education, Canada.

Halpern-Felsher, B., Cornell, J., Kropp, R., & Tschann, J. (2005). Oral versus vaginal sex among adolescents: Perceptions, attitudes, and behavior. *Pediatrics,* 115(4), 845–851.

King, A., Beazley, R., Warren, W., Hankins, C., Robertson, A., & Radford, J. (1988). *Canada Youth and AIDS Study.* Kingston, ON: Queen's University.

Mosher, W., Chandra, A., & Jones, J. (2005). Sexual behavior and selected health measures: Men and women 15–44 years of age, United States, 2002. Centers for Disease Control and Prevention. National Center for Health Statistics. *Vital and Health Statistics,* 362, 1–22.

Prinstein, M., Meade, C., & Cohen, G. (2003). Adolescent oral sex, peer popularity, and perceptions of best friends' sexual behavior. *Journal of Pediatric Psychology,* 28(4), 243–249.

Remez, L. (2000). Special report: Oral sex among adolescents: Is it sex or is it abstinence? *Family Planning Perspectives,* 32(6), 298–304.

Ruditis, P. (2005). *Rainbow Party.* New York: Simon and Schuster.

ISSUE 9

Is Comprehensive Sex Education for Adolescents Too Liberal?

YES: Aida Orgocka, from "Perceptions of Communication and Education About Sexuality Among Muslim Immigrant Girls in the US," *Sex Education* (October 2004)

NO: John Santelli et al., from "Abstinence and Abstinence-Only Education: A Review of U.S. Policies and Programs," *Journal of Adolescent Health* (vol. 38, 2006)

ISSUE SUMMARY

YES: Aida Orgocka, a gender and development expert at the University of Illinois, presents a qualitative study of Illinois mothers' and daughters' perceptions of the sexual health school curriculum from a Muslim perspective. The participants tended to find the sex education curriculum at odds with Muslim values such that many of the girls opted to forgo the school-based sexual health classes.

NO: John Santelli, a professor of clinical population, family health, and clinical pediatrics at the Mailman School of Public Health in Columbia University, and colleagues review current U.S. policies encouraging abstinence-only sexual health education and discuss the potential negative impact and ethical considerations arising from these policies on adolescent sexual practices.

$\mathbf{I}$n recent years, the U.S. federal government has substantially increased funding for abstinence-based education while simultaneously placing more restrictions on what other sexual health topics are covered by this funding. If a sex education curriculum discusses other options (e.g., the benefits of using condoms or other forms of birth control), the program would not be eligible for funding under these policies and programs. While sex educators agree that abstinence is the most effective means of preventing pregnancy, sexually transmitted infections (STIs), and HIV/AIDS, they acknowledge that a substantial proportion of youth engage in sexual activity during their teen years and that much of this occurs prior to marriage. Thus, sex educators tend to promote the use of comprehensive sex education curricula; this is sometimes called "abstinence plus." That is, abstinence is a part of the curriculum, but discussion of what methods students can use to prevent STIs and pregnancy *if* they become or are sexually active are also presented.

Sex education researchers conclude that comprehensive sexuality education programs sometimes have no impact on students' sexual behavior. However, when these programs do have an effect, research tends to find that participants are more likely to postpone first sexual intercourse to a later date, reduce frequency of intercourse and the number of sexual partners, increase contraceptive use, and have a lower teen pregnancy rate (Kirby, 2001, 2007). Thus, when comprehensive sex education programs have an effect, it is in the desirable direction.

In contrast, there has been little empirical evidence to support the efficacy of abstinence-only programs (Hauser, 2004). Also, the Waxman Report (December 2004), prepared for the U.S. House of Representative Committee on Government Reform, investigated 13 commonly used abstinence-only sexual health education curricula and concluded that 11 out of 13 programs contained unproven claims, subjective conclusions, or factual inaccuracies.

Advocates of abstinence-only programs come from a more morally based viewpoint. One of their arguments is that North American societies are pluralistic, and different perspectives may not be represented in the relatively more permissive sexuality education programs (i.e., comprehensive sex education curricula). Abstinence-only proponents fear that moral ideologies informing sexuality ideologies might be discounted by the more liberal curricula. For example, if the dominant sex education culture within a school curriculum endorses behaviors such as oral sex and masturbation as acceptable, this may be at odds with the moral and sexual teachings of a particular religious group. Thus, the sex education curriculum is seen as contradicting the particular religious value system and might be characterized as attempting to "indoctrinate" students into accepting an ideological system contravening the ideologies taught at home. In particular, Muslim students and parents often find the sex education curriculum dominated by Judeo-Christian ideology and values that are often deemed as culturally inappropriate (see Sanjakdar, 2004).

Santelli and colleagues present an analysis of abstinence and abstinence-only education policies in the United States. They present a variety of health-based reasons as to why comprehensive sex education—including abstinence discussions—is preferable to abstinence-only initiatives. They discuss the ethics of abstinence-only programs: (1) that abstinence-only violates students' rights to accurate sexual health information; (2) that they hold sexual minority (e.g., gay) students to a higher standard than heterosexual students; and (3) that they violate free choice and informed consent principles. Orgocka represents a somewhat opposing viewpoint by presenting a study of Muslim mothers and daughters who find that North American sex education is ideologically incompatible with their religious teachings regarding sexuality. As a result, these students may feel marginalized, and many elect to opt out of the school-based sex education.

YES

Aida Orgocka

Perceptions of Communication and Education About Sexuality Among Muslim Immigrant Girls in the U.S.

Introduction

For the past three decades, issues of sexuality education for adolescents have occupied the agendas of researchers and policy makers alike. And although one in five children in the US live in an immigrant-headed household, we know surprisingly little about the challenges these youths face in obtaining information about sexuality, including biological reproduction, sexual intercourse, and sexual pleasure. This is particularly so for young immigrant girls who, through their sexual behavior, bear the brunt of maintaining family honor and ethnic and religious integrity. Parental perceptions that knowledge about sexuality leads to promiscuous sexual activity create obstacles for young immigrant girls wanting to obtain information about reproductive health.

This . . . study [investigated] how the interaction between Muslim immigrant mothers and their daughters shaped the daughters' agency in negotiating decisions about sexual conduct. It examines sexuality communication and education among Muslim immigrant girls in the US as mediated by their mothers and school-based sexuality education (SBSE) classes.

Exploring the link between these two channels of information is particularly interesting if not essential. Among Muslims, parents are a main source for teaching youths about sexuality and moral values regarding sexual conduct. Because education about sexuality is gender segregated, mothers teach their daughters, and fathers teach their sons. For Muslim immigrant families, in particular, educating activities at home are considered a necessity to counter the dominant information children receive at school, through their peers and the media. Because Muslim mothers are considered responsible for girls' sexual conduct, discussion of issues related to sexuality takes the form of moral interdiction and limits on outside influences, including SBSE programs.

From *Sex Education*, vol. 4, no. 3, October 2004, pp. 255–271. Copyright © 2004 by Taylor & Francis, Ltd. Reprinted by permission via Rightslink.

Among religious Muslims, learning about sex in the school curriculum is viewed as part of a belief system that condones premarital sexuality rather than as a subject in the school curriculum. Although SBSE programs provide useful information regarding sexual health, skill-building and independent decision-making information pertaining to sexual conduct, they may be perceived as propagating information that contradicts what youths are taught at home. Giving youths the tools to have 'safe' premarital sex is contrary to Islam and Muslim code of behavior. Parents perceive that these classes particularly challenge transmission of Islamic values to young girls by teaching them to conceptualize decision-making regarding sexual conduct as a personal rather than a family matter. As a result, most Muslim immigrant parents object to their children participating in SBSE classes. Some mothers may favor sending girls to SBSE classes, but all feel particularly responsible for countering information that challenges the moral values learnt at home.

Because sexuality education for Muslim families is closely connected to heterosexual partnership and marriage, the study's assumption was that girls participating in this research were heterosexual and would eventually marry. Focus group and individual semi-structured interviews were used to explore [the question,] What are the perceptions of mothers and daughters regarding school-based sexuality education classes?

Methods

Participants

Thirty mothers (mean age = 43.17 . . .) and their 38 daughters (mean age = 16.59, . . .) were recruited through snowball sampling techniques and by frequently visiting the local mosques and Islamic centers in Illinois. Over 83% of the mothers had been in the US for more than 10 years. About 47% had received a college education and about 53% were homemakers. All mothers were married. Daughters were predominantly US born (76%) with the rest having migrated with their parents when they were very young (24%). One attended middle school and another was home schooled (6%), 71% attended high school (53% in local public high schools and 47% local private high schools), and 23% attended college. Praying was central to most mothers and daughters. Seventy-seven per cent of the mothers and 68% of the daughters prayed at least three times a day. More mothers than daughters wore *hijab* (veil) (63% vs. 32%). Both mothers and daughters engaged in other aspects of being Muslim including wearing modest clothing, reading the *Qur'an,* and participating in activities of Muslim community. In addition to extended family, schools, and individual reading and exploration, both mothers and daughters identified their parents as important sources of Muslim education.

Data Collection Strategies

. . . The main body of data for this paper is based on focus groups and semi-structured interviews. In addition to helping elicit sensitive and rich contextual information, these were considered as empowering strategies that allowed Muslim mothers and daughters to express and reflect upon their own personal perspectives. . . . [The] wording of questions was kept almost the same for both mothers and daughters.

Focus groups were used to gain research insights and increase understanding of group perspectives on communication and education about sexuality. They also served as a preliminary tool to help develop the semi-structured guide for the individual interviews that were conducted afterwards. . . . To gauge their perceptions about SBSE classes, both mothers and daughters initially rated how often girls should attend SBSE classes on a five point scale of '1 = never' to '5 = always', and then were asked to elaborate on the answer.

Procedure

. . . Four group discussions with the mothers and six group discussions with the daughters were conducted separately in English. Up to five participants participated in each group. They were homogeneously grouped in terms of socio-economic status, age, marital status, place of residence, religiousness, country of origin and length of stay in the USA (especially for the mothers). . . .

The individual semi-structured interviews were also conducted separately with each of the mothers and daughters in English. For those few participants who were not fluent in English, at their request, a key informant who was fluent in Arabic and English attended the interview sessions. In a few other instances the mothers requested that their daughters be part of the interview process to translate for them in case they did not understand. . . .

The recorded material was transcribed *verbatim*. The analysis focused on representing mothers' and daughters' perceptions through their accounts. . . . Codes were oriented toward participants' understandings of communication with each other, as well as their perceptions of SBSE classes. . . . Upon coding, I identified the themes that permeated the group discussions and the interviews. . . .

[In] this study I looked for convergence in emergent themes across a sample of group discussions rather than across participants within a group. Perspectives of individual mothers and daughters were the focus of analysis in the interview material. The expectation for this part of the analysis was that both mothers and daughters would see communication and education about sexuality differently due to different immigration, age and education experiences.

Results

Perceptions of School-Based Sexuality Education

[More] daughters [29%] than mothers [3%] were of the opinion that they should 'rarely' attend SBSE classes. In addition, more mothers [30%] than daughters [11%] agreed that daughters should 'always' attend these SBSE classes. Group discussions and individual interviews shed light on some of the reasons for these answers.

Mothers' perceptions.   A common concern for mothers was that the dominant socio-cultural environment was very suggestive and conductive to unregulated and unrestricted sexual activity. In the mothers' words, 'unbridled sexuality' is so pervasive in the US that they 'can't even realize it,' 'the ads, kissing, hugging, whatever you call it, sex.' Given this socio-cultural environment, mothers often commented that their daughters should attend SBSE classes to obtain the 'correct information.' While they did not approve whole-heartedly of their daughters' participation in SBSE classes because they thought the family should provide the sexuality education, mothers were concerned that the alternative source of information could be their daughters' peers whose knowledge, in their opinion, was usually cloaked in misinformation and age-related curiosity:

> I would rather them know that in a clinical manner than what they hear in the hallways. I personally would not like the school to play any role in sex education at all, but I know realistically that the people she is around are sexually active, some as early as the age of eight. I don't want her to be totally ignorant of what's going on, and unfortunately because of the society we live in she needs to be aware.

Some mothers agreed that SBSE classes provided important information, especially when this information was worded in a technical and scientific fashion. Mothers reported that sexuality education facilitated information that they otherwise would not have been able to give because they were never given such information and they did not have the proper knowledge and skills to discuss these issues. A mother recalled that 'even when I was having a baby, I didn't know what was happening to me, and my husband didn't know anything either.' Other mothers thought that it was useful that SBSE classes focused on the diseases that resulted from unprotected sex because 'if she [knows] and if she [learns] in school, she will not do it.'

Despite the usefulness of SBSE classes, mothers perceived that some of the contents of the classes were problematic. Mothers perceived that these classes, by discussing dating and premarital sexual relations, encouraged a lifestyle that was un-Islamic. Pointing to this concern, some of the mothers did not consent to their daughters attending sexuality education classes.

> She doesn't have to take a sex class. I didn't take any sex class and I am fine. So it is a natural thing, you catch up with the stuff . . . I still remember one of my friends, her kids, in school they teach about sex in fifth grade and I heard that her daughter came and told her mom they showed something about banana and how to give oral sex and stuff. I don't want them to know all that . . . Like the next thing they will say is 'OK, mom, I want to take a class where they can teach you different positions!' I don't want that.

Mothers also reported that the means through which sexuality information was shared was inappropriate. Mothers objected to the use of videos as didactic materials on account that showing these videos could lead to girls wanting to experiment with sex.

That mothers perceived SBSE classes to be pushing an un-Islamic lifestyle was a main motivator for mothers to counter the information that was given in these classes. A few mothers reported that they sat in the classes to ascertain that the material was 'decent.' They also engaged in additional conversations with their teenage daughters and countered material presented in SBSE classes with Islamic views on premarital sexuality.

Daughters' perceptions. Daughters echoed the mothers' concern that in the environment they live in 'whether you want it or not you get all the information about sex.' They learnt about sex in public school, on the street, through friends—both female and male—who carried condoms in their pockets and bragged that they were 'cool' because 'they are not virgin.' While the girls did not intend to engage in premarital sex, they agreed that SBSE classes provided them with information that they could use in the future. Rather than battle with the changes in their bodies, they learned to understand and interpret these changes. Furthermore, these classes taught girls how to deal with any consequences that came from surprise situations such as attacks from a sex offender.

A few girls reported that SBSE classes, by being informative, helped them challenge the value-laden information they received at home. Bringing a book home helped daughters facilitate a more open discussion with mothers who attempted to teach about sex and sexuality through scare tactics.

> You get some good information in these classes. All my mother would tell me, she would tell me like myths . . . hypothetical things, things that old ladies from generation to generation will tell her. Like 'Mom, that's not even true!' Like women born without a hymen . . . I told my mom, 'The nurses came in and they showed us how to put on the condom.' And she was like, 'Why are they teaching you how to do that?' Like 'Because there's girls that are already doing that mom!' She doesn't realize.

Despite the usefulness of these classes, some girls, like their mothers, perceived that some of the contents of the classes were problematic. A few girls perceived that SBSE classes were not sensitive to the religious and cultural differences of students attending those classes. By concentrating on students who planned to be involved in sexual activities before graduating from high school, these classes marginalized the experiences of those students that did not intend to involve in such activities:

> Maybe a sex education class should take into account that not everybody sitting there and watching the videos cares nothing about them. I think it was mostly geared towards Americans, maybe the Christian

point of view, and not take into account some people don't like to talk about it and don't know much about it. The levels of experience are different. But it was a kind of shock when I first had it, 'cause my parents didn't tell me. Most of my peers knew almost everything . . . They don't think it was a big deal and I did.

SBSE classes that discussed sexual relationships, also covered the consequences of unprotected sexual intercourse. However, girls perceived that these classes focused more than was necessary on warnings about diseases, infections and teenage pregnancy. Since Muslim girls participating in this study did not intend to engage in premarital sex, they found the material not only irrelevant but also distasteful. Three girls in the study defined sex as 'sick' and 'disgusting' and more had decided to not take SBSE classes.

Some girls suggested that the SBSE classes would be more useful if they were taught in gender-segregated classes. These would allow both male and female students to ask questions and not feel embarrassed because the other sex was present. SBSE classes had to also be age appropriate. Invariably, daughters recalled that they felt uncomfortable when their classmates giggled at the information being presented in class.

In the end, it is important to point out yet another observation. Muslim immigrant mothers and daughters participating in the study were not against sexuality education in principle. A few girls considered learning about sex and sexuality as part of their duty of being Muslim women. Learning about sex within the framework of Islam was for them, first and foremost, a religious requirement. An 18-year-old girl expressed this succinctly when she commented that 'as a Muslim, I should not be ashamed to discuss sex, or marriage, or issues of menstruation or anything, because we have the religious obligation to know this.'

Discussion

While the findings discussed here are restricted only to the researched group of Muslim immigrant mothers and daughters, themes may be extrapolated for work with Muslim and non-Muslim immigrant youth and their parents. Discussion of the study results focuses on [these] areas: . . . [a] sensitizing SBSE programs to the diversity of US populations; [b] implications for cooperation between parents and schools; and [c] implications for involvement of the community in youth's sexuality education. . . .

Sensitizing School-Based Sexuality Education

A good majority of the girls that had or were currently attending SBSE classes agreed that these classes were informative, especially when focusing on the anatomy of the female body. Topics such as body changes associated with biological maturity and menstruation were well explained. In fact, obtaining this information facilitated communication about sexuality between mothers and daughters and helped girls frame sexuality education as necessary within a larger perspective of premarital teenage pregnancy. Some mothers agreed that these classes were helpful to the daughters, since they did not have the scientific knowledge or the skills to talk to their daughters about sexuality. In fact, they indicated that as long as the SBSE classes were restricted to providing technical information through books they did not object.

While the SBSE classes provided useful information, some mothers had withdrawn their daughters from SBSE classes and some girls themselves did not express interest in attending these classes. Both mothers and daughters were dissatisfied with some of the contents and the way the classes were conducted. The majority of the girls that had attended SBSE classes perceived these classes to provide information in such a way that the choice to engage in sex was predetermined or assumed. As such, Muslim girls felt that these classes marginalized their experiences and decision to abstain from premarital sexual relationships. In fact, a few girls considered classes taught in this way a waste of time and energy. Mothers echoed these concerns and either prevented girls from attending these classes, or provided supplementary information within the Islamic framework to distance girls from experiences that these classes portrayed as normative for adolescents.

The other major dissatisfaction was that SBSE classes at times were a long series of warnings and diseases that came from unprotected sex. Muslim girls found unappealing such conceptualization of classes, and a few of them thought that they would engage in sex out of necessity to have babies only. Furthermore, both mothers and daughters agreed that most of this information was imparted at too early an age for girls. That some mothers and daughters disapproved of placing too much emphasis on unplanned pregnancies and sexually transmitted infections and diseases does not imply that SBSE classes should not cover these topics. The high rate of adolescent pregnancies and STDs makes imparting such information necessary. Furthermore, even if a person only has one partner, that partner may have had other experiences and that makes knowing the signs of an STI or STD imperative. However, it is possible that because these classes may have overemphasized the risks that came from unprotected sexual intercourse, they may have failed to describe sexuality as an integral part of developmental experience.

The objections mentioned here are not unique to Muslim immigrant populations. Aarons and Jenkins (2002) reported that Latino and African-American youth preferred clinics to schools for sex education and related services because the latter did not fit the reality of youths' lives. Ward and Taylor (1994) found that immigrant and minority youths perceived that SBSE classes failed to incorporate the reality that emotions related to sexuality are framed by cultural values and beliefs, that instructors were insensitive to youths' experiences and made assumptions about these youths based upon cultural stereotypes. While these findings may be skewed because only the perceptions of immigrant youths are reported, they suggest that sex educators face a challenging task in accomplishing the goal of reaching the diverse youths of America.

Fostering Collaboration Between Parents and Schools

Findings indicated that mothers were open to schools helping with education about sexuality. Most had reviewed and signed permission slips required for girls' participation in SBSE classes. Few took the initiative to reach out to schools and review the materials presented in these classes. That overwhelmingly mothers perceived that SBSE classes challenged the values imparted at home may evidence that mothers had a limited understanding of the contents and the manner in which information regarding sexuality was imparted in these classes.

To be sure, mothers play an active role in sexuality education and schools may help bridge the education experiences at home and school for immigrant youths. Sexuality educators may want to borrow from the experience of projects that address issues of achievement and English proficiency for immigrant youths. For example, Pecoraro and Magnuson (2001) suggest, among other strategies, that in order to better involve parents in school efforts to teach immigrant youths, schools need to build on what people already know from their experiences as parents and teachers in their home countries and create opportunities for parents to explore similarities and differences between new and native countries and to build bridges that will link the two experiences. Helping parents actively participate in the design of the sexuality education curricula as well as organizing classes for these parents may be two strategies for bringing parents closer to school and thus acquitting SBSE classes often perceived as challenging the transmission of family values.

Implications for Involvement of the Muslim Community

Muslim immigrant girls may have little knowledge about sexuality and may often be unprepared to deal with issues regarding sexuality and reproductive health. That girls may not be able to get information about sexuality through communication with mothers and/or sexuality education classes requires an exploration of other information venues. Two additional sources of information for Muslim girls and their parents could be registering/attending Islamic private schools and using resources offered by Islamic centers. Islamic schools shape their curricula within the parameters of Islam. Sexuality education is part of these curricula. A few girls in the study attended local private Islamic schools. They related that the classes were sex segregated and the curriculum was tailored to the students' ages. For example, actual explanations of intercourse within the framework of marriage were given to girls at the age of 17, the assumption being that these girls would soon marry. Although Islamic private schools address concerns of Muslim communities, only a fraction of Muslim families can afford to enroll their daughters in these schools.

Because most students attend public schools, the weight of supplementary sexuality education rests with the Islamic centers that overwhelmingly provide alternative education through Sunday schools. However, informal conversations with a few of the study's key informants suggested that no curriculum is in place to educate the young girls on issues of sexuality and marriage or to help parents discuss these issues. Islamic centers with such curricula have the potential to help both youth and their parents talk and learn about sexuality. Apart from brochures and booklets, these centers may help mothers become better sexuality educators by providing them with the information and skills necessary to talk not only about the technicalities but also the cognitive and affective dimensions of sexuality. Evaluation research on community efforts among other populations has shown that parent-training programs can significantly increase parents' knowledge and frequency of communicating with their adolescent children.

Islamic centers' efforts to serve Muslim youths have to be coupled with finding ways to attract these youths to their programs. About 40% of the girls participating in the study felt that they did not receive any information at the local Islamic center. Of the 50% who reported that they received information regarding women's duties and responsibilities at the Center, 30% were of the opinion that they received some instruction on how a woman dresses and behaves. Only 3% said they received information on spousal relationships. This is consistent with findings from other research that shows that one of the major complaints is that most Islamic centers just teach the *Qur'an,* but not about life or social values (Husain & O'Brien, 1999).

To attract more girls, Islamic centers may work with primarily non-governmental organizations (NGOs) that have gained experience from tackling issues of sexuality education. For example, Girls Incorporated, a nationally recognized NGO, has developed age-appropriate curricula (Preventing Adolescent Pregnancy) that help girls aged 9–18 and their parents deal with issues of learning about sexuality and making decisions accordingly. A three-year evaluation found that girls who had attended this program regularly were half as likely to have sex as girls who had participated less or not at all in the program. While not everything presented in this program has relevance for Muslim immigrant girls it should be borne in mind that these girls live in the US and are exposed to sexuality-related issues with the same intensity as their non-Muslim peers. Programs developed by Girls Incorporated can throw in relief concerns about how contemporary information about sexuality should be. Because such programs are well-versed in the challenges that US girls face regarding dealing with their own sexuality, they may be combined with Islamic tenets and be used to design curricula and didactic materials (brochures, videos) that provide supplementary information for young Muslim girls.

Future Directions

While this study focused on Muslim immigrant girls and their mothers, research also needs to target how Muslim immigrant adolescent boys obtain information regarding sexuality. Research shows that Muslim adolescent males may be more sexually active than Muslim adolescent females (Kulwicki, 1989). Therefore, learning about sexuality is an imperative for better sexual and reproductive health for them, too. Moreover, although fathers are supposed to serve as conduits of information regarding sexuality, they may play this role minimally. Research with other populations has shown that this task is particularly daunting for fathers since talking about sexuality requires establishing an intimate bond and that challenges the principles of traditional masculinity (Kirkman et al., 2001). These remarks warrant the importance of future studies in the field of understanding sexuality communication and education among immigrant male youths.

This research is not intended as a critique and/or evaluation of any particular sexuality education program. Its findings are based on perceptions of mothers and daughters and should be interpreted cautiously and not serve to dismiss the usefulness of SBSE classes. Worldwide, these programs aim to prevent and/or lower teenage pregnancy, inform about and reduce the chances of infection with STDs including HIV/AIDS, teach about the relationships between the sexes, provide an ethical framework for the expression of sexuality, and provide examples of healthy lifestyles, including a discussion of marriage relationships. These programs address biological, socio-cultural, psychological and spiritual dimensions of sexuality. Thus, it is imperative that the perceptions of educators and policy analysts should be taken into consideration.

Conclusion

This research explored Muslim immigrant girls' communication and education about sexuality as mediated by their mothers and SBSE classes. . . . The study . . . found that while SBSE classes were informative to girls, in participants' perceptions they marginalized Muslim immigrants girls' decisions and experiences to not engage in premarital sex by assuming that most adolescents engage in sex. This study's recommendation is that in order for SBSE programs to be effective they need to be characterized by cultural sensitivity to the diverse youth that need to obtain this information. Although SBSE may be attempting to address the various needs of immigrant youths, findings indicated that they have not yet adequately reached the Muslim community. Findings also showed that mothers and daughters were more open to sexuality education than indicated in the literature. Thus, further dialogue between schools and parents could be useful. Although surveying Islamic community efforts in educating young Muslim girls and their mothers was not part of this study, the limited sexuality-related knowledge girls received from communicating with their mothers and SBSE classes suggests that Islamic centers may be a potential venue through which girls and their mothers may obtain information about sexuality within the Islamic framework.

References

Aarons, S. J. & Jenkins, R. R. (2002) Sex, pregnancy, and contraception-related motivators and barriers among Latino and African-American youth in Washington, DC, *Sex Education*, 2, 5–30.

Husain, F. & O'Brien, M. (1999) *Muslim families in Europe: social existence and social care* (London, University of North London).

Kirkman, M., Rosenthal, D. A. & Feldman, S. S. (2001) Freeing up the subject: tension between traditional masculinity and involved fatherhood through communication about sexuality with adolescents, *Culture, Health & Sexuality*, 3, 391–411.

Kulwicki, A. (1989) *Adolescent health needs assessment survey: executive summary* (Office of Minority Health, Michigan Department of Public Health).

Pecoraro, D. & Magnuson, P. (Eds) (2001) *LEP parent involvement: a guide for connecting immigrant parents and schools* (St. Paul, MN, Minnesota State Department of Children, Families and Learning).

Ward, J. V. & Taylor, J. M. (1994) Sexuality education for immigrant and minority students: developing a culturally appropriate curriculum, in: J. M. Irvine (Ed.) *Sexual cultures and the construction of adolescent identities* (Philadelphia, PA, Temple University Press).

Abstinence and Abstinence-Only Education: A Review of U.S. Policies and Programs

This [paper] reviews key issues related to understanding and evaluating abstinence-only (AOE) or abstinence-until-marriage policies. We use the term AOE programs and policies to describe those that adhere to federal requirements (Table 1). We begin with background information on definitions of abstinence, initiation of sexual intercourse and marriage, physical and psychological health outcomes from these behaviors, and public support for abstinence and comprehensive sexuality education. Next, we review current federal policy and evaluations of abstinence education, including approaches to program evaluation and concepts of efficacy in preventing pregnancy and sexually transmitted infections (STIs). We then turn to the impact of AOE on other programs and the implications of AOE for specific

Table 1

Federal Definition of Abstinence-Only Education

Under Section 510 of the 1996 Social Security Act abstinence education is defined as an educational or motivational program which:

(A) has as its exclusive purpose, teaching the social, psychological, and health gains to be realized by abstaining from sexual activity

(B) teaches abstinence from sexual activity outside marriage as the expected standard for all school-age children

(C) teaches that abstinence from sexual activity is the only certain way to avoid out-of-wedlock pregnancy, sexually transmitted diseases, and other associated health problems

(D) teaches that a mutually faithful monogamous relationship in the context of marriage is the expected standard of human sexual activity

(E) teaches that sexual activity outside of the context of marriage is likely to have harmful psychological and physical effects

(F) teaches that bearing children out-of-wedlock is likely to have harmful consequences for the child, the child's parents, and society

(G) teaches young people how to reject sexual advances and how alcohol and drug use increases vulnerability to sexual advances

(H) teaches the importance of attaining self-sufficiency before engaging in sexual activity

populations such as youth who are sexually active (i.e., currently engaging in intercourse) and gay, lesbian bisexual, transgender, and questioning (GLBTQ) youth. Finally, we explore critical human rights issues raised by AOE, including the right to health information and the ethical obligations of health care providers and health educators. . . .

Definitions of Abstinence

Abstinence, as the term is used by program planners and policymakers, is often not clearly defined. Abstinence may be defined in behavioral terms, such as "postponing sex" or "never had vaginal sex," or refraining from further sexual intercourse if sexually experienced, i.e., ever had sexual intercourse. Other sexual behaviors may or may not be considered within the definition of "abstinence," including touching, kissing, mutual masturbation, oral sex, and anal sex. Self-identified "virgins" engage in a variety of non-coital genital activities. Sexual behavior among adolescents is often sporadic, and "secondary abstinence" is common.

Abstinence, as used in government policies and local programs, is also frequently defined in moral terms, using language such as "chaste" or "virgin" and framing abstinence as an attitude or a commitment. One study of abstinence-only program directors, instructors, and youth found that all groups defined abstinence in moral terms, such as "making a commitment" and "being responsible," as well as in more behavioral terms, such as not engaging in coitus.[1] Federal regulations for domestic AOE funding also adopt a moral and culturally specific definition of abstinence, requiring that abstinence education "teaches that a mutually faithful monogamous relationship in context of marriage is the expected standard of human sexual activity."

In understanding the ongoing debates about abstinence education, it is important to understand that although health professionals generally view abstinence as a behavioral issue or as a health issue, many advocates of AOE programs are primarily concerned with issues such as character and morality, based on their specific religious or moral beliefs. In this review, we have defined abstinence as abstinence from sexual intercourse and focused on abstinence as a public health issue, recognizing that many people view abstinence as a moral or religious issue.

Initiation of Sexual Intercourse and Marriage

Although abstinence until marriage is the goal of many abstinence policies and programs, few Americans wait until marriage to initiate sexual intercourse. Most Americans initiate sexual intercourse during their adolescent years. Recent data indicate that the median age at first intercourse for women was 17.4 years, whereas the median age at first marriage was 25.3 years. . . .

[Health] Outcomes for Adolescent Sexual Behaviors

Initiation of sexual intercourse in adolescence is accompanied by considerable risk of STIs and pregnancy. Adolescents have the highest age-specific risk for many STIs, and the highest age-specific proportion of unintended pregnancy in the United States. . . . Long-term sequelae of STIs can include infertility, tubal pregnancy, fetal and infant demise, chronic pelvic pain, and cervical cancer. A significant proportion of human immunodeficiency virus (HIV) infections appear to be acquired during adolescence. . . .

Although federal AOE funding language requires teaching that sexual activity outside of the context of marriage is likely to have harmful psychological effects, there are no scientific data suggesting that consensual sex between adolescents is harmful. . . . We are aware of no reports that address whether the initiation of adolescent sexual intercourse itself has an adverse impact on mental health. We also know little about whether purposively remaining abstinent until marriage promotes personal resiliency or sexual function or dysfunction in adulthood. . . .

Public Support for Abstinence and Comprehensive Sexuality Education

Public opinion polls suggest strong support for abstinence as a behavioral goal for adolescents.[2-3] These polls also indicate strong support for education about contraception and for access to contraception for sexually active adolescents.

Data from a recent nationwide poll of middle school and high school parents found overwhelming support for sex education in school; 90% believed it was very or somewhat important that sex education be taught in school, whereas 7% of parents did not want sex education to be taught.[3] Only 15% wanted an abstinence-only form of sex education. Parents thought it was appropriate to provide high school and middle school youth with broad information on sexual issues. . . . In these polls, most parents and most adolescents do not see education that stresses abstinence while also providing information about contraception as a mixed message.[2-3]

Current Federal Policy and Local Programs

Although the federal government began supporting abstinence promotion programs in 1981 via the Adolescent Family Life Act (AFLA), since 1996 there have been major expansions in federal support for abstinence programming and a shift to funding programs that teach only abstinence and restrict other information. These expansions include Section 510 of the Social Security Act in 1996, which was part of welfare reform, and Community-Based Abstinence Education projects in 2000, funded through an earmark in the maternal child health block grant for Special Projects of Regional and National Significance (SPRANS) program. The SPRANS program bypasses the 510 program's state approval processes and makes grants directly to community-based organizations. Eligible applicants include faith-based organizations. Both 510 and SPRANS programs prohibit disseminating information on contraceptive services, sexual orientation and gender identity, and other aspects of human sexuality. Section 510 provides an eight-point definition of abstinence-only education (Table 1) and specifies that programs must have as their "exclusive purpose" the promotion of abstinence outside of marriage and may not in any way advocate contraceptive use or discuss contraceptive methods except to emphasize their failure rates.

Since fiscal year (FY) 1997, programs funded under the AFLA have been required to comply with these Section 510 requirements. The initial implementation of 510 has allowed funded programs to emphasize different aspects of these eight points as long as the program did not contradict any of them. The Congressional intent of the SPRANS program was more rigid: to create "pure" abstinence-only programs, in response to concerns that states were using funds for "soft" activities such as media campaigns instead of direct classroom instruction and were targeting younger adolescents. Programs funded under SPRANS must teach all eight components of the federal definition, they must target 12–18-year-olds, and, except in limited circumstances, they cannot provide young people they serve with information about contraception or safer-sex practices, even with their own non-federal funds. Three states, including, most recently, Maine, have refused federal AOE funding given federal restrictions on providing information about contraception.

Federal funding for abstinence-only programs has increased from $60 million in FY 1998 to $168 million in FY 2005. Section 510 requires funded states to match three state dollars for every four federal dollars. Virtually all the growth in funding since FY 2001 (to $105 million in FY 2005) has come in the SPRANS program. In 2004, the administration of the 510 program and SPRANS program was moved administratively within the Department of Health and Human Services (DHHS), from the health-focused Maternal and Child Health Bureau (MCHB) to the Administration of Children and Families, the federal agency that promotes marriage and responsible fatherhood, reportedly in order "to enhance and coordinate similar youth programs within HHS." This move may also have reflected some Congressional dissatisfaction with MCHB's flexible implementation of the program.

Evaluations of Abstinence-Only Education and Comprehensive Sexuality Education Programs in Promoting Abstinence

To demonstrate efficacy, evaluations of specific abstinence promotion programs must address methodological issues including (1) clear definitions of abstinence. . . , (2) appropriate research design, (3) measurement issues including social desirability bias, and (4) the use of behavior changes as outcomes. Evaluations should also consider the use of biological outcomes such as STIs, in addition to behavioral measures. Experimental and quasi-experimental research designs can be used to avoid self-selection bias and to isolate program effect from changes in the individual due to increasing age or maturation. Biological outcomes such as STI incidence or prevalence may significantly improve the validity of program evaluations.

Two recent systematic reviews examined the evidence supporting abstinence-only programs and comprehensive sexuality education programs designed to promote abstinence from sexual intercourse.[4–5] These reviews employed similar scientific criteria in selecting studies for evaluation. Program evaluations had to have been conducted since 1980, conducted in the United States or Canada, targeted teens under age 18, used an experimental or quasi-experimental design, and measured behavioral effects such as timing of first intercourse. Kirby also included studies that measured impact on pregnancy or childbearing but did not measure sexual behavior.

Both reviews demonstrated that comprehensive sexuality education effectively promoted abstinence as well as other protective behaviors. Among 28 studies of comprehensive programs evaluated in the Kirby review, nine were able to delay initiation of sexual intercourse, 18 showed no impact, and one hastened initiation of sex. Manlove et al. identified three different types of comprehensive sexuality programs, and found that six of nine sex education programs delayed the onset of sex, compared with a control group, five of seven HIV/STI prevention programs delayed the onset of sex, and all four youth development programs delayed the onset of sex.

In contrast to the positive impact in delaying sexual intercourse seen with some comprehensive sexuality programs, Kirby found no scientific evidence that abstinence-only programs demonstrate efficacy in delaying initiation of sexual intercourse. Kirby found only three studies evaluating the impact of five different abstinence-only curricula that met minimal criteria for inclusion in the systematic review. No new study results have changed this conclusion (personal communication with Doug Kirby, November 2004). The more recent (2004) review by Manlove, reviewing many of the same studies, reached similar conclusions. Both Manlove and Kirby identified the lack of rigorously evaluated programs as a major problem in evaluating the effectiveness of abstinence-only education.

Non-peer-reviewed studies provide little support for the current federal support for abstinence-only programs. A review by Robert Rector identified 10 evaluations of AOE programs that appeared to demonstrate behavior change as a result of program participation.[6] However, few of these evaluations met the minimum scientific criteria listed above, and all contained flaws in methodology or interpretation of the data that could lead to significantly biased results. A review of 10 state program evaluations by Advocates for Youth found no evidence of an impact on adolescent sexual behavior.[7]

A rigorous national evaluation of abstinence-only education is currently being conducted by Mathematica Policy Research, Inc. with support from the DHHS's Office of the Assistant Secretary for Planning and Evaluation (OASPE). The second report from the Mathematica evaluation of first-year impacts of the programs did not include information on behavioral outcomes, reportedly given the short duration of follow-up. First-year impacts did include an increase in abstinence intentions (i.e., pledging to abstain from sex until marriage) and small effects on both norms supportive of abstinence and perceived consequences of teen and non-marital sex. No impacts were found for self-efficacy, self-esteem, or perceived self-control. A report on behavioral outcomes [was] planned . . . in 2005.

The minority staff of the Committee on Government Reform of the U.S. House of Representatives reviewed commonly used abstinence-only curricula for evidence of scientific accuracy. This report found that 11 of the 13 curricula contained false, misleading, or distorted information about reproductive health, including inaccurate information about contraceptive effectiveness, the risks of abortion, and other scientific errors. These curricula treat stereotypes about girls and boys as scientific fact and blur religious and scientific viewpoints.

Although counseling about abstinence is recommended as part of the American Medical Association's Guidelines for Adolescent Preventive Services, we found no published evaluations of clinical counseling to promote abstinence.

Concepts of Efficacy for Abstinence in Preventing Pregnancy and STIs

Abstinence from sexual intercourse has been described as fully protective against pregnancy and sexually transmitted infections. This is misleading and potentially harmful because it conflates theoretical effectiveness with the actual practice of abstinence. Abstinence is not 100% effective in preventing pregnancy or STIs as many teens fail in remaining abstinent. Moreover, some STIs may be spread via other forms of sexual activity, such as kissing or manual or oral stimulation. In addition to the program evaluations described above, attempts have been made to calculate the efficacy of abstinence in preventing pregnancy or STIs.

One approach has relied on notions from contraceptive efficacy research such as *method failure* or *perfect use* (i.e., theoretical or best use efficacy when a method is used perfectly, i.e., consistently and correctly) and *user failure* or *typical use* (i.e., effectiveness of a method as it is commonly used). However, efficacy trials of abstinence as a method of contraception that are comparable to contraceptive efficacy trials have not been conducted. The most useful data in understanding the efficacy of abstinence come from examination of the virginity pledge movement in the National Longitudinal Survey of Youth (Add Health). Virginity pledgers, like contraceptive users, are a self-selected group.

Add Health data suggest that many teens who intend to be abstinent fail to do so, and that when abstainers do initiate intercourse, many fail to protect themselves by using contraception.[8-9] Bearman and colleagues have examined the virginity pledge movement; they estimate that over 2.5 million adolescents have taken public "virginity pledges." They found that pledgers were more likely to delay initiation of intercourse, 18 months on average for adolescents aged 12–18 years. However, those pledgers who failed at abstinence were less likely to use contraception after they did initiate sexual intercourse. At six-year follow-up, the prevalence of STIs (chlamydia, gonorrhea, trichomoniasis, and human papillomavirus [HPV]) was similar among those taking the abstinence pledge and non-pledgers.[9] Although pledgers tended to marry earlier than non-pledgers, if married, most pledgers had vaginal intercourse before marriage (88%). Virtually all non-pledgers who had married had sex before marriage (99%). Although pledgers had fewer sexual partners compared to non-pledgers, they were less likely to report seeing a doctor for an STI concern and were less likely to receive STI testing.

Robert Rector of the Heritage Foundation has reanalyzed the Add Health data and severely criticized the Bruckner study in a recent presentation.[10] However, the Rector study has not undergone peer review and it, in turn, has been severely criticized for manipulating statistical norms for significance.[11] A serious flaw in this analysis was the use of self-reported STIs, instead of laboratory-reported infections as used in the Bruckner study. This is problematic given that many STIs are asymptomatic and pledgers were less likely to be tested for STIs.

Based on our review of the evaluations of specific AOE curricula and research on virginity pledges, user failure with abstinence appears to be very high. Thus, although theoretically completely effective in preventing pregnancy, in actual practice the efficacy of AOE interventions may approach zero.

Impact of Abstinence-Only Policies on Comprehensive Sexuality Education

. . . Although comprehensive sexuality education is broadly supported by health professionals, increasingly, abstinence-only education is replacing more comprehensive forms of sexuality education. In Texas, for example, the Texas Board of Education has decided to remove most information about contraception from new health education textbooks. Recent reports describe teachers and students being censured for responding to questions or discussing sexuality topics that are not approved by the school administrators, as well as restricting access to HIV/AIDS experts from the classroom, and censoring what experts and teachers can say in the classroom. The cancellation of Programs that Work from the Division of Adolescent and School Health at the Centers for Disease Control and Prevention, is another example. Programs that Work used a rigorous peer-reviewed process to identify programs that were effective in changing adolescent sexual risk behaviors; this cancellation is believed to be the result of the Centers for Disease Control and Prevention's (CDC) failure to identify any abstinence-only programs as effective. Likewise, Rep. Henry Waxman in a July 2005 letter to DHHS Secretary Michael Leavitt criticized an abstinence-inspired DHHS website (4parent.gov) as inaccurate and ineffective, promoting misleading and inaccurate information on STIs and condoms, and providing a narrow focus on abstinence. The website used content from the National Physicians Center for Family Resources, a supporter of AOE, instead of scientists from the National Institutes of Health (NIH) or CDC or physicians from leading professional organizations such as the American Academy of Pediatrics or Society for Adolescent Medicine.

Surveys on health educational practice in the United States provide further evidence of an erosion of comprehensive sexuality education. Data from the School Health Policies and Programs Study in 2000 found that 92% of middle and junior high schools and 96% of high schools taught abstinence as the best way to avoid pregnancy, HIV, and STDs. Only 21% of junior high and 55% of high school teachers taught the correct use of condoms. Between 1988 and 1999, sharp declines occurred in the percentage of teachers who supported teaching about birth control, abortion, and sexual orientation, and in the percentages who actually taught these subjects. For example, in 1999, 23% of secondary school sexuality education teachers taught abstinence as the only way to prevent pregnancy and STDs, compared with only 2% who had done so in 1988. In 1999, one-quarter of sex education teachers said they were prohibited from teaching about contraception.

Impact of Federal Abstinence Policies on Pregnancy and HIV Prevention Programs

Federal and state governments provide support for family planning programs, which are available to adolescents through Title X of the Public Health Service Act. Title X program guidelines stress that abstinence should be discussed with all adolescent clients. Starting in the FY 2004 service delivery grant announcements, Office of Population Affairs announced that program priorities for Title X grantees would include a focus on extramarital abstinence education and counseling, increasing parental involvement in the decisions of minors to seek family planning services, the reporting of statutory rape, and working with faith-based organizations. Thus, Title X grantees are now expected to focus on these new priorities, while continuing to provide condoms and other contraceptive services, STI and HIV prevention education, cancer screening, and other reproductive health services. These changes may weaken efforts to promote effective reproductive health services for adolescents and unmarried individuals who are sexually active.

Language stressing abstinence has also appeared in drafts of the CDC's Interim HIV Content Guidelines for AIDS-Related Materials. These

Guidelines require that "all programs of education and information receiving funds under this title shall include information about the harmful effects of promiscuous sexual activity and intravenous drug use, and the benefits of abstaining from such activities."

Abstinence-only policies by the U.S. government have also influenced global HIV prevention efforts. The President's Emergency Plan for AIDS Relief (PEPFAR), focusing on 15 countries in sub-Saharan Africa, the Caribbean, and Asia that have been severely affected by AIDS, requires grantees to devote at least 33% of prevention spending to abstinence-until-marriage programs. Human rights groups find that U.S. government policy has become a source for misinformation and censorship in these countries. U.S. emphasis on abstinence may also have reduced condom availability and access to accurate information on HIV/AIDS in some countries.

Abstinence-Only Education and Sexually Active Youth

Programs geared to adolescents who have not yet engaged in coitus systematically ignore sexually experienced adolescents, a group with specific reproductive health needs and who often require more than abstinence education. Sexually experienced teens need access to complete and accurate information about contraception, legal rights to health care, and ways to access reproductive health services, none of which are provided in abstinence-only programs.

Abstinence-Only Education and GLBTQ Youth

Abstinence-only sex education may have profoundly negative impacts on the well-being of gay, lesbian, bisexual, transgender and questioning (GLBTQ) youth. An estimated 2.5% of high school youth self-identify as gay, lesbian or bisexual, and more may be uncertain of their sexual orientation. However, as many as 1 in 10 adolescents struggle with issues regarding sexual identity. Abstinence-only sex education classes are unlikely to meet the health needs of GLBTQ youth, as they largely ignore issues surrounding homosexuality (except when discussing transmission of HIV/AIDS), and often stigmatize homosexuality as deviant and unnatural behavior. Homophobia contributes to health problems such as suicide, feelings of isolation and loneliness, HIV infection, substance abuse, and violence among GLBTQ youth.

Under Section 510 requirements, emphasis must be placed on heterosexual marriage as the only appropriate context for sexual relationships. Federal law and regulations limit the definition of marriage within the meaning of federally funded abstinence-only programs to exclude same-sex couples. With the exception of Massachusetts, no states offer legal marriage to gay and lesbian couples, and recently, 11 states have passed laws specifically barring same-sex marriage. Lifelong abstinence as an implied alternative holds GLBTQ youth to an unrealistic standard markedly different from that of their heterosexual peers.

The Human Right to Sexual Health Information

Paradoxically, although abstinence is often presented as the moral choice for adolescents, we believe that the current federal approach focusing on AOE raises serious ethical and human rights concerns. Access to complete and accurate HIV/AIDS and sexual health information has been recognized as a basic human right and essential to realizing the human right to the highest attainable standard of health. Governments have an obligation to provide accurate information to their citizens and eschew the provision of misinformation; such obligations extend to government-funded health education and health care services.

International treaties provide that all people have the right to "seek, receive and impart information and ideas of all kinds," including information about their health. The U.N. Committee on the Rights of the Child, the U.N. body responsible for monitoring implementation of the Convention on the Rights of the Child, and which provides authoritative guidance on its provisions, has emphasized that children's right to access adequate HIV/AIDS and sexual health information is essential to securing their rights to health and information.

Article 12 of the International Covenant on Economic, Social and Cultural Rights (ICESCR) specifically obliges governments to take all necessary steps for the *"prevention, treatment and control of epidemic . . . diseases,"* such as HIV/AIDS. The Committee on Economic, Social and Cultural Rights, the U.N. body responsible for monitoring implementation of the ICESCR, and which provides authoritative guidance on its provisions, has interpreted Article 12 to require the *"the establishment of prevention and education programmes for behaviour-related health concerns such as sexually transmitted diseases, in particular HIV/AIDS, and those adversely affecting sexual and reproductive health."*

The United Nations Guidelines on HIV/AIDS and Human Rights provide guidance in interpreting international legal norms as they relate to HIV and AIDS. These guidelines similarly call on states to *"ensure that children and adolescents have adequate access to confidential sexual and reproductive health services, including HIV/AIDS information, counseling, testing and prevention measures such as condoms,"* and to *"ensure the access of children and adolescents to adequate health information and education, including information related to HIV/AIDS prevention and care, inside and outside school, which is tailored appropriately to age level and capacity and enables them to deal positively and responsibly with their sexuality."* Access to accurate health information is a basic human right that has also been described in international statements on reproductive rights such as the Programme of Action of the International Conference on Population and Development—Cairo, 1994.

Overall, these international treaties and statements clearly define the important responsibility of governments to provide accurate and complete information on sexual health to their citizens.

Ethical Obligations of Health Care Providers and Health Educators

We believe that patients have rights to accurate and complete information from their health care professionals and that health care providers have ethical obligations to provide accurate health information. Health care providers may not withhold information from a patient in order to influence their health care choices. Such ethical obligations are part of respect for persons and are operationalized via the process of providing informed consent. Informed consent requires provision of all pertinent information to the patient. Similar ethical obligations apply to health educators. . . .

[We] believe that it is unethical to provide misinformation or to withhold information from adolescents about sexual health, including ways for sexually active teens to protect themselves from STIs and pregnancy. Withholding information on contraception to induce them to become abstinent is inherently coercive. It violates the principle of beneficence (i.e., do good and avoid harm) as it may cause an adolescent to use ineffective (or no) protection against pregnancy and STIs. We believe that current federal AOE is ethically problematic, as it excludes accurate information about contraception, misinforms by overemphasizing or misstating the risks of contraception, and fails to require the use of scientifically accurate information while promoting approaches of questionable value.

Summary and Authors' Commentary

Although abstinence from sexual intercourse represents a healthy behavioral choice for adolescents, policies or programs offering "abstinence only" or "abstinence until marriage" as a single option for adolescents are scientifically and ethically flawed. Although abstinence from vaginal and anal intercourse is theoretically fully protective against pregnancy and disease, in actual practice, abstinence-only programs often fail to prevent these outcomes. Although federal support of abstinence-only programs has grown rapidly since 1996, existing evaluations of such programs either do not meet standards for scientific evaluation or lack evidence of efficacy in delaying initiation of sexual intercourse.

Although health care is founded on ethical notions of informed consent and free choice, federal abstinence-only programs are inherently coercive, withholding information needed to make informed choices and promoting questionable and inaccurate opinions. Federal funding language promotes a specific moral viewpoint, not a public health approach. Abstinence-only programs are inconsistent with commonly accepted notions of human rights.

In many communities, AOE has been replacing comprehensive sexuality education. Federally funded AOE programs censor lifesaving information about prevention of pregnancy, HIV and other STIs, and provide incomplete or misleading misinformation about contraception. The federal government's emphasis on abstinence-only approaches may also be harming other public health efforts such as family planning programs and HIV prevention efforts—domestically and globally. Federally funded abstinence-until-marriage programs discriminate against GLBTQ youth, as federal law limits the definition of marriage to heterosexual couples.

Schools and health care providers should encourage abstinence as an important option for adolescents. "Abstinence-only" as a basis for health policy and programs should be abandoned.

References

1. Goodson P, Suther S, Pruitt BE, Wilson K. Defining abstinence: views of directors, instructors, and participants in abstinence-only-until-marriage programs in Texas. J Sch Health 2003;73(3):91–6.

2. Albert B. American Opinion on Teen Pregnancy and Related Issues 2003. Washington, DC: National Campaign to Prevent Teen Pregnancy, 2004.

3. Dailard C. Sex education: politicians, parents, teachers and teens. Issues Brief (Alan Guttmacher Inst) 2001(2):1–4.

4. Kirby D. Emerging Answers: Research Findings on Programs to Reduce Teen Pregnancy. Washington, DC: National Campaign to Prevent Teen Pregnancy, 2001.

5. Manlove J, Romano-Papillo A, Ikramullah E. Not Yet: Programs to Delay First Sex Among Teens. Washington, DC: National Campaign to Prevent Teen Pregnancy, 2004.

6. Rector RE. The Effectiveness of Abstinence Education Programs in Reducing Sexual Activity Among Youth. The Backgrounder #1533. Washington, DC: The Heritage Foundation, 2002.

7. Hauser D. Five Years of Abstinence-Only-Until-Marriage Education: Assessing the Impact. Washington, DC: Advocates for Youth, 2004.

8. Bearman PS, Bruckner H. Promising the future: virginity pledges and first intercourse. Am J Sociol 2001;106:859–912.

9. Bruckner H, Bearman PS. After the promise: the STD consequences of adolescent virginity pledges. J Adolesc Health 2005;36:271–8.

10. Rector RE, Johnson KA. Adolescent virginity pledges, condom use, and sexually transmitted diseases among young adults. Presented to the National Welfare Research and Evaluation Conference of the Administration of Children and Families, Washington, DC, June 14, 2005.

11. Ellenberg J. Sex and significance: how the Heritage Foundation cooked the books on virginity [cited 2005 Jul 29]. Available from: http://slate.msn.com/id/2122093/

POSTSCRIPT

Is Comprehensive Sex Education for Adolescents Too Liberal?

While there is little argument among practitioners, educators, and researchers about the importance of teaching abstinence as a viable, important component of school-based sexual health education, what other topics are to be taught—and in what framework they are to be presented—remains controversial. For example, condoms can be presented as highly effective—when used properly and consistently, condoms are 97 percent effective at preventing pregnancy (ideal or theoretical effectiveness rate; based on what is called "method failure"—condoms, as a method, fail only 3 percent of the time). On the other hand, condoms can be presented as having a high failure rate of 14 percent (i.e., only 86% effective). This is based on "typical" use rates—meaning that people may not use condoms correctly so that 14 out of 100 couples who report that they use condoms as their birth control method become pregnant within a year. This figure is based on "user failure"; people who do not use the method correctly introduce "user" error into the effectiveness of the birth control device. Thus, an educator can put her/his personal slant on the device by being either overly optimistic (i.e., condoms are extremely effective) or overly pessimistic (i.e., condoms are incredibly unreliable). Quite simply, the perspective of the educator colors the presentation of the information.

Morality is integrally linked to sex education—there is no sex education that is amoral or without a moral perspective. Where the difference lies is in the overarching framework. Theorists Shweder, Much, Mahapatra, and Park (1997) discuss different moral models to which people subscribe. Those who are in favor of comprehensive sexual health education might be considered as adopting an "ethic of autonomy," where the independence of the individual is highly respected. From this ethical perspective comes the "harm reduction" model. An example of a harm reduction intervention is needle exchange programs for intravenous drug users. The idea behind this is that an individual makes his/her own decisions—in this case to inject drugs—and that others cannot proscribe their behavior. What one can do is to make the behavior, as undesirable and/or repugnant as we find it, as safe as possible for the individual. Thus, by offering to exchange dirty needles for new, clean ones, we are reducing the harm the individual is doing to her/himself while respecting the individual's autonomy.

Another moral framework is the "ethic of divinity," whereby there is a "right" and a "wrong" way of behaving or acting. The wrong way is considered as contravening "natural law" or the way things *should* be. Sometimes natural law is viewed as going against nature, while other times it is viewed as going against the way God meant life to be. This is often shaped by the particular religious perspectives to which one subscribes. Using the intravenous drug use example, a person who subscribes to an ethic of divinity might argue that needle exchange programs subtly condone drug use and that "Just Say No" campaigns are more congruent with their ethical belief system. Drug use violates a natural law principle that one needs to treat the body "as a temple" (i.e., with respect). Using drugs violates this law; thus, one must do all that is possible to have the drug user discontinue the behavior.

Santelli and colleagues clearly come from an ethic of autonomy. They refer to misinformation or withholding of information as violating the *principle of beneficence* (i.e., do good and avoid harm). They clearly view comprehensive sex education curricula as congruent with their ethical framework. While Orgocka does not argue against comprehensive sex education, per se, her participants may represent people who oppose some of the comprehensive sexual education curricula that are viewed as contradicting, challenging, or even violating traditional family values (be these Islamic or those of other conservative religious minority groups). The family values perspective clearly fits within the "ethic of divinity" of Islam. For example, rules about sexual health have a strong impact on many areas of life in Islamic culture (e.g., prayers, bathing, marriage), and sexual health education is considered part of the purview of a correct religious upbringing (Sanjakdar, 2004).

Is there such a thing as a sexual health curriculum that satisfies all of these different ethical "camps"? Certainly, a curriculum will garner less objection with various facets if it can represent some aspect of all of the moral perspectives such that it respects autonomy but also demonstrates cultural sensitivity. A codicil: It should be noted that people rarely subscribe to one ethical framework "purely" without incorporating some ideology based on other ethical perspectives. So, is comprehensive sex education for adolescents too liberal? The answer is: It depends on one's framework.

References/Further Readings

Hauser, D. (2004). *Five years of abstinence-only-until-marriage education: Assessing the impact.* Washington, D.C.: Advocates for Youth.

Kirby, D. (2001). *Emerging answers: Research findings on programs to reduce teen pregnancy.* Washington, D.C.: National Campaign to Prevent Teen Pregnancy.

Kirby, Douglas B., Laris, B., & Rolleri, Lori (2007). Sex and HIV Education Programs: Their Impact on Sexual Behaviors of Young People Throughout the World. *Journal of Adolescent Health, 40*(3), 206–217.

Sanjakdar, F. (2004). The critical role of schools and teachers in developing a sexual health education curriculum for Muslim students. Paper presented at the Australian Association for Research in Education, Melbourne, Victoria, Australia. (ISSN 1324-9339). Available on the Web at: http://www.aare.edu.au/04pap-san04188.pdf.

Shweder, R.A., Much, N.C., Mahapatra, M., & Park, L. (1997). The "big three" of morality (autonomy, community, divinity) and the "big three" explanation of suffering. In A.M. Brant & P. Rozin (Eds.), *Morality and Health* (pp. 99–169). Florence, KY: Taylor & Frances/ Routledge.

The Waxman Report. (2004, December). "The content of federally funded abstinence-only education programs." Prepared for Representative Henry A. Waxman, US House of Representatives Committee on Government Reform. Minority Staff Special Investigations Division. Retrieved June 23, 2006 from: http://www.democrats.reform. house.gov/Documents/20041201102153-50247.pdf.

ISSUE 10

Does a Traditional or "Strong" Double Standard with Respect to Sexual Behavior Exist Among Adolescents?

YES: Mary Crawford and Danielle Popp, from "Sexual Double Standards: A Review and Methodological Critique of Two Decades of Research," *Journal of Sex Research* (February 2003)

NO: Michael J. Marks and R. Chris Fraley, from "The Sexual Double Standard: Fact or Fiction?" *Sex Roles* (February 2005)

ISSUE SUMMARY

YES: Mary Crawford, a psychology professor at the University of Connecticut, and her graduate student Danielle Popp present evidence suggesting the double standard that males are socially rewarded and females socially derogated for sexual activity exists among adolescents as it does among adults.

NO: Researchers Michael Marks and Chris Fraley oppose the above claim and suggest that there is little evidence that the traditional double standard exists among adolescents or even among adults.

"What do you call a girl with many sexual partners? A slut. What do you call a guy with many sexual partners? A stud." This quote, taken directly from students in a Psychology of Gender class, illustrates how easily young people can identify the key constructs involved in the sexual double standard. The sexual double standard, put simply, is that the same heterosexual behavior is judged differently depending on whether a male or a female is engaging in the behavior. That is, boys who are sexual are celebrated or rewarded for their behavior while girls who are similarly sexual are censured or punished for their behavior. While the "line" is arguable for what sexual behaviors by girls is acceptable, across times and social groups, girls and boys can identify what is and is not permissible vis-a-vis girls' sexual activity. For example, in the 1950s, a Catholic school girl whose skirt was too short and showed "too much leg" would have been branded as "loose." In contrast, sexual intercourse may be permissible for a girl of the 2000s *if* she is in a romantic relationship with a boy; otherwise, she may still be labeled as "loose" (i.e., in today's language, a slut, whore, etc.). Today's language may be different (e.g., "player") but the concepts remain the same.

Sociologist Ira Reiss was one of the first people to write about the sexual double standard from an academic viewpoint. In his classic 1967 work, *The Social Context of Premarital Sexual Permissiveness,* Reiss discussed the double standard in relation to premarital intercourse and divided the double standard into "orthodox" and "transitional" categories. The orthodox standard viewed premarital intercourse as permissible for males but not for females under *any* circumstance, while the transitional double standard viewed premarital intercourse as permissible for males under any circumstance and permissible for females but only if they were engaged or deeply in love. In the 1960s, Reiss optimistically predicted that North American society would move toward increasing sex-role equality and decreasing sexual double standards.

Research on the double standard continued into the 1970s and beyond. A meta-analysis by Oliver and Hyde (1993) found a gender difference in the endorsement of the sexual double standard. Reiss's 1960 studies found that men were more likely than women to endorse the double standard (while women were more likely to endorse total abstinence for all). In contrast, Oliver and Hyde found that women were more likely to endorse the double standard than men. This gender effect became stronger across the years. Thus, both men and women were becoming more permissive in their sexual attitudes, *but* men were dropping their endorsement of the double standard while women were moving from an abstinence-only attitude to a more double standard–based attitude. It is noteworthy that this gender difference in double standard endorsement was only moderate-to-small, which is not surprising as there is strong and consistent research that men are more sexually liberal than women (i.e., if we consider the double standard as a form of sexist sexual conservatism). Many different types of studies today seem to suggest that the sexual double standard was and is alive and well in the 1980s, 1990s, and 2000s, as is documented in the selection by Crawford and Popp.

In contrast, other researchers maintain that, while lay people believe that the sexual double standard exists and they are able to articulate the double standard easily, a sexual double standard does not exist in terms of its application to the evaluation of others. In their selection, Marks and Fraley interpret the existing research as failing to support the sexual double standard. Even in considering Reiss's 1967 data, students did not endorse the double standard to any great extent. In fact, only 25 percent endorsed a double standard (either orthodox or transitional; almost half (42 percent) endorsed abstinence from sexual intercourse for all). While reading the following selections, consider whether the evidence presented can be interpreted as supporting or refuting the existence of the sexual double standard.

YES  Mary Crawford and Danielle Popp

Sexual Double Standards: A Review and Methodological Critique of Two Decades of Research

Traditionally, men and women have been subjected to different "rules" guiding sexual behavior. Women were stigmatized for engaging in any sexual activity outside of heterosexual marriage, whereas for men such behavior was expected and rewarded. Boys had to "sow their wild oats," but girls were warned that a future husband "won't buy the cow if he can get the milk for free." Women were faced with a Madonna-whore dichotomy: They were either pure and virginal or promiscuous and easy. . . .

What follows is a review of evidence from a variety of research methods including experimental designs, ethnographies, interviews, focus groups, and linguistic analyses. . . .

Experimental Research

Experimental research has been used to examine individuals' preferences for partners and their beliefs about acceptable levels of sexual activity for males and females at varying relationship stages. Experimental methods have been used to examine both individual double standards and perceptions of societal double standards. Individual double standards have been examined using within-subject designs, in which participants are asked to answer questions or make judgments about the sexual behavior of either male or female targets and are immediately asked the same questions about targets of the other sex. Perceptions of societal double standards have been examined directly by asking participants whether or not societal double standards exist. Sexual double standards also can be inferred from experiments using between-subjects designs, in which one group of participants is asked about male targets, and another group is asked the same questions about female targets.

Within-Subject Designs: Measures of Individual Double Standards

Within-subject designs provide the purest test of double standards because the same participants respond to the same set of questions for each target.

From *Journal of Sex Research,* vol. 40, no. 1, February 2003, excerpts from pp. 13–26. Copyright © 2003 by Society for the Scientific Study of Sexuality. Reprinted by permission via Copyright Clearance Center.

We found only two within-subject experimental studies in our search of the literature. . . . Six hundred ninety Scottish teenagers . . . were asked to estimate how many sexual partners most 20-year-old women or men have had and to rate a hypothetical young woman or man who changes sex partners a number of times during the year. Respondents predicted that women would have had significantly fewer sexual partners than men. Further, for both religious men and nonreligious women, sexually active women were considered less popular among both sexes than sexually active men. Finally, women who changed sex partners a number of times during the year were rated as more irresponsible and as having less self-respect than men who engaged in the same behaviors.

Sprecher and Hatfield (1996) found that men endorsed a double standard for women and men who were dating casually (. . . dating less than one month) but not for women and men who were dating seriously (. . . almost one year) or who were pre-engaged (had seriously discussed the possibility of getting married). In the U.S., . . . undergraduates . . . completed a premarital sexual permissiveness scale for themselves, "a male," and "a female." The permissiveness scale asked participants to rate the acceptability of sexual intercourse at each of five dating stages (first date, casually dating, seriously dating, pre-engaged, and engaged). Male participants held significantly more permissive attitudes for a male (the total score for items referring to a male) than for a female. Men's endorsement of a double standard was strongest at the first date but also existed for intermediate dating stages. Overall, U.S. men reported greater endorsement of double standards than did U.S. women.

This study was part of a cross-cultural comparison of double standards in the U.S., Japan, and Russia. Of note in the Japanese and Russian samples, which also consisted entirely of [undergraduates], Russian students were more likely than U.S. students to show what the researchers termed a *traditional* double standard, especially at the first date, casual, and serious dating levels. Additionally, the greater endorsement of double standards by male participants than by female participants found in the U.S. sample was not found in the Russian and Japanese samples.

Between-Subjects Designs: Measures of Societal Double Standards

In between-subjects designs, each participant is presented with only one target; therefore, a direct measure of the double standard within the individual cannot be obtained. However, by comparing responses across participants by target sex, it is possible to determine whether, overall, women and men are judged differentially for engaging in the same behavior. . . .

Person-perception tasks allow researchers to examine the consequences of double standards on evaluations of males and females engaging in identical behavior. Evidence of double standards exists if women are evaluated differently than men for engaging in comparable levels of sexual activity under the same conditions.

Sprecher, McKinney, and Orbuch (1987) had . . . undergraduates . . . read a questionnaire ostensibly completed by another student. The questionnaire included manipulations for target sex, age at first coitus (16 or 21), and relationship stage at first coitus (a steady dating relationship that had lasted almost a year or a casual one that had lasted one week). Participants rated the fictional student on 23 bipolar scales that composed of four factors: Sexual and Other Values (e.g., sexually experienced, sexually liberal, liberal in sex-roles), Maturity and Intelligence (e.g., responsible), Positive Personality (e.g., likable), and Dominance (e.g., dominant, active, masculine). There was a main effect for target sex such that female targets received higher scores on the Sexual and Other Values scale and lower scores on the Maturity and Intelligence, Positive Personality, and Dominance scales. There were also significant interactions between target sex and relationship stage at first coitus (Positive Personality and Dominance) and between target sex and age at first coitus (Maturity and Intelligence, Positive Personality, Dominance). Although having first coitus in a non-committed relationship or at a young age had a negative effect on how both males and females were evaluated, the negative effect was greater for females. These results suggested that women were perceived more negatively than men for being more sexually experienced.

In a series of two studies, Oliver and Sedikides (1992) examined mate-selection preferences. . . . In Study 1, . . . undergraduates . . . were asked to complete a sexual permissiveness scale as they would want either a blind date or spouse to complete it. Both male and female participants preferred low levels of sexual permissiveness in both blind dates and spouses. Male participants preferred lower levels of sexual permissiveness in a spouse than in a blind date; there were no significant differences for female participants. In Study 2, . . . undergraduates read a sexual permissiveness scale ostensibly filled out by an opposite sex student who was either sexually permissive or sexually nonpermissive. Participants then rated the target on . . . Evaluation (e.g., morality) and Attraction (e.g., sexual attractiveness). Although the permissive target received lower evaluation ratings overall, female participants rated the male permissive target significantly more negatively than males rated the female permissive target. Male participants rated the female target as significantly more attractive when she was permissive than nonpermissive. Females rated the permissive male target as less desirable as both a spouse and a blind date. However, males rated the permissive female target as significantly less desirable for a spouse and significantly more desirable for a blind date than they rated the nonpermissive female target.

Milhausen and Herold's (1999) . . . female undergraduate participants . . . completed a questionnaire measuring both perceptions of a societal double standard and personal endorsement of double standards. . . . Findings indicated that participants overwhelmingly . . . believed that there is "a double standard for sexual behavior (a standard in which it is more acceptable for a man to have had more sexual partners than a woman)" (p. 363). Similarly, 93% of participants . . . believed that "women who have had many sex partners are judged more harshly than men who have had many sex partners" (p. 363). When asked to explain their answers, 49% of respondents mentioned women's being penalized for their sexual behavior, and 48% mentioned men's being rewarded for theirs. Additionally, 42% of participants believed that it is women who "judge women who have had sex with many partners more harshly" (p. 363). Personal endorsement of double standards was measured by asking participants to indicate on a 5-point scale whether they would encourage or discourage a male or female friend from dating someone who has had intercourse with more than 10 different partners. Results showed that women were more likely to discourage a female friend from dating a man who had 10 previous sexual partners than to discourage a male friend from dating a woman who had 10 previous partners.

A smaller group of studies . . . showed little or no support for double standards. Jacoby and Williams (1985) presented . . . undergraduates with five "sexual profiles" of opposite sex persons consisting of sets of answers to questions about sexual ideology and experience. Participants rated the dating and marriage desirability of the target in each profile. Findings indicated that there was no difference in the kinds of relationships in which sex was seen as acceptable for men and women and that no more than moderate sexual experience was desirable in either a male or a female dating or marriage partner. . . .

Mark and Miller (1986) asked . . . undergraduates . . . to read a supposed transcript of an interview with another student whose sex and sexual permissiveness (virgin, relationship sex, casual sex) were varied. After reading the transcript, participants rated the target on . . . [ten] factors: Poor Adjustment, Unconventional, Likable, Agreeable, Caring, Assertive, Immoral, Conforming, . . . Trusting [, and] Sexual (chaste-promiscuous, modest-immodest, nonseductive-seductive, moral-immoral). . . . Participants also completed . . . evaluations and mental health [questions]. Results indicated little support for sexual double standards. The only significant results were on the sexual and agreeable scales. Male participants judged female targets as more sexual than male targets if they engaged in casual sex. Liberal males and traditional females rated females who had had casual sex as marginally less agreeable than they rated males who had had casual sex.

Sprecher (1989) asked . . . undergraduates . . . to answer a premarital sexual permissiveness scale for 1 of 20 targets. Targets varied in gender, age, and relationship to the participant (i.e., a female or sister). The permissiveness scale asked participants to rate the acceptability of three sexual behaviors (heavy petting, sexual intercourse, and oral-genital contact) at four different relationship stages (first date, casually dating [dating less than 1 month], seriously dating [dating almost 1 year], and engaged). Although the findings did not support sexual double standards, they suggested that age (regardless of target sex) is important when evaluating sexual standards.

O'Sullivan (1995) had . . . undergraduate students . . . read a vignette about a target who varied in sex, number of past partners (low [2 for males and 1 for females] or high [13 for males and 7 for females]), and type of relationship (committed or noncommitted). . . . Male targets were rated somewhat less positively than female targets overall. Sexually experienced targets received the least positive evaluations, and targets in noncommitted sexual relationships were rated as [more negative. Little] evidence of double standards was found. Women did not receive more negative evaluations than men did when described as having had high numbers of past sexual partners in noncommitted relationships. . . .

Sprecher, Regan, McKinney, Maxwell, and Wazienski (1997) asked . . . undergraduate . . . students . . . to complete one of three versions of a mate-selection preference list consisting of 18 partner traits. The target's sexual experience was manipulated using three versions of the sexuality items: sexual chastity (no previous sexual partners), some sexual experience (few sexual partners), or considerable sexual experience (several previous partners). Sprecher et al. found no evidence of a heterosexual double standard, with participants reporting no differences in preference for level of sexual experience based on target sex.

Gentry (1998) asked participants . . . to read a portion of an interview with a fictional heterosexual . . . student focusing on relationships and sexuality. The target's sex, number of relationships (either an exclusive, monogamous sexual relationship or sexual relations with multiple partners), and level of sexual activity (above average, below average, or average) were manipulated. . . . Results showed that participants based their judgments about the targets on information about number of relationships and level of sexual activity rather than the target's sex.

Summary and Critique of Experimental Studies

Of the 11 studies reported in detail, 5 found evidence of sexual double standards. Only 2 of the 11 studies used within-subject designs; both of these found evidence of double standards.

Studies varied in the possible moderating variables they assessed. Only one study reported analyses based on target age; both target age and its interaction with target sex were significant (Sprecher et al., 1987). Seven reported analyses based on relationship stage; of these seven, three reported overall evidence of double standards. Additionally, all three found significant main effects of relationship stage and interactions between target sex and relationship stage. Two studies found that sexually active men were judged more harshly than were sexually active women. . . .

Experimental designs have several advantages for studying sexual attitudes. They allow the researcher to manipulate or control variables believed to influence double standards, such as relationship stage. Unlike any other method, they permit causal inferences to be drawn. Because they typically present participants with hypothetical scenarios and use paper-and-pencil measures of dependent variables, they are relatively easy to use with large samples, which yield more statistical power. Their decontextualized scenarios also allow participants to reflect on their attitudes without personal emotional involvement.

Offsetting these theoretical and practical advantages are several limitations. An intrinsic problem with statistical comparisons is that the null hypothesis of similarity can never be taken as proven, whereas hypotheses of differences can be assessed probabilistically. The statistical emphasis on significant differences may foster the "file drawer problem" in which studies reporting similarities in attitudes toward a target's behavior regardless of target sex may remain unpublished, leading to an overestimate of double standards.

Other limitations of experimental methods are not intrinsic but occur frequently in practice. For example, virtually all the experimental studies described in this review relied on convenience samples of North American . . . students. This is a serious limitation, not just because these samples are unrepresentative of the general population, but because they are unrepresentative in particular ways that are rarely discussed or even acknowledged by researchers. . . .

In designing experimental studies of double standards, researchers have occasionally confounded target sex and participant sex. . . . If women's evaluations of men differ from men's evaluations of women, the difference could be due to either participant sex or target sex. Participants might be endorsing different standards for women and men, or they might be endorsing a single standard, but one that is different for female and male participants. The former fits our definition of a double standard; the latter does not. However, even if individual women and men each hold a single standard, if the standard held by women is different from the standard held by men, heterosexual women and men could still be evaluated differently by potential partners. These complexities can be teased out by systematically varying, both participant sex and target sex.

Another theoretical and practical issue in experimental designs is that the conceptual and linguistic categories used to measure double standards are preformed by the experimenter. . . . [The] response categories available to participants may be inadequate to represent the variable under consideration. [Even] when the categories seem adequate, the method assumes that they have the same meaning to all participants and that the meaning ascribed to the category by participants is the same as that ascribed by the experimenter. . . .

Qualitative and Interpretive Designs

In contrast to experimental methods, qualitative studies more readily lend themselves to contextually sensitive phenomena. The questions they can address are more open-ended and diffuse, less abstract and hypothetical. Here we review studies using ethnographic, interview, focus group, and linguistic analyses.

Ethnographic Studies

Ethnographic researchers, by definition, attempt to capture the belief systems of a community through close and sustained observation. Therefore, individuals' accounts of their communities' norms and their own beliefs about sexuality may emerge as part of broader ethnographic studies not specifically focused on double standards.

Heterosexual double standards are salient in ethnographies of adolescent culture in U.S. middle schools. In a 3-year study, Eder, Evans, and Parker (1995) used a variety of data sources: They observed lunchtime activity, attended extracurricular activities, conducted individual and small group interviews, and recorded audio and video tapes of students' spontaneous conversations with peers. Within the middle school peer culture, girls (but never boys) sometimes were negatively labeled simply because they showed interest or assertiveness with respect to sexuality. Girls who initiated any kind of sexual overture (e.g., "making a pass") were labeled "bitches," "sluts," and "whores." The sanction against female sexual agency extended to wearing attractive clothing or makeup, which also could earn the label of whore. The routine use of sexual insults aimed at girls by boys, and to a lesser extent by girls, suggested that middle school students "do not believe that girls should be sexually active or have a variety of boyfriends, while such behaviors are viewed as normal and acceptable for boys" (p. 131). Eder et al. (1995) concluded, "labeling young girls in this manner becomes part of a continual attempt to limit their sense of sexual autonomy and identity" (p. 153).

Focusing on girls, Orenstein (1994) conducted a yearlong ethnographic study of two middle schools, one suburban, White, and affluent, the other urban, largely ethnic minority, and poor. Girls' accounts described their fear of the slut label and their shamed silence around sexual desire. Orenstein vividly captured how double standards can be communicated even in a sex education class. The teacher, Ms. Webster, is trying to illustrate the risk of sexually transmitted diseases:

> "We'll use a woman," she says, drawing the Greek symbol for woman on the blackboard. "Let's say she is infected, but she hasn't really noticed yet, so she has sex with three men."
>
> (As she draws symbols for men on the board) a heavyset boy in a Chicago Bulls cap stage whispers, "What a slut," and the class titters.
>
> "Okay," says Ms. Webster, who doesn't hear the comment. "Now the first guy has three sexual encounters in six months." She turns to draw three more women's signs, her back to the class, and several of the boys point at themselves proudly, striking exaggerated macho poses.
>
> "The second guy was very active, he had intercourse with five women." As she turns to the diagram again, two boys stand and take bows.
>
> During the entire diagramming process, the girls in the class remain silent. (p. 61)

Double standards have emerged in ethnographies of college students as well. Moffat (1989) studied peer culture on a university campus, focusing on sexual beliefs and attitudes and using a variety of methods. He conducted participant observation while "passing" as a student living in a men's dormitory, and he analyzed sexual autobiographies written by students in sexuality classes. He reported that the majority of students believed in heterosexual double standards and classified women into dichotomous categories of "good" women or sluts. Moffat characterized the attitudes of the male students he studied as follows:

> Men have the right to experiment sexually for a few years. There are a lot of female sluts out there with whom to so experiment. And once I have gotten this out of my system, I will then look for a good woman for a long-term relationship (or for a wife). (1989, p. 204)

Interview and Focus Group Studies

Individual interviews and focus group discussions are open-ended methods of self-report. In these settings, participants can express beliefs and attitudes in their own terms and provide contextual information to justify or explain their positions. One such study relied on interviews conducted with 55 adolescents, both boys and girls, with a mean age of 16 years (Martin, 1996). Participants were students at three high schools, one working-class public and two upper-middle-class private institutions. They were interviewed privately in the school setting for about an hour each. Questions assessed identity, self-esteem, and body image, as well as experiences with the physical changes of puberty, intimate relationships, and sexual intercourse. . . .

Both girls and boys distinguished between girls they called sluts, "hos," or "Sally off the street" and girls they called "regular" or "normal" girls, those who could become someone's girlfriend. Distinctions such as these were not made for boys. However, having sex was not enough to earn the label of slut. Instead, peers' distinctions were made based on whether the girl was "too young" or had "too many" partners. Martin concluded that "the double standard in sex is still firmly rooted in teenage culture" (pp. 85–86).

In addition to the double standards of peers, many girls perceived parental double standards. For example, one respondent who expressed confusion and guilt about her sexual activity reported that her boyfriend's mother categorized any girl who "slept with" a boyfriend or even used a tampon during menstruation as a slut. Martin's female participants appeared to "take the distinction of slut to heart and fear it." She concluded, "Regardless of its particular contextual meaning, the word slut holds a lot of power. Being called a slut or a ho—or feeling like one—is to feel degraded and dirty" (pp. 86–87).

In a study of attitudes toward condom use among 105 young (median age 18) drug users in Western Australia, both male and female participants were asked "What do young men think of young women who carry condoms?" and "What do young women think of young men who carry condoms?" (Loxley, 1996). Results showed discrepancies between participants' reports of the attitudes of people of their own sex and the other sex. Participants of each sex believed that those of the other sex held more negative attitudes than were actually reported (e.g., women thought men had more negative attitudes toward women than men actually reported having). This mismatch suggests that perceptions of societal double standards may influence behavior. However, the transparent within-subject design, with each participant being asked about both sexes' attitudes, may have induced unknown biases in responding. . . .

Other studies, using single-sex samples, also show that adolescents perceive and are affected by sexual double standards. Thompson (1995), using a snowball sampling technique and open-ended interviews, gathered stories from 400 girls representing a variety of geographical locations, class backgrounds, and ethnicities. . . . Thompson concluded that the heterosexual double standard remains "virulently alive and well" (p. 31) but that it is less absolute and more contextually negotiated than in the past. Girls described innumerable fine lines as to what constituted good and bad sexual behavior, lines that mapped local and individual constructions of sex and gender. They appeared to use these maps to define and orient themselves as "good girls," as opposed to "easy" girls or sluts.

A smaller study of 17 male college students (ages 18–22) used . . . transcripts from interviews (Fromme & Emihovich, 1998). These respondents endorsed a double standard that divided women into two groups. "Good women" were those who say no to casual sex or to intercourse early in a relationship; these women were seen as acceptable for longer term relationships. "Bad women" were those who had sex on a first date or sex with many partners. The authors noted that their respondents did not seem to recognize that they derogated women for behaviors they accepted for themselves, as in this comment:

> If I met a woman in a bar and had sex with her chances are I wouldn't call her because I wouldn't have any respect for her. Because if she did something like that . . . would I want someone like that for the rest of my life? No, of course not. (p. 174)

One other source of first-person accounts deserves mention. Espin (1997), drawing on her knowledge of Hispanic/Latin culture and on experiences as a therapist with Latina clients, notes that Hispanics in the U.S. continue to attribute a great deal of importance to female sexual purity. Particularly among the upper social classes, women's virginity before marriage is a cultural imperative, and women's sexual behavior is an important marker of a family's honor. Married women are expected to remain completely monogamous while accepting their husbands' extramarital sexual affairs. Indeed, experiencing sexual pleasure and gratification, even in marriage, may be interpreted as evidence of a lack of purity and virtue in women.

Using a focus group technique, Fullilove, Fullilove, Haynes, and Gross (1990) recruited low-income urban African American women to participate in small-group discussions of sexuality. The researchers reported data from six homogeneous groups, some comprised of adolescents and some of adult women. Participants spontaneously described a dichotomy of sexual roles for women: the "good girl/madonna" role and the "bad girl/whore" role. A comparable dichotomy did not exist for men. For the participants in this study, sexual intercourse outside marriage did not necessarily relegate a woman to the bad girl/whore category. Rather, bad women were those who engaged in casual sex or offered sex in return for money or drugs.

Ward and Taylor (1994), in a study of sexuality education for minority students, conducted homogeneous focus groups with urban adolescent boys and girls of six ethnic or cultural groups: Vietnamese, Portuguese, African American, White, Haitian, and Hispanic. Each group was facilitated by an adult from the relevant cultural background. Without exception, groups from all ethnic backgrounds described heterosexual double standards that were "limiting and oppressive to females" (p. 63). There were some variations across ethnic groups. For example, some groups stressed premarital chastity more than others did. However, contrasting expectations for females and males, with more restrictions on females' behavior, were clearly expressed in all groups.

The importance of local community norms is echoed in a study of 512 high school students (ages 15–19) from rural Australian small towns (Hillier, Harrison, & Warr, 1998). Using a combination of survey and focus group methods, participants' attitudes about safe sex were explored. Fourteen single-sex focus groups were conducted in seven towns, each led by a same-sex facilitator. Analyses of content and themes were conducted and "cross-verified by project members" (p. 18).

Participants judged many of the risks of having sex to be greater for young women than for young men. Chief among these was the "sullied reputation" risk, a pervasive concern expressed in every female focus group. Loss of one's reputation was perceived to lead to sexual harassment, loss of both female and male friends, shame, and alienation. Respondents made clear their belief that losing one's good reputation could happen quickly and easily in a small town where everyone's activities were known and talked about. The risk of a bad reputation was perceived by both sexes to apply only to girls. Such double standards were clearly captured in these remarks from two focus groups:

> Girl: They (boys) have a one-night stand and nothing happens. We're more in fear of getting labeled like a tart or a slut or something. Whereas the boys if they have it they don't get labeled . . . and we're more ashamed of it if we do.
> Boy: You do it for the feeling and to brag about it afterwards. (Hillier et al., 1998, p. 26)

The researchers concluded that when young women in these small towns had sexual intercourse, or even when others wrongly believed that they did, they risked losing friends, family, and the opportunity for future relationships. These risks were exacerbated by the fact that females were more socially defined through their relationships than males were. Therefore, the young women were unequally positioned with their sexual partners with respect to their power to negotiate.

Attitudes toward sexual risk taking also provided the impetus for a study of U.S. inner city youth (Stanton, Black, Kaljee, & Ricardo, 1993).

The primary method was focus groups, conducted with young people in two age groups (9–10 and 13–14), supplemented by interviews with parents and ethnographic background study. The focus group sample was drawn from patients at an urban pediatric clinic serving a largely low-income African American population.

Attitudes about girls' and boys' sexual activity seemed to be more similar than different in this population. High levels of sexual activity were perceived as normative for both sexes. One difference that did emerge was that sexual activity for even very young boys was socially accepted by peers and adults, whereas attitudes toward girls' sexual activity were more variable. Although some girls chose to abstain from sexual intercourse and reported that peers respected their choice, others reported a great deal of pressure to become sexually active. Moreover, participants agreed that girls who became pregnant received considerable positive attention and acceptance. Thus, these results suggest that peer pressure on boys strongly discouraged abstinence from intercourse. Although there was similar peer pressure on girls, at least some girls perceived abstinence as a viable option.

Taken together, these analyses of diverse ethnic and cultural groups suggest that contemporary sexual double standards are local and subcultural constructions rather than a universal mandate.

Language and Discourse Analyses

Language both reflects and reinforces social reality. Studies of terms for sexually active women and men show that such terms differ in frequency and connotation. The English language has many more terms describing women than men in specifically sexual ways, and the great majority of these are negative. In a study of slang from a U.S. university, almost 90% of the words for women and only 46% of the words for men had negative connotations. Many negative words for women described them as being very sexually active ("turboslut," "roadwhore," "skag," "wench"). There was only one term for very sexually active men ("Mr. Groin"), and it was not seen as unambiguously negative (Munro, 1989). In a language corpus from another university, Sutton (1995) found that students generated many negative words for women when asked simply to collect 10 slang terms that they and their friends used often. By far the largest category was terms denoting sexually active women: "bait," "beddy," "ho," "hooker," "hootchie," "scud," "skank ho," "slag," "slut," "tramp," and "whore" are examples. Sexually active women were also denoted by their genitals: "pelt," "slam hole," "stimey hole," and "tuna." The only comparable male term offered by students was "hoebuck" (a parallel to "hobag" but less negative in connotation). Thus, the linguistic resources available to assess the sexual behavior of women and men differ considerably and define women's (more than men's) morality and desirability in terms of their sexuality.

The only experimental study to include an open-ended question about language and sexuality was conducted by Milhausen and Herold (1999). Participants were asked what words they would use to describe a man or woman who has had many sexual partners. Two raters independently coded responses into categories. Virtually all the words listed for highly experienced men and women were deemed negative. Terms for men most often connoted sexual predation ("player") and promiscuity ("sleazy"). Terms for women most often connoted promiscuity ("slut") and psychological dysfunction ("insecure"). Milhausen and Herold tallied the number of negative terms applied to female and male targets. Finding no difference, they concluded that their linguistic analysis provided no support for double standards. All the participants in this study were women. . . .

Another recent study of language use showed that men are more likely to be portrayed positively and agentically in everyday talk about sex. Weatherall and Walton (1999) studied college students' metaphors for sexual activity by asking students to keep daily diaries of their sex talk for a week. Common types of metaphors were food and eating, animals, sport and games, and war and violence. Although most of these metaphors would seem to be potentially gender neutral, males were two and a half times more likely to be the actor in mundane talk about sexual activity. These linguistic data may reflect the double standard in agency and initiation that is a frequently recurring theme in qualitative and quantitative studies that assess attitudes about sexuality. . . .

Summary and Critique of Qualitative Studies

The majority of the ethnographies, interview and focus group studies, and linguistic analyses reviewed here found evidence for double standards, and sometimes indicated the influence of some of the same contextual factors shown in quantitative studies. As a group, the qualitative studies used a much more varied spectrum of participants with respect to ethnicity, race, social class, age, and social position than did the quantitative studies. Although there is no intrinsic reason that quantitative studies could not draw from diverse populations, this has not been the case in practice.

Qualitative researchers' use of diverse samples yields some benefits. It adds to the limited database of quantitative studies using college students and potentially can correct for some of the developmental and social biases introduced by over-relying on college sample. By drawing on participants from varying social positions, this research also helps portray the variety of socially constructed double standards. Open-ended methods have the potential to show the dynamic aspects of double standards: how they are conveyed in interaction and actively employed as a means of social control for both sexes. In the middle school sex education class described by Orenstein (1994), . . . both boys and girls were provided with models that might encourage them to incorporate sexual double standards into their value systems. Some boys engaged in macho posturing about high levels of male sexual activity, and some voiced negative labels for females who behaved similarly. These behaviors occurred without sanction from an authority figure and with approval from other students.

Of course, interpretive methods have their drawbacks, too. They are costly in terms of time. They require researchers who are members of the group being studied and/or highly trained in developing rapport and trust. Finally, unlike laboratory studies, they cannot manipulate variables to establish causality, and they cannot systematically examine the interaction of several factors.

There is potential for selection bias in choosing interpretive studies for a review, and this review is no exception. Because interpretive methods such as ethnographies may be very broad in scope, with the goal of capturing the ethos of a community, a narrow topic such as sexual double standards may be embedded in the (often book-length) report but not accessible by keyword or index searches. Another potential selection bias is that interpretive studies that look for but do not find evidence of double standards may not mention the topic in their reports, so that the published literature overrepresents the incidence of double standards. This is analogous to the file-drawer problem in quantitative studies. In this review, our criteria for including a qualitative study were necessarily less precise than our criteria for including a quantitative study. . . .

References

Eder, D., Evans, C. C., & Parker, S. (1995). *Gender and adolescent culture.* New Brunswick, NJ: Rutgers University Press.

Espin, O. M. (1997). *Latina realities: Essays on healing, migration and sexuality.* Boulder, CO: Westview Press.

Fromme, R. E., & Emihovich, C. (1998). Boys will be boys: Young males' perceptions of women, sexuality and prevention. *Education and Urban Society, 30,* 172–188.

Fullilove, M. T., Fullilove, R. E., Haynes, K., & Gross, S. (1990). Black women and AIDS prevention: A view towards understanding the gender rules. *The Journal of Sex Research, 27,* 47–64.

Gentry, M. (1998). The sexual double standard: The influence of number of relationships and level of sexual activity on judgments of women and men. *Psychology of Women Quarterly, 22,* 505–511.

Hillier, L., Harrison, L., & Warr, D. (1998). "When you carry condoms all the boys think you want it": Negotiating competing discourses about safe sex. *Journal of Adolescence, 21,* 15–29.

Jacoby, A. P., & Williams, J. D. (1985). Effects of premarital sexual standards and behavior on dating and marriage desirability. *Journal of Marriage and the Family, 47,* 1059–1065.

Loxley, W. (1996). "Sluts" or "sleazy little animals"?: Young people's difficulties with carrying and using condoms. *Journal of Community & Applied Social Psychology, 6,* 293–298.

Mark, M. M., & Miller, M. L. (1986). The effects of sexual permissiveness, target gender, subject gender, and attitude toward women on social perception: In search of the double standard. *Sex Roles, 15,* 311–322.

Martin, K. A. (1996). *Puberty, sexuality, and the self: Girls and boys at adolescence.* London: Routledge.

Milhausen, R. R., & Herold, E. S. (1999). Does the sexual double standard still exist? Perceptions of university women. *The Journal of Sex Research, 36,* 361–368.

Moffat, M. (1989). *Coming of Age in New Jersey.* New Brunswick, NJ: Rutgers University Press.

Munro, P. (1989). *Slang U.* New York: Harmony Books.

Oliver, M. B., & Sedikides, C. (1992). Effects of sexual permissiveness on desirability of partner as a function of low and high commitment to relationship. *Social Psychology Quarterly, 55,* 321–333.

Orenstein, P. (1994). *Schoolgirls: Young women, self-esteem, and the confidence gap.* New York: Doubleday.

O' Sullivan, L. F. (1995). Less is more: The effects of sexual experience on judgments of men's and women's personality characteristics and relationship desirability. *Sex Roles, 33,* 159–181.

Sprecher, S. (1989). Premarital sexual standards for different categories of individuals. *The Journal of Sex Research, 26,* 232–248.

Sprecher, S., & Hatfield, E. (1996). Premarital sexual standards among U.S. college students: Comparison with Russian and Japanese students. *Archives of Sexual Behavior, 25,* 261–288.

Sprecher, S., McKinney, K., & Orbuch, T. L. (1987). Has the double standard disappeared? An experimental test. *Social Psychology Quarterly, 50,* 24–31.

Sprecher, S., Regan, P. C., McKinney, K., Maxwell, K., & Wazienski, H. (1997). Preferred level of sexual experience in a date or mate: The merger of two methodologies. *The Journal of Sex Research, 34,* 327–337.

Stanton, B. F., Black, M., Kaljee, L., & Ricardo, I. (1993). Perceptions of sexual behavior among urban early adolescents: Translating theory through focus groups. *Journal of Early Adolescence, 13,* 44–66.

Sutton, L. A. (1995). Bitches and skankly hobags: The place of women in contemporary slang. In K. Hall & M. Bucholtz (Eds.), *Gender articulated: Language and the socially constructed self* (pp. 279–296). New York: Routledge.

Thompson, S. (1995). *Going all the way: Teenage girls' tales of sex, romance, and pregnancy.* New York: Hill and Wang.

Ward, J. V., & Taylor, J. (1994). Sexuality education for immigrant and minority students: Developing a culturally appropriate curriculum. In J. M. Irvine (Ed.), *Sexual cultures and the construction of adolescent identities* (pp. 51–68). Philadelphia: Temple University Press.

Weatherall, A., & Walton, M. (1999). The metaphorical construction of sexual experience in a speech community of New Zealand university students. *British Journal of Social Psychology, 38,* 479–498.

Michael J. Marks and
R. Chris Fraley

 **NO**

The Sexual Double Standard: Fact or Fiction?

In contemporary society it is widely believed that women and men are held to different standards of sexual behavior. As [many have] noted, "a man who is successful with many women is likely to be seen as just that—successful . . . [whereas] a woman known to have 'success' with many men is . . . likely to be known as a 'slut.'" The view that men are socially rewarded and women socially derogated for sexual activity has been labeled the *sexual double standard*.

The sexual double standard has received a lot of attention from contemporary critics of Western culture. Tanenbaum (2000), for example, has documented the harassment and distress experienced by adolescent girls who have been branded as "sluts" by their peers. Other writers have critiqued the way the media help to create and reinforce negative stereotypes of sexually active women and how these stereotypes may contribute to violence against women. Given the attention the sexual double standard has received in contemporary discourse, one might assume that behavioral scientists have documented the double standard extensively and elucidated many of the mechanisms that generate and sustain it. Despite much systematic research, however, there is virtually no consistent evidence for the existence of this allegedly pervasive phenomenon.

We have three objectives in this [paper]. Our first is to review briefly the empirical literature on the sexual double standard. As we discuss, research findings concerning the double standard do not strongly support its existence. Next, we discuss several methodological reasons why previous researchers may not have been able to document a double standard even if one exists. Finally, we report a study that was designed to determine whether the sexual double standard exists by rectifying the methodological limitations of previous studies.

Empirical Research on the Sexual Double Standard

The sexual double standard seems to be a ubiquitous phenomenon in contemporary society; one recent survey revealed that 85% of people believe that a double standard exists in our culture. The double standard is frequently

From *Sex Roles: A Journal of Research,* vol. 52, no. 3/4, February 2005, excerpts from pp. 175–186. Copyright © 2005 by Springer Science + Business Media. Reprinted by permission via Rightslink.

publicized by the media. For example, MTV, a popular cable television channel that specializes in contemporary culture, recently aired a program called "Fight for Your Rights: Busting the Double Standard" that was designed to convey the idea that a sexual double standard exists and that people should try to transcend it by exhibiting more egalitarian thinking.

Although the sexual double standard seems pervasive, empirical research does not necessarily show that people evaluate sexually active men and women differently. In fact, much of the literature reveals little or no evidence of a double standard. O'Sullivan (1995), for example, conducted a person perception study in which individual participants read vignettes of a male or female target who reported a high or low number of past sexual partners. Participants then evaluated the targets in domains such as likeability, morality, and desirability as a spouse. Although men and women who engaged in casual intercourse were evaluated more negatively than those whose sexual experiences occurred in committed relationships, a double standard was not found. Gentry (1998) also employed a person perception task and found that raters judged both male and female targets who had relatively few past sexual partners and who were in monogamous relationships more positively than targets who had a high number of partners and had frequent casual sex. Again, no evidence of a double standard was found. Sprecher et al. (1988) examined how appropriate certain sexual acts were for men and women of various ages. Although older targets received more permissive responses (i.e., they were allowed more sexual freedom), there were few differences in the standards used for men versus women for any age group.

Researchers have also documented many characteristics of respondents that influence attitudes toward sexuality, but few, if any, of these findings are consistent with a double standard. For instance, Garcia (1982) found that respondents' degree of androgyny was related to the sexual stereotypes they held. Androgynous participants (i.e., people who possess high levels of both masculine and feminine psychological traits) displayed a single standard, whereas gender-typed respondents (i.e., masculine men and feminine women) displayed a slight preference for female targets in the low-sexual experience condition. However, a preference for high-experience male targets over low-experience male targets was not found.

The number of sexual partners respondents have had also appears to influence their judgments of targets. Milhausen and Herold (1999), for example, found that women with many sexual partners were more tolerant of highly sexually active men than were women with few sexual partners. However, the interaction between target gender, target experience, and participant experience was not tested. The gender of the respondent has also been shown to influence views on sexuality. Women tend to hold sexual standards that are stricter than those of men, but do not necessarily apply those standards differently as a function of the gender of the person being evaluated.

In summary, although it appears that people *do* evaluate others with respect to the number of sexual partners those people have had, research does not consistently show that those evaluations differ for male and female targets. Even in situations in which men and women are evaluated differently, the associations usually vary only in magnitude, not in sign. In other words, there are some situations in which both women and men may be evaluated more negatively as the number of sexual partners they report increases, but this association is only slightly stronger for women than it is for men. As we will explain below, this pattern can be characterized as a "weak" rather than "strong" double standard. If the sexual double standard is as pervasive and powerful as many people believe, empirical research should reveal crossover interactions such that the association between sexual experience and evaluations is negative for women but positive for men.

Sexual Double Standard Research Methodology

Although the empirical literature would seem to suggest that the sexual double standard is not in operation, it may be the case that behavioral scientists have failed to tap it properly. Commonly used paradigms for studying the sexual double standard may have methodological limitations that prevent the double standard from emerging. If this is the case, changes are needed in the methodology used in sexual double standard research.

One limitation of past research is the likely existence of demand characteristics. For example, if a study explicitly requires participants to rate the appropriateness of certain sexual behaviors for men, immediately followed by identical questions regarding women, participants may try to answer either in an egalitarian manner or in a manner that is consistent with what they believe to be the norm. Given that many people have preconceived notions about the sexual double standard, it is important to minimize demand characteristics when researching attitudes toward sexuality.

A second limitation of past research involves the presentation of sexual activity in a valenced fashion. For example, some researchers have used materials that imply that premarital sexual intercourse "is just wrong" or have described a target as having a number of past sexual partners that is "a lot above average." This kind of language implies that there is something abnormal or inappropriate about the target's activity. Describing sexual activity with value-laden terms or implying that a person is involved in *any* behavior to an excess may lead to biased evaluations of that person, regardless of whether that person is male or female. If a sexual double standard exists, the use of these kinds of descriptors may occlude researchers' ability to document it clearly.

Finally, much of the past double standard research has not differentiated between attitudes and evaluations. *Attitudes* toward sexual behavior may include general beliefs about the norms of the culture, personal decisions about when sex is permissible, and the perceived appropriateness of certain sexual behaviors. *Evaluations* concern real judgments made about specific people who engage in sexual activity. Attitudes may be independent of the way people actually evaluate one another. Because of this, results concerning attitudinal differences (e.g., women hold less permissive sexual standards than men do) as evidence of the double standard's existence may conflict with results concerning evaluations of others' behavior. We believe that at the core of popular interest in the sexual double standard is the notion that men and women are evaluated differently depending on their sexual experience. Although the general attitudes that people hold about sexuality are of interest to psychologists, these attitudes may not be reflected in the actual evaluations that people make about one another. Therefore, it is imperative to focus on the evaluations that people make about specific individuals.

Overview of the Present Study

The objective of the present experiment was to determine whether people evaluate men and women differently based on the number of sexual partners they have had. To do this, we asked participants to rate a target on a number of evaluative dimensions. We manipulated both (a) the sex of the target and (b) the number of sexual partners reported by the target. This experiment was explicitly designed to rectify some of the limitations of previous research on the sexual double standard. For example, we focused on the evaluations people made about specific targets rather than general perceptions of social norms. We did not include valenced or biased descriptions of sexual activity (e.g., "promiscuous," "above average number of partners"). Moreover, we employed a between-subjects design to reduce potential demand characteristics. These features enabled us to draw attention away from the sexual focus of the study and allowed us to tap the way people evaluate others who vary in gender and sexual experience. . . .

Competing Hypotheses

If a traditional or "strong" sexual double standard exists, then as the number of sexual partners reported increases, male targets would be evaluated more positively and female targets more negatively. . . .

It is also possible that a "weak" double standard exists, such that both men and women are derogated for high levels of sexual experience, but to different degrees. . . . Finally, if there is no sexual double standard, then we would observe equivalent slopes for male and female targets. . . .

Method

Participants

. . . The . . . sample consisted of 144 undergraduates from a large midwestern university (44 men, 100 women) who participated in fulfillment of partial course credit. The mean participant age in this sample was 19.66 ($SD = 3.14$, range 18–30 years). . . .

Design

We employed a 2 (target sex) $\times$ 6 (number of partners: 0, 1, 3, 7, 12, or 19) between-subjects design. . . .

Procedure

A page (constructed by the experimenters) that contained five questions and the answers to those questions was given to the participants to read. Participants were told that the page was a section from a general public survey that had been completed by an anonymous individual. The page contained answers to questions such as "What are your hobbies?" and "How do you see yourself?" Information about the target's sexual experience was conveyed in response to the question "What is something not many people know about you?" The key phrase in the response was "I've had sex with [number] [guys/girls]. I don't really have much to say about it. It's just sort of the way I've lived my life."

After reading the page that contained the target's answers, participants were asked to rate 30 evaluative statements about the target. Participants rated each item on a *Disagree* [to] *Agree* [scale]. These items . . . power, intelligence, likeability, morality, quality as a date, quality as a spouse, physical appeal, and friendship [comprised] four evaluative factors: *values* . . . , *peer popularity* . . . , *power/success* . . . , and *intelligence*. . . .

Results

. . . [A statistical technique, called multiple regression was used to analyse the results.]

In the values domain, there was a main effect of number of sexual partners. . . . Targets with more partners were evaluated more negatively. . . . There was no main effect of target sex and no . . . interaction [of number of sexual partners and target sex].

In the domain of peer popularity, there was a main effect of number of sexual partners. . . . Targets with more partners were evaluated more negatively. . . . There was no main effect of target sex and no . . . interaction [of number of sexual partners and target sex].

In the domain of power/success, there were no main effects of target sex or number of sexual partners, although there was a tendency for participants to evaluate targets with many partners more negatively. . . . There was no . . . interaction [of number of sexual partners and target sex].

In the domain of intelligence, again there was a main effect of number of sexual partners. . . . Targets with more partners were evaluated more negatively. . . . There was no . . . interaction [of number of sexual partners and target sex].

Discussion

To date, there has been little evidence that women are evaluated more negatively than men for having many sexual partners. However, if the double standard exists, methodological limitations of previous research may have prevented it from emerging clearly. In the present research, we sought to provide a rigorous test of whether or not the sexual double standard exists by rectifying methodological limitations of previous studies. Our data reveal virtually no evidence of a traditional, or "strong," sexual double standard. . . .

These results . . . suggest that although the double standard may not operate in overall evaluations of persons, it may play a role in shaping perceptions of sexually active people in specific domains. Concerning the domain of intelligence, for example, engaging in frequent casual sex may not be a "smart" thing to do in light of the dangers of sexually transmitted diseases (especially AIDS). . . .

These results suggest that even after addressing some of the methodological limitations of previous research, traditional accounts of the sexual double standard do not appear to characterize the manner in which sexually active men and women are evaluated. This raises the question of whether the sexual double standard is more a cultural illusion than an actual phenomenon. If the double standard does not accurately characterize the manner in which people evaluate sexually active others, why does belief in it persist?

One possibility is that people are sensitive to our culture's "sexual lexicon." Many writers have observed that there are more slang terms in our language that degrade sexually active women than sexually active men. On the basis of such observations, people may conclude that a sexual double standard exists. However, one must be cautious when citing sexual slang as evidence of a double standard. It may be more valuable to consider the relative frequency of the use of slang terms than to consider solely the number of slang terms that exist. When Milhausen and Herold (2001) analyzed the frequency of sexual slang used to describe men and women in actual discourse, they found that the majority of men and women used negative terms to describe both sexually experienced men *and* women. They reported that a minority of men (25%) and women (8%) actually used words such as "stud" to describe sexually active men. Moreover, sexually active men were frequently described with words that fall into the category of *sexual predator* (e.g., "womanizer") or *promiscuous* (e.g., "slut," "dirty"). So although a difference exists in the *number* of sexual slang terms to describe men and women, it is not nearly analogous to the difference in the frequency of their *use* for men and women.

The confirmation bias may also help to explain why people believe that the sexual double standard exists. Confirmation bias refers to a type of selective thinking in which one tends to notice evidence that confirms one's beliefs and to ignore or undervalue evidence that contradicts one's beliefs. Confirmation biases may lead people to notice cases that are consistent with the double standard (e.g., a woman being referred to as a "slut") and fail to notice cases inconsistent with the double standard (e.g., a man being referred to as a "whore"). Because the vast majority of people believe that a sexual double standard exists, it is likely that people will process social information that seemingly corroborates the sexual double standard and will ignore information that refutes it. In short, although men and women may have an equal probability of being derogated (or rewarded) for having had many sexual partners, people may tend to notice only the instances in which women are derogated and men are rewarded. Attending to cases that are consistent with the double standard while ignoring cases inconsistent with it may create the illusion that the sexual double standard is more pervasive than it really is.

Limitations of the Present Study

Although we sought to correct some limitations of past research, other limitations remain. First, the statistical power of the student sample was low because of the relatively small sample size. . . .

Second, the results reported here may not generalize to populations outside of Western culture. Culture can be a powerful sculptor of sexual attitudes and behavior; the double standard may exist in one culture, but be absent from another. For instance, a review of the anthropological literature on sex and sexuality in Africa reveals much evidence of a double standard in African culture.

Third, this study, like much previous research, employs an experimental person perception paradigm. Studying the double standard in more naturalistic settings may reveal dynamics not otherwise tapped by more artificial methodologies. For example, observing "hot spots" where social interactions are possibly centered on sex (e.g., bars, locker rooms) may offer insight to the kinds of attitudes expressed concerning the sexual activity of men and women.

Finally, the present research is relatively atheoretical, partly because we believe that it is necessary to document the phenomenon of the double standard systematically (if it exists) before bringing theoretical perspectives to bear on it. Nonetheless, there may be theoretical perspectives that would help guide us in a more effective search for this phenomenon. For example, social psychological theory suggests that people tend to conform to social norms in the presence of others. Because there are strong gender norms concerning the appropriate sexual behavior of men and women, people may behave in accordance with these norms in social situations. Our study, like other studies on the double standard, only focused on individuals in nongroup situations. Social psychological theory suggests that social interaction in group contexts may be a necessary precondition for the emergence of the double standard.

Conclusions

In an effort to denounce the sexual double standard, contemporary authors, critics, and the media may actually be *perpetuating* it by unintentionally providing confirming evidence for the double standard while ignoring disconfirming evidence. Most accounts from these sources cite numerous cases of women being derogated for sexual activity, perhaps in an effort to elicit empathy from the audience. Empathy is a commendable (and desirable) goal, but these writings may also serve to embed the double standard in our collective conscious. Suggesting that a societal double standard is the basis of the derogation of women shifts focus away from those who are truly at fault—those who are engaging in or permitting sexual harassment and other forms of derogation.

In closing, we believe that it may be beneficial to shift the emphasis of sexual double standard research from the question of *whether* the double standard exists to *why* the double standard appears to be such a pervasive phenomenon when it really is not. By addressing this question, future researchers should be able to elucidate the disparity between popular intuitions and the research literature and open doors to novel avenues for our understanding of attitudes toward sexuality.

References

Garcia, L. T. (1982). Sex-role orientation and stereotypes about male-female sexuality. *Sex Roles, 8,* 863–876.

Gentry, M. (1998). The sexual double standard. The influence of number of relationships and level of sexual activity on judgments of women and men. *Psychology of Women Quarterly, 22,* 505–511.

Milhausen, R. R., & Herold, E. S. (1999). Does the sexual double standard still exist? Perceptions of university women. *Journal of Sex Research, 36,* 361–368.

Milhausen, R. R., & Herold, E. S. (2001). Reconceptualizing the sexual double standard. *Journal of Psychology and Human Sexuality, 13,* 63–83.

O'Sullivan, L. F. (1995). Less is more: The effects of sexual experience on judgments of men's and women's personality characteristics and relationship desirability. *Sex Roles, 33,* 159–181.

Sprecher, S., McKinney, K., Walsh, R., & Anderson, C. (1988). A revision of the Reiss Premarital Sexual Permissiveness Scale. *Journal of Marriage and the Family, 50,* 821–828.

Tanenbaum, L. (2000). *Slut!* New York: Harper Collins.

POSTSCRIPT

Does a Traditional or "Strong" Double Standard with Respect to Sexual Behavior Exist Among Adolescents?

The selections presented here both provide compelling cases for the existence of the double standard and the non-existence of the double standard. How a particular study is conducted seems to have an impact on whether a double standard effect is documented (or not). Could researchers be incorrectly measuring the sexual double standard or missing important components of how the double standard is conveyed? Both Marks and Fraley as well as Crawford and Popp would agree that classic social science research, whereby an experiment is conducted holding as many other variables constant as possible, may fail to capture a true double standard effect. It seems as if participants in these types of studies are not judging males and females differentially; participants seem to like "sexually permissive" individuals less, regardless of their gender. The double standard seems to be more evident in the qualitative research (e.g., ethnographies, interviews) reviewed by Crawford and Popp. When observing people in a more naturalistic setting, the double standard seems to be alive and well (e.g., the classroom example cited in Crawford and Popp is particularly compelling).

Another clever qualitative study was published recently that attempted to document subtle or covert sexual messages consistent with the sexual double standard. Aubrey (2004) content analyzed sexual messages conveyed in television dramas that were aimed at adolescents (e.g., Gilmore Girls, Dawson's Creek) and found that there was a trend that supported the sexual double standard such that women tended to be more likely to receive negative consequences (e.g., guilt, rejection) of sexual behavior. Also related to the double standard is the idea that "good girls" will not initiate sexual behavior. Aubrey assessed the results of female sexual initiation and found negative consequences were the more likely outcome when a woman initiated sex relative to when a man initiated sex. This conveys messages to both women and men: Women—do not initiate sex or bad things will ensue; and men—when women initiate sex, it may be dangerous for either or both of you. Also, this study found that men initiated sex much more often than women did; the message to youth may be that men are expected to be more sexually active and women are expected to be passive recipients. This is also an indirect sexual double standard-type message.

Whether a sexual double standard exists or not, people believe it exists. Milhausen and Herold (1999) found that 93 percent of their sample of university women agreed that the double standard exists. Does this belief have any potential impact on the sexuality of youth—particularly young women—in our society? Indeed, it is possible that women will be less prepared to have sex if they believe in the existence of the double standard. For example, one study cited by Crawford and Popp found that if a woman believed her male partner endorsed the double standard, she was less likely to provide a condom during intercourse. The belief in the double standard existence may also have an adverse effect on young women's views of themselves. They may evaluate their own sexual desires as undesirable and in conflict with societal standards. As a result, they may experience ambivalence about their sexuality (see Welles, 2005). It is possible that this contributes to women's greater negativity about sex relative to men.

The belief in the existence of the sexual double standard may be more important than the actual existence of the double standard. That is, maybe we do not evaluate others by the double standard but perhaps we adjust our behavior and assess ourselves in relation to our belief in this perceived "norm." In fact, Marks and Fraley (2006) conducted a follow-up study where they found evidence that people pay more attention to information that is consistent with their belief in the double standard and ignore information that contradicts the double standard. Thus, our own "confirmation bias" (i.e., the tendency to pay closer attention to social information that is consistent with our belief system and discount information that is inconsistent) may perpetuate the belief in the sexual double standard. Further, media such as television, news sources, and magazines may further endorse the existence of the sexual double standard (see Aubrey, 2004). If we make people aware of these personal and systemic biases, we may be able to counteract the effects of these beliefs—particularly when these effects may be detrimental to youth.

References/Further Readings

Aubrey, J. S. (2004). Sex and punishment: An examination of sexual consequences and the sexual double standard in teen programming. *Sex Roles, 50,* 505–514.

Double Standard, (DVD) (2002). CTV. Product information available at: http://www.mcintyre.ca/cgi-bin/search/mmiview.asp?ID=4736

Greene, K., & Faulkner, S. L. (2005). Gender, belief in the sexual double standard, and sexual talk in heterosexual dating relationships. *Sex Roles, 53*(3–4), 239–251.

Marks, M., & Fraley, R. C. (2006). Confirmation bias and the sexual double standard. *Sex Roles, 54*(1–2), 19–26.

Milhausen, R. R., & Herold, E. S. (1999). Does the sexual double standard still exist? Perceptions of university women. *The Journal of Sex Research,* 36, 361–368.

Muehlenhard, C. L., & Quackenbush, D. M. (1998). Sexual Double Standard Scale. In C. M. Davis, W. L. Yarber, R. Bauserman, G. Scherer & S. L. Davis (Eds.), *Handbook of sexuality-related measures* (pp. 186–188). Thousand Oakes, CA: Sage.

Oliver, M. B., & Hyde, J. S. (1993). Gender differences in sexuality: A meta-analysis. *Psychological Bulletin,* 114, 29–51.

Reiss, I. (1967). *The social context of premarital sexual permissiveness.* New York: Holt, Rinehart, and Winston.

Schleicher, S. S., & Gilbert, L. A. (2005). Heterosexual dating discourses among college students: Is there still a double standard? *Journal of College Student Psychotherapy,* 19(3), 7–23.

Welles, C. E. (2005). Breaking the silence surrounding female adolescent sexual desire. *Women & Therapy,* 28(2), 31–45.

White, E. (2001). *Fast girls: Teenage tribes and the myth of the slut.* New York: Scribner.

ISSUE 11

Is Female Sexual Orientation More Fluid than Male Sexual Orientation During Adolescence?

YES: Lisa M. Diamond, from "A New View of Lesbian Subtypes: Stable versus Fluid Identity Trajectories over an 8-year Period," *Psychology of Women Quarterly* (vol. 29, no. 2, 2005)

NO: Margaret Rosario, Eric W. Schrimshaw, Joyce Hunter, and Lisa Braun, from "Sexual Identity Development Among Lesbian, Gay, and Bisexual Youths: Consistency and Change Over Time," *The Journal of Sex Research* (February 2006)

ISSUE SUMMARY

YES: Lisa Diamond, an assistant professor of psychology and women's studies at the University of Utah, presents the results of an 8-year study that compared women who were "stable" versus "fluid" in their sexual orientation self-labeling and found that those who were "fluid" had more fluctuation in their physical and emotional attractions as well as sexual behavior and romantic relationships. She argues for acknowledging the important role of female plasticity in sexual orientation research.

NO: Researchers Rosario and colleagues oppose the hypothesis that females are more sexually fluid than males. They argue that female youth were less likely to change their sexual identity than males.

Often adults dismiss adolescent same-sex romantic or sexual relationships as "just a phase." This "phase" concept is reinforced in popular television shows where it is not uncommon to hear a joke about a woman who "tried it" in college—meaning she had sexual relations with another woman. In the following selection, Diamond makes a similar reference to this with the term "LUG" (lesbian until graduation). Within the lesbian community, one might hear jokes about "tourists visiting the Isle of Lesbos"—referring to women who are curious about sex with other women but who do not adopt a sexual minority identity label (e.g., lesbian, bisexual, or part of the women's community).

These anecdotal accounts illustrate the controversy surrounding women's sexual fluidity. The flexibility of women's—especially young women's—sexuality has been a question of interest since the sexual revolution; men's sexuality, in contrast, appears to be more stable.

Roy Baumeister's theory of erotic plasticity (2000, 2004) condends that women's sexuality is more plastic (i.e., can be more easily shaped by cultural, social, and environmental factors) and is more reactive to such external factors as historical events, socialization and peer influence, and other cultural determinants. In contrast, Baumeister contends that there is substantial evidence of the invariability of men's sexuality. As an example, Baumeister cites that the sexual revolution had a greater impact on women's sexuality—which changed a lot—than on men's sexuality—which changed very little. Thus, women's sexuality changed as a consequence of their social environment. Hypotheses can be derived from his theory, such as women who are exposed to positive gay/lesbian/bisexual environments would be more likely to consider or to engage in same-sex behavior while men would not be as likely to do so.

There are a number of explanations as to why this gender difference in erotic plasticity might exist. For example, differences in erotic plasticity may be based on power differences: Women tend to be in lower positions of social power, so flexibility is more adaptive (i.e., to please their more powerful male partners). Alternatively, men may have a stronger sex drive than women; a milder sex drive is more easily molded. Therefore, gender differences in erotic plasticity may be explained by either nature or nurture.

In his extensive review and theoretical paper, Baumeister (2000) considers studies of the bisexual behavior of women and men as evidence of women's greater erotic plasticity. In the following selection, Diamond applies Baumeister's theory by investigating adolescent women who initially identify as a sexual minority (i.e., as a lesbian or bisexual woman) and then relinquish that label (i.e., identifying as heterosexual or *not* as lesbian or bisexual). Diamond illustrates that there are "fluid" lesbians—these are women who, as youth, identify as lesbian but, across time, change their self-label (i.e., either reject the label lesbian for "no label" or identify as bisexual). She demonstrates that these "fluid" lesbians are distinctly different in terms of their physical and emotional attraction to other people as well as different with regard to their sexual behavior and romantic relationships compared to "stable" lesbians or "stable" bisexual women.

Rosario et al.'s study challenges the gender plasticity hypothesis by comparing both young men's and young women's sexual minority label relinquishment longitudinally. When you are reading these two selections, consider how the different methods (e.g., different time frames: 8 years versus 1 year and different comparison groups: women versus men and women) used by the researchers might account for the differences in the authors' conclusions.

YES

Lisa M. Diamond

A New View of Lesbian Subtypes: Stable versus Fluid Identity Trajectories over an 8-year Period

Although it is typically assumed that individuals with exclusive, early-appearing, and longitudinally stable same-sex attractions and behavior are the most common and representative "types" of sexual minorities, this does not appear to be the case. Recent representative studies of American adults (Laumann, Gagnon, Michael, & Michaels, 1994) and adolescents (French, Story, Remafedi, Resnick, & Blum, 1996; Russell & Seif, 2002) have found that individuals reporting nonexclusive attractions outnumber those reporting exclusive same-sex attractions, especially among women. Furthermore, psychophysiological research has documented that both lesbian-identified and heterosexual-identified women show genital arousal to both same-sex and other-sex visual sexual stimuli (Chivers, Rieger, Latty, & Bailey, 2004). Women also appear more likely to exhibit situational and environmental plasticity in sexual attractions, behavior, and identification (Baumeister, 2000; Diamond, 2000, 2003a). Collectively, such findings demonstrate that the distinction between lesbian, bisexual, and heterosexual women is one of degree rather than kind.

. . . In this article, I draw upon data collected from an 8-year longitudinal study of young sexual-minority women to explore the usefulness of a typology that focuses on change in lesbian identification over time. This research seeks to understand experiential and developmental differences between three types of sexual-minority women: those who maintain stable lesbian identifications once they come out, those who alternate between lesbian and nonlesbian labels after coming out, and those who never adopt lesbian labels, choosing instead to identify as bisexual or to reject identity labels altogether.

This approach represents a useful departure from previous research on lesbian identity development for two primary reasons. First, it takes fluidity between lesbian and bisexual identities and experiences—which has traditionally been treated as a source of error and ambiguity in sexual identity research—and treats it as a fundamental starting point for theorizing about typologies of female same-sex sexuality. Thus, whereas prior

From *Psychology of Women Quarterly*, vol. 29, no. 2, June 2005, excerpts from pp. 119–121, 122–124, 125–128. Copyright © 2005 by Blackwell Publishing, Ltd. Reprinted by permission.

studies of sexual identity have assumed that "lesbians," "bisexuals," and "heterosexuals" exist as stable, natural types, simply waiting to be tabulated and assessed, the present research treats such identities as potentially and meaningfully variable across the life span, and focuses on identifying the unique attributes of women who do or do not migrate between lesbian and nonlesbian identities over time.

Second, whereas extant research on sexual identity development focuses only on feelings and experiences that occur prior to "coming out" (e.g., earliest recollections of same-sex attractions, as in Savin-Williams, 1998), the present research focuses on trajectories of experience that occur after a woman has come out (at least among a subset of women who came out in their teens and early twenties). . . . This approach is particularly relevant for studying women's sexual identity development, given the extensive evidence that this process has a more variable time course and a broader set of situational triggers among women than among men (reviewed in Diamond, 1998; Savin-Williams & Diamond, 2000). Because the current research draws from 8 years of longitudinal data on adolescent and young adult sexual-minority women's attractions, identities, and behaviors, it provides a unique opportunity to examine "post-coming out" development as it unfolds over the course of adolescence and young adulthood, a period of time that is particularly apt for studies of transitions and adjustments in sexuality and identity.

The Potential Meaning of Identity Change

Note that I do not presume that a typology based on identity stability versus change is "better" or more accurate than the traditional lesbian/bisexual/heterosexual typology. Rather, my goal is to explore whether a typology that makes use of information about the consistency of a sexual-minority woman's identification over time can reveal meaningful patterns of sexual experience and development that might otherwise be obscured. For example, considering the accumulating evidence for fluidity and plasticity in both heterosexual and sexual-minority women's sexuality (Baumeister, 2000; Diamond, 2003b; Golden, 1996; Weinberg, Williams, & Pryor, 1994; Whisman, 1993), examining consistency may be a more effective way to examine how women construct and interpret their sexual self-concepts over time, particularly given the extant evidence that different women use markedly different criteria for labeling themselves lesbian versus bisexual (Golden, 1996; Rust, 1992, 1993). Some consider periodic attractions to men to be consistent with lesbian identification as long as they are not acted upon (Rust, 1992), whereas others maintain that periodic sexual contact with men is consistent with a lesbian label under certain circumstances (Diamond, 2000, 2003a).

Rather than viewing identity change as movement toward or away from a woman's "true" identity, the current approach considers some of the factors that might make some women more likely to exhibit identity stability than others. One possibility, for example, is that women with stable patterns of lesbian identification will show the most exclusive and consistent patterns of same-sex attractions and behavior, given that such patterns easily lend themselves to the culturally accepted definition of lesbianism. In contrast, women with predominant—but not exclusive— same-sex attractions, or attractions that fluctuate over time, might find it more difficult to maintain a consistent lesbian label, and might transition between lesbian and other labels depending on their environments, relationships, and circumstances.

Another intriguing possibility concerns women who feel that their attractions are focused on "the person and not the gender." There has been increasing documentation and discussion of this phenomenon in recent years (reviewed in Diamond, 2003b; see also Cass, 1990; Weinberg et al., 1994). Although some might presume that such women are "really" heterosexual, there is currently no basis on which to conclude that this particular pattern of experience is characterized by uniformly low same-sex attractions. Rather, such women might report predominant same-sex or other-sex attractions, depending on their current constellation of relationships. Either way, they might be particularly likely to exhibit change in identification over time, as their relationships change. Thus, focusing on trajectories of sexual identification, rather than single snapshots, might be particularly informative for understanding these women's experiences.

Finally, this perspective offers new ways to consider sexual development. For example, it has long been presumed that bisexual orientations have a different etiology and developmental trajectory than lesbian orientations. As Bell, Weinberg, and Hammersmith (1981) noted, "[bisexuality is] much less strongly tied to pre-adult sexual feelings. . . . Exclusive homosexuality tends to emerge from a deep-seated predisposition, while bisexuality is more subject to influence by social and sexual learning" (pp. 200–201). This plausible and widely held supposition is echoed in the long-standing colloquial distinction between *primary/born* lesbians, whose same-sex sexuality is presumed more essential, early-developing, and exclusive, and *elective/bisexual/political* lesbians, whose same-sex sexuality is presumed more subject to external influence (Burch, 1993; Ettore, 1980; Golden, 1994; Ponse, 1978). Yet framing this distinction in terms of bisexuality versus lesbianism may be misguided. Perhaps, instead, distinctions between "early-developing" and "late-developing" sexual-minority women have as much to do with the consistency of women's identification than their overall distribution of sexual attractions.

The Current Study

In the present research, these possibilities were investigated by directly comparing patterns of attraction and behavior in three groups of sexual-minority women: (a) those who have maintained consistent lesbian identifications over an 8-year period spanning the transition from late adolescence to young adulthood (denoted *stable lesbians*), (b) those who alternated between lesbian and nonlesbian labels during this time period (denoted *fluid lesbians*), and (c) those who never adopted lesbian labels, despite acknowledging and acting upon same-sex attractions (denoted *stable nonlesbians*). Although this typology is exploratory, the following tentative hypotheses are advanced:

1. Given the cultural emphasis on consistency and exclusivity in same-sex attractions and behavior as a primary criteria of lesbianism, stable lesbians will have reported both more exclusive and more consistent same-sex attractions and behavior over the 8 years of the study than fluid lesbians and stable nonlesbians.
2. Because documented instances of sexual fluidity often involve the experience of unexpectedly becoming attracted to—or involved with—specific individuals, regardless of their gender, fluid lesbians and nonlesbians will be more likely to report that their attractions are more oriented to the person and not their gender.
3. Stable lesbians will report earlier sexual identity milestones than fluid lesbians and nonlesbians (i.e, earlier attractions, sexual contact, sexual questioning, and identification). Additionally, given the cultural presumption that lesbianism is more intrinsic than bisexuality, stable lesbians will be more likely than fluid lesbians and stable nonlesbians to report that they were born with their sexuality and less likely to feel that their sexuality was influenced by their environment or by personal choice.

Method

Participants

Participants were 79 nonheterosexual women between the ages of 18 and 25 years old who were initially interviewed in person as part of a longitudinal study of sexual identity development among young women (Diamond, 1998, 2000, 2003a). . . . Three follow-up interviews were conducted by phone over the ensuing 8 years. . . .

At the beginning of each interview, each woman was asked, "How do you currently label your sexual identity to yourself, even if it's different from what you might tell other people? If you don't apply a label to your sexual identity, please say so." Lesbian- and bisexual-identified women were categorized according to their chosen identity labels. Women who declined to attach a label to their sexuality were classified as *unlabeled*. This included women who identified as "questioning" at the first interview. No women identified as questioning in subsequent interviews. Over the course of the study, 7 women described their sexual identity using alternative identity labels, such as "queer," "pansexual," or "polyamorous." When asked to describe what these labels meant, each of these women indicated that her underlying attractions were bisexual, but expressed reservations about the bisexual label because (a) it did not adequately describe the fluid and changing nature of their sexual feelings, and/or (b) it was associated with negative stereotypes, such as promiscuity. Because each of these women described her underlying attractions as bisexual, they were considered bisexual for categorization purposes. . . .

Procedures

Time 1 (T1) assessments were scripted, face-to-face interviews conducted with each woman by the primary investigator. . . . The primary investigator reinterviewed participants over the phone two years later (T2) and again after an additional three years (T3) and another additional three years (T4). The T2, T3, and T4 interviews followed a standard script reassessing the major variables assessed at T1. . . . The final T4 sample size was 79, consisting of 89% of the original respondents. None of the women who were recontacted declined to be reinterviewed. . . .

Measures

. . . T1 interviews assessed the age at which participants first consciously questioned their sexual identity, first experienced a same-sex attraction, first engaged in same-sex contact, and first openly adopted a sexual-minority identity. To assess same-sex attractions, women were asked at each interview to report the percentage of their total attractions that were directed toward the same sex on a day-to-day basis; separate estimates were provided for sexual versus emotional attractions. This yields an estimate of the relative frequency of same-sex versus other-sex attractions, regardless of the intensity of these attractions or the total number of sexual attractions experienced on a day-to-day basis. . . . To assess sexual behavior, participants were asked to report the total number of men and women with whom they engaged in sexual contact (defined as any sexually motivated intimate contact) between T1 and T2, between T2 and T3, and between T3 and T4. This information was translated into percentages, so that 100% represents exclusive same-sex behavior and 0% represents exclusive other-sex behavior. . . .

Finally, at T4 women were asked to rate, on a 1 to 5 Likert scale, their agreement with the following statements describing different aspects of sexual orientation and its development: "I'm the kind of person that's attracted to the person rather than their gender;" "I feel my sexuality is something I was born with;" "I feel my own sexuality has been influenced by my environment;" and "I feel my own lesbianism or bisexuality is something I chose."

Results

Women who identified as lesbian at each of the four assessment periods ($n = 18$) were designated as stable lesbians; those who have claimed both lesbian and nonlesbian labels at different points in the past 8 years ($n = 25$) were designated fluid lesbians; those who never adopted a lesbian label at any of the four assessments, and instead selected bisexual or unlabeled identities ($n = 36$), were designated stable nonlesbians. This categorization therefore combines nonlesbians who identify as bisexual with nonlesbians who are unlabeled. The decision to combine these groups was made on the basis of similarity in the bisexual and unlabeled women's overall patterns of attraction and behavior, documented in previous assessment of this sample (Diamond, 1998, 2000, 2003a), and to focus specifically on the relevance of changes in lesbian identification. . . .

Physical and Emotional Attractions

Hypothesis 1 predicted that across the 8 years of the study, stable lesbians would report the greatest and most consistent same-sex physical and emotional attractions. To test this hypothesis, an . . . analysis . . . (ANOVA) was conducted with identity group as the independent factor and self-reported percentages of same-sex physical attractions at T1, T2, T3, and T4 as the dependent variables. This analysis was then repeated with self-reported emotional attractions as the dependent variables. Both analyses detected a significant effect of identity group for physical attraction . . . and emotional attraction. . . . There was no . . . significant change in attractions across the four assessments. . . . As predicted, stable lesbians had the highest same-sex attractions and stable nonlesbians the least, with fluid lesbians intermediate between them. . . . To examine whether fluid lesbians were more similar to stable lesbians or stable nonlesbians, . . . comparisons were conducted using mean levels of attractions across the four assessments. . . . These analyses found that fluid lesbians had significantly greater physical and emotional same-sex attractions than did nonlesbians over the 8 years of the study . . . but significantly less same-sex physical attractions than did stable lesbians. . . . Thus, with respect to physical attractions, fluid lesbians appear to represent a fairly distinct group. Their emotional attractions, however, did not significantly differ from those of stable lesbians.

To test whether stable lesbians exhibited the most consistent attractions over time, absolute difference scores were conducted to represent changes in attractions from T1 to T2, T2 to T3, and T3 to T4. The mean of these absolute differences scores was then calculated to represent the overall magnitude of fluctuation in attractions across the 8 years of the study. An . . . analysis . . . (MANOVA) was conducted with identity group as the independent variable and mean fluctuations in physical and emotional attractions as the two dependent variables. There was a significant effect of identity group. . . . Stable lesbians showed significantly smaller fluctuations in physical and emotional attractions than both of the other groups . . . whereas fluid lesbians and stable nonlesbians did not differ.

Lastly, an analysis . . . was conducted to test for group differences in the degree to which women felt that their attractions were directed to "the person rather than their gender." There was a significant effect of identity group; . . . stable lesbians reported significantly less agreement with this statement ($M = 2.7$) than either fluid lesbians ($M = 3.7$) and nonlesbians ($M = 4.1$). . . . Fluid lesbians and nonlesbians did not differ from one another.

Sexual Behavior and Romantic Relationships

With regard to sexual behavior, it was predicted that across the 8 years of the study, stable lesbians would report the greatest percentage of same-sex sexual contact and stable nonlesbians the least, with fluid lesbians intermediate between them. This expectation was confirmed. . . . There was also a significant . . . decline in same-sex behavior across the 8 years of study. . . . This . . . decline was observed in all identity groups. . . .

A similar pattern of findings was observed for rates of participation in same-sex romantic relationships. As with same-sex sexual contact, the . . . analysis detected a significant effect of identity group. . . . These analyses found that fluid lesbians had significantly greater percentages of same-sex sexual contact and romantic relationships than did nonlesbians over the 8 years of the study . . . but significantly less than did stable lesbians. . . .

To test for differences in the magnitude of behavior/relationship change, absolute difference scores were calculated representing the total change in same-sex sexual contact and in same-sex romantic relationships from T1 to T4. . . . Stable lesbians had significantly less change in sexual behavior than both of the other groups . . . , but fluid lesbians and nonlesbians did not differ. . . .

Timing and Perceived Cause of Same-Sex Sexuality

A . . . test for identity group differences in the ages at which women reported (at T1) having experienced their first same-sex attractions, sexual questioning, same-sex sexual contact, and sexual-minority identification was conducted. There was no significant overall effect of identity group. . . . A test for identity group differences in the degree to which women felt that they were born with their sexuality, that their sexuality was influenced by their environment, and that their sexuality was something that they chose was conducted. Again, there was no significant overall effect of identity group. . . .

Discussion

This research adopted a new approach to studying sexual identity development by replacing the standard question—"how do lesbians differ from bisexuals in their attractions, behavior, and developmental histories"—with a question that presumes (rather than ignores or problematizes) longitudinal fluidity in identity. Specifically, this research examined how young sexual-minority women who maintained stable lesbian identifications over an 8-year period from late adolescence to young adulthood differed from young women who adopted inconsistent lesbian identifications and from women who maintained nonlesbian (i.e., bisexual or unlabeled) identifications. This study sought to explore the relevance of considering longitudinal consistency in identification as a marker of important sexual-developmental phenomena among sexual-minority women that might otherwise go unexplored.

Do stable lesbians, fluid lesbians, and stable nonlesbians make up distinct groups? The answer to this question is both yes and no. Perhaps one of the most important findings of this research is that the differences and similarities between these three groups were not consistent across all of the assessed phenomena. In some domains, fluid lesbians more closely resembled nonlesbians, and in other domains they were more similar to stable lesbians. Such discrepancies demonstrate the inadequacy of straightforward "lesbian/bisexual" categories for modeling variability in sexual-minority women's long-term identity development. In light of such findings, one might argue for an end to sexual categorization altogether, at least within the realm of social scientific research. Lesbian versus bisexual identity labels might be personally meaningful, but their scientific relevance for understanding the nature and development of female same-sex sexuality is increasingly unclear (see, e.g., Diamond, 1998). Yet, although replacing overarching sexual taxonomies with individualized, dimensional assessments of multiple sexual and emotional phenomena may be a more effective way to assess interindividual differences in same-sex sexuality, jettisoning all attempts at categorization seems unwarranted. Rather, the present research suggests the usefulness of exploring a range of alternative typologies. Not only might this approach serve to better elucidate the nature and development of different trajectories of same-sex experience over the life course, but it also makes explicit the degree to which all such typologies are relatively artificial and cannot be presumed to represent natural types.

Attractions and Behavior

The pattern of results regarding physical/emotional attractions and sexual/ romantic behavior confirms the expectation that women with nonexclusive attractions and behavior are less likely to maintain a stable lesbian identification over time, even when their attractions and behavior are predominantly oriented toward women. It is notable that in this regard, fluid lesbians emerged as a fairly distinct group, reporting more same-sex sexual attractions, contact, and romantic relationships than nonlesbians but less than stable lesbians. Over the 8 years of the study, fluid lesbians reported experiencing approximately 80% of their physical attractions for women and 70% of their sexual behavior with women, compared to 93% and 92%, respectively, among stable lesbians and 45% and 32%, respectively, among stable nonlesbians. Thus, their unique pattern of identity fluctuations directly corresponds to their liminal status in these domains.

The picture is somewhat different with regard to changes in attractions and behavior. Here, stable lesbians emerged as the distinct group, reporting smaller absolute fluctuations in their physical and emotional attractions from assessment to assessment (approximately 7 percentage points) than either fluid lesbians or nonlesbians (approximately 17 percentage points). Similarly, stable lesbians generally disagreed with the characterization "I'm the kind of person that is attracted to the person rather than their gender," whereas fluid lesbians and nonlesbians showed similar degrees of agreement with this characterization. The correspondence between this pattern of results and the findings regarding attraction/behavior change is particularly notable given prior research suggesting that "person-specific" attractions and relationships often catalyze abrupt—but sometimes tempo-rary—transitions in sexual experience and identity (Cassingham & O'Neil, 1993; Diamond, 2003b).

These findings have important implications for understanding the distinction between lesbian and bisexual orientations, which has become a topic of increasing debate (see Rust, 1992) given the increasing evidence for fluidity and plasticity in female sexuality (Baumeister, 2000). After all, if female sexuality is fluid, one might argue that we shouldn't bother distin-guishing between lesbians and bisexuals to begin with: Perhaps all lesbians are "potential bisexuals," and vice versa. Yet this would make sense only if all women appeared to be equally plastic in their sexuality, and the find-ings of this study suggest that this is not the case. Rather, some women appear to experience (and perceive the possibility for) greater change in their attractions and behaviors than others, and these women appear most likely to adopt nonlesbian labels or to change labels over time, even if they are predominantly attracted to women. . . .

Thus, whereas the conventional lesbian/bisexual/heterosexual typol-ogy concerns itself only with the degree of a woman's same-sex attrac-tions (exclusive/mixed/nonexistent), the present research suggests that we should consider the plasticity of a woman's same-sex sexuality (including identity, attractions, and behavior) as an orthogonal dimension. This plas-ticity, of course, would mean that there are fluid and stable subtypes of bisexuals and heterosexuals as well as lesbians. This understanding is an important point, as it challenges the common presumption that bisexual-ity is by definition a state of flexibility and plasticity. To the contrary, some bisexual women may experience their pattern of nonexclusive attractions as relatively stable, whereas others may experience the same pattern as flexible and situationally influenced. To understand the implications of such differences for women's subjective experiences of their sexuality and their identity over time, future research should systematically assess the degree of women's self-perceived sexual plasticity in concert with conven-tional assessments of their same-sex attractions and behavior.

Timing and Perceived Cause of Same-Sex Sexuality

Consideration of fluid versus stable subtypes of sexual-minority women raises obvious questions about whether the initial expression or long-term development of their sexuality differs. The results of this preliminary inves-tigation suggest few differences among stable lesbians, fluid lesbians, and nonlesbians with respect to the conventional sexual identity milestones of first same-sex attractions, first same-sex sexual contact, first sexual ques-tioning, and first sexual identification. Furthermore, these groups did not differ in their perceptions of the essential versus environmental/chosen nature of their sexuality: fluid lesbians, stable lesbians, and nonlesbians were equally likely to report feeling that they were born with their sexuality, that their sexuality had been influenced by their environment, and that they chose their sexuality. . . .

The fact that the distinction between stable versus fluid patterns of identification did not correspond with the distinction between essential and chosen/situational same-sex sexuality is counter to many common assumptions about the nature and development of lesbian and bisexual orientations, and suggests that when viewed from a life course perspective, initial sexual identity development and long-term sexual identity development are quite different processes that may be shaped by substantially different forces. This point is particularly notable given that prior research on sexual identity development has focused almost exclusively on the period of time before individuals first self-identify as sexual minorities, assuming that once this milestone is achieved, little subsequent development takes place. Not only is this supposition incorrect, but the present findings demonstrate that the types of sexual-developmental pathways women follow after coming out may tell us more about variability in the nature and experience of same-sex sexuality than the pathways women take to coming out. . . .

Conclusions

The alternative approach to sexual categorization taken in this article is not meant to replace traditional lesbian/bisexual/heterosexual distinctions, but to highlight the value of parsing the phenomenon of female same-sex sexuality in novel ways to reveal different facets of its nature and development. . . .

. . . The present research . . . demonstrates that the prevalence of plasticity and nonexclusivity in female sexuality does not mean that we must abandon all attempts to describe and explain systematic profiles of same-sex experience and development. Rather, by formulating and testing typologies that move beyond the traditional lesbian/bisexual distinction, and that take into account a longer time scale for the process of identity development, we can reveal novel and meaningful patterns of same-sex sexuality that productively challenge long-standing assumptions about subtypes of sexual-minority women. Such research can set the stage for provocative new investigations into the multiple ways that sexual-minority women's identities, attractions, relationships, and self-concepts change and intersect with one another at different stages of the life course.

References

Baumeister, R. F. (2000). Gender differences in erotic plasticity: The female sex drive as socially flexible and responsive. *Psychological Bulletin, 126,* 247–374.

Bell, A. P., Weinberg, M. S., & Hammersmith, S. K. (1981). *Sexual preference: Its development in men and women.* Bloomington, IN: Indiana University Press.

Burch, B. (1993). *On intimate terms: The psychology of difference in lesbian relationships.* Chicago: University of Illinois Press.

Cass, V. (1990). The implications of homosexual identity formation for the Kinsey model and scale of sexual preference. In D. P. McWhirter, S. A.

Sanders, & J. M. Reinisch (Eds.), *Homosexuality/heterosexuality: Concepts of sexual orientation* (pp. 239–266). New York: Oxford University Press.

Cassingham, B. J., & O'Neil, S. M. (1993). *And then I met this woman*. Freeland, WA: Soaring Eagle Publishing.

Chivers, M. L., Rieger, G., Latty, E., & Bailey, J. M. (2004). A sex difference in the specificity of sexual arousal. *Psychological Science 15*, 736–744.

Diamond, L. M. (1998). Development of sexual orientation among adolescent and young adult women. *Developmental Psychology, 34*, 1085–1095.

Diamond, L. M. (2000). Sexual identity, attractions, and behavior among young sexual-minority women over a two-year period. *Developmental Psychology, 36*, 241–250.

Diamond, L. M. (2003a). Was it a phase? Young women's relinquishment of lesbian/bisexual identities over a 5-year period. *Journal of Personality and Social Psychology, 84*, 352–364.

Diamond, L. M. (2003b). What does sexual orientation orient? A biobehavioral model distinguishing romantic love and sexual desire. *Psychological Review, 110*, 173–192.

Ettore, E. M. (1980). *Lesbians, women, and society*. London: Routledge.

French, S. A., Story, M., Remafedi, G., Resnick, M. D., & Blum, R. W. (1996). Sexual orientation and prevalence of body dissatisfaction and eating disordered behaviors: A population-based study of adolescents. *International Journal of Eating Disorders, 19*, 119–126.

Golden, C. (1994). Our politics and choices: The feminist movement and sexual orientation. In B. Greene & G. M. Herek (Eds.), *Lesbian and gay psychology: Theory, research, and clinical applications* (pp. 54–70). Thousand Oaks, CA: Sage.

Golden, C. (1996). What's in a name? Sexual self-identification among women. In R. C. Savin-Williams & K. M. Cohen (Eds.), *The lives of lesbians, gays, and bisexuals: Children to adults* (pp. 229–249). Fort Worth, TX: Harcourt Brace.

Laumann, E. O., Gagnon, J. H., Michael, R. T., & Michaels, F. (1994). *The social organization of sexuality: Sexual practices in the United States*. Chicago: University of Chicago Press.

Ponse, B. (1978). *Identities in the lesbian world: The social construction of self*. Westport, CT: Greenwood Press.

Russell, S. T., & Seif, H. (2002). Bisexual female adolescents: A critical analysis of past research and results from a national survey. *Journal of Bisexuality, 2*, 73–94.

Rust, P. R. (1992). The politics of sexual identity: Sexual attraction and behavior among lesbian and bisexual women. *Social Problems, 39*, 366–386.

Rust, P. R. (1993). Coming out in the age of social constructionism: Sexual identity formation among lesbians and bisexual women. *Gender and Society, 7*, 50–77.

Savin-Williams, R. C. (1998). ". . . And then I became gay": Young men's stories. New York: Routledge.

Savin-Williams, R. C., & Diamond, L. M. (2000). Sexual identity trajectories among sexual-minority youths: Gender comparisons. *Archives of Sexual Behavior, 29*, 419–440.

Weinberg, M. S., Williams, C. J., & Pryor, D. W. (1994). *Dual attraction: Understanding bisexuality*. New York: Oxford University Press.

Whisman, V. (1993). Identity crisis: Who is a lesbian anyway? In A. Stein (Ed.), *Sisters, sexperts, queers: Beyond the lesbian nation* (pp. 47–60). New York: Penguin.

Margaret Rosario et al.    **NO**

Sexual Identity Development Among Lesbian, Gay, and Bisexual Youths: Consistency and Change Over Time

The development of a lesbian, gay, or bisexual (LGB) sexual identity is a complex and often difficult process. Unlike members of other minority groups (e.g., ethnic and racial minorities), most LGB individuals are not raised in a community of similar others from whom they learn about their identity and who reinforce and support that identity. Rather, LGB individuals are often raised in communities that are either ignorant of or openly hostile toward homosexuality. Because sexual identity development is a process for which LGB individuals have been unprepared and which is contextually unsupported and stigmatized, it would seem that the process would be characterized by inconsistency or incongruence among its affective, cognitive, and behavioral components, such that behavior may not always coincide with affect or identity. However, psychological theory has long maintained that individuals seek to achieve congruence among affect, cognitions, and behaviors because incongruity generates psychological tension. Thus, same-sex oriented affect and behavior may lead individuals to adopt an identity consistent with such sentiments and behavior (e.g., as gay or lesbian). Similarly, identification as gay or lesbian may lead individuals to engage in sexual behaviors consistent with that identity. Indeed, the incongruence among gay identity and heterosexual behavior has been used to explain the eventual transition from heterosexual to homosexual behavior, so as to eliminate dissonance between identity and behavior. In this article, we examine consistency and change in LGB sexual identity, as well as the congruence between changes in identity and other aspects of sexuality (e.g., behavior, affect, and attitudes).

Sexual identity development for LGB individuals, also known as "the coming-out process," has received considerable attention, resulting in numerous theoretical models. These theoretical models, taken together, describe a process of identity formation and integration as individuals strive for congruence among their sexual orientation (i.e., sexual attractions, thoughts, and fantasies), sexual behavior, and sexual identity. Identity formation consists of becoming aware of one's unfolding sexual orientation, beginning to question whether one may be LGB, and exploring that emerging LGB

From *Journal of Sex Research*, vol. 43, no. 1, February 2006, excerpts from pp. 46–57. Copyright © 2006 by Society for the Scientific Study of Sexuality. Reprinted by permission via Copyright Clearance Center.

identity by becoming involved in gay-related social and sexual activities. Identity integration involves incorporating and consolidating a LGB identity. This is evident by the individual coming to accept a LGB identity, resolving internalized homophobia by transforming negative attitudes into positive attitudes, feeling comfortable with the idea that others may know about the unfolding identity, and disclosing that identity to others. Identity formation and integration are involved in a reciprocal process. They share some common components, such as gay-related social activities, that serve as both a facilitator and an outcome of identity development over time.

Research on Identity Formation and Integration

Research on the sexual identity development of LGB individuals has focused primarily on the age of various developmental milestones associated with identity formation. Although the studies generally support an overall linear trend from sexual attractions to sexual activity to self-identification as LGB at the group level, they also highlight considerable variability at the individual level. However, the studies are limited because they utilize retrospective reports that may bias results, given the tendency of people both to craft narratives consistent with their current condition and to minimize past fluctuations or changes. Thus, the retrospective design may overestimate the linear nature or consistency of the data. Developmental researchers have argued that LGB sexual identity development should be studied longitudinally and prospectively.

Only two longitudinal and prospective studies have examined changes in sexual identity over time, both of which were conducted among young women. Although no comparable studies exist on the sexual identity development of males, three longitudinal studies of young men have examined changes in sexual attractions. Taken together, the studies have found considerable consistency, as well as change, in sexual self-identification and attractions over time. For example, among 80 female youths, . . . Diamond (2000; 2003) found that 70% were consistent in their self-identification as lesbian, bisexual, or unlabeled after two years, and 50% were consistent after five years. An additional 15% transitioned to a lesbian or bisexual identity after two years, as did 14% after five years. Few youths transitioned from a lesbian, bisexual, or unlabeled identity to a straight identity. Among 216 behaviorally bisexual men (ages 18–30 years), Stokes and colleagues (1997) found that over the course of one year, 49% reported no changes in sexual orientation, 34% became more homosexually oriented, and 17% became more heterosexually oriented. Clearly, the consistency and change documented by these research studies must now be understood.

Prospective changes in LGB sexual identity would be expected to be influenced by aspects of earlier sexual identity formation, such as time since the occurrence of sexual developmental milestones. Sexual identity formation takes time because many LGB youths go through a period of sexual questioning, experimentation, and conflict before assuming and consistently self-identifying as LGB. Thus, we hypothesized that youths for whom more time has passed since reaching various sexual developmental milestones are more likely to report a sexual identity that is consistently LGB than youths who reached the milestones more recently. One study examining this hypothesis (Diamond, 2003) may have had too little statistical power to detect differences in the age of sexual developmental milestones between female youths maintaining an identity as lesbian or bisexual and those youths who changed to a straight or unlabeled identity.

Changes in LGB sexual identity would also be expected to correlate with other aspects of sexuality more broadly—specifically, sexual orientation and sexual behavior. Given congruence theory, we hypothesized that youths with a consistent gay/lesbian identity would have a sexual orientation that is more same-sex centered and would be more likely to report same-sex behaviors, but less likely to report other-sex behaviors than youths who, for example, recently transitioned from a bisexual identity to a gay/lesbian identity. Indeed, Diamond (2003) found that female youths who were consistent in their lesbian or bisexual identity reported more same-sex sexual attractions than peers who transitioned from a lesbian or bisexual identity to a heterosexual or unlabeled identity. Similarly, sexual behavior (e.g., number of female sexual partners) differed between those with a consistent sexual identity and those who relinquished their lesbian/bisexual identity. Unfortunately, no comparisons were made between the consistently lesbian and bisexual youths. Regardless, research among adults has not found a high level of congruity among aspects of sexuality. Perhaps external constraints, such as living in potentially hostile communities (e.g., rural settings) as compared with more supportive communities (e.g., urban environments), retard or impede congruence.

Finally, we hypothesized that changes in sexual identity would influence aspects of identity integration, given the need for congruence. . . . Although research has not examined this hypothesis longitudinally, cross-sectional research has found that differences in sexual identity were associated with differences in aspects of identity integration. In an earlier report on our sample, we found that youths who self-identified as gay/lesbian, as compared with bisexual, were involved in more gay-related social activities, endorsed more positive attitudes toward homosexuality, were more comfortable with other individuals knowing about their same-sex sexuality, and disclosed their sexual identity to more individuals. However, this past report neither examined changes in sexual identity nor investigated the longitudinal relations between changes in sexual identity and aspects of identity integration.

Gender

The individual variability in the age of sexual developmental milestones mentioned earlier has led researchers to critique linear models of development, particularly for women. Theorists have suggested that women are more likely than men to self-identify as bisexual and that women are more "fluid" or "plastic" in their sexual identity than men, although others dispute these claims because they consider the research inconclusive. The available evidence is mixed. Several studies have found that more female than male youths identified as bisexual. However, a large national study found that female youths were no more likely than male peers to identify as bisexual. In addition, studies have found some gender differences in the average age and order of various sexual developmental milestones, but not in all instances. Despite these findings, the potential role of gender on changes in sexual identity remains unexamined because the studies examining longitudinal changes in sexual identity development have been based on single-sex samples (e.g., Diamond, 2000; Stokes et al., 1997).

This Study

[We] examine consistency and change in sexual identity over time among LGB youths. Further, we examine how LGB youths who remain consistent in their sexual identity differ from those who have changed their sexual identity with respect to sexual identity formation (i.e., sexual developmental milestones, sexual orientation, and sexual behavior) and identity integration (i.e., comfort and acceptance of LGB identity, involvement in gay social activities, positive attitudes toward homosexuality, comfort with others knowing about their sexuality, and self-disclosure of identity to others). We hypothesized that youths who were consistent over time in a gay/lesbian identity would have been aware of their same-sex sexual orientation, been sexually active with the same sex, and been involved in gay-related social activities for a longer period of time than youths who had changed sexual identities. We also hypothesized that consistently identified gay/lesbian youths would have a current sexual orientation that is more same-sex centered, report a higher prevalence of recent sexual behavior with the same sex but a lower prevalence of recent sexual behavior with the other sex, and report higher levels of identity integration than youths who had changed sexual identities or consistently identified as bisexual. We also expected differences between consistently bisexual youths and those who had changed identities: we hypothesized that youths who had transitioned from a bisexual to a gay/lesbian identity were more likely than consistently bisexual youths to have a current sexual orientation that is more same-sex centered, report a higher prevalence of recent sexual behavior with the same sex but a lower prevalence of recent sexual behavior with the other sex, and evidence higher levels of identity integration. In addition, we examined potential gender differences in consistency and change in sexual identity, given the hypothesis in the literature that female youths are more fluid in their sexual identity than male peers.

Method

Participants

Male and female youths, ages 14 to 21 years, were recruited from organizations that serve LGB youths. . . . The final sample consisted of 156 youths (51% male) with a mean age of 18.3 years (SD = 1.65). . . .

Procedure

. . . Youths were administered a questionnaire by [a same-sex] interviewer at baseline and subsequent assessments 6 and 12 months later. . . .

Measures of Sexual Identity and Identity Formation

Sexual identity, sexual developmental milestones, sexual orientation, and sexual behaviors were assessed using the Sexual Risk Behavior Assessment—Youth (SERBAS-Y) for LGB youths. . . .

Sexual identity. . . . asking, "When you think about sex, do you think of yourself as lesbian/gay, bisexual, or straight?" . . . Items also assessed whether youths had ever thought they were really gay/lesbian or bisexual prior to the baseline assessment.

Psychosexual developmental milestones. . . . Youths were asked the ages when they were first attracted to, fantasized about, and were aroused by erotica focusing on the same sex. The mean age of these three milestones was computed to obtain a mean age of awareness of same-sex sexual orientation. . . .

Youths also were asked about the age when they first thought they "might be" gay/lesbian, when they first thought they "might be" bisexual, when they first thought they "really were" gay/lesbian, and when they first thought they "really were" bisexual. Finally, youths were asked about the age when they first engaged in any one of a several specific sexual activities (i.e., manual, digital, oral, anal-penile, vaginal-penile, and analingus) with the same sex and with the other sex. . . .

Sociosexual developmental milestones. [We] asked youths at baseline for the age when they first spoke or wrote to anyone (e.g., peer, counselor, teacher, coach, adult, switchboard) about homosexuality or bisexuality. We asked a similar series of questions with respect to ages when they first participated in various social or recreational gay-related activities (e.g., going to a gay bookstore or coffee house). . . .

Current sexual orientation. . . . Youths were asked the extent to which their recent sexual attractions, thoughts, and fantasies were focused on the same or the other sex (a) when in the presence of other individuals, (b) while masturbating, dreaming, or daydreaming, and (c) when viewing erotic material in films, magazines, or books. . . .

Recent sexual behaviors. [We] focused on whether youths reported any sexual activity (i.e., manual, digital, oral, anal-penile, vaginal-penile, and analingus) with the same sex or other sex.

Measures of Identity Integration

Involvement in gay-related activities. The prevalence of lifetime involvement in gay/lesbian-related social activities was assessed at baseline using [an 11-item] scale (e.g., going to a gay bookstore, gay coffee house, gay pride march, gay fair, gay club or bar). . . . At subsequent assessments, youths were asked about their involvement in the past 6 months (i.e., since their last assessment). . . .

Attitudes toward homosexuality. . . . eleven items (e.g., "My [homosexuality/bisexuality] does not make me unhappy") . . . assessed attitudes toward homosexuality. The mean of these items was computed at each assessment. . . .

Comfort with homosexuality. . . . twelve items (e.g., "If my straight friends knew of my [homosexuality/bisexuality], I would feel uncomfortable") . . . assessed comfort with others knowing the youth's sexuality. The mean of these items was computed for each time period. . . .

Self-disclosure of sexual identity to others.   Youths were asked at baseline to enumerate "all the people in your life who are important or were important to you and whom you told that you are (lesbian/gay/bisexual)." At subsequent assessments, youths were asked about the number of individuals to whom the youth had disclosed during the past six months (i.e., since the last assessment). The number of individuals reported was used as the indicator of self-disclosure to others. . . .

Certainty about, comfort with, and self-acceptance of sexuality.   At the 6-month and 12-month assessments, [we] asked youths who had self-identified as gay/lesbian, "How certain are you about being lesbian/gay at this point?" and asked the bisexual youths, "How certain are you about being bisexual at this point?" . . . "How comfortable are you with your lesbianism/gayness?" and asked the bisexual youths, "How comfortable are you with your lesbian/gay side?" [We] asked the gay/lesbian youths, "How accepting of your lesbianism/gayness are you?" and asked the bisexual youths, "How accepting are you of your lesbian/gay side?" We coded the prevalence of being very certain/comfortable/accepting (1) as compared to being less than very certain/comfortable/accepting (0) for each variable. . . .

Results

Sample-Level Sexual Identity Over Time

. . . Prior to the baseline assessment, nearly 40% of youths had self-identified only as gay/lesbian, an equal number had identified as gay/lesbian and bisexual, and one fifth identified exclusively as bisexual. Over the three subsequent assessments, the number of youths identifying as gay/lesbian increased, while the number of youths identifying as only bisexual decreased.

The examination of sexual identity over time ignores potential changes within youths of different sexual identities. . . . In general, youths either maintained their sexual identity or assumed a gay/lesbian identity over time. Youths who had identified as gay/lesbian at earlier times consistently identified as such at later times. Youths who had identified as both gay/lesbian and bisexual prior to baseline were approximately three times more likely to identify as gay/lesbian than as bisexual at subsequent assessments. Of youths who had identified only as bisexual at earlier assessments, 60–70% continued to identify as bisexual, while approximately 30–40% assumed a gay/lesbian identity over time.

Individual-Level Changes in Sexual Identity Over Time

As valuable as the aforementioned data may be, they are limited because the level of analysis is the sample rather than the individual. Sample-level data fail to address the critical issue of individual change in sexual identity. Therefore, at the individual-level of analysis, we created profiles for each youth of the change in sexual identity over the four longitudinal times, resulting in three major groups composed of youths who (a) consistently self-identified as gay/lesbian, (b) transitioned from bisexual to gay/lesbian identities, or (c) consistently self-identified as bisexual. [Few youths demonstrated] other patterns of change in sexual identity. . . .

Change in Sexual Identity: Univariate Relations

We [compared] the three LGB sexual identity groups (i.e., consistently gay/lesbian, consistently bisexual, and transitioned to gay/lesbian) with respect to the time since the youths experienced various psychosexual and sociosexual milestones of identity formation. The youths generally did not differ significantly on the time since reaching various psychosexual milestones, contrary to hypothesized expectations. However, as hypothesized, the youths did differ on time since reaching sociosexual milestones. Consistently gay/lesbian youths had their first discussion about same-sex sexuality with another individual and were involved in a gay-related social activity for at least a year longer than either of the other two groups of youths. . . .

As hypothesized, youths who consistently identified as gay/lesbian differed from consistently bisexual and transitioned youths on current sexual orientation and sexual behaviors. Consistently gay/lesbian youths reported both sexual orientation and sexual behaviors that were more same-sex centered than peers who transitioned to a gay/lesbian identity, and both of these groups of youths differed from peers who consistently identified as bisexual. Youths who consistently identified as gay/lesbian were more certain about, comfortable with, and accepting of their LGB identity than were peers who transitioned to a gay/lesbian identity or who consistently identified as bisexual. Furthermore, consistently gay/lesbian youths were involved in more gay-related social activities, endorsed more positive attitudes toward homosexuality, and were more comfortable with other individuals knowing about their homosexuality.

Gender and Age

. . . [Female] youths were over three times more likely than male youths . . . to identify consistently as gay/lesbian than to transition from a bisexual to a gay/lesbian identity. . . . Female youths also were less likely than male youths . . . to have transitioned from a bisexual to a gay/lesbian identity as compared with maintaining a bisexual identity. . . . Furthermore, female youths were no more likely than male youths to identify as consistently bisexual as compared with consistently gay/lesbian. . . . Youths who were consistently gay/lesbian were significantly older than youths who had transitioned to a gay/lesbian identity. . . .

Discussion

Although changes in sexual identity are possible over time, very little research has examined such changes—and none among both male and female youths. [We] found evidence of both considerable consistency and change in LGB sexual identity over time. Youths who identified as gay/lesbian prior to baseline were overwhelmingly consistent in this identity. In contrast, many youths who identified as bisexual or as both gay/lesbian and bisexual prior to baseline later identified as gay/lesbian. These findings suggest that, although there were youths who consistently self-identified as bisexual throughout the study, for other youths, a bisexual identity served as a transitional identity to a subsequent gay/lesbian identity.

[We] found three patterns of sexual identity over time: consistently gay/lesbian, transitioned from bisexual to gay/lesbian, and consistently bisexual. Of the youths, 72% consistently identified as gay/lesbian or bisexual over time. This finding of consistency is similar to past research (Diamond, 2000: 70%). . . .

Youths who changed sexual identities were hypothesized to report experiencing psychosexual and sociosexual milestones of identity formation more recently than youths whose sexual identity remained consistently gay/lesbian. For the psychosexual milestones, we found no support for this hypothesis. . . . One explanation for the null findings is that psychosocial factors (e.g., a family with strong anti-gay attitudes, experiences of ridicule, greater internalized homophobia) may delay some youths from developing a consistent LGB identity or may lead some youths to adopt a bisexual identity before identifying as gay/lesbian. For the sociosexual milestones, however, we found, as hypothesized, that among the consistently gay/lesbian youths, more time had passed since they experienced sociosexual milestones than was the case among consistently bisexual youths or youths who transitioned from a bisexual to gay/lesbian identity.

Consistent with social psychological theory regarding congruence among affect, cognition, and behavior, and as hypothesized, we found that changes in sexual identity were significantly and strongly associated with current sexual orientation and sexual behaviors. The differences in sexual orientation and sexual behavior between consistently gay/lesbian youths and youths who transitioned to a gay/lesbian identity suggest that, even after adopting a gay/lesbian identity, youths continued to harbor discrepancies between the new identity and subsequent sexual orientation and behavior. Indeed, the observed decrease in the magnitude of these differences over time suggests that even after the adoption of a gay/lesbian identity, transitioned youths continue to change their orientation and behavior to match their new sexual identity. The findings of congruence between sexual identity, orientation, and behavior appear, at first, to contrast with previous research on adults that has found that many individuals with same sex attractions and behavior do not identify as LGB. . . .

Changes in sexual identity were hypothesized to be associated with corresponding changes in aspects of the identity integration process. Indeed, we found that consistently gay/lesbian youths differed from youths who transitioned from bisexual to gay/lesbian identities. The differences indicated that even after youths self-identify as gay/lesbian, a great deal of change may continue to take place in many aspects of sexuality. Thus, acceptance, commitment, and integration of a gay/lesbian identity is an ongoing developmental process that, for many youths, may extend through adolescence and beyond.

As hypothesized, consistently bisexual youths scored significantly lower than consistently gay/lesbian youths on most markers of identity integration. These data may indicate that consistently bisexual youths take a longer period of time to form and integrate their sexual identity than do consistently gay/lesbian youths. The data also may indicate that consistently bisexual youths experience more cognitive dissonance than consistently gay/lesbian youths. Clearly, more research into the similarities and differences between bisexual and gay/lesbian youths is needed, with follow-up of samples through adolescence and perhaps into adulthood.

Considerable interest has been expressed in potential gender differences in sexual identity development. . . . [Female] youths were significantly more likely than male peers to identify consistently as gay/lesbian than to change identities. These findings challenge past research suggesting that the sexual identity of females is more fluid than that of males. . . . However, because studies of change in sexual identity have been conducted among single-sex samples of females (e.g., Diamond, 2000; 2003), any observed changes may have generated an impression of plasticity, when such a hypothesis could not be tested without comparable data on males. Another indicator of the fluidity hypothesis would be a higher prevalence of bisexuality among female than male youths. However, we found that female youths were no more likely to self-identify as consistently bisexual than were male youths. This finding, although at odds with some cross-sectional findings, is consistent with other cross-sectional findings. In addition, we found no gender differences in the relations between sexual identity and aspects of sexual identity formation or integration. These findings indicate a similar process of sexual identity development between male and female youths. Because this study is the first, to our knowledge, to have data on changes in sexual identity over time among both male and female youths, we advocate for more longitudinal research on gender differences in sexual identity.

The study findings are tempered by potential study limitations. First, our sample was recruited from gay-focused organizations and, therefore, the extent to which the findings generalize to a more heterogenous sample of LGB youths is unknown. However, given that the youths in the current sample were no more consistent in their sexual identity than lesbian and bisexual youths recruited from both gay and non-gay venues (Diamond, 2000), we do not believe this to be a major limitation. Second, the size of the sample was modest. However, it had sufficient power to detect a medium effect, and it was much larger than past research studies on changes in sexual identity. . . . Finally, we followed the youths prospectively for a single year. However, because the developmental task of adolescence is identity formation and integration and because adolescence extends through approximately age 25 in the United States, we advocate that future research follow individuals through their twenties, allowing researchers to obtain a more thorough understanding of the process of sexual identity development. Our data, although limited to a one-year follow-up period, lend support and provide a rationale for the importance of longitudinal assessments of sexual identity development.

References

Diamond, L. M. (2000). Sexual identity, attractions, and behavior among young sexual-minority women over a 2-year period. *Developmental Psychology, 36,* 241–250.

Diamond, L. M. (2003). Was it a phase? Young women's relinquishment of lesbian/bisexual identities over a 5-year period. *Journal of Personality and Social Psychology, 84,* 352–364.

Stokes, J. P., Damon, W., & McKirnan, D. J. (1997). Predictors of movement toward homosexuality: A longitudinal study of bisexual men. *The Journal of Sex Research, 34,* 304–312.

POSTSCRIPT

Is Female Sexual Orientation More Fluid than Male Sexual Orientation During Adolescence?

The gendered theory of erotic plasticity suggests that women are more sexually flexible than men and that this flexibility would extend to sexual orientation. A hypothesis derived from Baumeister's theory is women would be more fluid than men in terms of their sexual orientation and/or their sexual behavior (with same-sex and other-sex partners). For example, in the Kinsey surveys, it was found that lesbian women were more likely to have had sexual intercourse with men than gay men were to have had sexual intercourse with women. Several more recent studies have found this same pattern with lesbians exceeding gay men in terms of sexual behavior with other-sex partners. Also, more women than men identify as bisexual than exclusively homosexual, according to Baumeister.

Diamond's study speaks indirectly to Baumeister's theory. She demonstrates that 58% of her sample who initially identified as lesbian adopted different sexual orientation identity labels over the course of 8 years. This group differed significantly from the 42% of lesbians who were stable in their identity self-label across the 8 years in terms of physical and emotional same-sex attraction as well as same-sex behavior and romantic relationships. Stable lesbians had greater physical and emotional same-sex attraction and had more same-sex sexual contact and romantic relationships compared with fluid lesbians. Thus, the 'fluid lesbians' were really much more fluid than those who identified as lesbian consistently across the years. Diamond's main point is that simply accepting the label of lesbian at one point in time may not be sufficient to capture the nature of a woman's sexual orientation; there is a subset of self-identified lesbians who are likely to change over time.

Rosario et al.'s study speaks more directly to the hypotheses set out by Baumeister because they compare women to men. Contrary to the idea that women are more erotically plastic than men, Rosario et al. found that female youth were less likely to change identities over the year-long longitudinal study than were the male youth who participated. Also contrary to Baumeister's theory, the girls were no more likely than the boys to self-identify as bisexual as opposed to lesbian/gay. Their results suggest that males and females have similar sexual identity developmental processes, and women may not be more flexible than men.

Do these findings mean that the erotic plasticity theory should be discounted? There are a number of considerations that must be taken into account before we prematurely dismiss this theory. Diamond's results can be interpreted to support Baumeister's theory. However, her study involved older participants than those in the Rosario et al. study. Further, Diamond's longitudinal analysis lasted 5 years while Rosario et al.'s consisted of a 1-year follow-up. Perhaps female and male youth are equally erotically plastic, but once we head into emerging adulthood (e.g., early-to-mid 20s), women remain more sexually flexible, and men become more erotically fixed. Certainly, these two studies speak to the gendered theory of erotic plasticity; however, many more studies need to be conducted before we can accept or reject this theory. Another noteworthy point is that we know very little about the sexuality of bisexual individuals; in research studies, bisexual women tend to be categorized with lesbian women. As a result, our knowledge of the unique sexual development and processes of bisexual youth and adults is quite limited.

References/Further Readings

Baumeister, R. F. (2000). Gender differences in erotic plasticity: The female sex drive as socially flexible and responsive. *Psychological Bulletin, 126*(3), 347–374.

Baumeister, R. F. (2004). Gender and erotic plasticity: Sociocultural influences on the sex drive. *Sexual and Relationship Therapy, 19*(2), 133–139.

Baumeister, R. F., & Stillman, T. (2006). Erotic plasticity: Nature, culture, gender, and sexuality. In R. D. McAnulty & M. M. Burnette, (Eds.). *Sex and sexuality, Vol. 1: Sexuality today: Trends and controversies.* (pp. 343–359). Westport, CT: Praeger/Greenwood.

Carver, P. R., Egan, S. K., & Perry, D. G. (2004). Children who question their heterosexuality. *Developmental Psychology, 40*(1), 43–53.

Diamond, L. M. (2003). Was it a phase? Young women's relinquishment of lesbian/bisexual identities over a 5-year period. *Journal of Personality and Social Psychology, 84*(2), 352–364.

Diamond, L. M. (2006) The evolution of plasticity in female-female desire. *Journal of Psychology and Human Sexuality, 18*, 245–274.

Diamond, L. M. (2008). Female bisexuality from adolescence to adulthood: Results from a 10-year longitudinal study. *Developmental Psychology, 44*(1) 5–14.

Dickson, N., Paul, C., & Herbison, P. (2003). Same-sex attraction in a birth cohort: Prevalence and persistence in early adulthood. *Social Science and Medicine, 56*, 1607–1615.

Kinnish, K. K., Strassberg, D. S., & Turner, C. W. (2005). Sex differences in the flexibility of sexual orientation: A multidimensional retrospective analysis. *Archives of Sexual Behavior, 34*, 173–183.

Russell, S. T., & Seif, H. (2002). Bisexual female adolescents: A critical analysis of past research, and results from a national survey. *Journal of Bisexuality*, 2(2), 73–94.

Savin-Williams, R. C., & Ream, G. L. (2007). Prevalence and stability of sexual orientation components during adolescence and young adulthood. *Archives of Sexual Behavior*, 36, 385–394.

Internet References . . .

eNotAlone

eNotAlone provides information, book reviews, and advice on a variety of relationship issues including cyber-relationships, love relationships of teens, the impact of divorce and relationship dissolution on children, and parenting teens.

http://www.enotalone.com

Pew Internet & American Life Project

Funded by an independent nonprofit charitable trust, Pew produces reports that explore the impact of the internet on families, communities, daily life, education, health and civic & political life.

http://www.pewinternet.org

Child Trends: Social Science Research

Child Trends is an independent, nonpartisan research center focusing on children and youth with the goals of improving outcomes for children.

http://www.childtrends.org

Focus Adolescent Services

An independent entity, not affiliated with any private, public, or governmental organization, nor under the direction of any outside individual or groups, provides comprehensive information, and support for teen and family issues.

http://www.focusas.com

Advocates for Youth

A youth-serving organization that creates programs and advocates for policies that provide information on reproductive and sexual health.

http://www.advocatesforyouth.org

Equality Rules

A website created by the Government of Ontario designed to educate children and teens about the importance of healthy, equal, and respectful relationships. There is also a section for parents/guardians or teachers.

http://www.equalityrules.ca

Kids Help Phone

A well-known and valuable Canadian bilingual telephone service and web resource for youth.

http://www.kidshelpphone.ca

Relationships

*S*ocial relationships are critical in the growth, development, and behaviour of adolescents. There are many different types of relationships that are important to teens, including family ties, friendships, and romantic relationships. The following three issues address some aspect of the social relations of youth and the impact that these relationships have on adolescent development.

- Does Divorce or Disruption in Family Structure During Adolescence Have a Detrimental Effect on Development?

- Does Dating Impede Developmental Adjustment for Adolescents?

- Do Online Friendships Hinder Adolescent Well-Being?

ISSUE 12

Does Divorce or Disruption in Family Structure During Adolescence Have a Detrimental Effect on Development?

YES: Paul R. Amato, from "The Impact of Family Formation Change on the Cognitive, Social, and Emotional Well-Being of the Next Generation," *The Future of Children* (Fall 2005)

NO: Eda Ruschena et al., from "A Longitudinal Study of Adolescent Adjustment Following Family Transitions," *Journal of Child Psychology and Psychiatry* (vol. 46, no. 4, 2005)

ISSUE SUMMARY

YES: Sociology professor Paul Amato presents evidence that children growing up in stable, two-parent families are less likely to experience cognitive, emotional, and social problems than those who do not.

NO: Eda Ruschena, a psychologist at the Catholic Education Office in Melbourne, and her colleagues from the University of Melbourne claim that adolescents do not necessarily experience negative social, emotional, or psychological outcomes during family transitions.

$\mathbf{F}$amily structure has undoubtedly changed in the past 60 years. Marriage, for example, has become a less permanent institution, resulting in more divorces, more children of divorce, and subsequently more blended families. Just a few decades ago, most children in North America grew up in intact, two-parent families. This has changed, however, with increasing divorce rates. Since 1950, the divorce rate has almost doubled. In Canada, more than 70,000 divorces were granted in 2003 (Statistics Canada, 2006). In the United States, this number is considerably larger, with more than 950,000 divorces granted every year. The U.S. divorce rate in 2005 was 0.36 percent divorces per capita (National Vital Statistics Report, 2005). Predictions of first marriages ending in divorce are currently at 50 percent, and with 75 percent of these divorced people remarrying, blended families are becoming common. It is estimated that 40 percent of children will experience family divorce, and many will find themselves in blended families (Hetherington & Elmore, 2003).

Over the years, these changes in family structure have influenced the direction of research on this topic. Prior to the 1970s, the few studies that existed focused on the negative effects of family disruption, stating that children in such families and more specifically in families of divorce were at greater risk for maladjustment and delinquency. It was only when divorce rates started to climb at alarming rates in the late sixties and early seventies (i.e., increasing 113 percent between 1966 and 1976) that researchers began examining divorce in greater detail (Kelly, 2003). The focus, however, was still on divorced families as flawed families. There were no studies at the time comparing children of divorced families to children of never-divorced families. As a result, there was no evidence to support the argument that children of divorce were in fact worse off. Furthermore, longitudinal studies did not exist, making it impossible to distinguish between short-term and long-term outcomes.

In the 1980s, research on divorce continued to increase rapidly, addressing some of the limitations from the past. Researchers began examining children's overall adjustment, both short term and long term; however, studies remained one-sided and heavily focused on the negative effects. By the late 1980s, strides were finally being made toward identifying the risks and protective factors associated with both positive and negative outcomes. In addition, researchers began expanding the research on risk and resilience to identify environmental situations and circumstances that placed some children at greater risk for psychosocial maladjustment while protecting others from the long-term negative effects. The fact that some children and adolescents functioned well after divorce confirmed the importance of examining psychosocial well-being as well as environment.

What are the effects of divorce? Perhaps if children are not involved, divorce can be seen as a way of setting adults free from unhappy and/or abusive marriages. However, when a marriage dissolves and children are involved, there are consequences. Parent-child relationships change, living arrangements change, and financial situations change (Wallerstein & Lewis, 2004). For adolescents, these changes can be difficult, especially moving from neighborhoods or schools. But, do these adjustments have a detrimental effect on all adolescents? Many researchers report negative outcomes for all children but adolescents in particular, finding they are affected behaviourally, academically, emotionally, and socially. Others find that a disruption to family structure does not pose a threat to healthy adolescent development and that the majority of adolescents do not have long-term psychological adjustment problems. Opposing views continue to exist. Is the divorced or disrupted family a happy family with well-adjusted adolescents? Are adolescents from long-term, stable families better off emotionally and socially? These questions are addressed in the selections that follow.

Amato reports that while chronic conflict is damaging to children and adolescents, two-parent families are usually better. He argues that children growing up in stable, two-parent families are less likely to experience cognitive, emotional, and social problems than those who do not. Opposing this view, Ruschena and her colleagues claim that adolescents do not necessarily experience negative social, emotional, or psychological outcomes during family transitions.

YES

Paul R. Amato

The Impact of Family Formation Change on the Cognitive, Social, and Emotional Well-Being of the Next Generation

Perhaps the most profound change in the American family over the past four decades has been the decline in the share of children growing up in households with both biological parents. Because many social scientists, policymakers, and members of the general public believe that a two-parent household is the optimal setting for children's development, the decline in such households has generated widespread concern about the well-being of American children. . . .

My goal in this article is to . . . [address two] questions. First, how do children in households with only one biological parent differ in terms of their cognitive, social, and emotional well-being from children in households with both biological parents? Second, what accounts for the observed differences between these two groups of children? . . .

Research on the Effects of Family Structure on Children

The rise in the divorce rate during the 1960s and 1970s prompted social scientists to investigate how differing family structures affect children. Their research focus initially was on children of divorced parents, but it expanded to include out-of-wedlock children and those in other nontraditional family structures.

Parental Divorce

Early studies generally supported the assumption that children who experience parental divorce are prone to a variety of academic, behavioral, and emotional problems. In 1971, . . . Wallerstein and Kelly began an influential long-term study of 60 divorced families and 131 children. According to the authors, five years after divorce, one-third of the children were adjusting well and had good relationships with both parents. Another group

From *The Future of Children Journal,* vol. 15, no. 2, Fall 2005, pp. 75–96. Copyright © 2005 by Brookings Institution Press. Reprinted by permission.

of children (more than one-third of the sample) were clinically depressed, were doing poorly in school, had difficulty maintaining friendships, experienced chronic problems such as sleep disturbances, and continued to hope that their parents would reconcile.[1]

Despite these early findings, other studies in the 1970s challenged the dominant view that divorce is uniformly bad for children. For example, . . . Hetherington [et al. found that the] children with divorced parents exhibited more behavioral and emotional problems than did the children with continuously married parents. Two years after divorce, however, children with divorced parents no longer exhibited an elevated number of problems (although a few difficulties lingered for boys). Despite this temporary improvement, a later wave of data collection revealed that the remarriage of the custodial mother was followed by additional problems among the children, especially daughters.[2]

Trying to make sense of this research literature can be frustrating, because the results of individual studies vary considerably: some suggest serious negative effects of divorce, others suggest modest effects, and yet others suggest no effects. Much of this inconsistency is due to variations across studies in the types of samples, the ages of the children, the outcomes examined, and the methods of analysis. To summarize general trends across such a large and varied body of research, social scientists use a technique known as meta-analysis.

In 1991, . . . Keith and I published the first meta-analysis dealing with the effects of divorce on children.[3] Our analysis summarized the results of ninety-three studies published in the 1960s, 1970s, and 1980s and confirmed that children with divorced parents are worse off than those with continuously married parents on measures of academic success (school grades, scores on standardized achievement tests), conduct (behavior problems, aggression), psychological well-being (depression, distress symptoms), self-esteem (positive feelings about oneself, perceptions of self-efficacy), and peer relations (number of close friends, social support from peers). . . . Moreover, children in divorced families tend to have weaker emotional bonds with mothers and fathers than do their peers in two-parent families. These results supported the conclusion that the rise in divorce had lowered the average level of child well-being.

Our meta-analysis also indicated, however, that the estimated effects of parental divorce on children's well-being are modest rather than strong. We concluded that these modest differences reflect widely varying experiences within both groups of children. Some children growing up with continuously married parents are exposed to stressful circumstances, such as poverty, serious conflict between parents, violence, inept parenting, and mental illness or substance abuse, that increase the risk of child maladjustment. Correspondingly, some children with divorced parents cope well, perhaps because their parents are able to separate amicably and engage in cooperative co-parenting following marital dissolution.

In a more recent meta-analysis, based on sixty-seven studies conducted during the 1990s, . . . children with divorced parents, on average, scored significantly lower on various measures of wellbeing than did children with continuously married parents.[4] As before, the differences between the two groups were modest rather than large. Nevertheless, the more recent meta-analyses revealed that children with divorced parents continued to have lower average levels of cognitive, social, and emotional well-being, even in a decade in which divorce had become common and widely accepted. . . .

Children Born Outside Marriage

[Like] children with divorced parents, children who grow up with a single parent because they were born out of wedlock are more likely than children living with continuously married parents to experience a variety of cognitive, emotional, and behavioral problems. Specifically, compared with children who grow up in stable, two-parent families, children born outside marriage reach adulthood with less education, earn less income, have lower occupational status, are more likely to be idle (that is, not employed and not in school), are more likely to have a nonmarital birth (among daughters), have more troubled marriages, experience higher rates of divorce, and report more symptoms of depression.

A few studies have compared children of unmarried single parents and divorced single parents. Despite some variation across studies, this research generally shows that the long-term risks for most problems are comparable in these two groups. . . .

Although it is sometimes assumed that children born to unwed mothers have little contact with their fathers, about 40 percent of unmarried mothers are living with the child's father at the time of birth.[5] If one-third of all children are born to unmarried parents, and if 40 percent of these parents are cohabiting, then about one out of every eight infants lives with two biological but unmarried parents. Structurally, these households are similar to households with two married parents. And young children are unlikely to be aware of their parents' marital status. Nevertheless, cohabiting parents tend to be more disadvantaged than married parents. They have less education, earn less income, report poorer relationship quality, and experience more mental health problems.[6] These considerations suggest that children living with cohabiting biological parents may be worse off, in some respects, than children living with two married biological parents.

Consistent with this assumption, . . . Brown found that children living with cohabiting biological parents, compared with children living with continuously married parents, had more behavioral problems, more emotional problems, and lower levels of school engagement.[7] . . . Parents' education, income, psychological well-being, and parenting stress explained most—but not all—of these differences. . . .

The risk of relationship dissolution also is substantially higher for cohabiting couples with children than for married couples with children. For example, the Fragile Families Study indicates that about one-fourth of cohabiting biological parents are no longer living together one year after the child's birth.[8] . . .

Death of a Parent

Some children live with a single parent not because of divorce or because they were born outside marriage but because their other parent has died. Studies that compare children who experienced the death of a parent with children separated from a parent for other reasons yield mixed results. The Amato and Keith meta-analysis found that children who experienced a parent's death scored lower on several forms of well-being than did children living with continuously married parents. Children who experienced a parent's death, however, scored significantly *higher* on several measures of well-being than did children with divorced parents. McLanahan and Sandefur found that children with a deceased parent were no more likely than children with continuously married parents to drop out of high school. Daughters with a deceased parent, however, were more likely than teenagers living with both parents to have a nonmarital birth.[9] . . . [In summary,] these studies suggest that experiencing the death of a parent during childhood puts children at risk for a number of problems, but not as much as does divorce or out-of-wedlock birth.

Discordant Two-Parent Families

Most studies in this literature have compared children living with a single parent with a broad group of children living with continuously married parents. Some two-parent families, however, function better than others. Marriages marked by chronic, overt conflict and hostility are "intact" structurally but are not necessarily good environments in which to raise children. Some early studies compared children living with divorced parents and children living with two married but discordant parents. In general, these studies found that children in high-conflict households experience many of the same problems as do children with divorced parents. . . .

A more recent generation of long-term studies has shown that the effects of divorce vary with the degree of marital discord that precedes divorce. When parents exhibit chronic and overt conflict, children appear to be better off, in the long run, if their parents split up rather than stay together. But when parents exhibit relatively little overt conflict, children appear to be better off if their parents stay together. In other words, children are particularly at risk when low-conflict marriages end in divorce. In a twenty-year study, Alan Booth and I found that the majority of marriages that ended in divorce fell into the low-conflict group. Spouses in these marriages did not fight frequently or express hostility toward their partners. Instead, they felt emotionally estranged from their spouses, and many ended their marriages to seek greater happiness with new partners. Although many parents saw this transition as positive, their children often viewed it as unexpected, inexplicable, and unwelcome. Children and parents, it is clear, often have different interpretations of family transitions.

Stepfamilies

Although rates of remarriage have declined in recent years, most divorced parents eventually remarry. Similarly, many women who have had a nonmarital birth eventually marry men who are not the fathers of their children. Adding a stepfather to the household usually improves children's standard of living. Moreover, in a stepfamily, two adults are available to monitor children's behavior, provide supervision, and assist children with everyday problems. For these reasons, one might assume that children generally are better off in stepfamilies than in single-parent households. Studies consistently indicate, however, that children in stepfamilies exhibit more problems than do children with continuously married parents and about the same number of problems as do children with single parents. In other words, the marriage of a single parent (to someone other than the child's biological parent) does not appear to improve the functioning of most children.

Although the great majority of parents view the formation of a stepfamily positively, children tend to be less enthusiastic. Stepfamily formation is stressful for many children because it often involves moving (generally to a different neighborhood or town), adapting to new people in the household, and learning new rules and routines. Moreover, early relationships between stepparents and stepchildren are often tense. Children, especially adolescents, become accustomed to a substantial degree of autonomy in single-parent households. They may resent the monitoring and supervision by stepparents and react with hostility when stepparents attempt to exert authority. Some children experience loyalty conflicts and fear that becoming emotionally close to a stepparent implies betraying the nonresident biological parent. Some become jealous because they must share parental time and attention with the stepparent. And for some children, remarriage ends any lingering hopes that the two biological parents will one day reconcile. Finally, stepchildren are overrepresented in official reports of child abuse. . . .

Variations by Gender of Child

Several early influential studies found that boys in divorced families had more adjustment problems than did girls.[2] Given that boys usually live with their mothers following family disruption, the loss of contact with the same-gender parent could account for such a difference. In addition, boys, compared with girls, may be exposed to more conflict, receive less support from parents and others (because they are believed to be tougher), and be picked on more by custodial mothers (because sons may resemble their fathers). Subsequent studies, however, have failed to find consistent gender differences in children's reactions to divorce.

The meta-analyses on children of divorce provide the most reliable evidence on this topic. The Amato and Keith meta-analysis of studies conducted before the 1990s revealed one significant gender difference: the estimated negative effect of divorce on social adjustment was stronger for boys than girls. In other areas, however, such as academic achievement, conduct, and psychological adjustment, no differences between boys and girls were apparent.[3] In my meta-analysis of studies conducted in the 1990s, the estimated effect of divorce on children's conduct problems was stronger for boys than for girls, although no other gender differences were apparent.[4] Why the earlier studies suggest a gender difference in social adjustment and the more recent studies suggest a gender difference in conduct problems is unclear. Nevertheless, taken together, these meta-analyses provide some limited support for the notion that boys are more susceptible than girls to the detrimental consequences of divorce. . . .

Why Do Single-Parent Families Put Children at Risk?

Researchers have several theories to explain why children growing up with single parents have an elevated risk of experiencing cognitive, social, and emotional problems. Most refer either to the economic and parental resources available to children or to the stressful events and circumstances to which these children must adapt.

Economic Hardship

For a variety of reasons, . . . most children living with single parents are economically disadvantaged. It is difficult for poor single parents to afford the books, home computers, and private lessons that make it easier for their children to succeed in school. Similarly, they cannot afford clothes, shoes, cell phones, and other consumer goods that give their children status among their peers. Moreover, many live in rundown neighborhoods with high crime rates, low-quality schools, and few community services. Consistent with these observations, many studies have shown that economic resources explain some of the differences in well-being between children with single parents and those with continuously married parents.[9] Research showing that children do better at school and exhibit fewer behavioral problems when nonresident fathers pay child support likewise suggests the importance of income in facilitating children's well-being in single-parent households.[10]

Quality of Parenting

Regardless of family structure, the quality of parenting is one of the best predictors of children's emotional and social well-being. Many single parents, however, find it difficult to function effectively as parents. Compared with continuously married parents, they are less emotionally supportive of their children, have fewer rules, dispense harsher discipline, are more inconsistent in dispensing discipline, provide less supervision, and engage in more conflict with their children. Many of these deficits in parenting presumably result from struggling to make ends meet with limited financial resources and trying to raise children without the help of the other biological parent. Many studies link inept parenting by resident single parents with a variety of negative outcomes among children, including poor academic achievement, emotional problems, conduct problems, low self-esteem, and problems forming and maintaining social relationships. Other studies show that depression among custodial mothers, which usually detracts from effective parenting, is related to poor adjustment among offspring.[9] . . .

Exposure to Stress

Children living with single parents are exposed to more stressful experiences and circumstances than are children living with continuously married parents. . . . This results in feelings of emotional distress, a reduced capacity to function in school, work, and family roles, and an increase in physiological indicators of arousal.[11] Economic hardship, inept parenting, and loss of contact with a parent . . . can be stressful for children. Observing conflict and hostility between resident and nonresident parents also is stressful. Conflict between nonresident parents appears to be particularly harmful when children feel that they are caught in the middle, . . . and when one parent attempts to recruit the child as an ally against the other. Interparental conflict is a direct stressor for children, and it can also interfere with their attachments to parents, resulting in feelings of emotional insecurity.

Moving is a difficult experience for many children, especially when it involves losing contact with neighborhood friends. Moreover, moves that require changing schools can put children out of step with their classmates in terms of the curriculum. Children with single parents move more frequently than other children do, partly because of economic hardship . . . and partly because single parents form new romantic attachments. . . . Studies show that frequent moving increases the risk of academic, behavioral, and emotional problems for children with single parents.[9] For many children, . . . the addition of a stepparent to the household is a stressful change. And when remarriages end in divorce, children are exposed to yet more stressful transitions. . . .

Conclusion

. . . Research clearly demonstrates that children growing up with two continuously married parents are less likely than other children to experience a wide range of cognitive, emotional, and social problems, not only during childhood, but also in adulthood. Although it is not possible to demonstrate that family structure is the cause of these differences, studies that have used a variety of sophisticated statistical methods, including controls for genetic factors, suggest that this is the case. This distinction is even stronger if we focus on children growing up with two *happily married* biological parents.

. . . Compared with other children, those who grow up in stable, two-parent families have a higher standard of living, receive more effective parenting, experience more cooperative co-parenting, are emotionally closer to both parents (especially fathers), and are subjected to fewer stressful events and circumstances. . . .

[In summary, the] importance of increasing the number of children growing up with two happily and continuously married parents and of improving the well-being of children now living in other family structures is self-evident. Children are the innocent victims of their parents' inability to maintain harmonious and stable homes. . . .

Endnotes

1. Judith S. Wallerstein and Joan B. Kelly, *Surviving the Breakup: How Children and Parents Cope with Divorce* (New York: Basic Books, 1980).

2. E. Mavis Hetherington, "Divorce: A Child's Perspective," *American Psychologist* 34 (1979): 851–58; E. Mavis Hetherington, Martha Cox, and R. Cox, "Effects of Divorce on Parents and Children," in *Nontraditional Families*, edited by Michael Lamb (Hillsdale, N.J.: Lawrence Erlbaum, 1982), pp. 233–88.

3. Paul R. Amato and Bruce Keith, "Consequences of Parental Divorce for Children's Well-Being: A Meta-Analysis," *Psychological Bulletin* 10 (1991): 26–46.

4. Paul R. Amato, "Children of Divorce in the 1990s: An Update of the Amato and Keith (1991) Meta-Analysis," *Journal of Family Psychology* 15 (2001): 355–70.

5. Larry L. Bumpass and Hsien-Hen Lu, "Trends in Cohabitation and Implications for Children's Family Contexts in the United States," *Population Studies* 54 (2000): 29–41; Sara McLanahan and others, "Unwed Parents or Fragile Families? Implications for Welfare and Child Support Policy," in *Out of Wedlock: Causes and Consequences of Nonmarital Fertility*, edited by Lawrence L. Wu and Barbara Wolfe (New York: Russell Sage Foundation, 2001), pp. 202–28.

6. Susan Brown, "The Effect of Union Type on Psychological Well-Being: Depression among Cohabitors versus Marrieds," *Journal of Health and Social Behavior* 41 (2000): 241–55; Susan Brown and Alan Booth, "Cohabitation versus Marriage: A Comparison of Relationship Quality," *Journal of Marriage and the Family* 58 (1996): 668–78; Judith Seltzer, "Families Formed outside of Marriage," *Journal of Marriage and the Family* 62 (2000): 1247–68.

7. Susan Brown, "Family Structure and Child Well-Being: The Significance of Parental Cohabitation," *Journal of Marriage and the Family* 66 (2004): 351–67. For a general review of this literature, see Wendy Manning, "The Implications of Cohabitation for Children's Well-Being," in *Just Living Together: Implications of Cohabitation for Families, Children, and Social Policy*, edited by Alan Booth and Ann Crouter (Mahwah, N.J.: Lawrence Erlbaum Associates, 2002), pp. 21–152.

8. M. Carlson, Sara McLanahan, and Paula England, "Union Formation and Dissolution in Fragile Families," Fragile Families Research Brief, no. 4 (Bendheim-Thoman Center for Research on Child Wellbeing, Princeton University, January 2003); see also Sara McLanahan, "Diverging Destinies: How Children Are Faring under the Second Demographic Transition," *Demography* 41 (2004): 606–27.

9. Sara McLanahan and Gary Sandefur, *Growing Up with a Single Parent: What Hurts, What Helps* (Harvard University Press, 1994).

10. Valarie King, "Nonresident Father Involvement and Child Well-Being: Can Dads Make a Difference?" *Journal of Family Issues* 15 (1994): 78–96; Sara McLanahan and others, "Child Support Enforcement and Child Well-Being: Greater Security or Greater Conflict?" in *Child Support and Child Well-Being*, edited by Irwin Garfinkel, Sara McLanahan, and Philip K. Robins (Washington: Urban Institute Press, 1996), pp. 239–56.

11. L. I. Pearlin and others, "The Stress Process," *Journal of Health and Social Behavior* 22 (1981): 337–56; Peggy A. Thoits, "Stress, Coping, and Social Support Processes: Where Are We? What Next?" *Journal of Health and Social Behavior*, extra issue (1995): 53–79.

Eda Ruschena, Margot Prior,
Ann Sanson, and Diana Smart

 **NO**

A Longitudinal Study
of Adolescent Adjustment
Following Family Transitions

Divorce has become considerably more common in the West over the recent decades. The Australian Bureau of Statistics (2002) has projected that for a group of present-day newborn babies and based on 1997–1999 divorce rates, 32% of their future marriages will end in divorce. . . . Concomitant with these family changes there has been an increase in research focused upon adjustment outcomes for children. The overall picture remains unclear, however, with reviews of the large body of literature in this field finding inconsistent outcomes that are largely dependent upon methodological characteristics of individual studies. There is little doubt, though, that divorce brings a number of important stressors for children (Emery, 1999). The process of separation, of learning to alternate between households, of perhaps moving homes or schools, can be very challenging. Contact with the non-residential parent can be sporadic and may diminish over time (Emery, 1999). Whether children are survivors, winners, or losers, after their parents' divorce or remarriage, depends upon a large number of interconnected variables (Hetherington, 1989).

A majority of researchers focusing upon the effects of family transitions have examined behavioural, emotional and academic outcomes, with the reported outcomes appearing largely negative (Amato & Keith, 1991). . . .

Another central focus for research is how family structure and functioning affects and is affected by transitions. There is agreement that the relationship between the residential parent and the child can be a protective factor in terms of children's adjustment after divorce, but in reality there is often a decline in parenting quality after a family transition, with more inconsistent discipline and affection. A decline in post-divorce relationships between fathers and their children is common, although problems may also have been present prior to the divorce (Amato & Booth, 1996; Zill, Morrison, & Coiro, 1993) so a causal relationship should not be assumed.

Another theoretical stance contends that it is not the divorce per se which leads to poorer outcomes for children, but the influence of interparental conflict. Indirectly, conflict may diminish parents' emotional

From *Journal of Clinical Psychology,* vol. 46, no. 4, 2005, excerpts from pp. 353–363. Copyright © 2005 by Association for Child and Adolescent Mental Health. Reprinted by permission of Wiley-Blackwell.

energy and interfere with their ability to respond sensitively to their children's emotional needs. Parents in high conflict marriages engage in more erratic disciplinary practices and are more likely to use anxiety or guilt-inducing techniques to discipline their children than parents in low-to-moderate conflict marriages, according to Kelly (1998). Further, the very structure of the post-transition family can lead to poorer outcomes for children, with the absence of a biological parent (usually the father) and the attendant loss of resources (financial, emotional) being the most influential factors. Studies comparing children and adolescents from families that have experienced either parental death or divorce (Kiernan, 1992) have shown lower well-being for children affected by divorce compared to those who have lost a parent through death, suggesting an additional adverse mechanism operating in divorced families, other than simply parent loss.

Divorce often leads to deterioration in financial circumstances for families and this is associated with poorer outcomes for children (Emery, 1999; Rodgers, 1996). This may be partly due to the flow-on effects of economic losses, such as having to move schools or suburbs and losing contact with peers and familiar environments, further taxing the coping resources of children and adolescents already suffering emotional strain. In addition to being a predictor variable in adjustment outcomes, income can also be seen as a confounding variable, hence many studies of post-divorce outcomes controlling for the influence of income find differences between married and single-parent families reduced by about half, for measures such as school attainment, and by a lesser amount for internalising and externalising behaviour problems. However, considerable variance in children's adjustment between the two groups remains unexplained.

Additional family transitions such as remarriage of one or both parents and/or the addition of step-siblings can affect children's functioning. Number of marital transitions was associated with behavioural difficulties in longitudinal studies by . . . Hetherington and Clingempeel (1992), and difficulties were apparent in the stepfather–stepchild relationship and also in sibling relationships.

Gender and age of the child have also been implicated in variable outcomes in the family transitions literature. Many studies have observed significantly worse outcomes for boys rather than girls (Hetherington, Stanley-Hagan, & Anderson, 1989). Alternatively Zill et al. (1993) found no reliable interactions with gender on any of the measured variables in their study. . . . In terms of age at transition, developmental psychologists generally believe that the limited understanding of pre-school children leaves them more vulnerable to the effects of parental conflict and family disruption . . . (Hetherington & Clingempeel, 1992; Zill et al., 1993). On the other hand, later divorces may be more deleterious than earlier ones, perhaps because the developmental challenges of adolescence and young adulthood can compound the stress of family disruption. . . .

Temperament is another influential factor in terms of the impact of stressful life events upon children and adolescents. . . . [A] number of studies have uncovered associations between positive, outgoing, flexible temperamental attributes and improved outcomes after a family transition (Hetherington et al., 1989). . . .

Rationale for the Study

Few major research studies of outcomes after divorce have emanated from Australia. . . . A review of 25 Australian studies conducted from the 1970s until the 1990s (Rodgers, 1996) showed that as with international findings, many Australian researchers have found divorce to be associated with a range of adverse social and psychological outcomes, for adolescents and adults. However, research seemed patchy, . . . and many studies had problems related to a lack of statistical power. . . .

Longitudinal data offers many advantages for [the] research. The availability of data from the Australian Temperament Project (ATP) from 1983 to 2000 allowed us to examine two key questions using this approach. Firstly, we examined group differences between children who had experienced a family transition, that is, a parental separation, divorce or death, and those who had not, on outcome measures such as degree of family attachment, level of educational attainment, and behavioural measures of social competence and psychosocial maladjustment. We hypothesised that children experiencing separation and divorce would be at risk for poorer outcomes. Secondly, for those experiencing family transitions, we tested the potency of key variables identified in the literature . . . to predict better or worse adjustment.

Method

Participants

. . . This project began in 1983 when the mother of every infant aged four to eight months, who attended selected infant Welfare Centres in a specific two-week period, was invited to participate in the project. The total number of families recruited at the first stage of the research was 2,443. . . . From infancy onwards, at roughly 15–18-month intervals, families were contacted . . . with requests to complete questionnaires (13 data waves in all). . . .

By 2000, when the target participants were 17–18 years old, . . . 1,310 parents and 1,260 adolescents responded to the surveys. . . .

The data bank from the 18 years of this study was used to explore predictors of outcome for young people who at 17–18 years of age reported that their family had undergone a family transition during the child's lifetime.

Procedure

The ATP data bank was accessed for data on the sample from infancy to 17–18 years of age. In the year 2000, a separate questionnaire, independent of the main ATP survey, was also sent to a sub-sample of the ATP cohort (aged 17–18 years), relating to their experiences of family transitions.

This sub-sample [(n = 151)] was chosen by selecting those adolescents who answered affirmatively to questions in the ATP year 2000 survey about their experience of a marital separation, divorce, remarriage, or parental death during their lifetime. . . . One hundred and forty-nine participants from the general ATP database, whose families *had not* been through a transition (that is, a divorce, separation or death), provided the comparison group. . . .

Measures

Demographic information.   These data, collected at 17–18 years, via both the general ATP questionnaire and the separate Family Transitions Questionnaire, included information about the participant adolescent's gender, birth order, number of children in the family, living arrangements and geographic location. Participants were asked about transitions occurring over the ATP adolescent's lifetime, including whether parents had separated, divorced, died, or remarried, presence of step-siblings in the family, number of house and school moves over the ATP adolescent's lifetime, and the level of contact with the non-residential parent. Overall socioeconomic status (SES) was available for every data . . . using the mean of both parents' occupational and educational status. . . .

Behaviour problems.   A number of measures had been used to assess behaviour problem. . . . The Behar Pre-school Behaviour Questionnaire provided information on parent-reported problem behaviour at child age of three to four years. . . . Across ages five to twelve years, the Rutter Problem Behaviour Questionnaire was used to identify problem behaviours via parent ratings. . . . During the adolescent years (ages 13–14 and 17–18), the Revised Behaviour Problem Checklist was used to measure parent perceptions of behaviour problems, including different aspects of internalising and externalising behaviours. An adolescent self-report measure, with parallel sub-scales to the parent form, was adapted from the RBPQ by the ATP team. . . . At age 17–18, the Short Mood and Feelings Questionnaire was used to measure self-reported depressive symptoms, . . . and a short form of the Revised Manifest Anxiety Scale was used to measure self-reported anxious behaviours. . . .

Academic measures.   Total School Problems was a five-item . . . scale measuring both academic and behaviour problems at school at 17–18 years, as reported by parents. . . .

Measures of temperament.   Parents rated their ATP adolescent (at 17–18) on a number of temperament dimensions using the School Age Temperament Questionnaire. . . .

Family measures (at age 17–18).   The Parent's Overall Temperament Rating scale was an ATP measure that comprised one question, reflecting the parent's perception of how easy or difficult the child was when compared to other children of the same age. . . . *The Sibling Relationship scale* comprised ten questions . . . that rated intimacy and support, as well as conflict between the ATP adolescent and up to two siblings. . . . *Attachment to parents* was an adolescent-reported short form of the . . . Inventory of Parent Attachment that assessed the quality of the parent–adolescent relationship. . . . *The Parent–Adolescent Conflict scale* was a parent-completed short-form of the Prinz Conflict Behaviour Questionnaire covering aspects of the parent–adolescent relationship. . . . A *Parental Marital Conflict scale* was a retrospective parent-reported measure of inter-parental conflict over two time periods: between birth and twelve years, and from twelve years to the present. . . .

Peer relationship measure.   Antisocial Peer Associations was a six-question scale, . . . which measured parental reports of the degree to which their adolescent associated with substance-using and/or anti-social peers. The 15–16-year-old data were used for this study.

Social skills measures.   When the children were 11–12 and 13–14 years of age, parents and children completed the Social Skills Rating System. . . .

Family transition information.   The Family Transitions questionnaire . . . sought information about post-transition living arrangements, social support during and after the transition, contact with the non-residential parent, and details of further family changes that may have occurred since the original transition. This questionnaire also assessed the adolescent's feelings of regret, relief, and ambivalence in relation to the parents' separation. . . .

Results

1. Descriptive characteristics of the groups

The transitions group comprised those adolescents who at 17–18 years of age reported that their family had experienced a transition during the child's lifetime. They were compared with comparison group participants on a number of demographic variables. . . . On most factors, the two groups were found to be similar, although a greater number of transition group members lived independently from parents (7% versus 1% respectively).

Transitions experienced by participants included parental death, separation and divorce, remarriage of one or both parents, the addition of stepparents and/or step-siblings, as well as house moves and school changes directly resulting from these family transitions, with some respondents experiencing multiple transitions of the same type. . . . A one-way ANOVA showed the mean number of house moves to be significantly lower for those adolescents who did not experience a family transition. . . . A majority (63%) of those having experienced family transitions did not have step-siblings. The mean . . . age at which the transition occurred was eleven years old and almost half the sample experienced their transition during adolescence.

Data from the concurrent 17–18 years questionnaire . . . showed that almost half the respondents still saw their non-residential parent at least fortnightly. . . . Finally, respondents were asked about their satisfaction with their level of contact with the non-residential parent. Responses were split between those who indicated contact was insufficient and those who felt it to be satisfactory. Only a small number of respondents indicated that the degree of contact was too great.

2. *Between-group differences: Transitions groups versus comparison group participants*

Behaviour problems.   The first analysis examined whether negative consequences of family transitions were detectable in late adolescence (17 to 18 years of age). . . . Analyses of variance comparing groups on a composite score of parent- and teen-reported problem behaviours, and on internalising and externalising problems separately, showed no main effect of group type nor interaction effects between group and gender. Gender differences were found, however, in terms of overall problem behaviours . . . and internalising problems, [with girls reporting] greater difficulties. . . .

An ANOVA using the longitudinal data (from age 3–4 to 17–18) examined whether rates of problems were higher among those who came from a family that *would* experience a transition at some time over the course of the ATP. . . . There was no significant difference found between the transitions and comparison groups on this analysis at any point in time.

Differences in family factors.   Further analyses examined group differences in relation to: parents' evaluations of their relationship with the ATP adolescent, parental rating of the adolescent's overall ease or difficulty compared to peers, parent–child conflict, inter-parental conflict, and quality of the ATP adolescent's relationship with siblings. A MANOVA revealed no significant effects of gender alone or gender and group combined, but there was a significant main effect for group type. . . . Transitions group parents reported more conflict with their adolescent than comparison group parents. . . . Comparison adolescents also reported a better quality relationship with their reporting parent than transitions group adolescents, in terms of factors such as communication, trust, and lack of alienation. . . .

Differences in social skills.   No significant main effect of group type or interactive effect of group type and gender were found on the measures of social skills . . . from age 11 to 14. However, . . . [females] reported themselves to have significantly more empathy than their male counterparts, . . . and females were reported by both themselves and their parents to be significantly more cooperative. . . .

Academic differences.   There was no significant difference between groups on an overall school problems score measured at age 17–18. . . .

3. *Between group differences: Divorce group, parental death group and comparisons*

Thirty-one participants in the sample had experienced a parental death. They were compared with 50 randomly selected subjects whose parents had divorced and 50 randomly selected subjects who were still in their original families, to investigate the effect of type of family transition compared to no transition. . . . No significant differences were found between the three groups, on the following: overall behaviour problems and specific internalising or externalising problems at 17–18 years, composite behaviour problems across the ages from 3–4 to 17–18, family factors, and school problems at 17–18 years. . . .

4. *Predictors of outcomes: Analyses within the transitions group*

A number of linear regression analyses were performed within the transitions group to explore predictors of outcomes at age 17–18. Predictor variables included the following: gender, number of transitions during the participant's lifetime, number of years since the transition occurred, socioeconomic status, parent's overall rating of the ease or difficulty of the ATP adolescent, inter-parental conflict, parent-teen conflict, the adolescent's tendency to associate with antisocial peers, and concurrent temperament dimensions of reactivity, approach-withdrawal and persistence. . . .

Three separate regression analyses were performed predicting overall behaviour problems, externalising problems and internalising problems in the transitions group. Of all the variables listed above, the parent's overall rating of their adolescent as easy or difficult, the tendency to associate with antisocial peers, gender, and two dimensions of temperament (all at age 17–18) were significant predictors of more behaviour problems. . . .

5. *Analyses within the comparison group*

In order to explore whether these predictors of problem behaviour were unique to transition group adolescents, similar regression analyses (again at age 17–18) were repeated with the comparison group. As items such as years since transition and number of transitions clearly did not apply to this group, the regression analyses had fewer predictor variables, but were otherwise similar. Again, parent's overall rating and dimensions of temperament were significant predictors of behaviour problems. Socioeconomic status was also a predictor of higher internalising behaviour problems for the comparison group. . . .

6. *Comparisons with other ATP participants who were potential members of the transitions group*

Given that relatively few group differences were found between transitions and comparison group participants, it was important to check that the transitions group was representative of a community sample of adolescents who had experienced a family transition. Although the original ATP participants at 4–8 months old were carefully shown to be a representative community sample, there has been some attrition over time. Analyses were performed on a sample of data from 1983 (age 4–8 months) comparing the entire transitions sample ($N = 262$) with children who did not later participate in the 17–18-year-old survey wave, but whose families had previously reported experiencing a transition at some point during the project ($N = 121$). . . .

T-tests revealed that the transitions group's families were of significantly higher socio-economic status (SES) in 1983 compared to the non-participating group. . . . There were no significant differences on the total behaviour problems composite; the approach, rhythmicity, cooperation, activity–reactivity and irritability temperament dimensions; or the easy–difficult temperament scale at 4–8 months of age. Thus while the transitions group appeared to be a higher SES group than the non-participating group, and this may have influenced their continuance in the study, the two groups were similar on all aspects of functioning assessed at enrolment in the study.

Discussion

Using a large, longitudinal database, this research aimed to test the hypothesis that Australian adolescents whose families had experienced a family transition would have poorer outcomes in behaviour, well-being and family processes compared with adolescents living in their original families. . . .

Group Differences

Contrary to our hypothesis, there were no group differences on internalising, externalising and overall behaviour problems at 17–18 years, findings that contrast with those of many researchers in this field who have found that children and adolescents who have experienced transitions are significantly worse off in terms of behavioural adjustment (Amato & Keith, 1991). Longitudinal analyses did not reveal group differences in either overall or extreme problem behaviour scores. . . . For problem behaviour scores from age 3 to 18 years, transitions group participants scored similarly to their peers from intact families.

Most published studies in the family transitions literature tend to focus upon negative behavioural outcomes. In this study, positive behaviours in the domain of social competence were also examined. The two groups were again comparable on such dimensions as responsibility, cooperativeness, self-control and empathy.

Although the literature repeatedly points to a decline in academic functioning after family transition (Rodgers, 1996), the lack of significant differences between the ATP groups on this variable was also supported by qualitative interview data used in another, unreported part of this study. Most interviewees were dismissive of notions that their schoolwork was affected by parental divorce. Hence, overall, it appeared that the young people from the ATP were developing well both across time and at late adolescence. . . .

One possible reason for the lack of significant differences between the transitions and comparison groups could be that the transitions group was a particularly well-functioning one. Comparison of the current transitions group with another ATP subgroup which had earlier reported a family transition but had not participated in the 17–18-year data collection revealed modest but significant differences between the groups on family socio-economic background, but no differences on any of the measured aspects of child functioning. Thus it did not seem that this transitions group was an especially high-functioning one. . . .

It may also be that distinctive characteristics of Australian society are contributing to successful outcomes for these adolescents, although Rodgers (1996) dismissed the notion that Australia was somehow dissimilar from other countries in contributing to better adjustment outcomes after divorce, since the majority of Australian findings actually supported the concept of group differences. However, in Dunlop and Burns' work (1988) and now in this study, adolescents from families that have experienced transitions and those still in their original families appear to be functioning in very similar ways. Particular Australian factors such as the provision of social security benefits and legal enforcement of child maintenance payments may mitigate some of the more extreme financial hardship and life stress that can ensue after a family breakdown. Given that few significant differences were found between the transitions and intact groups, it is not surprising that the adolescents who had experienced a parental death were not differentiated from their peers on behavioural, academic, family and coping variables (Kiernan, 1992). . . .

Most of the significant main effects in this study involved gender. Girls experienced higher overall levels of behaviour problems and specifically, more internalising problems including anxiety and depression. These findings are consistent with much of the research into overall gender differences in psychological symptomatology. . . . Girls were also found to be more socially competent than boys in late childhood to early adolescence, which is also a normative finding (Prior et al., 2000). However, since there were no interactions between gender and group status, this effect cannot be ascribed to the effects of separation and divorce.

Predictors of Functioning

Parental rating of the ATP child's ease or difficulty compared to his or her peers consistently predicted higher problem behaviours. Over the years, this ATP-devised measure has been predictive for a variety of outcomes (Prior et al., 2000) and rather than being a measure of temperament as originally formulated, it appears to represent the level of ease and harmony in the parent–child relationship. Consistent with the findings of researchers such as Hetherington (1989), dimensions of temperament have proved significant in predicting behavioural outcomes in this study, as they have in much previous ATP research (Prior et at., 2000), with a lack of persistence or attentional self-regulation associated with externalising problems, and withdrawal, or shyness, associated with internalising problems, Despite the traditional emphasis placed on factors such as age at transition, years since transition, and contact with the non-residential parent, these factors did not contribute to the functional outcomes experienced by the adolescent. Of all the specifically transitions-related variables, only number of transitions experienced was (weakly) predictive of overall behaviour problems in the transitions group. . . .

The identified, significant predictors of behavioural outcomes were not unique to the transitions group. Personality factors such as dimensions of temperament and parent's overall ease/difficulty rating, rather than external, structural factors, were also associated with problem behaviour in the comparison group. The child's temperament would clearly have a powerful effect upon the type of relationship he or she has with a parent, which would in turn affect adjustment outcomes for the child. Dunlop and Burns (1988) showed that regardless of whether parents are together or apart, adolescents who have a warm and supportive relationship with at least one parent show better adjustment on a variety of measures than those who do not. For example, possessing the trait of persistence, i.e., the ability to follow through on a task even when circumstances are difficult, may enable a person to trial different coping strategies, if one proved to be unsuccessful, or to just keep persevering. Being able to approach others for help or to allow the approach of others is likely to be another factor involved in optimal coping. Social and personal networks can allow young people to access help during hardship. Moreover, children and adolescents with positive temperamental styles are more likely to have developed warm, supportive parental relationships that would be invaluable during any period of difficulty. . . .

Conclusion

. . . [The] current research is useful in portraying children and adolescents from transition families as functioning in similar ways to their peers from intact families. For this large Australian adolescent sample, the family transition has not necessarily negatively impacted on current social, emotional or psychological outcomes, although relationships with parents may have been negatively affected. For those with poorer behavioural outcomes, the most prominent contributing factors were dimensions of temperament and parent–child relationship quality, rather than structural determinants related to the transition itself. Although many studies in the literature have found significant negative effects, the results are often tempered by small effect sizes. That is, while a small group of children from disrupted families are often found to be functioning more poorly than peers from intact families, the vast majority are developing into competent human beings, functioning satisfactorily in most domains. This study highlights the resilience of many young people faced with personal and social upheaval.

References

Amato, P.R., & Booth, A. (1996). A prospective study of divorce and parent–child relationships. *Journal of Marriage and the Family*, 58, 356–365.

Amato, P. R., & Keith, B. (1991). Parental divorce and the well-being of children: A meta-analysis. *Psychological Bulletin*, 110, 26–46.

Australian Bureau of Statistics. (2002). *Marriages and divorces. Australia.* Catalogue No. 3310.0. Canberra.

Dunlop, R., & Burns, A. (1988). *Don't feel the world is caving in: Adolescents in divorcing families.* Melbourne: Australian Institute of Family Studies.

Emery, R.E. (1999). *Marriage, divorce and children's adjustment* (2nd edn). Thousand Oaks, CA: Sage.

Hetherington, E.M. (1989). Coping with family transitions: Winners, losers, and survivors. *Child Development,* 60, 1–14.

Hetherington, E.M., & Clingempeel, W. G. (1992). Coping with marital transitions: A family systems perspective. *Monographs of the Society for Research in Child Development*, 57 (2–3, Serial No. 227).

Hetherington, E.M., Stanley-Hagan, M., & Anderson, E. R. (1989). Marital transitions: A child's perspective. *American Psychologist,* 44, 303–312.

Kelly, J.B. (1998). Marital conflict, divorce and children's adjustment. *Child and Adolescent Psychiatric Clinics of North America*, 7, 259–271.

Kiernan, K. E. (1992). The impact of family disruption in childhood on transitions made in young adult life. *Population Studies*, 46, 213–234.

Prior, M., Sanson, A., Smart, D., & Oberklaid, F. (2000). *Pathways from infancy to adolescence: Australian Temperament Project 1983–2000.* Melbourne: Australian Institute of Family Studies.

Rodgers, B. (1996). Social and psychological wellbeing of children from divorced families: Australian research findings. *Australian Psychologist,* 31, 174–182.

Zill, N., Morrison, D.R., & Coiro, M.J. (1993). Long-term effects of parental divorce on parent–child relationships, adjustment, and achievement in young adulthood. *Journal of Family Psychology*, 7, 91–103.

POSTSCRIPT

Does Divorce or Disruption in Family Structure During Adolescence Have a Detrimental Effect on Development?

In examining the research on family structure, Amato argues that children growing up in a stable long-term two-parent family are less likely to have psychosocial problems during both childhood and adulthood. He concludes that the children who have stable family structures have a higher standard of living, receive better parenting, have stronger and more secure attachments to parents, and are exposed to fewer stressful events. Ruschena and colleagues, on the other hand, examined family transitions such as separation, divorce, remarriage, and death on children and adolescents and found no significant differences between groups on measures of behavioral and emotional adjustment, academic outcomes, and social competence. In other words, adolescents from disruptive family structures functioned the same as adolescents from intact families.

Supporting Amatos' argument, Sun and Li (2002) also found that children of divorce have lower scores on measures of well-being (i.e., academic functioning, locus of control, and self-esteem) compared to children of intact families. Although they reported that family resources could mediate the negative effects of disruption over time, the process essentially affected children continuously both before and after divorce.

Mavis Hetherington, on the other hand, supports the arguments of Ruschena and her colleagues, stating that 75–80 percent of children from divorced homes are coping well and certainly functioning in the normal range 20 years later (Hetherington & Kelly, 2002). Although Hetherington states, "Divorce is usually brutally painful to a child," she argues that "negative long-term effects have been exaggerated to the point where we now have created a self-fulfilling prophecy" (p. 7). An important point that Hetherington raises is that many children of divorce are "uncommonly resilient, mature, responsible, and focused."

So, which is it: Do adolescents suffer continuously, or do they fare well over time? Wallerstein and Lewis take a "middle of the road approach to this argument." They view divorce not so much as an acute stress from which the child recovers but instead a life-transforming experience that can have both positive and negative outcomes. From this perspective, instead of debating whether or not adolescents suffer, researchers should focus on finding ways to ensure the life experience is positive. What are the risk factors for a negative experience, and what are the protective factors leading to a positive experience? For example,

Wallerstein and Lewis identified grandparents as a protective factor, stating that children from divorced homes faired better if they had close stable grandparents. Children felt comforted by the models that the grandparents provided. On the other hand, a risk factor identified was mood and affect of the parents. Children who continued to suffer during adulthood often reported that it was difficult to move on if one parent remained lonely and unhappy.

Additional risk factors identified in the research include the initial separation such as the abrupt departure of one parent, continuing parent conflict after separation, ineffective or neglectful parenting, loss of important relationships such as extended family members, and financial/economic changes (Kelly, 2003). Protective factors identified by Kelly are competent custodial parents, effective parenting from the non-residential parent, and amicable versus high conflict relationship between the divorced parents. In summary, the outcomes for children and adolescents appear to be complex and dependent on many factors that can either have a detrimental effect on development or contribute to a positive outcome.

References/Further Readings

Hetherington, E. M., & Elmore, A. M. (2003). Risk and resilience in children coping with their parents' divorce and remarriage. In S. S. Luthar (Ed.), *Resilience and vulnerability: Adaptation in the context of childhood adversities* (pp. 183–212). Cambridge: Cambridge University Press.

Hetherington, E. M., & Kelly, J. (2002). *For better or for worse: Divorce reconsidered*. New York: Norton.

Kelly, J. B. (2003). Changing perspectives on children's adjustment following divorce: A view for the United States. *Childhood*, 10, 237–254.

National Vital Statistics Report, 2005, Volume 54. National Centre for Health Statistics, Hyattsville, MD. http://www.cdc.gov/nchs/products/pubs/pubd/nvsr/54/54-pre.htm.

Peris, T. S., & Emery, R. E. (2004). A prospective study of the consequences of marital disruption for adolescents: Predisruption family dynamics and postdisruption adolescent adjustment. *Journal of Clinical Child and Adolescent Psychology*, 33, 694–704.

Statistics Canada. (2006). Divorces by province and territory. CANSIM, table 053-0002, http://www40.statcan.ca/101/cst01/famil02.htm.

Sun, Y., & Li, Y. (2002). Children's well-being during parents' marital disruption process: A pooled time-series analysis. *Journal of Marriage and Family*, 64, 472–488.

Wallerstein, J. S., & Lewis, J. M. (2004). The unexpected legacy of divorce: Report of a 25-year study. *Psychoanalytic Psychology*, 21, 353–370.

ISSUE 13

Does Dating Impede Developmental Adjustment for Adolescents?

YES: Deborah P. Welsh, Catherine M. Grello, and Melinda S. Harper, from "When Love Hurts: Depression and Adolescent Romantic Relationships," in Paul Florsheim, ed., *Adolescent Romantic Relations and Sexual Behavior* (Lawrence Erlbaum, 2003)

NO: Wyndol Furman and Laura Shaffer, from "The Role of Romantic Relationships in Adolescent Development," in Paul Florsheim, ed., *Adolescent Romantic Relations and Sexual Behavior* (Lawrence Erlbaum, 2003)

ISSUE SUMMARY

YES: Researchers Welsh, Grello, and Harper, while not arguing that all teen romantic relationships are detrimental, demonstrate how such relationships can be a catalyst for teens who are at risk to develop depression.

NO: Wyndol Furman, a child clinical psychologist at the University of Denver, and Laura Shaffer make the case for areas where romantic relationships can impact teen development. While many of their arguments are speculative or supported only by correlational research, they make a compelling case for the benefits of teenage romances.

When should teens be allowed to date? Is this just inconsequential "puppy love"? Are these relationships good or bad for adolescents? Should adults attempt to dissuade teens from dating? These are questions that capture the debate about adolescent romantic relationships.

Dating is a key process for adolescents. Much of teens' time is spent attempting to date, talking about dating, actually dating, and recovering from dating relationships. Thus, teen romantic relationships seem like a normal part of adolescent development. Early developmental theorists in the 1950s, such as Harry Stack Sullivan and Erik Erikson, argued that dating in early and middle adolescence prepares the teen for developing mature, functional adult inter-personal relationships. However, little research has addressed the impact of romantic relationships on adolescent development. Rather, most research in the area of close adolescent relationships has focused on relationships with peers or parents.

Much of the research that does exist seems to focus on adolescent romantic relationships as a negative outcome; that is, romantic relationships are often viewed as part of a constellation of problem behavior such as early initiation of intercourse and other sexual activities, alcohol and substance use, parental defiance, and delinquency. Romantic relationships have been linked to stress experiences for adolescents. For example, research suggests that teens sometimes enter into romantic relationships for undesirable motivations such as to elevate their social status, to prove their "maturity," or to help them separate from their family. Teen romance can add to stress levels by interfering with friendships and parental relationships as well as perhaps distracting the adolescent from his/her academic achievement. Also, teen romantic relationships have been investigated as contributing to negative emotions that may lead to depression. Breaking up, in particular, can have a variety of negative effects on youth, including having a negative impact on the adolescent's self-image and self-worth, feeling undesirable, feelings of betrayal, and general sadness.

Less attention is focused on the many benefits of teen romantic relation-ships. For example, romantic partners are a significant source of social support for the adolescent, relationships are a source of strong positive emotions, and dating helps the adolescent become more autonomous. Romantic relationships can also be a means of developing better interpersonal skills and competencies, gaining status and popularity, and helping to solidify various social identities. Intrapersonally, the teen may develop a positive sense of self through dating (i.e., feel desirable, wanted, intimate) and positive self-regard. Research seems to suggest that affiliation, companionship, and friendship are critical components of romantic relationships for adolescent development.

Welsh, Grello, and Harper discuss what they call the "dark side" of adolescent romance. While these authors acknowledge the potentially positive aspects of teen romantic relationships, they present many of the potential pitfalls of such relationships and how these may lead at-risk individuals to depression, which can have an adverse impact on adolescent development. Furman and Shaffer, while acknowledging the potential pitfalls of teen romantic relationships, discuss the potential positive impact that such relationships can have, including facilitating identity development, enhancing peer and family relationships, providing positive sexual development, and encouraging academic achievement.

YES

Deborah P. Welsh, Catherine M. Grello, and Melinda S. Harper

When Love Hurts: Depression and Adolescent Romantic Relationships

The pervasiveness of depression along with the extremely serious psychological, social, and economic consequences it wreaks in our society makes it one of the most pressing mental health concerns of our time. Depression in adolescents is associated with detrimental consequences, including social impairment in family, peer, and romantic relationships, academic problems, suicide, and risk for future depressive episodes. Adolescence, particularly early to middle adolescence, is considered the pivotal time period during which overall rates of depression rise and gender differences in depressive symptoms emerge. Interestingly, this is also the time during which adolescents typically begin romantic relationships. Although romantic relationships clearly play a normative, healthful role in adolescent development for most adolescents . . ., this [paper] focuses on the dark side of adolescent romance. That is, we examine when romantic relationships may be detrimental to adolescent development and may be associated with the rise of depressive symptomatology as well as with the gender difference in depression that emerges during adolescence.

[We] first present . . . theoretical models explaining the etiology of adolescent depression and . . . theoretical models of adolescent romantic relationships. We attempt to integrate these perspectives in an effort to explain the link between romantic relationships and depressive symptomatology in adolescents. Our integrative model posits that a variety of individual characteristics may place certain adolescents at risk for developing depressive symptoms when exposed to the stressors inherent in romantic relationships. Second, we examine some of these stressors or challenges associated with different developmental stages of adolescents' romantic relationships. Finally, we [conclude with] practical implications. . . .

Models of Adolescent Depression

Most contemporary models of adolescent depression are multifaceted and include cognitive, interpersonal, socio-cultural, and biological components. . . . Some people respond to distressing feelings with a passive, ruminative style of coping that tends to promote further depressive symptoms while others use more active, distracting types of strategies that are more effective in interfering with the positive feedback cycle of depressive symptoms. Girls and women are more likely to ruminate in response to depressive feelings, while boys and men are more likely to use the more active, and adaptive, coping styles. . . . [The] challenge of mastering the new domain of developing and maintaining sexual/romantic relationships is the most prominent new hurdle experienced by adolescents.

Global interpersonal styles have also been suggested as an important component in developmental models of depression. . . . Interpersonally vulnerable individuals are preoccupied with the affection of others, with feelings of loneliness and helplessness, fear abandonment, desire intense closeness, and they have difficulty in expressing anger overtly. [When] individuals with this pattern of interpersonal vulnerability experience stressful events involving other people, intense feelings of interpersonal vulnerability are potentiated, and internalizing psychological disorders result. Once again, the role of adolescent romantic relationships is likely to serve as one of the most significant stressors for adolescents in this etiological model of depression. . . .

[Difficulties] in achieving individuation within parent–adolescent relationships may be reflected in later romantic relationships. These differences are manifested in maladaptive interpersonal behaviors that maintain and increase depressive symptoms in adolescents by exacerbating physiological stress responses to interpersonal conflict. . . . [One] style, wherein girls engage in interpersonal conflict but give up and concede to others, is [called agitated submission]. In contrast, boys with higher levels of depressive symptoms exhibit a behavioral pattern that is highly submissive, but low in conflict and more distancing [passive submission]. . . .

Adolescent romantic relationships play a significant role in these three models of adolescent depression. They provide the context in which precipitating ineffective cognitive coping strategies (e.g., rumination), potentiating feelings of interpersonal vulnerability, and/or ineffective behavioral coping are likely to manifest and be maintained.

Models of Adolescent Romantic Relationships

. . . Furman and Wehner (1994, 1997) . . . proposed a developmental theory of adolescent romantic relationships that builds upon attachment theory. A fundamental component of their theoretical model is the concept of "views," which refers to the preconceptions, beliefs, and expectations held by individuals about particular types of relationships. Furman and Wehner postulated that individual couple members' views of romantic relationships influence their patterns of interaction in their romantic relationships as well as the way they *interpret* the interactions that occur within those relationships. Thus, two members of the same dating couple may be involved in the same interaction and, due to differences in their views of romantic relationships, may interpret and respond to that interaction very differently. Furman and Wehner (1994, 1997) conceptualized individuals' views of romantic relationships as either *secure, dismissing,* or *preoccupied* in nature, similar to the categorization scheme used by attachment theorists. They asserted that individuals' views of romantic relationships are affected by romantic experiences and, in turn, affect adolescents' perceptions of their romantic experiences. Therefore, a correlation is expected between individuals' views of romantic relationships and their perceptions of the interaction occurring in their romantic relationships. In fact, empirical evidence [supports this].

. . . [One] of the key ways in which internal working models of past relationships influence adolescents' current romantic relationships is via their impact on expectations of attaining acceptance and avoiding rejection. [Adolescents develop] anxious or angry expectations of rejection as a result of a history of experiencing rejection from parents, peers, and romantic partners. These "rejection-sensitive" individuals possess a cognitive-affective processing system that becomes activated in social situations where rejection is possible, and influence the interpretation and course of their interactions in ways that confirm and maintain their rejection expectations. One way rejection-sensitive individuals may try to avoid rejection is by exercising self-silencing behaviors, including the suppression of their opinions, thus submerging their individual identity within the context of the romantic relationship. In our current project of high-school-aged adolescents, the Study of Tennessee Adolescent Romantic Relationships (STARR), we found that girls who reported the greatest loss of their sense of self in their romantic relationships were significantly more likely to report depressive symptoms when compared to all other adolescents. Interestingly, adolescent boys were twice as likely as girls to lose their sense of self in their romantic relationships. However, losing their sense of self in their romantic relationships did not seem to be problematic for the adolescent boys in the sample. There was no correlation between loss of self and depressive symptoms in boys.

In summary, . . . recent models of romantic relationship development highlight the importance of understanding the lenses that individual adolescents bring to their romantic relationships and the ways in which these lenses impact couple members' own perceptions of their interpersonal relationships and interactions. These models predict that individual qualities that adolescent couple members bring to their romantic relationships (i.e., their beliefs and expectations of relationships formed from their prior experiences of relationships) will be related to the nature of their current romantic relationships, their interactions within the context of these current romantic relationships, and their subjective understanding of these interactions. In a cyclical and self-fulfilling manner, adolescents' subjective understanding of their interactions impacts the nature of their interactions with their romantic partners which, in a recursive loop, further impacts their subjective understanding of those interactions.

Although these models were formulated to understand the normative development of adolescent romantic relationships, they have clear implications for the development of depression, especially when integrated with the models of depression discussed previously. For example, adolescents who transition to romantic relationships with insecure models of relationships and are highly sensitive to relational rejection will be likely to interpret their partners' behaviors in more negative ways, which will result with these individuals responding to their partners in less effective ways, such as self-silencing. . . .

Developmental Considerations of Romantic Relationships

. . . [The] similar timing between the increase in rates of depression, the emergence of gender differences in depression, and the onset of adolescent romantic relationships is probably not coincidental. Rather, theoretical and empirical evidence suggest that adolescent dating relationships may serve as a stressor facilitating depression, an interpersonal context in which maladaptive coping styles develop and are maintained, as well as a context in which symptoms of psychological distress become manifest. Our integrative model posits that a variety of individual characteristics may place certain adolescents at risk for developing depressive symptoms when exposed to the stressors inherent in romantic relationships. Some of the key individual characteristics differentiating deleterious romantic relationships from healthy normative development include gender (female), a ruminative cognitive style of coping, an interpersonally vulnerable style, an agitated submissive (girls) or passive submissive (boys) pattern of interpersonal behavioral coping, an insecure internal working model of relationships, rejection sensitivity, self-silencing behavior, and developmental level (e.g., premature commitment, premature transition to sexual intercourse). We argue that these elements gleaned from theories of depression and theories of romantic relationship development fit together to provide a framework for understanding the intersection between adolescents' romantic relationships and the emergence of adolescent depressive symptoms. We . . . now . . . [discuss] . . . specific aspects of romantic relationships that are particularly problematic for adolescents who . . . may be more vulnerable to the developmental challenges of romantic relationships.

Stressors Associated with the Romantic Relationship Context

Romantic relationships are the most affectively charged domain for adolescents, and, thus, are the single largest source of stress for adolescents. . . . In a high school sample, . . . girls attributed 34% of their strong emotions to real and fantasized romantic relationships and boys attributed 25% of their strong emotions to romantic relationships (Wilson-Shockley, 1995). The suggestion that romantic relationships accounted for between a quarter and a third of all middle teens' strong emotional states was quite impressive and far greater than any other single domain including school, family, or same-sex peer relationships. . . . Although the majority of these strong emotions attributed to romantic relationships were positive, a substantial minority (42%) were negative, including feelings of depression. . . .

In a recent empirical investigation of over 12,000 nationally representative adolescents between 12 and 17 years of age, Joyner and Udry (2000) examined the association between change in depressive symptoms over a 1-year period and involvement in a romantic relationship. They found that adolescents who became romantically involved during the year between data collection points showed more depressive symptoms than adolescents who were not romantically involved during the year. . . . [Females may be] more vulnerable to the detrimental impact of romantic relationships. Romantic relationships are a new domain for adolescents in which they must struggle to gain competence. It is probably not surprising that they occupy a disproportionately large portion of adolescents' thoughts and create more stress (both positive and negative) than any other domain. These studies provide strong and compelling empirical data to suggest that aspects of romantic relationships are stressful and related to depression in adolescents.

Adolescent romantic relationships have three developmental stages. There are different challenges associated with each stage of relationship development. In the first stage, *infatuation,* adolescents are concerned with whether or not the object of their attraction reciprocates their interest. . . . In the following sections, we examine [the] specific struggles associated with each of the developmental stages of adolescent dating: infatuation (stressor = unreciprocated love), dyadic dating stage (stressors = sexual behavior decision-making and infidelity), and the termination stage (stressor = breaking-up).

I. Infatuation Stage

Unreciprocated Love

Adolescents are clearly capable of experiencing romantic love. However, quite frequently, these feelings are one-sided and unreciprocated. The feelings of love for another can exist even when the adolescent has rarely or never spoken to the admired one [or] when the admired individual shows no interest in return. Fantasy can be strong, as many adolescents believe that the admired one returns the same feelings of admiration. When the fantasy is potent, adolescents frequently misinterpret signals from the admired individual. These misinterpretations can increase the adolescents' vulnerability to disappointment when the adolescent eventually discovers that the individual does not return the admiration.

Although adolescents typically report positive feelings during the pursuit of a relationship, when the rejection from unreciprocated adolescent love occurs, the rejected adolescent frequently reports decreased self-esteem and despair, increased humiliation and feelings of inferiority, and decreased feelings of desirability and attractiveness. These negative emotions are reportedly devastating and often enduring, as the adolescent not only has to deal with the personal rejection but the abandonment of the fantasy. Individuals who enter an unrequited love relationship who are rejection sensitive, have insecure attachment models, tend to ruminate, are interpersonally vulnerable, or have agitated submissive interpersonal patterns of interaction would be expected to be particularly prone to depressive symptoms following the rejection of an unreciprocated love relationship.

II. Dyadic Dating Stage

[If the interest is reciprocated, adolescents may move to the second stage of romantic relationships.]

Sexual Decision Making

Sexual behaviors are an important aspect of adolescents' romantic relationships. In fact, the incorporation of sexuality into relationships is the primary element that distinguishes romantic relationships from adolescents' other close relationships. Sexual intercourse, the primary and almost exclusive sexual behavior examined by researchers, has become a statistically normative behavior among adolescents. . . . Sexual activity is clearly prevalent in adolescent romantic relationships. The decision about what sexual activities should and will occur within the context of any given adolescent's romantic relationships and the sequella of those decisions, however, are often associated with a great deal of turmoil.

Adolescents report that peer pressure is one of the strongest motivations for engaging in sexual behavior, and peer group rejection or acceptance of sexual intercourse is very much related to adolescents' decisions to abstain or transition to sexual intercourse. The decision to have sexual intercourse is experienced differently by adolescent males and females, with females experiencing first intercourse significantly more negatively than males. It is likely that adolescents who are more vulnerable to depression, particularly interpersonally vulnerable adolescents and less securely attached or rejection sensitive adolescents, are especially susceptible to the power of peer pressure. In addition, these high-risk adolescents may look to sexuality to compensate for poor past relationships. Attachment style has been empirically associated with adolescent sexual behavior[;] insecurely attached adolescents are more sexually promiscuous, have sex more frequently, and engage in sexual behaviors at an earlier age. . . .

Sexual behaviors have been strongly linked with depression, especially in adolescent females. . . . This link is strongest in younger adolescents, suggesting that sexual intercourse may be a clearer marker of psychological distress when it occurs early or off-time rather than when it occurs at a more normative time. . . . Tubman, Windle, and Windle (1996) found evidence that premature sexual debut was associated with depression and that late transition to intercourse was associated with decreased self-esteem and poor social relationships. . . .

In an earlier project from our lab, we observed and interviewed 61 middle- to late-adolescent heterosexual couples in an intensive study of their communication processes, their relational and psychological functioning, and their sexual behavior. We found that distinct sexual behaviors were related in very different ways to the couple members' individual and relational functioning. Specifically, we found that the more affectionate sexual behaviors of handholding, kissing, and light petting were associated with more committed and more intimate relationships. Whether or not couples were engaging in sexual intercourse was not related to their individual or relational functioning. However, sexual intercourse was associated with couple members' perceptions of higher levels of interpersonal conflict in their videotaped conversations. Additionally, we found that couple members' experience of having power or control in their sexual decision making was related to psychological well-being in the adolescent females. Female couple members who felt that they had less voice than their boyfriends in decisions about sex reported lower self-esteem. These findings suggest that sexual behaviors and decision-making are related to adolescents' mental health.

In summary, sexual behaviors are associated with depressive symptoms in what is probably a bi-directional or cyclic fashion. That is, depressed adolescents are more likely to engage in sexual behaviors, specifically sexual intercourse, and these behaviors are likely to further exacerbate adolescents' depression. However, it is important to keep in mind that most of the literature on adolescent sexuality has operated from a deficit model, in which sexual behaviors (intercourse) are assumed to be a marker or symptom of psychological distress in adolescents. Thus, research operating from this deficit paradigm has focused on comparing adolescents who have had sexual intercourse with those who have not. This sort of investigation prevents an understanding of the diversity of adolescents' experiences about their sexuality. Further, by focusing exclusively on heterosexual intercourse as the definition of sexuality, the current research literature fails to capture the diversity of sexual behaviors experienced by heterosexual as well as gay and lesbian adolescents and the mental health implications of these behaviors. It is important for future research in this area to explore adolescent sexuality from a normative, developmental position that allows us to understand the meanings that adolescents ascribe to sexual behaviors and to their decisions about whether to engage in particular sexual activities. This approach will allow researchers to differentiate the adolescents for whom sexual behavior is symptomatic of psychological disturbance from those for whom sexual behavior is associated with healthy, developmentally appropriate exploration.

Infidelity

Heterosexual adolescents' romantic relationships are typically characterized by mutual expectations for emotional and sexual fidelity. . . . Investigations of heterosexual adolescents' attitudes toward sexual betrayal reveal very low tolerance of infidelity from both males and females. Adolescents typically define infidelity in terms of sexual behaviors, especially petting and intercourse. . . . In spite of strong personal as well as cultural heterosexual prescriptions for exclusive dyadic romantic relationships, extra-dyadic romantic involvement is extremely common during adolescence among heterosexual and gay youth. . . .

[The] extremely high degree of sexual betrayal identified among adolescent romantic couples in spite of strong personal attitudes and cultural prescriptions about the unacceptability of infidelity may stem from competing and conflicting developmental demands of adolescence. Two of the most important developmental tasks of adolescence include identity development and intimacy development. Adolescents' search for identity is facilitated by exploration, including multiple romantic partners. To the extent that the perception of oneself as sexually and socially desirable is important to adolescents' developing identities, opportunities for greater sexual experiences that promote positive self-image will be difficult to resist. These developmental needs conflict, however, with adolescents' need to develop the capacity to maintain intimate, committed, enduring relationships. . . .

Unfaithfulness in a romantic relationship can be particularly devastating to adolescents who value exclusivity as they experience the violation as a loss of trust and loyalty in addition to the loss of the romantic partner. Adolescents express the belief that when a partner cheats, the relationship is irreparably damaged. Most adolescent romantic relationships do not survive infidelity and are typically terminated once the transgression is exposed, and both partners appear to experience a range of negative emotions. . . .

The guilt and confusion over violating one's personal values along with the feelings of excitement experienced in conjunction with the infidelity may lead certain unfaithful adolescents toward depression. Likewise, the loss of trust, loss of relationship, and the feelings of personal undesirableness experienced by the partner cheated on can also initiate a negative spiral of depression in vulnerable youth. . . .

III. Termination Stage

Breaking Up

Breaking up with a romantic partner is common. . . . The termination of these emotionally intense relationships is often traumatic for heterosexual as well as for gay and lesbian adolescents and clearly amplifies an adolescent's vulnerability for depression. Gay, lesbian, and heterosexual couples have not been found to differ in either their reasons for dissolving a relationship or on the levels of distress caused by the breakup. Several investigations have found that females are especially susceptible to depressive symptomatology immediately following the dissolution of a romantic relationship.

Most studies have found that initial distress following the breakup of a romantic relationship is high and then subsides as time passes. However, for some adolescents, especially female adolescents, the pain can endure. . . . Mearns (1991) . . . found evidence linking clinical depression with recent romantic relationship dissolution, particularly for females. . . .

Another explanation for the gender difference in the impact of romantic relationship termination may be a consequence of the intensity of emotion, commitment, and investment in the relationship. Although males report falling in love more frequently and at younger ages than females, females report experiencing more commitment and more passionate feelings towards their partners. Studies have consistently demonstrated that increased commitment leads to increased relationship investment. . . . [The] intensity of distress following the dissolution of a romantic relationship is dependent on the amount of investment the individual had in the relationship. Thus, females' tendency to be more committed and have more investment in their romantic relationships, possibly in conjunction with their greater tendency to use less adaptive cognitive and interpersonal coping strategies, may contribute to the greater incidence of depression they experience following the termination of their romantic relationships.

There is evidence that the impact of relationship termination may depend on who initiates the breakup as well as the availability of alternative resources and social support. The partner who initiates the termination of the relationship suffers less initial emotional distress following the breakup than the aggrieved partner. The initiator of a desired breakup has more control over the breakup and therefore, has had more time to mentally prepare for the loss of the relationship. The initiator of a desired breakup is also likely to be the less committed member of the couple and is more likely to have alternative options. The partner who feels responsible for the problems that led up to the breakup, especially when this partner is female, often experiences strong distress along with guilt and self-blame following the relationship termination. Psychological distress following relationship dissolution subsides when adolescents begin new romantic relationships. This may stem from the increased self-esteem adolescents experience as a result of feeling renewed desirability, from the reparation of adolescents' fragile developing sense of personal identity which may be located within a relational domain, or from the resumption of day-to-day interactions, goals, and plans that were interrupted by the breakup. Social support in general facilitates recovery and adjustment following romantic relationship dissolution in the long run, although social support does little to relieve the initial distress of breaking up.

Conclusion

Taken together, the available theoretical and empirical evidence supports a link between adolescent romantic relationships and the development of depressive symptomatology. Programs and policies designed to address the profound problem of adolescent depression should target adolescent romantic relationships as a key component. Intervention/prevention strategies need to be designed at multiple levels of influence including interventions focused on impacting adolescents directly as well as programs aimed at influencing those who work with and care for adolescents. . . .

We have argued for a link between developmental models of depression and developmental models of adolescent romantic relationships. We have provided . . . evidence that suggests that certain cognitive and interpersonal strategies utilized by some adolescents, particularly female adolescents, along with insecure internal representations of interpersonal relationships put these adolescents at risk for developing depressive symptoms during their adolescent years. This risk may be expressed in the form of depression when these at-risk adolescents are faced with certain relational challenges common to adolescents as they learn to develop and maintain mature romantic relationships. We have recommended that depression prevention and intervention programs incorporate developmental theories and findings regarding adolescent romantic relationships with interpersonal and cognitive theories of depression in an attempt to change the ways in which adolescents interact within their romantic relationships, how they view their relationships, and how they cope with the challenging aspects of those relationships in order to promote healthier individual and relational functioning.

References

Furman, W., & Wehner, E. A. (1994). Romantic views: Toward a theory of adolescent romantic relationships. In R. Montemayor, G. R. Adams, & T. P. Gullotta (Eds.), *Personal relationships during adolescence* (pp. 168–195). Thousand Oaks, CA: Sage.

Furman, W., & Wehner, E. A. (1997). Adolescent romantic relationships: A developmental perspective. In S. Shulman & W. A. Collins (Eds.), *New directions for child development: Romantic relationships in adolescence: Developmental perspectives* (pp. 21–36). San Franciso: Jossey-Bass.

Joyner, K., & Udry, R. (2000). You don't bring me anything but down: Adolescent romance and depression. *Journal of Health and Social Behavior, 41,* 369–391.

Mearns, J. (1991). Coping with a breakup: Negative mood regulation expectancies and depression following the end of a romantic relationship. *Journal of Personality and Social Psychology, 60*(2), 327–334.

Tubman, J. G., Windle, M., & Windle, R. C. (1996). The onset and cross-temporal patterning of sexual intercourse in middle adolescence: Prospective relation with behavioral and emotional problems. *Child Development, 67,* 327–343.

Wilson-Shockley, S. (1995). *Gender differences in adolescent depression: The contribution of negative affect.* Unpublished master's thesis, University of Illinois at Urbana-Champaign.

**Wyndol Furman and
Laura Shaffer**

The Role of Romantic Relationships in Adolescent Development

Most of us would characterize our adolescent romantic relationships as short-lived and superficial. In some respects, this description is correct. Most adolescent relationships only last a few weeks or months; it is unlikely that these relationships have the depth and complexity that characterize long-term committed relationships.

At the same time, the characterization of these relationships as short and superficial is incomplete. These relationships are central in adolescents' lives. They are a major topic of conversation among adolescents. Real or fantasized relationships are the most common cause of strong positive and strong negative emotions—more so than friendships, relationships with parents, or school. Moreover, adolescents are not the only ones who see these relationships as significant. The formation of romantic relationships is often thought to be one of the important developmental tasks of adolescence, and these relationships have significant implications for health and adjustment.

Not only are adolescent romantic relationships significant in their own right, but . . . they play an important role in shaping the general course of development during adolescence. In particular, adolescents face a series of tasks that include (a) the development of an identity, (b) the transformation of family relationships, (c) the development of close relationships with peers, (d) the development of sexuality, and (e) scholastic achievement and career planning. In the sections that follow, we describe how romantic relationships may play a role in each of these key developmental tasks.

Three caveats are warranted. First, the research primarily has been conducted with heterosexual adolescents in Western cultures, and we know little about gay, lesbian, and bisexual relationships or romantic relationships in other cultures. Second, even the existing literature on Western heterosexual romantic relationships is limited. The question of what impact they have on development has received almost no attention. Thus, our comments are often speculative and will need to be tested empirically. Finally, the effects of romantic relationships vary from individual to individual. As will be seen repeatedly, the specific impact they have is likely to depend heavily on the nature of the particular experiences.

Romantic Relationships and Identity Development

According to Erikson, the key developmental task of adolescence is the development of identity. During early adolescence, there is a proliferation of self representations that vary as a function of the social context. That is, early adolescents develop a sense of themselves with their mothers, fathers, friends, romantic partners, and others. Sometimes their different selves may contradict one another, but such contradictions are usually not acknowledged. In middle adolescence, they begin to recognize such seeming contradictions in their conceptions of themselves, and may be conflicted or confused. By late adolescence, many of them are able to integrate the seeming contradictions into a coherent picture.

Romantic experiences may play a role in the development of a sense of self or identity in two ways. First, adolescents develop distinct perceptions of themselves in the romantic arena. They do not simply have a concept of themselves with peers, but have different self-schemas of themselves with the general peer group, with close friends, and in romantic relationships. Romantic self-concept is related to whether one has a romantic relationship and to the quality of that relationship, suggesting that romantic experiences may affect one's sense of self in the romantic domain. Thus, adolescents who have had positive experiences may think of themselves as attractive partners, whereas those who have had adverse romantic experiences may have little confidence in their ability to be appealing partners or have successful relationships.

Second, romantic experiences and romantic self-concept may also affect one's global self-esteem. This effect is poignantly expressed in one of our teen's reflections about her romantic experiences, including those with an abusive partner. "Hum, what have I gained? (6 sec.pause). I feel I haven't gained like a lot, but I feel like I lost a lot. I lost my self-respect. I don't respect myself. It's like I feel like I have no self-esteem, no self-control, no nothing." Consistent with her comments, romantic self-concept has been empirically found to be substantially related to self-worth. Romantic self-concept is also related to one's self-concept in other domains, particularly physical appearance and peer acceptance.

Although global self-esteem and perceived competence in various domains are fundamental aspects of self-representations, the concept of identity entails more than these. In the process of developing an identity, adolescents acquire moral and religious values, develop a political ideology, tentatively select and prepare for a career, and adopt a set of social roles, including gender roles. Romantic relationships may facilitate the development of these facets of identity. . . . On the other hand, sometimes romantic relationships may hinder the identity development process. For example, parenthood—a potential consequence of romantic involvement—is thought to have a detrimental effect on adolescents' normative exploration of identity because of the constant demands and responsibilities it entails. Unfortunately, we can only speculate about how romantic relationships may facilitate or hinder identity development, as we have little empirical data about the role they may play. We know that peers and friends influence adolescents' attitudes and behaviors, but as yet, the specific influence of romantic relationships or romantic partners simply has not been examined.

One particularly promising domain to study is gender-role identity. According to the gender intensification hypothesis, early adolescence is a period in which gender-related expectations become increasingly differentiated. Girls are expected to adhere to feminine stereotypes of behavior, whereas boys are expected to adhere to masculine stereotypes. It is commonly thought that the emergence of dating may be one of the most powerful factors contributing to the intensification of conventional gender roles. Romantic partners, as well as other peers, may reinforce or punish different gender-related behaviors or roles; certainly adolescents are likely to act in ways that they think might make them more attractive to members of the other sex. Of course, different romantic partners are likely to have different expectations regarding gender roles, and one's own experiences in romantic relationships would be expected to affect one's concepts of gender roles.

The Transformation of Family Relationships

During adolescence, relationships with parents and other family members undergo significant changes. . . . Romantic relationships may play a role in these transformations of family relationships in several ways. At the most basic level, adolescents spend less time with family members and more time with the other sex or in romantic relationships as they grow older. Those who have romantic relationships spend less time with family members than those who are not currently involved with someone.

Romantic relationships are also a common source of conflict and tension in the family. . . . Dating and romantic relationships are topics in which parents and adolescents have different expectations and both are invested in exercising jurisdiction. . . . In other instances, . . . conflicts with family members may lead some adolescents to seek out romantic relationships to escape family problems. . . .

[Parents] may have ambivalent feelings about their children's romantic relationships. For example, mothers report being both joyful that their daughters are happy, and yet sometimes jealous and aware of the loss of an exclusive tie. Similarly, the satisfaction of seeing their sons mature can be counterbalanced by the realization that they are growing up and eventually leaving the household. . . . A serious relationship can be seen as an intrusion or threat to the family. . . .

Although conflict and ambivalent feelings about romantic relationships may occur commonly, these should not be overstated. In popular stereotypes, adolescence is thought of as period of great strife between parents and peers, but in fact, peer and parental influences are typically synergistic. We believe that the same synergism may be characteristic of romantic relationships and family relationships. . . .

The links between supportive behavior in relationships with romantic partners and parents are complicated. As adolescents grow older, they are more likely to turn to a boyfriend or girlfriend for support [and] less likely to seek support from their parents. The early phases of the transition from a parent as the primary attachment figure to a romantic partner may begin in adolescence, particularly in late adolescence. Specifically, adolescents may begin to turn to their partners or peers for a safe haven, although their parents are likely to remain as their primary secure base.

[The] amount of support in the two types of relationships at any particular age is positively correlated. Perhaps the ability to be supportive in one relationship carries over to the other relationship. Having a supportive romantic relationship (vs. just any romantic relationship) may also have a positive effect on one's general emotional state, which in turn may foster positive interactions in the home. Thus, although romantic relationships can be a source of strain on relationships with parents, they may have some positive effects on these relationships in other instances.

The Development of Close Relationships with Peers

Concomitant with the changes in the family throughout adolescence are significant changes in peer relationships. . . . Over the course of adolescence, they increasingly turn to their peers for support as these relationships become more intimate in nature. . . .

Adolescent romantic relationships may contribute to adolescents' peer relations in several ways. . . . [Adolescents] spend increasing amounts of time with their peers, and these changes in the sheer frequency of interaction primarily occur in interactions with the other sex or in romantic relationships. One function such interactions serve is affiliation. These affiliative interactions are both stimulating and utilitarian in nature. Such interchanges provide opportunities for reciprocal altruism, mutualism, and social play. Adolescents may develop their capacities to cooperate and co-construct a relationship. Moreover, the interactions are very rewarding in nature, as spending time with the other sex or having a romantic relationship is associated with positive emotionality.

The presence of such romantic relationships is also likely to influence the relationships one has with other peers. A boy/girlfriend becomes part of the adolescent's network and, in a significant minority of instances, remains part of the network even after the romantic element of the relationship has dissolved. He or she may introduce the teen to other adolescents. If the relationship becomes more serious, the social networks of the two overlap more as mutual friendships develop. . . .

Just as the impact on family relationships varies, romantic relationships' effects on peer relations do also. For example, three different patterns of relations between the peer group and romantic relationships [have been] identified. . . . In some cases the peer group became less salient as the romantic relationship was given priority. Sometimes, the choice between peers and romantic relationships was a source of conflict between the adolescent and the peers or partner. Finally, sometimes the peer group relations remained unchanged by the presence of the new relationship.

Romantic relationships can also affect one's standing in the peer group, as dating in Western cultures has traditionally served the functions of status grading and status achievement. Dating a particularly attractive or popular person could improve one's popularity or reaffirm that one is popular. . . .

Additionally, adolescents are likely to date those who share similar interests, attitudes, and values to theirs. Their dating selections may reinforce the reputation they have or identify the crowd they are seen as being part of. That is, their peers are likely to think they are similar to the individuals they are dating.

Finally, although double standards of sexual behavior are much less striking than they used to be, ethnographic work suggests that having sexual intercourse can still enhance boys' status in the peer group, whereas it may jeopardize the status of girls in at least some peer groups. Similarly, having a serious romantic relationship can lead to ridicule and jeopardize one's status in some peer groups where members of the other sex are simply seen as objects for sexual conquest.

[Romantic] relationships . . . can affect friendships in particular. . . . Often a romantic partner becomes the best friend, displacing the old friend.

Regardless of whether romantic relationships do or do not displace a friendship, it seems likely that the experiences in friendships and romantic relationships may influence each other. Both forms of relationships entail intimate disclosure, support seeking and giving, and mutuality. The skills that these require appear likely to carry over from one type of relationship to the other. . . .

Sexual Development

The development of sexuality is another key task in adolescence. As adolescents' bodies begin to mature in reproductive capacities, their sexual desires increase. Most adolescents begin to experiment with sexual behavior, and gradually develop some comfort with their sexuality. . . .

It almost seems unnecessary to say that romantic relationships play a key role in the development of sexuality. Certainly, sexual behavior often occurs in brief encounters, as adolescents "hook-up" with each other for an evening. Additionally, sexual behaviors, particularly mild forms of sexual behavior, commonly occur with friends with whom adolescents are not romantically involved. Nevertheless, casual or committed romantic relationships are primary contexts for sexual behavior and learning about sexuality. The majority of adolescents first have intercourse with someone they are going steady with or know well and like a lot. Moreover, most teenagers are selective about with whom they have intercourse. . . .

Aside from the idea that romantic relationships are a primary context for the development of sexuality, we know remarkably little about the specific role these relationships play. In fact, we know more about the influence of peers and parents than about romantic partners. Yet, it is difficult to believe that the partner and the nature of the relationship do not play critical roles in determining sexual behavior and in determining what is learned from the experiences.

Some descriptive information exists on the characteristics of sexual partners. For example, . . . [adolescents] are also more likely to have sexual intercourse for the first time with someone who is already sexually active than someone who is not. . . . [The] modal reason given for first having intercourse is to have the partner love them more. These findings suggest that the characteristics of the partner and one's feelings about the partner are critical determinants of sexual behavior, but we still know little about the particulars.

In part, the absence of information about the role of romantic relationships may reflect the field's focus on sexual intercourse, contraception, and pregnancy and their demographic correlates. The field has emphasized these components because of the significance they have for health. Yet, an understanding of adolescent sexuality requires a broader perspective. Bukowski, Sippola, and Brender (1993) proposed that the development of a healthy sense of sexuality includes: (a) learning about intimacy through interaction with peers, (b) developing an understanding of personal roles and relationships, (c) revising one's body schema to changes in size, shape, and capability, (d) adjusting to erotic feelings and experiences and integrating them into one's life, (e) learning about social standards and practices regarding sexual expression, and (f) developing an understanding and appreciation of reproductive processes. We believe that one's romantic relationships are likely to be one of the primary, if not the primary context, for learning about most of those facets of sexuality. Romantic relationships provide a testing ground not only for the how of sexual behavior but also for the what and when. They provide a context in which adolescents discover what is attractive and arousing. Adolescents learn what they like in their partners and what partners tend to like. They learn to reconcile their sexual desires, their moral values, and their partners' desires.

Finally, a critical facet of sexual development is the establishment or solidification of sexual orientation. Much of the existing research on adolescent sexuality and romantic relationships has focused on heterosexual adolescents, but current estimates indicate that approximately 10% of youth in the U.S. will consider themselves gay, lesbian, or bisexual at some point in their lives. Many sexual minority youth become aware of their same-gender attractions in early to mid-adolescence. . . . The majority . . . date heterosexually. Adolescents who are questioning their sexual orientation often find that these relationships help them determine or confirm their sexual preferences.

Scholastic Achievement and Career Planning

Around the beginning of adolescence, students in the United States make a transition from elementary school to middle school or junior high. In middle adolescence, they move on to high school. Some continue on to colleges or vocational schools in late adolescence, whereas others complete their formal education when they graduate from high school, and still others drop out of middle school or high school. Similar educational transitions occur in other Western societies. What is common across Western cultures, at least, is that the emphasis on academic learning increases with age, and students began to take increasingly different paths. . . .

[Early] involvement in romantic relationships has been linked with poorer scholastic achievement. In fact, romantic involvement and sexual behavior have been found to be negatively correlated with academic achievement throughout adolescence. Such associations could exist because those who are less academically oriented may be more likely to develop romantic relationships, or because romantic relationships may have an adverse effect on school achievement.

The time spent with a romantic partner could distract from schoolwork, but we suspect that any such effect may be highly dependent on the characteristics of the partner and the nature of the relationship. . . . That is, some partners may detract from school, but others may promote achievement by studying together, helping with homework, encouraging achievement, or providing support. . . .

Romantic partners may also influence career plans and aspirations. They can serve as comrades with whom to share ideas and dreams. They may encourage or discourage particular careers or educational plans. Developing a committed relationship, deciding to get married, or having a child is also likely to affect the plans for the future. . . . [Romantic] relationships may have either benefits or drawbacks for career plans, depending on the particular circumstances.

Clinical and Educational Implications

Our discussion of the role of romantic relationships in adolescent development has a number of implications for clinicians, educators, and parents. Perhaps the most obvious is how important romantic relationships can be in adolescents' lives. Not only are they central in the eyes of adolescents, but we have described the impact they may have on adolescent development.

Often, however, adults tend to downplay the significance of these relationships. Parents may tease their teens about a romantic relationship, or dismiss it as "only puppy love" and try to discourage them from getting too romantically involved as adolescent. In part, such reactions are understandable. . . . Romantic experiences entail a number of risks, such as pregnancy, sexual victimization, and violence. As valid as these parental concerns may be, however, they miss the point to some degree. Even if the relationships are relatively superficial, they are phenomologically quite important, and as we have suggested, may contribute to adolescent development. Thus, although parental monitoring of adolescent romantic experiences seems highly desirable, some sensitivity to the significance of the relationships for youth seems important as well. Disparaging or derogating a teen's relationship is not likely to be an effective parenting strategy. . . .

In general, those working with adolescents would want to consider the role romantic experiences play in different aspects of development. For example, sex education programs may want to consider the role relationships play in sexual behavior, and not just focus on anatomy and contraceptive practices. Similarly, because the romantic domain is an important one in identity development, clinicians working with adolescents who are struggling with identity issues may want to consider how these issues are enacted in relationships. Clinicians and parents should also be sensitive to the role romantic experiences may play in the process of redefining relationships with family members or peers. . . .

Conclusions

Although we have tried to make the case that romantic relationships may influence the course of adolescent development, . . . evidence is quite limited. Not only has relatively little research been conducted on these relationships in adolescence, but also the existing work has been guided primarily by models in which these relationships are treated as outcomes. For example, most research . . . seems to implicitly be guided by the idea that friendships or family relationships affect romantic relationships. The studies, however, are all correlational, and in most cases, the data are gathered at one time point. Thus, it is at least theoretically possible that the causal influences are in the other direction, or in both directions.

The limitations in our data bases cannot be corrected by simply recognizing that correlation does not imply causation. In designing our research, we need to consider deliberately how romantic relationships may impact other adolescent relationships or facets of development. This point is nicely illustrated in the literature on parental reactions to dating relationships. Some studies suggested that parental support is associated with increased or continued involvement in a dating relationship (Lewis, 1972), whereas other work suggested that romantic relationships could be enhanced by parental interference—the Romeo and Juliet effect (Driscoll, Davis, & Lipetz, 1972). The issue here is not that the findings are contradictory, however, but that the work had only considered the idea that parents may shape their offsprings' romantic relationships. Little consideration was given to the idea that late adolescents may also be attempting to shape their parents' impressions of the relationship and thus, may modify their own interactions with their parents. Leslie, Huston, and Johnson (1986), however, found that the vast majority of late adolescents monitor the information they provide about their romantic relationships, and have made multiple efforts to influence their parents' opinions about the romantic relationships. The parents, too, had often communicated either approving or disapproving reactions. Thus, by considering the idea that the paths of influence may be bi-directional, the investigators provided a better understanding of the process than if they had simply tested a unidirectional model.

It is also important to remember that the effects of romantic experiences may not be salutary. We have focused mainly on how romantic relationships may contribute to the normative developmental tasks of adolescence, but there are risks as well. Approximately 20% to 25% of young women are victims of dating violence or aggression. Adolescent romantic break-ups are one of the strongest predictors of depression, multiple-victim killings, and suicidal attempts or completions (Brent et al., 1993; Fessenden, 2000; Joyner & Udry, 2000; Monroe et al., 1999). Most incidents of sexual victimization are perpetrated by a romantic partner. The sexual activity that commonly co-occurs with romantic involvement places adolescents at risk for sexually transmitted diseases or becoming pregnant.

Perhaps the critical point is that the impact of romantic experiences is likely to vary from individual to individual. In the various sections . . . , we have tried to emphasize how not only the existence of a romantic relationship, but the quality of that relationship or the timing of the involvement may determine what the outcome of the experience will be. . . . [The] characteristics of the partner will also influence the nature of the romantic experience and its impact.

The emphasis on the variability of romantic experiences points out the need to identify the critical processes that are responsible for any impact that romantic experiences have. It may not be the simple presence of a relationship, but instead certain features or experiences that occur within the relationship that determine the outcome. . . .

Finally, in order to understand the impact of romantic relationships, we will need to understand the context in which they occur. The nature of these experiences [varies] as a function of the social and cultural context in which they occur. Conversely, we need to separate out the specific influence of romantic experiences from related experiences. . . . [It] had been shown that peer relationships in general had an impact on development, but as yet, nobody had examined the specific impact of romantic relationships. Although romantic relationships certainly share many features with other forms of peer relations, they also have some distinct features that may lead them to have a different impact than other peer relationships.

In summary, we have tried to discuss how romantic relationships may contribute to various facets of adolescent development, including the development of an identity, the transformation of family relationships, the development of close relationships with peers, the development of sexuality, and scholastic achievement and career planning. The evidence is consistent with the idea that romantic experiences may play a role in these various domains, but the evidence is still limited. . . .

References

Brent, D. A., Perper, J. A., Moritz, G., Baugher, M., Roth, C., Balach, L., & Schweers, J. (1993). Stressful life events, psychopathology, and adolescent suicide: A case control study. *Suicide and Life-Threatening Behavior, 23,* 179–187.

Bukowski, W. M., Sippola, L., & Brender, W. M. (1993). Where does sexuality come from? In H. E. Barbaree, W. L. Marshall, & D. R. Laws (Eds.), *The juvenile sex offender* (pp. 84–103). New York: Guilford.

Driscoll, R., Davis, K. E., & Lipetz, M. E. (1972). Parental interference and romantic love: The Romeo and Juliet effect. *Journal of Personality and Social Psychology, 24,* 1–10.

Fessenden, F. (2000, April 9). They threaten, seethe, and unhinge, then kill in quantity. *New York Times,* p. 1.

Joyner, K., & Udry, J. R. (2000). You don't bring me anything but down: Adolescent romance and depression. *Journal of Health and Social Behavior, 41,* 369–391.

Leslie, L. A., Huston, T. L., & Johnson, M. P. (1986). Parental reactions to dating relationships: Do they make a difference? *Journal of Marriage and the Family, 48,* 57–66.

Lewis, R. (1972). A developmental framework for the analysis of premarital dyadic formation. *Family Process, 11,* 16–25.

Monroe, S. M., Rohde, P., Seeley, J. R., & Lewinsohn, P. M. (1999). Life events and depression in adolescence: Relationship loss as a prospective risk factor for first onset of major depressive disorder. *Journal of Abnormal Psychology, 108,* 606–614.

POSTSCRIPT

Does Dating Impede Developmental Adjustment for Adolescents?

Based on both readings, it is clear that adolescent romantic relationships are important to teens and their development. While these relationships typically lack the seriousness and commitment levels involved in many adult romantic relationships, they should not be dismissed as "puppy love." Well over half of teens have had a romantic relationship in the past year and a half (see Bouchey & Furman, 2003) and these relationships appear to be of critical importance in teens' social lives.

Based on Welsh, Grello, and Harper, it is possible that these relationships can have a detrimental impact on the development of teens—particularly those who are at risk of depression. For the at-risk teen, the relationship may be a causal factor in the depression because of the potential negative events that can occur within the dating scenario (e.g., cheating, breakups, rejection) coupled with dysfunctional interpersonal styles (e.g., submissive response to conflict). Alternatively, a depressed individual may enter a romantic relationship in an attempt to distract him/herself from other unpleasant environmental events (e.g., child-parent conflict). There are many stages within the relationship cycle that may be interpreted negatively and may trigger depression by the depression-prone individual.

Furman and Shaffer's article depicts a more optimistic perspective on teen dating and its potential impact on development. The romantic relationship may have a variety of positive effects on the adolescent's identity development, family relationships, peer relations, sexual development, and scholastic achievement. While acknowledging the potential risks of teen dating (e.g., violence, unexpected pregnancy, depression), there are many positive growth experiences inherent in teen dating both intra- and interpersonally. The developmental impact on an adolescent who is dating is likely very complex, depending on an interaction of the individual, the situation, and the environment in which the dating occurs. Sadly, we do not know a lot about these possible "normal" dating sequences.

Clinicians, educators, and researchers need to develop better explicated theories of the normal progress of adolescent romantic relationships. Simply knowing that an adolescent is involved in a romantic relationship tells us little about needed intervention (e.g., to help prevent negative outcomes such as depression or relationship violence). Being able to predict which types of teens and which types of romantic relationships have negative consequences for the adolescent seems imperative for efforts to help these youth have positive growth experiences rather than experience detrimental outcomes. This is an area of adolescence that is in dire need of further research.

Also, it is important not to draw conclusions about adolescent romances without adequate information. In an interview with the online publication, *Hypography: Science for Everyone,* Wyndol Furman was asked to comment on a study that found that adolescents in romantic relationships were more depressed, more likely to engage in delinquency, and more prone to alcohol abuse than adolescents who did not date (Joyner & Udry, 2000). He was quoted as saying that "It's not like romantic relationships hold only danger for teens, without any benefits. . . . I don't buy that, any more than the idea that driving a car is only dangerous. There are risks, but are you going to give up your car?"

References/Further Readings

Adolescent lovers studied (14 February 2001). *Hypography: Science for Everyone.* http://www.hypography.com/article.cfm?id=29888.

Bouchey, H. A., & Furman, W. (2003). Dating and romantic experiences in adolescence. In G. R. Adams & M. D. Berzonsky (Eds.), *Blackwell handbook of adolescence* (pp. 313–329). Malden, MA: Blackwell.

Florsheim, P. (Ed.). (2003). *Adolescent romantic relations and sexual behavior: Theory, research, and practical implications.* Mahwah, NJ: Erlbaum.

Furman, W. (2002). The emerging field of adolescent romantic relationships. *Current Directions in Psychological Science,* 11(5), 177–180.

Joyner, K., & Udry, J. R. (2000). You don't bring me anything but down: Adolescent romance and depression. *Journal of Health and Social Behavior,* 41, 369–391.

ISSUE 14

Do Online Friendships Hinder Adolescent Well-Being?

YES: **Lauren Donchi and Susan Moore,** from "It's a Boy Thing: The Role of the Internet in Young People's Psychological Wellbeing," *Behavior Change* (vol. 21, no. 2, 2004)

NO: **Patti M. Valkenburg and Jochen Peter,** from "Online Communication and Adolescent Well-Being: Testing the Stimulation Versus the Displacement Hypothesis," *Journal of Computer-Mediated Communication* (vol. 12, 2007)

ISSUE SUMMARY

YES: Psychologists Lauren Donchi and Susan Moore suggest that adolescent boys who rate their online friendships as very important are more likely to have lower self-esteem and to be lonely. Those with more face-to-face friendships are higher on self-esteem and less lonely.

NO: Professors Patti Valkenburg and Jochen Peter, in the Amsterdam School of Communications Research at the University of Amsterdam, argue that online communication enhances well-being through its positive effect on time spent with friends and quality of friendships.

In recent years, the Internet has increasingly assumed an important role in everyday life. In 2005, 67.9 percent of households had at least one regular Internet user. This was up from 64 percent in 2003 and 59 percent in 2002 (Statistics Canada, 2004). In the United States, rates are similar with 68 percent of the population using the Internet on a regular basis (Pew Internet Report, 2005a). In both countries, usage is very dependent on children and adolescents. Homes with unmarried children under age 18 have the highest rates of Internet use with more and more children and adolescents using it as a means of communication (e.g., email, instant messaging and chat rooms). More specifically, 87 percent of American adolescents between the ages of 12 and 17 have Internet access (Pew Internet Report, 2005b). Of these, more than 90 percent reported using email on a regular basis, approximately 50 percent reported using instant messaging and 22 percent reported participating in online chat rooms. Not surprisingly, these statistics are age dependent. In other words, adolescent use increases with age, such that

43 percent of 10–11-year olds versus 86 percent of 16–17-year olds use instant messaging (IM) programs such as MSN (Pew Internet Report, 2004).

Instant messaging and chat rooms are ways of sending instant real-time messages to other online users. It is a rapidly growing way of communicating especially among today's adolescents. The text-based messages between two or more individuals who are simultaneously online are generally informal (i.e., without punctuation and often with grammatical errors). In addition to text messaging, users can view each other as they chat (e.g., using a webcam), send or receive files, and play games. Many youth are also using their cell phones to text message while away from their computer. With so many youth using MSN and other online communication programs, it seems pertinent to examine the effects on psychosocial development. Are these online relationships healthy?

Past research has found that face-to-face communication and participation in social groups have a positive effect on level of social support, probability of having fulfilling personal relationships, self-esteem, commitment to social norms, and overall psychological well-being. Because the Internet permits for communication and social interaction, time spent online can facilitate communication with distant friends and relatives. It can also facilitate conversation with friends close by without having to plan for get-togethers (Parks & Roberts, 1998).

Although positive outcomes such as these have been reported, it has been argued that the benefits depend on the quality of the online relationships as well as what adolescents are giving up to spend time chatting online. In other words, cyber-friendships may not be of the same quality as face-to-face friendships and time spent online is time not spent elsewhere such as engaging in sports and social activities. Taking this argument further, one could worry that Internet communication encourages isolation as well as the formation of superficial relationships with strangers. There is also the danger that children and adolescents will become prey for Internet pornography and/or pedophiles that use the Internet to establish intimate relationships with children. This is undoubtedly a concern for parents. With the current statistics on adolescent Internet usage, it is the right time to examine these issues and ask the following questions: What exactly are the dangers of the Internet and more specifically online communications or cyber friendships on adolescent development? Are there benefits to this type of communication? Do males and females similarly experience the positive and negative effects of Internet communication use? And, finally, are online relationships healthy relationships?

These important questions are addressed in the selections that follow. In the first selection, Lauren Donchi and Susan Moore suggest that adolescent boys who rate their online friendships as very important are more likely to experience the negative effects of cyber relationships. In the second selection, Patti Valkenburg and Jochen Peter report that adolescents mainly use IM for online communication and use it to communicate with existing friends. They argue that such communication is beneficial and does not negatively impact well-being.

YES

**Lauren Donchi and
Susan Moore**

It's a Boy Thing: The Role of the Internet in Young People's Psychological Wellbeing

. . . In Australia, 37% of all households currently have Internet access and this percentage is continuing to rise (Australian Bureau of Statistics, 2001). However, while the majority of Australians (61%) have some access to the Internet, the largest single grouping of users is teenage children. Males, particularly younger males, are more frequent users than females, although Odell, Korgen, Schumacher and Delucchi (2000) argue that the gender gap is closing quickly. Given these statistics, it would not be surprising to hear that the Internet has a marked effect on social life. . . .

One way to assess the relationships between social wellbeing and Internet use among young people is to examine the role that online and offline (face-to-face) friendships play in the alleviation of loneliness and the maintenance or development of self-esteem. . . . While it is well known that friendship is important to wellbeing, is this importance specific to face-to-face friends? . . .

Another variable of importance in examining wellbeing in Internet-use relationships is the actual time spent online. Longer amounts of time could be interpreted as relatively antisocial, and may reduce possibilities for social learning and social reinforcement in 'real-life' situations. On the other hand, if the time is spent engaged in Internet relationships, social learning and social rewards may still be available. Thus, in this study, we investigated the associations between time spent on the Internet (in different pursuits including personal communication, entertainment and information-seeking), number and importance of online and offline friendships, and social wellbeing.

This study focuses on Internet use and social relationships of young people in the 15 to 21 years age group, . . . a time in which friendship and peer-group belongingness is particularly salient to psychosocial development. . . . Peer interactions present opportunities for adolescents to develop the social competencies and social skills required for participation in adult society. Research affirms that peer friendships are important for maintaining psychological health and that peer-relationship difficulties

From *Behaviour Change*, vol. 21, no. 2, 2004, pp. 76–89. Copyright © 2004 by Susan M Moore. Reprinted by permission of the author.

are likely to be a source of stress to young people that leads to feelings of loneliness (Demir & Tarhan, 2001; Parkhurst & Asher, 1992). . . .

While adolescent social relations typically take place in face-to-face settings, the introduction of communication applications on the Internet (e.g., email, chatrooms, Usenet newsgroups), . . . has led to the suggestion that Internet networks may also function as important social networks for users. Some support for this view is provided by Parks and Floyd (1996), who . . . found that nearly two-thirds of respondents had formed personal relationships with people they had met via an Internet newsgroup. . . . Further, a study by the Pew Internet and American Life Project (2001) . . . found that Internet communication was an essential feature of young people's social lives and had partially replaced face-to-face interactions. So while the Internet enables people to form online social networks, whether these online friendships can provide a substitute for face-to-face friendships in assisting development towards social maturity and psychological wellbeing is an open question. . . .

Disturbing signs that the Internet fosters loneliness in users first emerged in a longitudinal study conducted by Kraut and colleagues (Kraut et al., 1998; Kraut & Mukopadhyay, 1999) . . . [who] found that after controlling for initial-outcome variables, greater use of the Internet was associated with increased loneliness. They also found that teenagers used the Internet for more hours than adults and increases in Internet use were associated with larger increases in loneliness for teenagers than for adults. These findings were somewhat controversial, and the study was criticized for methodological reasons (small sample; no control group without access to the Internet). . . .

Since the publication of Kraut et al.'s (1998) . . . study that claimed 'using the Internet adversely affects psychological wellbeing' (p. 1028), social scientists have shown . . . interest in the Internet. However, much of the available research . . . has produced mixed results.

Some research has substantiated claims that Internet use is associated with reduced psychological wellbeing. For example, Armstrong, Phillips and Saling (2000) examined Internet use and self-esteem levels . . . [and found] that more time spent on the Internet was associated with lower self-esteem.

[On the other hand, a] recent longitudinal study conducted by Shaw and Gant (2002) [investigating] Internet use, loneliness and self-esteem . . . found that over the course of the study, during which subjects chatted anonymously on the Internet, participants' loneliness decreased and self-esteem increased.

Other research has [also] shed doubt on the association between Internet use and psychological wellbeing. Gross, Juvonen and Gable (2002) found that time online was not associated with loneliness. They surveyed 130 adolescents between the ages of 11 and 13 years. . . . Kraut and colleagues (2002) [in] . . . a second longitudinal study . . . found no overall relationship between Internet use and loneliness or self-esteem. However, they [did report] that Internet use was associated with better outcomes for extroverts (i.e., decreased loneliness and increased self-esteem) and worse outcomes for introverts (i.e., increased loneliness and decreased self-esteem). Hence in [their] study, individual characteristics served as important moderating variables between internet use and psychological wellbeing. . . . In sum, while much research has studied the relationship between Internet use and psychological wellbeing, the available data is equivocal.

One reason for the mixed findings regarding Internet use and loneliness may be that while evidence points to the importance of employing a multidimensional concept of loneliness, there is little available research which links more complex conceptions of loneliness to Internet use. Most studies have employed the UCLA Loneliness Scale, which has come to be viewed as the standard scale to assess loneliness, measuring it as a global construct. One exception was Weiss (1973), who distinguished between emotional loneliness and social loneliness. Emotional loneliness is characterised by a feeling of abandonment, emptiness and apprehension due to the absence of a close, intimate attachment. Social loneliness refers to the feeling of boredom and marginality due to the lack of belonging to a social network or community. Weiss argues that relief from emotional loneliness requires the formation of an attachment relationship that promotes a sense of emotional security, whereas remediation from social loneliness requires being accepted as a member of a friendship network that provides a sense of social integration.

The association between Internet use and Weiss's (1973) bimodal theory of loneliness was examined by Moody (2001), who compared 166 university students' self-reported Internet use to their social and emotional loneliness and to their friendship networks both on the Internet and on a face-to-face basis. Moody developed the Social Network Scale to assess the latter. His findings revealed that while students who spent more time on the Internet communicating with friends were likely to have higher rates of emotional loneliness, they were less like to experience social loneliness than those who spent less time on the Internet communicating with friends. Moody concluded that the psychological effects of Internet use are more complex than previous studies have indicated. His findings suggest that by limiting the face-to-face component of social interaction, emotional loneliness might occur despite high Internet use, providing some individuals with a sense of social integration and thus lowered social loneliness.

Following Moody's (2001) lead, the present study employed Weiss's (1973) distinction between emotional and social loneliness in studying the associations between Internet use, social networks and psychological wellbeing. Furthermore, in keeping with previous research, global loneliness (as measured by the UCLA scale) and self-esteem were also used as measures of psychological wellbeing. The study distinguished between time spent on different activities on the Internet, and used measures of social networks which included, but were not limited to, number of friends. . . . In short, this study examined the relationships between wellbeing, time spent on the Internet, and social networks, including online and offline (face-to-face) networks. Patterns of relationships were examined separately for the sexes because of previous research suggesting differences in the ways young men and young women use the Internet, even though differences in the amount of time spent on the Internet by males and females are closing (Odell et al., 2000).

Method

Participants

There were 336 participants, aged 15 to 21 years in the sample (114 males and 222 females). This included 110 [secondary school students (mean age 16.16) and] 226 university-based [students (mean age 18.55)]. . . .

Materials

The questionnaire consisted of sections designed to measure demographic variables (gender, age, education level), Internet use, social networks, loneliness and self-esteem.

Measuring Internet use   In order to assess the amount of time young people spend on the Internet on an average day, respondents were presented with a list of Internet activities. Thirteen of the activities related to three categories of Internet use: interpersonal communication (4 items; e.g., 'visiting chat rooms'), entertainment (5 items; e.g., 'searching for things of personal interest') and information (4 items; e.g., 'finding articles and references'). For each Internet activity, participants were asked to indicate in minutes the time spent on each activity 'on an average day'. . . .

Measuring social networks   Respondents use of the Internet and face-to-face relations for communicating with friends was measured using the 12-item Social Network Scale (Moody, 2001). . . . Respondents were asked to indicate how well each item described them on a 5-point Likert scale. . . .

In order to assess the number of friends young people regularly communicate with on the Internet and on a face-to-face basis, participants were asked to answer two questions: 'How many friends do you talk to regularly on the Internet?' and 'How many friends do you talk to regularly on a face-to-face basis?'

Measuring loneliness   The UCLA Loneliness Scale was used to measure loneliness conceptualized as a global, unidimensional construct. . . . The 20-item scale has 10 descriptive feelings of loneliness and 10 descriptive feelings of satisfaction with social relationships. . . .

[The] . . . 10-item Emotional and Social Loneliness Scale . . . was used to measure loneliness conceptualized as a multidimensional construct. The scale comprises two 5-item subscales that distinguish between emotional loneliness (e.g., 'I don't have a special love relationship') and social loneliness (e.g., 'Mostly, everyone around me seems like a stranger'). . . .

Measuring self-esteem The measure used to obtain an assessment of self-esteem was Form A of the 16-item Texas Social Behaviour Inventory. . . .

Results

Gender Differences in Internet Use

. . . Males and females spent similar lengths of time on the Internet on an average day engaged in personal communication: female mean—65.4 minutes, male mean—68.7 minutes; and information-seeking: female mean—56.5 minutes, male mean—59.1 minutes. However, males spent significantly longer using the Internet for entertainment on an average day, in fact, about twice as much time as females: female mean—63.9 minutes, male mean—121.6 minutes. . . . In addition, males said they had more regular Internet friends than females. . . . For face-to-face regular friendships the trend was reversed, with females indicating more friendships. . . . The sexes did not differ on the importance they attached to either Internet or face-to-face friendships.

Relationships between Online and Face-to-Face Friendships

. . . The numbers of friends on- and offline were positively associated for both sexes; the more friends in one domain, the more in the other (they may indeed be an overlapping set). An interesting gender difference occurred for the scales measuring perceived importance of the two domains; for females these two scales were unrelated, suggesting that online and offline networks were not developed at the expense of one another. For males, these two scales were negatively associated, suggesting that the young men in this study tended to emphasise one domain over the other.

Network Group Differences on Wellbeing

The number of regular face-to-face friends (face-to-face friends) and number of regularly-communicated-with online friends (online friends) were divided at their respective medians into high and low face-to-face and high and low online friendship groups. A four-way multivariate analysis of variance was conducted with gender (male, female), education level (school, university), face-to-face friendship group (high, low) and online friendship group (high, low) as the independent variables. The dependent variables were the four measures of wellbeing: general loneliness (UCLA loneliness score), social loneliness, emotional loneliness and self-esteem.

The main effects of gender . . . and face-to-face friendship group . . . were significant; other main effects did not show significant group differences. . . .

Males were significantly more socially lonely than females, . . . and males were also significantly more emotionally lonely than females. . . . The trends for the males in the sample to have lower self-esteem and score higher on the UCLA loneliness scale than females were not statistically significant.

Not surprisingly, face-to-face friendship group was also related to the wellbeing measures. Specifically, those with more face-to-face friends had higher self-esteem than those in the low face-to-face friendship group. . . . The high friendship group was also less socially lonely, . . . and less generally lonely on the UCLA scale than the low face-to-face friendship group. . . .

There were gender-by-friendship group interactions for both online and face-to-face friendship groups. . . . [Females] with more online friends were higher on self-esteem and lower on loneliness than females with fewer online friends, but . . . the opposite was true for males. Higher numbers of online regular friendships seemed to militate against self-esteem and be related to greater loneliness for males. . . .

For face-to-face friendships, the effects on wellbeing were in the same direction for males and females, but they were stronger for males. [Those] with more face-to-face friendships were higher on self-esteem and less lonely, with males showing greater extremes of loneliness and low self-esteem than females, and wellbeing as more strongly associated with face-to-face friendships for males than for females.

Predicting Wellbeing from Number of Friends (On- and Offline), Social Network Importance (On- and Offline) and Time Spent on the Internet

Regressions were conducted (separately for males and females) to assess whether the set of variables including number of online and face-to-face friends, perceived importance of online and face-to-face networks and time spent on the Internet predicted wellbeing (self-esteem and 3 measures of loneliness). None of the potential predictor variables were correlated at greater than .6. . . . Correlations . . . showed a pattern for girls of significant positive correlations between wellbeing and face-to-face friendship indicators, and weak or nonsignificant correlations between wellbeing and online friendship indicators. There were no significant correlations between time spent on the Internet and wellbeing for girls. For boys, the correlations between wellbeing and face-to-face friendship indicators were significant and positive and between wellbeing and both time spent on the Internet and online friendship indicators were significant and negative. . . .

The regressions show a similar pattern of findings to the MANOVA, in the sense that the results for males suggest a greater implication of Internet use in loneliness and lower self-esteem. While the importance associated with face-to-face friendships and, to some extent, the number of face-to-face friends were the strongest predictors of loneliness and self-esteem, online relationship activity was also consistently associated with well being for males, but in a negative direction. In other words, young men who rated their online friendship networks as very important were more likely to have lower self-esteem and to be lonely. None of the measures of the time spent online (for communication, entertainment or information-related activities) were significant predictors of wellbeing.

Discussion

The present study supported previous research suggesting that young males would spend more time on the Internet on an average day than young females (Kraut & Mukopadhyay, 1999; Odell et al., 2000). Both sexes indicated that they spent large amounts of time with this medium, three hours per day for girls and four for boys. While these times may have been overestimated due to the form of measurement used (assessing minutes per average day across several categories of activity), they do suggest some cause for concern. The gender gap had closed for the Internet activities of personal communication and information-seeking, but was still very much in evidence for Internet entertainment, an activity on which boys spent about two hours per day—twice as long as the girls. In addition, boys had more Internet friends and fewer face-to-face friends than girls, although the total friendship numbers were equal. Boys who ascribed high importance to their Internet friends tended to estimate their face-to-face networks as less important, while girls rated the importance of their Internet and face-to-face friendships similarly. The picture that emerges is of young people spending long hours at the computer, with boys in particular limiting their time for face-to-face interactions and, to some extent, discounting these. Time available for offline activities is thus reduced, particularly for boys. How do these findings relate to wellbeing?

Young people reported that the number of face-to-face friendships were clearly related to wellbeing, with more friends associated with higher self-esteem and lower social and general loneliness. These effects were stronger for boys, indicating that offline friends were particularly important as markers of wellbeing for them. In addition, while online friendships were associated with better wellbeing for girls, the opposite was true for boys. Higher numbers of regular online friendships amongst boys were related to lower self-esteem and greater loneliness. In the regressions, offline friendship number and perceived importance positively predicted wellbeing for both sexes, while online friendship number and importance negatively predicted wellbeing for boys only. These effects of friendship patterns swamped any relationships between wellbeing and time spent online.

Thus, the answer to the question of whether online social interactions can substitute for (or enhance) offline face-to-face friendships for young people during adolescence and early adulthood appears to be a definite 'no' for boys. There is a great deal of evidence that peer relations play an important role in promoting adolescent and youth social–emotional development, act as a buffer against loneliness and enhance self-esteem (e.g., Demir & Tarhan, 2001; Parkhurst & Asher, 1992). This study suggests a need for young men to experience a significant proportion of these peer relationships in the real-world domain. Those young men who strongly emphasise the importance of their online relationships may be cutting off options for psychosocial development through the give and take of face-to-face friendships. This may be a result of lack of social confidence and poor social skills leading to avoidance of real-world friendships with all their difficulties. Or it may be that the nature of Internet relationships (e.g., possibilities for anonymity and role-playing, reduced need to 'work at' friendships) can undermine skills needed in face-to-face relationships. Or, more simply, online friendships may reduce time available for offline friendships which appear to have a greater potential to relate positively to wellbeing. Kraut and colleagues (1998) speculated that negative effects of Internet use could result from both the displacement of social activities and of strong ties. According to this view, the time an individual spends online might interrupt or replace time they had previously spent engaged in real-life social activities. Furthermore, by using the Internet, an individual may be substituting their better real-life relationships or 'strong ties', which are thought to lead to better psychological outcomes, for artificial online relationships or 'weak ties'.

Girls, on the other hand, seem to have developed mechanisms by which their online activity does not interfere with offline friendships, and may even enhance it. For girls, more friendships either on- or offline related to positive indicators of wellbeing. This may relate in part to the fact that girls spend less time on the Internet altogether. In addition, when they do access the Internet, around one-third of this time is devoted to personal communication activities, some of which may involve relating to friends who are substantially of the face-to-face type. Boys, on the other hand, spend only about one-quarter of their time in such activities, preferring to engage in Internet entertainment, games and so on, which have a greater potential to be socially isolating.

It has been suggested that the lack of clarity in the literature to date regarding the association between wellbeing and Internet use may relate to issues surrounding the measurement of wellbeing (Moody, 2001). We used 4 measures and, in particular, were able to test out Moody's (2001) idea that time spent on the Internet communicating with friends would be related to higher emotional, but not higher social, loneliness. This was not the case. In fact, all wellbeing measures were negatively related to Internet focus (time spent on the Internet, Internet friendships, and their perceived importance) for boys. For girls, the relationships between Internet activity and measures of loneliness were weakly negative or nonexistent. Thus boys appear to be disadvantaged both socially and emotionally by their reliance on Internet friendships, while social and emotional advantage is associated with online and offline friendships for girls, and offline friendships for both sexes. . . .

References

Armstrong, L., Phillips, J.G., & Saling, L.L. (2000). Potential determinants of heavier Internet usage. *International Journal of Human-Computer Studies, 53,* 537–550.

Australian Bureau of Statistics. (2001). *Use of the Internet by householders, Australia: Catalogue No. 8147.0,* Canberra: Author.

Demir, A., & Tarhan, N. (2001). Loneliness and social dissatisfaction in Turkish adolescents. *Journal of Psychology, 135,* 113–124.

Gross, E.F., Juvonen, J., & Gable, S.L. (2002). Internet use and wellbeing in adolescence. *Journal of Social Issues, 58,* 75–91.

Kraut, R., Kiesler, S., Boneva, B., Cummings, J., Helgeson, V., & Crawford, A. (2002). Internet paradox revisited. *Journal of Social Issues, 58,* 49–74.

Kraut, R., & Mukopadhyay, T. (1999). Information and communication: Alternative uses of the Internet in households. *Information Systems Research, 10,* 287–304.

Kraut, R., Patterson, M., Lundmark, V., Kiesler, S., Mukopadhyay, T., & Scherlis, W. (1998). Internet paradox: A social technology that reduces social involvement and psychological well-being? *American Psychologist, 53,* 1017–1031.

Moody, E.J. (2001). Internet use and its relationship to loneliness. *CyberPsychology & Behaviour, 4,* 393–401.

Odell, P., Korgen, K., Schumacher, P., & Delucchi, M. (2000). Internet use among female and male college students. *CyberPsychology & Behaviour 3,* 855–862.

Parkhurst, J.T., & Asher, S.R. (1992). Peer rejection in middle school: Subgroup differences in behaviour, loneliness, and interpersonal concerns. *Developmental Psychology, 28,* 231–241.

Parks, M.R., & Floyd, K. (1996). Making friends in cyberspace. *Journal of Communication, 46.* . . .

Pew Internet & American Life Project. (2001). *Teenage life online: The rise of the instant-message generation and the Internet's impact on friendships and family relationships.* . . .

Shaw, L.H., & Gant, L.M. (2002). In defense of the Internet: The relationship between Internet communication and depression, loneliness, self-esteem, and perceived social support. *CyberPsychology & Behavior, 5,* 157–171.

Weiss, R.S. (1973). *Loneliness: The experience of emotional and social isolation.* Boston, MA: The MIT Press.

Patti M. Valkenburg
and Jochen Peter

 **NO**

Online Communication and Adolescent Well-Being: Testing the Stimulation Versus the Displacement Hypothesis

Introduction

Opportunities for adolescents to form and maintain relationships on the Internet have multiplied in the past few years. Not only has the use of Instant Messaging (IM) increased tremendously, but Internet-based chatrooms and social networking sites are also rapidly gaining prominence as venues for the formation and maintenance of personal relationships. In recent years, the function of the Internet has changed considerably for adolescents. Whereas in the 1990s they used the Internet primarily for entertainment, at present they predominantly use it for interpersonal communication (Gross, 2004).

The rapid emergence of the Internet as a communication venue for adolescents has been accompanied by diametrically opposed views about its social consequences. Some authors believe that online communication hinders adolescents' well-being because it displaces valuable time that could be spent with existing friends. . . . Adherents of this displacement hypothesis assume that the Internet motivates adolescents to form online contacts with strangers rather than to maintain friendships with their offline peers. Because online contacts are seen as superficial weak-tie relationships that lack feelings of affection and commitment, the Internet is believed to reduce the quality of adolescents' existing friendships and, thereby, their well-being.

Conversely, other authors suggest that online communication may enhance the quality of adolescents' existing friendships and, thus, their well-being. Adherents of this stimulation hypothesis argue that more recent online communication technologies, such as IM, encourage communication with existing friends (Bryant, Sanders-Jackson, & Smallwood, 2006). Much of the time adolescents spend alone with computers is actually used to keep up existing friendships (Gross, 2004; Valkenburg & Peter, 2007). If

From *Journal of Computer-Mediated Communication,* vol. 12, issue 4, 2007, excerpts from pp. 1169–1182. Copyright © 2007 by International Communication Association. Reprinted by permission of Blackwell Publishing, Ltd and Patti M. Valkenburg and Jochen Peter.

adolescents use the Internet primarily to maintain contacts with their existing friends, the prerequisite for a displacement effect is not fulfilled. . . .

Several studies have investigated the effect of Internet use on the quality of existing relationships and well-being. Some of these studies used depression or loneliness measures as indicators of well-being; others employed measures of life-satisfaction or positive/negative affect. The studies have provided mixed results: Some have yielded results in agreement with the displacement hypothesis. Others have produced results in support of the stimulation hypothesis. . . .

At least one omission in earlier research may contribute to the inconsistent findings regarding the Internet-well-being relationship. Most research to date has been descriptive or exploratory in nature. The studies investigate direct linear relationships between Internet use and one or more dependent variables, such as social involvement, depression, or loneliness. Hardly any research has been based on a-priori explanatory hypotheses regarding *how* Internet use is related to well-being. More importantly, there is no research that contrasts opposing explanatory hypotheses in the same study. . . .

The main aim of this study is to fill the gap in earlier research and pit the predictions of the displacement hypothesis against those of the stimulation hypothesis. By empirically studying the validity of the processes proposed by the two hypotheses, we hope to improve theory formation and contribute to a more profound understanding of the social consequences of the Internet. In fact, the two hypotheses are based on the same two mediators. Both hypotheses state that online communication affects adolescents' well-being through its influence on (1) their time spent with existing friends and (2) the quality of these friendships. However, the displacement hypothesis assumes a negative effect from online communication on time spent with existing friends, whereas the stimulation hypothesis predicts a positive relationship between these two variables. The two opposing hypotheses are stated below.

> **H1a:** Online communication will reduce time spent with existing friends.
> **H1b:** Online communication will enhance time spent with existing friends.

. . . Neither hypothesis predicts a direct relationship between online communication and well-being. Rather, both suggest that the influence of online communication on well-being will be mediated by the quality of friendships. There is general agreement that the quality of friendships is an important predictor of well-being. Quality friendships can form a powerful buffer against potential stressors in adolescence (Hartup, 2000), and adolescents with high-quality friendships are often more socially competent and happier than adolescents without such friendships. Based on these considerations, we hypothesize that if online communication influences well-being, it will be through its influence on the quality of existing friendships. Our second hypothesis, . . . therefore states:

> **H2:** Adolescents' quality of friendships will positively predict their well-being and act as a mediator between online communication and well-being.

However, the relationship between online communication and the quality of friendships may also not be direct. Both the displacement and stimulation hypotheses assume that time spent with existing friends acts as a mediator between online communication and the quality of friendships. Based on these assumptions, we hypothesize an indirect relationship between online communication and the quality of friendships, via the time spent with existing friends:

> **H3:** Adolescents' time spent with friends will predict the quality of their friendships and act as a mediator between online communication and the quality of friendships.

Type of Online Communication: IM Versus Chat

In earlier Internet effects studies, the independent variable Internet use has often been treated as a one-dimensional concept. This may be another important reason why the findings of these studies are so mixed. Many studies only employed a measure of daily or weekly time spent on the Internet and did not distinguish between different types of Internet use, such as surfing or online communication. . . .

It is quite possible that daily time spent on the Internet does not affect one's well-being, whereas certain types of Internet use do have such an effect. In this study, we focus on the type of Internet use that is theoretically most likely to influence well-being and the quality of existing friendships: online communication. We believe that if the Internet influences well-being, it will be through its potential to alter the nature of social interaction through the use of online communication technologies. In this study, well-being is defined as happiness or a positive evaluation of one's life in general (Diener, Suh, Lucas, & Smith, 1999).

Online communication in itself is a multidimensional concept. We focus on two types of communication that are often used by adolescents: IM and chat in public chatrooms. Both types of online communication are synchronous and often used for private communication. However, they differ in several respects. First, whereas chat in a public chatroom is often based on anonymous communication between unacquainted partners, IM mostly involves non-anonymous communication between acquainted partners (Valkenburg & Peter, 2007). Second, whereas chat is more often used to *form* relationships, IM is typically used to *maintain* relationships (Grinter & Palen, 2004). Although there is no previous research on the social consequences of IM versus chat, it is entirely possible that these two types of online communication differ in their potential to influence the quality of existing friendships and well-being. . . . The second aim of our study is to investigate the differential effects of IM versus chat on well-being and the two mediating variables. Because previous research does not allow us to formulate a hypothesis regarding these differential effects of different types of online communication, our research question asks:

> **RQ1:** How do the causal predictions of the displacement and stimulation hypothesis differ for IM and chat in a public chatroom?

Method

Sample

In December 2005, an online survey was conducted among 1,210 Dutch adolescents between 10 and 17 years of age (53% girls, 47% boys). Sampling and fieldwork were done by Qrius, a market research company in Amsterdam, the Netherlands. . . . The sample was representative of Dutch children and adolescents who use the Internet in terms of age, gender, and education. . . . Adolescents were notified that the study would be about Internet and well-being and that they could stop participation at any time they wished. . . . Completing the questionnaire took about 15–20 minutes.

We preferred an online interviewing mode to more traditional modes of interviewing, such as face-to-face or telephone interviews. There is consistent research evidence that both adolescents and adults report sensitive behaviors more easily in computer-mediated interviewing modes than in non-computer-mediated modes. . . . Therefore, the response patterns in our study may have benefited from our choice of a computer-mediated interviewing mode as far as more intimate issues, such as the quality of friendships and well-being, are concerned.

Measures

IM Use

We measured adolescents' IM use with four questions: (a) "On *weekdays* (Monday to and including Friday), how many days do you usually use IM?" (b) "On the *weekdays* (Monday to and including Friday) that you use IM, how long do you then usually use it?" (c) "During *weekends* (Saturday and Sunday), how many days do you usually use IM?" The response options were: (1) *Only on Saturday;* (2) *Only on Sunday;* (3) *On both days;* and (4) *I do not use IM on the weekends.* If respondents selected response options 1 to 3 in the question on IM weekend use, they were asked the following question for Saturday and/or Sunday: (d) "On a Saturday (a Sunday), how long do you usually use IM?" Respondents' IM use per week was calculated by multiplying the number of days per week that they used IM (range 0 through 7) by the number of minutes they used it on each day. . . . The mean time spent with IM per week was 15 hours and 15 minutes (SD = 21 hours and 10 minutes).

Chat Use

We measured respondents' chat use in the same way as their IM use. Using the same four questions, we asked the respondents to evaluate how much time per week they used chat in public chatrooms. The mean time spent with chat per week was 1 hour and 23 minutes (SD = 7 hours and 30 minutes).

Time Spent with Friends

Time spent with existing friends was measured with three items that were adopted from the companionship subscale of Buhrmester's (1990) Network of Relationship Inventory. We first asked respondents to think of the friends they know from their offline environment, such as from school and the neighborhood. Then we asked them three questions: (a) "How often do you meet with one or more of these friends?," (b) "How often do you and these friends go to places and do things together?," and (c) "How often do you go out and have fun with one or more of these friends?" Response options ranged from 1 (*never*) to 9 (*several times a day*). The three items loaded on one factor, which explained 69% of the variance (Cronbach's alpha = .76; $M = 5.78$; $SD = 1.65$).

Quality of Friendships
The quality of existing friendships was measured with the relationship satisfaction (three items), approval (three items), and support (three items) subscales of Buhrmester's (1990) Network of Relationship Inventory. We asked respondents to think of the friends they know from their offline environment, such as from school and the neighborhood. Example items were: (1) "How often are you happy with your relationship with these friends?" (satisfaction), "How often do these friends praise you for the kind of person you are?" (approval), and (3) "How often do you turn to these friends for support with personal problems?" Response options ranged from 1 (*never*) to 5 (*always*). The nine items were averaged to form a quality of friendship scale (Cronbach's alpha = .93; $M = 3.44$; $SD = 0.72$).

Well-Being
We used the five-item satisfaction with life scale developed by Diener, Emmons, Larsen, and Griffin (1985). Examples of items of this scale are "I am satisfied with my life" and "In most ways my life is close to my ideal." Response categories ranged from 1 (*agree entirely*) to 5 (*disagree entirely*) and were reversely coded. Cronbach's alpha for the scale was .88, which is comparable to the alpha of .87 reported by Diener et al. (1985).

Results

Time Spent with IM and Chat
Respondents spent significantly more time per day on IM than on chat. Specifically, they spent on average two hours and 11 minutes per day on IM and on average 12 minutes per day on chat. This greater amount of time spent on IM suggests that if any effect of the Internet is to be expected, it will occur through the use of IM. However, to verify this claim, we test the separate effects of IM and chat in the subsequent analyses.

Online Communication with Existing Friends
We also investigated the assumption in this and earlier studies that IM is most often used to communicate with existing friends, whereas chat in a public chatroom is more often used to communicate with strangers. This assumption was supported. Ninety-one percent of the respondents indicated that they "often" to "always" used IM to communicate with

existing friends. Thirty-seven percent of the respondents indicated that they "often" to "always" used chat to communicate with existing friends.

Pitting the Displacement Hypothesis against the Stimulation Hypothesis

Following the displacement and stimulation hypothesis, we did not assume a direct relationship between online communication and well-being. Rather, we expected that the direct relationship between online communication would be mediated by the time spent with existing friends and the quality of these friendships. . . . In line with our expectations, neither IM nor chat use was directly related to well-being. However, the results do suggest a mediated positive effect of IM use and, to a lesser extent, a positive mediated effect of chat use on well-being through the time spent with friends and the quality of friendships.

We used a formal mediation analysis to test our hypotheses. In recent years, several approaches to examining indirect or mediated effects have been discussed. The most widely used approach is the causal steps approach developed by Judd and Kenny (1981). . . . The causal steps approach has recently been criticized, first because it does not provide a statistical test of the size of the indirect effects, and second because the requirement that there must be a significant direct association between the independent and dependent variable is considered too restrictive.

The problems inherent in the causal steps approach are solved in the intervening variable approach proposed by MacKinnon and his colleagues (MacKinnon, Lockwood, et al., 2002), which was used in the present study. The first step in this approach is to run a regression analysis with the independent variable predicting the mediator. The second step is to estimate the effect of the mediator on the dependent variable, after controlling for the independent variable. However, because we hypothesized that two (rather than one) intervening variables would mediate the effect of online communication on well-being, we used a four-step procedure to test for mediation.

In the first step, the independent variable (online communication) predicted the first intervening variable (time spent with friends). In the second step, the first intervening variable (time spent with friends) predicted the second intervening variable (quality of friendships), while controlling for the independent variable (online communication). In the third step, the first intervening variable (time spent with friends) predicted the second intervening variable (quality of friendships), and in the fourth and final step, the second intervening variable (quality of friendships) predicted well-being, while controlling for the first intervening variable (time spent with friends). . . .

. . . The first mediation analysis shows that time spent with IM was positively related ($\beta = .15$, $p < .001$) to the time spent with existing friends, a result which supports the stimulation hypothesis and our H1b. The opposite displacement hypothesis expressed in H1a, which predicted a negative path between these two variables, was not supported. The regression analysis showed that time spent with chat was not significantly related to time spent with friends ($\beta = .02$, n.s.). This implies that the first condition for mediation was not met in the case of time spent with chat. In other words, the causal predictions of the two hypotheses (H1a and H1b) only applied to IM, but not to chat. Therefore, the subsequent mediation analyses were only conducted for time spent with IM.

Our second hypothesis stated that the quality of friendships would positively predict well-being and act as mediator between time spent with friends and well-being. This hypothesis was supported. . . . The second mediation analysis shows that the quality of friendships significantly predicted well-being ($\beta = .16$, $p < .001$), even when the first mediating variable (time spent with friends) was controlled. The fact that time spent with friends remained a significant predictor ($\beta = .13$, $p < .001$) of well-being when the quality of friendship was controlled indicates that the mediation of quality of friendship was only partial. Finally, in support of our third hypothesis, time spent with friends acted as a full mediator between time spent with IM and the quality of friendships. . . .

We tested the significance of the indirect effects by means of a formula developed by Sobel (1982). If the Sobel test leads to the critical z-value of 1.96, the mediator carries the influence of the independent variable to the dependent variable. . . . The z-value for the first mediation analysis was 5.03, $p = .001$; the z-value for the second mediation analysis was 4.98, $p = .001$. These significant z-values indicate that both the time spent with friends and the quality of friendships are valid underlying mechanisms through which the effect of IM on well-being can be explained.

Discussion

The aim of this study was to test the validity of two opposing explanatory hypotheses on the effect of online communication on well-being: the displacement hypothesis and the stimulation hypothesis. Both hypotheses assume that online communication affects adolescents' well-being through its influence on their time spent with existing friends and the quality of those friendships. However, the displacement hypothesis assumes a negative effect from online communication to time spent with existing friends, whereas the stimulation hypothesis predicts a positive relationship between these variables.

We used formal mediation analyses to test the validity of the two mediating variables. Our results were more in line with the stimulation hypothesis than with the displacement hypothesis. We found that time spent with IM was positively related to the time spent with existing friends. In addition, the quality of friendships positively predicted well-being and acted as a first mediator between time spent with IM and well-being. Finally, we found that time spent with friends mediated the effect of time spent with IM on the quality of friendships.

However, the positive effects of our study held only for the time spent with IM and not for time spent with chat in a public chatroom. IM and chat seem to have very different functions for adolescents. In line with earlier studies, we found that the majority of adolescents use IM to talk with their existing friends. Chat in a public chatroom is less often used by adolescents. However, when utilized, adolescents primarily seem to chat with strangers. It is important for future research to differentiate between the uses of online communication technologies. . . .

Overall, our study suggests that Internet communication is positively related to the time spent with friends and the quality of existing adolescent friendships, and, via this route, to their well-being. These positive effects may be attributed to two important structural characteristics of online communication: its controllability and its reduced cues. . . . Studies have shown that these characteristics of online communication may encourage intimate self-disclosure (e.g., Valkenburg & Peter, 2007), especially when adolescents perceive these characteristics of Internet communication as important (Valkenburg & Peter, 2007). Because intimate self-disclosure is an important predictor of reciprocal liking, caring, and trust, Internet-enhanced intimate self-disclosure may be responsible for a potential increase in the quality of adolescents' friendships. . . .

References

Bryant, J. A., Sanders-Jackson, A., & Smallwood, A. M. K. (2006). IMing, text messaging, and adolescent social networks. *Journal of Computer-Mediated Communication*, **11**(2), article 11. . . .

Buhrmester, D. (1990). Intimacy of friendship, interpersonal competence, and adjustment during preadolescence and adolescence. *Child Development*, **61**(4), 1101–1111.

Diener, E., Emmons, R. A., Larsen, R. J., & Griffin, S. (1985). The satisfaction with life scale. *Journal of Personality Assessment*, **49**, 71–75.

Diener, E., Suh, E. M., Lucas, R. E., & Smith, H. L. (1999). Subjective well-being: Three decades of progress. *Psychological Bulletin*, **125**(2), 276–302.

Grinter, R. E., & Palen, L. (2004). Instant messaging in teen life. *Proceedings of the 2002 ACM Conference on Computer Supported Cooperative Work (CSCW '02)*. . . .

Gross, E. F. (2004). Adolescent Internet use: What we expect, what teens report. *Journal of Applied Developmental Psychology*, **25**(6), 633–649.

Hartup, W. W. (2000). The company they keep: Friendships and their developmental significance. In W. Craig (Ed.), *Childhood Social Development: The Essential Readings* (pp. 61–84). Malden, MA: Blackwell.

Judd, C. M., & Kenny, D. A. (1981). Process analysis: Estimating mediation in treatment evaluations. *Evaluation Review*, **5**(5), 602–619.

MacKinnon, D. P., Lockwood, C. M., Hoffman, J. M., West, S. G., & Sheets, V. (2002). A comparison of methods to test mediation and other intervening variable effects. *Psychological Methods*, **7**(1), 83–104.

Sobel, M. E. (1982). Asymptotic intervals for indirect effects in structural equations models. In S. Leinhart (Ed.), *Sociological Methodology* (pp. 290–312). San Francisco: Jossey-Bass.

Valkenburg, P. M., & Peter, J. (2007). Preadolescents' and adolescents' online communication and their closeness to friends. *Developmental Psychology,* **43**(2).

POSTSCRIPT

Do Online Friendships Hinder Adolescent Well-Being?

Lauren Donchi and Susan Moore assessed the relationship between psychological well-being and Internet use among adolescents, focusing on time spent online as well as the differences between face-to-face and online friendships. Their results indicated that females with more online friends were higher on self-esteem and lower on loneliness than females with few online friends. The opposite however was true for males. Specifically, the more the online friends, the lower the self-esteem and the greater the loneliness for males.

Patti Valkenburg and Jochen Peter, on the other hand, found that psychological well-being was not harmed because of online friends. The majority of adolescents use instant messaging (IM) to communicate with existing friends. The authors tested the displacement hypothesis (online communication is with strangers, removes time with existing friends, and has a negative effect on well-being) against the stimulation hypothesis (enhances quality of existing friendships and has a positive effect on well-being). They found support for the stimulation hypothesis: "Internet communication is positively related to the time spent with friends and the quality of existing friendships, and, via this route, to their well-being."

These two selections contribute to our understanding of online friendships and address our concerns in several ways. Online friendships can be unhealthy for boys especially if they are socially anxious. The results reported by Donchi and Moore support previous research findings such as those by Moody (2001) who found that high levels of Internet use were associated with high levels of emotional loneliness as measured by a sense of emptiness brought on by the absence of intimate relationships. Moody argued that emptiness was a result of too much time online, removed from face-to-face peer interaction. Mazalin and Moore (2004), also supporting the negative effects of online communications, found that participating in chat rooms was associated with less mature identity status and higher levels of social anxiety for males. They argue that because the peer group plays an important role in adolescent development (i.e., Social Learning Theory), the diminished proximity of the peer group limits social learning and hence has a negative effect on development. According to Erikson's theory, healthy adolescent development leads to a strong sense of self and a strong identity. If development is impaired, an adolescent is at risk for a weak sense of self and a less mature identity. The gender differences found with respect to online friendships could imply that males are more vulnerable with respect to the formation of a healthy identify and a sense of self. Males may need more face-to-face friendships than females in order to establish a strong sense of self. It is recommend that this be examined in future studies.

The positive outcomes reported by Valkenburg and Peter, whereby adolescents use online communications to further strengthen face-to-face friendships can be linked to the "rich get richer model" proposed in previous studies (Kraut et al. 1998; 2002). Kraut & colleagues argue that individuals who are highly sociable and have strong support systems get more social benefit from online communication. In other words, for extraverts, they found that using the Internet was associated with increases in community involvement, better self-esteem, and decreases in negative effect such as loneliness and depression. Those who are already comfortable in social situations can take away the many benefits of Internet communication (e.g., strengthening offline relationships).

Kraut et al. further argue that introverts, who are anxious and/or lonely, are more likely to communicate online rather than face-to-face to avoid physical proximity. For these individuals and perhaps for boys more than girls, online friendships can do more harm than good, especially if they are forming friendships with strangers. McKenna and Bargh (1999) found that socially-anxious and lonely individuals were more likely to form very close intimate friendships on the Internet. For these individuals, the Internet replaced face-to-face interactions. However, as the online relationship strengthened, McKenna and Bargh found the more likely it was these socially anxious individuals would integrate their online friendships into their offline lives. If the online "friends" are predators, this could be dangerous for the vulnerable anxious adolescent. Apart from the risk of forming relationships with dangerous strangers, there could also be concern that socially-anxious adolescents are forming electronic friendships with the machine, instead of healthy peer friendships. This could interfere with learning effective social skills.

References/Further Readings

Gross, E., Juvonen, J., & Gable, S. (2002). "Internet use and well-being in adolescence." *Journal of Social Issues, 58*(1), 75–90.

Kraut, R., Patterson, M., Lundmark, V., Kiesler, S., Mukhopadhyay, T., & Scherlis, W. (1998). Internet paradox: A social technology that reduces social involvement and psychological well-being. *American Psychologist, 53*, 1017–1031.

Kraut, R., Kiesler, S., Boneva, B., Cummings, J., Helgeson, V., & Crawford, A. (2002). Internet paradox revisited. *Journal of Social Issues, 58*, 49–74.

Mazalin, D., & Moore, S. (2004). Internet use, identity development and social anxiety among young adults. *Behaviour Change, 21*, 90–102.

McKenna, K.Y.A., & Bargh, J.A. (1999). Causes and consequences of social interaction on the Internet. A conceptual framework. *Media Psychology*, 1, 259–270.

Moody, E.J. (2001). Internet use and its relationship to loneliness. *Cyber Psychology and Behavior*, 4, 393–401.

Parks, M., & Roberts, L. (1998). Making MOOsic: The development of personal relationships on line and a comparison to their off-line counterparts. *Journal of Social and Personal Relationships*, 15, 517–537.

Pew Internet and American Life Project (2004). How Americans use instant messaging. http://www.pewinternet.org/pdfs/PIP_Instantmessage_Report.pdf

Pew Internet and American Life Project (2005a). Internet Tracking Survey. http://www.pewinternet.org/pdfs/PIP_Broadband_questionnaire.pdf

Pew Internet and American Life Project (2005b). The Internet at school. http://www.pewinternet.org/PPF/r/163/report_display.asp

Statistics Canada (2004). Household Internet Use Survey. http://www.statcan.ca/daily/english/040708/d040708a.htm

Internet References . . .

Bullying.org

A website, created by W. Belsey in response to school shootings in Colorado and Alberta in 1999, designed to raise awareness about bullying, support individuals who have been bullied, and help organizations respond to bullying.

http://www.bullying.org

www.cyberbullying.org

This website, is a collection of valuable resources, facts about cyberbullying, and examples of cyberbullying.

http://www.cyberbullying.org
http://www.cyberbullying.ca

Kidsmart

This is a UK internet safety program website designed for kids, teachers, and caregivers produced by the children's internet charity, Childnet International.

http://www.kidsmart.org.uk

Cybertip!.ca

Cybertip!.ca is Canada's tipline for reporting online sexual exploitation of children and youth funded by federal and provincial governments as well as private organizations and is run by Canadian Centre for Child Protection.

http://www.cybertip.ca

Office of Juvenile Justice and Delinquency Prevention

The Office of Juvenile Justice and Delinquency Prevention develops and implements effective programs for juveniles.

http://www.ojjdp.ncjrs.org

Youth Justice Renewal

The Department of Justice maintains this website with information regarding the Youth Criminal Justice system in Canada. The website outlines the Youth Criminal Justice Act, & provides research and reports on a variety of youth justice topics.

http://canada.justice.gc.ca/eng/pi/yi-jj/index.html

The Children Left Behind Project

The Children Left Behind Project is a joint initiative of the Indiana Youth Services Association and the Center for Evaluation and Education Policy. The aim of this website is to share research findings on the use and effect of school suspension and expulsion.

http://ceep.indiana.edu/ChildrenLeftBehind
http://www.ceep.indiana.edu/equity

Problem Behaviors

*T*here are many areas where adolescent behavior can cause problems for the developing teen. This area of study is sometimes called abnormal adolescent psychology or the sociology of juvenile delinquency. By studying these behaviors, we can attempt to prevent problems before they occur and intervene when problems do occur. What is defined as a "problem" or an antisocial behavior can change depending on the social, political, and economic climate of the time. The following part deals with two issues of adolescent problems that are currently hot topics in antisocial adolescent behavior.

- Should Adolescents Who Commit Serious Offenses Be Tried and Convicted as Adults?

- Are Girls Bigger Bullies than Boys?

ISSUE 15

Should Adolescents Who Commit Serious Offenses Be Tried and Convicted as Adults?

YES: Daniel P. Mears, from "Getting Tough with Juvenile Offenders: Explaining Support for Sanctioning Youths as Adults," *Criminal Justice and Behavior* (April 2001)

NO: Laurence Steinberg and Elizabeth S. Scott, from "Less Guilty by Reason of Adolescence: Developmental Immaturity, Diminished Responsibility, and the Juvenile Death Penalty," *American Psychologist* (December 2003)

ISSUE SUMMARY

YES: Daniel Mears, an associate professor for the College of Criminology and Criminal Justice at Florida State University, reports that for serious offenses, there is widespread support for sanctioning youths as adults. He points to a conservative group, fearful of crime, worrying about social order and public safety.

NO: Laurence Steinberg, distinguished university professor at Temple University, and Elizabeth Scott, law professor at the University of Virginia, argue that adolescents often lack the capabilities to make mature judgments, control impulses, and resist coercion from peers and therefore should not be held to the same standards of criminal conduct as adults.

Not much more than a century ago, little distinction was made between how children and adults were tried and convicted. This changed, however, when child development researchers recognized the time between childhood and adulthood as a distinct period of development. As such, child advocacy groups argued that children and adolescents should be removed from adult courts and prisons. This led to the first juvenile court in the United States in 1899 and the Juvenile Delinquent's Act of 1908 in Canada. These changes to the justice system were based on arguments of providing care and custody to vulnerable children with a focus on rehabilitation and reintegration.

For over 50 years, both systems ran smoothly. It was not until the 1960s when the recognition and protection of children's legal rights were questioned. Child welfare groups argued that juveniles within the system were not being rehabilitated and were being given long and cruel sentences. By the 1970s, following several class-action lawsuits alleging cruel and unusual punishment, governments reexamined the way youth were tried, convicted, and rehabilitated, resulting in the U.S. 1974 Juvenile Justice and Delinquency Prevention Act (JJDPA) and Canada's 1984 Young Offenders Act (YOA). Both acts, focusing on children's rights, rehabilitation, and reintegration, mandated that juveniles be protected and cared for and not be placed in adult jails. The JJDPA is still in effect in the United States, while the YOA was replaced in 2003 with the Youth Criminal Justice Act (YCJA). The change in Canada was made to address the escalating incarceration rates that had been higher than other Western countries. Custody in Canada is now reserved for violent offenders and serious repeat offenders.

Although the JJDPA and YCJA addressed the rehabilitation of youth, problems continue to exist. As youth violence and crime rates rose through the 1980s and 1990s, there was public demand for a "get tougher" approach to juvenile crime. Public perception was that the JJDPA and YCJA protected youth too much, resulting in higher crime rates and compromised social order. In the United States, this "get tougher" approach resulted in government action and in the majority of states having laws making it easier to try young juveniles in adult criminal court. For example, the youngest in American history was Michigan's Nathaniel Abraham. In 1999, he was 11 when he was charged and prosecuted as an adult for murder (Tuell, 2002). Interestingly, youth crime rates have dropped since the mid-1990s.

If adolescents can be tried and convicted as adults, can they also be executed like adults? In the United States, the answer is yes. Every nation in the world prohibits the execution of juvenile offenders, except for the United States, where only 13 U.S. jurisdictions prohibit the execution of juveniles (Tuell, 2002). Between 1973 and 2003, 2.6 percent (22 of 859) of the total executions in the United States were juvenile offenders. How are these decisions made? Who essentially decides which juveniles to transfer to adult court and on what factors do they consider in the decision? In the United States and in Canada, judicial waiver (i.e., one method of transfer to adult court) is initiated by the prosecutor, decided by the judge, and usually based on age, criminal history, seriousness of offense, likelihood to rehabilitate, and threat to the public. Is this the right way to deal with young offenders? Should adolescents who commit serious offenses be tried and convicted as adults? Should the decision be based on public opinion, threat to society, seriousness of the crime, or age and maturity of the defendant? How do we balance the individuals' rights against those of society?

These questions will be addressed in the selections that follow. Steinberg and Scott argue that juveniles cannot be held blameworthy for their crimes in the same way as adults because of cognitive and psychosocial deficits resulting in immature decision making, vulnerability to external pressure, and unformed character. Daniel Mears, on the other hand, argues that there is support for sanctioning juveniles as adults. He points to a conservative group, fearful of crime, worrying about social order and public safety.

327

YES

Daniel P. Mears

Getting Tough with Juvenile Offenders: Explaining Support for Sanctioning Youths as Adults

In recent years, getting tough with juvenile offenders has become a prominent focus of reforms and political campaigns (Roberts & Stalans, 1998).
Central to these efforts has been the increased expansion of laws enabling
youths to be transferred from juvenile to criminal court, especially for the
commission of violent and drug offenses (Torbet & Szymanski, 1998). This
trend clearly runs counter to the *parens patriae* (state as parent) foundation
of the juvenile court, in which rehabilitation and the "best interests" of the
child were viewed as being of paramount importance (Feld, 1999). It also
runs counter to public opinion in America, which generally holds that rehabilitation, particularly for juveniles, should be a central feature of sanctioning (Roberts & Stalans, 1998, p. 52). Indeed, survey research consistently
reveals considerable support among Americans for investing in nonpuni-
tive, rehabilitative sanctioning, especially where youths are concerned
(Stalans & Henry, 1994). Given recent expansions in juvenile transfer laws,
the question thus emerges as to the link between support for rehabilitative
sanctioning and transfer of youths to adult court. The more general question is, Who supports sanctioning youths as adults and why?

Although substantial research has been conducted on public opinion and punishment, much of it remains primarily descriptive, prompting
calls for more nuanced and theoretical analyses. The situation is particularly acute in the area of public attitudes about juvenile justice (Stalans &
Henry, 1994), especially given the transfonnation of the juvenile court in
recent years to an increasingly criminal-like institution (Feld, 1999). Taking
these observations as a point of departure, this article has the following
three goals: (a) to focus attention on theorizing and explaining views toward sanctioning youths in adult courts, (b) to examine specific factors
that to date have not been sufficiently addressed in the context of juvenile
justice sanctioning, and (c) to investigate specific mechanisms, including
marital status and political orientation, through which a rehabilitative
philosophy of punishment may affect support for sanctioning youths as
adults. The latter focus stems from what appears to be an emerging tension

From *Criminal Justice and Behavior,* vol. 28, no. 2, April 2001, excerpts from pp. 206–226.
Copyright © 2001 by Sage Publications. Reprinted by permission via Rightslink.

between conservative "tough love" approaches (e.g., George W. Bush's recent calls for "compassionate conservatism"; see Lardner & Walsh, 1999) and more liberal/traditional rehabilitative emphases. . . .

Support for Sanctioning Youths in the Adult Justice System

Despite the considerable research focused on public attitudes toward juvenile justice, much of this research has focused primarily on use of the death penalty for youths, rehabilitative sanctioning, funding for treatment and vocational training, and fear of victimization (Schwartz et al., 1993). One notable exception is Schwartz et al.'s national study of demographic factors associated with support for trying juveniles in adult court and sentencing them to adult prisons. They found that the profile of those most likely to support sanctioning youths as adults for selling illicit drugs or committing property or violent crimes consisted primarily of males, persons approaching middle age, African American parents, and those who are fearful of being the victim of violent crime. However, they did not assess the role of philosophy of punishment or political or religious orientation or of factors such as income or marital status, each of which previous research suggests may be related to punitiveness (Jelen, 1998). Moreover, contextual factors such as public disorder, urbanization, and crime rates, which research on the death penalty and fear of crime has highlighted as being of potential importance (Taylor, Scheppele, & Stinchcombe, 1979), remain largely unexamined in studies of support for sanctioning youths as adults.

Perhaps of more immediate importance than assessing whether such factors indeed are related to support for more punitive sanctioning of youths is the need to understand better why and how. In the context of juvenile justice, a focus on rehabilitative attitudes toward sanctioning is particularly warranted, given the foundation of the juvenile court on the idea of rehabilitation and the best interests of the child. One avenue by which to explore this relationship is to examine links between rehabilitative orientations and whether an individual is married. The latter distinction is important because marriage can be viewed as reflecting a commitment to mainstream conventional values, particularly those bearing on the notion of the sacredness of childhood. As Plissner (1983) has noted, "married people are more likely . . . to have, or to expect, children and, if so, to take a benign view of authority and a dim view of social disorder" (p. 53).

In theorizing possible linkages, two competing possibilities present themselves. On one hand, those who are married may adhere more strongly to conventional societal values (Plissner, 1983), which may contribute to their viewing youthful offenders as young adults. In turn, this view may temper the influence of a rehabilitative philosophy of punishment and enhance a nonrehabilitative, more punitive orientation. On the other hand, those who are married may be more likely to view youthful offenders as less culpable for their behavior, which may enhance the influence of a rehabilitative philosophy of punishment while diminishing that of a punitive orientation. Finally, insofar as an interaction exists between sanctioning philosophy and marital status, the question emerges as to whether it can be explained by reference to political ideology. The latter clearly is linked to sentencing policy formation generally (Roberts & Stalans, 1998) as well as to marital status not broadly but for specific political issues, thus raising the possibility that sanctioning philosophy and marital status may be linked to political orientation.

Method

Data

The data for this study came from the National Opinion Survey of Crime and Justice (NOSCJ). . . . Three dependent variables were examined: Juveniles should be tried as adults if charged with (a) selling illegal drugs, (b) committing a property crime, or (c) committing a violent crime. Each of these variables was coded 1 (*agree* or *strongly agree*) or 0 (*neutral, disagree, or strongly disagree*) to focus on the issue of who actively supports adult sanctioning of youths. . . .

Three sets of independent variables were used in the analyses: sociodemographic, attitudinal, and contextual factors. Sociodemographic factors included age as well as age squared (to examine curvilinearity in the effect of age), . . . race, . . . annual household income, . . . education, . . . marital status, . . . and number of people in household. . . .

Attitudinal factors included political ideology, which was coded dichotomously to emphasize conservative ideological orientations (1 = conservative, 0 = moderate or liberal), as well as views on parents having legal responsibility for their children's actions, . . . religious denomination (1 = conservative Protestant, 0 = other), and rehabilitative philosophy of sanctioning juveniles (1 = rehabilitation, 0 = other). For religion, respondents were given denominational categories from which to choose; those who listed a specific denomination were coded as conservative Protestant if they described themselves as being Christian, evangelical, embracing the "full gospel," or as belonging to any of the following: Apostolic, Assembly of God, Baptist, Church of Christ, Church of the Nazarene, Faith United, Jehovah's Witness, Mormon, Pentecostal, Reformed Church, or Unity. For punishment philosophy, . . . "other" included three options from which respondents could choose as representing the main purpose of punishing juveniles: deterrence, incapacitation, and retribution. The contrast thus was between rehabilitative and nonrehabilitative approaches to sanctioning.

Finally, contextual factors included a public disorder index . . . composed of views about eight items (trash and litter, neighborhood dogs running loose, graffiti, vacant houses and unkempt lots, unsupervised youths, noise, people drunk or high in public places, and abandoned cars and car parts); urbanization . . . and state-level juvenile (ages 10 to 17) property and violent crime rates (number of arrests per 100,000 persons ages 10 to 17). . . .

Design and Analyses

Given the considerable attention state legislatures have given to violent and drug offenses, the analyses center on three types of offenses (selling illegal drugs, property crime, and violent crime) rather than a composite measure of attitudes toward sanctioning youths as adults. Also, because the focus of this article is on examining support for or against sanctioning youths as adults, the dependent variables have been coded dichotomously. . . .

Results

. . . [There] is slight evidence of a curvilinear relationship between age and support for more punitive (i.e., adult-like) sanctioning of youths who engaged in property crime, with support declining until middle age and increasing thereafter. . . . [For] property offending, . . . males were more likely than females to support more punitive sanctioning when juveniles committed this type of offense. Those who had higher incomes were somewhat more likely to support more punitive sanctioning of juveniles when the offense involved selling drugs, whereas those who were married were more likely to support harsher sanctioning when the crime involved a violent offense. By contrast, both higher levels of education and adherence to a rehabilitative philosophy of punishment consistently were associated with a reduced likelihood of supporting the sanctioning of youths as adults, regardless of offense. . . . [Many] of the other identified factors . . . were either unassociated with or inconsistently associated with support for more punitive sanctioning, including race, . . . the number of people in a household (significant only for violent crime), adherence to a conservative political ideology or to the belief that parents should be held legally responsible for their children's actions, affiliation with a conservative Protestant denomination, perception of public disorder, and living in an urbanized area (significant only for selling illegal drugs) or in a state with higher juvenile property and violent crime rates. . . .

[The] effect of sanctioning philosophy on support for sanctioning youths as adults varied depending on whether an individual was married. . . . [Those] most supportive of sanctioning youths as adults were married and adhered to a nonrehabilitative philosophy of punishment, whereas those least supportive were married and adhered to a rehabilitative philosophy of punishment.

In attempting to account for the interaction between philosophy of punishment and marital status, it was theorized that an individual's political ideology might play a role and perhaps even eliminate any observed interactive relationship. To test this hypothesis, a three-way interaction term was created using rehabilitative philosophy (R), being married (M), and conservative ideology (C) as constituent terms. . . .

The only model for which a three-way interaction effect surfaced was support for adult-like sanctioning of youths who sold illegal drugs. . . .

In the two-way interaction model, . . . the effect of being married increased the predicted probability that a nonrehabilitative philosophy would result in support for adult-like sanctioning of youthful drug dealers. . . . Conversely, among those adhering to a rehabilitative philosophy of punishment, being married only marginally affected the probability of supporting more punitive sanctioning. In the three-way interaction model for selling illegal drugs, the initial difference identified in the two-way interactive model was not eliminated but rather was differentially present among different groups. . . . That is, being married increased the probability of supporting more punitive sanctioning among those adhering (a) to a conservative political orientation and a rehabilitative philosophy of punishment . . . or (b) to a nonconservative political orientation and a non-rehabilitative philosophy of punishment. . . .

Discussion

Findings from this research parallel that of other research (Schwartz et al., 1993). . . . When the offense was property crime, slight evidence of a curvilinear relationship between age and support for sanctioning youths as adults emerged, with the greatest support among the youngest and oldest age groups. For this same offense, males were more likely than females to support more punitive sanctioning of youths. By contrast, an effect of income emerged only for youths tried for selling illegal drugs, with wealthier individuals more likely to support punitive sanctioning. Nonetheless, some general patterns consistently emerged across the three types of offenses examined in this study (selling illegal drugs, committing property crime, or committing violent crimes): Support for sanctioning youths as adults was greater among the married, and it was markedly lower among the better educated and adherents to a rehabilitative philosophy of punishment. In addition, few if any direct effects were evident for race, number of people in household, conservative political ideology, belief that parents should be legally responsible for their children's actions, conservative Protestantism, perception of public disorder, or living in an urbanized area or in a state with higher juvenile property and violent crime rates.

The fact that there is relatively widespread support for adult-like sanctioning of youths tried for selling illegal drugs or committing property or violent crimes and that, for the most part, this support cuts across many sociodemographic groups, contexts, and political ideologies, is striking. It does not belie the fact that widespread support also exists for rehabilitation, especially for youths. However, it does suggest the prevalence of a tough love approach to juvenile sanctioning that perhaps always has underlain the juvenile court but that today clearly is more pronounced (Feld, 1999; Roberts & Stalans, 1998; Schwartz et al., 1993) and is, it appears, independent of juvenile crime rates (Taylor et al., 1979). That certain factors, including marital status and philosophy of punishment, exert an influence that seemingly is independent of political ideology suggests also that views about punishment to some extent transcend political boundaries. . . .

In examining potential interactive effects, several notable patterns arose. First, an interaction between philosophy of punishment and marital status was evident across offenses. Specifically, among those with a non-rehabilitative orientation, the married were considerably more likely than the nonmarried to support sanctioning youths as adults; by contrast, marital status exerted little differential influence among those with a rehabilitative orientation. Second, a three-way interaction between philosophy of punishment, marital status, and political ideology surfaced but only for the crime of selling illegal drugs. Specifically, among those holding political orientations and philosophies of punishment that were inconsistent (e.g., a conservative political orientation coupled with a rehabilitative philosophy), being married significantly increased punitiveness.

The initial two-way interaction suggests that being married enhances a nonrehabilitative orientation, thus generating more support for tougher sanctioning of youths. This accords with the idea that those who are married have a greater stake in conventional mainstream societal values (Plissner, 1983) and therefore may be more likely to be threatened by affronts to society. The image thus is one of a group (i.e., those who are married and who adhere to punitive philosophies of punishment) that is especially fearful of crime and its potential consequences and, as a result, is more likely to view juveniles as young adults who warrant adult-like sanctioning. . . .

Given that crime and social disorder have been prominent concerns among conservatives, the question is whether the observed interaction can be explained by reference to political ideology. The three-way interactive models provided tentative support for this possibility, but only for the offense of selling illegal drugs: Being married significantly increased the probability of supporting more punitive sanctioning of youthful drug dealers, but only among those adhering to inconsistent political and punishment orientations. One potential explanation for this finding . . . is that holding a consistent set of beliefs in essence may "trump" any effect of being married. By contrast, holding an inconsistent set of beliefs may lead those who are married to tend toward a more punitive punishment philosophy and, in turn, to support more punitive sanctioning of youths. . . .

The interactive effects of sanctioning philosophy, marital status, and political ideology suggest the intriguing possibility that calls for tough love approaches to sanctioning—most recently and prominently the compassionate conservatism promoted by George W. Bush (Lardner & Walsh, 1999)—have a basis not only in conservative politics but in broader social and philosophical trends in society. The fact that a three-way interaction emerged only for selling illegal drugs lends potential support to this view, especially given the long-standing concern in the United States about the role of drugs in undermining social order. More generally, the interactive effects suggest that our knowledge to date about how exactly different groups view sanctioning and its effect merits renewed attention. . . .

Conclusion

Recent increases in more punitive, adult-like laws for juvenile sanctioning raise questions about the extent to which and why there is public support for such laws. Thus, this article has focused broadly on exploring previously identified factors, including those that have been less systematically examined, and, more specifically, on explicating the interactive role of sanctioning philosophy, marital status, and political orientation in support for sanctioning youths as adults. These issues are important because juvenile sanctioning has become a pressing social issue nationally (Torbet & Szymanski, 1998). However, they also provide a unique opportunity to understand better the basis on which the juvenile court has been transformed from an informal, rehabilitative institution founded on the notion of *parens patriae* to a formal, punitive-based institution that increasingly resembles the criminal justice system (Feld, 1999).

Clearly, public support for sanctioning youths as adults is widespread and cuts across many sociodemographic groups and social settings. . . .

Beyond these observations, there are critical issues that require closer scrutiny if we are to understand better who supports sanctioning youths as adults and, to the extent that they do, why. Such understanding is important not only for its own sake but to provide policy makers with insight into the kinds of policies that reflect public sentiment. Foremost among these issues is the understanding that public opinion is neither monolithic nor simple. As Roberts (1992) has written, "Public perceptions of offenders . . . are complex and far from unidimensional" (p. 138). As but one example, the support for trying juveniles in adult court for commission of select offenses should not be taken as support for adult sentencing. Indeed, Schwartz et al. (1993) found that although the "public prefers having juveniles accused of serious crimes (felonies) tried in adult criminal courts . . . [they do] not favor giving juveniles the same sentences as adults or sentencing them to adult prisons" (p. 24). Moreover and as noted earlier, research consistently shows that the public supports rehabilitative programming, especially of youths (Roberts, 1992).

Echoing calls from others for closer attention to support for tougher sanctioning of juveniles (Roberts & Stalans, 1998; Stalans & Henry, 1994), findings from this article suggest the need for considerably more attention to studying the relationship between philosophy of punishment and other factors. . . . For example, previous research has emphasized the role of fear of crime and of having children (Schwartz et al., 1993), but there are many other situational and social contextual factors that remain to be examined closely, including the role of victimization of family or friends, views toward the potentially mitigating influence of a youth's history of abuse, media coverage of crime, age composition of a given area, unemployment rates, religious heterogeneity, and so forth (Stalans & Henry, 1994). . . .

In short, there is much empirical and theoretical work to be done to further our understanding of public support for sanctioning youths as adults. Given the profound changes to the juvenile court in recent years (Feld, 1999), there is a compelling need for such work. Indeed, if the juvenile justice system is to develop on a more rational basis or at least is to reflect accurately public opinion, the complexity behind their views will require more realistic and nuanced accounts. On the 100th anniversary of the first juvenile court in the United States, it is none too soon to begin developing a sounder foundation for juvenile justice policy.

References

Feld, B.C. (1999). *Bad kids: Race and the transformation of the juvenile court.* New York: Oxford University Press.

Jelen, T.G. (1998). Research in religion and mass political behavior in the United States: Looking both ways after two decades of scholarship. *American Politics Quarterly, 26,* 110–134.

Lardner, G., Jr., & Walsh, E. (1999, October 24). George W. Bush: The Texas record; Compassion collides with the bottom line. *The Washington Post,* p. A1.

Plissner, M. (1983). The marriage gap. *Public Opinion, 6,* 53.

Plutzer, E., & McBurnett, M. (1991). Family life and American politics: The "marriage gap" reconsidered. *Public Opinion Quarterly, 55,* 113–127.

Roberts, J.V. (1992). Public opinion, crime, and criminal justice. In M. H. Tonry (Ed.), *Crime and justice: A review of research* (Vol. 16, pp. 99–180). Chicago: University of Chicago Press.

Roberts, J.V., & Stalans, L.J. (1998). Crime, criminal justice, and public opinion. In M. H. Tonry (Ed.), *The handbook of crime and punishment* (pp. 31–57). New York: Oxford University Press.

Schwartz, I.M., Guo, S., & Kerbs, J.J. (1993). The impact of demographic variables on public opinion regarding juvenile justice: Implications for public policy. *Crime & Delinquency, 39,* 5–28.

Stalans, L.J., & Henry, G.T. (1994). Societal views of justice for adolescents accused of murder: Inconsistency between community sentiment and automatic legislative transfers. *Law and Human Behavior, 18,* 675–696.

Taylor, D.G., Scheppele, K.L., & Stinchcombe, A.L. (1979). Salience of crime and support for harsher criminal sanctions. *Social Problems, 26,* 411–424.

Torbet, P.M., & Szymanski, L. (1998). *State legislative responses to violent juvenile crime: 1996–1997 update.* Washington, DC: Department of Justice, Office of Juvenile Justice and Delinquency Prevention.

Laurence Steinberg and
Elizabeth S. Scott

 **NO**

Less Guilty by Reason of Adolescence: Developmental Immaturity, Diminished Responsibility, and the Juvenile Death Penalty

Since 1990, only a handful of countries in the world . . . have executed individuals whose crimes were committed when they were juveniles. Twenty-one states in the United States allow the execution of individuals under the age of 18, and in most of these states, adolescent offenders as young as 16 can be sentenced to death (Streib, 2002). The United States Supreme Court has held that the death penalty is unconstitutional for youths who are under 16 at the time of their offense (*Thompson v. Oklahoma*, 1998) but has declined to categorically prohibit capital punishment for 16- and 17-year-olds. . . .

The juvenile death penalty is a critically important issue in juvenile crime policy, but it is not our sole focus in this article. We are interested in the broader question of whether juveniles should be punished to the same extent as adults who have committed comparable crimes. Capital punishment is the extreme case, but in practical effect, it is not the most important one in an era in which youth crime policy has become increasingly punitive. The question of whether juveniles should be punished like adults is important to discussions about sentencing guidelines, the transfer of juvenile offenders into the adult criminal justice system, and the incarceration of juveniles in adult facilities (Fagan & Zimring, 2000). High-profile murder cases, like those involving Lee Malvo [the 17-year-old Washington-area serial sniper,] or Lionel Tate, the Florida 14-year-old who was sentenced to life in prison for killing a playmate during a wrestling match, generate public attention to these matters, but questions about the appropriate punishment of juvenile offenders arise in many less visible cases, including those involving nonviolent crimes such as drug selling.

In this article, we draw on research and theory about adolescent development to examine questions about the criminal culpability of juveniles. Recent shifts in juvenile justice policy and practice toward the harsher treatment of youthful offenders are grounded in concerns about

From *American Psychologist,* vol. 58, no. 12, December 2003, excerpts from pp. 1009–1018. Copyright © 2003 by American Psychological Association. Reprinted by permission via Rightslink.

public protection and the belief that there is no good reason to exercise leniency with young offenders. This view rejects the conventional wisdom behind traditional juvenile justice policy and challenges those who support reduced punishment for juveniles to justify a separate, more lenient justice regime for young offenders. We accept this challenge, and we argue that emerging knowledge about cognitive, psychosocial, and neurobiological development in adolescence supports the conclusion that juveniles should not be held to the same standards of criminal responsibility as adults. . . .

Excuse and Mitigation in the Criminal Law

The starting point for our argument is the core principle of penal proportionality . . . (Bonnie, Coughlin, & Jeffries, 1997). Proportionality holds that fair criminal punishment is measured not only by the amount of harm caused or threatened by the actor but also by his or her blameworthiness. Thus, the question we address is whether, and in what ways, the immaturity of adolescent offenders is relevant to their blameworthiness and, in turn, to appropriate punishment for their criminal acts. Answering this question requires a careful examination of the developmental capacities and processes that are relevant to adolescent criminal choices, as well as the conditions and circumstances that reduce culpability in the criminal law (Scott & Steinberg, 2003).

As a preliminary matter, it is important to distinguish between excuse and mitigation, two constructs that are distinct within the law but that are often blurred in laypersons' discussions of crime and punishment. In legal parlance, *excuse* refers to the complete exculpation of a criminal defendant; he or she bears no responsibility for the crime and should receive no punishment. Not surprisingly, defenses that excuse actors altogether from criminal liability are very narrowly drawn. For example, crimes committed under extreme duress may be excused—one who acts with a gun to one's head, for instance—whereas crimes committed under less stressful conditions would not (Robinson, 1997). Unlike excuse, which calls for a binary judgment—guilty or not guilty—*mitigation* places the culpability of a guilty actor somewhere on a continuum of criminal culpability and, by extension, a continuum of punishment. Thus, mitigation is a consideration when a harmful act is sufficiently blameworthy to meet the minimum threshold of criminal responsibility, but the actor's capacities are sufficiently compromised, or the circumstances of the crime sufficiently coercive, to warrant *less* punishment than the typical offender would receive. For example, mental illness that distorts an individual's decision making, but that is not severe enough to support an insanity defense, can reduce the grade of an offense or result in a less punitive disposition (Bonnie et al., 1997).

The public debate about the criminal punishment of juveniles is often heated and ill-informed, in part because the focus is typically on excuse when it should be on mitigation. It is often assumed, in other words, that the only alternative to adult punishment of juveniles is no punishment at all—or a slap on the hand. Instead, we argue that the developmental immaturity of adolescence mitigates culpability and justifies more lenient punishment, but that it is not, generally, a basis for excuse. . . . That is, a juvenile offender, owing to his or her developmental immaturity, should be viewed as *less* culpable than a comparable adult offender, but not as an actor who is without any responsibility for the crime. . . .

Criminal law doctrine takes account of excuse and mitigation in many ways in calculating the seriousness of offenses and the amount of punishment that is appropriate. For example, [defense factors] such as duress, insanity, and self-defense recognize that actors can cause the harm of the offense but be less culpable than the typical offender—or, in extreme cases, not culpable at all (Robinson, 1997). . . .

[Factors] that reduce criminal culpability can be grouped roughly into three categories. The first category includes endogenous impairments . . . in the actor's decision-making capacity [i.e., mental illness, MR, extreme distress] that affect his or her choice to engage in criminal activity (Kadish, 1987). . . .

Under the second category, culpability is reduced when the external circumstances faced by the actor are so compelling that an ordinary (or "reasonable") person might have succumbed to the pressure in the same way as did the defendant (Morse, 1994). . . .

The third category of mitigation includes evidence that the criminal act was out of character for the actor. . . . For example, a reduced sentence might result if the crime was a first offense; if the actor expressed genuine remorse . . . or, more generally, if the criminal act was aberrant in light of the defendant's established character traits and respect for the law's values (United States Sentencing Commission, 1998).

Developmental Immaturity and Mitigation

Each of the categories of mitigation described in the previous section is important to an assessment of the culpability of adolescents who become involved in crime, and each sheds light on differences between normative adolescents and adults. First, and most obviously, adolescents' levels of cognitive and psychosocial development are likely to shape their choices, including their criminal choices, in ways that distinguish them from adults and that may undermine competent decision making. Second, because adolescents' decision-making capacities are immature and their autonomy constrained, they are more vulnerable than are adults to the influence of coercive circumstances that mitigate culpability for all persons, such as provocation, duress, or threat. Finally, because adolescents are still in the process of forming their personal identity, their criminal behavior is less likely than that of an adult to reflect bad character. Thus, for each of the sources of mitigation in criminal law, typical adolescents are less culpable than are adults because adolescent criminal conduct is driven by transitory influences that are constitutive of this developmental stage.

Deficiencies in Decision-Making Capacity

It is well established that reasoning capabilities increase through childhood into adolescence and that preadolescents and younger teens differ substantially from adults in their cognitive abilities (Keating, 1990). . . . Although few psychologists would challenge the assertion that most adults have better reasoning skills than preadolescent children, it is often asserted that, by mid-adolescence, teens' capacities for understanding and reasoning in making decisions roughly approximate those of adults (Furby & Beyth-Marom, 1992). . . . However, . . . there is good reason to question whether age differences in decision making disappear by mid-adolescence. . . . Laboratory studies that are the basis of the assertion that adolescents' reasoning ability is equivalent to that of adults are only modestly useful in understanding how youths compare with adults. . . . In typical laboratory studies of decision making, individual adolescents are presented with hypothetical dilemmas under conditions of low emotional arousal and then asked to make and explain their decisions. In the real world, and especially in situations in which crimes are committed, however, adolescents' decisions are not hypothetical, they are generally made under conditions of emotional arousal (whether negative or positive), and they usually are made in groups. In our view, it is an open and unstudied question whether, under real-world conditions, the decision making of mid-adolescents is truly comparable with that of adults.

More important, even when teenagers' cognitive capacities come close to those of adults, adolescent judgment and their actual decisions may differ from that of adults as a result of psychosocial immaturity. Among the psychosocial factors that are most relevant to understanding differences in judgment and decision making are (a) susceptibility to peer influence, (b) attitudes toward and perception of risk, (c) future orientation, and (d) the capacity for self-management. Whereas cognitive capacities shape the *process* of decision making, psychosocial immaturity can affect decision-making *outcomes*. . . .

There is considerable evidence that the four dimensions of psychosocial maturity described in the previous paragraph continue to develop during the adolescent years. First, substantial research supports . . . that . . . teenagers are more responsive to peer influence than are adults. Studies in which adolescents are presented with hypothetical dilemmas in which they are asked to choose between an antisocial course of action suggested by their peers and a prosocial one of their own choosing indicate that susceptibility to peer influence increases between childhood and early adolescence as adolescents begin to individuate from parental control, peaks around age 14, and declines slowly during the high school years (Steinberg & Silverberg, 1986). Peer influence affects adolescent judgment both directly and indirectly. . . . [Adolescents] make choices in response to direct peer pressure. . . . More indirectly, adolescents' desire for peer approval . . . affects their choices, even without direct coercion. . . .

Second, it is well established that over an extended period between childhood and young adulthood, individuals become more future-oriented.

Studies in which individuals are asked to envision themselves or their circumstances in the future find that adults project out their visions over a significantly longer time frame than do adolescents (Nurmi, 1991). . . . There are at least two plausible explanations for this age difference in future orientation. First, owing to cognitive limitations in their ability to think in hypothetical terms, adolescents simply may be less able than adults to think about events that have not yet occurred. . . . Second, the weaker future orientation of adolescents may reflect their more limited life experience. For adolescents, a consequence 5 years in the future may seem very remote in relation to how long they have been alive; teens may simply attach more weight to short-term consequences because they seem more salient to their lives (Gardner, 1993).

Third, adolescents differ from adults in their assessment of and attitude toward risk. In general, adolescents use a risk–reward calculus that places relatively less weight on risk, in relation to reward, than that used by adults. When asked to advise peers on making a potentially risky decision, . . . adults spontaneously mentioned more potential risks than did adolescents (Halpern-Felsher & Cauffman, 2001). . . .

A number of explanations for this age difference have been offered. First, youths' relatively weaker risk aversion may be related to their more limited time perspective, because taking risks is less costly for those with a smaller stake in the future (Gardner & Herman, 1990). Second, . . . considerable evidence indicates that people generally make riskier decisions in groups than they do alone (Vinokur, 1971); there is evidence both that adolescents spend more time in groups than do adults and, as noted earlier, that adolescents are relatively more susceptible to the influence of others.

Fourth, . . . the widely held stereotype that adolescents are more impulsive than adults finds some support in research on developmental changes in impulsivity and self-reliance over the course of adolescence. As assessed on standardized self-report personality measures, impulsivity increases between middle adolescence and early adulthood and declines thereafter, and gains in self-management skills take place during early, middle, and late adolescence (Steinberg & Cauffman, 1996). . . . [Adolescents] have more rapid and more extreme mood swings . . . than adults, which may lead them to act more impulsively. Taken together, these findings indicate that adolescents may have more difficulty regulating their moods, impulses, and behaviors than do adults.

Most of the developmental research on cognitive and psychosocial functioning in adolescence measures behaviors, self-perceptions, or attitudes, but mounting evidence suggests that at least some of the differences between adults and adolescents have neuropsychological and neurobiological underpinnings. . . . [Studies] of brain development during adolescence, and of differences in patterns of brain activation between adolescents and adults, indicate that the most important developments during adolescence occur in regions that are implicated in processes of long-term planning, the regulation of emotion, impulse control, and the evaluation of risk and reward. For example, changes in the limbic system around puberty may stimulate adolescents to seek higher levels of novelty and to take more risks and may contribute to increased emotionality and vulnerability to stress (Dahl, 2001). At the same time, patterns of development in the prefrontal cortex, which is active during the performance of complicated tasks involving long-term planning and judgment and decision making, suggest that these higher order cognitive capacities may be immature well into late adolescence (Geidd et al., 1999).

At this point, the connection between neurobiological and psychological evidence of age differences in decision-making capacity is indirect and suggestive. However, the results of studies using paper-and-pencil measures of future orientation, impulsivity, and susceptibility to peer pressure point in the same direction as the neurobiological evidence, namely, that brain systems implicated in planning, judgment, impulse control, and decision making continue to mature into late adolescence. Thus, there is good reason to believe that adolescents, as compared with adults, are more susceptible to influence, less future oriented, less risk averse, and less able to manage their impulses and behavior, and that these differences likely have a neurobiological basis. The important conclusion for our purposes is that . . . like offenders who are mentally retarded and mentally ill, adolescents are less culpable than typical adults because of diminished decision-making capacity. . . .

Moreover, like offenders who are mentally retarded, there is good reason to believe that the deficiencies of adolescent judgment are [biological in origin.] . . . [During] adolescence, immature judgment is likely no more subject to the volitional control of the youth than is the poor judgment of adults who are mentally retarded.

Heightened Vulnerability to Coercive Circumstances

. . . As we noted earlier, criminal culpability can be reduced on the basis of circumstances that impose extraordinary pressures on the actor. The criminal law does not require exceptional fortitude or bravery of citizens and, in general, recognizes mitigation where an ordinary (or in legal parlance, "reasonable") person might have responded in the same way as the defendant under similar circumstances. In evaluating the behavior of an adolescent in responding to extenuating circumstances, however, the correct basis for evaluation is not comparison of the actor's behavior with that of an "ordinary" adult but rather with that of an "ordinary" adolescent (Scott & Steinberg, 2003).

Because of their developmental immaturity, normative (i.e., "ordinary") adolescents may respond adversely to external pressures that adults are able to resist. If adolescents are more susceptible to *hypothetical* peer pressure than are adults . . . , it stands to reason that age differences in susceptibility to *real* peer pressure will be even more considerable. Thus, it seems reasonable to hypothesize that a youth would succumb more readily to peer influence than would an adult in the same situation. Similarly, if adolescents are more impulsive than adults, it may take less of a threat to provoke an aggressive response from a juvenile. And, because adolescents are less likely than adults to think through the future consequences of their actions, the same level of duress may have a more disruptive impact on juveniles' decision making than on that of adults. . . .

Recent evidence on age differences in the processing of emotionally arousing information supports the hypothesis that adolescents may tend to respond to threats more viscerally and emotionally than adults (Baird, Gruber, & Fein, 1999), but far more research on this topic is needed.

Unformed Character as Mitigation

In addition to the mitigating effects of adolescents' diminished decision-making capacity and greater vulnerability to external pressures, youthful culpability is also mitigated by the relatively unformed nature of their characters. As we have noted, the criminal law implicitly assumes that harmful conduct reflects the actor's bad character and treats evidence that this assumption is inaccurate as mitigating of culpability. For most adolescents, the assumption *is* inaccurate, and thus their crimes are less culpable than those of typical criminals.

The emergence of personal identity is an important developmental task of adolescence and one in which the aspects of psychosocial development discussed earlier play a key role. As documented in many empirical tests of Erikson's (1968) theory of the adolescent *identity crisis*, the process of identity formation includes considerable exploration and experimentation over the course of adolescence. . . . Often this experimentation involves risky, illegal, or dangerous activities like alcohol use, drug use, unsafe sex, and antisocial behavior. For most teens, these behaviors are fleeting; they cease with maturity as individual identity becomes settled. Only a relatively small proportion of adolescents who experiment in risky or illegal activities develop entrenched patterns of problem behavior that persist into adulthood (Farrington, 1986). Thus, making predictions about the development of relatively more permanent and enduring traits on the basis of patterns of risky behavior observed in adolescence is an uncertain business. At least until late adolescence, individuals' values, attitudes, beliefs, and plans are likely to be tentative and exploratory expressions rather than enduring representations of personhood. Thus, research on identity development in adolescence supports the view that much youth crime stems from normative experimentation with risky behavior and not from deep-seated moral deficiency reflective of "bad" character. . . .

In view of what we know about identity development, it seems likely that the criminal conduct of most young wrongdoers is quite different from that of typical adult criminals. Most adults who engage in criminal conduct act on subjectively defined preferences and values, and their choices can fairly be charged to deficient moral character. This cannot be said of typical juvenile actors, whose behaviors are more likely to be shaped by developmental forces that are constitutive of adolescence. To be sure, some adolescents may be in the early stages of developing a criminal identity and reprehensible moral character traits, but most are not. Indeed, studies of criminal careers indicate that the vast majority of adolescents who engage in criminal or delinquent behavior desist from crime as they mature into adulthood (Farrington, 1986). Thus the criminal choices of typical young offenders differ from those of adults not only because the choice, *qua* choice, is deficient as the product of immature judgment, but also because the adolescent's criminal act does not express the actor's bad character.

The notion that individuals are less blameworthy when their crimes are out of character is significant in assessing the culpability of typical young offenders. In one sense, young wrongdoers are not like adults whose acts are less culpable on this ground. A claim that an adult's criminal act was out of character requires a demonstration that his or her established character is good. The criminal choice of the typical adolescent cannot be evaluated in this manner because the adolescent's personal identity is in flux and his or her character has not yet stabilized. However, like the adult offender whose crime is mitigated because it is out of character, adolescent offenders lack an important component of culpability—the connection between a bad act and a bad character. . . .

Developmental Immaturity, Diminished Culpability, and the Juvenile Crime Policy

The adolescent who commits a crime typically is not so deficient in his or her decision-making capacity that the adolescent cannot understand the immediate harmful consequences of his or her choice or its wrongfulness, as might be true of a mentally disordered person or a child. Yet, in ways that we have described, the developmental factors that drive adolescent decision making may predictably contribute to choices reflective of immature judgment and unformed character. Thus, youthful criminal choices may share much in common with those of adults whose criminal behavior is treated as less blameworthy than that of the typical offender, because their criminal behavior is out of character, their decision-making capacities are impaired by emotional disturbance, mental illness, or retardation, or their criminal choices were influenced by unusually coercive circumstances.

If, in fact, adolescent offenders are generally less culpable than their adult counterparts, how should the legal system recognize their diminished responsibility? An important policy choice is whether immaturity should be considered on an individualized basis, as is typical of most mitigating conditions, or as the basis for treating young law violators as a separate category of offenders (Scott & Steinberg, 2003).

We believe that the uniqueness of immaturity as a mitigating condition argues for the adoption of, or renewed commitment to, a categorical approach, under which most youths are dealt with in a separate justice system, in which rehabilitation is a central aim, and none are eligible for the ultimate punishment of death. Other mitigators—emotional disturbance and coercive external circumstances, for example—affect criminal choices with endless variety and have idiosyncratic effects on behavior;

thus, individualized consideration of mitigation is appropriate where these phenomena are involved. . . .

Ongoing research on the links between brain maturation and psychological development in adolescence has begun to shed light on why adolescents are not as planful, thoughtful, or self-controlled as adults, and, more importantly, it clarifies that these "deficiencies" may be physiological as well as psychological in nature. Nevertheless, we are a long way from comprehensive scientific understanding in this area, and research findings are unlikely to ever be sufficiently precise to draw a chronological age boundary between those who have adult decision-making capacity and those who do not. Some of the relevant abilities (e.g., logical reasoning) may reach adultlike levels in middle adolescence, whereas others (e.g., the ability to resist peer influence or think through the future consequences of one's actions) may not become fully mature until young adulthood.

Many perspectives can inform debates about youth crime policy and the juvenile death penalty, but surely one should be the science of developmental psychology. Psychologists have much to contribute to discussions about the underpinnings, biological bases, and developmental course of the capacities and competencies relevant to criminal culpability and to the appropriateness of capital punishment for juveniles. Especially needed are studies that link developmental changes in decision making to changes in brain structure and function, and studies that examine age differences in decision making under more ecologically valid conditions.

In our view, however, there is sufficient indirect and suggestive evidence of age differences in capacities that are relevant to criminal blameworthiness to support the position that youths who commit crimes should be punished more leniently than their adult counterparts. Although, as we have noted, the definitive developmental research has not yet been conducted, until we have better and more conclusive data, it would be prudent to err on the side of caution, especially when life and death decisions are concerned. The Supreme Court has repeatedly emphasized that the death penalty is acceptable punishment only for the most blameworthy killers (*Gregg v. Georgia*, 1976; *Lockett v. Ohio*, 1978). All other developed countries have adopted a policy that assumes that adolescents, because of developmental immaturity, simply do not satisfy this criterion. The United States should join the majority of countries around the world in prohibiting the execution of individuals for crimes committed under the age of 18.

References

Baird, A., Gruber, S., & Fein, D. (1999). Functional magnetic resonance imaging of facial affect recognition in children and adolescents. *Journal of the American Academy of Child and Adolescent Psychiatry, 38,* 195–199.

Bonnie, R., Coughlin, A., & Jeffries, J. (Eds.). (1997). *Criminal law.* New York: Foundation Press.

Dahl, R. (2001). Affect regulation, brain development, and behavioral/emotional health in adolescence. *CNS Spectrums, 6,* 1–12.

Erikson, E. (1968). *Identity: Youth and crisis.* New York: Norton.

Fagan, J., & Zimring, F. (2000). *The changing borders of juvenile justice: Transfer of adolescents to the criminal court.* Chicago: University of Chicago Press.

Farrington, D. (1986). Age and crime. In M. Tonry & N. Morris (Eds.), *Crime and justice: An annual review of research* (pp. 189–217). Chicago: University of Chicago Press.

Furby, L., & Beyth-Marom, R. (1992). Risk taking in adolescence: A decision-making perspective. *Developmental Review, 12,* 1–44.

Gardner, W. (1993). A life-span rational choice theory of risk taking. In N. Bell & R. Bell (Eds.), *Adolescent risk taking* (pp. 66–83). Newbury Park, CA: Sage.

Gardner, W., & Herman, J. (1990). Adolescents' AIDS risk taking: A rational choice perspective. In W. Gardner, S. Millstein, & B. Wilcox (Eds.), *Adolescents in the AIDS epidemic* (pp. 17–34). San Francisco: Jossey-Bass.

Gregg v. Georgia, 428 U.S. 153 (1976).

Giedd, J., Blumenthal, J., Jeffries, N., Castllanos, F., Liu, H., & Zijdenbos, A., et al. (1999). Brain development during childhood and adolescence: A longitudinal MRI study. *Nature Neuroscience, 2,* 861–863.

Halpern-Felsher, B., & Cauffman, E. (2001). Costs and benefits of a decision: Decision-making competence in adolescents and adults. *Journal of Applied Developmental Psychology, 22,* 257–273.

Kadish, S. (1987). Excusing crime. *California Law Review, 75,* 257–296.

Keating, D. (1990). Adolescent thinking. In S. S. Feldman & G. R. Elliot (Eds.), *At the threshold: The developing adolescent* (pp. 54–89). Cambridge, MA: Harvard University Press.

Lockett v. Ohio, 438 U.S. 586 (1978).

Morse, S. (1994). Culpability and control. *Pennsylvania Law Review, 142,* 1587–1660.

Nurmi, J. (1991). How do adolescents see their future? A review of the development of future orientation and planning. *Developmental Review, 11,* 1–59.

Robinson, P. (1997). *Criminal law.* New York: Aspen.

Scott, E., & Steinberg, L. (2003). Blaming youth. *Texas Law Review, 81,* 799–840.

Steinberg, L., & Cauffman, E. (1996). Maturity of judgment in adolescence: Psychosocial factors in adolescent decision-making. *Law and Human Behavior, 20,* 249–272.

Steinberg, L., & Silverberg, S. (1986). The vicissitudes of autonomy in early adolescence. *Child Development, 57,* 841–851.

Streib, V. (2002). *The juvenile death penalty today: Death sentences and executions for juvenile crimes, January 1, 1973–November 15, 2002* [Unpublished report]. . . .

Thompson v. Oklahoma, 487 U.S. 815 (1998).

United States Sentencing Commission. (1998). *United States sentencing guidelines manual: Section 5K2.20.* Washington, DC: Author.

Vinokur, A. (1971). Review and theoretical analysis of the effects of group processes upon individual and group decisions involving risk. *Psychological Bulletin, 76,* 231–250.

POSTSCRIPT

Should Adolescents Who Commit Serious Offenses Be Tried and Convicted as Adults?

Steinberg and Scott address the issue of culpability or blameworthiness. They explain the factors that reduce culpability among adolescents, which they argue should reduce the grade of an offense and subsequently the punishment. The adolescent cognitive and psychosocial characteristics described include immature decision making because of still-developing cognitive capacities, greater vulnerability to external pressures such as peer coercion, and a still-developing identity resulting in tentative values, attitudes, and beliefs. Because of these factors, Steinberg and Scott recommend a separate justice system for adolescents with a focus on rehabilitation, more lenient punishments, and laws prohibiting their execution.

Mears does not necessarily argue against Steinberg and Scott but instead addresses the public opinion of sanctioning youth as adults. Public opinion is strong when it comes to implementing laws and policies and as such, it is necessary to know who supports the "tough love" approach and why. He reports that a conservative group comprised of married individuals with a philosophy of punishment is more likely to support transfer of youth to adult court, especially for serious offenses. This conservative group with conventional mainstream values is especially fearful of crime and its potential consequences, such as the threat to public safety and social disorder. The argument here is one of collective rights.

Many brain researchers support Steinberg's argument stating that structurally, the brain is still growing and maturing during adolescence. Jay Giedd of the National Institute of Mental Health (NIMH) considers 25 the age at which the brain has reached maturity, especially in the areas of the frontal lobe, the region responsible for planning, reasoning, and impulse control. Because the adolescent brain is not fully developed, adolescents are more prone to erratic behaviour driven by emotions and are not as morally culpable as adults. Fried & Reppucci (2001) also support this view, arguing that throughout adolescence, judgment is impaired because "the development of several psychosocial factors that are presumed to influence decision making lags behind the development of the cognitive capacities that are required to make mature decisions" (p. 45).

U.S. law views decision making differently than what is stated above. Essentially, past the age of 14 years, adolescents are competent decision makers under the informed-consent model as long as they are of average or above-average intelligence and can make a knowing, voluntary, intelligent decision (Ambuel & Rappaport, 1992). Steinberg and Scott, however, argue that the informed-consent model is inadequate because it overemphasizes the cognitive components at the expense of the non-cognitive components (e.g., social factors such as peer influence) that may influence mature judgment and sound decision making. Adolescents at 14 may or may not have the cognitive capacity necessary to make good choices, and therefore deciding on an exact age for informed consent or transfer to adult court is impossible. Steinberg and Scott recommend that adolescents who are being considered for transfer to adult court undergo psychological testing to determine their level of maturity.

Jon Sparks, a lawyer in California and past chief of police in Arizona, supports the findings by Mears. He argues that juveniles should be tried as adults if they commit serious crimes such as rape, robbery, or murder, regardless of their age, because children should know at a very young age that "if they do the crime, they will do the time." He further states that many young offenders think the juvenile justice system is a joke, knowing they will not receive harsh punishments. He agrees with them, stating that justice is served only when a juvenile is handled as an adult http://www.newdawnpublishing.com/article_2.htm.

Support for sanctioning youth as adults was also documented by Moon, Wright, Cullen, and Pealer (2000). They found that the majority of respondents in their study favored juvenile capital punishment, often for young offenders. More respondents, however, preferred alternative sentencing options such as life in prison without parole or life in prison with work requirements. Although somewhat dated, a public opinion pole in 1996 also showed that Americans in general supported the transfer of juveniles who have committed serious crimes to adult court (Triplett, 1996).

The arguments are well laid out with respect to trying and convicting youth in adult court when they commit serious crimes. Do lenient penalties protect the public? Are harsh adult penalties fair for an adolescent who lacks the cognitive capacities to reason and make decisions effectively? Should policies reflect public sentiment? Are individual rights more important than collective rights, or how can we balance the two?

References/Further Readings

Ambuel, B., & Rappaport, J. (1992). Developmental trends in adolescents' psychological and legal competence to consent to abortion. *Law and Human Behavior, 16*, 129–154.

Beckman, M. (2004). Crime, culpability, and the adolescent brain. *Science, 305*, 596–599.

Butts, J., & Mitchell, O. (2000). Brick by brick: Dismantling the border between juvenile and adult justice. *Criminal Justice, 2*, 167–213.

Fried, C. S., & Reppucci, N. D. (2001). Criminal decision making: The development of adolescent judgment, criminal responsibility, and culpability. *Law and Human Behavior, 25*, 45–61.

Giedd, J. N. (2004). Structural magnetic resonance imaging of the adolescent brain. *Annals of the New York Academy of Science,* 1021, 77–85.

Grisso, T., Steinberg, L., Woolard, J., Cauffman, E., Scott, E., Graham, S., Lexcen, F., Reppucci, N. D., & Schwartz, R. (2003). Juveniles' competence to stand trial: A comparison of adolescents' and adults' capacities as trial defendants. *Law and Human Behavior,* 27, 333–363.

Kennedy, D. (1997). Let's hold juveniles responsible for their crimes. National Policy Analysis: A Publication of the National Center for Public Policy Research, 166. http://www.nationalcenter.org.

Mears, D. P., Hay, C., Gertz, M., & Mancini, C. (2007). Public opinion and the foundation of the juvenile court. *Criminology,* 45(1), 223–257.

Moon, M. M., Wright, J. P., Cullen, F. T., & Pealer, J. A. (2000). Putting kids to death: Specifying public support for juvenile capital punishment. *Justice Quarterly,* 17, 663–684.

Office of Juvenile Justice and Delinquency Prevention. (1999). Juvenile justice: A century of change. Washington DC: Office of juvenile Justice.

Shook, J. J. (2005). Contesting childhood in the US justice system: The transfer of juveniles to adult criminal court. *Childhood,* 12, 461–478.

Statistics Canada. (1997 through 2000). Youth Court Statistics. Ottawa: Canadian Centre for Justice Statistics.

Streib, V. L. (2003). The juvenile death penalty today: Death sentences and executions for juvenile crimes, January 1, 1973–June 30, 2003. http://www.law.onu.edu/faculty/streib.

Triplett, R. (1996). The growing threat: Gangs and juvenile offenders. In T. J. Flanagan & D. R. Longmire (Eds.). *Americans view crime and justice: A national public opinion survey* (pp. 137–150). Thousand Oaks, CA: Sage.

Tuell, J. A. (2002). *Juvenile offenders and the death penalty.* Child Welfare League of America. National Center for Program Standards and Development. Washington, DC.

ISSUE 16

Are Girls Bigger Bullies than Boys?

YES: Melanie J. Zimmer-Gembeck, Tasha C. Geiger, and Nicki R. Crick, from "Relational and Physical Aggression, Prosocial Behavior, and Peer Relations: Gender Moderation and Bidirectional Association," *Journal of Early Adolescence* (November 2005)

NO: Christina Salmivalli and Ari Kaukiainen, "'Female Aggression' Revisited: Variable- and Person-Centered Approaches to Studying Gender Differences in Different Types of Aggression," *Aggressive Behavior* (vol. 30, 2004)

ISSUE SUMMARY

YES: Melanie Zimmer-Gembeck, an assistant professor of psychology at Griffith University in Australia, and her colleagues report gender differences in levels of relational aggression, which is a type of bullying. In early adolescence, girls are more relationally aggressive than boys. The authors argue that girls may use relational aggression to gain and keep friends.

NO: Christina Salmivalli, professor of applied psychology, and psychologist Ari Kaukiainen, both from University of Turku, argue that boys use all types of aggression more than girls in early adolescence. This included direct aggression, verbal aggression, and indirect or relational aggression.

In recent years, bullying has become increasingly more serious among today's youth. Conflict and misunderstanding are part of normal development. As cognitive capacities become more sophisticated, adolescents learn to argue. This is part of gaining independence and learning to think for themselves. Bullying, however, introduces risk to normal development.

Bullying is a relationship problem, defined as a subset of aggression occurring when one or more individuals verbally, physically, and/or psychologically harass another person (Olweus, 1997). Olweus also states that there are three core characteristics of bullying: It is aggressive behavior, it occurs over time, and it involves a power imbalance. With respect to the aggressive behavior, bullying also involves physical aggression (e.g., hitting, punching, pushing), verbal aggression (e.g., name-calling, insulting, yelling obscenities), and the more psychological form of aggression often referred to as indirect, relational, or social aggression. Indirect, relational, or social aggression can each be defined differently, yet each has similar characteristics with respect to the type of manipulation involved.

Indirect aggression is defined as a "type of behavior in which the perpetrator attempts to inflict pain in such a manner that he or she makes it seem as though there is no intention to hurt at all" (Bjoörkqvist, Österman & Kaukiainen, 1992, p. 118). Essentially, it's a "behind-the-back" aggression. A related term is "stabbing in the back." Relational aggression is defined as behaviors that hurt others by damaging relationships or feelings (Crick & Grotpeter, 1995). This type of mainly covert aggression is about the endpoint, where the goal is to disrupt friendships. Social aggression is also focused on the endpoint and is defined as the "manipulation of group acceptance through alienation, ostracism, or character defamation" (Cairns, Cairns, Neckerman, Ferguson, & Gariépy, 1989, p. 323). Social aggression involves damaging another's self-esteem and/or social status. Indirect, relational, and social aggression have the following characteristics in common: gossiping, spreading rumors, ignoring, deliberately leaving someone out of a group, turning others against others, embarrassing others in public, performing practical jokes, and sending abusive phone calls (Archer & Coyne, 2005).

There is evidence that physical and verbal aggressions decline in early adolescence, at the same time as the more covert types escalate. Research has indicated that between the ages of 8 and 18, physical aggression declines in both males and females, whereas indirect aggression increases significantly between 8 and 11 years of age and then starts to decline. There is the argument that with the development of social intelligence, direct physical and verbal aggressions are replaced with indirect, relational, or social aggression (Björkqvist et al., 1992). The decline in physical and verbal aggressions after age 11 can also be linked to adolescent moral and cognitive development. Essentially, with advanced cognitions and moral reasoning, adolescents make better choices (e.g., aggression is unacceptable), have enhanced perspective-taking skills, and they have more mature conflict resolution (i.e., talking it through versus using aggression). Development is gradual and individual; therefore, the decline in physical aggression and the initial increase followed by a decrease in relational aggression will be different for each individual and dependent on a number of factors.

During this transition, are girls as aggressive as boys? Do they bully as much as boys? Past research has reported males to be bigger bullies and more aggressive than females. However, findings indicate that while girls engage in fewer acts of physical aggression, they engage in equal if not higher levels of indirect, relational, or social aggression (Moretti, Catchpole, & Odgers, 2005). Does this make them as aggressive as boys? During adolescence, do boys continually engage in more aggressive acts than girls? These questions will be addressed in the selections. Melanie Zimmer-Gembeck and her colleagues report gender differences in levels of aggression during early adolescence, while Christina Salmivalli and Ari Kaukiainen argue that boys use all types of aggression more than girls in early adolescence.

YES ↵

**Melanie J. Zimmer-Gembeck,
Tasha C. Geiger, and Nicki R. Crick**

Relational and Physical Aggression, Prosocial Behavior, and Peer Relations Gender Moderation and Bidirectional Associations

Relationships among children, and children's reputation and status in the peer group, are important for social and emotional development. Being held in positive regard by peers has been associated with future social competence and relatively fewer behavioral problems. Furthermore, in numerous studies, peer rejection has been consistently associated with later individual maladjustment, such as learning difficulties, poor academic achievement, loneliness and depressive symptoms in childhood, and mental health problems and criminality in adolescence and adulthood.

Because children's status with their peers is one of the most robust indicators of maladjustment, both cross-sectional and prospective studies have been conducted to investigate why some children and adolescents are more preferred by peers than other children. In particular, researchers have focused on whether children's own behaviors predict acceptance and rejection by peers. Convincing evidence has emerged showing that children's physically aggressive behaviors are predictive of rejection by the peer group. . . .

Few longitudinal studies of behavior and peer relationships have followed children as they [age.] . . . This is an important question to address as the progression from childhood into early adolescence is a time marked by significant change in the nature and form of peer groups and friendships. . . .

Peer Status, Children's Behaviors, and Gender

A . . . key objective . . . was to investigate gender differences in associations between peer status and children's behaviors (gender moderation). Physical and relational aggression and prosocial behavior were the behaviors examined. . . . [In] addition to physical aggression, relational aggression and prosocial behavior were measured . . . to expand the study of children's behavior, peer status, and gender.

From *Journal of Early Adolescence*, vol. 25, no. 4, November 2005, excerpts from pp. 421–452.

Relational aggression.   Relational aggression involves "behaviors that harm others through damage (or threat of damage) to relationships or feelings of acceptance, friendship, or group inclusion." For example, relational aggression includes the use of social exclusion to harm others. . . . [Relational] aggression and related behaviors have been found to increase around early adolescence (about age 11 through 12). As desires for intimacy and exclusivity in relationships increase from late childhood to early adolescence, some young people may increasingly use relationally aggressive strategies rather than physical aggression to harm others or influence their relationships. In past studies of early adolescents, relational aggression has been more common than physical aggression, and relational aggression has been associated with poorer peer relationships. . . .

Prosocial behavior.   There have been recent appeals to expand the study of peer interactions by placing more emphasis on positive behaviors during the transition into adolescence. A link has been established between prosocial behavior and peer acceptance, with prosocial children being more accepted by their peers. . . .

Social preference and social impact.   Social preference and social impact were the measures of peer status in the current study. . . . Social preference has been referred to as a measure of likability and peer acceptance, whereas social impact been referred to as a measure of prominence and visibility in the peer group. . . . [Likability], dominance, and prominence in the peer group [become] increasingly salient in adolescence after a transition to middle school. . . .

Gender moderation hypotheses.   . . . [We] expected that gender would moderate associations between peer status and children's behaviors. First, the association between physical aggression and social preference was expected to be greater among males than females. . . .

Second, associations between relational aggression and social preference and between relational aggression and social impact were expected to be stronger for girls than for boys. With regards to peer preference, we expected that engagement in relational aggression in Grade 3 will be associated with lower peer preference in early adolescence because these behaviors can violate the emphasis on trust that is becoming more salient and characteristic of peer relationships during this transitional period. Yet previous research findings have shown that relational aggression is associated with lower peer preference for girl (but not for boys), after physical aggression was taken into account. Earlier relational aggression was also expected to be associated with greater social impact in early adolescence as . . . one motivation for relational aggression may be to increase dominance and prominence in the peer group. A recent study found associations between relational aggression and social impact among girls (Lease, Kennedy, & Axelrod, 2002). Using a combination of reports of who is popular and who is liked, girls who were popular but not as well liked were more relationally aggressive. It appears that relationally aggressive girls can have more social impact in the peer group but be less preferred when compared to girls who are less relationally aggressive. However, overall, we did anticipate that relational as well as physical aggression would have independent effects on later social preference and impact for both genders. . . .

Finally, we expected . . . earlier prosocial behavior would predict later peer status, and earlier social preference and impact would be associated with prosocial behavior by early adolescence. We expected these associations to be stronger among females as compared to males. . . .

Three-Year Stability of Peer Status and Children's Behaviors

In addition to examining the associations between peer status and children's behaviors and the moderation of these associations by gender, a final aim of the current study was to examine the stability of social preference, social impact, and children's behaviors across a 3-year interval spanning entry into adolescence and a middle school environment. A particular interest was in the 3-year stability of relationally aggressive behavior. . . .

Method

Participants

Children participated in sociometric assessments in their classrooms in Grades 3 (T1) and 6 (T2). . . . The longitudinal sample for this study consisted of [458] children who completed assessments at T1 and T2. . . .

Procedure

Peer nominations were collected in Grades 3 and 6. . . . Children were supplied with alphabetized rosters of their classmates and nomination forms. Each child on a roster was assigned an identification number. Students used identification numbers to nominate three classmates (male or female) for each item. . . .

Measures

Social preference and impact. Students nominated the three classmates they liked most and the three classmates they liked least. Peer acceptance scores for each child were calculated by summing liked most nominations. Peer rejection scores for each child were calculated by summing liked least nominations. . . . Social preference and social impact scores were computed as acceptance score minus rejection score and acceptance score plus rejection score, respectively. . . . Hence, social preference is the extent to which children are liked versus disliked by peers (assessed as peer acceptance minus peer rejection), whereas social impact reflects a child's visibility in the peer group (assessed as peer acceptance plus peer rejection). . . .

Children's aggression and prosocial behavior. . . . The physical aggression scale contained three items: "classmates who hit, kick, or punch others at school," "kids who push and shove others around," and "kids who tell others that they will beat them up unless kids do what they say." The relational aggression scale contained five items, including "kids who try to make another kid not like a certain person by spreading rumors about them or talking behind their backs"; "kids, who when they are mad at a person, get even by keeping that person from being in their group of friends"; "people who, when they are mad at a person, ignore the person or stop talking to them"; "kids who let their friends know that they will stop liking them unless the friends do what they want them to do"; and "people who try to exclude or keep certain people from being in their group when doing things together (like having lunch in the cafeteria or going to the movies)." The prosocial behavior scale contained three items, including "people who say or do nice things for other classmates," "kids who help others join a group or make friends," and "people who try to cheer up other classmates who are upset or sad about something.". . .

Results

Gender Differences . . .

. . . In Grades 3 and 6, girls were more preferred by peers than boys, and boys had slightly more social impact than girls in Grade 6. Females were more prosocial than males, whereas males were more physically aggressive than females. No significant gender difference was obtained in relational aggression in third grade, but by sixth grade, females were significantly more relationally aggressive than boys. . . .

Social Preference

. . . *[Children's] behavior and social preference, and gender moderation.* In Grade 3, . . . [aggressive behavior (including relational aggression)] was negatively associated, and prosocial behavior was positively associated with social preference for boys and girls. In Grade 6, children's behaviors and social preference were intercorrelated with only one exception for boys and three exceptions for girls. In Grade 6, relational aggression was not associated with prosocial behavior in either gender, and relational and physical aggression scores were not significantly associated with social preference among females. . . .

In Grade 3, the positive association between relational and physical aggression was stronger for boys than girls, and the positive association between prosocial behavior and preference was weaker among boys than girls. In Grade 6, . . . the negative associations between relational aggression and social preference and between physical aggression and social preference were stronger among boys than girls.

... *[Children's] behavior, social preference, and gender moderation [across time.]* ... [In] Grade 3, relational aggression was negatively associated with later social preference, and this association was only significant among girls. . . . [Social] preference in Grade 3 predicted children's behaviors within Grade 6. Children who were more preferred in Grade 3 were less often nominated as relationally . . . and physically aggressive and more often nominated as prosocial in Grade 6. . . . [There were no] significant gender differences [across time]. . . .

Social Impact

... *[Children's] behavior and social impact, and gender moderation.* In Grade 3, all children's behaviors and social impact scores were significantly intercorrelated for boys and girls with the exception of prosocial behavior and social impact for boys and physical aggression and social impact for girls. In Grade 6, with the exception of physical aggression and social impact among boys, children's behaviors and social impact were significantly intercorrelated. . . . [Aggressive (including relational aggression)] and prosocial behaviors were positively associated with social impact. . . .

In Grade 3, the positive association between relational aggression and social impact, and the positive association between physical aggression and social impact were stronger among boys than girls. The positive association between prosocial behavior and impact was weaker among boys than girls in both Grade 3 and Grade 6.

... *[Children's behaviors, social preference, and gender moderation [across time].* . . . Physical aggression in Grade 3 predicted social impact only among boys, whereas relational aggression in Grade 3 predicted later social impact only among girls. Prosocial behavior in Grade 3 was positively associated with social impact in Grade 6 for boys and girls.

Conversely, children with higher social impact scores in Grade 3 were more often nominated as aggressive in Grade 6, but the [social] impact in Grade 3 and relational aggression in Grade 6 was not significant for girls. Additionally, the influence of social impact on later physical aggression was significant and stronger among boys than girls.

Discussion

Researchers have identified some of the correlates of peer status, and this work has revealed the significant role of peer reputation in the social development of children. However, few empirical investigations have had the opportunity to examine the independent effects of boys' and girls' physical aggression, relational aggression, and prosocial behavior on social preference and impact from childhood to early adolescence. Evidence exists concerning the negative influence of physical aggression on peer status, but the present investigation illustrated the additional importance of relational aggression and prosocial behavior as well as the gender of the child when explaining children's concurrent and future status with peers. Not only do children's aggressive and prosocial behaviors predict future peer relations, but the balance of being liked and disliked by classmates is important for shaping future aggressive and prosocial behaviors when interacting with peers.

. . . Associations Between Children's Behavior and Peer Relations [Across Time]

. . . *Social preference.*   Peer social preference, where high scores indicate being highly liked and rarely disliked by others . . . seemed to have a [great] influence on children's later physical aggression, relational aggression, and prosocial behaviors . . . among both boys and girls. Preference scores in Grade 3 predicted all later behaviors among boys and all behaviors with the exception of relational aggression among girls. These results concur with [the idea] that positive peer experiences are important for learning appropriate social skills such as negotiating conflict and helping others as well as indicating that the lack of these opportunities may be detrimental to interactions with schoolmates. . . .

Social impact.   . . . [Analyses] of peer social impact, where high scores indicate a higher level of like and dislike by peers . . . supported a gender normative hypothesis with behaviors more commonly associated with boys (physical aggression) linked to later social impact for boys and behaviors more commonly associated with girls (relational aggression) linked more strongly to later social impact for girls. Gender normative aggressive behaviors appear to be having an [effect] on status with other children at the transition from childhood to early adolescence. . . .

[Social] impact in Grade 3 also predicts children's aggressive behaviors in Grade 6. Earlier social impact is associated with increasing physical aggression for all children and relational aggression among boys only. Yet the association between earlier social impact and later physical aggression is stronger among boys compared to girls. Peers are increasingly noticing children with relatively more negative or positive behaviors, and this recognition seems to play a role in maintaining and escalating children's, especially boys', aggressive behaviors.

Aggression, peer status and gender.   Although previous research has consistently found negative associations between physical aggression and rejection and acceptance by peers, when both physical and relational aggression are considered, the current findings show that it is girls' relational aggression, and not physical aggression, that predicts both social preference and impact 3 years later. In contrast, . . . associations between social impact and physical aggression were stronger among boys as compared to girls. Additionally, the associations between earlier social preference and impact and later relational aggression were significant among boys, but not girls. Together, findings suggest that aggression may partly escalate among boys between Grades 3 and 6 as a reaction to their peer experiences rather than vice versa. Girls may use relational aggression for reasons other than as a response to their peer status, such as gender socialization or arising from their greater focus on dyadic friendship interactions. In other words, girls' relational aggression emerges and, in turn, affects their peer status; boys' aggression may be more of an outcome of their peer status and associated peer experiences. However, this interpretation of the findings is speculative. . . .

. . . Associations and Gender . . .

. . . [Relational] aggression and physical aggression co-occurred among boys and girls, but this was more likely among boys than girls. Thus, boys who have the highest physical aggression scores are often the same boys who have the highest relational aggression scores. However, the correlation between relational and physical aggression was not as strong for girls, indicating that these two forms of aggression do not as strongly covary among girls. These findings indicate that it continues to be important for researchers interested in aggression and gender to include separate assessments of relational and physical aggression. . . .

Among males, aggression (physical and relational) was consistently associated with social preference and impact in both Grade 3 and Grade 6. Among females, the impact of physically and relationally aggressive behaviors on their peer status changed with age. Aggressive behaviors were increasingly reflected in girls' peer social impact scores (like and dislike scores combined) rather than only in lower peer social preference scores (like scores net of dislike scores). These findings are supportive of other evidence that aggression can be associated with social dominance and liking by some peers, and dislike by other peers, especially in early adolescence. For example, Crick and Grotpeter (1995) found that relationally aggressive children (in Grades 3 to 6) are more likely than nonrelationally aggressive children to be classified as controversial (highly liked and disliked by others). Others (Henington, Hughes, Cavell, & Thompson, 1998; Salmivalli, Kaukiainen, & Lagerspetz, 2000) have reported that relational aggression is associated with higher status with some peers, especially in adolescence. Relational aggression may be increasingly used as a strategy to gain and keep friends at this time of heightened peer interactions. . . .

Stability of Children's Behaviors and Peer Relations

[An] objective of this investigation was to examine the 3-year stability of all constructs with particular focus on relational aggression and girls. It was clear that children's early social behavior, including relational aggression, and reputations established with classmates tend to accompany children into early adolescence even after they change schools and classrooms. . . . In the current study, social preference scores were somewhat more stable than impact scores, but there was moderate 3-year stability in physical aggression, relational aggression, and prosocial behavior. . . .

Gender Differences and Relational Aggression

There have recently been questions regarding whether relational aggression is more prevalent among females or males (for reviews on this topic see Geiger et al., 2004; Underwood, Galen, & Paquette, 2001). The current study findings regarding relational aggression by gender and age are important to consider in conjunction with these questions. We found that gender differences in levels of relational aggression differed depending on children's age. There was no gender difference in relational aggression among third grade children (about age 9); however, by sixth grade (about age 12), girls were more relationally aggressive than their male peers. Findings are consistent with that of Bjoerkqvist and colleagues (Bjoerkqvist, Lagerspetz, & Kaukiainen, 1992) who reported that gender differences in indirect aggression did not occur until about age 10. However, because girls have been found to be more relationally aggressive than boys as early as preschool (see Geiger et al., 2004), firm conclusions await further research. . . . [Gender] differences in relational aggression may depend on the measurement techniques used at different ages (e.g., peer nominations, observations). Gender differences in relational aggression are sometimes found when using observational or teacher report measures but not as often found when using peer nominations. The current studies relied on one reporting source: classmates. This may have resulted in slightly inflated associations. . . .

Summary and Conclusion

. . . It is important to consider gender, relational aggression, and prosocial behavior in addition to the more commonly studied behavior of physical aggression when investigating stability and change in peer status during childhood and adolescence. Furthermore, differential results across the two gender-moderation models presented here indicate the importance of examining both social preference and social impact as distinct constructs. Doing so allowed a more complete understanding of the age-related and gendered interface between children's positive and negative behaviors when interacting with peers and schoolmates' perceptions of others as liked or disliked members of the group.

References

Bjoerkqvist, K., Lagerspetz, K.M., & Kaukiainen, A. (1992). Do girls manipulate and boys fight? Developmental trends in regard to direct and indirect aggression. *Aggressive Behavior, 18,* 117–127.

Crick, N.R., & Crotpeter, J.K. (1995). Relational aggression, gender, and social-psychological adjustment. *Child Development, 66,* 710–722.

Geiger, T.C., Zimmer-Gembeck, M.J., & Crick, N.R. (2004). The science of relational aggression: Can we guide intervention? In M. M. Moretti, C. Odgers, & M. Jackson (Eds.), *Girls and aggression: Contributing factors and intervention strategies, Perspectives in law and psychology series* (pp. 27–40). New York: Kluwer.

Henington, C., Hughes, J.N., Cavell, T.A., & Thompson, B. (1998). The role of relational aggression in identifying aggressive girls and boys. *Journal of School Psychology, 36,* 457–477.

Lease, A.M., Kennedy, C.A., & Axelrod, J.L. (2002). Children's social constructions of popularity. *Social Development, 11,* 87–109.

Salmivalli, C., Kaukiainen, A., & Lagerspetz, K. (2000). Aggression and sociometric status among peers: Do gender and type of aggression matter? *Scandinavian Journal of Psychology, 41,* 17–24.

Underwood, M.K., Galen, B.R., & Paquette, J.A. (2001). Top ten challenges for understanding gender and aggression in children: Why can't we all just get along? *Social Development, 10,* 248–266.

Christina Salmivalli and
Ari Kaukiainen

"Female Aggression" Revisited: Variable- and Person-Centered Approaches to Studying Gender Differences in Different Types of Aggression

Introduction

During recent decades, increasing attention has been drawn to subtle forms of aggression, in which the perpetrator harms the target person by damaging or manipulating his/her relationships or status in the peer group rather than by making any overt (physical or verbal) attacks. Such forms of aggression have been referred to as indirect, relational, or social aggression. Each of these concepts emphasizes slightly different aspects of, or strategies by which, the harm is delivered. . . . In the present paper, we refer to the above forms of aggression as *indirect*.

When studies on indirect forms of aggression started to emerge, it was a common argument that while boys are more directly (i.e., physically and/or verbally) aggressive than girls, girls in turn use more indirect forms of aggression than boys. Since then, this statement has been taken more or less as a universal truth, even if the evidence seems to be far from conclusive.

What seems quite clear now is that females use more indirect than direct, at least physical, aggression, and in proportional terms, i.e., when expressed as proportions of the total aggression scores, girls may even use more indirect aggression than boys. For instance, Österman et al. [1998] found that 55 per cent of all aggression used by 8-year-old girls was indirect, while the corresponding proportion for boys was 26 per cent (among the 11- and 15-year-old adolescents, the proportions were 41 per cent and 52 per cent for girls vs. 23 per cent and 20 per cent for boys, respectively).

It might, however, be premature to say that 'the claim that human males are more aggressive than females appears to be false,' or that indirect aggression would be an exclusively 'female' type of aggression.

Already among the early studies, there were some that found few or no gender differences in indirect aggression, while some even found that

From *Aggressive Behavior,* vol. 30, no. 2, March/April, 2004, pp. 158–163. Copyright © 2004 by International Society for Research on Aggression (ISRA). Reprinted by permission of John Wiley & Sons, Inc.

boys used more indirect aggression than girls. These findings were, however, generally ignored in the ongoing academic debate, which was dominated by the view of females being more indirectly aggressive than males. There are, again, some recent studies showing very mixed patterns of findings regarding the use of indirect aggression. Underwood [2002], studying different subtypes of gender exclusivity and social aggression in children (10 to 14 years old), found no gender difference in verbal social aggression towards a provoking playmate in a laboratory setting, while girls showed more nonverbal, i.e., facial and gestural social aggression, than boys. On the other hand, there was a trend for boys to report using more relational aggression toward others than girls. Preliminary results from a meta-analysis by Scheithauer and Petermann [2002] showed no gender difference in the use of indirect, or what they call 'unprototypical' aggression across 70 studies. However, the effect sizes found varied according to age: adolescent girls, for instance, showed more this type of aggression than boys.

The aim of the present report is to participate in the ongoing discussion about gender differences in aggression by presenting results based on questionnaire data from three age groups in middle childhood and adolescence. In addition to comparing the mean scores of boys and girls on different types of aggression, we took a person-oriented approach and formed clusters with different 'aggression profiles' [using a technique called cluster analysis]. In the latter approach, individuals' value profiles rather than their scores on single variables are taken into consideration, and the person (with his/her unique combination of values on the relevant variables) is the central unit of analysis.

We were looking for two kinds of manifestations of 'female aggression.' If indirect aggression is typical of females, this would become apparent, first, in girls scoring higher than boys on indirect (while not on physical and verbal) aggression. Another manifestation of female indirect aggression would be the identification of a group of highly aggressive girls employing indirect, rather than direct aggressive strategies.

Method

The participants were 526 children (274 girls, 252 boys) from 22 school classes in two towns in Finland. They were from three grade levels, aged 10, 12, and 14 years. Aggression was measured by . . . a peer- and self-report procedure in which children evaluated all their same-sex classmates, as well as themselves, in terms of their use of direct physical (e.g. hits, kicks), direct verbal (e.g. yells, insults), and indirect aggression (e.g. says bad things behind the other's back, tries to get the others to dislike the person), on a five-point scale ranging from 0 = 'never' to 4 = 'very often'.

Results

[Analyses] (with both self- and peer-reports of physical, verbal, and indirect aggression as dependent variables) were conducted across all age groups and in each age group separately [and] were significant at the $p = .000$ level in all cases. Across age groups, *boys used all three types of aggression more than girls,* with only one exception: in self-reported indirect aggression, the difference between boys and girls was not significant. Looking at the three age groups separately, boys were again, in most cases, significantly more aggressive than girls. In indirect aggression, however, a significant gender difference was found only among the 10-year-old children, and only in peer reports.

[A] cluster analysis was performed with the . . . peer-reported scores on the three aggression scales [used] for forming the clusters. Five ["clusters"] with different aggression profiles were identified. According to . . . analyses, . . . the members of these clusters differed significantly from each other in self-, as well as peer-reported physical, verbal, and indirect aggression. . . .

Girls and boys were not evenly distributed in the clusters. . . . There were more boys than would have been expected by chance in [the extremely aggressive group] and [the high direct aggressive group], which were characterized by extremely high scores on all kinds of aggression [(the extremely aggressive group) and] high score on direct aggression [, respectively]. Girls on the other hand, were overrepresented in [. . . the low aggressive group and the high indirect aggressive group.] The former cluster was a group of nonaggressive children. The latter consisted of children with very high scores on indirect, above-average scores on verbal, and average scores on physical aggression. *All 36 children in this cluster were girls.* This suggests that even if girls are not—when comparing the average scores of all girls and all boys—more indirectly aggressive than boys are, there is a group of girls who are very aggressive, and predominantly indirectly so.

Discussion

While there seems to be clear evidence of boys being more physically (and perhaps verbally) aggressive than girls, a debate is going on regarding the gender difference—or lack of it—in indirect/social/relational aggression [Crick and Grotpeter, 1995; Lagerspetz and Björkqvist, 1994; Underwood et al., 2001]. In the present study, boys and girls in middle childhood and adolescence were compared with respect to 1) their average scores on direct, verbal, and indirect aggression, and 2) their 'aggression profiles', i.e., their combinations of values on the three aggression scales. Comparing the mean scores of boys and girls on the different types of aggression used (direct physical, direct verbal, and indirect), all the differences found showed boys being more aggressive than girls. The differences were largest in physical aggression, somewhat smaller in verbal aggression, and smallest, or in many cases non-existent in indirect aggression.

The person-oriented approach, however, revealed two cluster groups in which girls were overrepresented: the nonaggressive group, and the indirectly aggressive group. This suggests that, first, girls are nonaggressive as compared with boys, and second, highly aggressive girls rarely use all types of aggression to any great extent. There is a group of highly aggressive girls whose use of aggression was *predominantly indirect*. When boys were aggressive, on the other hand, they either tended to prefer direct (physical and verbal) strategies or to use quite high levels of *all kinds of aggression*. The latter is in line with Scheithauer and Petermann's [2002] finding that boys showed a combination of direct and indirect aggression more often than girls.

Should indirect aggression be called 'female aggression' at all? In the light of our data [as well as several other studies, see Galen and Underwood, 1997; Tomada and Schneider, 1997; Österman et al., 1998] we argue that it should not, at least in the sense of girls being, on average, more indirectly aggressive than males. But, perhaps in the sense that for a group of highly aggressive girls, it is the predominant way of being aggressive, we can talk about 'female aggression'.

From the methodological point of view, we suggest that studies of psychosocial adjustment and direct and indirect aggression might benefit from a person-oriented approach. Although direct and indirect aggression are highly intercorrelated, their common variance is often neglected when studying associations between indirect aggression and adjustment. For instance, direct aggression is rarely controlled for, when predicting concurrent or longitudinal adjustment from indirect aggression. It would be enlightening to see whether students in our [high indirect aggressive group] . . . suffer from adjustment difficulties, or whether they are in fact relatively well-adjusted. Unfortunately, our data do not allow such observations.

References

Crick N, Grotpeter J. 1995. Relational aggression, gender, and social-psychological adjustment. Child Dev 66:710–722.

Galen B, Underwood M. 1997. A developmental investigation of social aggression among children. Dev Psychol 33:589–600.

Lagerspetz K, Björkqvist K. 1994. Indirect aggression in girls and boys. In: Huessmann R, editor. Aggressive Behavior. Current perspectives. New York: Plenum Press.

Österman K, Björkqvist K, Lagerspetz K, Kaukiainen A, Landau S, Fraczek A, Caprara G. 1998. Crosscultural evidence of female indirect aggression. Aggr Behav 24:1–8.

Scheithauer H, Petermann F. 2002. Indirect/social/relational aggression in children and adolescents: A meta-analysis of gender- and age-specific differences. Paper presented in the XV world meeting of International Society for Research on Aggression, 28–31 July 2002, Montreal, Canada.

Tomada G, Schneider B. 1997. Relational aggression, gender, and peer acceptance: Invariance across culture, stability over time, and concordance among informants. Dev Psychol 33:601–609.

Underwood M. 2002. Developmental differences in friendship exclusivity and social aggression from middle childhood through early adolescence. Paper presented in the XV world meeting of International Society for Research on Aggression, 28–31 July 2002, Montreal, Canada.

Underwood M, Galen B, Paquette J. 2001. Top ten challenges for understanding gender and aggression in children: Why can't we all just get along? Soc Dev 10:248–266.

POSTSCRIPT

Are Girls Bigger Bullies than Boys?

Melanie Zimmer-Gembeck and colleagues examined the association between aggression and peer acceptance. In doing so, they found gender differences with respect to physical aggression, relational aggression, and prosocial behavior. More specifically, they argue that although young adolescent boys (i.e., grade 6) are more physically aggressive, girls of the same age are more relationally aggressive. Given that both physical aggression and relational aggression are forms of bullying, these results indicate that girls bully as much as boys, just in a different way. Instead of hurting their victims physically, they hurt them psychologically.

Christina Salmivalli and Ari Kaukiainen examined gender differences in direct (both physical and verbal) and indirect aggression during early adolescence. According to their results, boys use all three types of aggression more than girls. Differences were largest in physical aggression, smaller in verbal aggression, and smallest in indirect aggression. Cluster analyses revealed that, overall, girls are nonaggressive compared to boys and that highly aggressive girls rarely use all three types of aggression to any great extent, compared to highly aggressive boys.

In support of Zimmer-Gembeck, Geiger, and Crick's argument, Viljoen et al. (2005), in their sample of male and female adolescent offenders, found that a higher proportion of females compared to males were involved in some form of bullying; however, the nature of bullying differed across genders. Significantly more males than females used both physical and verbal bullying, whereas significantly more females used only verbal and more indirect forms of bullying. To summarize, females bullied more but tended to use only verbal and indirect aggression. Björkqvist et al. (1992) suggest that the cognitive and verbal superiority of girls might explain why indirect aggression is more common among them. Moretti, Catchpole, and Odgers (2005), in reviewing the literature, also support the findings of Zimmer-Gembeck, Geiger, and Crick. They report that social and relational forms of aggression are as common or more common in girls compared with boys, and such behavior may be used to secure high social status. They also report that the initial gains in social dominance are short-lived and that many are likely to be rejected if the aggression continues.

In support of the argument that boys bully more than girls, Peets and Kikas (2006), in a very similar study to Salmivalli and Kaukiainen, found that "boys, compared with girls, tended to manage their anger and conflict by using all the aggressive strategies more frequently, which indicates that aggression, regardless of the forms it takes, belongs to the behavioral repertoire of boys rather than girls" (p. 75). In a review of research studies using peer nominations (a typical method for relational aggression), Archer and Coyne (2005) also found that girls were not always more relationally aggressive than boys; however, girls used relational aggression more than physical aggression, and boys used more physical versus relational aggression. These differences were small during preadolescence, larger between 8 and 11 years of age, and peaking thereafter. Scheithauer and Petermann (2002) also found that adolescent boys compared to adolescent girls used more direct as well as indirect aggression. Finally, Tiet, Wasserman, Loeber, McReynolds, & Miller (2001) found that there were no significant differences between girls' and boys' relational aggression; however, boys were significantly more physically aggressive than girls, perhaps indicating that overall, boys are bigger bullies.

The above arguments provide evidence that both boys and girls engage in multiple forms of hurtful behavior. The debate is whether or not the amount of bullying is equal regardless of whether it is direct or indirect. Boys are more physically aggressive than girls; however, the findings are mixed as to whether girls engage in more relational aggression than boys. More specifically, it may be that when we think about social or verbal aggression, we access the most typical "social aggressor." Based on Salmivalli and Kaukiainen, this would involve girls (recall the highly indirectly aggressive cluster of all girls and no boys); thus, we may overestimate all girls' social aggression. Those who are highly socially aggressive are usually girls, but this does not mean that all girls are highly socially aggressive. This is called the "availability heuristic bias."

Adolescent aggression—and more specifically, bullying—is a serious problem for today's youth. Students who are bullied are more likely to have both physical and emotional problems lasting into adulthood. Adolescents who bully are also at risk for long-term problems such as being rejected by their peer group, academic failure, and criminal behavior. Given these negative effects both for the bully and the victim, this issue deserves continued attention in the research.

References/Further Readings

Archer, J. (2004). Sex differences in aggression in real-world settings: A meta-analytic review. *Review of General Psychology*, 4, 291–322.

Archer, J., & Coyne, S. M. (2005). An integrated review of indirect, relational, and social aggression. *Personality and Social Psychology Review*, 9, 212–230.

Archer, J., & Côté, S. (2005). Sex differences in aggressive behavior: A developmental and evolutionary perspective. In R.E., Tremblay, W. W. Hartup, & J. Archer (Eds). *Developmental Origins of Aggression.* (pp. 425–443). New York: Guilford.

Björkqvist, K., Österman, K., & Kaukiainen, A. (1992). The development of direct and indirect aggressive strategies in males and females. In K. Björkqvist & P. Niemelä (Eds.), *Of Mice and Women. Aspects of Female Aggression* (pp. 51–64). San Diego, CA: Academic Press.

Cairns, R. B., Cairns, B., Neckerman, H., Ferguson, L., & Gariépy, J. (1989). Growth and aggression: 1. Children to early adolescence. *Developmental Psychology, 25*, 320–330.

Crick, N. R., & Grotpeter, J. (1995). Relational aggression, gender, and social-psychological adjustment. *Child Development, 66*, 710–722.

Graves, K. N. (2007). Not always sugar and spice: Expanding theoretical and functional explanations for why females aggress. *Aggression and Violent Behavior, 12*(2), 131–140.

Hawley, P. H., Little, T. D., & Card, N. A. (2008). The myth of the alpha male: A new look at dominance-related beliefs and behaviors among adolescent males and females. *International Journal of Behavioral Development, 32*(1), 76–88.

Li, Q. (2006). Cyberbullying in schools: A research of gender differences. *School Psychology International, 27*(2), 157–170.

Moretti, M. M., Catchpole, R. E. H., & Odgers, C. (2005). The dark side of girlhood: Recent trends, risk factors and trajectories to aggression and violence. *The Canadian Child and Adolescent Psychiatry Review, 14*, 21–25.

Olweus, D. (1997). Bully/victim problems in school: Facts and intervention. *European Journal of Psychology of Education, 12*, 495–510.

Peets, K., & Kikas, E. (2006). Aggressive strategies and victimization during adolescence: Grade and gender differences, and cross-informant agreement. *Aggressive Behaviour, 32*, 48–79.

Scheithauer, H., & Petermann, F. (2002). Indirect/social/relational aggression in children and adolescents: A meta-analysis of gender- and age-specific differences. Paper presented in the XV world meeting of International Society for research on Aggression, July 2002, Montreal, Canada.

Scheithauer, H., Hayer, T., Petermann, F., & Jugert, G. (2006). Physical, verbal, and relational forms of bullying among German students: Age trends, gender differences, and correlates. *Aggressive Behavior, 32*(3), 261–275.

Tiet, Q. Q., Wasserman, G. A., Loeber, R., McReynolds, L. S., & Miller, L. S. (2001). Developmental and sex differences in types of conduct problems. *Journal of Child and Family Studies, 10*, 181–197.

Viljoen, J. L., O'Neill, M. L., & Sidhu, A. (2005). Bullying behaviors in female and male adolescent offenders: Prevalence, types, and association with psychological adjustment. *Aggressive Behavior, 31*, 521–535.

Vitaro, F., Brendgen, M., & Barker, E. D. (2006). Subtypes of aggressive behaviors: A developmental perspective. *International Journal of Behavioral Development, 30*(1), 12–19.

Yubero, S., & Navarro, R. (2006). Students' and teachers' views of gender-related aspects of aggression. *School Psychology International, 27*(4), 488–512.

Internet References . . .

parentstv.org

Maintained by the Parents Television Council, an advocacy organization, this website is constructed to aid in discouraging the increasingly graphic sexual themes and dialogue, depictions of gratuitous violence, and profane/obscene language on television during the hours when children are more likely to be viewing.

http://www.parentstv.org

American Academy of Child and Adolescent Psychiatry: Facts for Families

The American Academy of Child and Adolescent Psychiatry has a subpage entitled Facts for Families that has a number of research-based Fact Sheets regarding the impact of media on children and youth.

http://www.aacap.org/cs/root/facts_for_families/facts_for_families

National Literacy Trust

While devoted to literacy, this UK website contains a listing of abstracts of scholarly journal articles that pertain to the impact of television on adolescents' cognitive outcomes such as academic achievement.

http://www.literacytrust.org.uk

Entertainment Software Rating Board

This website was created by the Entertainment Software Rating Board, a non-profit, self-regulatory body that independently assigns ratings, enforces guidelines, and helps ensure responsible online privacy practices for the interactive entertainment software industry. This website provides concise and impartial information about the content and age-appropriateness of video games along with tips for parents about parental control.

http://www.esrb.org

Common Sense Media

Common Sense Media describe themselves as a non-partisan, not-for-profit organization dedicated to providing trustworthy information and tools, as well as an independent forum, so that families can have a choice and a voice about the media they consume.

http://www.commonsensemedia.org

Parents' Choice

The Parents' Choice Foundation bills itself as the nation's oldest nonprofit guide to quality children's media and toys (1978). Parents' Choice reviews books, toys, music, television, software, videogames, websites, and magazines for children and families of all achievements and backgrounds.

http://www.parents-choice.org

Media

*M*edia such as television, internet, and video play a large role in the lives of children and adolescence. Media is fun and adolescents spend a great deal of time engaging with media. Media such as television and video games are sometimes referred to as "the other parent" in children's lives. Some people believe that media use by children has a profound impact on their social, emotional, and physical development. What is key is identifying if such an impact exists and whether any influence on youth is positive or negative in terms of their lives. The following three issues address different media's impact on different adolescent developmental outcomes.

- Does Sex on TV Negatively Impact Adolescent Sexuality?

- Do Video Games Impede Adolescent Cognitive Development?

- Are Social Networking Sites (SNSs), Such a Facebook, a Cause for Concern Among Adolescents?

ISSUE 17

Does Sex on TV Negatively Impact Adolescent Sexuality?

YES: Rebecca L. Collins et al., from "Watching Sex on Television Predicts Adolescent Initiation of Sexual Behavior," *Pediatrics* (September 3, 2004)

NO: Rebecca L. Collins et al., from "Entertainment Television as a Healthy Sex Educator: The Impact of Condom-Efficacy Information in an Episode of *Friends*," *Pediatrics* (November 5, 2003)

ISSUE SUMMARY

YES: Rebecca Collins and colleagues from the RAND Corporation present evidence from a longitudinal survey that adolescents who viewed more sexual content at baseline were more likely to initiate intercourse and progress to more advanced sexual activities during the subsequent year.

NO: Collins and colleagues in an earlier study suggested that entertainment television can also serve as a healthy sex educator and can work in conjunction with parents to improve adolescent sexual knowledge.

$\mathbf{A}$lthough parents, schools, and the church play an important role in guiding and educating children and adolescents, the mass media, particularly television, has a very important influence on socialization. The negative effects of violence on television have long been studied with consistent findings indicating that exposure to violence is a risk factor for engaging in violent behaviours. More recently, the impact of sex on television has emerged as a "hot topic" in research. Why is that so? Two reasons come to mind: first, our understanding of the relationship between the media and behaviour, and second, the increase in sexual content on television.

The Kaiser Family Foundation (*Sex on TV 4*, 2005) reports that sexual content currently appears in 70 percent of all television programs. This rate increased from 56 percent in 1998 and 64 percent in 2002. Gone are the Mary Tyler Moore days of single beds and casual touching. Sexual content today is defined as talk about sex such as virginity and love; sexual behaviours such as flirting, kissing, and oral sex; and sexual intercourse—either implied or depicted. Of the programs with sexual content, 68 percent include talk about sex (up from 54 percent in 1998), 35 percent include sexual behaviours (versus 23 percent in 1998), and the remaining 11 percent include scenes in which sexual intercourse is either depicted or strongly implied (up from 7 percent in 1998). Primetime shows in particular have very high rates of sexual content, and these rates also continue to rise (77 percent in 2005 versus 68 percent in 1998 and 71 percent in 2002).

With these alarming statistics, concerns arise as to the type of information adolescents are getting about sex, especially with respect to safe sex and risky sexual behaviours. The Kaiser Foundation reports that of the 20 most popular shows for teens, only 10 percent of those with sexual content include information about risks (e.g., emotional/physical consequences) and/or responsibilities (e.g., contraception). Two-thirds of these messages have been interpreted by the Kaiser Foundation as minor or inconsequential, and of the shows that involve adolescent characters, only 23 percent include messages about sexual risks or responsibilities. On a positive note, the majority (89 percent) of sexual intercourse acts involve characters age 25 or older who have an established relationship with their partner. Does all this sex on TV affect adolescent sexuality and sexual activity? Before addressing this question, an examination of adolescent sexual behaviours warrants attention.

Nearly two-thirds of adolescents in North America will have had sexual intercourse before graduating from high school. More than a third of sexually active adolescents report not using a condom the last time they had sexual intercourse, and one-third of all females under the age of 20 become pregnant. An alarming 4 million teens contract a sexually transmitted infection (STI) each year, and adding to this, approximately 50 percent of all new HIV infections occur among adolescents under the age of 25 (Centers for Disease Control and Prevention, 2002). Although intercourse is common among today's youth, most report they wish they had waited before having sex. This could indicate that many are having sex before they are ready (Martino et al., 2005). Early intervention in itself is a risk factor for acquiring an STI and/or pregnancy. What factors contribute to early initiation? This brings us back to the question stated above: Is the media and in particular television a contributing factor?

According to the Kaiser report, 83 percent of parents believe sex on TV contributes to early sexual behaviour. Interestingly, the majority of adolescents surveyed agree. Given that television is an important source of information, it is imperative that we understand the effects the messages have on sexual behaviours. Does the exposure have a positive or negative influence on sexual socialization? Does sex on TV shape an adolescents conception of reality? Does sex on television teach our youth that sexual intercourse comes before love? Does it teach them risks and responsibilities? Does sex on TV essentially shape adolescent sexuality?

In the selections that follow, a group of researchers from the RAND Corporation present two sides to this argument. In the first study, they found that watching high levels of sex on television doubled the next-year likelihood of initiating intercourse. In the second selection, the same authors argue that sex on TV can serve as a healthy sex educator and can work in conjunction with parents to improve adolescent sexual knowledge.

371

YES

Rebecca L. Collins et al.

Watching Sex on Television Predicts Adolescent Initiation of Sexual Behavior

A key period of sexual exploration and development occurs during adolescence. During this time, individuals begin to consider which sexual behaviors are enjoyable, moral, and appropriate for their age group. Many teens become sexually active during this period; currently, 46% of high school students in the United States have had sexual intercourse.[1] Although intercourse among youths is common, most sexually active teens wish they had waited longer to have sex,[2] which suggests that sex is occurring before youths are prepared for its consequences. . . . [Furthermore, unplanned] pregnancies and STDs are more common among those who begin sexual activity earlier.[3]

Therefore, early sexual initiation is an important health issue. This raises the question of why individuals become sexually involved at younger ages. What factors hasten sexual initiation, and what factors delay its onset? There are many well-documented predictors of age of intercourse initiation, both social and physical. However, 1 factor commonly cited by parents and policy makers as promoting sex among teens has received little systematic scientific investigation, namely, television (TV). There is good scientific reason to think that TV may be a key contributor to early sexual activity. Sexual behavior is strongly influenced by culture,[4] and TV is an integral part of US teen culture. . . . [Sexual] messages [on TV] are commonplace, according to a scientific content analysis of a representative sample of programming from the 2001–2002 TV season. Sexual content appears in 64% of all TV programs; those programs with sexual content average 4.4 scenes with sexually related material per hour. Talk about sex is found more frequently (61% of all programs) than overt portrayals of any sexual behavior (32% of programs). Approximately 1 of every 7 programs (14%) includes a portrayal of sexual intercourse, depicted or strongly implied.[5]

This high-dose exposure to portrayals of sex may affect adolescents' developing beliefs about cultural norms. TV may create the illusion that sex is more central to daily life than it truly is and may promote sexual

From *Pediatrics*, vol. 114, no. 3, September 3, 2004, pp. e280–e289. Copyright © 2004 by American Academy of Pediatrics. Reprinted by permission.

initiation . . . , a process known as media cultivation.[6] Exposure to the social models provided by TV also may alter beliefs about the likely outcome of engaging in sexual activity. Social learning theory predicts that teens who see characters having casual sex without experiencing negative consequences will be more likely to adopt the behaviors portrayed.[7] Although televised sexual portrayals can theoretically inhibit sexual activity when they include depictions of sexual risks (such as the possibility of contracting an STD or becoming pregnant), abstinence, or the need for sexual safety, this type of depiction occurs in only 15% of shows with sexual content. In other words, only ~1 of every 7 TV shows that include sexual content includes any safe sex messages, and nearly two-thirds of these instances (63%) are minor or inconsequential in their degree of emphasis within the scene.[5] As a result, sexual content on TV is far more likely to promote sexual activity among US adolescents than it is to discourage it. . . .

Previous work demonstrated links between viewing of sexual content on TV and attitudes toward sex, endorsement of gender stereotypes likely to promote sexual initiation, and dissatisfaction with virginity, as well as a wide range of perceptions regarding normative sexual behavior.[8] In addition to these studies, 2 groundbreaking articles published in the early 1990s examined the question of whether exposure to sex on TV influences adolescent sexual behavior. The studies found positive associations between any lifetime intercourse and TV viewing among adolescents, but methodologic limitations rendered the results inconclusive.[9,10] . . .

[The present study was] designed to [further] test the effects of TV sexual content on adolescent sexual initiation [while correcting previous methodologic problems.] We examined the effects of exposure to TV sexual content overall, exposure to TV depictions of sexual risks or sexual safety, and exposure to TV portrayals of sexual behavior versus talk about sex. Although TV producers and the general public have expressed concern regarding both sexual talk and sexual behavior, portrayals of behavior have typically been the focus of such attention. Given the potential applications of our research, we considered it important to determine whether this emphasis is well placed. Social learning theory predicts that observation of either sexual talk or sexual behavior will influence teens to have sex, as long as the portrayed consequences are not negative, but the theory does not address whether the magnitudes of these effects will differ.[7] Finally, we examined the effects of hours spent viewing TV, independent of content. Some theory and research argue that any time spent watching TV affects sexual behavior,[6,10] whereas other research suggests that only programs with known sexual content have an influence.[7,9] . . .

We hypothesized that adolescents exposed to greater amounts of sexual content on TV would initiate intercourse sooner and would progress more quickly to higher levels of noncoital activity. However, we expected that exposure to portrayals of sexual safety or the risks that accompany sexual activity would be associated with a delay in sexual advancement. . . .

Methods

Procedure

We conducted a national telephone survey in spring 2001 and reinterviewed the same group 1 year later, in spring 2002. The survey measured TV viewing habits, sexual knowledge, attitudes, and behavior, and a large set of demographic and psychosocial variables shown to predict sexual behavior or TV viewing habits in previous research. . . .

Enrolling adolescents in a telephone survey that assesses sexual behavior requires care and sensitivity. All households were sent a letter describing the study before telephone contact, so that they could carefully consider their participation. At the time of the baseline telephone interview, we briefly surveyed the parents, to determine the household composition and to measure the parents' sexual attitudes. An adolescent participant was then randomly selected from among all household members in the age range of 12 to 17 years. Parental consent for the adolescent's participation and then the adolescent's assent were obtained before the interview. . . .

Sample

. . . [A] sample of 1762 adolescents, 12 to 17 years of age, . . . participated in both interviews. This longitudinal sample was 48% female, 77% white, 13% African American, 7% Hispanic, and 4% Asian or other race. . . . Seventeen percent had ever had intercourse at baseline and 29% at the follow-up assessments. . . .

Measures

Exposure to Sexual Content on TV

Three measures reflected the content of TV viewed at baseline, ie, exposure to sexual content, exposure to portrayals of sexual risks or the need for safety, and relative exposure to sexual behavior versus talk about sex. These measures were based on a set of 23 programs. . . . After eliminating movies, sports, game shows, and specials (1-time airings), we included 15 of the 20 programs on the top 10 list for 1 of the 4 groups. Five additional broadcast programs and 3 cable programs that were known (on the basis of prior content analyses) or expected (on the basis of reviews in the popular press) to contain high levels of sexual content were also included in the list. The final list included programs appearing on broadcast networks and basic and premium cable channels and encompassed animated and live action shows, reality shows, sitcoms, and dramas. As part of the baseline survey, teens indicated the frequency with which they watched these 23 programs during the previous TV season ("since school started last fall") on a 4-point scale, ranging from "never" to "every time it's on." We derived the exposure measures by multiplying the self-reported viewing frequency for each program by 1 of 3 indicators of the average content in an episode of that program and summing across programs.

Methods developed by Kunkel et al,[5] as part of a much larger study of TV sexual content, were used to determine the sexual content in a sample of episodes for the 23 programs. . . . Coders unitized the episodes into distinct scenes, indicating the presence of any of the following: 1) sexual behavior: physical flirting, passionate kissing, intimate touch, intercourse implied, or intercourse depicted; 2) sexual talk: talk about own/others' plans or desires, talk about sex that has occurred, talk toward sex, expert advice, or other; or 3) talk or behavior depicting risks or the need for safety in regard to sexual activity: abstinence, waiting to have sex, portrayals mentioning or showing condoms or birth control, and portrayals related to acquired immunodeficiency syndrome, STDs, pregnancy, or abortion. . . .

For each TV series studied, the amount of sexual content was calculated as the average number of scenes per episode containing a major focus on sexual behavior plus the average number of scenes containing a major focus on talk about sex. . . . The proportion of sexual content that included sexual behavior was measured by dividing the average number of scenes that contained a major focus on sexual behavior by the average number of scenes with any sexual content for each episode. Risk and safety content was calculated as the average number of scenes per episode containing any such portrayal, whether the focus was major or minor. . . .

Average Hours of TV Viewing
We measured time spent watching TV with a set of 5 items assessing hours of viewing on various days of the week and at different times of day. Responses were averaged to create a continuous indicator of average viewing time.

Sexual Behavior
Questions assessed behavior with someone of the opposite sex. Intercourse experience at both the baseline and follow-up assessments was measured with the item "Have you ever had sex with a boy/girl? By sex we mean when a boy puts his penis in a girl's vagina" (yes/no). . . . We measured lifetime levels of noncoital experience with a scale developed for this study. . . . Adolescents indicated whether they had ever 1) kissed,* 2) "made-out" (kissed for a long time), 3) touched a breast/had their breast touched,* 4) touched genitals/had their genitals touched, or 5) given or received oral sex. Items with an asterisk were asked of all youths, and the others were asked only if the response to the item listed immediately before it was yes. . . .

Covariates
[A number of covariates were measured as part of the baseline interview. These included gender, race/ethnicity, age, educational expectations, overall mental health, religiosity, self-esteem, deviance, and sensation seeking. In addition, indicators of social environment known to predict initiation of coitus were also measured. These included age of friends, living arrangements,

parents' education, parental monitoring, mother's work status, and parental discipline norms.]

Analyses

Preliminary Analyses

. . . Our preliminary analyses tested simple associations between the baseline TV viewing variables and sexual behavior. Because youths who see more sex on TV are also youths who watch more TV overall and who therefore see more sexual risk and safety content, the TV variables are best understood in the context of one another. We thus examined all 4 TV variables simultaneously in these tests. We also tested whether other respondent characteristics might explain any relationship between viewing sexual content and behavior, by examining bivariate associations between these characteristics and sex-heavy TV viewing at the baseline evaluation, intercourse initiation by the follow-up interview, and advancement in the level of noncoital behavior by the follow-up interview.

Our key analyses were a pair of multivariate regression equations including all TV viewing variables and all covariates as predictors of changes in sexual behavior from the baseline assessment to the follow-up assessment. A final pair of equations incorporated interaction terms, to test for differences in the associations between TV exposure and sexual behavior change as a function of age (<15 years vs ≥15 years of age), gender (male versus female), and race/ethnicity. . . .

Results

Before controlling for other variables, a diet of TV high in sexual content at baseline was strongly related to initiation of intercourse and advancement of noncoital activity levels in the following year. TV exposure to relatively more depictions of sexual behavior than talk were unrelated to either behavior, and although higher levels of overall viewing were negatively correlated with sexual advancement, these relationships did not reach statistical significance. However, TV exposure to the risks of sex was related to less progression in noncoital behavior. . . .

The factors that were positively associated with initiation of intercourse among virgins were older age, having older friends, getting low grades, engaging in deviant behavior, and sensation-seeking. Those associated with a lower probability of intercourse initiation were parental monitoring, parent education, living with both parents, having parents who would disapprove if the adolescent had sex, being religious, and having good mental health. Only 1 additional variable predicted changes in noncoital activity; exposure to risk or safety portrayals was related to a lower level of noncoital activity. Variables that were not predictive of either outcome were gender, race, self-esteem, educational aspirations, and mother's work outside the home.

[Most] of the variables predictive of later sex were also correlated at baseline with a sex-heavy TV diet, and most correlations were in the same direction as those observed for sexual activity. These variables could potentially account for the relationships between exposure to sexual content and sexual activity observed. To test for TV effects independent of such factors, we entered all of the bivariate predictors of intercourse initiation or noncoital stage into our models as covariates. We also included the gender and race variables in multivariate analyses, because they were central to planned tests for subgroup differences. The resulting models were excellent predictors of the outcome variables. A concordance or c statistic, scaled so that 50% corresponds to chance and 100% corresponds to perfect prediction, indicated that respondents' initiation of intercourse was correctly predicted 79% of the time and their advances in noncoital behavior were correctly predicted 90% of the time. . . .

The significant coefficient for sexual content in these models indicates that, after more than a dozen other predictors of sexual behavior were taken into account, exposure to TV sexual content remained a strong predictor of intercourse initiation among those who were virgins at the first interview. Exposure to sexual content was also strongly predictive of progressing noncoital activity. . . . [The] likelihood of intercourse initiation [was] approximately double for the high-exposure group, across all ages studied. . . . The probability of initiating breast touching was ~50% higher and the probability of initiating genital touching was almost double in the high-exposure group. . . .

After other factors were controlled statistically, greater relative exposure to behavior remained unassociated with later sexual behavior. We also found no significant association between exposure to portrayals of sexual risk and/or safety and later sexual behavior and no association between average hours of TV viewing and sex in these multivariate models.

Many of the other respondent characteristics that were bivariate predictors of intercourse initiation remained significant in the multivariate model, including older age, having mostly older friends, lower parent education, not living with both parents, less parental monitoring, less religiosity, poor mental health, sensation-seeking personality, deviant behavior, and low school grades. Only a small subset of these factors predicted noncoital activity in the multivariate model. Other than viewing sexual content, older age and less parental monitoring predicted advancing noncoital activity.

The effects of TV viewing were largely similar across demographic groups, with a few key exceptions. . . . African Americans with high levels of exposure to sexual risk and safety portrayals were less likely to have intercourse, whereas the sexual behavior of individuals from all other races combined was not related to such exposure. . . . This race interaction was also significant for noncoital activity. . . . African Americans were less likely to advance their noncoital activity level with exposure to sexual risk and safety portrayals, whereas changes in the activity levels of other races were not related to such exposure. . . .

The model predicting noncoital sex also produced a significant interaction between gender and total hours of TV viewing. . . . More time spent watching TV delayed noncoital activity among male subjects but had no effect among female subjects. . . .

Discussion

We observed substantial associations between the amount of sexual content viewed by adolescents and advances in their sexual behavior during the subsequent year. Youths who viewed 1 SD more sexual content than average behaved sexually like youths who were 9 to 17 months older but watched average amounts of sex on TV. This effect is not insubstantial. Predicted probabilities showed that watching the highest levels of sexual content effectively doubled the next-year likelihood of initiating intercourse and greatly increased the probability of advancing 1 level in noncoital activity. In other words, after adjustment for other differences between high and low viewers of sexual content, 12-year-olds who watched the highest levels of this content among youths their age appeared much like youths 2 to 3 years older who watched the lowest levels of sexual content among their peers. The magnitude of these results are such that a moderate shift in the average sexual content of adolescent TV viewing could have substantial effects on sexual behavior at the population level.

It is noteworthy that the association between viewing sexual content and intercourse initiation appeared to be much stronger before our introduction of covariates to the model. The finding that these factors reduce the effects of TV viewing on behavior demonstrates the importance of including such controls in future research. The majority of factors we examined in our work predicted both viewing of sexual content and advances in sexual behavior. Nonetheless, when we controlled statistically for these associations, the relationship between exposure to TV sex and later sexual behavior remained substantial, indicating that it could not be explained by any of the variables in our study. Relationships between viewing sexual content and advancing sexual behavior were not attributable to the effects of developing sexual behavior on selective viewing of sexual content. Our analyses controlled for adolescents' level of sexual activity at baseline, rendering an explanation of reverse causality for our findings implausible.

This result replicates and extends the findings of Brown and Newcomer.[9] Those authors found the same pattern of association with a sex-heavy TV diet in their research, but they could not clearly eliminate third-variable and reverse-causality explanations. We also extend their result by showing that it holds for noncoital sexual behaviors, across an age span of 5 years.

We did not find an association between sexual behavior and average hours of TV viewing. . . . Our result . . . undercuts cultivation theory, which suggests that TV content is homogeneous enough that overall viewing should predict sexual outcomes. Although the process of media cultivation may well take place, content is not as uniform as it was when the theory was proposed, which perhaps explains why the prediction was not supported. We observed a nonsignificant but suggestive negative coefficient for hours of viewing predicting noncoital sex (with other variables controlled). This would be consistent with a "babysitter effect" often attributed to TV, in which youths who spend more time viewing have less time to engage in problem behaviors.

We obtained the predicted relationship between exposure to portrayals of sexual risk or the need for sexual safety and delay of sexual behavior, but only among African American youths. . . . It may be that African Americans are more likely to use TV as a source of sexual information than are other groups. Other studies suggested that African Americans watch more TV and interpret sexual content differently.[11] However, we know of no theory that explains those findings, or our own, and we think that this is an important area for future research.

Portrayals of sexual talk and sexual behavior appear to have similar effects on youths. This is not surprising from a theoretical standpoint. Social learning theory posits that information is gleaned from what others say about a behavior as well as what they do, because both indicate social approval or disapproval of the activity in question. It apparently makes little difference whether a TV show presents people talking about whether they have sex or shows them actually having sex. Both affect perceived norms regarding sex, and thus sexual behavior.

Finally, we found that a number of factors were predictors of the transition to intercourse, consistent with previous work. However, there were fewer multivariate predictors of noncoital sex. This indicates the need for greater study of such behaviors, which may be increasingly common among adolescents as they struggle to become sexually active in a way that they perceive to be safe and/or preserving of virginity.

A limitation of this research was our inability to control for adolescent interest in sex or sexual readiness before TV viewing. Youths who are considering coital or noncoital activities that they have not yet enacted may watch more sex on TV (e.g., to get information or to satisfy desires). They may subsequently engage in these sexual activities sooner but as a result of their higher levels of interest, not as a result of their TV exposure. . . .

Other limitations appear to be based on the sensitive nature of our research topic. Although rates of intercourse were within the expected range at the follow-up evaluation, they were somewhat low at the baseline evaluation, which suggests that some participants were not initially honest about their sexual experience. . . .

Finally, although TV accounts for more of children's time than any other medium, the sexual content in films, music, and magazines is also likely to hasten sexual advancement. Therefore, it will be important to address these other contributions to sexual socialization in both future research and interventions. Indeed, we should note that, because TV viewing of sexual content is probably related to exposure to sex in other media, our results may reflect at least partially the influence of music, magazines, or movies. . . .

With these limitations in mind, our findings have clear implications. Reducing the amount of sexual talk and behavior on TV or the amount of time that adolescents are exposed to this content is likely to appreciably delay the initiation of both coital and noncoital sexual activities. Increasing the percentage of portrayals of sexual risk and safety, relative to other sexual content, might also inhibit early sexual activity, particularly among African American youths. However, reducing exposure to sexual content on TV may be difficult. An option that does not require altering TV content or adolescents' viewing habits has met with some success in other areas. Parents who view violent programs with their children and discuss their own beliefs regarding the behavior depicted may be able to reduce the effects of positively portrayed aggressive content on their children's behavior.[12] This process may also help limit the negative effects of sexual portrayals that do not contain risk information. . . .

References

1. Centers for Disease Control and Prevention. Trends in sexual risk behaviors among high school students: United States, 1991–2001. *MMWR Morb Mortal Wkly Rep.* 2002;51:856–859.

2. National Campaign to Prevent Teen Pregnancy. *With One Voice* 2002: America's Adults and Teens Sound Off About Teen Pregnancy. Washington, DC: The National Campaign to Prevent Teen Pregnancy; 2002.

3. Koyle P, Jensen L, Olsen J. Comparison of sexual behaviors among adolescents having an early, middle and late first intercourse experience. *Youth Soc.* 1989;20:461–476.

4. Nathanson C. *Dangerous Passage: The Social Control of Sexuality in Women's Adolescence.* Philadelphia, PA: Temple University Press; 1991.

5. Kunkel D, Eyal K, Biely E, et al. *Sex on TV3: A Biennial Report to the Kaiser Family Foundation.* Menlo Park, CA: The Henry J. Kaiser Foundation; 2003. . . .

6. Gerbner G, Gross M, Morgan L, Signorielli N. Living with television: the dynamics of the cultivation process. In: Bryant J, Zillman D, eds. *Perspectives on Media Effects.* Hillsdale, NJ: Lawrence Erlbaum Associates; 1986:17–40.

7. Bandura A. *Social Foundations of Thought and Action: A Social Cognitive Theory.* Englewood Cliffs, NJ: Prentice Hall; 1986.

8. Buerkel-Rothfuss N, Strouse J. Media exposure and perceptions of sexual behaviors: the cultivation hypothesis moves to the bedroom. In: Greenberg B, Brown J, Buerkel-Rothfuss N, eds. *Media, Sex and the Adolescent.* Cresskill, NJ: Hampton Press; 1993.

9. Brown JD, Newcomer SF. Television viewing and adolescents' sexual behavior. *J Homosex.* 1991;21:77–91.

10. Peterson JL, Moore KA, Furstenberg FF Jr. Television viewing and early initiation of sexual intercourse: is there a link? *J Homosex.* 1991;21:93–118.

11. Brown JD, Schulze L. The effects of race, gender, and fandom on audience interpretations of Madonna's music videos. *J. Commun.* 1990;40:88–102.

12. Donnerstein E, Slaby R, Eron L. The mass media and youth aggression. In: Eron LD, Gentry JH, Schlegel P, eds. *Reason to Hope: A Psychosocial Perspective on Violence and Youth.* Washington, DC: American Psychological Association; 1994:219–250.

Rebecca L. Collins et al.  **NO**

Entertainment Television as a Healthy Sex Educator: The Impact of Condom-Efficacy Information in an Episode of *Friends*

Forty-six percent of all high school students in the United States have had sex, and rates of sexually transmitted diseases and unintended pregnancy are high among these youth.[1] One factor thought to contribute to adolescent sexual risk is television.[2] It has been argued that television has become a sex educator to America's children, usurping the role of parents. Seven of ten primetime network programs contain sexual content, and the average primetime show with such content contains six scenes with sex per hour.[3] This high prevalence of sexual content has raised concern, in part, because of fear that the lessons taught by television are inaccurate and that, even when it is accurate, television is providing information more appropriately conveyed by parents. However, the same reasoning that supports these concerns can be used to argue that television is sometimes a healthy sex educator and may aid parents rather than usurp their roles.

The idea that television presents a distorted picture of sexuality is strongly supported by content analyses. Sex is largely portrayed on television as a casual activity, without health or other life consequences. The vast majority of scenes with sexual content fail to depict the responsibilities concomitant with sexual activity or to note the risks of pregnancy and contraction of sexually transmitted diseases.[3] Nonetheless, portrayals of sexual risk and responsibilities are sometimes present on television. Such portrayals were included in 15% of programs with sexual content in the 2001 to 2002 season and in 34% of shows with sexual content that involve teen characters.[3] This raises the possibility that television can be a healthy sex educator, teaching valuable lessons to adolescent audiences by modeling responsible behavior or pointing out the consequences that can result from careless sexual activity.[4] Consistent with this notion, 60% of teens participating in a recent survey said that they learned about how to

From *Pediatrics*, vol. 112, no. 5, November 2005, pp. 1115–1121. Copyright © 2005 by American Academy of Pediatrics. Reprinted by permission.

say "no" to a sexual situation by watching television, and 43% said they learned something from television about how to talk to a partner about safer sex.[5]

Clearly, parents are able to put information about sexuality in a context appropriate to family beliefs, values, and culture, which may differ from the television mainstream. However, the concern that television is usurping parents' role as sex educators can also be countered. Rather than substituting for parents, television may act as a catalyst to conversation, giving parents and their children an entrée to topics they find difficult to broach with one another. Thirty-three percent of 15- to 17-year-olds report that they have had a conversation about a sexual issue with one of their parents because of something they saw on television.[5] These conversations not only give parents a chance to provide their own input on sexual health issues, but also give them an opportunity to challenge any negative media messages and to reinforce positive messages. Thus, television may promote the role of parents as sex educators, rather than undermine it.

This article explores these positive opportunities for sex education via the entertainment media by studying the impact of one episode of the sitcom *Friends* that contained information about sexual risk. . . . The episode focuses on a pregnancy resulting from condom failure. It was part of the season's main story line, in which . . . Rachel experiences an unplanned pregnancy as a result of a single night of sex with Ross . . . (her former boyfriend). In the episode, Rachel tells Ross about the pregnancy for the first time. Ross responds with disbelief and exclaims "but we used a condom!" A statement that "condoms are only 97% effective" appears in this scene and also a subsequent one, reinforcing the condom use and condom failure elements of the story. Thus, the possibility of condom failure and the resulting consequence of pregnancy . . . could potentially have had a powerful effect on young people's sexual knowledge.

Other studies of health information contained in entertainment programming (sometimes termed "edu-tainment") suggest that this may have occurred. . . . For example, information about family planning was conveyed to large numbers of Africans as part of existing entertainment programming and apparently changed health behavior as a result[6]. . .

These studies show . . . that it is possible to deliver health messages to a very large audience through edu-tainment. They also indicate a potential for influencing health-related awareness, knowledge, and beliefs in this manner. We expected to observe such effects for the *Friends* episode. We hypothesized that adolescent *Friends* viewers would demonstrate enhanced awareness of condom failure. . . . We also expected a substantial percentage of viewers to report learning something about condoms as a result of the episode. . . .

[We] expected to find that many adolescents changed their beliefs about condom efficacy as a result of the episode, because the events portrayed might provide new information, inspire a search for information, or spur discussion regarding the issue of condom efficacy. Because the information conveyed in the *Friends* episode was fairly complex, we did not expect viewers' condom-efficacy beliefs to be changed in a single direction. Like much information regarding sexual health, the condom message in the episode communicated that the outcome of condom use is uncertain. It (accurately) indicated that condoms are very effective and should be used if one has sex, and also that condoms cannot be relied on with absolute certainty, so even protected sex should involve a careful decision. . . . [We] expected the *Friends* episode to have a mixed effect on perceptions of condom efficacy among adolescents, precipitating changes toward both enhanced and reduced perceived efficacy. . . .

We also hypothesized that the *Friends* episode would provoke conversation about the show between adolescent viewers and their parents, and result in discussions of pregnancy and condom efficacy that might not otherwise have occurred. . . .

We expected any interactions with parents that occurred to moderate the impact of the *Friends* episode. Previous research indicates that children who watch programming with their parents are differentially influenced by the content they see, as are children who discuss media content with their parents.[7] This process, termed mediation, sometimes counteracts media effects and sometimes enhances them, depending on whether parents agree with the media message. We expected the *Friends* condom-efficacy episode to more strongly affect adolescents who watched with their parents, who discussed the episode with their parents, or who discussed condom efficacy with their parents as a result of seeing the episode. . . .

Finally, although we expected the aforementioned effects, we also anticipated that many teens exposed to the episode would fail to process or retain the sexual health information it contained. . . . [We] hypothesized and tested for a few additional moderators that might determine who is most strongly affected. First, we predicted that all program effects (on condom awareness, condom beliefs, and talking to parents) would be stronger for more regular *Friends* viewers. Regular viewers are more likely to attend closely to the program, identify with the characters, and think later about its content. Second, we predicted that effects of the *Friends* episode would be greater among younger and sexually inexperienced adolescents, because they would have less real-life experience on which to draw. . . .

Methods

Sample

Respondents were drawn from the larger group of [adolescents (12–17 years)] in the Rand Television and Adolescent Sexuality study (TAS). . . . The TAS surveys asked about television-viewing habits, demographic and psychosocial characteristics, sexual attitudes, beliefs, knowledge, and behavior.

. . . For this study, we sampled all 648 respondents who were regular *Friends* viewers at TAS baseline, defined as teens who watch *Friends* "a lot" or "every time.". . . [of the 648, 506 were available for interviews. . . .

completion rate of 78%]. . . . Most analyses for this study focused on the 323 adolescents who reported seeing the episode and a subset of 155 of adolescents whose viewership could be confirmed with an additional question about the episode's content. . . . In one additional statistical test, the analysis sample consisted of the 472 *Friends* survey participants (305 self-reported and 150 confirmed viewers) who were surveyed at the TAS follow-up.

The TAS sample slightly underrepresented Hispanics, and slightly overrepresented two-parent households, compared with the nation as a whole. . . . [Confirmed] viewers were more likely to be female, to come from somewhat more educated families, and to be current regular viewers of *Friends*.

Procedures

. . . Fifty percent of participants were interviewed within 3 weeks of the air date . . . , and the remainder were interviewed within 4 weeks of the air date. . . . Median time between TAS baseline and the *Friends* survey was 6 months, as was the median time from the *Friends* survey to TAS follow-up.

Measures

Viewership of *Friends* and of the episode of interest were established at the outset of the *Friends* interview. We began with a short introduction informing respondents that we were interested in their responses to a recent episode of *Friends*. We then repeated the item from the TAS survey that was used to select our sample: "How often do you watch the television show *Friends*? (never, once in a while, a lot, every time it's on)." To assess whether respondents saw the key episode, we asked two questions: "Did you see the episode a few weeks ago when Rachel told Ross she's pregnant?" and "Did you see the episode where Phoebe and Joey got the fire department to break down Monica and Chandler's door?" The latter event took place during the condom-efficacy episode, but was unrelated to the plot. Respondents who reported seeing the pregnancy episode were classified as self-reported viewers. The subset who also reported seeing the fire department episode were classified as confirmed viewers. . . .

Among both self-reported and confirmed viewers, we assessed interpretation and recall of the key reproductive health information with a set of three items: "According to the episode, did Ross and Rachel use a condom when they had sex?," "What percent of the time did the *Friends* episode say condoms work in preventing pregnancy, from zero to 100%?," and "Which comes closer to the main message you took from this episode: lots of times condoms don't prevent pregnancy, or condoms almost always prevent pregnancy?". . . There was a wide range of responses to the percent-effectiveness question. Based on the distribution, we recoded it to a dichotomous measure reflecting responses of >95% but <100% versus all other responses. . . . Responses to the question about whether Ross and Rachel used a condom were coded to reflect "yes" versus all other responses.

We assessed the effects of the episode on condom beliefs with three measures, based on two items in the *Friends* survey. To tap perceived learning, we asked, "In thinking about that episode, did you learn anything new about condoms that you didn't know before? . . . To measure changes in perceived condom efficacy we asked, "In real life, how effective are condoms for preventing pregnancy?". . . This same item had been asked in the earlier TAS survey. We derived a dichotomous variable that reflected any change in condom-efficacy beliefs versus no change from a comparison of responses to the item at these 2 time points. Using the same repeated item, we also assessed the direction of belief change among those with any change, creating a dichotomous indicator of reduced perceptions of condom efficacy (less effective versus more effective).

Parental mediation surrounding the episode was tapped with a set of four items. Coviewing was assessed with, "When you watched the *Friends* episode in which Rachel told Ross she was pregnant, were you with a parent or other adult?" Parental discussion was assessed with three items: "Did you talk with a parent or another adult about that episode?," "Because of that episode, did you talk to a parent or another adult about how effective condoms are in preventing pregnancy?," and "Did you talk with a parent or another adult about whether it's good or bad that Rachel is pregnant, or did you not talk about this?"

We drew some additional data from the Rand TAS survey. For comparison with the *Friends* survey item concerning discussions of condom effectiveness, we drew responses to the baseline item: "Have you talked with a parent about condoms in the last 12 months (yes/no)?" Respondent gender, race/ethnicity, age in years, and experience with sexual intercourse (yes/no) were also measured with the TAS baseline survey and used in the present analyses. Finally, we asked respondents to the TAS followup, "What percent of the time do you think condoms work in preventing pregnancy, from zero to 100%?" . . .

Results

The pregnancy episode may have reached more than half of teen *Friends* watchers in our sample of frequent viewers: Sixty-four percent recalled seeing the episode where Rachel told Ross she is pregnant. However, we could confirm viewership among only 27% of those surveyed (ie, this percentage also reported seeing the fire-department episode). Most of those who saw the episode (59% of self-reported and 54% of confirmed viewers) interpreted its message as "lots of times, condoms don't prevent pregnancy.". . . A substantial minority of self-reported viewers (32%) remembered that the episode described Ross and Rachel as having used a condom when they had sex. The majority of confirmed viewers (65%) recalled this information. Fifteen percent of self-reported and 31% of confirmed viewers recalled that the episode said condoms were between 95% and 100% effective.

From 10% to 17% of viewers said they learned something new about condoms from the episode. About half of adolescents in both viewer groups rated the effectiveness of condoms differently than they had in the TAS survey 6 months before. Among these individuals, perceptions of condom effectiveness changed in both directions (more or less effective) about equally often. This was true regardless of how viewership was defined. . . . When asked as part of our earlier survey, most adolescents saw condoms as very or somewhat effective, and this was still true after the *Friends* episode.

Forty percent of those who reported watching the episode said they watched with an adult. From 16% to 24% of viewers talked with an adult about the episode, ≈10% talked with an adult about Rachel's pregnancy, and ≈10% talked with a parent or other adult about condom effectiveness because of the episode. Reactions to the episode were modified by viewing or discussing it with an adult. We tested for these effects among both confirmed and self-reported viewers; results were very similar. For simplicity, we present only confirmed-viewer effects. In this group, we found that teens who watched the condom episode with an adult (versus those who watched alone or with another youth) were twice as likely to recall that condoms were said to be between 95% and 100% effective. . . . Those who watched with an adult were also far more likely to talk to an adult about the episode. . . . Coviewing was not related to changes in condom beliefs or self-reports of learning something new about condoms. . . . Almost half (47%) of adolescents who discussed the episode with an adult recalled that condoms were described as >95% effective, nearly twice the number who remembered this information among those who did not talk with an adult. . . . Many adolescents who talked about the episode with an adult reported talking about condom effectiveness (31%), and many (33%) talked about Rachel's pregnancy. These percentages were substantially higher than those observed among adolescents who didn't specifically discuss the *Friends* episode with adults. . . .

Participants who had a condom-effectiveness discussion with an adult as a result of watching *Friends* were more than twice as likely to say they learned something new about condoms from the episode. . . . This was the only group in the study who may have experienced a directional change in their condom beliefs. Among those who changed their perceptions of condom efficacy after the episode, 75% of teens who talked to an adult about condom efficacy came to see condoms as more effective, whereas only 35% of those who did not discuss condoms with adults came to see condoms as more effective. . . . Surprisingly, discussions of condom effectiveness were unrelated to the likelihood of remembering that condoms were described as between 95% and 100% effective. . . .

To test whether the episode had enduring effects on viewers' condom-related knowledge, we examined responses to the condom efficacy item in the TAS follow-up survey. At TAS follow-up, 24% of self-reported and 30% of confirmed viewers rated condoms as 95% to 100% effective. In comparison, only 18% of the *Friends* sample who did not see the condom episode (before the *Friends* survey) rated condoms as 95% to 100% effective at follow-up. . . .

To explore the generalizability of the effects observed, we tested for differences between frequent and occasional viewers within our sample. . . . [We] found that 72% of frequent viewers versus 21% of occasional viewers recalled that Ross and Rachel used a condom, . . . and that frequent viewers who changed their condom beliefs were less likely than occasional viewers to view condoms as less effective than they had 6 months previously. . . .

Discussion

. . . Entertainment television is often presumed to have an exclusively negative influence on America's adolescents and is sometimes blamed for high rates of sexual activity, sexually transmitted disease, and unplanned pregnancy in this group. The jury is still out on whether television has such effects. Clearly, television is saturated with sexual content but empirical evidence that such content affects adolescent sexual behavior is still preliminary.[8,9] Although sexual content may eventually prove to affect sexual behavior, this study suggests that television can also be a positive force in the sex education of youth and has the potential to affect a broad cross section of teens. Television can teach the risks and responsibilities that accompany sexual activity in a way that books, pamphlets, and classroom instruction cannot, by portraying the experiences of sexually active individuals with whom adolescents identify. This vivid illustration of sexual consequences is hard to come by in other ways, because information about specific individuals' condom use is rarely available in real life. Entertainment television also has the advantage of being able to model socially responsible behavior without explicitly advocating it. Advocacy messages can produce resistance among adolescents.

A second key set of findings addresses the role of parents in this educational process. Forty percent of adolescent viewers watched the episode with an adult, and from 16% to 24% discussed it with an adult. Both of these factors served to reinforce the educational value of the show's content, helping teens to retain the information about how often condoms work. The 10% of viewers who were catalyzed by the episode into having a discussion of condom efficacy with an adult were also more likely to say they learned something new from the show. These interactions with adults apparently emphasized the effectiveness of condoms, more so than condom failure, because adolescents who reported them were the only group to see condoms as more effective than they had previously. The role of parents in altering television's impact is noteworthy and is consistent with research showing that parents and adults can enhance learning from educational programming.[10]

Although it would certainly be a bad idea for television to substitute entirely for traditional sources of sex education, television may supplement and enhance the effects of information from other sources. In this study, television served this role by instigating discussions of condom efficacy between teens and their parents, opening the door for sex education within the family. Analyses exploring whether conversations resulting from the episode were occurring among adolescents and parents who had already talked about condom use revealed that discussions of condom efficacy as a result of viewing were unrelated to prior conversations on the topic. This suggests that the program reopened some existing channels of communication, providing the opportunity for reinforcement of prior education by parents, and also helped some families to broach the topic for what may have been the first time. We assume that more discussion is positive, especially from parents' perspective, although we recognize this may not be true in all cases.

We observed few effects of the *Friends* episode on participants' condom-efficacy beliefs. Approximately 40% of viewers changed their beliefs from what they had been a few months earlier, when we last surveyed them. These changes could be real effects of viewing the condom episode if the program led to a search for more information about condom efficacy, or questioned adolescents' preexisting beliefs. However, these changes could also reflect instability in beliefs or their measurement over time that would have been observed regardless of episode viewing. We also observed little directional change in beliefs. Here we expected to find little change, because the complexity of the condom efficacy message could lead some adolescents to see condoms as more effective, and others as less. There was, however, a single exception to this null result: those who talked with parents about condom efficacy because of the *Friends* episode apparently came to see condoms as more effective. As noted, the episode accurately indicated both that condoms are effective and that condoms occasionally fail. Thus, parents could use the presented information to reinforce either or both of these messages. Although the episode itself did not sway teens either way on the issue, our finding concerning discussions with adults suggests that parents who talked to their kids may have emphasized condom effectiveness, rather than fallibility. This finding also reinforces the point that television may assist parents in their roles as sex educators, rather than substitute for them. Parents appear to have used the episode as a springboard for expression of their own views.

Although we did not observe strong effects of the *Friends* episode on condom beliefs, this should not be taken to indicate that television has little influence on sexual knowledge. Although the show we studied is one with which adolescents strongly identify, we looked at only one episode, and, as we have noted, the information it contained was ambiguous in its implications. Our finding that many young viewers retained the basic message about condoms and the more specific condom facts presented, even after 3 to 4 weeks, suggests that if sexual risk and responsibility portrayals were more prevalent on television and addressed subjects where the facts are less complex, the effects observed might well be powerful. A number of organizations are currently working to achieve this. The National Campaign to Prevent Teen Pregnancy and the Henry J. Kaiser Family Foundation currently work with television writers and producers to help them embed health messages in their entertainment programming.[4]. . .

Conclusions

The American Academy of Pediatrics has recommended that the broadcast industry adopt guidelines for responsible sexual content. The *Friends* episode studied herein would almost certainly meet these guidelines because of its portrayal of condom use. And our findings indicate that exposure to the program did have important educational effects. . . . Our results [also] suggest that families should . . . watch and discuss television together. . . . Finally, pediatricians should be notified by producers of entertainment programming when educational material is going to air on programs popular with youth. This would allow them to discuss the content with their patients and their parents.

References

1. Trends in sexual risk behaviors among high school students: United States, 1991–2001. *MMWR Morb Mortal Wkly Rep.* 2002;51:856–859.

2. Steyer JP. *The Other Parent: The Inside Story of the Media's Impact on Our Children.* New York, NY: Atria Books; 2002.

3. Kunkel D, Eyal K, Biely E, et al. *Sex on TV3: A Biennial Report to the Kaiser Family Foundation.* Santa Barbara, CA: Kaiser Family Foundation; 2003.

4. Brown JD, Keller SN. Can the mass media be healthy sex educators? *Fam Plann Perspect.* 2000;32:255–256.

5. Kaiser Family Foundation. *Teens, Sex and TV.* Menlo Park, CA: Kaiser Family Foundation; 2002.

6. Piotrow P, Rimon JG, Winnard K, et al. Mass media family planning promotion in three Nigerian cities. *Stud Fam Plann.* 1990;21:265–274.

7. Desmond RG, Singer JL, Singer DG, Calam R, Colimore K. Family mediation patterns and television viewing: young children's use and grasp of the medium. *Hum Commun Res.* 1985;11:461–480.

8. Brown JD, Newcomer SF. Television viewing and adolescents' sexual behavior. *J Homosex.* 1991;21:77–91.

9. Peterson JL, Moore KA, Furstenberg FF Jr. Television viewing and early initiation of sexual intercourse: is there a link? *J Homosex.* 1991;21:93–118.

10. Austin EW. Exploring the effects of active parental mediation of television content. *J Broadcast Electronic Media.* 1993;37:147–158.

POSTSCRIPT

Does Sex on TV Negatively Impact Adolescent Sexuality?

It is interesting that research conducted by the RAND Corporation found conflicting evidence for the effects of sex on TV. On the one hand, they present evidence that adolescents who viewed high levels of sexual content were more likely to initiate intercourse and progress to more advanced sexual activities during the subsequent year. They also reported that exposure to "talk about sex" on TV was associated with the same risks as exposure to sexual behaviour. In the second selection, however, the same researchers argued that sex on television could work in conjunction with parents to improve adolescent sexual knowledge and behaviours. Specifically, youth who watched sexual content on television with an adult and later discussed the content with an adult were more likely to benefit from the information than youth who did not watch with an adult or discuss the content with an adult. Why the conflicting reports? Upon examining the articles in more detail, one can find possible explanations.

In the first study, African American youths who watched content that included risks and responsibilities were less likely than other ethnic groups to initiate intercourse in the subsequent year. In the second selection, the content focused predominantly on risk factors, specifically contraception failure. In combining the findings from these two articles, it could be argued that when risk and responsibility factors are addressed in the sexual content, positive outcomes are possible. When sexual content involves sexual behaviours and intercourse without addressing risk and responsibility, negative outcomes result. In other words, adolescents with still-developing cognitive capacities may not be able to go beyond "the immediate messages" in the content. If sex is portrayed as irresponsible and enjoyable, adolescents process it as such and have a desire to imitate. On the other hand, when risks are addressed, they recognize the importance of safe sex. Furthermore, having an adult present during the program (i.e., a mature perspective) further enhances the adolescent's ability to interpret the messages effectively. Given that only 10 percent of popular teen programs include sexual content addressing risks and responsibilities might explain the negative outcomes in some studies. The positive outcomes may be explained in terms of specific content (i.e., risks and responsibilities) as well as the presence of an adult to support understanding. Further research is needed to clarify this issue.

References/Further Readings

Brodie, M., Foehr, U., Rideout, V., Baer, N., Miller, C., Flournoy, R., & Altman, D. (2001). Communicating health information through the entertainment media. *Health Affairs*, 20, 192–199.

Brown, J. D., & Keller, S. N. (2000). Can the mass media be healthy sex educators? *Family Planning Perspectives*, 32, 255–256.

Brown, J. D., & Witherspoon, E. M. (2002). The mass media and American adolescents' health. *Journal of Adolescent Health*, 31, 153–170.

Centers for Disease Control and Prevention. (2002). Trends in sexual risk behaviors among high school students—United States, 1991–2001. *Morbidity and Mortality Weekly Report*, 51, 856–859.

Kaiser Family Foundation Report. (2005). Sex on TV 4. The Henry J. Kaiser Family Foundation. Menlo Park, CA. http://www.kff.org.

Martino, S. C., Collins, R. L., Kanouse, D. E., Elliott, M., & Berry, S. H. (2005). Social cognitive processes mediating the relationship between exposure to television's sexual content and adolescents' sexual behaviour. *Journal of Personality and Social Psychology*, 89, 914–924.

Eyal, K., Kunkel, D., Biely, E. N., & Finnerty, K. L. (2007). Sexual socialization messages on television programs most popular among teens. *Journal of Broadcasting and Electronic Media*, 51 (2), 316–336.

Tolman, D. L., Kim, J. L., Schooler, D., & Sorsoli, C. L. (2007). Rethinking the associations between television viewing and adolescent sexuality development: Bringing gender into focus. *Journal of Adolescent Health*, 40, 84.e9-84.e16.

Ward, L. M., & Friedman, K. (2006). Using TV as a guide: Associations between television viewing and adolescents' sexual attitudes and behavior. *Journal of Research on Adolescence*, 16(1), 133–156.

ISSUE 18

Do Video Games Impede Adolescent Cognitive Development?

YES: Philip A. Chan and Terry Rabinowitz, from "A Cross-Sectional Analysis of Video Games and Attention Deficit Hyperactivity Disorder Symptoms in Adolescents," *Annals of General Psychiatry* (vol. 5, 2006)

NO: Jing Feng, Ian Spence, and Jay Pratt, from "Playing an Action Video Game Reduces Gender Differences in Spatial Cognition," *Psychological Science* (vol. 18, no. 10, 2007)

ISSUE SUMMARY

YES: Philip Chan, from Lifespan at Rhode Island Hospital, and Terry Rabinowitz, from the University of Vermont College of Medicine, report a significant association between playing video games and inattention and may lead to problems in school.

NO: Jing Feng, Ian Spence, and Jay Pratt, from the University of Toronto, report that playing video games can enhance spatial attention, which have been associated with success in mathematics and science courses.

Not surprising, research on adolescent cognition and intelligence focuses on the many variables in their lives that could have an impact on their developing brains. It has been documented in many studies how the media influences adolescent thinking and hence behavior. For example, as discussed in Issue 4, perceptions of body image, followed by eating and exercising behaviors, are greatly influenced by the media. A recent focus in the research is how different media forms can have a positive impact on cognition and contribute to performance gains at school and work. In particular, the relationship between playing video games and cognition is receiving much attention.

Video games were first introduced in 1958 with *Tennis for Two,* followed by *Spacewar* in 1961. The more popular *Pong* was released in 1972. This was the first generation of this new form of entertainment. Soon after, adventure games were introduced, followed by role playing games. Although the first games appeared mainly in video arcades, the home computer and smaller consoles brought them into people's homes. By the 1980s, online gaming and handheld liquid crystal display (LCD) games were introduced, and when the successful Nintendo Entertainment System emerged in 1985, gaming became a very popular form of entertainment. The 1990s saw the beginning of Internet gaming with real-time strategy (RTS) games where players were able to compete against each other online. First-person shooter games (FPS) also became popular during the 1990s. FPS is defined as a type of game with a first-person view, where the player maneuvers through a 3-D world, using the computer or television screen to see through the eyes of their character. The character's weapon and part of his/her hand is shown, almost always centered around the act of aiming and shooting at objects and/or the enemy (Schneider, Lang, Shin, & Bradley, 2004; Wikipedia, 2008).

By the end of the 1990s, Sony had introduced the PlayStation, and became a strong contender against Nintendo in the game industry. The twenty-first century continues to see advancements in technology and game sophistication, leading to more realistic and immersive games. This contributes to a more capturing and addictive form of entertainment. In fact, the video game industry has become so popular in recent years that it now rivals the film industry as the most profitable entertainment industry. Such success is due, in part, to the increasing number of people playing video games. It therefore comes as no surprise that research on the effects of playing video games has increased substantially in the last decade.

Most research has focused on the negative effects that video games have on social and emotional development, such as the relationship between violent video game play (e.g., *Mortal Kombat* and the *Grand Theft Auto* series) and aggressive and violent behaviors. Barlett, Harris, and Baldassaro (2007) reported a significant increase in hostility and aggression with increased play of a violent FPS video game. Uhlman and Swanson (2004) reported similar findings where individuals playing an FPS for 10 minutes attributed more aggressive actions and traits to themselves. Contrary to these negative findings, Ferguson (2007) in a meta-analysis of the research on video game violence effects found no support for either a correlational or causal relationship between violent game play and actual aggressive behavior. These mixed findings have led researchers to examine other variables that may be affected by video-game playing.

An area of research receiving increasing attention is the relationship between playing video games and cognitive development. More specifically, researchers are examining the impact of playing video games on attention span, executive functioning, and performance at school and work. As with the research on social and emotional development, the findings regarding cognitive development are mixed. Is it possible that playing video games and perhaps violent games enhances cognitive functioning? Or, does prolonged play have a negative impact on cognitive development and as such contribute to poor performance in school and work?

In the selections that follow, Philip Chan and Terry Rabinowitz argue that playing video games for more than one hour a day leads to inattention, which can have a negative impact on school performance. On the other hand, Jin Feng, Ian Spence, and Jay Pratt argue that playing video games and, in particular, FPS games require intense attentional resources which can result in superior spatial ability.

YES

Philip A. Chan and
Terry Rabinowitz

A Cross-Sectional Analysis of Video Games and Attention Deficit Hyperactivity Disorder Symptoms in Adolescents

Background

The Internet and other media types are reported to have important social and mental health effects in adolescents. The association between television viewing and obesity, attention disorders, school performance, and violence has been reported [1]. Likewise, recent studies on obsessive Internet use called "Internet Addiction" have shown negative effects on social health [2]. A significant relationship between Internet use and attention deficit hyperactivity disorder (ADHD) has also been shown in elementary school children. Other studies have reported the similarities between computer video game addiction and pathological gambling or substance dependence [3].

The effect of video games on adolescents is not well characterized despite a growing body of evidence demonstrating their addictive nature and popularity [4]. Indeed, video game use may exceed that of television use in children. . . . Most studies of mental health and media use did not specifically examine video games, but included them as a subset of television or Internet use. One extensively studied area is the content of video games and their relationship to subsequent aggressive behavior in children [5]. . . .

Despite recent negative attention, some studies have shown possible positive effects of video games on development. One study by Li et al. found a positive association between motor development and cognitive behavior in preschool age children [6]. Other studies have reported that previous computer game experience enhances laparoscopic simulator performance in physicians [7]. In addition, video games are more frequently being used as adjuncts to learning and training in various settings, including medical education [8].

The term "video games" does not always differentiate between console and Internet/computer video games but instead, suggests a loose clustering. Console video games include Nintendo, Sony Playstation, Microsoft

From *Annals of General Psychiatry*, 5:16, October 2006, excerpts from pp. 2–5, 10. Copyright © 2006 by Philip A. Chan. Reprinted by permission of the author.

Xbox, and others. Internet video games refer to computer games played online in a community setting with other players. Although similar in nature, several important differences exist. Console games can be played with other people, but most games are "single player" and are meant to be played alone. Internet games however, are designed for "multi-player" use and are played with others online, usually at distant sites. Console games are less expensive than Internet games, and do not require a computer. The genre of video games played on the Internet versus console games also differs in content. Console game themes include sports, action, strategy, family, puzzle, role-playing games, and simulation, while video game themes designed for Internet use are more specific and are mainly action and strategy. . . .

The relationship between video games and ADHD is unknown. The incidence of ADHD continues to rise and is a significant challenge on medical, financial, and educational resources. ADHD is a complex disorder that often requires input from the affected child or adolescent, teachers, parents, and physicians in order to be diagnosed correctly and treated successfully. The Conners' Parent Rating Scale (CPRS) [9] is the most widely used instrument to aid in the diagnosis of children with ADHD. . . .

This study examined the relationship between video game use and symptoms of ADHD. Other parameters studied included body mass index (BMI), school grades, work, detentions, and family situation.

Method

Design and Procedures

. . . Subjects were recruited from a local high school in Vermont. . . . Surveys were distributed to all 9th and 10th grade students at the school (n = 221). The survey included sections for students . . . and parents . . . to complete independently. . . . The final subject pool comprised 144; 72 each from parents and students. Original power calculations were based on a reported 10% prevalence of psychiatric disorders in the adolescent population and called for a total of 200 students for a power of 0.80. However, statistically significant results were reached after analysis of 144 completed questionnaires and led us to conclude that the study could be terminated at that point.

Measures

Time spent playing videos games, watching television, or using the Internet was assessed using a time scale of less than one hour, one to two hours, three to four hours, or greater than four hours. The student survey material included Young's Internet Addiction Scale, modified for video game use (YIAS-VG; internal consistency, alpha = 0.82) [10]. . . . The questions reflect the negative impact of video games on social functioning and relationships including excessive video game use, neglecting work and social life, anticipation, lack of control, and salience. Parents were surveyed using the Conners' Parent Rating Scale (CPRS; internal consistency, r = 0.57). The CPRS divides behavior into four categories: oppositional, hyperactivity, inattention, and ADHD. Other items included gender, family situation, exercise per week, detentions in the last month, work, and academic performance. Family situation was defined as either living with married parents or living with one parent who was divorced or separated. Academic performance was assessed by overall grade point average and last grade earned in both mathematics and English classes. . . .

Data Analysis

The dependent variables reported in numerical format (BMI, grades, YIAS-VG, CPRS) were analyzed using the student's t-test and the Mann-Whitney test. . . . Data reported as "yes/no" (sex, work, detentions, exercise, and family situation) was analyzed using the chi-square test. . . . Time spent playing video games, watching television, and using the internet was the independent variable. The time intervals compared were for student who spent less than one hour or greater than one hour on a particular activity. . . .

Results

The study cohort comprised 72 students; 31 males and 41 females in the ninth and tenth grade. Average age was 15.3 ± 0.7 years. . . . Almost 32% of students worked and 89% had parents who were married. Ten students had at least one detention in the last month and two students were involved in a physical fight in the last year. Four students consumed alcohol and one student reported daily smoking. Two students reported a diagnosis of ADHD and four reported having depression and/or anxiety.

The mean BMI for adolescents who watched less than one hour of television per day was 20.28 ± 2.33 and 22.11 ± 4.01 for those who watched more than one hour of television (p = 0.017). . . . There was a trend towards a higher BMI for adolescents spending more than one hour playing video games, but these results were not significant. No association was found between BMI and time spent on the Internet.

Students who played video games for more than one hour had significant increases in scores on the YIAS-VG (p < 0.001 for console and Internet video games). Other activities were associated with a trend toward increased YIAS-VG, but were not significant.

There was a significant increase in inattentive (p ≤ 0.001 for both Internet and console video games) and ADHD (p = 0.018 and 0.020 for console and Internet games, respectively) behavior in those who played video games for more than one hour. . . . No significant association was found between the hyperactivity or oppositional components of the CPRS and video game use. No significant relationship was found in any of the four categories and Internet or television use.

There was a trend toward lower grades in students who surf the Internet and play video games for more than one hour, but these results were not significant. . . . However, significantly lower grades were found between students who play video games for more than one hour and overall grade point average (GPA, p = 0.019 and 0.009 for console and Internet games, respectively).

Males were significantly more likely than females to spend greater than one hour a day playing console or internet video games (p < 0.001 and p = 0.003, respectively). Twenty males reported playing video games for more than one hour a day versus only one female adolescent reported playing internet video games for more than one hour. There was no significant relationship between gender and time spent watching television or on the Internet. We also found no significant association between time spent on any media form and students who worked, had married parents, received more detentions per month, or exercised more frequently.

Discussion

ADHD among children and adolescents has been attributed to both genetic and environmental factors. Of the media influences, only excessive Internet use has been reported to be associated with ADHD. The diagnosis of ADHD relies on input from teachers, parents, and physicians. This study found an increase in ADHD and inattention symptoms in adolescents who play video games for more than one hour a day.

The prevalence of ADHD in adolescents is reported to be 4–7%. This study found a prevalence of 8.3% based on a reported diagnosis by a parent. It was not possible to determine the actual diagnosis of ADHD based only on the raw scores of the CRPS. More or more severe symptoms of inattention and ADHD behavior were found in students who played video games for more than one hour, but further study is needed to more clearly understand the association between video games and ADHD. It is unclear whether playing video games for more than one hour leads to an increase in ADHD symptoms, or whether adolescents with ADHD symptoms spend more time on video games.

This study found no association between video games use and oppositional or aggressive behavior. Previous research has shown a positive correlation between violence in video games and aggressive behavior [1,5]. It is possible that video games only lead to this type of behavior in groups prone to violent behavior or in conjunction with other forms of violence in media. The power of this study was not designed to detect such differences, thus no inferences can be made.

The effect of television viewing on BMI has been reported in several studies. We found a significant association between increased BMI and watching television for more than one hour. Playing video games for more than one hour was not associated with an increase in BMI. Previous studies found a significant relationship between BMI and video games in younger populations. Our findings suggest this association may persist into early adolescence.

Time on the Internet was not associated with increased BMI; a trend towards decreasing BMI was found in adolescents who use the Internet for more than one hour. Our findings suggest that current recommendations to limit television and video game times for children should be followed.

Both console and Internet video games were associated with an increase in addiction scores as measured by YIAS-VG. The YIAS-VG assesses the degree to which video games negatively impact different social factors including daily activities, relationships, sleep, and daily thoughts. The increase in YIAS-VG scores imply that playing video games for more than one hour a day does have a negative impact on relationships and daily activity. We did not define a cutoff on the YIAS-VG to identify "excessive" video game use but the scores in our cohort were not high enough to be considered as evidence of "Internet Addiction" [4,10].

GPA was lower in those who played video games for more than one hour. Even though this study cohort had a relatively high overall GPA, the difference between an "A" (less than one hour of video games) versus a "B" (more than one hour of video games) is a significant change in grade. For students who are less academically proficient, this may be especially important. There was also a trend towards a lower GPA in students who watch television for more than one hour. Excessive television has been reported to be associated with poor school performance.

This investigation found that playing console and Internet video games for more than one hour a day has negative social and academic effects in adolescents. This association does not depend on being "addicted" to video games or playing for excessive time periods. Furthermore, there was no difference between playing video games on the Internet or on a console system. The intensive nature of video games is likely to cause this time dependent relationship between video games and behavior disorders, regardless of whether it is over the Internet or on a console system.

Several limitations of the study exist. This cross-sectional comparison of video games and ADHD does not allow for cause-effect relationships to be established. Therefore, it is impossible to say whether playing video games leads to an increase in ADHD symptoms, or if adolescents with more ADHD symptoms tend to spend longer times playing video games. Prospective studies to examine this relationship more closely are certainly justified. The subject cohort was also not representative of all groups. The large majority of students who responded to the survey were Caucasian, not involved with drugs or alcohol, had married parents, and did well in school. Thus, the association between video games and ADHD in other cohorts cannot be inferred. This study was designed to analyze adolescents who spent more than one hour of time playing video games. It would be interesting to examine the latter cohort in more detail to determine if there is a linear relationship between time spent playing video games and ADHD symptoms or academic performance, or if some other relationship exists among those who spend excessive time on these activities.

Conclusion

To our knowledge, this is the first study to find an association between video game use and ADHD symptoms in adolescents. . . .

References

1. Browne, K. D., & Hamilton-Giachritsis, C 2005: The influence of violent media on children and adolescents: A public-health approach. *Lancet*, **365**(9460): 702–710.

2. Shapira, N. A., Goldsmith, T. D., Keck, P. E. Jr., Khosla, U. M., & McElroy, S. L. 2000: Psychiatric features of individuals with problematic Internet use. *J Affect Disord*, **57**(1–3): 267–272. .

3. Tejeiro Salguero, R. A., Moran, R. M. 2002: Measuring problem video game playing in adolescents. *Addiction*, **97**(21): 1601–1606.

4. Johansson, A., & Gotestam, K. G. 2004: Internet addiction: Characteristics of a questionnaire and prevalence in Norwegian youth (12–18 years). *Scand J Psychol*, **45**(3): 223–229.

5. Gentile, D. A., Lynch, P. J., Linder, J.R., & Walsh, D.A. 2004: The effects of violent video game habits on adolescent hostility, aggressive behaviors, and school performance. *J Adolesc*, **27**(1): 5–22.

6. Li, X., & Atkins, M. S. 2004: Early childhood computer experience and cognitive and motor development. *Pediatrics*, **113**(6): 1715–1722.

7. Enochsson, L., Isaksson, B., Tour, R., Kjellin, A., Hedman, L., Wredmark, T., & Tsai-Fellander, L. 2004: Visuospatial skills and computer game experience influence the performance of virtual endoscopy. *J Gastrointest Surg*, **8**(7): 876–882. discussion 882.

8. Latessa, R., Harman, J. H. Jr., Hardee, S., & Scmidt-Dalton, T. 2004: Teaching medicine using interactive games: Development of the "stumpers" quiz show game. *Fam Med*, **36**(9): 616.

9. Conners, C. K., Sitarenios, G., Parker, J. D., & Epstein, J. N. 1998: The revised Conners' Parent Rating Scale (CPRS-R): Factor structure, reliability, and criterion validity. *J Abnorm Child Psychol*, **26**(4): 257–268.

10. Widyanto, L., & McMurran, M. 2004: The psychometric properties of the internet addiction test. *Cyberpsychol Behav*, **7**(4): 443–450.

Jing Feng, Ian Spence, and Jay Pratt  **NO**

Playing an Action Video Game Reduces Gender Differences in Spatial Cognition

T here is ample evidence that attentional processes are intimately involved in higher-level tasks in spatial cognition. Functional neuroimaging has linked mental rotation tasks to selective attention and the spatial distribution of attention; the right posterior parietal cortex (PPC) is strongly activated during tasks involving attention and mental rotation. Indeed, Coull and Frith (1998) have hypothesized that the right posterior parietal lobe (particularly the inferior parietal lobule) is involved in fundamental low-level attentional processes that "act as the lowest common denominator for many types of cognitive processes" (p. 185). Studies of visual neglect (Halligan, Fink, Marshall, & Vallar, 2003) also indicate that there is a close connection between selective spatial attention and the parietal lobes. Furthermore, the right PPC is important for selective spatial attention (Yantis & Serences, 2003), and it seems that an essential function of PPC is to shift attention among items in memory in order to keep them active (Lepsien & Nobre, 2006). This shifting of attention is likely critical for superior performance in mental rotation tasks.

Boys have always played different games than girls, and early recreational activities have often been cited as a major cause of gender differences in adult spatial cognition. In recent years, improvements in performance on a variety of high-level spatial tasks have been associated with playing video games (e.g., Law, Pellegrino, & Hunt, 1993). Because spatial attentional capacity is an important component of visual cognition, players who develop enhanced spatial attentional ability as a result of playing first-person shooter action games (Green & Bavelier, 2003, 2006) may also realize benefits in higher-level spatial cognition.

The first-person shooter action games that are appealing to boys, however, are not so attractive to girls (Quaiser-Pohl, Geiser, & Lehmann, 2006). Thus, boys may realize benefits in spatial attention that are largely denied to their female counterparts, who participate in such action games in much smaller numbers. The present study is the first to systematically investigate possible gender differences in low-level spatial attentional processes and their likely effects on higher-level spatial cognition.

From *Psychological Science*, vol. 18, no. 10, October 2007, excerpts from pp. 850–855. Copyright © 2007 by Association for Psychological Science. Reprinted by permission of Blackwell Publishing, Ltd.

Our first experiment investigated group differences—including gender differences—in spatial attention. In our second experiment, we explored the possibility that group differences in both low-level and higher-level spatial cognition might be modified. . . .

Experiment 1

In Experiment 1, we examined group differences in spatial attention for groups defined by gender, video-game-playing experience, and chosen field of study. We used the useful-field-of-view (UFOV) task to measure spatial attention. This well-established paradigm assesses the ability to detect, localize, and identify a target, and assesses the spatial distribution of attentional resources over a wide field of view (Edwards et al., 2005).

Method

Subjects

Undergraduates at the University of Toronto, Canada ($N = 48$; age range: 19–30 years), participated for course credit or compensation of $10/hr. The basic design was a between-subjects $2\times2\times2$ balanced factorial with 6 replications per cell. The factors were gender (male vs. female), video-game-playing experience (players vs. nonplayers), and field of study (arts vs. science). The players reported playing action video games for more than 4 hr per week, and the nonplayers reported no video-game play within the past 3 or more years. The science students were majoring in mathematics, physics, chemistry, biology, computer science, neuroscience, psychology (cognitive and neuroscience area), and cognitive science. The arts students were majoring in English literature, French, art history, fine arts, sociology, political science, economics, psychology (social area), and history. . . .

Stimuli

The stimuli were presented in an invisible circular area (63° in diameter) centered on a uniform light-gray screen. Each trial began with a centered, unfilled fixation square with a dark-gray border (3° × 3°). The fixation square was presented for 600 ms and then augmented by the stimulus display, which consisted of 24 similar distractor squares, each uniquely localized at an eccentricity of 10°, 20°, or 30° in one of eight equally spaced directions. On each trial, one randomly selected distractor square was replaced by the target, a dark-gray filled square (1.5° × 1.5°) surrounded by an unfilled circle with a dark-gray circumference (3° × 3°). The distractors were unfilled squares with dark-gray borders (3° × 3°), identical to the fixation square. When the target was located at an eccentricity of 10°, the stimulus display was presented for 10 ms; this duration was increased to 30 ms for eccentricities of 20° and 30°, to maintain a reasonable level of difficulty. After presentation of a task and then a response cue, subjects indicated in which of the eight possible directions the target had appeared.

Results and Discussion

Players were much superior (77% vs. 58%) to nonplayers, on average, $F(1, 40)$ = 34.38, $p_{rep} > .99$, $\eta^2 = .46$. There was also an effect of eccentricity, but no interactions involving eccentricity were significant. These findings replicate Green and Bavelier's (2003) UFOV results. . . . The science students outperformed the arts students (72% vs. 63%), $F(1, 40) = 6.99$, $p_{rep} = .95$, $\eta^2 = .15$, which suggests that students with superior attentional capacities may be drawn to careers in science. On average, males made more correct responses than females (71% vs. 64%), $F(1, 40) = 5.03$, $p_{rep} = .91$, $\eta^2 = .11$; most of this effect was due to the gender difference (64% vs. 52%) in the nonplayers, least significant difference in the means = 12% *(SE* = 5%), $p_{rep} = .94$. This experiment demonstrates—for the first time—a gender difference in spatial selective attention. Because the gender difference was much smaller in the players group than in the non-players group (and was not statistically significant in the players group), our second experiment was designed to determine whether or not the gender difference in spatial selective attention could be modified by training with a video game.

Experiment 2

In Experiment 2, we compared spatial attention and cognition in men and women before and after 10 hr of action-video-game training. A control group trained for 10 hr with a non-action game. Spatial attention was measured with the UFOV task used in Experiment 1. In addition, we assessed higher-level spatial abilities using a mental rotation test. We expected to find enhanced MRT performance as a by-product of improvements in spatial attentional capacity after training. Moreover, we expected that if the gender difference in selective attention was reduced after action-game training, the gender difference in MRT performance would also be reduced.

Method

Subjects

Twenty undergraduates (none of whom had participated in Experiment 1) were recruited. Six males and 14 females (age range: 18–32 years) participated and received $50 in compensation. All subjects reported no video-gaming experience during the preceding 4 years. Ten same-gender pairs were formed by matching individuals as closely as possible on their pretest scores in the UFOV task and MRT. One member of each pair was allocated at random to the experimental (action game) group, and the other member of the pair was assigned to the control (non-action game) group.

Tests

The UFOV task was as described in Experiment 1. The MRT used an AutoCAD-redrawn version of the Vandenberg and Kuse (1978) items. The 24 MRT items were presented in the normal order during the pretest. At posttest, the sequence was randomly reordered to make it difficult for subjects to recall their previous answers. Subjects had 3 min to complete as many items as possible.

Training
The experimental group was trained using *Medal of Honor: Pacific Assault,* which was chosen because it is similar to the games typically played by players in Experiment 1 and because it has been used before in attention training studies (Green & Bavelier, 2003). This game is a 3-D first-person shooter game that requires intense visual monitoring and attentional resources. The control group played *Ballance,* a 3-D puzzle game that involves steering a ball through a hovering maze of paths and rails with obstacles such as seesaws, suspension bridges, and pendulums.

Procedure
Subjects completed a pretest (UFOV task and MRT), 10 hr of individually supervised training with a video game (conducted in sessions of 1 to 2 hr in our laboratory within a maximum period of 4 weeks), and then a post-test (UFOV task and MRT). We had not originally planned a follow-up testing session; however, we were able to contact and retest all 20 subjects after an average interval of about 5 months (16–24 weeks).

Results and Discussion

After training, all subjects in the experimental group reported better shooting accuracy than when they started. Two subjects in the control group reached the maximum possible level of performance, and the others were very close to the maximum. Thus, both groups achieved substantial mastery of the games on which they were trained.

UFOV Task
Performance on the UFOV task showed no significant interactions involving eccentricity, so we collapsed the means over that factor. Because the follow-up data were collected 5 months (on average) after the main experiment was completed, these data were not included in the formal statistical analyses (analyses of variance). . . .

An improvement in UFOV was observed in the experimental group, but not in the control group. Performance of subjects who had trained with the action game improved substantially (from 61% to 74%), whereas there was no significant difference between pretest and posttest in the control group (from 61% to 63%). This finding replicates Green and Bavelier's (2003) finding that playing an action video game enhances spatial attention. However, the females benefited more (from 55% to 72%) than the males (from 68% to 78%), $F(1, 8) = 14.79$, $p_{rep} = .97$, $\eta^2 = .65$, and although the females did not quite reach the same level as the males, the posttest means were not statistically distinguishable (least significant difference, $p = .14$).

The 5-month follow-up means differed by gender. In the experimental group, the females maintained their level of performance, and the males increased their level by a small amount. However, 2 males in the experimental group had continued to play action video games in the interim (no other subjects had continued to play); this anomaly likely contributed to the improvement in the follow-up mean for males.

MRT

A square-root transformation of the number of correct items on the MRT was used to stabilize variance. Both males and females in the experimental group improved, but there was no significant change from pretest to post-test in the control group, $F(1, 16) = 7.33$, $p_{rep} = .94$, $\eta^2 = .31$; furthermore, the improvement in the experimental group was larger for females (2.0 to 2.7) than for males (2.9 to 3.2), $F(1, 8) = 5.193$, $p_{rep} = .87$, $\eta^2 = .39$, and the performance of the females on the posttest was indistinguishable from that of the males in the control group. Although the gender difference on the MRT was not eliminated, its size was much reduced. . . .

General Discussion

Playing an action video game can differentially enhance males' and females' performance on spatial tasks: Females showed larger improvements than males, such that prior gender differences were virtually eliminated (UFOV task) or reduced (MRT). Both males and females (with no prior video-gaming experience) in Experiment 2 either reached or closely approached the average UFOV performance of players in Experiment 1, and follow-up testing suggests that these gains were persistent. This finding is remarkable and implies that the underlying processes in the brain are qualitatively different from those in more typical cases of skill acquisition through practice—generally these show decay if there is no continued practice to maintain the level of skill.

Improvement in MRT performance as a function of training is not a novel finding. What is new here is that the improvement in MRT performance paralleled the improvement in UFOV and that the females realized greater gains in both tasks. This result supports our contention that MRT performance depends, at least in part, on lower-level capacities in spatial attention. Our study differs from previous training studies in another respect: Because our control group received a treatment (training on a non-action game), our results clarify the training effects of particular video games on MRT performance. Some previous studies found that video-game practice had little or no effect (e.g., Peters et al., 1995), implying that improved performance on spatial tasks after video-game practice may depend on the kinds of spatial abilities that are needed in the game and in the spatial task (Ogakaki & Frensch, 1994). Our data support this contention: We found no improvement in either UFOV or the MRT after training with a non-action game. Non-action games may be less likely to have a beneficial effect because they do not sufficiently exercise spatial attentional capacities.

Spatial abilities—including mental rotation ability—have been associated with success in mathematics and science courses (Delgado & Prieto, 2004), performance on standardized tests, and the choice of mathematics and science as majors in college. Although superior performance on tasks of spatial ability, such as the MRT, is strongly associated with success in the mathematical and engineering sciences, one does not *cause* the other. Rather, both are supported by lower-level cognitive capacities, and our data suggest that selective attention and the ability to distribute attention spatially are critically important building blocks of spatial cognition. Our second experiment has shown that spatial attentional capacity and a higher-level spatial function may be improved simultaneously by appropriate training.

Superior spatial ability is related to employment in engineering and science, and females, who typically score lower than males on tests of spatial skills, are underrepresented in these fields, with worldwide participation rates as low as one in five. Given that our first experiment and others (e.g., McGillicuddy-De Lisi & De Lisi, 2002) have shown that particular cognitive capacities are associated with educational and career choices, training with appropriately designed action video games could play a significant role as part of a larger strategy designed to interest women in science and engineering careers (Quaiser-Pohl et al., 2006). Non-video-game players in our study realized large gains after only 10 hr of training; we can only imagine the benefits that might be realized after weeks, months, or even years of action-video-gaming experience.

References

Castel, A.D., Pratt, J., & Drummond, E. (2005). The effects of action video game experience on the time course of inhibition of return and the efficiency of visual search. *Acta Psychologica, 119,* 217–230.

Coull, J.T., & Frith, C.D. (1998). Differential activation of right superior parietal cortex and intraparietal sulcus by spatial and nonspatial attention. *NeuroImage, 8,* 176–187.

Delgado, A.R., & Prieto, G. (2004). Cognitive mediators and sex-related differences in mathematics. *Intelligence, 32,* 25–32.

Edwards, J.D., Vance, D.E., Wadley, V.G., Cissell, G.M., Roenker, D.L., & Ball, K.K. (2005). Reliability and validity of useful field of view test scores as administered by personal computer. *Journal of Clinical and Experimental Neuropsychology, 27,* 529–543.

Green, C.S., & Bavelier, D. (2003). Action video game modifies visual selective attention. *Nature, 423,* 534–537.

Green, C.S., & Bavelier, D. (2006). Effect of action video games on the spatial distribution of visuospatial attention. *Journal of Experimental Psychology: Human Perception and Performance, 32,* 1465–1478.

Halligan, P.W., Fink, G.R., Marshall, J.C., & Vallar, G. (2003). Spatial cognition: Evidence from visual neglect. *Trends in Cognitive Sciences, 7,* 125–133.

Law, D.L., Pellegrino, J.W., & Hunt, E.B. (1993). Comparing the tortoise and the hare: Gender and experience in dynamic spatial reasoning tasks. *Psychological Science, 49,* 35–40.

Lepsien, J., & Nobre, A.C. (2006). Cognitive control of attention in the human brain: Insights from orienting attention to mental representations. *Brain Research, 1105,* 20–31.

McGillicuddy-De Lisi, A., & De Lisi, R. (Eds.). (2002). *Biology, society, and behavior: The development of sex differences in cognition.* Westport, CT: Ablex.

Ogakaki, L., & Frensch, P.A. (1994). Effects of video game playing on measures of spatial performance: Gender effects in late adolescence. *Journal of Applied Developmental Psychology, 15,* 33–58.

Peters, M., Laeng, B., Latham, K., Jackson, M., Zaiyouna, R., & Richardson, C. (1995). A redrawn Vandenberg and Kuse mental rotations test: Different versions and factors that affect performance. *Brain and Cognition, 28,* 39–58.

Quaiser-Pohl, C. Geiser, C. & Lehmann, W. (2006). The relationship between computer-game preference, gender, and mental-rotation ability. *Personality and Individual Differences, 40,* 609–619.

Vandenberg, S.G., & Kruse, A.R. (1978). Mental rotations: Group tests of three-dimensional spatial visualization. *Perceptual and Motor Skills, 47,* 599–604.

Yantis, S., & Serences, J.T. (2003). Cortical mechanisms of space-based and object-based attentional control. *Current Opinion in Neurobiology, 13,* 187–193.

POSTSCRIPT

Do Video Games Impede Adolescent Cognitive Development?

Academic performance and educational success is a goal for many youth and certainly a goal that parents have for their children. Enhancing cognitive development therefore is on the minds of parents and educators. While at school, children are engaged in tasks that contribute to cognitive development. Outside of school, however, there is concern that children are not engaged in activities that further develop their cognitive capacities. An activity receiving much attention is video-game playing. While some parents and educators criticize video-game playing and especially violent action games, others believe they can benefit children. The two selections for this issue are excellent examples of these opposing views.

Jing Feng, Ian Spence, and Jay Pratt found that playing an action FPS video game (*Medal of Honor: Pacific Assault*) can enhance cognitive development, in particular spatial attention and mental rotation ability. Their findings are important, especially for women, who showed larger improvements on spatial tasks than men. Feng et al. argue that superior spatial ability is associated with engineering and science and women more than men avoid these careers. They conclude that playing an action video game could enhance cognitive development while at the same time increase interest in science and engineering for women. Feng et al.'s conclusions support previous studies showing a positive correlation between video-game playing and tests of attention (Andrews and Murphy, 2006; Green & Bavelier, 2003).

Philip Chan and Terry Rabinowitz, on the other hand, reported negative effects of video-game playing on attention and performance. They examined the relationship between time spent playing video games (both console and Internet) and academic functioning. Their results indicated that adolescents who played a video game for more than one hour a day had significantly lower grade point averages and lower scores on the inattention component of an ADHD measure. They concluded that playing video games can contribute to inattention and increase problems at school. For children with ADHD, video games can intensify their symptoms. Chan and Rabinowitz's recent research and conclusions contradict previous findings. Future research is strongly recommended to either support the findings reported by Chan and Rabinowitzs' or to further support the positive outcomes of playing action video games. In the meantime, these selections raise awareness of the effects (both positive and negative) that action video games can have on cognitive development.

References/Further Readings

Andrews, G., & Murphy, K. (2006). Does video-game playing improve executive function? In Michael A. Vanchevsky (Ed.), *Frontiers in cognitive psychology* (pp. 145–161). New York: Nova Science Publishers, Inc.

Barlett, C. P., Harris, R. J., & Baldassaro, R. (2007). Longer you play, the more hostile you feel: Examination of first-person shooter video games and aggression during video game play. *Aggressive Behaviour,* 33, 486–497.

Ferguson, C. J. (2007). Evidence for publication bias in video game violence effects literature: A meta-analytic review. *Aggression and Violent Behavior,* 12, 470–482.

Green, C. S., & Bavelier, D. (2003). Action video-game modifies visual selective attention. *Nature,* 423, 534–537.

Schneider, E., Lang, A., Shin, M., & Bradley, S. (2004). Death with a story: How story impacts emotional, motivational, and physiological responses to first-person shooter video games. *Human Communication Research,* 30, 361–375.

Uhlmann, E., & Swanson, J. (2004). Exposure to violent video games increases automatic aggressiveness. *Journal of Adolescence,* 27, 41–52.

ISSUE 19

Are Social Networking Sites (SNSs), such as Facebook, a Cause for Concern among Adolescents?

YES: Ralph Gross and Alessandro Acquisti, from "Information Revelation and Privacy in Online Social Networks (The Facebook Case)," *In Proceedings of the 2005 ACM Workshop on Privacy in the Electronic Society,* ACM Press, New York (2005)

NO: Nicole B. Ellison, Charles Steinfield, and Cliff Lampe, from "The Benefits of Facebook 'Friends': Social Capital and College Students' Use of Online Social Network Sites," *Journal of Computer-Mediated Communication* (vol. 12, 2007)

ISSUE SUMMARY

YES: Ralph Gross, and Alessandro Acquisti, Carnegie Mellon University, argue that participation in social networking sites, such as Facebook, exposes users to both physical and cyber risks.

NO: Researchers Nicole Ellison, Charles Steinfield, and Cliff Lampe from the Department of Telecommunication, Information Studies, and Media, at Michigan State University present evidence suggesting a strong positive association between Facebook and social capital, self-esteem, and life satisfaction.

The ways in which adolescents communicate with and maintain friends have become more complex in recent years. Gone are the days where face-to-face or phone conversations are the norm. Adolescents today are using modern technology to interact with their friends and acquaintances. In particular, social networking sites (SNSs) have become increasingly popular.

Social networking sites are open or semi-open public systems (Valkenburg, Peter, & Shouten, 2006) where anyone can join at any time (open) or an individual is invited to join by another member (semi-open). There are numerous SNSs available and although they all have features in common, they vary as a function of purpose. For example, *Match.com* is a dating site, *Bookcrossing.com* is an interest site, and *Friendster, MySpace,* or *Facebook* are friendship sites. The focus of this Taking Sides issue is on friendship sites such as *Facebook*, which started in 2004 as a Harvard-only SNS (Cassidy, 2006). The initial goal of Facebook at Harvard (and later at other universities) was to support college/university networks. It has since spread to the point where users can connect with all friends, regardless of location, as well as friends they have lost touch with from childhood, high school, university, previous workplaces, and/or previous communities. Not only do users connect and stay in touch with each other but they can also view personal information about each other. With Facebook, for example, users create a very detailed, unique profile typically containing name, email address, personal address, phone number, school affiliation, major, gender, religion, hometown, birthdate, sexual orientation, relationship status, interests, job/occupation, favorite music, favorite books, favorite movies, friend network, and photos.

A user's Facebook site with his/her profile is called a homepage or "wall" and they as well as their "friends" can post messages there. The messaging feature can either be private (similar to email) or public (all who have access to the user's profile can read the posted messages). In addition to the personal information on each homepage, users can add modules ("applications" such as interest groups, travel logs, or photo albums), and/or join networks (organized by city, school, workplace etc.). The photo album application is very popular because users can share photos from recent events and travels. In addition, users can identify all other people in their photos (called tagging). This permits any user with access to the album to view and share pictures of people who are tagged. All applications and networks added can be viewed by those with access to the user's profile unless the user specifically denies access.

Once a Facebook is setup, a user can add friends or have others add them. This is done with a message such as "Susan has added you as a friend on Facebook. We need to confirm that you are, in fact, friends with Susan." Each new "friend" is added to the user's Friends list. This list is then visible to anyone who has access to the user's profile, resulting in somewhat of a popularity contest. As a result, users will increase their Friends list by adding distant acquaintances and sometimes complete strangers.

There is little doubt that Facebook is convenient and effective for keeping in touch with "friends"; however, there are concerns about Facebook as well. First, it is argued that it is addictive. With an increasing number of adolescents using Facebook, a Friends list can include as many as several hundred "friends." This equates into many hours reading homepages and writing on walls. Second, there are privacy concerns with information being displayed on these homepages. Although Facebook includes numerous tools available to protect privacy, many users are not using the tools. While it has been reported that the majority of users feel "safe" displaying personal information, they in fact have "zero privacy" (Regan, 2003). Specifically, Facebook administrators have access to a database about who knows who, and how they know them.

The issues surrounding SNSs have increasingly led to more research examining their impact on adolescent well-being. Are friendships enhanced with Facebook? Are Facebook users at risk for privacy attacks? Are employers using Facebook to check up on employees? Are online social networks healthy? Ralph Gross and Alessandro Acquisti provide evidence for the dangers of having and using social network sites. On the other hand, Nicole Ellison, Charles Steinfield, and Cliff Lampe present evidence suggesting that Facebook can build and maintain social capital, self-esteem, and life satisfaction.

**Ralph Gross and
Alessandro Acquisti**

Information Revelation and Privacy in Online Social Networks (The Facebook Case)

1. Evolution of Online Networking

In recent years online social networking has moved from niche phenomenon to mass adoption. Although the concept dates back to the 1960s . . ., viral growth and commercial interest only arose well after the advent of the Internet. The rapid increase in participation in very recent years has been accompanied by a progressive diversification and sophistication of purposes and usage patterns across a multitude of different sites. . . .

While boundaries are blurred, most online networking sites share a core of features: through the site an individual offers a "profile"—a representation of their sel[ves] (and, often, of their own social networks)—to others to peruse, with the intention of contacting or being contacted by others, to meet new friends or dates (Friendster, Orkut), find new jobs (LinkedIn), receive or provide recommendations (Tribe), and much more.

It is not unusual for successful social networking sites to experience periods of viral growth with participation expanding at rates topping 20% a month. Liu and Maes estimate in [5] that "well over a million self-descriptive personal profiles are available across different web-based social networks" in the United States, and Leonard, already in 2004, reported in [4] that world-wide "[s]even million people have accounts on Friendster. [...] Two million are registered to MySpace. A whopping 16 million are supposed to have registered on Tickle for a chance to take a personality test."

The success of these sites has attracted the attention of the media and researchers. The latter have often built upon the existing literature on social network theory to discuss its online incarnations. In particular . . . issues of trust and intimacy in online networking; . . . participants' strategic representation of their selves to others; and . . . harvesting online social network profiles to obtain a distributed recommender system.

In this paper, we focus on patterns of personal information revelation and privacy implications associated with online networking. Not only are the participation rates to online social networking staggering among

From *Proceedings of the ACM Workshop on Privacy in the Electronic Society,* WPES 2005, pp. 71–80. Copyright © 2005 by Association for Computing Machinery. Reprinted by permission. http://doi.acm.org/10.1145/1102199.1102214.

certain demographics; so, also, are the amount and type of information participants freely reveal. Category-based representations of a person's broad interests are a recurrent feature across most networking sites [5]. Such categories may include indications of a person's literary or entertainment interests, as well as political and sexual ones. In addition, personally identified or identifiable data (as well as contact information) are often provided, together with intimate portraits of a person's social or inner life.

Such apparent openness to reveal personal information to vast networks of loosely defined acquaintances and complete strangers calls for attention. We investigate information revelation behavior in online networking using actual field data about the usage and the inferred privacy preferences of more than 4,000 users of a site catered to college students, the Facebook. Our results provide a preliminary but detailed picture of personal information revelation and privacy concerns (or lack thereof) in the wild, rather than as discerned through surveys and laboratory experiments. . . .

2. Information Revelation and Online Social Networking

While social networking sites share the basic purpose of online interaction and communication, specific goals and patterns of usage vary significantly across different services. . . .

First, the pretense of identifiability changes across different types of sites. The use of real names to (re)present an account profile to the rest of the online community may be *encouraged* . . . in . . . Facebook, that aspire to connect participants' profiles to their public identities. The use of real names may be tolerated but filtered in dating/connecting sites like Friendster. . . . Or, the use of real names and personal contact information could be openly *discouraged,* as in pseudonymous-based dating websites like Match.com. . . .

Second, the type of information revealed or elicited often orbits around hobbies and interests. . . . These include: semi-public information such as current and previous schools and employers . . .; private information such as drinking and drug habits and sexual preferences and orientation . . .; and open-ended entries. . . .

Third, visibility of information is highly variable. In certain sites (especially the ostensibly pseudonymous ones) any member may view any other member's profile. . . . Such visibility tuning controls become even more refined on sites which make no pretense of pseudonymity, like the Facebook.

And yet, across different sites, anecdotal evidence suggests that participants are happy to disclose as much information as possible to as many people as possible. . . .

2.1 Social Network Theory and Privacy

. . . The application of social network theory to the study of information revelation (and, implicitly, privacy choices) in online social networks highlights significant differences between the offline and the online scenarios.

First, offline social networks are made of ties that can only be loosely categorized as weak or strong ties, but in reality are extremely diverse in terms of how close and intimate a subject perceives a relation to be. Online social networks, on the other side, often reduce these nuanced connections to simplistic binary relations: "Friend or not" [1]. . . .

Second, while the number of strong ties that a person may maintain on a social networking site may not be significantly increased by online networking technology, . . . "the number of weak ties one can form and maintain may be able to increase substantially, because the type of communication that can be done more cheaply and easily with new technology is well suited for these ties" [2] (p. 80).

Third, while an offline social network may include up to a dozen of intimate or significant ties and 1000 to 1700 "acquaintances" or "interactions" . . . [2] . . ., an online social networks can list hundreds of direct "friends" and include hundreds of thousands of additional friends within just three degrees of separation from a subject.

This implies online social networks are both vaster and have more weaker ties, on average, than offline social networks. . . . Hence, trust in and within online social networks may be assigned differently and have a different meaning than in their offline counterparts. . . .

2.2 Privacy Implications

Privacy implications associated with online social networking depend on the level of identifiability of the information provided, its possible recipients, and its possible uses. Even social networking websites that do not openly expose their users' identities may provide enough information to identify the profile's owner. This may happen, for example, through face re-identification. . . . Since users often re-use the same or similar photos across different sites, an identified face can be used to identify a pseudonym profile with the same or similar face on another site. Similar re-identifications are possible through demographic data, but also through category-based representations of interests that reveal unique or rare overlaps of hobbies or tastes. . . .

To whom may identifiable information be made available? First of all, . . . the hosting site, that may use and extend the information (both knowingly and unknowingly revealed by the participant) in different ways. . . . Second, the easiness of joining and extending one's network, and the lack of basic security measures . . . at most networking sites make it easy for third parties . . . to access participants data without the site's direct collaboration. . . .

How can that information be used? . . . Risks range from identity theft to online and physical stalking; from embarrassment to price discrimination and blackmailing. . . .

While privacy may be at risk in social networking sites, information is willingly provided. Different factors are likely to drive information revelation in online social networks. The list includes signalling . . . [2], because the perceived benefit of selectively revealing data to strangers may appear larger than the perceived costs of possible privacy invasions; peer pressure and herding behavior; relaxed attitudes towards . . . personal privacy; incomplete information . . .; faith in the networking service or trust in its members; myopic evaluation of privacy risks; or the service's own user interface.

We do not attempt to ascertain the relative impact of different drivers in this paper. However, in the following sections we present data on actual behavioral patterns of information revelation and inferred privacy attitudes in a college-targeted networking site. . . .

3. The Facebook.Com

Many users of social networking sites are of college age [1], and recent ventures have started explicitly catering . . . to specific colleges (e.g., the Facebook.com . . .).

College-oriented social networking sites provide opportunities to combine online and face-to-face interactions within an ostensibly bounded domain. This makes them different from traditional networking sites: they are communities based "on a shared real space." . . .

Since many of these sites require a college's email account for a participant to be admitted to the online social network of that college, expectations of validity of certain personal information provided by others on the network may increase. Together with the apparent sharing of a physical environment with other members of the network, that expectation may increase the sense of trust and intimacy across the online community. And yet, since these services can be easily accessed by outsiders . . . and since members can hardly control the expansion of their own network . . ., such communities turn out to be more *imagined* than real, and privacy expectations may not be matched by privacy reality.

The characteristics mentioned above make college-oriented networking sites intriguing candidates for our study of information revelation and privacy preferences. In the rest of this paper we analyze data gathered from the network of Carnegie Mellon University (CMU) students enlisted on one of such sites, the Facebook.

The Facebook . . . validates CMU-specific network accounts by requiring the use of CMU email addresses for registration and login. Its interface grants participants very granular control on the searchability and visibility of their personal information. . . . The default settings . . . are set to make the participants profile *searchable* by anybody else in any school in the Facebook network, and make its actual content *visible* to any other user at the same college. . . .

The Facebook is straightforward about the usage it plans for the participants' personal information: . . .its privacy policy reports that the site *will* collect additional information about its users. . . . The policy also reports that participants' information may include information that the participant has not knowingly provided (. . . IP address), and that personal data may be shared with third parties.

3.1 Access Tools

In June 2005, we separately searched for all "female" and all "male" profiles for CMU Facebook members using the website's advanced search feature and extracted their profile IDs. . . . We then downloaded a total of 4540 profiles— virtually the entire CMU Facebook population at the time of the study.

3.2 Demographics

The majority of users of the Facebook at CMU are undergraduate students (3345 or 73.7% of all profiles). This corresponds to 62.1% of the total undergraduate population at CMU. Graduate students, staff and faculty are represented to a much lesser extent (6.3%, 1.3%, and 1.5% of the CMU population, respectively). The majority of users is male (60.4% vs. 39.2%). . . . The vast majority of users (95.6%) falls in the 18–24 age bracket. Overall the average age is 21.04 years. . . .

3.3 Types and Amount of Information Disclosed

. . . CMU users of the Facebook provide an astonishing amount of information: 90.8% of profiles contain an image, 87.8% of users reveal their birth date, 39.9% list a phone number (including 28.8% of profiles that contain a cellphone number), and 50.8% list their current residence. The majority of users also disclose their dating preferences (male or female), current relationship status (single, married, or in a relationship), political views (from "very liberal" to "very conservative"), and various interests (including music, books, and movies). A large percentage of users (62.9%) that list a relationship status other than single even identify their partner by name and/or link to their Facebook profile. . . .

Across most categories, the amount of information revealed by female and male users is very similar. A notable exception is the phone number, disclosed by substantially more male than female users (47.1% vs. 28.9%). *Single* male users tend to report their phone numbers in even higher frequencies, thereby possibly *signalling* their elevated interest in making a maximum amount of contact information easily available. . . .

3.4 Data Validity and Data Identifiability

The terms of service of the site encourage users to only publish profiles that directly relate to them and not to other entities, people or fictional characters. In addition, in order to sign up with the Facebook a valid email address of one of the more than 500 academic institutions that the site covers has to be provided. This requirement, along with the site's mission of organizing the real life social networks of their members, provides incentives for users to only publish accurate information. . . .

. . . Determining the accuracy of the information provided by users on the Facebook . . . is nontrivial for all but selected individual cases. We therefore restrict our validity evaluation to the measurement of the manually determined *perceived* accuracy of information on a randomly selected subset of 100 profiles.

. . . We manually categorized the names given on Facebook profiles as being one of the following:

1. Real Name
   Name appears to be real.
2. Partial Name
   Only a first name is given.
3. Fake Name
   Obviously fake name.

. . . We found 89% of all names to be realistic and likely the true names for the users (for example, can be matched to the visible CMU email address provided as login), with only 8% of names obviously fake. The percentage of people that choose to only disclose their first name was very small: 3%. . . .

As comparison, 98.5% of the profiles that include a birthday actually report the *fully identified* birth date (day, month, and year). . . .

The vast majority of profiles contain an image (90.8%). . . . While there is no explicit requirement to provide a facial image, the majority of users do so. In order to assess the quality of the images provided we manually labelled them into one of four categories:

1. Identifiable
   Image quality is good enough to enable person recognition.
2. Semi-Identifiable
   The profile image shows a person, but due to the image composition or face pose the person is not directly recognizable. . . .
3. Group Image
   The image contains more than one face and no other profile information . . . can be used to identify the user in the image.
4. Joke Image
   Images clearly not related to a person. . . .

. . . In the majority of profiles the images are suitable for direct identification (61%). Overall, 80% of images contain at least some information useful for identification. Only a small subset of 12% of all images are clearly not related to the profile user. . . .

. . . Facebook users typically maintain a very large network of friends. On average, CMU Facebook users list 78.2 friends at CMU and 54.9 friends at other schools. 76.6% of users have 25 or more CMU friends, whereas 68.6% of profiles show 25 or more non-CMU friends. . . .

3.5 Data Visibility and Privacy Preferences

For any user of the Facebook, other users fall into four different categories: friends, friends of friends, non-friend users at the same institution and non-friend users at a different institution. By default, everyone on the Facebook appears in searches of everyone else, independent of the searchers' institutional affiliation. In search results the users' full names . . . appear along with the profile image, the academic institution that the user is attending, and the users' status there. The Facebook reinforces this default settings by labelling it "recommended" on the privacy preference page. Also by default the full profile (including contact information) is visible to everyone else at the same institution.

Prior research . . . has shown that users tend to not change default settings [6]. . . .

We tested how much CMU Facebook users take advantage of the ability the site provides to manage their presentation of sel[ves]. By creating accounts at different institutions, and by using accounts with varying degree of interconnectedness with the rest of the CMU network, we were able to infer how individual users within the CMU network were selecting their own privacy preference.

We first measured the percentage of users that changed the search default setting away from being searchable to everyone on the Facebook to only being searchable to CMU users. . . . Only 1.2% of users (18 female, 45 male) made use of this privacy setting.

. . . We then evaluated the number of CMU users that changed profile visibility by restricting access to CMU users. We used the list of profile IDs currently in use at CMU and evaluated which percentage of profiles were fully accessible to an unconnected user (not friend or friend of friend of any profile). Only 3 profiles (0.06%) . . . did not fall into this category.

. . . We can conclude that only a vanishingly small number of users change the . . . default privacy preferences. In general, fully identifiable information such as personal image and first and last name is available to anybody registered at any Facebook member network. Since the Facebook boasts a 80% average participation rate among undergraduate students at the hundreds of US institutions it covers, and since around 61% of our CMU subset provides identifiable face images, it is relatively easy for anybody to gain access to these data. . . . In other words, information suitable for creating a brief digital dossier consisting of name, college affiliation, status and a profile image can be accessed for the vast majority of Facebook users by anyone on the website. . . .

Additional personal data—such as political and sexual orientation, residence address, telephone number, class schedule, etc.—are made available by the majority of users to anybody else at the same institution, leaving such data accessible to any subject able to obtain even temporary control of an institution's single email address.

4. Privacy Implications

It would appear that the population of Facebook users we have studied is, . . . quite oblivious, unconcerned, or just pragmatic about their personal privacy. Personal data is generously provided and limiting privacy preferences are sparingly used. Due to the variety and richness of personal information disclosed in Facebook profiles, their visibility, their public linkages to the members' real identities, and the scope of the network, users may put themselves at risk for a variety of attacks on their physical and online persona. . . .

4.1 Stalking

. . . Facebook profiles include information about residence location, class schedule, and location of last login. A students' life during college is mostly dominated by class attendance. Therefore, knowledge of both the residence and a few classes that the student is currently attending would help a potential stalker to determine the user's whereabouts. In the CMU population 860 profiles fall into our definition of this category (280 female, 580 male). . . . Since our study was conducted outside of the semester (when many students might have deleted class information from their profiles) we speculate this number to be even higher during the semester.

A much larger percentage of users is susceptible to a form of cyberstalking using the AOL instant messenger (AIM). Unlike other messengers, AIM allows users to add "buddies" to their list without knowledge of or confirmation from the buddy being added. Once on the buddy list the adversary can track when the user is online. In the CMU population 77.7% of all profiles list an AIM screen name for a total of more than 3400 users.

4.2 Re-identification

. . . It has been shown previously that a large portion of the US population can be re-identified using a combination of 5-digit ZIP code, gender, and date of birth. The vast majority of CMU users disclose both their full birthdate (day and year) and gender on their profiles (88.8%). For 44.3% of users (total of 1676) the combination of birthdate and gender is unique within CMU. In addition, 50.8% list their current residence, for which ZIP codes can be easily obtained. Overall, 45.8% of users list birthday, gender, and current residence. . . .

In a related study we were able to correctly link facial images from Friendster profiles without explicit identifiers with images obtained from fully identified CMU web pages using a commercial face recognizer. . . . As shown in Section 3.4 a large number of profiles contain high quality images. At CMU more than 2500 profiles fall in this category. . . .

An additional re-identification risk lies in making birthdate, hometown, current residence, and current phone number publicly available at the same time. This information can be used to estimate a person's social security number and exposes her to identity theft.

The first three digits of a social security number reveal where that number was created. . . . The next two digits are group identifiers, which are assigned according to a peculiar but predictable temporal order. The last four digits are progressive serial numbers.

When a person's hometown is known, the window of the first three digits of her SSN can be identified with probability decreasing with the home state's populousness. When that person's birthday is also known, and an attacker has access to SSNs of other people with the same birthdate in the same state as the target . . ., it is possible to pin down a window of values in which the two middle digits are likely to fall. The last four digits (often used in unprotected logins and as passwords) can be retrieved through social engineering. Since the vast majority of the Facebook profiles we studied not only include birthday and hometown information, but also current phone number and residence (often used for verification purposes by financial institutions and other credit agencies), users are exposing themselves to substantial risks of identity theft.

4.3 Building a Digital Dossier

The privacy implications of revealing personal and sensitive information (such as sexual orientation and political views) may extend beyond their immediate impact, which can be limited. Given the low and decreasing costs of storing digital information, it is possible to continuously monitor the evolution of the network and its users' profiles, thereby building a digital dossier for its participants. College students, even if currently not concerned about the visibility of their personal information, may become so as they enter sensitive and delicate jobs a few years from now—when the data currently mined could still be available.

4.4 Fragile Privacy Protection

One might speculate that the *perceived* privacy protection of making personal information available only to members of a campus community may increase Facebook users' willingness to reveal personal information. However, the mechanisms protecting this social network can be circumvented. Adding to this the recognition that users have little control on the composition of their own networks (because often a member's friend can introduce strangers into that member's network), one may conclude that the personal information users are revealing even on sites with access control and managed search capabilities effectively becomes *public* data.

The Facebook verifies users as legitimate members of a campus community by sending a confirmation email containing a link with a seemingly randomly generated nine digit code to the (campus) email address provided during registration. Since the process of signing up and receiving the confirmation email only takes minutes, an adversary simply needs to gain access to the campus network for a very short period of time. . . .

. . . Social engineering is a well-known practice in computer security to obtain confidential information by manipulating legitimate users. . . . Implementation of this practice on the Facebook is very simple: just ask to be added as someone's friend. The surprisingly high success rate of this practice was recently demonstrated by a Facebook user who, using an automatic script, contacted 250,000 users of the Facebook across the country and asked to be added as their friend. According to [3], 75,000 users accepted: thirty percent of Facebook users are willing to make all of their profile information available to a random stranger and his network of friends. . . .

5. Conclusions

Online social networks are both vaster and looser than their offline counterparts. It is possible for somebody's profile to be connected to hundreds of peers directly, and thousands of others through the network's ties. Many individuals in a person's online extended network would hardly be defined as actual friends by that person; in fact many may be complete strangers. And yet, personal and often sensitive information is freely and publicly provided.

In our study of more than 4,000 CMU users of the Facebook we have quantified individuals' willingness to provide large amounts of personal information in an online social network, and we have shown how unconcerned its users appear to privacy risks: while personal data is generously provided, limiting privacy preferences are hardly used; only a small number of members change the default privacy preferences, which are set to maximize the visibility of users profiles. Based on the information they provide online, users expose themselves to various physical and cyber risks, and make it extremely easy for third parties to create digital dossiers of their behavior.

These risks are not unique to the Facebook. However, the Facebook's public linkages between an individual profile and the real identity of its owner, and the Facebook's perceived connection to a physical and ostensibly bounded community (the campus), make Facebook users a particularly interesting population for our research.

6. References

1. d. boyd. Friendster and publicly articulated social networking. In *Conference on Human Factors and Computing Systems (CHI 2004)*, April 24–29, Vienna, Austria, 2004.

2. J. Donath and d. boyd. Public displays of connection. *BT Technology Journal*, 22:71–82, 2004.

3. K. Jump. A new kind of fame. *The Columbian Missourian*, September 1, 2005.

4. A. Leonard. You are who you know. *Salon.com*, June 15, 2004.

5. H. Liu and P. Maes. Interestmap: Harvesting social network profiles for recommendations. In *Beyond Personalization - IUI 2005*, January 9, San Diego, California, USA, 2005.

6. W. Mackay. Triggers and barriers to customizing software. In *Proceedings of CHI'91*, pages 153–160. ACM Press, 1991.

Nicole B. Ellison, Charles
Steinfield, and Cliff Lampe

The Benefits of Facebook "Friends:" Social Capital and College Students' Use of Online Social Network Sites

Introduction

Social network sites (SNSs) . . . allow individuals to present themselves, articulate their social networks, and establish or maintain connections with others. These sites can be oriented towards work-related contexts (e.g., LinkedIn.com), romantic relationship initiation (the original goal of Friendster.com), connecting those with shared interests such as music or politics (e.g., MySpace.com), or the college student population (the original incarnation of Facebook.com). Participants may use the sites to interact with people they already know offline or to meet new people. The online social network application analyzed in this article, Facebook, enables its users to present themselves in an online profile, accumulate "friends" who can post comments on each other's pages, and view each other's profiles. Facebook members can also join virtual groups based on common interests, see what classes they have in common, and learn each others' hobbies, interests, musical tastes, and romantic relationship status through the profiles. . . .

Online SNSs support both the maintenance of existing social ties and the formation of new connections. Much of the early research on online communities assumed that individuals using these systems would be connecting with others outside their pre-existing social group or location, liberating them to form communities around shared interests, as opposed to shared geography (Wellman et al., 1996). A hallmark of this early research is the presumption that when online and offline social networks overlapped, the directionality was *online to offline*—online connections resulted in face-to-face meetings. . . .

Although this early work acknowledged the ways in which offline and online networks bled into one another, the assumed online to off-line directionality may not apply to today's SNSs that are structured both to

From *Journal of Computer-Mediated Communication*, vol. 12, issue 4, July 2007, excerpts from pp. 1143–1148, 1150–1153, 1155–1164. Copyright © 2007 by International Communication Association. Reprinted by permission of Blackwell Publishing, Ltd and the authors: Nicole Ellison, Charles Steinfield, and Cliff Lampe.

articulate existing connections and enable the creation of new ones. However, because there is little empirical research that addresses whether members use SNSs to maintain existing ties or to form new ones, the social capital implications of these services are unknown. . . .

Literature Review

Social Capital: Online and Offline

Social capital broadly refers to the resources accumulated through the relationships among people. . . . Bourdieu and Wacquant (1992) define social capital as "the sum of the resources, actual or virtual, that accrue to an individual or a group by virtue of possessing a durable network of more or less institutionalized relationships of mutual acquaintance and recognition" (p. 14). . . .

Social capital has been linked to a variety of positive social outcomes, such as better public health, lower crime rates, and more efficient financial markets (Adler & Kwon, 2002). According to several measures of social capital, this important resource has been declining in the U.S. for the past several years (Putnam, 2000). When social capital declines, a community experiences increased social disorder, reduced participation in civic activities, and potentially more distrust among community members. Greater social capital increases commitment to a community and the ability to mobilize collective actions. . . .

For individuals, social capital allows a person to draw on resources from other members of the networks to which he or she belongs. These resources can take the form of useful information, personal relationships, or the capacity to organize groups. Access to individuals outside one's close circle provides access to non-redundant information, resulting in benefits such as employment connections. Moreover, social capital researchers have found that various forms of social capital, including ties with friends and neighbors, are related to indices of psychological well-being, such as self esteem and satisfaction with life (Helliwell & Putnam, 2004).

Putnam (2000) distinguishes between bridging and bonding social capital. The former is linked to what network researchers refer to as "weak ties," which are loose connections between individuals who may provide useful information or new perspectives for one another but typically not emotional support. . . . Alternatively, bonding social capital is found between individuals in tightly-knit, emotionally close relationships. . . .

Social Capital and the Internet
The Internet has been linked both to increases and decreases in social capital. Nie (2001), for example, argued that Internet use detracts from face-to-face time with others, which might diminish an individual's social capital. However, this perspective has received strong criticism. . . .

Recently, researchers have emphasized the importance of Internet-based linkages for the formation of weak ties, which serve as the foundation of bridging social capital. Because online relationships may be supported by technologies like distribution lists, photo directories, and search capabilities, it is possible that new forms of social capital and relationship building will occur in online social network sites. Bridging social capital might be augmented by such sites, which support loose social ties, allowing users to create and maintain larger, diffuse networks of relationships from which they could potentially draw resources. . . .

Based on this prior work, we propose the following hypothesis:

> **H1:** Intensity of Facebook use will be positively associated with individuals' perceived bridging social capital.

In Putnam's (2000) view, bonding social capital reflects strong ties with family and close friends, who might be in a position to provide emotional support or access to scarce resources. Williams (2006) points out that little empirical work has explicitly examined the effects of the Internet on bonding social capital. . . . It is clear that the Internet facilitates new connections, in that it provides people with an alternative way to connect with others who share their interests or relational goals. These new connections may result in an increase in social capital. . . . However, it is unclear how social capital formation occurs when online and offline connections are closely coupled, as with Facebook. Williams (2006) argues that although researchers have examined potential losses of social capital in offline communities due to increased Internet use, they have not adequately explored online gains that might compensate for this. We thus propose a second hypothesis on the relationship between Facebook use and close ties:

> **H2:** Intensity of Facebook use will be positively associated with individuals' perceived bonding social capital.

Online social network tools may be of particular utility for individuals who otherwise have difficulties forming and maintaining both strong and weak ties. Some research has shown, for example, that the Internet might help individuals with low psychological well-being due to few ties to friends and neighbors (Bargh & McKenna, 2004). . . . For this reason, we explore whether the relationship between Facebook use and social capital is different for individuals with varying degrees of self-esteem . . . and satisfaction with life. . . . This leads to the two following pairs of hypotheses:

> **H3a:** The relationship between intensity of Facebook use and bridging social capital will vary depending on the degree of a person's self esteem.
>
> **H3b:** The relationship between intensity of Facebook use and bridging social capital will vary depending on the degree of a person's satisfaction with life.
>
> **H4a:** The relationship between intensity of Facebook use and bonding social capital will vary depending on the degree of a person's self esteem.
>
> **H4b:** The relationship between intensity of Facebook use and bonding social capital will vary depending on the degree of a person's satisfaction with life.

Maintained Social Capital and Life Changes

Social networks change over time as relationships are formed or abandoned. Particularly significant changes in social networks may affect one's social capital, as a person moves from the geographic location in which their network was formed and thus loses access to those social resources. Putnam (2000) argues that one of the possible causes of decreased social capital in the U.S. is the increase in families moving for job reasons; other research has explored the role of the Internet in these transitions. . . . Wellman et al. (2001), for example, find that heavy Internet users rely on email to maintain long distance relationships, rather than using it as a substitute for offline interactions with those living nearby.

Some researchers have coined the term "friendsickness" to refer to the distress caused by the loss of connection to old friends when a young person moves away to college (Paul & Brier, 2001). . . . We therefore introduce a measure focusing specifically on the maintenance of existing social capital after this major life change experienced by college students, focusing on their ability to leverage and maintain social connections from high school.

. . . We call this concept "maintained social capital." In keeping with the thrust of our prior hypotheses about the role of Facebook and bridging social capital, we propose the following:

> H5: Intensity of Facebook use will be positively associated with individuals' perceived maintained social capital.

Method

A random sample of 800 Michigan State University . . . undergraduate students was retrieved from the MSU registrar's office. All 800 students were sent an email invitation, . . . with a short description of the study, information about confidentiality and incentives, and a link to the survey. . . . A total of 286 students completed the online survey, yielding a response rate of 35.8%. . . . (34% male; 66% female), age (mean = 20.1, s.d. = 1.64), year in school (mean = 2.55, s.d. = 1.07), local (55% on campus; 45% off campus) vs. home residence (91% in-state; 9% out-of-state), ethnicity (87% white; 13% non-white), a measure of internet use (mean = 2 hrs, 56 mins. per day, s.d. = 1.52), and whether respondents were Facebook members or not (94% vs. 6%).

Measures . . .

Facebook Intensity

The Facebook intensity scale (Cronbach's alpha = .83) was created in order to obtain a better measure of Facebook usage than frequency or duration indices. This measure includes two self-reported assessments of Facebook behavior: . . . the number of Facebook "friends" and the amount of time spent on Facebook on a typical day. This measure also includes a series of Likert-scale attitudinal questions designed to tap the extent to which the participant was emotionally connected to Facebook and the extent to which Facebook was integrated into her daily activities. . . .

Facebook Usage: Elements in Profile and Perceptions of Who Has Viewed Profiles
We asked respondents to indicate which of several salient aspects of the profile (such as relationship status, high school, and mobile phone number) they included when constructing their profile. The instrument asked respondents to indicate who they thought had viewed their profile, such as high school friends, classmates, or family members. . . .

Use of Facebook to Meet New People vs. Connect with Existing Offline Contacts
In order to further investigate whether usage was more motivated by prior offline contacts or the potential to form new online contacts, we developed several items reflecting each of these paths. In the former case, the items measured whether respondents used Facebook to look up someone with whom they shared some offline connection, such as a classmate or a friend (Cronbach's alpha = .70). In the latter case, our instrument included several items that tapped the use of Facebook to make new friends without any reference to an offline connection, but these did not correlate highly, and our final analysis incorporated only a single item measure: using Facebook to meet new people.

Self-Esteem
Self-esteem was measured using seven items from the Rosenberg self-esteem scale (Rosenberg, 1989). The answers to these questions were reported on a 5-point Likert scale and exhibited high reliability (0.87).

Satisfaction with Life at MSU
The scale of satisfaction with life at MSU was adapted from the Satisfaction with Life Scale (SWLS) (Diener, Suh, & Oishi, 1997), a five-item instrument designed to measure global cognitive judgments of one's life. We amended each item slightly to refer specifically to the MSU context, on the assumption that restricting participants was more appropriate given our hypotheses and more likely to elicit accurate answers. The reliability test for this 5-point Likert scale showed a relatively high reliability (0.87). . . .

Bridging Social Capital
This measure assessed the extent to which participants experienced bridging social capital. . . . According to Williams (2006), "members of weak-tie networks are thought to be outward looking and to include people from a broad range of backgrounds. The social capital created by these networks generates broader identities and generalized reciprocity" (n.p.). We (e.g., I feel I am a part of the MSU community) therefore adapted five items from Williams' (2006) bridging social capital subscale and created three additional items intended to measure bridging social capital in the MSU context to create our bridging social capital scale (Cronbach's alpha = .87). One item, "MSU is a good place to be," was included because it loaded on the same factor and tapped into an outcome of bridging social capital.

Bonding Social Capital

Bonding was assessed using five items from the bonding subscale of the Internet social capital scales (e.g., there are several people at MSU I trust to solve my problems) developed and validated by Williams (2006). Responses were reported on a five-point Likert scale. These items were adapted to the MSU context (Cronbach's alpha = .75).

Maintained Social Capital

This original scale was inspired by our pilot interviews, media coverage of Facebook, and anecdotal evidence that suggested that keeping in touch with high school friends was a primary use of Facebook. These items were adapted from traditional measures of social capital which assess an individual's ability to mobilize support or action (Cronbach's alpha = .81) but focus on the ability to get assistance from a *previously inhabited* community (e.g., it would be easy to find people to invite to my high school reunion).

Findings

. . . In a short period of time, Facebook has garnered a very strong percentage of users on college campuses. In our sample, 94% of the undergraduate students we surveyed were Facebook members. We investigated whether members and non-members differed significantly along various demographic characteristics, but we lacked confidence in these findings given the extremely low number of non-Facebook users. The remainder of our analyses are based only on data from Facebook members.

Facebook members report spending between 10 and 30 minutes on average using Facebook each day and report having between 150 and 200 friends listed on their profile. . . . Respondents also report significantly more Facebook use involving people with whom they share an offline connection, . . . than use involving meeting new people (t = 26.14, p < .0001).

. . . Nearly all Facebook users include their high school name in their profile (96%), suggesting that maintaining connections to former high school classmates is a strong motivation for using Facebook. Not surprisingly, 97% report that high school friends had seen their profile. Ninety percent or more also reported that other friends as well as people in their classes had seen their profile, further suggesting an offline component to Facebook use.

. . . Students view the primary audience for their profile to be people with whom they share an offline connection. This is suggested as well by the responses to items about how they use Facebook. Mean scores for the offline-to-online scale were significantly higher than those for the single-item online-to-offline measure (p < .0001). This suggests that students use Facebook primarily to maintain existing offline relationships. . . .

In order to explore our research hypotheses regarding the relationship between Facebook use and the various forms of social capital, we conducted regression analyses. In each regression, we controlled for demographic, subjective well-being and Internet use factors, in order to see if usage of Facebook accounted for variance in social capital over and above these other independent variables.

In order to test Hypothesis 1, we first investigated the extent to which demographic factors, psychological well-being measures, and general Internet use predicted the amount of bridging social capital reported by students; the adjusted R^2 for this model was .38. We then entered the Facebook intensity variable, which raised the adjusted R^2 to .43. An additional pair of analyses further explored whether Facebook intensity interacted with the self-esteem and satisfaction with MSU life scales. . . . After first controlling for demographic factors, psychological well-being measures, and general Internet use, the extent to which students used Facebook intensively . . . contributed significantly (scaled beta = .34, p < .0001), supporting Hypothesis 1. . . . We also explored whether gender and year in school interacted with Facebook intensity. . . . These interactions were not significant. . . .

Overall, our independent factors accounted for nearly half of the variance in bridging social capital. The results suggest that Facebook is indeed implicated in students' efforts to develop and maintain bridging social capital at college. . . . Among the psychological measures, the extent of students' satisfaction with life at MSU was strongly correlated with bridging social capital (scaled beta = .66, p < .0001).

To explore Hypotheses 3a and 3b, the interaction between Facebook use and the psychological measures was examined. Both hypotheses are supported. Students reporting low satisfaction and low self-esteem appeared to gain in bridging social capital if they used Facebook more intensely, suggesting that the affordances of the SNS might be especially helpful for these students.

. . . Bonding social capital was also significantly predicted by the intensity with which students used Facebook (scaled beta =.37, p < .001 in model 2). Other factors that related to bonding social capital were ethnicity (being white, scaled beta = .16, p < .01, model 2), year in school (scaled beta = .22, p < .01, model 2), living on campus (scaled beta = .13, p < .01, model 2), self-esteem (scaled beta = .23, p < .01, model 2), and satisfaction with MSU life (scaled beta = .40, p < .001, model 2). General Internet use was not a significant predictor of bonding social capital, and the interactions between Facebook use and the two psychological measures were not significant. As in the bridging social capital analysis, gender and year in school did not interact significantly with Facebook use in predicting bonding social capital. . . . Overall, the included variables accounted for almost one quarter of the variance in students' reported bonding social capital.

Finally, entering only (model 3) our control factors accounted for 13% of the variance in maintained social capital. Adding Facebook intensity raised the R^2 to .17 and revealed the same strong connection to Facebook intensity (scaled beta = .36, p < .001), even after controlling for the number of years at college . . . and general Internet use. Interestingly, general Internet use was also a significant predictor of maintained social capital (scaled beta = .26, p < .05). . . . Ethnicity (being white, scaled beta = .23, p < .001) and self-esteem (scaled beta = .30, p < .001) were the other significant variables in this regression. . . . Together, the independent variables accounted for 16% to 17% of the variance in the maintained social capital measure.

Discussion

Returning to our original research question, we can definitively state that there is a positive relationship between certain kinds of Facebook use and the maintenance and creation of social capital. . . . Facebook appears to play an important role in the process by which students form and maintain social capital, with usage associated with all three kinds of social capital included in our instrument. . . .

Our participants overwhelmingly used Facebook to keep in touch with old friends and to maintain or intensify relationships characterized by some form of offline connection. . . . Facebook provided a way to keep in touch with high school friends and acquaintances. . . . This offline to online movement differs from the patterns observed by early researchers examining computer-mediated communication and virtual communities. Due to the structure of the site, which blocks entry to those without a school email address and then places individuals into communities based on that email address, Facebook serves a geographically-bound user base.

Our first dimension of social capital—bridging—assessed the extent to which participants were integrated into the MSU community, their willingness to support the community, and the extent to which these experiences broadened their social horizons or worldview. Our findings suggest that certain kinds of Facebook use . . . can help students accumulate and maintain bridging social capital. . . .

Participants' reports about who is viewing their profile provide insight into this dynamic. . . . Students report that the primary audiences for their profiles are high school friends and people they know from an MSU context. This implies that highly engaged users are using Facebook to crystallize relationships that might otherwise remain ephemeral. Haythornthwaite (2005) discusses the implications of media that "create latent tie connectivity among group members that provides the technical means for activating weak ties" (p. 125). Latent ties are those social network ties that are "technically possible but not activated socially" (p. 137). Facebook might make it easier to convert latent ties into weak ties, in that the site provides personal information about others, makes visible one's connections to a wide range of individuals, and enables students to identify those who might be useful in some capacity (such as the math major in a required calculus class), thus providing the motivation to activate a latent tie. These weak ties may provide additional information and opportunities, which are expressed as dimensions of bridging social capital that speak to interaction with a wide range of people and the more tolerant perspective this might encourage. Facebook seems well-suited to facilitate these experiences, in that detailed profiles highlight both commonalities and differences among participants.

We also found an interaction between bridging social capital and subjective well-being measures. For less intense Facebook users, students who reported low satisfaction with MSU life also reported having much lower bridging social capital than those who used Facebook more intensely. The same was true for self-esteem. Conversely, there was little difference in bridging social capital among those who reported high satisfaction with life at MSU and high self-esteem relative to Facebook use intensity. One explanation consistent with these interaction effects is that Facebook use may be helping to overcome barriers faced by students who have low satisfaction and low self-esteem. Because bridging social capital provides benefits such as increased information and opportunities, we suspect that participants who use Facebook in this way are able to get more out of their college experience. . . .

Bonding social capital was also predicted by high self-esteem, satisfaction with university life, and intense Facebook use, although overall, the regression model predicting bonding social capital accounted for less of the variation for this dependent variable than for bridging social capital. However, Facebook appears to be much less useful for maintaining or creating bonding social capital, as indicated by the fact that the bonding model only accounted for 22% of the variance (versus 46% in the bridging social capital models). We might expect Facebook usage to have less of an impact on bonding than bridging social capital given the affordances of this service. It can lower barriers to participation and therefore may encourage the formation of weak ties but not necessarily create the close kinds of relationships that are associated with bonding social capital. Yet the strong coefficient for Facebook intensity suggests that Facebook use is important for bonding social capital as well. . . .

Finally, Facebook intensity predicted increased levels of maintained social capital, which assessed the extent to which participants could rely on high school acquaintances to do small favors. For college students, many of whom have moved away for the first time, the ability to stay in touch with these high school acquaintances may illustrate most clearly the "strength of weak ties." These potentially useful connections may be valuable sources of new information and resources. Additionally, the ability to stay in touch with these networks may offset feelings of "friendsickness," the distress caused by the loss of old friends. . . .

Our empirical results contrast with the anecdotal evidence dominating the popular press. Although there are clearly some image management problems experienced by students as reported in the press, and the potential does exist for privacy abuses, our findings demonstrate a robust connection between Facebook usage and indicators of social capital, especially of the bridging type. . . .

The strong linkage between Facebook use and high school connections suggests how SNSs help maintain relations as people move from one offline community to another. It may facilitate the same when students graduate from college, with alumni keeping their school email address and using Facebook to stay in touch with the college community. . . . Colleges may want to explore ways to encourage this sort of usage.

References

Adler, P., & Kwon, S. (2002). Social capital: Prospects for a new concept. *Academy of Management Review,* 27(1), 17–40.

Bargh, J., & McKenna, K. (2004). The Internet and social life. *Annual Review of Psychology,* 55(1), 573–590.

Bourdieu, P., & Wacquant, L. (1992). *An Invitation to Reflexive Sociology.* Chicago: University of Chicago Press.

Diener, E., Suh, E., & Oishi, S. (1997). Recent findings on subjective well-being. *Indian Journal of Clinical Psychology,* 24(1), 25–41.

Haythornthwaite, C. (2005). Social networks and Internet connectivity effects. *Information, Communication, & Society,* 8(2), 125–147.

Helliwell, J. F., & Putnam, R. D. (2004). The social context of well-being. *Philosophical Transactions of the Royal Society,* 359(1449), 1435–1446.

Nie, N. H. (2001). Sociability, interpersonal relations, and the Internet: Reconciling conflicting findings. *American Behavioral Scientist,* 45(3), 420–435.

Paul, E., & Brier, S. (2001). Friendsickness in the transition to college: Precollege predictors and college adjustment correlates. *Journal of Counseling and Development,* 79(1), 77–89.

Putnam, R. D. (2000). *Bowling Alone.* New York: Simon & Schuster.

Rosenberg, M. (1989). *Society and the Adolescent Self-Image* (Rev. ed.). Middletown, CT: Wesleyan University Press.

Wellman, B., Haase, A. Q., Witte, J., & Hampton, K. (2001). Does the Internet increase, decrease, or supplement social capital? Social networks, participation, and community commitment. *American Behavioral Scientist,* 45(3), 436.

Wellman, B., Salaff, J., Dimitrova, D., Garton, L., Gulia, M., & Haythornthwaite, C. (1996). Computer networks as social networks: Collaborative work, telework, and virtual community. *Annual Review of Sociology,* 22, 213–238.

Williams, D. (2006). On and off the 'net: Scales for social capital in an online era. *Journal of Computer-Mediated Communication,* 11(2).

POSTSCRIPT

Are Social Networking Sites (SNSs), such as Facebook, a Cause for Concern among Adolescents?

Social networking sites (SNSs) have rapidly become popular as ways for adolescents to form and maintain relationships. As such, there is increasingly more debate regarding the impact (both positive and negative) of their use on adolescent well-being. While some researchers criticize SNSs, such as Facebook, as being addictive, invasive, and exposing, others believe SNSs can enhance healthy adolescent relationship formation. The two selections for this issue are excellent examples of these opposing views.

Ellison, Steinfield, and Lampe provide evidence for the social benefits of Facebook such that it can be used to maintain and enhance offline friendships. In particular, the researchers argue that users of Facebook are adding people they know to their network of friends more than using the site to form new relationships. This is particularly important as adolescents move away from home. Facebook gives them a venue where they can maintain previous relationships rather than losing touch. Ellison and associates further argue that Facebook use has a positive impact on well-being in that it enhances self-esteem. Supporting the positive benefits of SNSs are findings from Pew research where it was found that 91% of the teens using SNSs such as Facebook do so to enhance offline friendships (Lenhart & Madden, 2007).

Ralph Gross and Alessandro Acquisti on the other hand point out the negative impact of using Facebook. In particular they focus on privacy violations and personal safety. One of the main problems with Facebook according to Gross and Acquisti is the disregard for controlling personal information that the users of Facebook exhibit. As such, users are at risk both offline (e.g., stalking) and online (e.g., identity theft). Although users have numerous tools available to them to protect their privacy, the majority do not enable the privacy settings. This puts them at risk for not only stalking and identity theft, but also cyber-bullying. Further support for the concerns raised by Gross and Acquisti can be found in the articles by Hodge (2006) and Stone (2006).

References/Further Readings

Boyd, D. M., & Ellison, N. B. (2008). Social network sites: Definition, history, and scholarship. *Journal of Computer-Mediated Communication*, 13, 210–230.

Cassidy, J. (2006). Me media: How hanging out on the Internet became big business. *The New Yorker, 82*(13), 50.

Hargittai, E. (2008). Whose space? Differences among users and non-users of social network sites. *Journal of Computer-Mediated Communication, 13*, 276–297.

Hodge, M. J. (2006). The fourth amendment and privacy issues on the "new" Internet: Facebook.com and MySpace.com. *Southern Illinois University Law Journal, 31*, 95–123.

Lenhart, A., & Madden, M. (2007). Teens, privacy, & online social networks. *Pew Internet and American Life Project Report.* Retrieved July 9, 2008 from http://pewinternet.org/pdfs/PIP_Teens_Privacy_SNS_Report_Final.pdf

Regan, K. (2003). Online privacy is dead—What now? *E-Commerce Times.* January 2. http://www.ecommercetimes.com/story/20346.html

Stone, B. (2006). Web of risks: Students adore social-networking sites like Facebook, but indiscreet postings can mean really big trouble. *Newsweek*, August 27, 2006.

Valkenburg, P. M., Peter, J., & Shouten, A. P. (2006). Friend networking sites and their relationship to adolescents' well-being and social self-esteem. *CyberPsychology and Behavior, 9*(5), 584–590.

Contributors to This Volume

EDITORS

B.J. RYE is an associate professor of psychology and human sexuality as well as the director (currently on leave) of the Sexuality, Marriage, and Family Studies program at St. Jerome's University at the University of Waterloo in Waterloo, Ontario, Canada. Dr. Rye teaches such courses as Introduction to Human Sexuality, The Psychology of Gender, and The Psychology of Sexual Orientation. Her research focuses on attitudes toward sexual minority groups (e.g., attitudes toward gay and lesbian parenting, persons with HIV/AIDS, transgender individuals, and intersex people). She has also evaluated the efficacy of sexual health education programs and interventions, as well as investigated sexual health behavior practices from social psychological perspectives. Her writings have appeared in such journals as *AIDS & Behavior, The Journal of Sex Research, and Health Psychology*. Dr. Rye sits on the editorial board of *The Canadian Journal of Human Sexuality*. She received her PhD in social psychology from the University of Western Ontario, with a specialization in human sexuality.

MAUREEN DRYSDALE is an assistant professor of psychology and acting director of the Sexuality, Marriage, and Family Studies program at St. Jerome's University at the University of Waterloo in Waterloo, Ontario, Canada. She is also an associate with the Waterloo Centre for the Advancement of Co-operative Education. Dr. Drysdale teaches courses in adolescence, educational psychology, child abnormal psychology, and problem behaviors in the classroom. Her research interests include the many factors that impact academic achievement and, more specifically, problem behaviors in the classroom (e.g., autism, ADHD, conduct problems, depression, and eating disorders). She also researches adolescent transitions, such as high school–to–postsecondary and postsecondary-to-work transitions. She has presented her research findings at numerous professional conferences (SRA, CPA, AERA, WACE) and published in journals such as *The Journal for Students Placed at Risk* and the *Journal of Cooperative Education*. Dr. Drysdale received her PhD in educational psychology from the University of Calgary, specializing in human development and learning.

AUTHORS

ALESSANDRO ACQUISTI is an assistant professor of information technology and public policy at the H. John Heinz III School of Public Policy and Management at Carnegie Mellon University. He is a member of the CMU Usable Privacy and Security Laboratory, a member of CMU Privacy Technology Center, and a member of CMU Cylab. His research interests are economics of privacy and information security, economics of computers and AI, agents economics, computational economics, ecommerce, cryptography, anonymity, and electronic voting.

WILLIAM P. ADELMAN is a physician and a member of the Department of Adolescent Medicine at the National Naval Medical Center in Bethesda, Maryland.

NANCY E. ADLER is a professor of medical psychology at the University of California–San Francisco, director of the Health Psychology Program, director of the Center for Health and Community and vice chair in the Department of Psychiatry. Her research interests are the impact of socioeconomic status on health, and why individuals engage in health-damaging behaviors and how their understanding of risk affects their choices.

SHARON ALLEN is chairman of the board of directors of Deloitte LLP. She currently serves on the President's Export Council and is a member of the Women's Leadership Board at the John F. Kennedy School of Government at Harvard.

PAUL R. AMATO is a professor of sociology at Pennsylvania State University.

TAMIKA L. ANDERSON is a public health nurse and child care nurse consultant with the Davidson County Health Department in Lexington, North Carolina.

SANDRA H. BERRY is a professor and the senior director of the RAND Corporation's Survey Research Group and co-director of the RAND Health Center for the Study of HIV, STDs, and Sexual Behavior. She specializes in instrument design, in implementation of complex field procedures and experimental designs, and in data collection in unusual settings.

LISA BRAUN is a pediatrician at the Children's Hospital–Michigan.

SANDRA A. BROWN is an associate clinical professor in the Department of Psychiatry at the University of California. Her research interests are neuropsychological correlates of learning disabilities in children and adolescents, and clinical teaching and supervision of pre- and post-doctoral interns and fellows in psychology.

WILLIAM BURKE is a professor and the vice chair of the Department of Psychiatry at the University of Nebraska Medical Center in Omaha, Nebraska. He is the director of the Division of Geriatric Psychiatry, and heads the Psychopharmacology Research Consortium. His principal research interests are in the psychopharmacological treatments of psychiatric disorders.

PHILIP A. CHAN is from the Department of Internal Medicine at Rhode Island Hospital.

TERESA STANTON COLLETT is a professor of law at the University of St. Thomas School of Law. She is an elected member of the American Law Institute. She speaks on the topics of marriage, religion, and bioethics.

REBECCA L. COLLINS is a professor at the RAND Graduate School and senior behavioral scientist of the RAND Corporation. Her recent research involves media effects on health risk behavior, including a national study exploring associations between exposure to sexual content on television and adolescent sexual attitudes and behavior and a study of the effects of alcohol advertising on underage drinking.

JOY K. CRAWFORD is a doctoral candidate at the University of Washington in the Human Development and Cognition area of Educational Psychology.

MARY CRAWFORD is a professor in the University of Connecticut Department of Psychology. Her research interests are gender and communication, feminist research methods, and gender and cognition.

NICKI R. CRICK is the director of the Institute of Child Development and a professor at the University of Minnesota. Her research team has focused recently on the study of relational aggression.

ERIN CRUISE is an instructor of nursing at Radford University in Virginia.

RAYMOND DE KEMP is a researcher with Radboud University in the Netherlands.

LISA M. DIAMOND is an associate professor of psychology and gender studies at the University of Utah. She studies the emotional dynamics of attachment relationships between romantic partners and family members, and how they influence health-related physiological processes. She also studies the longitudinal development of same-sex sexuality in women.

LAUREN DONCHI has a bachelor's degree with honors from Swinburne University in Melbourne, Australia. She is a registered psychologist with a strong background in schools and education and is currently employed by the Department of Education & Training to provide psychology services within a network of schools in outer eastern Melbourne.

MARC N. ELLIOTT is a senior statistician with the RAND Corporation. His recent work involves consumer evaluations of Medicare and hospitals, and health disparities for small racial/ethnic groups.

ANDRE J.A. ELFERINK is a clinical epidemiologist and a member of the Dutch Medicines Evaluation Board of the Netherlands.

NICOLE E. ELLISON is an assistant professor in the Telecommunication, Information Studies, and Media department at Michigan State University.

Her research interests are social network sites, self-presentation in on-line dating environments, issues of privacy and security in online environments, deception in online dating profiles, and the use of blogs and wikis in the classroom.

GRAHAM EMSLIE is a professor and the chief of adolescent psychiatry at UT Southwestern and Children's Medical Center of Dallas. His research interests are in the areas of conducting efficacy and effectiveness trials with medications and psychotherapy for children and adolescents with depression, anxiety disorders, and attention-deficit disorder. He is also involved with developing and evaluating medication algorithm protocols for children and adolescents with depression.

RUTGER C.M.E. ENGELS is a professor and researcher in the Netherlands.

JING FENG is a Ph.D. candidate at the University of Toronto.

R. CHRIS FRALEY is an associate professor in the Department of Psychology at the University of Illinois at Urbana-Champaign. His research interests are attachment theory and close relationships; personality organization, dynamics, and development; social cognition and affect regulation; evolutionary psychology; and dynamic modeling, simulation, and psychological methods.

WYNDOL FURMAN is a child clinical psychology professor with the Department of Psychology at the University of Denver. His interests are centered around the study of close relationships in childhood and adolescence. He is the director of the Relationship Center in the Psychology Department of the University of Denver, where he studies children's and adolescents' relationships with different people. He is the co-editor of *The Development of Romantic Relationships in Adolescence* (Cambridge University Press, 1999).

TASHA C. GEIGER is a pediatrics faculty member at the University of Rochester Medical Center, Division of Developmental Disabilities. Her primary research interest is autism spectrum disorders.

CHRISTINE C. GISPEN-DE WIED is a medical researcher at the KNAW Research Information Centre in the Netherlands. She is also the clinical coordinator at the pharmacotherapeutical group of the Dutch Medicines Evaluation Board of the Netherlands.

CATHERINE M. GRELLO is a clinical psychologist. Her areas of expertise include anxiety disorders, borderline personality disorder, divorce issues, intimacy issues, mood disorders, parenting issues, personality disorders, and relationship issues.

RALPH GROSS is a Ph.D. candidate at Carnegie Mellon University. He is interested in computer vision methods for people identification.

KAREN HANSON is a professor of philosophy at Indiana University, Bloomington. Her research interests are in philosophy of mind, ethics, aesthetics, and American philosophy.

DUANE A. HARGREAVES is a researcher in the School of Psychology at Flinders University. His current research is on media influences on adolescent body image.

MELINDA S. HARPER is a clinical psychologist with Charlotte Psychotherapy and Consultation Group in Charlotte, North Carolina. She specializes in treatment of adolescents and young adults.

DOROTHY HATSUKAMI is a professor in the department of Psychiatry at the University of Minnesota. She is also co-leader of the Prevention and Etiology Research Program. She is a member of the Carcinogenesis and Chemoprevention Research Program, adjunct professor with the Division of Epidemiology and Community Health and Department of Psychology, and director of the Transdisciplinary Tobacco Use Research Center.

JOYCE HUNTER is co-director of the Community Collaboration Core at the HIV Center for Clinical and Behavioral Studies, New York State Psychiatric Institute and Columbia University. She is also principal investigator of the Working It Out Project, a community-based HIV prevention research project for gay, lesbian, and bisexual adolescents.

SARAH B. HUNTER is an associate behavioral scientist with the RAND Corporation. She researches substance-abuse prevention.

SHARON JAYSON is a journalist with *USA Today*.

SUE JENSEN is at the Department of Psychiatry, University of Minnesota, Minneapolis, Tobacco Use Research Center.

KIRK A. JOHNSON is a visiting fellow at The Heritage Foundation in Washington, D.C. He recently returned from 13 months spent in Iraq as the Deputy Director for Assessments in the Joint Strategic Planning and Assessment office at the U.S. Embassy in Baghdad.

DIANE C. JONES is an associate professor of Educational Psychology at the University of Washington.

DAVID E. KANOUSE is a senior behavioral scientist with the RAND Corporation. His areas of expertise are HIV, STDs, and sexual behavior.

ARI KAUKIAINEN is a lecturer in the Department of Psychology at the University of Turku. His research interests are learning difficulties, aggression, bullying, and social skills, and how they are connected to each other.

CHRISTOPHER J. KRATOCHVIL is an associate professor in the Depart ment of Psychiatry and a member of the graduate faculty at the University of Nebraska Medical Center (UNMC). He is also assistant director of the Psychopharmacology Research Consortium at UNMC. His research interests include pharmacotherapy of attention-deficit/hyperactivity disorder, treatment of pediatric depression, and genetics of psychiatric disorders.

DALE KUNKEL is professor of communication at the University of Arizona. Kunkel studies children and media issues from diverse perspectives, including television effects research as well as assessments of media industry content and practices.

CLIFF LAMPE is an assistant professor at Michigan State University. His research interest is the structure and effects of many-to-many interactions that occur online.

FRITS J. LEKKERKERKER is a specialist in internal medicine, endocrinology and clinical pharmacology. For more than 15 years, he has been the chairman of the Dutch Medicines Evaluation Board.

MAUREEN LYON is a licensed clinical psychologist and assistant research professor in pediatrics at George Washington University Medical Center, in the Division of Adolescent and Young Adult Medicine at Children's National Medical Center in Washington, D.C.

JOHN MARCH is professor of psychiatry and chief of child and adolescent psychiatry at Duke University Medical Center. Though based formally in the Department of Psychiatry and Behavioral Sciences, Dr. March also holds faculty appointments at the Duke Clinical Research Institute and in the Department of Psychology: Social and Health Sciences. His research interests include anxiety, obsessive-compulsive and tic disorders, developmental psychopharmacology, clinical trials methods, psychometrics/instrument development, and CNS mechanisms of treatment response.

MICHAEL J. MARKS is a researcher affiliated with the Social-Personality Division at the University of Illinois at Urbana-Champaign. His current research includes examining the impact of social interaction on the sexual double standard, exploring whether seeking confirming information (confirmation bias) leads to perception of the double standard, and constructing a theoretical perspective on the double standard.

ALEXANDER McKAY is research director for the Sex Information and Education Council of Canada.

DANIEL P. MEARS is an associate professor in the Florida State University College of Criminology and Criminal Justice. He conducts basic and applied research on social programs and policies, focusing on crime causation, juvenile and criminal justice, and effective crime prevention and intervention strategies.

ANGELA MIU is a senior programmer analyst with the RAND Corporation.

SUSAN MOORE is a social psychologist and a research professor in the Department of Psychology at Swinburne University in Melbourne, Australia. Her research interests include adolescent sexuality and risk-taking, attitude research, and beliefs about romance and love.

LAUREN R. NOYES is director of research projects at The Heritage Foundation in Washington, D.C. Her areas of expertise are welfare, education, and family issues.

AIDA ORGOCKA is a gender and development expert at the University of Illinois. She is a member of the Global Migration and Gender Network.

MARY A. OTT is an assistant professor at Indiana University School of Medicine.

GEERTJAN OVERBEEK is a researcher with Radboud University in the Netherlands.

EMILY J. OZER is an assistant professor at the University of California, Berkeley. Her research interests are school- and community-based interventions, promotion of mental and physical health among adolescents, violence prevention, and trauma and post-traumatic stress disorder.

JOCHEN PETER is an associate professor in the Amsterdam School of Communications Research at the University of Amsterdam. His research focuses on the consequences of adolescents' Internet use for their sexual socialization and psychosocial development.

DANIELLE POPP is an assistant professor in the Florida Atlantic University Department of Psychology. She conducts research in the areas of social perception, interpersonal expectancies, and social influence.

JAY PRATT is a professor in the Department of Psychology at the University of Toronto. His research interests include visual cognition, attention, aging, eye movements, and motor control.

MARGOT PRIOR is a professor at the University of Melbourne. She has been a lecturer, clinician, and researcher in the field of family and child development for more than 30 years at Monash, LaTrobe, and Melbourne Universities. Her research interests include autism, learning difficulties, communication disorders, and social inequalities in children's health and well-being.

TERRY RABINOWITZ is associate professor of psychiatry and of family medicine, University of Vermont College of Medicine, and director of the Psychiatric Consultation Service and director of Telemedicine, Fletcher Allen Health Care, Burlington, Vermont.

ROBERT E. RECTOR is a senior research fellow with the Heritage Foundation in Washington, D.C. His areas of expertise are welfare, poverty, and marriage.

JENNIFER ROGERS is a Ph.D. candidate in the department of sociology at the University of California, Santa Barbara.

MARGARET ROSARIO is an associate professor in psychology. Her research interests are concerned with the multidimensional interfaces of identity, and the influence of exposure to community violence on a host of adaptational and health-related outcomes. Potential mediators and moderators of these relations are of critical interest.

JERRY R. RUIS is a member of the Dutch Medicines Evaluation Board of the Netherlands.

EDA RUSCHENA is a psychologist at the Catholic Education Office in Melbourne.

JOSEPH J. SABIA is an assistant professor in the department of Housing and Consumer Economics at the University of Georgia.

CHRISTINA SALMIVALLI is a professor of applied psychology at the University of Turku. Her research interests are peer relations in childhood, bullying and victimization, and social cognition and social adjustment.

ANN SANSON is the network coordinator of the Australian Research Alliance for Children & Youth, Melbourne Office (Research Network). She is a professor and assists Professor Fiona Stanley in her role as the research network convenor. Ann is responsible for the further development of the network particularly in relation to enhancing the capacity for collaborative initiatives.

JOHN SANTELLI is a pediatrician and adolescent medicine specialist who recently joined the School of Public Health at Columbia University. He has conducted research in the areas of HIV/STD risk behaviors, programs to prevent STD/HIV/unintended pregnancy among adolescents and women, school-based health centers, clinical preventive services, and research ethics.

REBECCA SCHLEIFER is a researcher with the HIV/AIDS and Human Rights Program, Human Rights Watch, New York.

RON H.J. SCHOLTE is a researcher in the Netherlands.

ERIC W. SCHRIMSHAW is a researcher with Columbia University, New York.

ELIZABETH S. SCOTT teaches family law, property law, criminal law, and children and the law. She has written extensively on marriage, divorce, cohabitation, child custody, adolescent decision making, and juvenile delinquency. Her research is interdisciplinary, applying behavioral economics, social science research, and developmental theory to family/juvenile law and policy issues. She was the founder and co-director of the University of Virginia's interdisciplinary Center for Children, Families and the Law.

LAURA SHAFFER is a graduate student at the University of Denver. She is interested in researching late-adolescent sexual relationships.

DIANA SMART is a research fellow at the Australian Institute of Family Studies and the project manager for the Australian Temperament Project. Her research interests include adolescent and youth development, transitions to young adulthood, developmental pathways and transition points, and fostering social competence and social responsibility.

IAN SPENCE is a professor in the Department of Psychology at the University of Toronto. Current research projects include the effective use of color in scientific visualization, the role of color in visual memory, individual differences in spatial cognition, and the navigation of dynamic information displays such as Web sites.

LAURENCE STEINBERG is a professor of psychology at Temple University. He is currently director of the John D. and Catherine T. MacArthur Foundation Research Network on Adolescent Development and Juvenile Justice. He is president-elect of the Division of Developmental Psychology of the American Psychological Association.

CHARLES STEINFIELD is a professor and chairperson in the Department of Telecommunication, Information Studies, and Media at Michigan State University. His research focuses on the organizational and social impacts of new communication technologies.

JITSCHAK G. STOROSUM is a member of the Dutch Medicines Evaluation Board of the Netherlands and the psychiatric department of the Academic Medical Center in Amsterdam, the Netherlands.

DANIEL SUMMERS is a specialist in adolescent medicine at the Mount Sinai Adolescent Health Center of Mount Sinai School of Medicine in New York.

MARIKA TIGGEMAN is a professor of psychology at Flinders University. Her expertise includes body image, eating disorders, media effect on body image, dieting, and diet.

JEANNE TSCHANN is a professor at the University of California, Santa Cruz. Her primary research interest is the study of personal relationships and their influence on health-related outcomes among children and adolescents.

PATTI M. VALKENBURG is a professor in the Amsterdam School of Communications Research and director of the Center for Children, Adolescents, and the Media. Her research interests include children's and adolescents' likes and dislikes of entertainment, their development as consumers, and the emotional and social effects of television and the Internet.

CORNELIUS F.M. VAN LIESHOUT is a researcher in the Netherlands.

BARBARA J. VAN ZWIETEN is one of the two Dutch regulators on the Committee for Proprietary Medicinal Products and a member of the Dutch Medicines Evaluation Board of the Netherlands.

BENEDETTO VITIELLO is a psychiatrist specializing in psychopharmacology and treatment research. He has been with the National Institute of Mental Health since 1989.

JOHN WALKUP is an associate professor of psychiatry and behavioral sciences, Division of Child and Adolescent Psychiatry, Johns Hopkins Medical Institutions in Baltimore, Maryland. He currently serves as the deputy director of the Division of Child and Adolescent Psychiatry and is the principal investigator of the National Institute of Mental Health funded Johns Hopkins Research Unit of Pediatric Psychopharmacology and Psychosocial Interventions. Dr. Walkup is the author of a number of articles and book chapters on psychopharmacology, Tourette's syndrome, and obsessive compulsive disorder and other anxiety disorders.

BRUCE WASLICK is an associate of the Baystate Medical Center in Massachusetts.

ELIZABETH WELLER is attending psychiatrist with child and adolescent psychiatry at The Children's Hospital of Philadelphia. Her professional interests are depression, mania, bereavement, bipolar disorder, and psychopharmacology.

DEBORAH P. WELSH is an associate professor in the Department of Psychology at the University of Tennessee. Her research interests are adolescent romantic relationships and adolescent interactions with family members.

TAMAR WOHLFARTH is a clinical assessor of the Dutch Medicines Evaluation Board in the Netherlands.

MELANIE J. ZIMMER-GEMBECK is an associate professor in the School of Psychology at Griffith University–Gold Coast Campus. Her research areas include the interface of children's and adolescents' relationships with peers and individual development, the development of the self-system, relational aggression, externalizing behaviors and internalizing symptoms, intervention programs for children and adolescents, statistical methods for analyzing change, coping with stress, and parenting.